SIGN AND DESIGN

DUMBARTON OAKS SYMPOSIA AND COLLOQUIA

SIGN AND DESIGN

Script as Image in Cross-Cultural Perspective
(300–1600 CE)

Edited by

BRIGITTE MIRIAM BEDOS-REZAK
AND JEFFREY F. HAMBURGER

DUMBARTON OAKS RESEARCH LIBRARY AND COLLECTION
WASHINGTON, D.C.

© 2016 Dumbarton Oaks

Trustees for Harvard University, Washington, D.C.

All rights reserved.

Printed in the United States of America by Sheridan Books, Inc.

LIBRARY OF CONGRESS CIP DATA

Sign and Design: Script as Image in Cross-Cultural Perspective (300–1600 CE)
(Symposium) (2012 : Dumbarton Oaks)
Sign and design : script as image in cross-cultural perspective (300–1600 CE) /
edited by Brigitte Miriam Bedos-Rezak and Jeffrey Hamburger.
pages cm. — (Dumbarton Oaks symposia and colloquia)
Papers from the symposium Sign and Design: Script as Image in Cross-Cultural
Perspective (300–1600 CE), October 12–14, 2012, Dumbarton Oaks Research Library
and Collection, Washington, D.C.
Includes bibliographical references and index.
isbn 978-0-88402-407-1 (alk. paper)
1. Writing in art—Congresses.
2. Writing and art—History—Congresses.
3. Picture-writing—History—Congresses.
4. Monograms—History—Congresses.
5. Illumination of books and manuscripts, Medieval—Congresses.
6. Signs and symbols—Religious aspects—Congresses.
I. Bedos-Rezak, Brigitte, editor.
II. Hamburger, Jeffrey F., 1957–, editor.
III. Title.
NX650.W75S54 2012
411—dc23
2015000842

www.doaks.org/publications

Book design and composition: Melissa Tandysh
Managing editor: Joel Kalvesmaki

CONTENTS

ACKNOWLEDGMENTS

I N ADDITION TO THANKING OUR CONTRIBUTORS FOR THE CARE WITH which they prepared and revised their papers, it remains only to thank emphatically Dumbarton Oaks and, in particular, its director, Jan Ziolkowski, his incredibly efficient executive assistants, Francisco Lopez and Raquel Begleiter, and the publications department for their hospitality, guidance, and support during both the conference and the preparation of this volume. This has been an immensely complicated undertaking, which also benefited from the constructive input of external reviewers. Without the initiative, efficiency, and insight of these dedicated individuals, our designs would have remained desires.

ABBREVIATIONS

AA	*Archäologischer Anzeiger*
AER	*De antiquis ecclesiae ritibus libri*, ed. E. Martene, 4 vols. (Anvers, 1736–1738)
AH	*Art History*
AI	*Ars islamica*
AJA	*American Journal of Archaeology*
AJP	*American Journal of Philology*
ArtB	*Art Bulletin*
ArtLomb	*Arte lombarda*
bBer	Babylonian Talmud, tractate Berakhot
BIE	*Bulletin de l'Institut d'Égypte*
Bm	Bibliothèque municipale
BMGS	*Byzantine and Modern Greek Studies*
BMMA	*Bulletin of the Metropolitan Museum of Art*
BMQ	*The British Museum Quarterly*
BnF	Bibliothèque nationale de France
BSl	*Byzantinoslavica*
BSOAS	*Bulletin of the School of Oriental and African Studies*
bYoma	Babylonian Talmud, tractate Yoma
BZ	*Byzantinische Zeitschrift*
CahArch	*Cahiers archéologiques*
CahCM	*Cahiers de civilisation médiévale, X^e–XIIe siècles*
CCCM	Corpus Christianorum Continuatio Mediaevalis
CCSL	Corpus Christianorum, series latina
CIFM	*Corpus des inscriptions de la France médiévale*
CPh	*Classical Philology*
DACL	*Dictionnaire d'archéologie chrétienne et de liturgie*
Δελτ.Χριστ.Ἀρχ.Ἑτ.	*Δελτίον τῆς Χριστιανικῆς ἀρχαιολογικῆς ἑταιρείας*
DOP	*Dumbarton Oaks Papers*
DOS	Dumbarton Oaks Studies
EME	Early Medieval Europe
Ἐπ.Ἑτ.Στερ.Μελ.	*Ἐπετερὶς ἑταιρείας Στερεοελλαδικῶν μελετῶν*
EphL	*Ephemerides liturgicae*
ErJb	*Eranos-Jahrbuch*
FS	*Frühmittelalterliche Studien*
GBA	*Gazette des beaux-arts*
HSCPh	*Harvard Studies in Classical Philology*
IEJ	*Israel Exploration Journal*
IRAIK	*Izvestiia Russkogo arkheologicheskogo instituta v Konstantinople*

JbAC	*Jahrbuch für Antike und Christentum*
JBL	*Journal of Biblical Literature*
JJS	*Journal of Jewish Studies*
JÖB	*Jahrbuch der Österreichischen Byzantinistik*
JÖBG	*Jahrbuch der Österreichischen Byzantinischen Gesellschaft*
JQR	*Jewish Quartly Review*
JRA	*Journal of Roman Archaeology*
JRS	*Journal of Roman Studies*
MarbJb	*Marburger Jahrbuch für Kunstwissenschaft*
MGH Poetae	Monumenta Germaniae historica, Poetae latini medii aevi
MGH SS	Monumenta Germaniae historica, Scriptores
MGH Ep	Monumenta Germaniae historica, Epistolae
MM	F. Miklosich and J. Müller, *Acta et diplomata graeca medii aevi–sacra et profana* (Vienna, 1860–1890)
NABU	*Nouvelles Assyriologiques Brèves et Utilitaires*
NC	*The Numismatic Chronicle*
Νέος Ἑλλ.	*Νέος Ἑλλενομνήμων*
n. st.	new style (calendral)
ODB	*The Oxford Dictionary of Byzantium*
PG	Patrologiae cursus completus, Series graeca, ed. J.-P. Migne (Paris, 1857–66)
PL	Patrologiae cursus completus, Series latina, ed. J.-P. Migne (Paris, 1844–80)
PLP	*Prosopographisches Lexikon der Palaiologenzeit*
RBén	*Revue bénédictine*
RBK	*Reallexikon zur byzantinischen Kunst*, ed. K. Wessel (Stuttgart, 1963–)
REB	*Revue des études byzantines*
REI	*Revue des études islamiques*
RES	*Revue des études slaves*
SBN	*Studi bizantini e neoellenici*
TM	*Travaux et mémoires*
WSt	*Wiener Studien*
VizVrem	*Vizantiiskii vremennik*
ZKunstg	*Zeitschrift für Kunstgeschichte*
ZPapEpig	*Zeitschrift für Papyrologie und Epigraphik*
ZRVI	*Zbornik radova Vizantološkog instituta*

Introduction

BRIGITTE MIRIAM BEDOS-REZAK
JEFFREY F. HAMBURGER

LIKE THE INTERNATIONAL CONFERENCE HELD AT DUMBARTON OAKS
(Washington, D.C., 12–14 October 2012) from which it stems, this book addresses the pictorial dimension of writing systems from cross-cultural and multidisciplinary perspectives. Our
volume details premodern attitudes toward and manipulations of script that testify to a vivid engagement with the generative power of the letter as a graphic entity with spatial and plastic potential.
Historians, including specialists in art and literature, paleographers, and anthropologists, consider
imagistic scripts of the ancient and medieval Near East, Europe, Byzantium, and Latin America,
and within Jewish, polytheistic, Christian, and Muslim cultures.[1] They engage with pictographic,
ideographic, and logographic writing systems, as well as with alphabetic scripts. In the premodern
period, writing was effected by the human hand and consisted of a set of meaningful marks inscribed
on or in stone, metal, wax, papyrus, parchment, and paper, to mention only the most common possibilities. The dynamic of the dialectic between the material and immaterial took on a particular
tension in the realm of religion, where the natural and supernatural coexist in an infinite variety of
ways across cultures.[2]

In the age of digital media, the word *script* refers first and foremost, not to the form lent to letters,
but instead to a computer program designed to carry out a particular task. The act of writing, in turn,
involves technical processes enabled by electronic equipment that generate a digital matrix of zeros
and ones to be projected onto screens as text. These transmutations of numeral inscription into legible
writing constitute a fundamental break from earlier analog technologies, which neither the printing
press nor the typewriter displaced despite their mechanization of writing. As computers increasingly
dominate all forms of textual and iconographic production, a widespread nostalgia for and interest in
older, more personalized forms of writing, such as autography, calligraphy, glyphs, graffiti, and even
tattoos, have developed. Nonetheless, recent scholarship on handwriting in the age of the Internet
and digital media points out that handwriting has never disappeared in the wake of new technologies and eloquently conveys the extent to which writing remains a manual craft associated with

---

1 Comprehensive coverage was, of course, impossible. Dumbarton Oaks specializes in western, Byzantine, and Latin American
civilizations, and gave our project its geographic and cultural framework.

2 For Christianity, both eastern and western, see the essays gathered in Stéphanie Dianne Daussy et al., eds., *Matérialité et imma-
térialité dans l'église au Moyen Age* (Bucharest, 2012).

functional practices, social significance, and aesthetic categories.[3] This volume, therefore, is not an exercise in romantic recovery.

In other ways, however, our topic could not be more traditional. The relationship between script and image has long been a staple of scholarship, which has probed the manner and meaning of its dynamics in terms of equivalency, complementarity, and polarity.[4] Social scientists researching the invention of writing have tended to conclude that writing developed from images. Scholars of Common Era, Abrahamic, religious cultures point out that in Judaism, Islam, and Christianity, whether in the Byzantine east or in the Latin west, text and image have always had an uneasy coexistence. We have built on and benefited from this rich trove of scholarship, but we have also departed from it in the spirit of exploration and experimentation.

Without discounting previously established frameworks, this volume marks a shift away from an interest in text and image to a concern for the dialogic role of image in writing. As a result, our working notion of imagistic lettering sets aside the traditional binary so as to engage the interactive grouping of support, space, letter, image, and word, a quintet in which each component relates to the other without absorbing or being subsumed by it. Each component, therefore, exceeds the others in its signifying processes, destabilizing iconic, medial, and linguistic referentiality, and thereby challenging representational (mimetic transparency) and signifying (linguistic transparency) arrangements.

We suggest that in imagistic scripts the causal or inferential work of representation gives way to the coexistence of medium, colors, forms, graphic signs, lines, and traces, where interrelationships are a matter of shared situational arrangements. In such a conception of mixed mediality, premodern, iconic letterforms suggest an understanding of writing as gesturing and of reading as gazing, and compel consideration of the co-signification of sign forms. To this extent, imagistic lettering is analogous to a rebus, albeit one that eschews phonetic or syllabic resolutions.[5] Script-images form hybrid signs, whose effect inheres in a suspension of meaning that opens up the system of representation and signification within the contexts in which they were produced and circulated. The exploration of such systems proceeds in three main directions, each of which constitutes a specific section of this volume. In introducing these sections, however, we must acknowledge the rhizomatic nature of our topic, the ways in which it resists the demands of clarity and defies the strict categorization of outline. We have therefore made a point of indicating relevant connections between all essays independent of their organization in thematic parts.

The Iconicity of Script

The concept of a rhizome is inimical to the search for origins.[6] Indeed, the origins of writing are considered by Anne-Marie Christin in support of her main contention, in the broad chronological and geographic approach she has pursued, that writing should be emancipated from its subjection to speech.[7] She argues that the legible issued from the visible, not from a linguistic mode of communication. Christin's analysis dwells on the ideogram, and she demonstrates that alphabetic scripts, which she presents as secondary to and reinvented from the ideogram, require different forms of analysis.

3 Sonya Neef, José van Dijck, and Eric Ketelaar, eds., *Sign Here: Handwriting in the Age of New Media* (Amsterdam, 2006), 7–9.

4 Of these, *ut pictura poesis* is only the most familiar. Ekphrasis is another. Variations on the text-image paradigm extend to include oppositions between oral and written, hearing and seeing, and, in the Latin West, Latin and the vernaculars—a hierarchy of languages, both spoken and written, that vary in terms of the relationship to visual forms of expression. A sampling of the most recent studies includes Laura Kendrick, *Animating the Letter: The Figurative Embodiment of Writing from Late Antiquity to the Renaissance* (Columbus, 1999); Jeffrey F. Hamburger, ed., *The Iconicity of Script: Writing as Image in the Middle Ages*, special issue of *Word and Image* 27, no. 3 (2011); idem, *Script as Image* (Leuven, 2014); and Anna Contadini, *Arab Painting: Text and Image in Illustrated Painted Manuscripts* (Leiden, 2010).

5 The inspiration for this simile comes from Georges Didi-Huberman, *Devant l'image* (Paris, 1990), 176–77.

6 Gilles and Felix Guattati, *Mille Plateaux* (Paris, 1980), trans. Brian Massumi as *A Thousand Plateaus* (Minneapolis, 1987).

7 Anne-Marie Christin, *L'image écrite ou la déraison graphique* (Paris, 1995; repr. 2001).

142

143

*IN ILLUMINATED MANUSCRIPTS, FOR EXAMPLE.

Nevertheless, she maintains that all forms of writing share operational modes linked to their generic iconicity.

A modern comic book might seem an unlikely place to turn for insight into the history of iconic letters. However, Scott McCloud (b. 1960), a historian of comics as well as a comic strip artist in his own right, notes that comics stand in a tradition that extends back to the Middle Ages and beyond. An opening from his *Understanding Comics* offers a condensed history of pictorial scripts and related forms of representation (Intro. fig. 1).[8] In the beginning, maintains McCloud, was the image; as noted by his comic persona, speaking from within a cartouche-like frame, "the earliest words were,

in fact, stylized pictures." The pictorial writing systems that fill the frame around him emphasize this point: to the left, Egyptian hieroglyphs; to the right, Aztec glyphs; and at the bottom, Mayan (as found in the Dresden Codex, the oldest extant book written in the Americas).[9] Using examples ranging from cuneiform to Chinese characters, this unusually learned comic traces the history of script as it became ever more abstract, noting that, "in time, most modern writing would come to represent sound only and lose any lingering resemblance to the visible world." With the advent of printing, at least

INTRO. FIG. 1.
Scott McCloud, *Understanding Comics* (New York, 1993), 142–43.
Photo courtesy of Harper Collins Publishing.

8 Scott McCloud, *Understanding Comics* (New York, 1993), 142–43.

9 For the identification of the passage from the Dresden Codex (p. 50), we are indebted to Alexandre Tokovinine of Harvard University, who notes that vis-à-vis the original, some of the glyphs are out of order. For a freely available facsimile of the codex, visit http://digital.slub-dresden.de/werkansicht/dlf/2967/1/cache.off (accessed 1 March 2015).

in the West, "the written word took a great leap forward . . . but where," asks McCloud, "had all the pictures gone?" In a footnote elaborating on this proverbial "blackening of the page," he notes that illuminated manuscripts, in which words and pictures continued to coexist, represent an exception to the trend.

One could offer many glosses or corrections to McCloud's encapsulated account. In the comic, the translation of a steer's head and stalks of wheat remains fanciful, all the more so as even in the adjoining historical examples, most of the pictographs represent not things, but syllables. In its basic outline, McCloud's summary is accurate, but only to a point. In the western tradition, that point, predictably, marks the retreat from naturalistic modes of representation that began in the latter part of the nineteenth century, a retreat that became a rout in the face of the modernist challenge to tradition. Outside the academic spheres of history and anthropology, a literary and artistic movement for the emancipation of writing from speech crystallized in the nineteenth century around Stéphane Mallarmé (1842–1898). From Pablo Picasso on, whether in the art of Paul Klee (1878–1940), Jasper Johns (b. 1930), or Cy Twombly (1928–2011), writing once again forms part of the pictorial process

(or, conversely, picturing once again can be conceived as a form of writing).

Cy Twombly's series *Notes from Salahah*, dated 2005–2007, provides but one of many examples (Intro. fig. 2).[10] At first glance, Twombly's broad painterly scrawl looks like a child's classroom prank, a meaningless meander filling a blackboard-like panel with jagged spirals that leave no room for meaningful signs. Twombly's horizontal vortices reference the automatic writing of the surrealists, but they also hark back to the vatic power of premodern calligraphy, when writing embodied the movement of the hand and seemingly channeled the spirit that informed it. The Evangelist Mark in the Carolingian Ebbo Gospels can be seen as a medieval Twombly, no less firmly rooted in dreams of the classical than his modern alter ego, but, like him, embodying a translation into figural calligraphy that hovers between exacting precision and tremulous excitement (Intro. fig. 3). In Twombly's modern

10 Kirk Varnedoe, *Cy Twombly: A Retrospective* (New York, 1994); Catherine Bernard, "Cy Twombly: l'écriture en/ au miroir," *Revue française d'études américaines* 46 (1990): 269–81; Richard Leeman, "Roland Barthes et Cy Twombly: Le 'champ allusif de l'écriture'," *Rue Descartes* (2001): 61–70; and Jon Bird, "Indeterminacy and (Dis)order in the Work of Cy Twombly," *Oxford Art Journal* 30 (2007): 486–504.

work, the artist, made present by the exaggerated gestural language of his brush strokes, takes the place of the scribe, whose divine inspiration is a source of power. Twombly referred to his works in this vein as "pseudo-writing." This term could no less be applied to the regimented series of wounds decorating the pages of a fifteenth-century English devotional manual, which offers, in its combination of line and drips (one is tempted to invoke the splatter of schlock horror), a mesmerizing dialogue between reason and emotion, painterly precision and visceral gesture (Intro. fig. 4).[11]

Twombly is just one of many modern artists who invite their viewers to reconsider the relationship between text and image, text as image, and image as text. Klee is another such artist; his often-cited statement "art does not reproduce the visible; rather, it makes visible,"[12] provides a precedent for Anne-Marie Christin, who in this volume outlines a process whereby visual scrutiny of surfaces leads to an interrogation of their observable traces and to an interpretation, and not an enunciation, of these traces' systemic organization. Christin upholds the richness of ideogrammatic writings, which mobilize graphic forms, lines, and supports to reconstitute verbal

INTRO. FIG. 3.
Evangelist Mark,
Ebbo Gospels, Épernay.
Bm, ms. 1, fols. 90v–91r.

Photo courtesy of the
Bibliothèque nationale
de France.

11 The growing literature on this idiosyncratic manuscript is indicative of increased interest not only in the aesthetic of the abject, but also in pictorial scripts; see Marlene Villalobos Hennessy, "Aspects of Blood Piety in a Late-Medieval English Manuscript," in *History in the Comic Mode: Medieval Communities and the Matter of Person*, ed. Rachel Fulton and Bruce W. Holsinger (New York, 2007), 182–91; eadem, "The Social Life of a Manuscript Metaphor: Christ's Blood as Ink," in *The Social Life of Illumination: Manuscripts, Images, and Communities in the Late Middle Ages*, ed. Joyce Coleman, Mark Cruse, and Kathryn A. Smith (Turnhout, 2013), 17–52;

and Hamburger, *Script as Image*, 20. On the actual use of pseudoscript in premodern Europe, particularly in Italy, see Alexander Nagel, "Twenty-Five Notes on Pseudoscript in Italian Art," *RES: Anthropology and Aesthetics* 59–60 (2011): 228–48.

12 Paul Klee, *Schöpferische Konfession*, ed. Kasimir Edschmid (Berlin, 1920), trans. in idem, "Creative Credo," in *Theories of Modern Art: A Source Book by Artists and Critics*, ed. Herschel B. Chipp (Berkeley, 1968), 182–86.

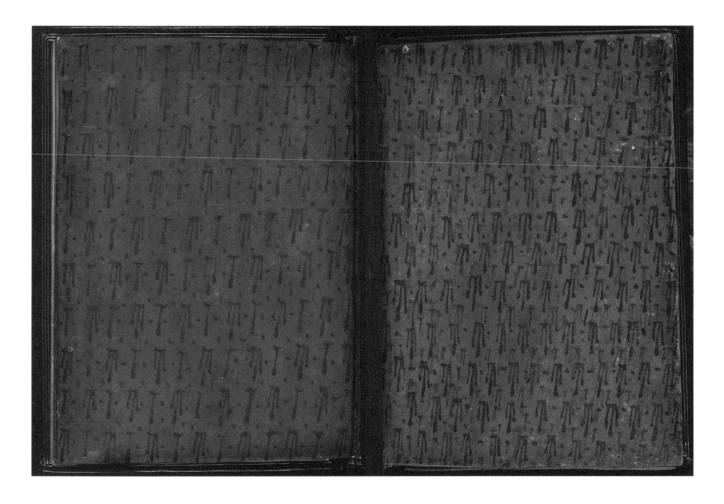

INTRO. FIG. 4.
*The Wounds of
Christ*, Psalter and
Rosary of the Virgin,
England (Kent),
ca. 1480–1490s.
London, British
Library, Egerton MS.
1821, fols. 7v–8r.

Photo © The British
Library Board.

meaning, and contrasts them with the impoverished alphabetic encoding system that mediates the logocentric cultures of western societies and Abrahamic religions.

Logocentricity provides the foil against which the interrelationship of sign and design in scripts has to be discussed and from which this relationship needs to be distinguished. In the Christian world, the dominant theory of theologians, powerfully claimed by the colonial Spaniards in Latin America discussed by Thomas Cummins, contrasted alphabetic writing with depiction, and scripture with picture. They insisted on the superiority of writing, arguing that alphabetical writing was immaterial and transparent, not calling attention to itself but leading to the sounds of words, which in turn represented thought. It was in part for this reason that the dedication ceremonies for churches, analyzed by Didier Méhu, literally inscribed the alphabet within and even onto the building, making it one with the liturgical manuscripts

employed to carry out the rite inside its walls. The papers in this volume all work to demonstrate the tenuous nature of this iconoclastic theory of writing, which derives from the classical taste of highly influential early Christian Fathers such as Jerome (d. 420) and Augustine (d. 430).[13] Classical aesthetics had their origins in Greek rhetorical theories about the proper use of words, whereby words were to serve argument, not to seduce the listener by calling attention to themselves and provoking admiration for stylistic ornaments that displayed the bodily form of language. To Jerome's classical taste, the ideal inscription of Holy Scripture should draw so little attention to itself as to be nearly transparent. He famously ranted against religious texts written in silver on purple-dyed pages or with decorated and enlarged letters. For him, these manuscripts called attention to the image

13 According to E. H. Gombrich, *The Sense of Order: A Study in the Psychology of Decorative Art* (Ithaca, 1979), 19–20.

BRIGITTE MIRIAM BEDOS-REZAK AND JEFFREY F. HAMBURGER

of writing to the detriment of the meaning. Witness the symbolic significance later attached to the use of dyes and metallic pigments in illuminated manuscripts, Jerome did not succeed in suppressing patrons and scribes' efforts to embellish the letter, while the rise of Christian image worship profoundly influenced the way texts and scriptures were presented.[14] Texts took on texture; writing had incarnational presence as well as theological import.

However interwoven image and writing are with visualization and interpretation, the relationship of this texture to speech and language must be addressed. In her study of Aztec pictography, Elizabeth Hill Boone emphasizes the relative independence of pre-Hispanic Aztec pictograms from language. Nevertheless, Boone's analysis bears particularly on those instances in which Aztec figural images were made to accommodate speech acts, namely, a device known as the speech scroll. Speech scrolls emerging from the mouths of rulers, supernatural beings, or animals had a complex relationship with language. As secondary graphemes associated with primary figures, they constitute a sign characterizing the figures thus depicted as rulers. Particularized by affixes, they express verbal action, transforming the medium of their configuration, from a stable space of meaningful ideoplastic figures to a lively stage of dramatic action and interaction among animated beings. Ultimately, linear strings of sequenced glyphs, whether arranged in speech scrolls or not, display a rhetorical structure. Although early colonial manuscripts, in particular pictorial catechisms, were more likely to contain a sustained presence of glyphs organized in linguistic streams, Boone gives evidence that preconquest pictography was open to linguistic rhythms and patterning even before the

alphabetic system of the West influenced pictographic syntax.

The encounter between the Pre-Columbian graphic systems of Mexico and Peru and the alphabetic system of Spain is central to Tom Cummins's examination of the mutually supportive cultural processes at work in imperial conquest, such as printing and evangelization, or translation and instruction. Cummins shows that indigenous languages were tolerated and used by colonial administrators. It was the transcription of these languages that became the target of intense Spanish activity and ideological productivity. Even when confronted by a hieroglyphic system that was fundamentally logographic, such as Mayan writing, the Spaniards rendered it into alphabetic texts, as they did with all pre-Columbian writing. When glyphs were preserved, they were accompanied by explanatory captions, almost as if their function was to illustrate the alphabetic text rather than to be translated by it. Both Boone and Cummins note that Pre-Columbian Mesoamerican writing systems could have accommodated syllabic rendering and Spanish words. Against a background of the continuing use of Pre-Columbian spoken languages for religious and administrative purposes, the banishment of the earlier writing systems and their systematic substitution by the alphabet constructed, in the guise of remedy, a demonstration of the incommensurability between pictography and the alphabetic letter. Moreover, the superiority of the alphabet was demonstrated in practice, as letters seemed capable of inscribing all languages. This bias in favor of letters was not new in the West. In fact, one of its colonial exponents, the Spanish Jesuit José de Acosta (1539–1600), reminded his readers that the Second Council of Nicaea (787) had established that "pictures are a book for the illiterate."[15] The council was reiterating a dictum famously enunciated by Pope Gregory I the Great (d. 604), which, though variously and often dubiously interpreted, retained a vital currency well into the sixteenth century during the Council of Trent (1545–1563). As made clear by Cummins's reading of Acosta and other contemporary texts, in particular alphabet books, the promotion of the alphabet underscored the

14 For examples, see John M. Burnam, "The Early Gold and Silver Manuscripts," *CPh* 6 (1911): 144–55; Thomas Lentes, "*Textus Evangelii*: Materialität und Inszenierung des *textus* in der Liturgie," in *"Textus" im Mittelalter: Komponenten und Situationen des Wortgebrauchs im schriftsemantischen Feld*, ed. Ludolf Kuchenbuch and Uta Kleine, Veröffentlichungen des Max-Planck-Instituts für Geschichte 216 (Göttingen, 2006), 132–48, at 137–38; and Herbert L. Kessler, "The Eloquence of Silver," in *L'allégorie dans l'art du Moyen Âge: Formes et fonctions; Héritages, créations, mutations; Actes du colloque du RILMA, Institut Universitaire de France (Paris, INHA, 28–29 mai 2010)*, ed. Christian Heck (Turnhout, 2011), 49–64.

15 See full citation in Cummins, pp. 96–97.

inferiority of "illiterate" Native Americans. It also articulated the divine significance of the letter, said to flesh out words in the same way that Christ incarnated the Logos, able to bridge absence and to render present. The imposition of the alphabet in the Americas thus combined the substantiation of a specific ideology of writing and the inscription of Spanish imperial rule within a framework of salvific history.

Remarkably, early modern advocates of the superiority of the letter, whether Catholic or Protestant, seem to have been unable to make their point without embellishing letters with various bodily and natural figures or subsuming them within graphic signs, such as the monogram of Christ. Monograms painted on the walls of sixteenth-century Mexican public buildings offered monumental inscriptions parallel to the monograms carved on medieval western and Byzantine churches.[16] Both fostered a dynamic between visual and legible perceptions of the inscribed word.

The Byzantine epigrams that are the subject of Ivan Drpić's essay also appear in monumental settings, though they are also found on icons, reliquaries, and personal ornaments. In short, such epigrams were a pervasive part of Byzantine visual and literary culture. In contrast with Antony Eastmond, who elsewhere in this volume argues that Byzantine inscriptions at times bordered on the illegible, thereby creating independent aesthetic effects, Drpić, in parallel with Irene Winter's discussion of the legibility of cuneiform inscriptions, observes that whatever their material substrate, the lettering of epigrams remained letters. They might be elongated or differently sized, elegant ligatures might join them, and niello might fill them, yet at no point do letters mix with or morph into images, nor was their fundamental legibility compromised. In arguing for the sensory perception of epigrammatic poetry as an aesthetic and material artifact, Drpić stresses the Byzantine sensitivity to letters qua letters in terms of their ornamental, cosmetic value. Poetic epigrams functioned as a form of *kosmos* through the transformative power of scripted letters to animate their supports and to index

sacred and supernatural spaces. In this context, literary and calligraphic forms operated as dialogic constituents of the epigram, itself a hybrid production whose poetics were iconic, emerging both from letters and from text. Serving to commemorate or celebrate, evaluate or explain, praise or perpetuate the memory of the dead, epigrams lent voice not only to donors but also to objects. As Drpić observes, although numerous epigrams have been transmitted in anthologies, in their original forms they would have been as much physical as textual artifacts. Scale, setting, and materials conditioned their performance; and the reader's body would have entered into dialogue with the speaking presence of another, whether that of the donor, poet, or monument. Rhetorical craft and physical ornamentation accessible to sight and touch became interwoven, each elaborating, evoking, and explaining the other in ways that appealed directly to the sensory experience of the viewer. In Drpić's analysis, the term *kosmos*, meaning "order," but also "adornment," "decoration," and "beauty," assumes central importance and can serve as much to characterize the reader's response as the inherent qualities of the object-text itself. In this context, *kosmos* refers less to the entirety of creation—the subject of the initial in the Carolingian Moutier-Grandval Bible at the center of Herbert Kessler's contribution—than to principles of design that inform the perception of artificial, man-made objects as well as natural ones. To adorn such objects, especially icons, was not simply to mask them, but also to manifest their inherent participation in the beauty and magnificence of the divine. Kosmos, far from superficial and superfluous, in the way modernity often defined ornament, honors the object. The epigrams that "clothe" the object mediate between object and viewer, and between object and logos. Epigrams not only adorned icons, they both expressed and possessed their own iconic dimension. In elite Byzantine cultural practice, adorning sacred objects acquired special status as a way of demonstrating piety and largesse.

In Byzantium, letters and their refined inscription sufficed to endow epigrams with a material and ornate dimension. Beatrice Fraenkel's examination of the autograph signs used by medieval notaries to authenticate their documents, however, exposes a signatory practice

16 See in this volume the essays of Debiais (135–52) and Eastmond (219–36).

in which letters were insufficient. When they were used in notarial signs, letters formed less personal names than graphic arrangements. Often notarial signs eschewed letters altogether, becoming pure designs. Recourse to such signs predominated from the thirteenth century to the sixteenth century, ultimately disappearing upon the official enforcement of the signature as the definitive authenticating sign. Fraenkel, however, seeks to revise and redirect the teleological approach, which posits that notarial signs and signs of documentary validation in general are merely exotic forerunners of the signature.[17]

Fraenkel transports us, as did Ghislain Brunel in the paper he delivered at the conference,[18] to the medieval world of European chanceries and writing bureaus, whose scribal responsibilities privileged the production of official, authentic, and authoritative documents. Notarial marks were part of the mechanisms for documentary authorization, together with seals and such graphic designs as monograms, *rotae*, crosses, and illegible *signa* in various letterlike shapes. All these signs of validation share the common trait of deploying an (icono)graphic component within the expression of personal identity and commitment. Whether fully graphic or not, notarial marks were pictorial and drawn, whereas the notaries' names were written as part of a document's text. In some few cases, which are of particular interest to Fraenkel, names and signa combined to form rebus-signatures. In such signatures, names appear as both text and image. Written names of notaries referenced individuals, advancing no further claims as to their status or authority. Names drawn as rebuses included surnames, often derived from common nouns, and facilitated their integration into a traditional system of personal nomenclature that, prior to the thirteenth century, had been based solely upon the use of baptismal names. If rebus-signatures focused upon and favored strategies of naming, then graphic marks, in their imitation and recuperation of the ambient emblematic of power, associated notaries with the users and bearers of such particular emblems. When notaries took the papal or episcopal *rota* or a heraldic device found in a ruler's coat of arms as an element of their own marks, these images created a figural horizon of recognition that placed them among high-ranking authorities. Imagistic notarial marks thus enabled participation in an empowering emblematic context, one that even extended to the supernatural. In their alignment of letters, graphic points, and geometric motifs, notarial marks resemble the figures or notes of Solomon's *Ars Notoria*. Both notarial and "notorial" graphic elements appear to enforce a principle of nonrepresentability, at once linguistic and iconographic, in their effort to actualize power and authority.

Text: Imaging the Ineffable

Magic and notarial marks could thus be said to operate outside the sphere of representation as a conduit for that which cannot be represented. Herbert Kessler's essay elucidates such an approach by considering in exacting detail a single historiated initial from a Carolingian manuscript, the Moutier-Grandval Bible (ca. 840). Easily overlooked in favor of the manuscript's magnificent, full-page frontispieces, the opening letter to John's first epistle proves no less complex in its figurative sources and strategies. The letter doubles as a cosmological diagram, drawing on a rich tradition of cosmological imagery extending back to antiquity, and glossing the first principle outlined in John's Gospel: the world issued from the word, from Christ Logos who has coexisted with the Father since the beginning of time. This letter, as a cosmological image, thus participates in a broader conception of kosmos, albeit different than that developed in Ivan Drpić's contribution. In unraveling the complex genesis and iconography of an unusually complicated initial, Kessler's analysis reveals how multivalent geometric forms, above all the circle, lend it shape and inform its content. As in Carolingian sacramentaries, the initial in the bible demonstrates an interplay of letter and sign that takes on theological dimensions, enacting for the viewer the interaction of the physical and spiritual in Christ's two natures and, above all, in the Eucharist. The initial therefore serves as an instrument of initiation, not just edification; it has a performative dimension. In

17 Béatrice Fraenkel, *La signature: Genèse d'un signe* (Paris, 1992).

18 See a summary of Brunel's paper below, pp. 13–14.

his attention to the dynamic communication between the shape of letters and the figures they incorporate, Kessler perceives that these initials form the textual materiality of God's temporal revelation and incarnation, even as they delineate blankness, the space of the invisible, triune, and eternal God.

In his examination of southern French and northern Spanish monumental chrismons of the Romanesque period, Vincent Debiais shows that the imbrication of letters and spaces within Pyrenean chrismons also displays and plays with the mystery of the Christian God. Chrismons, the monogrammatic arrangements of letters that express Christological identity (chirho: XP; alpha-omega: A-Ω; Christos: XPS) play on two alphabetic registers, the Greek and the Latin. For example, by forcing a Latin reading of the Greek construction "XP, A," some chrismons produce the word *pax*. However, readers are specifically directed, by means of an external epigraphic inscription, to see in this word a Trinitarian symbol, with each letter referring to a person of the Trinity. The movement from (Greek) letters to (Latin) words to abstract images subsumes the semantics of linguistics within a perpetual semiosis of divine eternity. Inscribed within circles that symbolize the entire universe, chrismons enacted the godlike attribute of absolute self-referentiality while eschewing imagistic and semantic representation. Debiais's selection of Romanesque chrismons from the Pyrenean region shows that they supported a variety of strategies by which to associate letters and words with a ceaseless deferral of meaning, and to locate divine self-referentiality within that very inability of letters and words to have a stable meaning of their own. It is in their broken, translated, and hijacked form that letters mean "Christ," and signify him as the source and end of all meaning. Thus, on some chrismons, the lines of the chi-rho deconstruct the Christological name by serving in the formation of other words, like *lex*, *lux*, *pax*, and *rex*, or in the drawing of a cross. The effect is not only of continuous script but also of script as a background to the large chi-rho, which alone emerges at a scale that reaches the limits of the circle. The play of foreground and background and the different visual trajectories delineated by the letters'

formation of various words animate the chrismon. The chrismon was expected to impregnate a space with sacredness and protection, as a sign of the living God used during ceremonies of church dedication and placed at the entrance of churches. Though sometimes accompanied by textual inscriptions, chrismons were not simply texts, and though sometimes including images, chrismons were not simply images. Suspended between the possibility of naming and the possibility of representing, they were a medial conduit for the ineffable quality of Christ's divinity.

From the mid-thirteenth century onward, the Jews of medieval central Europe subscribed eagerly to the artistic formulae pioneered by Christians in their books, buildings, and artifacts. The lavish decoration of Hebrew liturgical books and bibles, however, stopped short of any inclusion of anthropomorphic representations of God. Yet, as shown by Katrin Kogman-Appel, Ashkenazi illuminated prayer books (*mahzorim*) show that Jewish book designers took up the challenge of representing the divine. Their strategy focused on the treatment of the names of God (*Adon*, *El*, and others), which are typically the opening words of the liturgical poems (*piyyutim*) contained in the mahzorim and read on specific Jewish holidays. Each holiday and its set of piyyutim celebrate and commemorate particular historical moments or seasons of the Jewish calendar, and when a *piyyut* is introduced by a decorated word panel, the panel's iconographic program depicts scenes relevant to the holiday with which it is associated. Within these scenes, the letters forming God's name are etched in gold and form dramatic shapes, but it is less their grandiose beauty than their situation within the iconographic programs they occupy that rendered God's presence visually palpable. Thus, to focus on one of the illuminations (from the Leipzig Mahzor, ca. 1310) discussed by Kogman-Appel, the word *El*, "God," appears in an illustration of the piyyut connected with the additional Torah reading specific to Shabbat Shekalim (Shemot 30:11–16). Both the piyyut and the Torah portion describe the offerings by Israelites of a half-shekel for the construction and maintenance of the Tabernacle. Building upon the biblical text, the piyyut links the monetary offering to atonement for sins. In the Leipzig Mahzor the scale that evaluates monetary contributions and the repentance required to attain forgiveness is balanced upon the ligature aleph-lamed, which forms the word *El*. The letters are thus a structural part of the represented object, and as such they are integral to the very construction of the image. They acquire figural import from their building and scaffolding function. The performance of these letters, however, is not figuration but actualization. They anchor and organize the representational images among which they appear to be "consequent upon the divine immersion in lettristic plenitude."[19]

Whereas in Christian iconography letters forming the name of God, such as the chi-rho monogram studied by Debiais, invite multidirectional reading, making alphabetic writing a figural conduit for multiple meaning, in Jewish iconography the Hebrew letters remain fixed and intrinsic to the divine name, with their numerical and other valences the preserve of abstract thinking and mystic experience. In his discussion of Islamic calligraphy, İrvin Cemil Schick devotes some of his analysis to poems and mystical texts, which praise the letters formed by the beloved's face or man's stature. Significantly, in the case of the latter, the letters drawn by the human silhouette shape the word, but not the image of, God. Poetry thus inscribes letters within form, a design that is also found in calligraphic works. Pictorial calligraphies in particular enclose Qur'anic verses, prayers, dedications, and other texts within the shape of a bird, lion, horse, or ship. The comparative dimension provided by the essays gathered in this volume makes it possible to note that while Islamic letters can inhabit an image, Jewish letters remain letters, and Christian letters can be inhabited by images. In considering the question of script as image, Schick positions the prominence of ornamental writing in Muslim culture within the broader context of Islamic art, where figurative images abound on wall paintings, miniatures, textiles, and metalwork. Calligraphy was not a matter of compensating either for the alleged Islamic

ban on representational art or for an absence of images. In fact, the injunction that sacred spaces should not be decorated forbids both images and writing, which suggests that script and image belonged to the same world. However, there was a general understanding that making images of living creatures was a blasphemous emulation of God's creation, but writing, which was conceived as an emanation of God's power, inscribed objects within the God-ordered world of Islam and thus marked them with their true identity. Calligraphic inscriptions, as an embodiment of God's word, bridged the world between man and God. Calligraphic images, as containers of written inscriptions, reveal God's signs hidden in his creation. From Schick's perspective, the very centrality of writing in Muslim perception of divine creation and revelation accounts for the rich and sustained calligraphic dimension of Arabic script. The meaning of such calligraphy thus extends beyond, though does not necessarily eschew, the legible. Significantly, in some inscriptions written language becomes iconic, with the letters shaped so as to depict forms that the word itself connotes. This overlap of phonological and graphological spheres is analogous to onomatopoeia.[20] It is also an extreme case of visual punning, and Schick's inclusion of more traditional puns in his discussion of calligraphic inscriptions shows the extraordinary range of Islamic calligraphic works, which, as forms of worship, sites of sublime beauty, and expressions of humor, opened and enriched the lines of communication between man and God and between man and man.

Performativity:
Iconic Script and the Body

Irene Winter's paper looks at examples of monumental and miniature epigraphy from the ancient Near East, focusing on objects from the public sphere in which script appears both in and on the image. In her analysis, size is less significant than the mode of address, in this case to a public

---

19 This felicitous expression was found in Jed Rasula and Steve McCaffery, eds., *Imagining Language: An Anthology* (Cambridge, Mass., 1998), 328.

20 Christian Hempelmann and Andrea C. Samson, "Visual Puns and Verbal Puns: Descriptive Analogy or False Analogy?" in *New Approaches to the Linguistics of Humor*, ed. Diana Popa and Salvatore Attardo (Galati, 2007), 180–96.

viewership, therefore small-scale luxury objects are also included. Winter identifies a "lapidary style," in which cuneiform writing was executed with special attention to legibility and regularity. The morphology of script inevitably changed over long periods of time—changes that can themselves be construed as having semantic content.[21] Winter's emphasis, however, falls on certain constants of official practice, in particular the purposeful clarity that marks public inscriptions, a clarity that makes the entire tradition and forms part of their signifying process. In contrast to the element of playfulness found in other scribal and epigraphic traditions, cuneiform conformed to a canon in which the distinction between textual signs and figural imagery was upheld. Winter's analysis suggests analogies to Drpić's argument concerning the integrity of letterforms in Byzantine inscriptions. Viewed against the formal invention found in other traditions, however, such stability need not be regarded as normative, but rather as the conscious articulation of a particular set of values. Charting changes in this lapidary style over a period of three thousand years, Winter argues for the need to undertake an independent analysis of text and image before seeking to understand their interaction as part of a broader semantic field. Carved inscriptions, let alone the act of writing, carried authority, even for the overwhelming majority of the populace who could not read. Winter concludes that the lettering on monuments addressed to a large public required regularization, which in turn constitutes a principle of design within the lapidary style that serves as a sign in its own right no matter the content of the monumental inscriptions for which it was used.

Antony Eastmond's contribution offers a contrast to those practices, whether ancient or modern, that insist on a degree of adherence to legibility. His topic is the Byzantine monogram, a special instance of the imbrication of text and image that is predicated on the obscured legibility of the letterforms it amalgamates. Monograms record acts of piety, donation, patronage, and euergetism (the doing of good deeds); they mark objects and monuments, yet often defy

decipherment. They conceal as much as they reveal, thereby adding mystery to meaning. As observed by Eastmond, they signify by virtue of their form rather than by conveying information, or rather, their form itself constitutes the information. In keeping with Winter's insistence on formal modes of address informing the presentation of script in public, Eastmond also emphasizes the extent to which monograms, despite their personal character, formed part of a pervasive public discourse. Placement shapes their meaning. Monograms also create a stratification of their audience into those who are able to decipher their contents and those who cannot, but who nonetheless would be impressed by their material splendor and sophistication. Eastmond traces a shift from message to medium in which texts become images, especially in public viewing contexts. Contrasting apprehension with comprehension, Eastmond identifies the monogram as a special case in which design dominates, but in doing so generates novel forms of signification.

In her essay on the historiated and decorated initials in the late eighth-century Gellone Sacramentary, one of the earliest western medieval manuscripts to employ what in later centuries became the commonplace device of incorporating figures or narrative into the forms or spaces of letters, Cynthia Hahn further explores the dialectic between visibility and legibility (or, conversely, the inscrutable and the illegible). Appropriate to the function of a sacramentary (the book that contained the texts required by the celebrant for the performance of the mass), the decorated word takes on a body or, better, bodies, undergoing a continuous process of performative transmogrification analogous to the transformation of substances at the heart of the Eucharistic ritual. Far from serving simply as place markers or symbolic images, the decorated letters participate in the act of praying itself and lend it a shape and structure. The pliant forms of the letters augment, rather than encumber, the efficacy of the sacramental petitions they accompany. As noted by Hahn, the images enhance the reader/viewer's understanding of sacred ritual not simply by lending literal articulation to its spoken formulas, but by lending them visual and corporeal presence, all the more appropriate in light of the Eucharistic function of the

---

21 On this topic, see Stephen D. Houston, ed., *The Shape of Script: How and Why Writing Systems Change* (Santa Fe, 2012).

INTRO. FIG. 5.

Charter of King Charles V, in which the king certifies that he gifted his brother, John, duke of Berry, with a fragment of the True Cross. Paris, January 1372. Paris, Archives nationales, AE II 393.

Photo ARCHIM, with kind permission of the Archives nationales.

ceremonies in which they participate. In the pages of the Gellone Sacramentary, textual culture presents itself as material culture.

The performative dimensions of script assume center stage in Didier Méhu's discussion of the church dedication rite articulated in pontificals, in which the Greek and Latin alphabets were inscribed in or written on the floor of the new church. Like other contributors, in particular Hahn, Méhu emphasizes the visual elaboration and ornamentation of script, in this case in the liturgical manuscripts that describe the Dedication ceremony. Script, as understood by Méhu and, he argues, by the medieval scribes who produced pontificals, does more than merely convey information; it opens the door to imagination and conceptualization in ways that lend the textual content resonance. Méhu subsequently relates the legible forms of letters to the loaded concept of *figura*, from which the modern term "figuration" derives. By tracing the changing figuration of the ritual, including its presentation in a variety of formal scripts, in the manuscripts that outlined the ceremony from the eighth century to the end of the first millennium, Méhu charts changing understandings

of vision and visuality in a clerical context. In Méhu's analysis, a given pontifical's *mise-en-page* does not simply serve to order information, it structures the celebrant's understanding of the ritual and hence takes on its own ritual dimension. The codex is not just a container, it is a site of cognition and a shaper of cognitive process.

As with Fraenkel's presentation, Ghislain Brunel's conference paper (not included in this volume) explored the imaging of letters and names within administrative texts, in particular the royal charters issued by the kings of France from the late thirteenth century onward.[22] Performativity was crucial to such charters, as they were expected to enforce the king's will in the spheres of law, politics, and economics. Since the early Middle Ages, graphic marks and image-bearing seals had contributed an iconic affirmation that royal diplomas and their contents had

22 Ghislain Brunel's work on royal decorated charters has appeared in Brunel, *Images du pouvoir royal: Les chartes décorées des Archives nationales* (Paris, 2005), and Ghislain Brunel and Marc H. Smith, eds., "Les chartes ornées dans l'Europe romane et gothique," special edition of *Bibliothèque de l'Ecole des chartes* 169, no. 1 (2011).

been duly authorized by the king.[23] The imagistic turn in the layout and design of late medieval documents, however, particularly targeted initial letters, conflating them with the emblematic, heraldic, and physiognomic portraits of the charters' authors and actors.[24] Letters formed the stage for entire scenes of granting, bestowing, and transferring power, as their visual script duplicated both the dispositions of the decorated charters and the traditional, recognizable array of royal ideological imagery (Intro. fig. 5).[25] While visually embodied, illuminated letters presented charters as royal scripture. Imbued with the king's power and continuing presence, their literal illustration of documentary dispositions suggests an aesthetic iteration of diplomatic discourse, a recapitulation that situated textual dispositions within the spatial circumstances of their occurrences. Thus, the decorated letter mediates, and indeed translates, the impact and reception of words. In so doing, illuminated charters manifested the power of the letter, at once the necessary component of words and discourse and an index of their referential axes.

Epilogue: Lifelines and the Life of Lines

One cannot smoke a painting of a pipe, however realistically it might be depicted. One can, however, read painted letters. Painted letters are as real as written letters, and it is not possible to distinguish between the two forms in the way that an artifactual pipe fundamentally differs from its painted image.[26] With this incisive observation, Tim Ingold cuts through the knots that philosophers have, since Michel Foucault,[27] laboriously tightened around René Magritte's painting *Ceci n'est pas une pipe*. Whereas Foucault insisted that Magritte's work illustrated the incommensurable natures of word and image, between the said and the seen, Ingold demonstrates the protean nature of letters, celebrating their expressive potential beyond linguistic and discursive boundaries. Every letter is but a representation of itself, and as such it may be drawn and written, at once script and image. In modern epistemologies, overestimations of both writing and the importance of images have led to a separation between drawing and writing.[28] Yet, when writing cannot be clearly distinguished from the art of drawing and sculpting letters, as in the calligraphic and epigraphic products of Hebrew, Arabic, Greek, and Latin script presented in this volume, writing must be understood as a handicraft, and the perception of written texts may shift from an emphasis on linguistic compositions to a recognition of the work of the hand.[29] One of the goals of this volume is to pause before considering the reference, meaning, or agency of scripted material so as to capture the moment when the hand drew the letters, remembering them not only as shapes but also as gestures of devotion, worship, ritualistic performance, public statement, and cosm(et)ic illumination. In Aztec scrolls, scribes traced speech acts with lines and signs that track rhythms and movements rather than forms.[30] Byzantine monograms engage visibility, or representational arrangements, but they challenge readability, or the signifying arrangement.[31]

Is it therefore redundant to speak of script as image? Only to a point. The essays gathered in this volume compel a recognition that there were in fact different categories of imagistic

23 An analysis of early medieval French sealing practice, with relevant bibliography, is given in Brigitte M. Bedos-Rezak, *When Ego Was Imago: Signs of Identity in the Middle Ages* (Leiden, 2011), 75–94.

24 Recent studies of French royal illuminated charters include, in addition to those cited at note 22, Brigitte M. Bedos-Rezak, "Image as Patron: Convention and Invention in Fourteenth-Century France," in *Patrons and Professionals in the Middle Ages*, ed. Paul Binski and Elizabeth A. New, Harlaxton Medieval Studies 22 (Donington, UK, 2012), 216–36; Stephen Perkinson, *The Likeness of the King: A Prehistory of Portraiture in Late Medieval France* (Chicago and London, 2009), 231–38.

25 The charter illustrated in fig. 5 (January 1372, n. st.) contains King Charles V's certification that he made a gift of a fragment of the True Cross to his brother, John, duke of Berry. The charter's initial letter K is composed of the full standing figure of a crowned king, delivering with his right hand a cross to a kneeling recipient and holding with his extended left arm an angel playing viol. The charter is illustrated, transcribed, translated from Latin into French, and analyzed in Brunel, *Images du pouvoir royal*, 170–74, acte no. 25.

26 Tim Ingold, *Being Alive: Essays on Movement, Knowledge, and Description* (Florence, Ky., 2011), 177, 182–83, 195.

27 Michel Foucault, *Ceci n'est pas une pipe: Deux lettres et quatre dessins de René Magritte* (Montpellier, 1973), chapter 6.

28 Ingold, *Being Alive*, 177, 182–83, 195.

29 Ibid., 295.

30 See Boone, chap. 2.

31 See Eastmond, chap. 11.

INTRO. FIG. 6.

Augustine, *De doctrina christiana*, twelfth century. Cambrai, Bm, ms. 559, fol. 40v.

Photo IRHT, Base Enluminures, with kind permission of the Bibliothèque municipale of Cambrai. Médiathèque d'Agglomération de Cambrai. Cliché CNRS-IRHT.

letters.[32] Historiated initials not only frame or contain figural scenes, they form part of an overall *mise-en-page* from which both the initial and the scene derive additional significance. Lettered images (or imaged letters), which provide performance cues to readers, warp to inflect and create discursive meaning. Animated letters, formed by human, animal, vegetal, and artifactual bodies, are physically and semantically s(t)imulated by their components.[33] The lettristic letter remains a letter, however beautifully executed: referentially rigid, it can be a locus of mystical visions and speculations. Letters rendered as geometric symbols are aniconic and conceptual, with a capacity for negotiating the relationship between the physical and metaphysical. Granted that all premodern letters were the result of handiwork, there seems to emerge a division among alphabetic letters between those that change shape and those that remain more rigidly standardized. A shape-shifting letter becomes a unicum, contaminated by materiality and de-signed so that its abstract, conventional meaning is superseded and its signifying efficacy redirected away from the phonetic and toward the visual, the physical, and the gestural. Letters inscribed calligraphically remain within the phonetic economy of conventional meaning. Their calligraphy draws attention to their aesthetic and other formal qualities, and as such they operate visually, endowing the words they shape with extralinguistic meaning. The alphabetic letter, thus, may not be so very far from the ideogram.[34]

32 As noted by Ben C. Tilghman, "The Shape of the Word: Extralinguistic Meaning in Insular Display Lettering," in Hamburger, *Iconicity of Script*, 292–308, at 293, who distinguishes the historiated initial, the animated letter, and the geometric aniconic letter.

33 We borrow this expression from the title of Kendrick's book, *Animating the Letter*.

34 This point is made in Christin, *L'image écrite ou la déraison graphique*, 5, where the author states that the effectiveness of writing, whether ideographic or alphabetic, derives

The imaginative appeal of letters as contiguous to life forces is evident in their designs as humans, birds, fish, and plants. The hand-drawn imagistic letter had the perceived advantage of a mimetic and indexical connection with things and with the body. It speaks not of words but of physical presence, not as an arbitrary character but as a trace left by a hand. In the early eighth-century Echternach Gospels, we even see initial letters ending in spiral designs that look like human fingerprints.[35] Such letters mimic the human body, presenting themselves as traces of physical contact and perpetuating bodily lines. As a living force, the letter could even be perceived as a killer. Scholars of premodern Christian cultures tell us that not only did these groups harbor a distrust of images but also of words and letters. Christian readings of Scripture sought spiritualized interpretations that might cut through the "killing letter" (2 Cor. 3:6) of the Old Testament texts to liberate their spiritual sense. In a twelfth-century manuscript of Augustine's *De doctrina christiana,* a carefully designed letter H introduces the fourth book (Intro. fig. 6),[36] in which Augustine

explains that a literal interpretation of Scripture subjects understanding to the flesh, killing the soul and reducing man to a beast. The upright of the H is formed by the soft, exposed, human body; a dragon's body fashions the curves of the letter. The human being has been beaten by the dragon and shows early signs of bestiality (his feet have turned to claws) even as he struggles against the dragon and liberates a small dove, perhaps the spirit of the letter.[37]

Thus, there remains a medieval conundrum about writing: on the one hand, anything that complicated the function of the letter as sign of the sound of a spoken word, any deformation of the letter's shape through the incorporation of pictorial signs, might be perceived as inappropriate by certain medieval intellectuals. On the other hand, alphabetic writing could be experienced as empty and anonymous, in the sense that it presumed to substitute a sign and a signification different from the signified subject. And yet a third perception, especially of the Abrahamic, religions of the book, was that the written word was divinely released. Whatever the ambiguities of letters and of images, they all issued from the gestural act of drawing lines that double as life lines.

from the fact that writing is an image. Cf. C. Sirat, *Writing as Handwork* (Turnhout, 2006).

35 BnF, Lat. 9389, fol. 177r; illustrated and discussed in Kendrick, *Animating the Letter,* 18.

36 Cambrai, Bm, ms. 559, fol. 40v; illustrated in Kendrick, *Animating the Letter,* 133, fig. 63.

37 See the excellent analysis of Kendrick, in *Animating the Letter,* 133.

The Iconicity of Script

Visible/Legible

An Iconic Typology of Writing

ANNE-MARIE CHRISTIN[†]

TRANSLATED BY STEFANIE GOYETTE

W HAT PLACE MUST BE GIVEN TO THE LETTERS OF OUR GRECO-LATIN alphabet in relation to other signs of writing, if we consider exclusively their *visual* aspect? This is a question that I have asked myself, not about the scripted letter, but about the printed letter.[1] The response is the same in both cases: no attempt has been made to consider the letter as a visual sign, or, to put it even more frankly, the concept of the letter as a visual entity does not exist. The letter necessarily possesses a figure, but this figure finds itself neutralized and nullified by the purely linguistic concept that rules it. Were not the shapes of Greek letters borrowed from the Phoenicians proof that their form has no specificity or relevance in and of itself? The Greek alphabet would even come to symbolize the vanity of the systems that preceded it, all of which were burdened by image and by decorative frivolities, and from which it was possible to extract a minimalist design. At least, this was the point of view of linguists and semioticians in the 1970s, whose theory echoes others disseminated throughout Western history. The most radical among these theories belongs to the Romans, who were convinced that their writing was a "representation of the word," or, in a certain sense, its reflection. We know what destructive forces followed in the wake of such a conviction, ravaging the very analysis of the image itself and condemning this analysis to structural dissection in order to "make sense."

The first cause to be defended in such a context is that of the *support* of the image or text, to demonstrate that such support is not the "open window through which history can be observed," as Leon Battista Alberti wrote in his treatise *On Painting*, but rather a concrete and reactive presence, the principal factor in the legibility of the written.[2] This is what I attempted to prove for a long time, before turning to the letter and the question of the "figure."[3] Today, the problem arises in a different

---

1 [Translator's note: An earlier synthesis of the argument presented here appeared in French in Anne-Marie Christin, "Pour une typologie iconique de l'écriture: L'Imaginaire lettré," *Inmunkwahak: The Journal of the Humanities* (Institut des Humanités de l'Université Yonsei à Séoul) 99 (2013): 5–32.]

2 Leon Battista Alberti, *De pictura* (1435); French translation by Jean Louis Schefer, *De la peinture* (Paris, 1992).

3 The argument defended here represents the latest stage of my research on writing and its iconic origins, a project born from a critical reflection on the diverse theories of writing current in the 1970s. The initial findings of my research can be found in *L'image écrite ou la déraison graphique* (Paris, 1995; repr. 2001), followed by *Poétique du blanc: Vide et intervalle dans la civilisation de l'alphabet* (Paris, 2000; repr. 2009), and *L'invention de la figure* (2011). See also "The First Page," trans. Sarah Linford, *European Review* 8, no. 4 (October 2000): 457–66, http://www.ceei.univ-paris7.fr/07_ressource/01/document/the_first_page.pdf (accessed 16 January 2015); and "From Image to Writing," in *A History of Writing, From Hieroglyph to Multimedia*, ed. A.-M. Christin (Paris, 2002), 8–14,

setting, and presents itself in a new way. In the great debate that currently pits the defenders of a "humanist" conception of art—originating in the Italian Renaissance—against those who advocate opening art to other cultural models, following Aby Warburg and certain anthropologists, it is surprising to note that the plural nature of writing systems is never discussed or even mentioned. The fact that writing played a determining role in the elaboration of the idea of "civilization," whence the very notion of "art" was deduced, is recognized by all. The role of writing was explicitly noted in the Renaissance by Alberti himself, who suggested apprenticeship in writing as a training model for painters:

> I should like youths who first come to painting to do as those who are taught to write. We teach the latter by first separating all the forms of the letters which the ancients called elements. Then we teach the syllables, next we teach how to put together all the words. Our pupils ought to follow this rule in painting. First of all they should learn how to draw the outlines of the planes well. Here they would be exercised in the elements of painting. They should learn how to join the planes together. Then they should learn each distinct form of each member and commit to memory whatever differences there may be in each member.[4]

For contemporary anthropologists, the notion of "primitive art," inherited from Franz Boas, cannot be understood except in opposition to the art of written culture. Yet this written culture, whether exalted or challenged, must be that of the West, since the notion of art itself is born of it. Such a concept is foreign to, for example, Chinese and Japanese cultures. The conception of writing to which these cultures gave birth must therefore be fundamentally different from the system that is practiced the West: the alphabet. Yet no scholars affirm that this is the case.

Nevertheless, the fact is that this alphabet, which Alberti used as a model for painting as if it constituted a universal system (an opinion one could still reasonably hold in his time), and which modern-day devotees of primitive art continue to promote indirectly, is the system least suited for the image. In relation to the ideogram—whether it be Egyptian, Chinese, or Mayan—which, in order to reconstitute a verbal meaning, plays with its graphic forms, its lines, and its relationship with the surface on which it is inscribed, the letter of the Greco-Latin alphabet is effectively nothing more than the graphic transcription of a phoneme. It is the figure of an element (*stoicheion*), according to the definition proposed by Plato in the *Theaetetus*, which was then continually taken up in Greece and in the Latin world, in parallel with *gramma* or *littera*. Moreover, it should be noted that *stoicheion* is the same term used by Alberti in *On Painting*. What lessons might the letter have to offer us on the image, particularly on the subject of "art"? The only "iconic" imperative to which the letter must submit itself is that of being distinctive. With regard to the layout of letters in text, their linear succession—necessary to make verbal sense of the text's phonetic substrate and to suggest by analogy the continuity of a statement—makes a limited, even reductive, use of the physical space offered by its support. The iconic space is first and foremost a place of random crossings and multiple poles formed by the ascenders, descenders, and other physical features of letters, determined as much by the material of the surface (stone, paper, screen, etc.) as by the necessity of visual expression. This space can certainly welcome the artificial, even dictatorial, currents of the alignment of the letters reflecting the thread of a statement; but this rigidity is foreign to the vocation of the writing space itself.

With these competing goals in mind, we can better understand why, first, the opposition between oral and written cultures initially appeared in the civilization of the alphabet: it

---

originally published as *Histoire de l'écriture: De l'idéogramme au multimedia* (Paris, 2001; 2nd ed., Paris, 2012).

4 Leon Battista Alberti, *On Painting*, trans. John R. Spencer (New Haven, 1970). For the French, see Schefer, *De la peinture* (n. 2 above), 217: "Je voudrais que ceux qui débutent dans l'art de peindre fassent ce que je vois observé par ceux qui enseignent à écrire. Ils enseignent d'abord séparément tous les caractères des éléments, apprennent ensuite à composer les syllabes, puis enfin les expressions. Que nos débutants suivent donc cette méthode en peignant. Qu'ils apprennent séparément d'abord le contour des surfaces—que l'on peut dire les éléments de la peinture—, puis les liaisons des surfaces, enfin les formes de tous les membres."

is here that such opposition finds its theoretical reason for being and its justification. The written alphabet is the graphic version of the oral; we owe this belief to the Romans. Second, such a summary analysis cannot be fully credited, since it ignores the writing systems of two-thirds of the planet. Most of these excluded writing systems display a subtle complementarity between the oral and the iconic, whence "primitive art" must have drawn—and must still draw—a great part of its inspiration, and of which the alphabet is an orphan. This second observation leads to a third. Even though painters were frustrated and disappointed with alphabetic motifs, they also found in them a space of experimentation and an exceptional richness, since they were free to reintroduce letters into the universe of the visible where their place was unknown and still unexplored. Thus, it is not the system of the alphabetic letter but its practice that we must investigate if we want to address its visual values and situate them among those of other writing systems. To return to Plato, the letter must be imagined as *eikon* (created image), not as *eidolos* (appearance), to understand the originality and the necessity of its visual functions.

In his 1972 article in the *Dictionnaire encyclopédique des sciences du langage*, Tzvetan Todorov attempted a linguistic typology of writing. This typology misunderstood writing's visual aspect, artificially linking its genesis to the "determinatives" (or "keys")—which can be deciphered but not pronounced—on the pretext that "such a categorization evidently presupposes a logical analysis of language," or risks affirming that "all logography is born from the impossibility of a generalized iconic representation." Nevertheless, the article concludes by expressing the necessity of elaborating "a *grammatology*, or science of writing," in which one task would be to establish "a typology of graphic principles and techniques."[5] Though interesting, the enunciative rigor of linguistic categories has no equivalent in the world of images. On the contrary, what characterizes images is their heterogeneous combination of a support, which has multiple

origins, and of more or less enigmatic figures. This will be demonstrated below. As for the messages that these images may be charged with delivering, their meaning rests above all on the interpretation of the viewer. Here, the recipient is in charge. Stéphane Mallarmé understood this well: "The poet . . . awakens, in writing, the master of ceremonies of everyone's private feast day."[6] In the magic of written text, the act of writing is less important than that of reading, and the spoken word has no power.

Visible/Legible

It seems to me that a visual typology must be approached though an examination of the written phenomenon from the perspective of its legibility. "Visible" and "legible" are parallel and closely linked to one another; their differences lie only in the particular application of each term. "Visible" refers to a process, to the general and spectacular mode of "becoming visible." It is of the order of *revelation*. "Art does not reproduce the visible, it makes visible": it is with this formula that Paul Klee opened the era of contemporary art.[7] The "legible" also stems from revelation, but in a more specific way, through the combination of a visible that is immediately accessible with a more elusive reference, which also renders the visible more familiar. The revelation that the legible offers is not on the order of amazement or surprise, but of reminiscence. While the visible owes its efficacy and its allure to the enigmatic effect engendered by novelty, the legible draws its power from the mnemonic association that arises between the visual dispositive, which at first seems accidental or gratuitous, and the graphic structure that causes meaning to be abruptly discovered or rediscovered within it. It is certainly not by chance that the spectacle of the starry sky and the visual

5 Translation of Tzvetan Todorov, "Écriture," in Oswald Ducrot and Tzvetan Todorov, *Dictionnaire encyclopédique des sciences du langage* (Paris, 1972), 249–56.

6 "Le Poëte . . . éveille, par l'écrit, l'ordonnateur de fêtes en chacun." Stéphane Mallarmé, "Stages and Pages," in *Divagations*, trans. Barbara Johnson (Cambridge, Mass., 2007), 163. Translation of Stéphane Mallarmé, "Planches et feuillets," in *Divagations* (1897), Gallimard, coll. "Poésie" (Paris, 1976), 230.

7 Paul Klee, *Schöpferische Konfession*, ed. Kasimir Edschmid (Berlin, 1920), trans. in idem, "Creative Credo," in *Theories of Modern Art: A Source Book by Artists and Critics*, ed. Herschel B. Chipp (Berkeley, 1968), 182–86.

rationality imposed on it by the organization of the constellations haunted the first civilizations of writing, and that they located nearly all their foundational myths in the stars.

But space and its graphic networks are not the only components of the legible. Also in play is the intelligence of the journey, very different from the purely verbal intelligence of history. While the modalities of this reading were still ambiguous in the painting of Nicolas Poussin, Paul Valéry made them explicit:

> The painter disposes colored pigments on a plane and he must use their lines of separation, thicknesses, harmonies, and contrasts to express himself. The spectator only sees a more or less faithful representation of flesh, gesture, landscape, things he might see through the window of a museum . . . I believe, notwithstanding, that the surest method of judging a painting is to begin by identifying nothing, and then to proceed step by step to make a series of inductions that is necessitated by the presence at the same moment of a number of colored spots within a given order to rise from metaphor to metaphor, from supposition to supposition, to a knowledge of the subject—sometimes only to a consciousness of pleasure—that one has not always had to begin with.[8]

Examples, both literary and pictorial, can also be found in Eugène Fromentin, Paul Verlaine, or Paul Klee—such examples of this journey of visual intelligence are founded as much on

imagination as on observation.[9] Even more important for this hypothetical argument is the confirmation added by the specialists of prehistory, particularly Denis Vialou in his article opening the new edition of the *Histoire de l'écriture*.[10]

The Inscribed before the Written

One of the principal objectives of Vialou's article is to show that the surface of inscription is not sufficient to define the support on which man carved or drew his first figures. Such a support must also, and more importantly, be defined by the natural context in which it is situated. Everything begins at this point in the history of images: a given society's choice of a particular place to stage the creation of an image or a text. This choice of space is likely influenced by chance, such as a stopping point in a journey, but also represents the discovery of a suitable surface. The subterranean cave wall, for example, is a particular surface within a particular space that may be offered to the gaze of all or accessible only to certain individuals. This unity of space, surface, shelter, and temporality that produces the image incites other journeys, whether physical or purely visual, to be created or appropriated. Prehistoric paintings are not born of an artist's whim or by chance, they participate intimately in the profound movement of social and cultural innovation that marks the true beginning of the human adventure: "The emergence of systems of graphic representation accompanies and amplifies social and economic changes," emphasizes Vialou.

> Societies render themselves autonomous in relation to their original cultural roots. . . . Prehistoric art affirms their identity and symbolizes the appropriation of their territories. . . . The more new spaces that are conquered or acquired by a growing number of

---

8   "Le peintre dispose sur un plan des pâtes colorées dont les lignes de séparation, les épaisseurs, les fusions et les heurts doivent lui servir à s'exprimer. Le spectateur n'y voit qu'une image plus ou moins fidèle de chairs, de gestes, de paysages, comme par quelque fenêtre du mur du musée. . . . Je crois cependant que la méthode la plus sûre pour juger une peinture, c'est de n'y rien reconnaître d'abord et de faire pas à pas la série d'inductions que nécessite une présence simultanée de taches colorées sur un champ limité, pour s'élever de métaphores en métaphores de suppositions en suppositions à l'intelligence du sujet, parfois à la simple conscience du plaisir, qu'on n'a pas toujours eu d'avance." Paul Valéry, "Introduction to the Method of Leonardo da Vinci," in *Selected Writings,* trans. Malcom Cowley (New York, 1950), 89–107, at 104. Paul Valéry, *Introduction à la méthode de Léonard de Vinci* (Paris, 1894; repr. 1957), 53–54.

9   For a more detailed commentary of the process of visual appropriation, see my chapter "Enigmes du parcours," in *L'invention de la figure,* 51–72.

10   Trans. of Denis Vialou, "L'inscrit, avant l'écrit," in *Histoire de l'écriture,* ed. Anne-Marie Christin (Paris, 2001; repr. 2012), 16–24.

differentiated societies, the more territories tend to be marked and thus delimited.[11]

One of the consequences of this move toward sociocultural autonomy and diversification consisted in the selection of particular supports for the image:

> The open range of specificities for parietal spaces, buildings, or furniture shows their active, explicit implications, in terms of graphic construction, or their implicit significance, in the realm of the perception of graphic spaces. There is no case where the relations between the works and their ground are neutral. The parietal space is thus constitutive of the graphic space; stated in a different way, graphic space allows representations and their grounds to communicate with one another.[12]

Prehistoric man did not decide to inscribe a figure on stone because it is a stable, durable material. This was not his priority. What was important to him in the first place was to orient a surface toward the human life around it and to give it a status related to the human presence evolving before it. The initial function of this inscribed figure was to introduce a socialized visual coherence into the natural order, into the interior of a space or of a place, a coherence that a human group wanted to associate to it. The purpose was also to borrow material from this space. The inscribed figure was born from its support not only because of this space's screenlike ability to recede into invisibility as it transformed all trace or form into revelatory vision but also because it was a physically identifiable presence, a provocation to the gaze and to the hand. The screen itself incited the creation of forms for which it could be the instigator. Here, space and time belong first to the stone upon which they are drawn and reinvented. Moreover, the figure that takes form there, far from appearing as the substitute of an absent reality, is full of reality itself. But it is a reality that owes everything to abstraction, or more specifically to the illusion of abstraction, as if prehistoric man better appreciated the lessons of the stone than those of the living nature that he recreated: the continuity of the line, like the realism that a modern gaze expects from it, was not at all important to him. Further still, as Vialou points out, the first figurative inscriptions are fragmentary and discontinuous:

> In most cases, animal figuration is reduced to an anatomical segment, head, horns or antlers, paws or hooves. . . . These synecdoches attest a superior degree of the figurative abstraction that characterizes the animal art of Prehistory, even while the stylistic expression of the Magdalanian bestiary would lead us to expect an exceptionally high level of naturalism.[13]

First Generation: Writing Invented

These graphic synecdoches render the appearance of writing conceivable, the graphic figure constituting a kind of preconceived interface—and an ideal interface—between language and image, even before it was possible to imagine

11 "L'émergence des systèmes de représentations graphiques accompagne et amplifie (les) changements sociaux et économiques. . . . Les sociétés s'autonomisent par rapport à leur enracinement culturel originel. . . . L'art préhistorique affirme leur identité et symbolise l'appropriation de leurs territoires. . . . Plus de nouveaux espaces sont conquis ou acquis par un nombre croissant de sociétés différenciées, plus les territoires ont tendance à être davantage marqués et donc délimité." Denis Vialou, "Images préhistoriques: Écritures par défaut?" in *Actes du Forum International d'Inscriptions, de calligraphies et d'écritures dans le monde à travers les âges, 24–27 Avril 2003, Bibliotheca Alexandrina*, ed. Ismail Serageldine (Alexandria, 2007), 28–31.

12 "L'éventail ouvert des spécificités des espaces pariétaux, immeubles ou mobiliers, montre leurs implications actives, explicites, dans la construction graphique, ou implicites dans la perception des espaces graphiques. En aucun cas, les relations entre les œuvres et leurs supports ne paraissent neutres. L'espace pariétal est donc constitutif de l'espace graphique; autrement dit, l'espace graphique met en correspondance spatiale les représentations avec leurs supports." Ibid., 32.

13 "Très souvent, la figuration animale est réduite à un segment anatomique, tête, cornes ou ramures, pattes ou sabots. . . . Ces synecdoques témoignent d'un degré supérieur de l'abstraction figurative qui caractérise l'art animalier de la Préhistoire, plus généralement que ne le fait accroire l'expression stylistique du bestiaire magdalénien d'un exceptionnel haut niveau naturaliste." Vialou, "L'inscrit, avant l'écrit," 18. [Editor's note: In prehistoric art, the Magdalenian culture (ca. 15,000–10,000 BCE) refers to a late period of the Upper Paleolithic in western Europe, during which cave painting received its most exquisite treatment, as exemplified by the parietal art, pictographs, and drawings found in Lascaux (France) and Altamira (Spain).]

a program capable of putting them together. To later inventors, this interface made available a fragmentation of representation, assuring graphic autonomy to the figure in relation to reality, completed by the critical suggestion of its outline (choice of profile or frontal view, etc.). The interface also proposed, simultaneously, the corollary of this fragmentation: the ability to combine the elements that it selected and united, which could then become bearers (or not) of a new meaning. This graphic conjunction was used in the service of mythological visual memory. It was possible to substitute words and language for drawing, which would be the case with writing. This is why the fantastic figure was first in the order of graphic creation: because figural creation arises from the fantastic.

This malleability of the figure, its openness to the imaginary, endowed it with an exceptional capacity for welcoming that which was foreign to it. It also made "writing" possible, since the notion of combining image with language did not yet exist, and consequently graphism was itself open to the imaginary. Attesting to this is the determining role that the genesis of the first writing systems played—in particular in Egyptian and Mayan civilizations—in the iconic transposition of the names of gods or important persons. In these cases, written language was a kind of homage rendered to the invisible world where the spoken word has no place, but whence revelation, power, and the possibility of divination are born. The fact that most of these names were composed of sentences or of fragments of a sentence helped to inspire the idea that a transfer was possible from one mode of expression to the other, from the verbal formula to the iconic assemblage.[14]

There are other types of intermediary practices at work between writing and "raw" image and language. Writing combines image and language in sentences and in texts. But their connection consists of precarious formulas that leave all autonomy to the language to exploit

some of its symbolic values in a merely incidental fashion and to apply these to the image. It is not possible to give a status to such attempts, or even to identify criteria that could define such a status. Yet some paths are offered to us in historical writings by way of certain strategies to which these writings owe their first appearance, which we might term "signs of beginning." For example, it is clear that the variable, changeable potentialities of the ideogram—going from the logogram to phonogram or determinative—derive from its initial and polyvalent vocation as a figure. Egyptian hieroglyphic writing is rich in such slippages, born of an accumulation of meanings that have different origins but that all converge in the same figure.[15] It can thus be legitimately deduced that, in the context of oral cultures, every iterative, polysemous figure is charged with a value as a type of pregraphemic "sign." This phenomenon seems widespread in Dogon culture, if we can judge by the tracings made by Geneviève Calame-Griaule and Pierre-Francis Lacroix.[16] This is the case for the sinusoidal line (or line of chevrons). There are an impressive number of diverse interpretations to which this line lends itself: "It is at once the symbol of water, of the snake, of light, of the word, of germination, of weaving, etc." All these interpretations, however, are assembled around a single core of meaning: "In a more general sense, the line of chevrons is the symbolic representation of the concept of undulating movement in the form of a spiral; this element is common to all of the sign's possible meanings, which should be classified as belonging to the same symbolic category."[17]

14 A comparative analysis of the different modalities of transcription of the proper name in civilizations of the ideogram and of the alphabet can be found in Anne-Marie Christin, ed., *L'écriture du nom propre,* Actes du colloque du Centre d'étude de l'écriture et de la Bibliothèque nationale de France (Paris, 1998).

15 In particular, see Pascal Vernus, "Ecriture du rêve et écriture hiéroglyphique," in "L'instance de la lettre," special issue of *Littoral* 7, no. 8 (1983): 27–32.

16 Geneviève Calame-Griaule and Pierre-Francis Lacroix, "Graphies et signes africains," *Semiotica* 1, no. 3 (1969): 256–72; repr. in Simon Battestini, ed., *De l'écrit africain à l'oral, le phénomène graphique africain* (Paris, 2006), 273–290.

17 Ibid. (*Semiotica* [1969]: 270): "'Elle est le symbole à la fois de l'eau, du serpent, de la lumière, de la parole, de la germination, du tissage, etc.' Toutes ces interprétations se rassemblent pourtant en un seul noyau de sens: 'D'une façon plus générale, la ligne de chevrons est la représentation symbolique du concept de mouvement ondulatoire en forme de spirale, qui est l'élément commun à toutes les significations possibles du signe et leur vaut d'être classées dans la même catégorie symbolique.'"

The conclusion to which this statement leads the two authors reflects the confusion that may have afflicted the observers of "non-written" cultures in a scholarly context (the article dates from 1969), which was dominated by linguistics and the alphabetic model, such as it was understood by Ferdinand de Saussure (1857–1913). However, their conclusion also constitutes a completely new way of thinking about writing and its origins:

> It should be noted that here we are dealing with a system proceeding in a direction diametrically opposed to that of a true writing system, the latter generally participating in a pictographic stage before arriving at a simplified sign that is more or less emptied of its concrete content. The concern is different; for the Dogon, as for the Bambara, the drawing was a preliminary study in the creation of the world; the divine's sketch (*dessin du divin*) of a thing precedes that thing's existence, just as a thought is elaborated in the mind before being expressed in speech.[18]

The invention of writing, which proceeds in long stages depending on the civilization—in Egypt, five hundred years separate the appearance of noun phrases and the constitution of a true hieroglyphic system—has nowhere caused the image to be eliminated completely, or even set aside. On the contrary, each culture bears witness to the emergence of a form of iconic reinvention related to its writing system and to the dominant mode of communication—verbal or visual. This reinvention itself privileges one aspect or another of the image: ground, figure, or graphic style. In Mesopotamia, where the verb is dominant, written text and image border on and complete one another on the same support following certain norms, the history of which would be an invaluable discovery. Jean-Marie Durand made a first analysis of this subject in 1979.[19] In Egypt, the figure retains the values proper to it, whatever the nature—be it textual or iconic—of the inscription that receives it. Recourse to the rebus rests upon this multivalence, as Pascal Vernus has shown.[20] In China, the story is different yet again, perhaps owing to the fact that the "line" is conceived as a natural property by which man can only be inspired:

> In ancient times, Pao Xi reigned over the world. Raising his eyes, he gazed upon the shapes in the sky and, lowering his eyes, he contemplated the phenomena on the earth. He considered the marks (*wen*) visible on the bodies of birds and animals, as well as the advantageous placements offered by the earth.... He then began to create the eight trigrams in order to communicate with the power of the infinite Potency.[21]

Further, the path of calligraphy, newly forged by Chinese letters, is undoubtedly the most sophisticated writing system of all. It is at the origin of a form of visual creation stemming from the third generation of writing.

Second Generation: Writing Reinvented

The relationships between the first and second generations of writing belong to the order of opposition, even of rupture. These terms must not be confused. The succession from one to the other has no chronology except the order of filiation that links the second system to that from which it was born; it is not necessarily inscribed in a historical continuum. Egyptian and Mayan

---

18 Ibid., 270: "Il est à remarquer que nous avons affaire ici à un système procédant dans un sens diamétralement opposé à celui d'une véritable écriture, celle-ci partant généralement du stade pictographique pour aboutir à un signe simplifié et à peu près vidé de son contenu concret. La préoccupation est en effet différente; chez les Dogon, comme pour les Bambara, le dessin a été une étude préliminaire dans la création du monde; le tracé du divin d'une chose précède son existence, de même que la pensée s'élabore dans l'esprit avant de s'exprimer par la parole."

19 See Jean-Marie Durand, "Texte et image à l'époque néo-assyrienne," in *Dire, Voir, Ecrire: Le texte et l'image*, special issue of *Textuel* 6 [= *Textuel 34/44*] (1979): 15–22.

20 I refer here specifically to the articles written by Pascal Vernus for my *Histoire de l'écriture*: "Les écritures de l'Egypte ancienne" and "Adaptation de l'écriture au monument," 52–73.

21 "Dans les temps anciens, Pao Xi régna sur le monde. Levant les yeux, il contempla les figurations qui sont dans le ciel et, baissant les yeux, contempla les phénomènes qui sont sur la terre. Il considéra les marques (*wen*) visibles sur le corps des oiseaux et des animaux ainsi que les dispositions avantageuses offertes par la terre.... Il commença alors à créer les huit trigrammes afin de communiquer avec le pouvoir de l'Efficience infinie." *Zhouyi, Xici*, II, §2, cited by François Jullien, "A l'origine de la notion chinoise de littérature," *Extrême-Orient-Extrême-Occident* 3 (1983): 48.

hieroglyphics, separated from one another by two millennia, belong to the same first generation of writing systems, just as the Greek alphabet, which appeared in the eighth century BCE, and the Japanese system, which gained its autonomy about twenty centuries later, both belong to the second. What the second-generation writing systems have in common, and what essentially characterizes them, is that they are born from societies in which writing participates in an official and institutional fashion in the cultural environment and its memory in the same way as oral language and the image. All second-generation writing is, by its nature and by principle, metawriting. It does not result from an objective or logical process. This is because all reinvention of writing responds first to specific sociocultural and linguistic needs. It is also because these new writing systems continue to participate in the unstable, vagabond, simultaneous universe of the legible/visible. Whether a written language is always deciphered or is only seen without being understood, as must have long been the case with the hieroglyphic system for users of the Greek and then Latin alphabets, first-generation writing inevitably intervenes as a partner, objective or imaginary, in verbo-visual communication and in the creation of iconic and textual systems that succeeded it. The art of memory is a notable example of these involuntary reinterpretations of a system that was no longer understood, but which people attempted to appropriate long afterward.[22]

A particularly revelatory parallel can be posited between the Japanese system and the Greco-Latin alphabet. While the latter broke away from the systems that preceded it by transforming writing into a pure "phonological code," the former chose not only to remain within the circle of influence belonging to Chinese ideography, but also to distinguish itself by respecting the principle of its duality through visual escalation. The

entire history of the Japanese system shows that it allows, or even solicits, mixing Chinese ideograms (*kanji*) with the syllabaries of Japanese origin (*katakana* and *hiragana*). As a whole, the Japanese system provides keys for complementary reading without excluding foreign systems, such as the alphabet, in the case of citations. Another revealing trait is that while opting for the phonetic transparence of the syllabary for the transcription of their language, the Japanese endeavored to maintain transparency in the expressive mobility proper to written language. Katakana and hiragana, if they are pronounced the same way, nonetheless still reveal two different messages when read in graphic form. The first retains the rigidity of Chinese written style—currently used only for the transcription of foreign words or names—while the second, which appeared in the eleventh century, is inspired by the fluid calligraphic "grass-writing," and further accentuates this style's suppleness to underscore the originality of Japanese writing.

Beginning in the sixteenth century Western and Japanese civilizations came into contact with one another several times, and in each culture artists attempted to take the discoveries of the other as inspiration, without always being successful. This interaction allows us to better perceive the impact that the practice of a given writing system and the visual expertise that it engenders can have on the artistic production associated with it. While the distinctive function of the alphabetic letter led the West to endow its pictorial representation with the brutal illusion of *trompe l'oeil*,[23] Japan developed its own manner of blending and combining paintings, poems, and fans in the form of assemblages—or *harimaze*—placed on album pages and folding screens. With Ando Hiroshige (1797–1858), harimaze was raised to the status of a kind of original woodblock print. It also seems certain that the mobility of Japanese writing played a role in the creation of fans with multiple viewing possibilities, a practice which dates to the same era as the invention of hiragana (eleventh century). The great era of Japanese painting

22 It is known that the Greeks maintained regular relations with Egypt beginning in the sixth century BCE (for their colony in Naucratis). The hieroglyphic origins of the art of memory seem to have escaped the notice of Frances Yates, *The Art of Memory* (Chicago, 1966); French translation by Daniel Arasse, *L'Art de la mémoire* (Paris, 1975). I develop this subject further in the chapter "La mémoire blanche," in *Poétique du blanc* (Paris, 2009), especially 123–32.

23 On this subject, I permit myself to refer the reader to my chapter "La lettre et le réel" in Christin, *L'invention de la figure*, 73–96.

on screens in the sixteenth century, a practice closely related to painting fans, had its European equivalent in painting characterized by a central vanishing point, an "open window on history," whose theory is formalized at around the same time in reference to the alphabet.[24]

Third Generation: The Lettered Imagination

In the prolongation of first- or second-generation systems, but without focusing in this case on the invention of new systems, certain atypical creations emerged in literate circles. Such creations participate explicitly in the written, but expand their range outside the constraining domain of pure linguistics, becoming a type of return to the legible and to archaic sources in the pursuit of novel textual and aesthetic effects. The cultural effects of these systems were often lasting and profound. Chinese calligraphy is the most remarkable example of these creations, as much for the iconic richness of its style as for the powerful and innovative combinations that it introduced between nature and written texts through the technique of literati landscape painting.

The *Six Gentlemen* scroll, painted by Ni Zan in 1345, provides a particularly salient example of the three elements of literati landscape and their mutual powers of translation. Vertical or curved strokes, playing on the diverse possible nuances of the ink and inspired by calligraphic techniques, permit us to identify six different types of trees in the foreground rising higher than the far-off horizon, beyond which distant mountains can be seen. Integrated within the composition, the open central area of the scroll is transformed into space, depth, and water. But it still remains a support for writing, just as the stroke of the brush remains that of calligraphy, attested by the poems framing the landscape like so many textual figures. These figures are signs of another element of imagination: a description attracting the gaze to one or another aspect

of the painting, like the name, "gentlemen," which is given to the trees that appear in Huang Gongwang's poem, itself inscribed just above the images of these trees. The scroll is simultaneously a landscape and a support for poetry; real and imaginary are commingled in unique, white, mute matter. The scroll is a human work animated with "breath," the *ki*, which provides its creative force, but it is also the primordial vastness of space before creation.[25]

The entire history of the western book since the dawn of the manuscript is guided by the desire to rediscover this visual material of the written renounced by the alphabet but indispensable to its reading: illuminations, abbreviations, glosses, calligraphic strategies—these all seek to reintroduce an absent visibility to writing. The domain is at once immense and multitudinous. The notion of third-generation writing, as a new instrument of analysis, would allow us to better posit the richness and diversity of medieval creations.

In the transitional years at the end of the fifteenth century and at least by the beginning of the sixteenth century, humanist reading was confronted by three important discoveries: Egyptian hieroglyphs, printing (xylographic then typographic), and finally the literary affirmation of the vernacular languages and their circulation. These gave birth to two forms of third-generation writing. The first is inscribed in the continuity of the manuscript tradition: it is the rebus. Certainly, the messages contained in these rebuses are brief and modest, on the order of proverb, but they are no different from Mesopotamian or Egyptian proper nouns: they all translate the concern for visual expression, for the transmission of particular verbal formula through vision. In both cases, the desire to

---

24 A volume of collected essays on Japanese screens, under the provisional title *Par la brèche des nuages: Les paravents japonais,* which I edited, will appear in a French-English edition published by Flammarion. One of the major goals of this book is comparing the civilization of the painting and of the alphabet to that of the Japanese screen and mixed writing.

25 An echo of this technique can be found in Japan, in the attempt at an *ashide* (writing in the form of bulrushes) syllabary, in which the text is dispersed across a landscape. Marked by a ludic and popular point of view, yet another style, the *moji-e,* would take off somewhat later. These images in writing combine the calligraphic suppleness of *kana* with the figurative allusions of kanji. See Claire-Akiko Brisset, *A la croisée du texte et de l'image: Paysages cryptiques et poèmes cachés (ashide) dans le Japon classique et médiéval,* Collège de France, Institut des hautes études japonaises (Paris, 2009), and Marianne Simon-Oikawa, "Des images en écriture," in Christin, ed., *Histoire de l'écriture,* 153–55.

communicate the formula in parallel with and in a different manner from these two levels is added to the concern for visual expression. Only the motivation governing this choice differentiates the two concerns. As soon as the visual goals of "the inventors of writing" caused the statement of a proper noun to benefit from the surreal and enigmatic prestige of images, the rebus occupied itself with a double version of the same message, stemming in part from parody.

The appearance of typography seriously undermined the rebus. Recourse to movable type made possible the simultaneous and reasoned orchestration on the same page of multiple types of alphabets—capitals, minuscule, or italics—according to a principle comparable to that of the hiragana and the katakana, quite different from the capricious and experimental iconic imaginary of the manuscripts. In introducing the image at the heart of this textual marquetry, the emblem stands at the origin of a novel textual formula of figurative writing, since it is combined in close relation with the letter to second-generation writing systems. The poster designers of the nineteenth century pushed the experiment even further, inspired in part by Japanese woodblocks. "The poster, with its pithy phrases, invading the newspaper—it often makes me dream, like a new mode of speaking," wrote Mallarmé in the 1890s.[26] Is it not tempting to conclude that, inexorably, new technologies and computer science have begun to lay the foundation for a revolution of the same order? More than ever, the place of the legible in the image deserves to hold our attention.

26 "L'affiche, lapidaire, envahissant le journal—souvent elle me fit songer comme devant un parler nouveau." Stéphane Mallarmé, *La Musique et les Lettres* (1895), in *Igitur, Divagations, Un coup de dés* (Paris, 1976), 367. Translation in Christine Poggi, *In Defiance of Painting: Cubism, Futurism, and the Invention of Collage* (New Haven, 1992), 276.

Select Bibliography

In addition to the entries below, see the publications of the Centre d'étude de l'écriture et de l'image (CEEI), described and summarized at http://www.ceei.univ-paris7.fr/06_publication/index.html. Articles from *Textuel* refer to the journal maintained by the U.F.R. Sciences des textes et documents that has appeared under other names and titles, including *Textuel 34/44* and *Cahiers Textuel*.

Buschinger, Philippe, ed. "Écriture et typographie en Occident et en Extrême-Orient." *Textuel* 40 (2001).

Christin, Anne-Marie. "Narration and Visual Thought: Philippe Clerc's *Revues-Images*." Translated by Judith E. Preckshot. In *Conjunctions, Verbal-Visual Relations*, edited by Laurie Edson, 131–57. San Diego, 1996.

———. "A Picture-Poem from *Mains libres*." *Shantih* (Fall–Winter 1975): 19–21.

———. "Text and Image." Translated by Barbara Wright. *European Review* 3, no. 2 (1995): 119–29.

———. "Towards a Theory of Mixed Messages: The Experience of *l'immédiate*." Translated by Susan L. Rogers. *Word & Image* 3, no. 4 (October–December 1987): 292–304.

———. "A Visionary Book: Charles Nodier's *l'Histoire du roi de Bohême et de ses sept châteaux*." *Visible Language* 19, no. 4 (Autumn 1985): 462–82.

Christin, Anne-Marie, ed. *Dire, Voir, Ecrire: Le texte et l'image*, special issue of *Textuel* 6 (1979).

———. "Écrire, voir, conter." *Textuel* 25 (1993).

———. *L'Écriture du nom propre*. Actes du colloque international du Centre d'étude de l'écriture et de la Bibliothèque nationale de France. Paris, 1998.

———. *Écritures II*. Paris, 1985.

———. *Écritures III: Espaces de la lecture*. Actes du colloque de la Bibliothèque publique d'information, Centre Georges Pompidou, et du Centre d'étude de l'écriture, Université Paris 7. Paris, 1988.

———. "Écritures paradoxales." *Textuel* 17 (1985).

———. *Écritures, systèmes idéographiques et pratiques expressives*. Actes du colloque international de l'Université Paris 7. Paris, 1982.

———. "L'espace et la lettre." *Cahiers Jussieu* 3 (1977).

———. *Histoire de l'écriture: De l'idéogramme au multimedia*. Paris, 2001; 2nd ed., Paris, 2012.

———. *A History of Writing: From Hieroglyph to Multimedia*. Paris, 2002. [translation of previous]

Christin, Anne-Marie, and Atsushi Miura, eds. "La lettre et l'image: Nouvelles approches." *Textuel* 54 (2007).

Fraenkel, Béatrice, ed. *Illettrismes, Écritures IV*. Actes du colloque de 1991. Paris, 1994.

Prassoloff, Annie, and Danielle Hébrard, eds. "L'appropriation de l'oral." *Textuel* 7 (1990).

Renonciat, Annie, and Marianne Simon-Oikawa, eds. *La pédagogie par l'image en France et au Japon*. Rennes, 2009.

Sakai, Cécile, and Anne Kerlan-Stephens, eds. *Du visible au lisible: texte et image en Chine et au Japon*. Arles, 2006.

Simon-Oikawa, Marianne, ed. *L'Ecriture réinventée: formes visuelles de l'écrit en Occident et en Extrême-Orient*. Paris, 2007.

Pictorial Talking

The Figural Rendering of Speech Acts and Texts in Aztec Mexico

E L I Z A B E T H   H I L L   B O O N E

THE PICTOGRAPHIC WRITING SYSTEM EMPLOYED BY THE AZTECS AND their neighbors in central and southern Mexico in the centuries before the Spanish conquest (1521 CE) challenges our notions of writing and reading and our assumptions about image making and interpretation. The practitioners and users of Mexican pictography conceptualized it as a graphic system that recorded knowledge. It was developed not to replicate visually perceived forms in two dimensions, but to encode and preserve concepts and data with clarity and precision; for Pre-Columbian Mexicans it occupied the cultural category of writing, which in other cultures was and is occupied by alphabetic or hieroglyphic scripts. As the Franciscan friar Motolinia noted in 1541, Mexican pictography was "their way of writing, supplying their lack of an alphabet by the use of symbols."[1]

Except in appellatives, however, pictography does not usually record sounds and words, as do other writing systems; rather it is a semasiographic system that conveys meaning directly to the reader/viewer by means of graphic marks that signify within the conventions of its own system.[2] Its position as writing in a cultural sense, and as not-quite-writing in the sense that it does not generally record spoken language, puts it at odds with other glottographic (language-based recording) systems. Linguists and epigraphers looking to understand "the linguistic underpinnings that characterize the writing systems of the world" set aside pictography because it does not have the goal of recording speech or "meaningful sound."[3] The study of pictography draws on a different set of analytical tools than

1 Motolinia [Toribio de Benavente], *Motolinia's History of the Indians of New Spain*, ed. and trans. Francis Borgia Steck (Washington, D.C., 1951), 74.

2 From the Greek *semasia* or "meaning," as articulated by Ignace J. Gelb, *A Study of Writing* (Chicago, 1963), 11; Geoffrey Sampson, *Writing Systems* (Stanford, 1985), 26; and Elizabeth Hill Boone, "Introduction: Writing and Recording Knowledge," in *Writing without Words: Alternative Literacies in Mesoamerica and the Andes*, ed. Elizabeth Hill Boone and Walter Mignolo (Durham, 1994), 15, 18–22. Scholars who describe the glottographic nature (and phoneticism) of Mexican pictography concentrate only on the signs for personal names and places. See, for example, Henry B. Nicholson, "Phoneticism in the Late Pre-Hispanic Central Mexican Writing System," in *Mesoamerican Writing Systems*, ed. Elizabeth P. Benson (Washington, D.C., 1974), 1–46; Hanns J. Prem, "Aztec Writing," in *Epigraphy: Supplement to the Handbook of Middle American Indians*, vol. 5, ed. Victoria R. Bricker (Austin, 1992), 53–69; Alfonso Lacadena, "Regional Scribal Traditions: Methodological Implications for the Decipherment of Nahuatl Writing," *The PARI Journal* 8, no. 4 (2008): 1–23; Marc Zender, "One Hundred and Fifty Years of Nahuatl Decipherment," *The PARI Journal* 8, no. 4 (2008): 24–37; and Gordon Whittaker, "The Principles of Nahuatl Writing," *Göttinger Beiträge zur Sprachwissenschaft* 16 (2008): 47–81.

3 Stephen Houston, John Baines, and Jerrold Cooper, "Last Writing: Script Obsolescence in Egypt, Mesopotamia, and Mesoamerica," *Comparative Study of Society and History* 45 (2003): 430.

does the study of language-based, glottographic systems. Whereas analysis of glottographic systems, including the appellatives of Mexican pictography, relies on linguistic and epigraphic approaches that parse images into logograms (word signs) and phonograms (phonetic indicators and phonetic complements that specify reading value), analysis of pictography more generally employs the iconographic reading of conventional signs, an understanding of the context of their appearance, and a syntactic analysis of their spatial arrangement.[4]

Equally, pictography fits poorly within the cultural category of art and image making. Its figural images and symbols represent neither perceived forms nor idealized beings and structures within a picture plane. Rather, like letters and words, they signify by convention and operate within the complex graphic structure of an otherwise neutral, flat plane. Although pictography does employ figural images, these images are to be read conventionally and symbolically— more as glyphs than as depictions. In this way, pictography, although highly figural, stands in contrast to the mimetic figuration of Europe and Asia. Pictography thus complicates discussions of both writing and artistic practice in a global sense.

In this volume, which explores the unity and complementarity of script and image, the point of reference for most authors is script. The question for many is not when image becomes script, but how and why scripts are or become iconic, how they function as extralinguistic signifiers, or how figural images complicate and extend their semantic range. I approach the unity of sign and design from a different vantage, for the material I study is both a tightly structured collection of images and a script. My point of reference is the system of figural images, and my goal

is to look at the issues raised when such iconic images, which ordinarily function as nonlinguistic signs, are required to stretch beyond their normal state in order to record speech acts. Since Mexican pictography was not designed to render speech acts, when it does, this exertion pushes the boundaries of the pictographic canon.

My effort to find the linguistic in pictography resonates with, but inverts, the arguments of most of the other essays, which target the extralinguistic content of scripts. We all, however, are concerned with the complex signification of marks on specially prepared and framed surfaces. As Anne-Marie Christin points out, the letter of script is by nature both visible (as a graphic mark) and legible (as an expression of language) (see chap. 1). It is the visibility of the marks that extends their meaning beyond language. The monogram of Christ analyzed by Vincent Debiais, for example, becomes an autonomous symbol, syntactically functioning nominally or descriptively, as do some symbols in Mexican pictography (see chap. 7). The Byzantine epigrams examined by Ivan Drpić qualify the objects of their material support and structure human interaction with these objects, just as do iconic bands around Aztec monuments (see chap. 3). Thomas Cummins and I both approach the semiotic systems of indigenous Americans prior to the conquest and as they transitioned to alphabetic writing, but our perspectives and goals differ (see chap. 5). Whereas he features the wholesale absorption of Pre-Columbian signs into the literary corpus of the Roman alphabet, standing for Christian civilization and cultural superiority, I track adaptive changes within Mexican pictography itself as a system in flux.

Pictography usually represents speech by means of speech scrolls, which can be embellished graphically to characterize or specify the content of that speech. With or without the speech scrolls, pictography can also employ images to specify the content of speech acts and can replicate linear voicings of concepts and data. In this article I explore pictorial talking by looking first at the function and nature of speech scrolls. Then I analyze the content of speech acts as that content is signified graphically. Finally, I focus on sequential streams of iteration: linear streams of glyphs that parallel and cue spoken

4 For analysis of pictography, see Mary Elizabeth Smith, *Picture Writing from Ancient Southern Mexico: Mixtec Place Signs and Maps* (Norman, Okla., 1973); eadem, "The Mixtec Writing System," in *The Cloud People: Divergent Evolution of the Zapotec and Mixtec Civilizations*, ed. Kent V. Flannery and Joyce Marcus (New York and London, 1983), 238–45; Maarten Jansen, "Mixtec Pictography: Conventions and Contents," in Bricker, ed., *Epigraphy*, 20–33; and Elizabeth Hill Boone, *Stories in Red and Black: Pictorial Histories of the Aztecs and Mixtecs* (Austin, 2000). For analysis of glottographic systems, see Smith, "Mixtec Writing System," and note 2.

discourse. My attention moves from the simplest graphic indication of speech to the longest and most complex, and from pre-Hispanic Mexican pictography to its transformation in the early colonial period into a script capable of recording Catholic doctrinal orations with subtlety and nuance. Prior to this, however, it is useful to outline some of the principal features of pictography as an extralinguistic graphic system.

Mexican Pictography

Mexican pictography is like so many other writing systems in being composed of flat conventional marks that are arranged on a specially prepared discrete surface according to specific conventions. These special surfaces can be of stone, ceramic, or wood, but they are usually the flat planes of portable books. Meaning is conveyed both by the marks themselves and by their placement relative to each other on the plane. The marks are figural and are representational to the extent that they usually bear some resemblance or overt visual reference to what they signify, but they are not illusionistically realistic in describing optically perceived form. Like alphabetic written words, they are graphic abstractions of entities, qualities, events, times, locations, and sometimes sounds. These marks are spatially organized in a great variety of configurations, depending on the structural principles that govern the grammars of different literary genres.

Most pictographic signs are based on human and animal forms, sometimes fused together or with a variety of interchangeable parts, and are represented in a manner that displays the most characteristic features of the form and allows it to hold the most information. Max Verworn coined the term *ideoplastic* to describe such figures in early Egyptian and non-western art, meaning that the rendered form accords with the idea of the original form rather than its optical image; this term applies well to Mexican pictography.[5] An ideoplastic image is a stable and inert rendering of form that is understood and known rather than seen. Such is the

conventionally posed figure of the water goddess Chalchiutlicue (Jade Her Skirt) in a divinatory manual, where she is patron of a *trecena*, or thirteen-day period (fig. 2.1).[6] The figure's legs, arms, and head are simply attached to a profile torso without any effort to render the junctures anatomically. Thus the figure can be called paratactic, having discrete parts that are joined together without conjunctive transitions.[7] The fingers of the hands and the toes of the feet are not distinguished left from right. Her accoutrements—headdress, back device, nose ornament, earrings, elaborate pectoral, *huipil* (blouse), skirt, sandals, and the implements she holds forth—are all rotated so as best to represent their components and characteristics.

The complex pictographic image is also accretive and agglutinative, being composed of multiple visual elements that are added to a core. Chalchiutlicue's human form is an armature upon which are layered her many physical attributes and accoutrements. Agglutination is a principal characteristic of the grammar of Nahuatl, the language of the Aztecs, which relies on nominal and verbal words constructed into sentence words by adding multiple affixes to a stem.[8] This same packing on of separate meaningful elements to build a message can also be seen in pictography, and we should recognize that many complex pictographic images, such as this water goddess, likely function as figural sentences.

The relationship between these marks and what they signify belongs to the treacherous realm of iconography. Pictography has a sliding scale of indexicality, extending from the relatively straightforward picture on one end to the graphic articulation of nearly unfathomable metaphoric meaning on the other end. Within this scale one encounters representational abstractions of various sorts, symbols that

---

5 Max Verworn, *Ideoplastische Kunst: Ein Vortrag* (Jena, 1914).

6 *Codex Borbonicus, Bibliothèque de l'Assemblée Nationale–Paris (Y120)*, ed. Karl A. Nowotny and Jacqueline de Durand-Forest (Graz, 1974), 5

7 From the Greek *paratassein*, "to arrange side by side," as employed by Gerhard Krahmer to characterize early Egyptian figures painted or carved in relief: Krahmer, *Figur und Raum in der Ägyptischen und Griechisch-archaischen Kunst*, Hallesches Winckelmannsprogramm 28 (Halle, 1931), 8–10.

8 J. Richard Andrews, *Introduction to Classical Nahuatl* (Austin, 1975), xii.

FIG. 2.1.

The trecena governed by Chalchiutlicue covering the days 1 Reed through 13 Serpent, pictured with their supernatural patrons. Codex Borbonicus, p. 3. Paris, Bibliothèque de l'Assemblée nationale français, ms. Y.120.

Photograph courtesy of the Bibliothèque de l'Assembelée nationale.

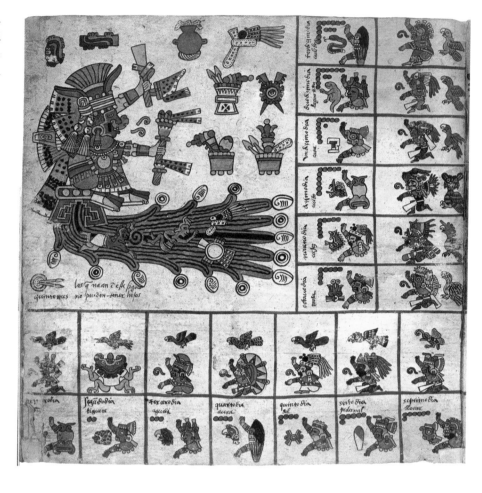

are linked to their referents only by convention, various levels of synecdoche and metonymy, and, of course, metaphors of varying complexity. For example, the headdress of unspun cotton in the upper right of Chalchiutlicue's panel signifies the presence and forces of Tlazolteotl (Filth Goddess, patroness of weavers, who absolved one's sexual transgressions). To the right of Chalchiutlicue are ceramic vessels containing bloodletters, human hearts, and particular herbs, all qualified as especially precious by the addition of a conventionally rendered flower; they signify the kinds of offerings required to activate particular prophetic forces. By convention and allusion, pictography easily conveys a great range of data and thought, including entities, qualities and states of being, places, abstract concepts, actions and events, temporalities, appellatives, and the sounds of language. Each of the major literary genres—histories, divinatory almanacs, and protocols for ritual—has its own pictorial conventions.

The Codex Mendoza, for example, contains an Aztec victory chronicle, featuring in figure 2.2 the reign of the ruler Ahuitzotl (Water Beast).[9] On the left, the signs that identify the years of his reign run sequentially in conjoined rectangular frames from top to bottom: from 8 Reed through 10 Rabbit, each sign is composed of a number of disks and one of four year signs. The signifier for the ruler Ahuitzotl appears center left, between the year signs and the third row of glyphs. His status and occupation as ruler are conveyed by his seated posture on a reed mat, the pointed turquoise diadem on his head, and the small speech scroll to the right of his mouth; the speech scroll signifies his title of *tlatoani*, or speaker. We identify the individual as Ahuitzotl because of the name sign attached

9 Elizabeth Hill Boone, "The Aztec Pictorial History of the Codex Mendoza," in *The Codex Mendoza*, vol. 1, ed. Frances F. Berdan and Patricia R. Anawalt (Berkeley and Los Angeles, 1992), 35–54, 152–53.

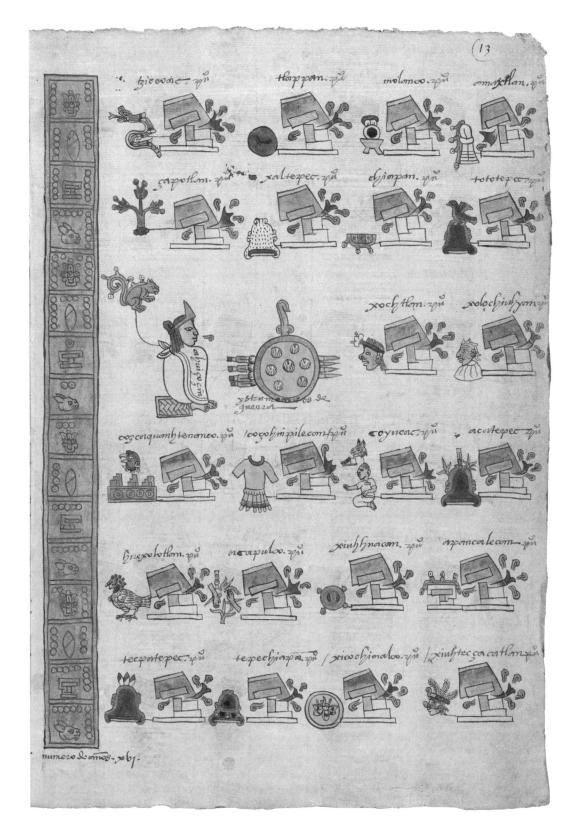

FIG. 2.2.
The reign and
victories of the ruler
Ahuitzotl. Codex
Mendoza, fol. 13r.
Oxford, Bodleian
Library, MS. Selden
3134
Photograph courtesy of
the Bodleian Library,
Oxford University.

to his head: a rodentlike beast with the convention for water running along its back and tail. In the center of the page, a conventional symbol for war—a shield backed by horizontal spears and a vertical spear-thrower—marks the presentation as a message of victory. All around are the defeated polities, identified by their place signs and by burning temples with their roofs askew. Not all these polities had their temples burned, however; the burning temple is simply one of the conventions for indicating conquest and defeat.

The spatial syntax of this presentation is largely diagrammatic. The strip of year signs, the ruler, and the symbol for war are fixed in their respective locations—they appear this way for all rulers' reigns—with the conquests displayed in rows.[10] The space or plane of the page thus carries associative powers, for it effectively creates a set by linking similar, syntactically equivalent items (the conquered polities) to the ruler and his reign. This plane is also qualified temporally, for it is restricted to the sixteen-year period of 8 Reed to 10 Rabbit. A similarly diagrammatic and temporally bounded presentation is the large panel featuring the goddess Chalchiutlicue (see fig. 2.1), which carries prognosticative information for the trecena beginning with the day 1 Reed and ending on 13 Serpent. The panel encloses and unites the graphic elements of the predictive assemblage. In the divinatory panel of figure 2.1, the elements arrayed around the image of Chalchiutlicue are conceptualized as carrying equal weight, just as the conquests of Ahuitzotl are in the Codex Mendoza. The spatial field of the set implicitly compares them with each other and states their shared participation in the meaning of the aggregate.

Another genre of pictographic record—which efficiently interweaves time, place, and event, but exploits a linear rather than a diagrammatic structure—is the *res gestae* genealogical history of the Mixtec screenfold books. An example is the Codex Selden, a section of which features events during the reign of Lady 6 Monkey of Añute (fig. 2.3).[11] This pictorial

record organizes its content as a linear flow along registers that track back and forth in a boustrophedon pattern that begins at the bottom of each page. Series of events, usually ordered chronologically, compose this flow. The events of Lady 6 Monkey's story begin at the right side of the bottom register with a statement of her birth, which is conventionally signified by a seated adult woman with a red umbilical cord joining her rump to a round, yellow placenta. Lady 6 Monkey is here identified, as are all the protagonists in the Mixtec pictorial histories, by her birthday calendrical name; in this case it is 6 Monkey (six disks and the day sign Monkey), which is attached to her head by a line. She wears as a poncho her personal name, Serpent Quechquemitl. This birth statement of Lady 6 Monkey "Serpent Quechquemitl" then participates in a subsequent event: her consultation with an aged male named 10 Lizard. The space around the 6 Monkey image functions in two ways. First, it serves simply to define her birth statement. Second, the space to the right creates an experiential space that joins her with 10 Lizard in a meeting that must have taken place at a single (but here unspecified) location and time.

In the second register (above), attention shifts to Lady 6 Monkey's father, Lord 10 Eagle "Jaguar," who successfully defends Añute from an attack by Lord 3 Lizard "Hair of Jade," whose invasion is marked by the road with footprints under his feet. Both warriors hold round shields and stone-faced swords, but 10 Eagle grasps the submissive 3 Lizard by the hair in a gesture of conquest. Behind 10 Eagle, Añute ("Place of Sand") is glyphically signified by a hill sign that is qualified by a human mouth (a phonetic complement carrying the sound "a") with a curl of sand emitting from it. A band of clouds across the top of the hill sign characterizes Añute as a highland town among the clouds.[12] The precise

10 The arrangement of the conquests is not yet known to be meaningful, as they are given in a different order in cognate documents: Boone, "Aztec Pictorial History," 38–39.

11 For readings of the story of Lady 6 Monkey, see Alfonso Caso, *Interpretación del Códice Selden 3135 (A.2) / Interpretation*

of the Codex Selden 3135 (A.2) (Mexico City, 1964), 32–37; Boone, *Stories in Red and Black*, 70–77; Maarten Jansen and Gabina Aurora Pérez Jiménez, *La dinastía de Añute: Historia, literatura e ideología de un reino mixteco* (Leiden, 2000), 124–44.

12 The place sign of this polity, formerly called Belching Mountain because the sand from the mouth had been read as a belch, was correctly identified as Añute by Mary Elizabeth Smith, "The Codex Selden: A Manuscript from the Valley of Nochixtlán?" in Flannery and Marcus, eds., *Cloud People*, 248–55.

FIG. 2.3.
The first page narrating the story of Lady 6 Monkey of Añute, reading from the bottom up. Codex Selden, p. 6. Oxford, Bodleian Library, MS. Selden 3135.

Photograph courtesy of the Bodleian Library, Oxford University.

date of this battle is given to the right: the day 4 Wind (mouth mask of wind god) in the year 4 House (the year marked by the AO sign that signifies year). Although 6 Monkey's birth is noted succinctly, her father's defense of Añute is stated in greater detail, with the particulars of place, date, and attacker included, and it occupies most of a register. Space is elastic in these res gestae histories according to the amount of detail being recorded.

Other events in the 6 Monkey story follow in this manner. All the participants are identified by their calendrical and personal names, and the events are clearly articulated by means of well-known conventions. Place signs locate these events, while specific dates provide temporal control when needed. The Mixtec res

gestae history, with its sequential action, range of diverse events, secure dating, and multiple personae, approximates in narrative richness and structure histories of the western European tradition. Although its vocabulary is highly figural and its syntax is spatial, it is a graphic form that aligns more clearly with western writing than with western pictorial representation.

Whether organized diagrammatically or linearly, pictographic texts are founded on the figural image and the meaning it conventionally carries within a specific genre, organizational structure, spatial field, and cohort of images. The sounds of spoken language are consciously cued in appellatives, where they function as phonetic indicators and complements to help identify the correct word, such as the image of a human mouth to signal the "a" in Añute in the Codex Selden. Pictography is a writing system beautifully designed to record concepts and data of an extralinguistic nature, a system particularly well adapted to functioning across languages in the multilingual world of Late Post-Classic central and southern Mexico (ca. 1300–1521 CE).

Speech acts do appear in pictography, although exceptionally, when speech is a requisite feature of the message. Pictography represents speech by adding one or more scrolls indicating speech in front of a figure's mouth, by qualifying the scrolls according to the nature of the utterance, and by assembling discrete images to establish the contents of speech acts. A key element is the speech scroll, a phoneme of pictography that signifies within a range of meanings that are embraced by the notion of "speech" but yields different specific meanings depending on context.

The Speech Scroll

In pictography, speech scrolls appear as signs that can function adjectivally, nominally, or verbally. Usually they are secondary graphemes, or signs, attached to or associated with a principal grapheme that is figurally shaped as a being of some sort: human, supernatural, or animal. An example is the ruler Ahuitzotl in the Codex Mendoza (see fig. 2.2), where the speech scroll represents the ruler's title tlatoani (speaker) in Nahuatl. This image of Ahuitzotl is not a picture of him speaking; rather, it is a sign complex that employs the attributes that signify this ruler (his name sign, turquoise diadem, speech scroll, and seated position on the woven mat throne). The scroll here is an adjectival qualifier rather than a verbal construct. Speech scrolls qualify rulers' images in this manner throughout the Codex Mendoza and in several other Aztec pictorials. After the conquest, speech scrolls were even used to characterize Spanish officials as leaders, or tlatoani equivalents.[13]

FIG. 2.4. Sign for "holy kingdom" in a pictorial catechism. Paris, Bibliothèque nationale de France, mexicain 399, fol. 4r, line 5.

Photograph courtesy of the Bibliothéque nationale de France.

In the divinatory almanac of figure 2.1, the figure that represents Chalchiutlicue is also qualified with a scroll, as are the rain gods who govern another thirteen-day period two pages later.[14] Throughout the manuscript speech scrolls also accompany the smaller images of the Lords of the Day (the thirteen supernaturals who govern the thirteen numerical coefficients of the day signs), pictured in individual

13   Speech scrolls mark rulers in the Codex Boturini, p. 2 (José Núñez Corona, ed., *Antigüedades de Mexico* [Mexico City, 1964], 2: pl. 2); Codex Aubin, fols. 70r–78r (Walter Lehmann and Gerdt Kutscher, eds., *Geschichte der Azteken: Der Codex Aubin und verwandte Dokumente* [Berlin, 1981], pls. 284–92); and Codex Xolotl in instances where the figures are clearly not meant to be read as speaking (Charles Dibble, ed., *Codíce Xolotl*

[Mexico City, 1980], maps 1–7), although many scrolls in the Codex Xolotl represent active speech as well. The Codex Osuna of 1565 employs the scroll to characterize both indigenous and Spanish rulers, and in one instance (34r) rulership is signified with only the royal diadem and a set of two speech scrolls (Vicente Cortes Alonso, ed., *Pintura del gobernador, alcaldes y regidores de México* [Mexico City, 1973–76]). For speech scrolls as markers of Moctezuma and other rulers, see also Patrick Hajovsky, *On the Lips of Others: Moteuczoma's Fame in Aztec Monuments and Rituals* (Austin, 2015), ch. 5.

14   No other trecena patrons have such speech scrolls, and the reason for this distinction is unclear. However, Tepeyolotl in his jaguar manifestation, patron of the third trecena, has scrolls of smoke coming from his mouth, and Xolotl, patron of the sixteenth trecena, and Xochiquetzal, patroness of the nineteenth trecena, have emerging from their mouths both a flint knife and a cord or stream that ends in a flower motif. Although Eduard Seler, *Commentarios al Códice Borgia* (Mexico City, 1964), 2:222, read these knife-flower combinations as a reference to bloodletting, Ferdinand Anders, Maarten Jansen, and Luis Reyes García, *El Libro del Cihuacoatl: Homenaje para el año del Fuego Nuevo; Libro explicativo del llamado Códice Borbónico* (Mexico City, 1991), 164, 176, interpret them as speech that employs both flowery, happy, and beautiful words and words of knives, death, and sacrifice.

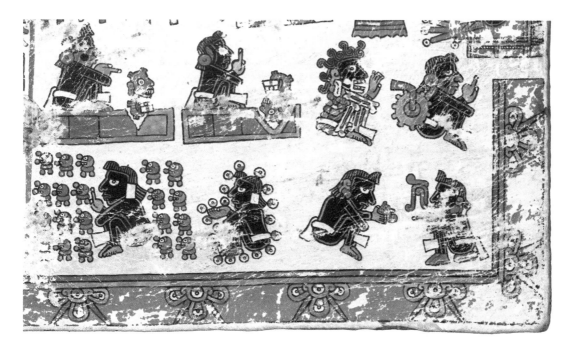

FIG. 2.5.
The opening section
of the Codex Vienna,
p. 52. Vienna,
Österreichische
Nationalbibliothek,
Codex Vindobonensis
Mexicanus 1.

Photograph courtesy
of the Österreichische
Nationalbibliothek.

cells surrounding the central panel.[15] I believe we should read these scrolls as metaphoric qualifiers, similar to those that identify earthly rulers. They likely characterize the figures as rulers of a sort, for these figures represent the very forces that govern the fates associated with each day.

The indexical link between the speech scroll and rulership was strong enough to endure for generations after the Spanish conquest of Mexico and the semiotic disruption it occasioned. A pictorial transcription of the Catholic catechism that was painted sometime between 1591 and the mid-seventeenth century, for example, employed the speech scroll for its metaphoric properties. When the author of the catechism rendered the statement in the Paternoster that refers to Christ's kingdom in heaven, he used an abstracted speech scroll to represent the kingdom, and he qualified it as holy by adding a small cross (fig. 2.4). Here the speech scroll retained its old indigenous meaning, and it functions in the pictorial text as a noun for rulership. The scroll

continued to serve as a spatially static and graphically stable sign that functions either adjectivally or nominally to reference "speakership" or "rule."

When the scroll is embellished or compounded, however, it detaches from this metaphoric meaning and becomes more properly a sign of an activity or an action. The scroll approximates real speech that flows from the mouth. The opening passage of the Mixtec cosmogony in the Codex Vienna, for example, begins in the lower right corner of its first page with a couplet (fig. 2.5).[16] Two generic male figures painted a priestly or supernatural black initiate by their actions all the creative acts that follow. The first male, on the right, has a compound speech scroll of three curls colored turquoise, red, and green (the original green now faded to brown). The preciosity of this triad of colors, as well as the multiplicity of scrolls, signifies an embellished, elaborated utterance, which we read as song or a ritual, speechlike prayer.[17]

15   Even the earth lord Tlaltecuhtli, whose horizontally gaping mouth would seem incompatible with a speech scroll, has one in trecenas 3, 4, and 6–9 in the Codex Borbonicus. Speech scrolls also issue from the mouths of the Lords of the Day in the Tonalamatl Aubin, from the same pictographic tradition, but no other supernaturals in the Tonalamatl Aubin have them. Eduard Seler, *The Tonalamatl of the Aubin Collection: An Old Mexican Picture Manuscript in the Paris National Library (Manuscrits Mexicains Nos. 18–19)* (London, 1901), 26.

16   Otto Adelhofer, ed., *Codex Vindobonensis Mexicanus 1: Österreichische Nationalbibliothek Wien* (Graz, 1963), discussed in Boone, *Stories in Red and Black*, 89–96; and Elizabeth Hill Boone, *Cycles of Time and Meaning in the Mexican Books of Fate* (Austin, 2007), 13–14.

17   Green pigments derived from plants were fugitive, turning brown or tan over time. This is why the palettes of the Codices Bodley, Borgia, Selden, Vaticanus B, and Vienna today lack green and are instead dominated by reds, yellows, and various shades of tan.

The second figure leans forward and releases powdered tobacco from his hands. These males do not represent actual humans—in fact, at this point in the genesis story, humans do not exist—rather they signify the first ritual acts of song and offering that will bring the Mixtec world into being. The human form functions here only as a graphic vehicle that allows the painter to render the speech scrolls. The scrolls, despite their curves and volutes, are stable signs that function semantically as nominal verb forms, representing song or singing, prayer or praying.

The stability of the scroll as nominal sign begins to dissolve into animation when the scroll signifies more specific speech acts. With specificity, the scroll becomes semantically more verbal than nominal. Its new active role as a verb also transforms the image to which it is attached. It energizes the image, forcing the static sign of a human figure to metamorphose into a more active being who emits the scroll.

We see this in another trecena of the divinatory manuscript discussed earlier, this one governed by the patrons Huehuecoyotl (Old Coyote) on the right and Ixtlilton (Little Black Face) on the left (fig. 2.6). Huehuecoyotl retains the conventional pinwheel pose of supernatural patronage, and his speech scrolls might seem conventional as well, if not for the singing drummer opposite him. The drummer has his arms outstretched so his hands can slap the great kettle drum, and from his mouth comes a linear series of speech scrolls. Two ordinary ones lead to a great and wondrously embellished scroll, the most elaborate found in the pictographic corpus. The body of this great scroll is pattered with *ihuitl* designs, the pairs of white curls that look a bit like a percent sign. The ihuitl signifies the days of the ritual calendar and their prophetic forces—the days and the fates attached to them.[18] Atop the scroll is a large, multilayer flower, rendered conventionally, which further qualifies the oration as flowery speech, formal and ritual speech of the most elegant kind, the speech of poetry and prayer. Together the flower and the ihuitl signs identify this as a ritual utterance about prophecy and the fates.

This great speech scroll, as the culmination of the other scrolls, reads as real speech in action. The active quality of this speech then begins to transform the figures and the space they inhabit. There is a dramatic tension here between the principal figures as static signs and as active beings that together produce sound. As the principal and secondary patrons of this trecena, they remain stable forces surrounded by the set of glyphs that help signify the fates of this week. But the speech acts animate the images and transform them into individuals singing. We read these images much differently than we read Ahuitzotl in the victory chronicle or Chalchiutlicue in this same manuscript. In the words of our editors, Brigitte Bedos-Rezak and Jeffrey Hamburger, what elsewhere was reading (the reading of signs) has now become gazing (see Introduction). The act of recognizing marks and interpreting their meaning within a graphic notational system has become more like the act of viewing things, in this case sentient beings participating in a shared activity, who are rendered figurally on a field. Here the sign is energized.

This, of course, changes the syntactic properties of the field itself. When figures participate together like this in a common activity or shared experience, their action creates a more forceful and specific kind of spatial field. The field between and around them takes on the character of experiential or dramaturgical space, which binds them together temporally and geographically. The field of the panel is still the aggregative space that unites all the figures and glyphs as a set of prognosticative forces, but the space between the drummer and Huehuecoyotl is charged with more specific, locational meaning, uniting them in a physical space, a space activated by the speech scroll. The configuration has taken on the quality of a scene rather than a set of neutral signs. This will also be true of other examples discussed below.

Content of Speech Acts

The drummer's speech is richly characterized as divinatory, elaborate, and elegant, although we are not given more of its particulars. With some other speech acts, the authors provide more specificity. The content of speech can be signified by affixes to the scroll and by separate independent glyphs.

Several speech acts are included in the story of Lady 6 Monkey in the Codex Selden, introduced earlier. Lady 6 Monkey's life story involves battling forces hostile to Añute, marrying, and giving birth to royal heirs. In the top register of page 6 (see fig. 2.3), an extended speech scroll visualizes the action and event of her betrothal. She and her intended husband, 11 Wind "Bloody Jaguar" (6 Monkey on left and 11 Wind to her right), are pictured seated on low jaguar-skin stools facing the supernatural Lady 9 Grass of Chalcatongo (Skull Place).[19] From Lady 9 Grass a long speech scroll reaches across to 11 Wind, over and around his name sign, to reach the head of 6 Monkey and join the two. The scroll here is not embellished with detail, but its extension and the historical context of the meeting tell of its content.[20]

Later in the narrative 6 Monkey sends two ambassadors to enemy towns, as recorded on the top two registers of page 7 (fig. 2.7). The

---

19   The painter inadvertently omitted one of the disks of Lord 11 Wind's calendrical name.

20   This meeting with Lady 9 Grass at Chalcatongo is also recorded in several other pictorial histories: Codices Colombino 3ab–4ab, Bodley 35b–36b, and Zouche-Nuttall 44. See Ferdinand Anders, Maarten Jansen, and Gabina Aurora Pérez Jiménez, *Crónica Mixteca: El rey 8 Venado, Garra de Jaguar, y la dinastía de Teozacualco-Zaachila* (Mexico City, 1992), 184–86; Manuel Hermann Lejarazu, *Códice Colombino: Una nueva historia de un antiguo gobernante* (Mexico City, 2011), 94–99.

---

18   Boone, *Stories in Red and Black*, 35, 253; Boone, *Cycles of Time and Meaning*, 88–95.

FIG. 2.7.

Registers narrating
Lady 6 Monkey's
rebuffed diplomatic
mission to two enemy
polities and her
consultation with
Lady 9 Grass about
war. Codex Selden,
p. 7ab. Oxford,
Bodleian Library 3135,
Arch Selden A.2.

Photograph courtesy of
the Bodleian Library,
Oxford University.

ambassador at the lower left carries in his back-pack 6 Monkey's metaphoric person in the form of her head with her calendrical name attached, while the ambassador to the right (near the center of the register) carries the leafy stalks that symbolize her royal authority. The ambassadors are confronted by the lords of the two polities, who are pictured on the right side of the register in a pose of aggression on top of their place signs. Flint knives, conventionally rendered by pointed lozenges half-colored red, are attached to their speech scrolls; the knives inform the reader that they speak cutting, hostile, or insulting words.[21]

In the next register, 6 Monkey again visits Lady 9 Grass at Chalcatongo. Facing each other, they talk of war. The content of this conversation is represented in the set of glyphs between them. From bottom to top we see a round war shield backed by a bloody spear, a fire drilling

board (perhaps a reference to burning the enemies' temples), a bound volute and two sets of wavy lines that elsewhere signify war or combat, and at the top the chevron path that signifies enemy.[22] The historian does not record who said what, only the subject of the communication. Perhaps because this communication lacks speech scrolls, the human figures and the glyphs between them remain static as signs. We are given a statement that 6 Monkey and 9 Grass met at Chalcatongo and discussed and decided on war in its various aspects. War does ensue, and 6 Monkey is victorious.

Elsewhere, the presence of speech scrolls personalizes the interaction between conversants. In an Aztec migration history, the Codex Boturini, the historian records an episode when the Aztecs were living as vassals under Coxcoxtli (Pheasant), the ruler of Culhuacan. Coxcoxtli sent Aztec warriors to battle the rival Xochimilca (people of Xochimilco), during which time the Aztecs cut

21 Jansen and Pérez Jiménez, *Dinastía de Añute*, 134–35, have interpreted this episode slightly differently, describing the stony speech as a warning shouted to Lady 6 Monkey that she was destined to be "killed by a knife." They opine that 6 Monkey misinterpreted this speech and attacked and killed the two men. This interpretation of the speech's content does not change the fundamental nature of the speech act. Another instance of a qualified speech scroll appears in the Codex Zouche-Nuttall, p. 20, where Lord 10 Rain appears in the context of the funeral of two who had died in the so-called War of Heaven; his speech scroll is topped with the day sign 7 Flower, which is the calendar name of another who had died in the War of Heaven. The calendar name and context strongly suggest he spoke about Lord 7 Flower: Boone, *Stories in Red and Black*, 58–59, 256.

22 For the chevron band, see Smith, *Picture Writing*, 33. The wavy lines are paired with the chevron band in the context of war in the Codices Becker I 7a, 8b; Bodley, 9a, 10b, 22a, 28b; Colombino, 10a; and (as part of personal names) Zouche-Nuttall, 8, 57. Alfonso Caso, ed., *Códice Alfonso Caso: La vida de 8-Venado, Garra de Tigre (Colombino-Becker I)* (Mexico City, 1996); idem, *Interpretación del Códice Bodley 2858 / Interpretation of the Codex Bodley 2858* (Mexico City, 1960); and Nancy P. Troike, ed., *Codex Zouche-Nuttall, British Museum, London (Add. MS. 39671)* (Graz, 1987). Jansen and Pérez Jiménez, *Dinastía de Añute*, 135, suggest the wavy lines refer to the trembling of the earth.

off the ears of the defeated warriors and brought the ears back to Coxcoxtli in sacks. Detailed on a single page in the Codex Boturini (fig. 2.8), the story is also recounted in chronicles written alphabetically after the conquest.[23] On the left, a communication between Coxcoxtli and two Aztec vassals is indicated by a gesture and speech scrolls; the glyphs between them convey its content. From top to bottom the glyphs are the place name of Xochimilco (Flower Field, its sign being a rectangular patch of ploughed field with two conventionalized flowers on top), the shield-and-club symbol for war, and the sack, to which Coxcoxtli points. An additional war symbol is connected by a dotted line to one of the Aztecs' speech scrolls, as if to emphasize that both sides are participating in the conversation about war. The specific instructions to sever the ears are pictured as part of another speech act at the far right. Here, glyphs of the ruler's diadem and two severed ears are linked by a dotted line to a warrior holding up an obsidian blade toward the face of a presumed warrior from Xochimilco; the blade is the instrument with which the ears are to be cut. These instructions are quite literal: "cut off the ears of the Xochimilca for the ruler [Coxcoxtli]."

These glyphs that signify with some specificity the content of Aztec and Mixtec conversations are arranged in stacks or short sets, effectively making use of available space. But there is little sense of meaningful sequence. They signify the basic semantic elements of the speech acts but not their rhetorical structure. One of the most prominent qualities of audible speech, however, is its insistent sequentiality, a factor of its inherent

temporality. One hears speech in the order in which it is uttered, and although certain words, phrases, and intonations may dominate as one listens and reflects on what is heard, one cannot know the full content of a voiced speech act until that act is finished. One cannot skip around or skim it, as one might skim or speed-read a written text; one cannot access both the beginning and the end at the same time. Only when speech is rendered graphically is there a potential to access the full sequence practically simultaneously.

Streams of Iteration

Since Mexican pictography is designed to record concepts and data rather than speech itself, graphic flows of spoken information are very rare. But streams of iteration do occur on occasion, and their features can be telling. Such streams often include a greater number of glyphic elements to index the data of the speech than do the single glyphs and glyphic clusters discussed earlier. The streams also retain something of the rhetorical structure of speech acts, especially its linear sequentiality. They can be accompanied by speech scrolls or not.

The Codex Xolotl, a political history of the Valley of Mexico in the fifteenth century, contains a number of vocal streams, more, in fact, than any other pictorial in the Aztec tradition. A group of three such streams issued by the tyrant Tezozomoc (Angry Stone) in map 7 exemplifies the totality (fig. 2.9).[24] Although much of Tezozomoc's image at the left has been abraded, enough remains to recognize a cloaked figure seated on a high-backed throne and facing

FIG. 2.8.
The episode during which Aztec warriors brought the severed ears of the Xochimilca in sacks back to the ruler Coxcoxtli. Codex Boturini, p. 21, top. Mexico, Biblioteca Nacional de Antropología, Colección de Codices 35–38.

Photograph courtesy of CONACULTA, Instituto de Nacional de Antropología e Historia.

23 Diego Durán, *The History of the Indies of New Spain*, trans. Doris Heyden (Norman, Okla., 1994), 114.

24 Explicated by Dibble, *Códice Xolotl*, 89–92.

FIG. 2.9.
The tyrant
Tezozomoc issues
three streams of
speech, which flow
left to right from
his seated figure.
Codex Xolotl, map 7.
Paris, Bibliothèque
nationale de France,
mexicain 1–10.

Photograph courtesy
of the Bibliothèque
nationale de France.

right, and, to the left, his name sign: a conventionalized stone with curls of anger or agitation rising above it. Three vocal streams begin with Tezozomoc and run to the right. Tezozomoc is not in conversation with anyone; rather, these three speech streams are directives, designed to reach a variety of ears.

The topmost stream is shortest. It begins with the familiar symbol for war (a round shield backed by an obsidian edged club), followed by the ethnic name for the Acolhua people (the combination of water [*a*] and arm [*acolli*]) and then the place sign for the polity of Ecatepec (a bean [*e*], dotted scrolls of wind [*ehecatl*], and the number three [*yei*]). The Acolhua and Ecatepec signs work as phonetic rebuses. This speech declares war against the Acolhua people of Ecatepec; footprints subsequently carry its message off to Tezozomoc's armed warriors (not shown in fig. 2.9), who are in the process of capturing their Acolhua counterparts.

Tezozomoc's aggression against the Acolhua continues in the second and third streams of speech. The second records the tyrant's humiliating directive that Lord Ixtlilxochitl (Eye Flower) order his people, the Acolhua, to weave cotton mantles for Tezozomoc. Two speech scrolls begin this stream, which continues with the woven mat throne of rulers (an indirect reference to Ixtlilxochitl as ruler), the Acolhua

ethnic sign, a striped bale of cotton, and a square mantle. Tezozomoc's aggression then escalates, as the third and longer stream calls for the assassination of Ixtlilxochitl and the implied defeat of six Acolhua polities allied to him. Following two speech scrolls, the historian has painted Ixtlilxochitl's name sign (an eye topped by a flower) pierced by an arrow to signify his murder, then two more speech scrolls that lead to the glyph of a head with closed eyes (signifying death), followed by the Acolhua glyph and the place signs of the allied polities.[25]

As in the conversations about war in the Mixtec Codex Selden and the conversations about severed ears in the Aztec Codex Boturini, these streams of iteration are composed of glyphs that provide the essential data of the communication. But here the glyphs are sequenced according to what we can suppose to have been the linguistic expression of these speech acts. The directive for the Acolhua to make cotton mantles, for example, has the mantles, the end product of the order, as its last glyph. Similarly, the death of Ixtlilxochitl in the third and longest stream must come before the allies whose defeat implicitly follows. These streams of iteration

25 These polities are: Huexotla, Cohuatlinchan, Cohuatepec, either the Acolhua ethnic sign again or the town of Acolhuacan, Chicuhnauhtla, and Otompan. Dibble, *Códice Xolotl*, 92.

FIG. 2.10.

Sun Stone of
Moctezuma
Ilhuicamina. Mexico,
Museo Nacional de
Antropología, MNA
10-393459.

Reproduction authorized
by CONACULTA,
Instituto Nacional de
Antropología e Historia.

read like the rebus texts they are, here from left to right. Their linearity requires that long, narrow spaces be created on the page to accommodate them. The spaces occupied by these streams cannot be characterized as experiential, for they do not define location. Rather they are perhaps better described as linguistic corridors, which are attached to and issue out from the figure of the tyrant Tezozomoc. They are not unlike the kinds of verbal streams that appear in some late Gothic and early Renaissance paintings, often within banderoles, to introduce alphabetic texts of spoken words into an otherwise mimetic scene.

The sequentiality and glyphic composition of these rebus texts, plus their left-to-right reading order, suggest pictography's transformation after the conquest as it moved toward approximating western writing.[26] As an early colonial document, the Codex Xolotl exhibits more pictorial talking than any other codex, and it is unique in having long rebus texts spoken by individuals. The streams of iteration register information that personalizes Tezozomoc and the other protagonists

to an extent not seen in any other pictorial history, and the linguistic corridors complicate the diagrammatic structure of the history.

New research reveals, however, that sequential streams of glyphs related to language are more than a post-conquest phenomenon. The great Sun Stone carved in the mid-fifteenth century for the fifth Aztec emperor Moctezuma Ilhuicamina (Moctezuma I) has two such streams running around the top and bottom of its circumference (fig. 2.10). The cylindrical monument, measuring 2.24 meters in diameter, is a gladiatorial stone, to which captive warriors were tied for ritual combat before being put to death. Featuring the sun disk on its top surface and the Aztec conquests of eleven polities on its cylindrical sides, the stone uniquely frames these conquests not with sky and earth bands, like the similar Stone of Tizoc, but with two bands of repeating motifs. These have been interpreted as generally related to human sacrifice.[27] Rochelle

26 Elizabeth Hill Boone, "The Death of Aztec Pictography," in *The Disappearance of Writing Systems*, ed. John Baines, John Bennet, and Stephen Houston (London, 2008), 253–86, esp. 269–71.

27 For the iconography of the Sun Stone, see Felipe Solís Olguín, "El temalacatl-cuauhxicalli de Moctezuma Ilhuicamina," in *Azteca Mexica: Las culturas del México antiguo*, ed. José Alcina Franch, Miguel León-Portilla, and Eduardo Matos Moctezuma (Barcelona, 1992), 225–32; idem, "Monuments of Sun Worship," in *The Aztec Calendar and Other Solar Monuments*, ed. Eduardo Matos Moctezuma and

FIG. 2.11.

Motifs on the Sun
Stone of Moctezuma
Ilhuicamina.
Reading left to
right, top: bones,
heart, skull, cipactli;
middle: flint, hand,
bundle; bottom:
encircled cross,
encircled X shape.

Drawing by
Anne Bomalaski.

bones   heart   skull   cipactli

flint   hand   bundle

encircled cross   encircled X shape

Collins and I have recently argued that this cluster is specifically associated with the bellicose deity Tezcatlipoca, patron of rulers. More relevant to the topic here, however, is the complex patterning of the motifs, which is rhythmic and reflects the discourse structure of Nahuatl high speech.[28] Although the bands lack speech scrolls, they are extraordinary examples of pictographic texts that parallel and likely call forth ritual speech acts.

The bands have well-defined sequences of nine motifs: seven are iconic, representing objects—crossed bones, heart, skull, *cipactli* (crocodile), flint knife, severed hand, and bundle of kindling—that carry generalized meanings related to death, sacrifice, offering, and the earth (fig. 2.11). Two abstract circular motifs—an encircled cross and an encircled X shape—which

have not been found elsewhere in Aztec art, function on the stone as syntactic indicators, although they may carry other meanings as well. The sequence of these motifs follows regular and repeating patterns that compose the graphic equivalent of verses and lines, as in poetry. The organization of motifs on the bands of the Sun Stone of Moctezuma Ilhuicamina, sequenced as they appear on the stone, left to right, appears below:

Top Band
   (+) bones heart skull cipactli
   (×) flint hand bundle
   (×) bones heart skull cipactli
   (×) flint hand bundle
   (×) bones skull cipactli heart hand flint
      bundle

   (+) bones skull cipactli heart flint bundle
   (×) bones skull cipactli heart flint bundle
   (+) bones skull
   (×) heart cipactli
   (×) flint hand bundle
   (×) bones heart skull cipactli
   (×) flint hand bundle

Felipe Solís Olguín (Mexico City, 2004), 76–153; and Eduardo Matos Moctezuma, "La Piedra del Tízoc y la del antiguo Arzobispado," in *Escultura monumental mexica*, ed. Eduardo Matos Moctezuma and Leonardo López Luján (Mexico City, 2009), 291–326.

28 Elizabeth Hill Boone and Rochelle Collins, "The Petroglyphic Prayers on the Sun Stone of Motecuhzoma Ilhuicamina," *Ancient Mesoamerica* 24, no. 2 (2013): 1–17.

Bottom Band

> (+) bones heart skull cipactli flint hand
>   bundle
>
> (+) bones heart skull cipactli flint hand
>   bundle
>
> (+) bones heart skull cipactli
> (×) flint hand bundle
> (×) bones heart skull cipactli
> (×) flint hand heart bundle
>
> (+) bones flint cipactli hand bundle
>
> (+) bones heart skull flint cipactli hand
>   bundle
>
> (+) bones heart skull flint cipactli hand
>   bundle

The encircled cross, represented as (+) above, marks the beginning of a verse, and the encircled X shape, represented as (×), marks a new line. Each band begins with an encircled cross. The first verse proceeds: bones, heart, skull, cipactli. The next line reads: flint, hand, bundle. The next line: bones, heart, skull, cipactli; and the next: flint, hand, bundle. These sequences repeat like a chorus. The top band ends with same couplet with which it began: bones, heart, skull, cipactli; flint, hand, bundle. There are similar repetitions with variations on the bottom band. The bands organize the motifs in rhythmic patterns that employ various forms of parallelism characteristic of Nahuatl poetry, such as duplication, duplication with variation, and the conjoining and separation of sets of motifs.[29] Each band opens and closes with couplets. The top band and the bottom band also relate to each other as complementary presentations that share some rhythmic features but vary others. The motifs are structured much like Nahuatl poetic discourse as it was recorded alphabetically after the conquest.

The bands are petroglyphic prayers or exhortations, rendered in visual rather than vocal terms. They are not configured as linguistic streams spoken by a specific individual recorded in a document; rather they stand permanently as graphic cues to an oration that could have been voiced by those viewing the stone. In this way the bands qualify the stone, as do the epigrams that run across monuments discussed in this volume by Ivan Drpić (chap. 3).

The Sun Stone of Moctezuma Ilhuicamina negates some common assumptions about pictography, notably that it eschews speech and the strict linearity characteristic of other scripts. The bands on the Sun Stone demonstrate that prayers could be manifested graphically and carved in stone. They also show that the graphic code of pictography can parallel the linguistic code of Nahuatl even more than previously supposed.[30] This suggests that we should look more closely at other patterns and arrangements in pictography to see where rhetorical structures may be shared with Nahuatl, beyond agglutination. The linguistic streams that appear in the Codex Xolotl may reflect the influence of alphabetic writing, with its linearity and sequentiality, but it is clear from Moctezuma's Sun Stone that pictography was already open to linear discourse.

The potential for pictography to record specific speech acts, to become more like word writing, was fulfilled after the Spanish conquest, when indigenous converts to Christianity were called upon to record the doctrinal laws and texts of the Catholic catechism. These converts created alphabetic catechisms in indigenous languages, and they transcribed the catechism into figures and symbols (fig. 2.12). Some thirty pictorial catechisms have survived, dating from perhaps as early as the late sixteenth century and continuing to the nineteenth century.[31]

29 Ángel María Garibay K., *Historia de la literatura náhuatl*, 2 vols. (Mexico City, 1971), 1:65–73; and Miguel León-Portilla, "*Cuicatl y tlahtolli*, las formas de expresión en náhuatl," *Estudios de Cultura Náhuatl* 16 (1986): 13–108, esp. 29–32.

30 In a posthumously published article about Teotihuacan writing, Pierre Colas distinguished between glyphs or individual signs that appear within speech scrolls (as infixes) and those that are affixed to or outside the scrolls, which he found to be discrete sets. He concluded that infix signs are semasiographic and affixed signs are either semasiographic or glottographic. Colas's analysis of graphic space offers a useful starting point for understanding Teotihuacan imagery: "Writing in Space: Glottographic and Semasiographic Notation at Teotihuacan," *Ancient Mesoamerica* 22 (2011): 13–25.

31 Overviews are John Glass, "A Census of Middle American Testerian Manuscripts," in *Handbook of Middle American Indians*, ed. Robert Wauchope and Howard F. Cline (Austin, 1975), 14, 281–96; and Anne Normann, "Testerian Codices:

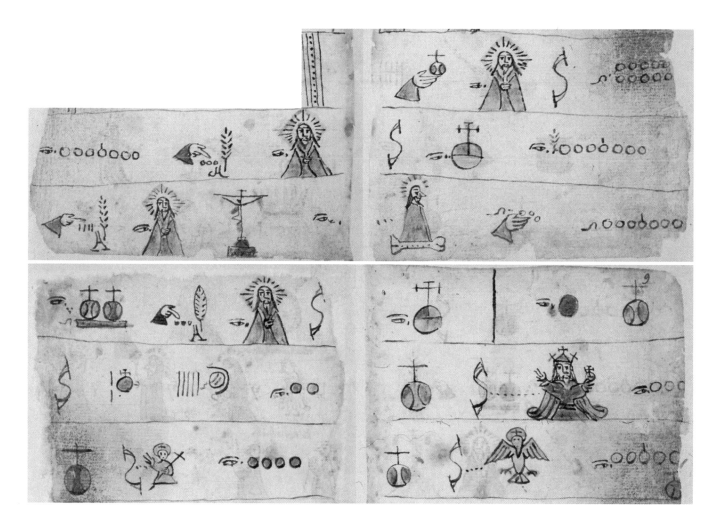

Their images retain the conventional ideoplastic character of preconquest pictograms, and, like both pictography and alphabetic writing, they occupy a flat neutral surface. Like alphabetic texts and the images of Mixtec genealogical histories, the figures appear sequentially in registers. As in pictography, this surface extends across the interior gutter of facing pages, and although the images usually read left to right, some catechisms follow the back-and-forth boustrophedon tracks of the indigenous tradition. Although almost all the images signify as ideograms for their referents, a few manuscripts employ phonograms and phonetic qualifiers.[32]

The imagery and symbolism of the figures are drawn from the iconographies of both indigenous Mexico and Catholic Europe.

Although pictographic catechisms form a heterogeneous corpus, they all share their glyphic character and their loyalty to the canonical texts. A catechism in the Bibliothèque nationale de France (mexicain 399) is more phonetic and more verbal than the others, and it specifically cues a Nahuatl rather than a Spanish or

Hieroglyphic Catechisms for Native Conversion in New Spain" (Ph.D. diss., Tulane University, 1985). See Justino Cortés Castellanos, *El catecismo en pictogramas de Fr. Pedro de Gante* (Madrid, 1987), for a study of one of the best-known examples.

32 Recent studies are Bérénice Gaillemin, "Images mémorables pour un texte immutable: Les catéchismes pictographiques

testériens (Mexique, XVIᵉ–XIXᵉ siècles)," *Gradhiva: Revue d'anthropologie et d'histoire des arts* 13 (2001): 205–25; Louise Burkhart, "The 'Little Doctrine' and Indigenous Catechesis in New Spain," *Hispanic American Historical Review* 94, no. 2 (2014): 167–206; Elizabeth Hill Boone, "El discurso en imágenes: La producción azteca de textos cristianos," in *Homenaje a Alfredo López Austin*, ed. Eduardo Matos Moctezuma and María Teresa Uriarte (Mexico City, forthcoming); and Elizabeth Hill Boone, Louise Burkhart, and David Távarez, *Painted Words: Nahua Catholicism, Politics, and Memory in the Atzaqualco Pictorial Catechism* (Washington, D.C., forthcoming), chaps. 2–3.

Latin text.[33] An excerpt from the beginning of the Articles of the Faith (fig. 2.12) exemplifies the features of the manuscript well. The catechism employs a number of specific conventions: a circle divided horizontally and vertically in the manner of medieval *mappamundi* and topped by a cross represents the concept of deity or divinity, *teotl* in Nahuatl. A different circle with two vertical, curved elements topped by a cross signifies the concept of belief. An S stands for the word *Dios*. The frontal face or bust of a bearded male surrounded by an aura represents the phrase "our lord" or *totecuyo* in Nahuatl. A set of parallel lines represents "many" or "all," and a ball with oblique hatching within an arc, representing a ball of thread, signifies the concept of doing or making. Small eyes cue the Nahuatl affix *in*. The text of the articles begins thusly:

Here are the beliefs (articles of faith), of our lord (*in totecuyo*), God (*Dios*) There are fourteen.

Seven, pertain to (to him are counted), our lord, God, as a deity (*inic teotl*), and (*ihuan*) seven

Pertain to, our lord, Jesus Christ, as a man (Christ's humanity signified by the bone). Here are, the seven

Beliefs, that pertain to, our lord, God, as a deity. The first one, I believe in,

God, only one, all maker (maker of all things). The second one, I believe in, God, the Supreme Being. The third one,

I believe in, God, the Child. The fourth, I believe in, God, the Holy Spirit.

The author of this catechism does more than convey the content of the Articles of Faith; he conveys the verbal text that pronounces the Articles. These pictorial catechisms were created not solely to convey the essential meanings of the doctrinal precepts but also to remind their users of the verbal stream of words in a doctrinal text. Pictography here has become a servant of alphabetic writing, as an alternative script to record verbal texts otherwise written in letters and words. Such pictographic catechisms were highly prized by their owners, who considered

their traditional signs truer to their indigenous sensibility and thus more fully theirs. The pictographic catechism represents pictography's closest approximation to the kind of sequential discourse that glottographic writing systems record. It records via images the stream of words that exist in a canonical textual statement, and it does so with some precision.

—⁓—

Pictography's relation to speech and language is clearly complex and dynamic. Not intended to record language linguistically, it can nonetheless record the act of speaking and the content of speech acts when that data is requisite for the larger message. The speech scroll is a key factor, for it can function as an adjectival sign, a nominal sign, and as an active verb. By referencing speech (*tlatolli*) and speakership (*tlatoani*), the scroll serves as a glyphic metaphor for rule. It signifies earthly rulers, and in the Codex Borbonicus it characterizes the supernatural rulers of the thirteen days in a trecena, the Lords of the Days. Embellished and made more specific by the addition of affixes, however, the speech scroll becomes animated. This now-verbal scroll approximates real speech and conveys by its qualifiers the content of particular speech acts. Its verbal nature enlivens the figures with which it is associated, converting an otherwise figural sign into an image that, although still conventionalized, is now mimetic to a degree. This speaking sign more closely approximates a representation of a sentient being who is speaking. One interprets these speaking figures less as signs to be read and more as active figures to be viewed. For us, the process of reading has become closer to the process of observing.

Although pictography does not often detail the content of speech acts, when it does it employs glyphic images to reference the fundamental data being conveyed. The great speech scroll in the Codex Borbonicus is qualified by its size and the addition of ihuitl and flower signs, which together call forth the heightened quality of sacred speech. Speech scrolls usually accompany the glyphic content of speech acts, but they are not always required. In the Codex Selden, for example, when Lady 6 Monkey and

33 Boone, Burkhart, and Távarez, *Painted Words.*

Lady 9 Grass discuss war, their poses and juxtaposition, as well as the historical context of the meeting, are sufficient to signify the verbal discourse.

Mexican pictography comes closest to other writing systems when it organizes individual glyphs into streams of iteration, linear sequences of images that convey the content of speech acts. These appear especially in early colonial manuscripts and likely reflect pictography's response to the influence of alphabetic writing. The complex sequences of glyphs that run along the framing bands of the Sun Stone of Moctezuma I, however, demonstrate that the range of pictographic practice before the conquest was greater than previously supposed. These sequences have been interpreted as petroglyphic prayers, the lithic equivalent of voiced orations permanently fixed on the monument. The Sun Stone's glyphic sequences, which replicate the rhetorical structure of high Nahuatl speech, suggest that we should look more closely at pictography and oration as being governed by some of the same discursive structures. This kind of sequential, glyphic presentation before the conquest also foreshadowed later expressions of individualized speech and catechistic texts that developed in the early colonial period.

Chrysepes Stichourgia

The Byzantine Epigram as Aesthetic Object

IVAN DRPIĆ

ODERN LEXICA DEFINE AN EPIGRAM AS "A SHORT POEM ENDING IN A witty or ingenious turn of thought."[1] In Byzantium, however, neither brevity nor witticism was a defining feature of an epigram. Derived from the preposition *epi*, meaning "on" or "upon," and the verb *graphein*, "to write," the word *epigramma* simply means "inscription." Perfectly in accordance with this etymology, the epigram in Byzantine usage is defined primarily by its real or potential inscriptional use and denotes either a verse inscription written on an object or a poem accompanying a piece of literature.[2] Usually written in dodecasyllable, the medieval Greek equivalent of the ancient iambic trimeter,[3] epigrams could appear on a wide range of objects, from fortification walls and church façades to icons and reliquaries, tombs, articles of personal adornment, and even coins. Their role varies considerably depending on the occasion or the function of the object at hand. Dedicatory epigrams commemorate acts of munificence and philanthropy, signal ownership, accompany pious gifts, or vocalize prayers to holy figures. Epitaphs displayed at tombs preserve and perpetuate the memory of the dead among the living. Some verses praise, evaluate, describe, explain, or comment on the object to which they are attached. Others, directly engaging the spectator, may variously serve to dramatize the act of viewing, provide moral exhortation and guidance, or enhance the spectator's emotional response. The number of Byzantine epigrams that can still be seen in situ is considerable. A recent assessment counts some twelve hundred verse inscriptions preserved from the period 600 to 1500.[4] Complementing this sizable corpus are hundreds of epigrams that have come down to us through manuscript anthologies. Taken together, the inscriptional and manuscript evidence leaves no doubt that the symbiosis and synergy between the physical object and the inscribed verse was a common phenomenon in the Byzantine world.

---

1   The quoted definition comes from John A. Simpson et al., eds., *The Oxford English Dictionary* (Oxford, 1989), s.v. "epigram."

2   See Marc Lauxtermann, *Byzantine Poetry from Pisides to Geometres: Texts and Contexts* (Vienna, 2003), 26–34, 131–32; and Andreas Rhoby, *Byzantinische Epigramme auf Fresken und Mosaiken* (Vienna, 2009), 37–45.

3   On dodecasyllable, see Paul Maas, "Der byzantinische Zwölfsilber," *BZ* 12 (1903): 278–323; Wolfram Hörandner, "Beobachtungen zur Literarästhetik der Byzantiner: Einige byzantinische Zeugnisse zu Metrik und Rhythmik," *BSl* 56 (1995): 279–90, at 285–89; Marc Lauxtermann, "The Velocity of Pure Iambs: Byzantine Observations on the Metre and Rhythm of the Dodecasyllable," *JÖB* 48 (1998): 9–33; and Andreas Rhoby, "Vom jambischen Trimeter zum byzantinischen Zwölfsilber: Beobachtung zur Metrik des spätantiken und byzantinischen Epigramms," *WSt* 124 (2011): 117–42.

4   Rhoby, *Byzantinische Epigramme auf Fresken und Mosaiken*, 51. This figure does not include epigrams on seals.

Defined by its inscriptional use, the Byzantine epigram is a twofold entity, simultaneously a literary composition and a material artifact—a painted, carved, hammered, embroidered, nielloed, or otherwise manufactured string of letters. The following example may serve to highlight this duality. Toward the end of the first decade of the fourteenth century, Manuel Philes, the most prolific poet of the late Byzantine era, composed an epigram at the behest of an aristocratic patron by the name of Maria Doukaina Komnene Branaina Palaiologina Tarchaneiotissa.[5] The epigram was intended for a funerary chapel that served as the burial place for her husband, the *protostrator* Michael Tarchaneiotes Doukas Glabas.[6] The verses give voice to the grieving widow who, in an imaginative and emotionally suffused passage, addresses the deceased as follows (vv. 14–21):

Ὡς ὄστρεον γοῦν ὀργανῶ σοι τὸν τάφον
ἢ κόχλον, ἢ κάλυκα κεντρώδους βάτου,
μάργαρέ μου, πορφύρα, γῆς ἄλλης ῥόδον·
εἰ καὶ τρυγηθὲν ἐκπιέζῃ τοῖς λίθοις,
ὡς καὶ σταλαγμοὺς προξενεῖν μοι δακρύων·
αὐτὸς δὲ καὶ ζῶν, καὶ θεὸν ζῶντα βλέπων,
ὡς νοῦς καθαρὸς τῶν παθῶν τῶν ἐξ ὕλης,
τὸν σὸν πάλιν θάλαμον εὐτρέπιζέ μοι.

I construct this tomb for you like a pearl oyster shell, or a shell of the purple dye, or a bud upon a thorny brier. O my pearl, my purple, my rose of another land, even though, being plucked, you are pressed by the stones, so as to cause me sheddings of tears. Yet you yourself, both living and beholding the living God, as a spirit pure from material passions, prepare again for me your chamber.[7]

Philes's poem is one of the rare examples of an epigram preserved both in the manuscript record

and in situ. The verses are copied, for instance, in a massive, mid-fourteenth-century, two-volume miscellany of classical and Byzantine authors now in the University Library in Uppsala.[8] The relevant folio 172v (fig. 3.1) is certainly not without visual interest. The controlled calligraphic hand with the occasional flourish, the use of red ink for the title and the initial alpha, a balanced *mise-en-page* with spacious margins—all these elements appeal to the eye, contributing to a compelling presentation of the text. Nonetheless, the epigram's visual dimension in the Upsaliensis is clearly secondary. Embedded in a learned anthology, Maria's lament is here presented primarily as a self-contained literary composition, yet another item in the discursive universe of Greek writing.

The reading and viewing experience of the epigram is radically different when we encounter this poem in the physical setting for which it was originally composed, namely, a marble cornice running along the façades of the funerary chapel in the former monastery of the Virgin *Pammakaristos* in Istanbul (fig. 3.2).[9] Placed not much above eye level, the rhythmical lines of Maria's lament can be easily read from the ground. Far from being a self-contained literary piece, the epigram here acquires a powerful material presence. Large majuscule letters are carved

5 The epigram has been published in Emmanuel Miller, ed., *Manuelis Philae carmina ex codicibus Escurialensibus, Florentinis, Parisinis et Vaticanis* (Paris, 1855–57), 1:117–18, no. CCXXIII.

6 On this couple, see Ioannes G. Leontiades, *Die Tarchaneiotai: Eine prosopographisch-sigillographische Studie* (Thessalonike, 1998), nos. 32 and 38; *PLP*, nos. 27504 and 27511 (= 4202).

7 Trans. Alexander van Millingen, *Byzantine Churches in Constantinople* (London, 1912), 159, with minor modifications. Unless otherwise indicated, all translations from the Greek in this essay are my own.

8 On this manuscript, see Gustav H. Karlsson, ed., *Codex Upsaliensis Graecus 28: Geschichte und Beschreibung der Handschrift nebst einer Nachlese von Texten* (Stockholm, 1981). Incidentally, this is not one of the manuscripts consulted by Emmanuel Miller for his edition of Philes (above n. 5). The Upsaliensis preserves a slightly different version of the epigram. Line 14, e.g., here reads: "ὡς ὄστρεον δ' οὖν ὀργανῶ σοι τὴν στέγην." The same reading is attested in the inscriptional version of the epigram, on which see below.

9 On the funerary chapel of the Pammakaristos monastery, see Hans Belting, Cyril Mango, and Doula Mouriki, *The Mosaics and Frescoes of St. Mary Pammakaristos (Fethiye Camii) at Istanbul* (Washington, D.C., 1978); Arne Effenberger, "Zur Restaurierungstätigkeit des Michael Dukas Glabas Tarchaneiotes im Pammakaristoskloster und zur Erbauungszeit des Parekklesions," *Zograf* 31 (2006–7): 79–94; and Vasileios Marinis, *Architecture and Ritual in the Churches of Constantinople: Ninth to Fifteenth Centuries* (New York, 2014), 191–98. For the inscription on the cornice, see especially van Millingen, *Byzantine Churches*, 157–60; Amy Papalexandrou, "Text in Context: Eloquent Monuments and the Byzantine Beholder," *Word & Image* 17, no. 3 (2001): 259–83, at 276–77; and Andreas Rhoby, *Byzantinische Epigramme auf Stein: Nebst Addenda zu den Bänden 1 und 2* (Vienna, 2014), 661–66, no. TR76.

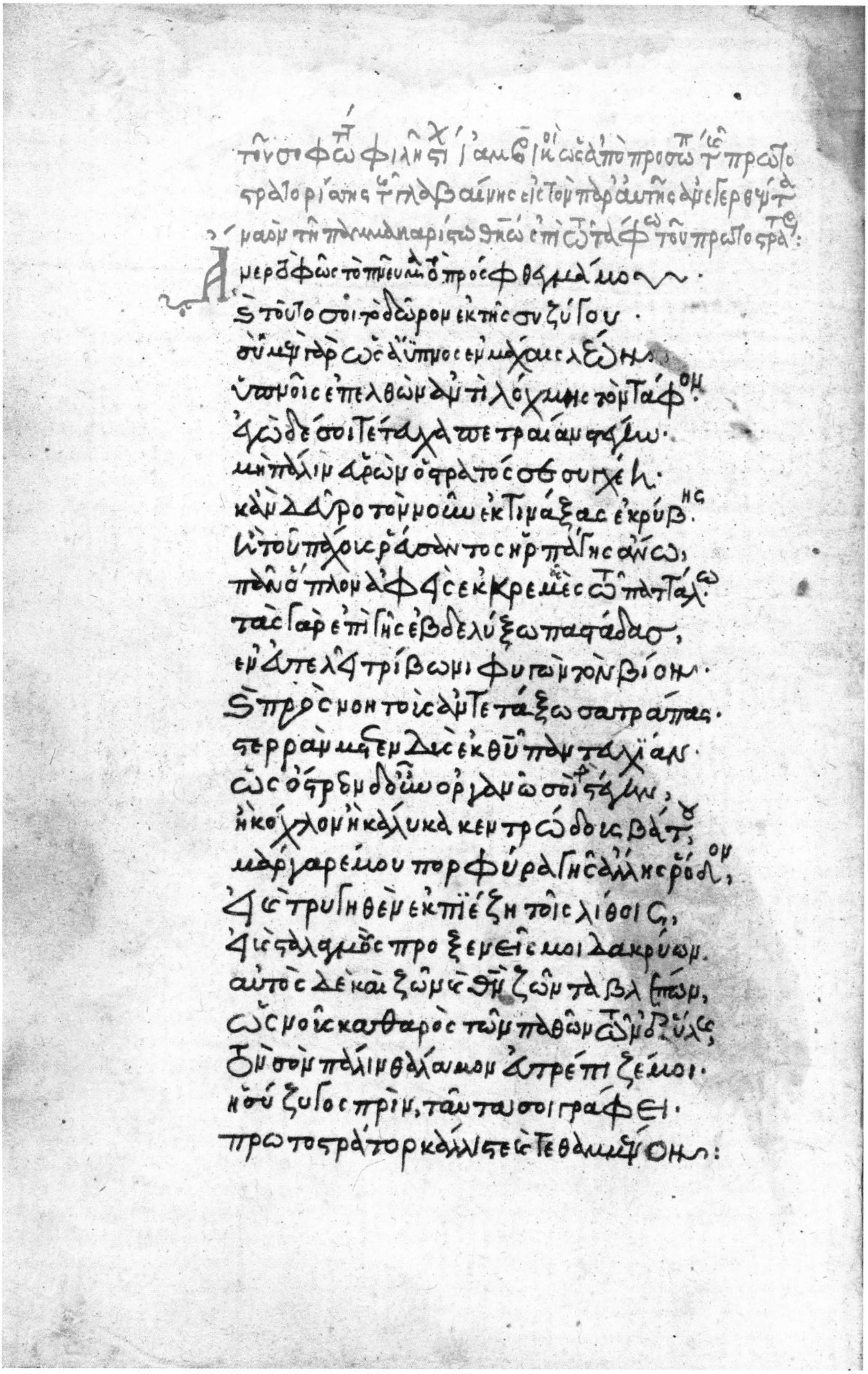

FIG. 3.1.
Epigram by Manuel
Philes on the
funerary chapel of
the monastery of the
Virgin Pammakaristos
in Constantinople,
Uppsala, University
Library, Cod. gr.
28, fol. 172v, mid-
fourteenth century.

Photo: Uppsala,
University Library.

FIG. 3.2.
Detail of the verse inscription on the funerary chapel of the former monastery of the Virgin Pammakaristos (Fethiye Camii), Istanbul, early fourteenth century.

Photo: Cyril Mango, courtesy of Image Collections and Fieldwork Archives, Dumbarton Oaks Research Library and Collection, Washington, D.C.

in relief along the face of the cornice, which is set at an angle and thus projects into space. The string of elegantly proportioned letters produces a controlled linear movement structured by a concatenation of dominant vertical strokes. Contributing to the inscription's ornamental quality is the generous use of ligatures as well as the occasional alteration of letters of different size, with one letter nestled within or growing out of another. The material presence of the epigram is further intensified not only through its integration with the structural and decorative system of the façades, but also through the interaction between the spectator and the marble verses. To fully experience the epigram, the inquisitive visitor to the chapel is forced to move along its richly textured stone and brick walls. In medieval times, this bodily experience would have been further enhanced through vocal recitation, as such metrical inscriptions were commonly read aloud.[10]

The stone inscription displayed on the chapel's façades opens Philes's poetry to sensory apprehension. Materialized in marble and experienced through oral performance and movement in space, the mournful dodecasyllables of Maria's lament acquire the status of a self-consciously aesthetic object—the epigram becomes an artifact. In what follows, I wish to explore the aesthetic dimension of epigrammatic poetry in Byzantine culture. I use the term *aesthetic* in a specific—one could say pre-Kantian—sense as referring to the domain of sensory perception and materiality. The term here embraces the visual, material, and other extralinguistic aspects of an inscribed text. The aesthetic dimension of the epigram, I argue, was not only recognized and appreciated by the Byzantines, but it also constituted a desired, if not requisite, feature of the inscribed verse. Epigrams were meant to be viewed as much as read; they appealed to the eye no less than to the mind. While the use of inscriptions as instruments of extralinguistic communication and signification is a phenomenon shared across historical and geographical boundaries (see, for example, Debiais and Winter, chaps. 7 and 10

10 On the practice of reading aloud in Byzantium, see Herbert Hunger, *Schreiben und Lesen in Byzanz: Die byzantinische Buchkultur* (Munich, 1989), esp. 125–29; Papalexandrou, "Text in Context," 259–83; Lauxtermann, *Byzantine Poetry*, esp. 55–56; Guglielmo Cavallo, *Leggere a Bisanzio* (Milan, 2007), esp. chap. 5; Amy Papalexandrou, "Echoes of Orality in the Monumental Inscriptions of Byzantium," in *Art and Text in Byzantine Culture*, ed. Liz James (Cambridge, 2007), 161–87; and Diether R. Reinsch, "Stixis und Hören," in

Πραχτιχά του ϛ′ Διεθνούς Συμποσίου Ελληνιχής Παλαιογραφίας, ed. Basiles Atsalos and Nike Tsirone (Athens, 2008), 1:259–69.

respectively), my aim in this essay is to unpack a culturally specific conceptualization of the aesthetics of the inscribed word. I focus not so much on Byzantine epigraphic practice as on the cultural discourse behind it. To explore how and why the epigram was conceived as an aesthetic object in Byzantium, I take my lead from a passage found in a twelfth-century source, a monody composed by Niketas Eugeneianos on the occasion of the death of his friend, and most likely also his teacher, the poet Theodore Prodromos.[11] The significance of this source lies in the fact that it offers us a rare instance in which a Byzantine author comments on the value and effects of epigrammatic poetry.

Celebrating the literary accomplishments of the dead poet, midway through the monody Eugeneianos sets out to praise Prodromos's panegyrics in hexameter and then turns to another genre in which Prodromos excelled, namely, epigrams (vv. 150–59):

> Καὶ κόσμον ἐκλέλοιπας σεπτῶν εἰκόνων·
> κοσμούμεναι γὰρ ἐκ λίθων καὶ μαργάρων
> ὡς κόσμον εἶχον ἐντελῆ σου τοὺς στίχους,
> καὶ κόσμος ἦν ἄντικρυς ἡ στιχουργία
> τοῦ κοσμοποιοῦ μαργάρου τῶν εἰκόνων.
> Ποῖον τὶ δυσθέατον ὑπὲρ τοὺς τάφους,
> ὧν ἐν πόνοις τίθησι καὶ κλῆσις μόνη;
> Ἠγαλλόμην δὲ τοῖς τάφοις ὡς νυμφίοις
> χιτῶνα χρυσόστικτον ἠμφιεσμένοις
> τὴν χρυσεπῆ σου καὶ σοφὴν στιχουργίαν.

You have left behind the adornment of the holy icons. For, being adorned with [precious] stones and pearls, they also had your verses as a perfect adornment. Truly the poetry of the pearl that adorned the icons [i.e., Prodromos] was a [form of] adornment. What is more disagreeable to gaze upon than the tombs, the very mention of which causes pain? Yet I took great pleasure in the tombs, which, like bridegrooms, were clothed in the golden words of your learned poetry as if in a garment embroidered with gold.

Prodromos, whom Eugeneianos likens to a pearl, has departed from this world, leaving behind his verses, epigrams affixed to icons and epitaphs displayed at tombs. Praising these two categories of poetic inscription, Eugeneianos dwells not so much upon their literary merit—this is, of course, implied—but stresses their visual aspect. As a perfect adornment, Prodromos's verses inscribed upon icons are juxtaposed with precious stones and pearls. Furthermore, the golden words of his learned epitaphs are explicitly conceived as things to be gazed upon and admired, artifacts that afford sensory pleasure through their physical appearance, transforming gloomy tombs into sumptuously arrayed bridegrooms. Eugeneianos, in other words, admires the inscribed verses penned by the dead poet not only for their literary content, but also for their aesthetic appeal as objects.

The author's enthusiastic appraisal of the visual dimension of Prodromos's epigrams must have been informed in part by contemporary epigraphic practice. Beginning in the eleventh century, Byzantine inscriptions became increasingly ornate.[12] The simplicity, clarity, and regularity of the former epigraphic style gave way to a taste for decorative effects. The uniformity of the uncial gradually broke down under the intrusion of cursive forms, accents, and breathing

---

11   Eugeneianos composed three monodies dedicated to Prodromos. One is in prose: Louis Petit, "Monodie de Nicétas Eugéneianos sur Théodore Prodrome," *VizVrem* 9 (1902): 446–63, at 452–63. The other two are verse monodies, one written in dodecasyllable and the other in hexameter: Carlo Gallavotti, "Novi Laurentiani codicis analecta," *SBN* 4 (1935): 203–36, at 222–31. The passage discussed below comes from the monody in dodecasyllable (ibid., 222–29). On Prodromos, see Wolfram Hörandner, *Theodoros Prodromos: Historische Gedichte* (Vienna, 1974); Alexander Kazhdan, "Theodore Prodromus: A Reappraisal," in *Studies on Byzantine Literature of the Eleventh and Twelfth Centuries* (Cambridge, 1984), 87–114; and Nikolaos Zagklas, "Theodore Prodromos: The Neglected Poems and Epigrams (Edition, Translation and Commentary)" (Ph.D. diss., University of Vienna, 2014), esp. chap. 1. On Eugeneianos and his relationship with Prodromos, see Alexander P. Kazhdan, "Bemerkungen zu Niketas Eugenianos," *JÖBG* 16 (1967): 101–17; and Michael J. Kyriakis, "Of Professors and Disciples in Twelfth [*sic*] Century Byzantium," *Byzantion* 43 (1973): 108–19.

12   See Cyril Mango, "Byzantine Epigraphy (4th to 10th Centuries)," in *Paleografia e codicologia greca: Atti del II Colloquio internazionale*, ed. Dieter Harlfinger et al. (Alessandria, 1991), 1:235–49, esp. 246; "Epigraphy," *ODB* 1:712; Phlora Karagianne, "Παρατηρήσεις στη χρήση της μικρογράμματης γραφής στις βυζαντινές επιγραφές (10ος–14ος αι.)," in Atsalos and Tsirone, eds., *Πρακτικά*, 2:681–88; and Rhoby, *Byzantinische Epigramme auf Stein*, 75–79. See also Hunger, *Schreiben und Lesen*, 129.

marks; abbreviations and ligatures proliferated; and playful combinations of letters, one growing out of another or placed within or above it, became common. Nonetheless, legibility never fell victim to ornamental exuberance. Moreover, although the fusion of image and letter—for instance, in the form of the figural or historiated initial[13]—was part of the Byzantine graphic repertoire, imagistic scripts were never used for inscriptions displayed on artifacts and buildings. Despite increasing interest in decorative flourishes, Byzantine epigrams carefully maintained the graphic integrity of text. Their legibility may have been occasionally diminished, but was hardly ever compromised.

Unfortunately, none of the icons and tombs for which Prodromos composed epigrams has been preserved. Yet it is safe to assume that the verses placed upon them were lettered in a decorative style characteristic of contemporary epigraphy. While the quoted passage from Eugeneianos's monody seems to register an awareness of and sensitivity to the visual effects of this style, it bears emphasizing that the author's praise of the aesthetic dimension of Prodromos's epigrams is not formulated in generic terms. Rather, it employs very specific language and imagery, which call for closer scrutiny. Notable in this regard is the prominence of the theme of adornment, or—to use the word employed by Eugeneianos—the theme of *kosmos*. The choice of this word, which, along with its cognates, appears no fewer than five times in the quoted excerpt, is not accidental. Kosmos is a semantically pregnant term.[14] Its primary meaning is "order" and, by extension, "the ordered world"

or "universe," but it can also mean "adornment," "decoration," and "beauty." In Byzantine textual sources dealing with what we now call works of art and architecture, the term is encountered in a variety of contexts. Kosmos can refer to any kind of enhancement or elaboration that goes beyond the purely functional or structural aspects of a work, anything that elicits a sense of wonder and joy in the spectator or imparts value on account of its material opulence, elegant arrangement, or technical virtuosity.[15] In Eugeneianos's monody, however, the term is used in a very specific, almost technical sense. It refers to precious-metal and often bejeweled frames, revetments, and various kinds of appliqués affixed to icons.[16] The

13 See, most recently, Emma Maayan Fanar, *Revelation through the Alphabet: Aniconism and Illuminated Initial Letters in Byzantine Artistic Imagination* (Geneva, 2011), with further bibliography. See also the contributions by Kessler and Hahn in this volume.

14 For the history and meaning of the word *kosmos*, see Hans Diller, "Der vorphilosophische Gebrauch von κόσμος und κοσμεῖν," in *Festschrift Bruno Snell* (Munich, 1956), 47–60; Jula Kerschensteiner, *Kosmos: Quellenkritische Untersuchungen zu den Vorsokratikern* (Munich, 1962); and Aryeh Finkelberg, "On the History of the Greek ΚΟΣΜΟΣ," *HSCPh* 98 (1998): 103–36. See also Pierre Chantraine, *Dictionnaire étymologique de la langue grecque: Histoire des mots* (Paris, 1999), s.v. "κόσμος." On kosmos, see in addition the seminal essay on ornament by Ananda K. Coomaraswamy, "Ornament," *ArtB* 21 (1939): 375–82.

15 Countless examples may be cited, but see Jan Olof Rosenqvist, *The Life of St. Irene, Abess of Chrysobalanton: A Critical Edition with Introduction, Translation, Notes, and Indices* (Uppsala, 1986), 2–4 (variously manufactured pictures and wall paintings as kosmos); the testamentary rule of Neophytos, abbot of the monastery of Docheiariou on Mount Athos (ca. 1118), in *Actes de Docheiariou*, ed. Nicolas Oikonomidès (Paris, 1984), 96 (liturgical cloths and vessels as kosmos); Inmaculada Pérez Martin, ed. and trans., *Miguel Ataliates: Historia* (Madrid, 2002), 164 (columns, annexes, vestibules, and other spaces auxiliary to the main body of a church as kosmos; marble revetment as kosmos); *Basilika* 59.3.7, in *Basilicorum libri LX*, series A, ed. Herman J. Scheltema and Nicolaas van der Wal, 8 vols. (Groningen, 1955–88), 7:2724 (the founder's tomb and portrait in a church as kosmos); and especially the *ekphrasis* of the Metropolis at Serres by Theodore Pediasimos, in Paolo Odorico, "L'ekphrasis de la metropole de Serrès et les miracles des saints Théodore par Théodore Pediasimos," in *Ναός περικαλλής: Ψηφίδες ιστορίας και ταυτότητας του Ιερού Ναού των Αγίων Θεοδώρων Σερρών*, ed. Basilike Penna (Serres, 2013), 127–54, at 133–34, which presents a veritable mélange of different types of kosmos. For the use of the term *kosmos* and its cognates in the context of the arts of the book, see Basile Atsalos, "Termes byzantins relatifs à la décoration des manuscrits grecs," in *I manoscritti greci tra riflessione e dibattito*, ed. Giancarlo Prato (Florence, 2000), 2:445–511, at 447–56.

16 For the adornment of icons, see André Grabar, *Les revêtements en or et en argent des icônes byzantines du Moyen Âge* (Venice, 1975); Nancy Patterson Ševčenko, "Vita Icons and 'Decorated' Icons of the Komnenian Period," in *Four Icons in the Menil Collection*, ed. Bertrand Davezac (Houston, 1992), 57–69; Irina A. Sterligova, *Dragotsennyi ubor drevnerusskikh ikon XI–XIV vekov: Proiskhozhdenie, simvolika, khudozhestvennyi obraz* (Moscow, 2000); Titos Papamastorakis, "The Display of Accumulated Wealth in Luxury Icons: Gift-Giving from the Byzantine Aristocracy to God in the Twelfth Century," in *Byzantine Icons: Art, Technique and Technology*, ed. Maria Vassilaki (Heraklion, 2002), 35–47; Jannic Durand, "Precious-Metal Icon Revetments," in *Byzantium: Faith and Power (1261–1557)*, ed. Helen C. Evans (New York, 2004), 243–51; Glenn Peers, *Sacred Shock: Framing Visual Experience in Byzantium* (University Park, Pa., 2004),

practice of adorning icons, relics, Gospel books, and other sacred objects with precious materials was well established in Byzantium, but it was in the eleventh century and later that such costly adornments came to be consistently designated as kosmos. In inventories, wills, and acts of donation, the term and its derivatives—*holokosmetos, kekosmemenos, enkekosmemenos,* and others—became a standard way of distinguishing objects, primarily icons, adorned with precious materials from the unadorned ones.[17] The kosmos of an adorned icon can be limited to a frame or nimbus, or spread across the icon's background or even across its entire surface (fig. 3.3). Occasionally, details of the costume or objects held by the depicted holy figure may be highlighted by revetment. Only exceptionally does the revetment expand to cover exposed parts of the flesh—a praying hand, for instance. In the case of relics, kosmos can take different forms: a sumptuous casket in which a relic is enshrined, for instance, or a few strips of gilded silver affixed to a saint's skull or finger bone. The kosmos of a Gospel book normally takes the form of a luxury binding, while that of a chalice may be in the shape of a precious-metal mount for the cup, embellished with gems and enamels.

By the twelfth century, adornment emerged as a culturally significant gesture in Byzantium. To add kosmos to a sacred object—an icon, in particular—became the quintessential, if not normative, manifestation of piety and largesse among the Byzantine elite.[18] Eugeneianos's claim that the epigrams penned by Prodromos constitute a form of kosmos in their own right must be seen as a corollary of the unprecedented importance attached to this gesture in the contemporary aesthetic discourse and devotional practice.

To fully elucidate the Byzantine understanding of kosmos and how it operates is beyond the scope of this essay, but I do want to make some general remarks relevant to the subject at hand.[19] Kosmos is, by definition, relational: it exists in

chap. 5; Annemarie Weyl Carr, "Donors in the Frames of Icons: Living in the Borders of Byzantine Art," *Gesta* 45 (2006): 189–98; Brigitte Pitarakis, "Les revêtements d'orfèvrerie des icônes paléologues vus par les rédacteurs d'inventaires de biens ecclésiastiques: Les icônes de l'église de la Vierge Spèlaiôtissa de Melnik (Bulgarie)," *CahArch* 53 (2009–10): 129–42; and Bissera V. Pentcheva, *The Sensual Icon: Space, Ritual, and the Senses in Byzantium* (University Park, Pa., 2010), esp. 198–208, 211–22.

17 The relevant documents include the inventory of the monastery of Xenophon on Mount Athos in an act of 1089, in *Actes de Xénophon*, ed. Denise Papachryssanthou (Paris, 1986), 59–75, no. 1, at 72; the inventory of the monastery of Saint John the Theologian on Patmos (1200), in Charles Astruc, "L'inventaire dressé en septembre 1200 du trésor et de la bibliothèque de Patmos: Édition diplomatique," *TM* 8 (1981): 15–30, at 20–21; an act of donation of 1240 concerning the monastery of the Holy Trinity in Thessalonike, in *Actes de Lavra*, ed. Paul Lemerle et al. (Paris, 1970–82), 2:1–4, no. 70, at 3; the inventory of the monastery of the Virgin *Boreine* near Byzantine Philadelphia (1247), in *Actes de Vatopédi*, ed. Jacques Bompaire et al. (Paris, 2001–6), 1:136–62, no. 15, at 157; the *typikon* of the convent of the *Bebaia Elpis* in Constantinople (between ca. 1285 and 1300, with revisions and additions from the 1330s and later), in Hippolyte Delehaye, *Deux typica byzantins de l'époque des Paléologues* (Brussels, 1921), 18–105, at 92–94, 102; the will of the *skouterios* Theodore Sarantenos (1325), in Bompaire et al., *Actes de Vatopédi*, 1:344–61, no. 64, at 355; the inventory of the monastery of the Virgin *Spelaiotissa* at Melnik (1365), in ibid., 2:299–304, no. 120, at 303; the inventory of the monastery of the Virgin *Gabaliotissa* at Vodena (1375), in Lemerle et al., *Actes de Lavra*, 3:105–7, no. 147, at 106–7; the list of belongings of Manuel Deblitzenos in an act of 1384, in Oikonomidès, ed., *Actes de Docheiariou*, 258–65, no. 49, at 264; an act of the patriarch Anthony IV of 1392, in Lemerle et al., *Actes de Lavra*, 3:122–24, no. 152, at 123; the inventory of Hagia Sophia in Constantinople (1396), in MM, 2:566–70, no. DCLXXXVI, at 567–68; and the inventory of the monastery of the Virgin *Eleousa* near Stroumitza (most likely 1449), in Louis Petit, "Le Monastère de Notre-Dame de Pitié en Macédoine," *IRAIK* 6 (1900): 1–153, at 118–19. See also the entry on kosmos in the online database *Artefacts and Raw Materials in Byzantine Archival Documents / Objets et matériaux dans les documents d'archives byzantins*, ed. L. Bender et al., http://elearning.unifr.ch/apb/typika/synthese/369, accessed 1 March 2015.

18 Nowhere is this phenomenon better documented than in epigrammatic poetry. In the twelfth century, adornment—especially in relation to icons—emerged as a pivotal theme in Byzantine dedicatory epigrams and, by implication, in the realm of artistic patronage that these texts were intended to commemorate. It is noteworthy that, while the language and imagery of kosmos are all but absent from the corpus of epigrams dating from the period between the ninth and the eleventh century, they are a staple in later Byzantine epigrammatic poetry. Even a cursory perusal of the relevant editions makes this clear: Roberto Romano, *Nicola Callicle: Carmi* (Naples, 1980); Hörandner, *Theodoros Prodromos*; Emmanuel Miller, "Poésies inédites de Théodore Prodrome," *Annuaire de l'Association pour l'encouragement des études grecques en France* 17 (1883): 18–64; Spyridon Lambros, "Ὁ Μαρκιανὸς κῶδιξ 524," *Νέος Ἑλλ.* 8 (1911): 2–59, 123–92; Konstantin Horna, "Die Epigramme des Theodoros Balsamon," *WSt* 25 (1903): 165–217; Miller, ed., *Manuelis Philae carmina*; Emidio Martini, ed., *Manuelis Philae carmina inedita ex cod. C VII 7 Bibliothecae nationalis Taurinensis et cod. 160 Bibliothecae publicae Cremonensis* (Naples, 1900); and Domenico Bassi, "Sette epigrammi greci inediti," *Rivista di filologia e d'istruzione classica* 26 (1898): 385–98.

19 For a fuller discussion, see Ivan Drpić, "*Kosmos* of Verse: Epigram, Art, and Devotion in Later Byzantium" (Ph.D. diss., Harvard University, 2011).

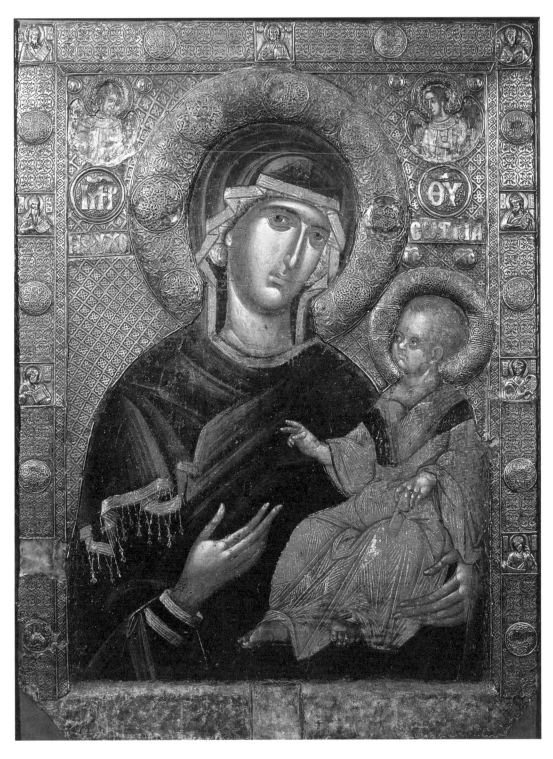

FIG. 3.3.   Adorned icon of the Virgin *Psychosostria* ("Soul-Saving") and Christ Child, early fourteenth century, Gallery of Icons, Ohrid.

Photo: Gianni Dagli Orti / The Art Archive at Art Resource, N.Y.

relation to the object that it adorns. Kosmos is also adjectival: not only does it enhance the object, but it can also inflect and empower it, or alter the object's status, function, and meaning. In fact, the object and its kosmos may be said to stand in a symbiotic relationship, in which the latter is not so much an adjunct, but a critical constituent of the former. Consequently, kosmos is perhaps best described in terms of "parergonality," as defined by Derrida in *The Truth in Painting*.[20] Like the Derridian *parergon*, kosmos operates within a liminal space between the essential and auxiliary, the intrinsic and extrinsic. Kosmos, finally, acts as a mediator between the object and the viewer. It can variously frame, stage, structure, and organize the appearance of the object. But through the accumulation and layering of precious substances and the resulting effect of material and sensory abundance, if not overload, kosmos can also externalize and make manifest the object's inner qualities—its sanctity, for instance.

Returning to Eugeneianos's claim that Prodromos's verses represent a form of adornment, we may ask, in what sense does a poetic inscription adorn the object upon which it is placed? How does the Byzantine epigram function as kosmos? The silver-gilt reliquary casket in the treasury of San Marco in Venice (fig. 3.4) may help us formulate an answer to this question.[21] Variously dated from the eleventh to the first half of the fifteenth century, the casket once enshrined relics of the four martyrs of

Trebizond in Asia Minor—Eugenios, Aquila, Kanidios, and Valerianos—who are depicted on the lid receiving their crowns of martyrdom from the enthroned Christ. A verse inscription running in two horizontal bands along the reliquary's four sides gives voice to the anonymous commissioner of this precious object.

Ὑμεῖς μὲν οὐ πτήξαντες αἱμάτων χύσεις
μάρτυρες ἠθλήσατε πανσθενεστάτως·
τοὺς τῆς ἑῴας ἀκλινεῖς στύλους λέγω,
τὸ λαμπρὸν εὐτύχημα Τραπεζουντίων,
πρώταθλον Εὐγένιον ἅμα δ᾽ Ἀκύλαν
Οὐαλλεριανόν τε σὺν Κανιδίῳ.
Καὶ τὴν ἀμοιβὴν τῶν ἀμετρήτων πόνων
ὁ Χριστὸς αὐτός ἐστιν ὑμῖν παρέχων·
καὶ γὰρ δίδωσι τοὺς στεφάνους ἀξίως.
Ἐγὼ δ᾽ ὁ τάλας πλημμελημάτων γέμων
ὑμᾶς μεσίτας τῆς ἐμῆς σωτηρίας
τίθημι φυγεῖν τὴν καταδίκην θέλων.

You martyrs did not fear to shed your blood but contended with all your might; I am speaking of the unbending pillars of the East, the gleaming good fortune of the Trapezuntines, the prizewinner Eugenios together with Aquila, Valerianos, and Kanidios. And Christ himself is providing you with the reward of your immeasurable labors; for he is giving out the crowns that you deserve. And I, wretched that I am, filled with sin, make you intercessors for my salvation in my desire to escape condemnation.[22]

From the Byzantine point of view, the silver-gilt casket acted as a kosmos for the now-missing relics of the four Trapezuntine martyrs. The same can be said of the verses placed upon it. Much like this precious box, the epigram itself served to frame, embellish, and amplify the holy remains, as well as to communicate their spiritual power and significance. It did so in a two-fold capacity: first as a poetic composition and second as a material artifact, a visually compelling string of boldly incised, nielloed letters, set off against a gilded background.

Granted that it is crafted with words skillfully arranged and intertwined according to the

20   Jacques Derrida, *The Truth in Painting*, trans. Geoff Bennington and Ian McLeod (Chicago, 1987).

21   On the casket, see Hans R. Hahnloser, ed., *Il Tesoro di San Marco*, vol. 2, *Il tesoro e il museo* (Florence, 1971), cat. no. 33 (Anatole Frolow); Jan Olof Rosenqvist, "Local Worshipers, Imperial Patrons: Pilgrimage to St. Eugenios of Trebizond," *DOP* 56 (2002): 193–212, at 210–11; and Evans, ed., *Byzantium: Faith and Power*, cat. no. 74 (Brandie Ratliff). For the verse inscription on the casket, see especially Alice-Mary Talbot, "Epigrams in Context: Metrical Inscriptions on Art and Architecture of the Palaiologan Era," *DOP* 53 (1999): 75–90, at 83–84; and Andreas Rhoby, *Byzantinische Epigramme auf Ikonen und Objekten der Kleinkunst: Nebst Addenda zu Band 1 'Byzantinische Epigramme auf Fresken und Mosaiken'* (Vienna, 2010), 260–62, no. Me85. The casket has been commonly dated to the fourteenth or the first half of the fifteenth century, but the paleography of the inscription suggests an earlier, eleventh- or twelfth-century date. See André Guillou, *Recueil des inscriptions grecques médiévales d'Italie* (Rome, 1996), 93–94, no. 91; and Rhoby, *Byzantinische Epigramme auf Ikonen*, 260.

22   Trans. Talbot, "Epigrams in Context," 84.

FIG. 3.4.
Reliquary casket of
the Four Martyrs
of Trebizond,
eleventh/twelfth or
fourteenth/fifteenth
century, Treasury of
San Marco, Venice.

Photo: Cameraphoto
Arte, Venice / Art
Resource, N.Y.

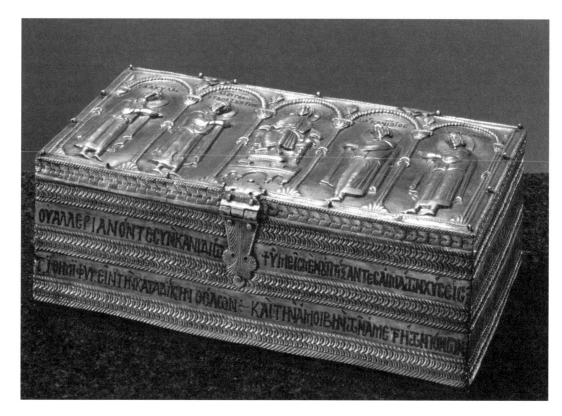

rules of prosody and rhetoric, a poetic inscription may adorn the object it accompanies as a literary text, or *logos*.[23] This notion explains in part the justaposition of verses with gems and pearls in Eugeneianos's eulogy of Prodromos's epigrams. In Byzantium, literary works were often celebrated by comparison with pieces of jewelry. In an epigram on the collection of homilies of Saint John Chrysostom, known characteristically as *Margaritai* ("Pearls"), the eleventh-century poet Christopher of Mitylene pictures the *logoi* of the gold-mouthed preacher as pearls rolling off his lips.[24] The same conceit appears in nonreligious contexts. In one of his letters, the great polymath Michael Psellos speaks of his literary products as "ἐλλόβια λογικὰ καὶ

περιδέραια γνωστικὰ καὶ περιτραχήλιοι κόσμοι καὶ ἐπιστήθιοι" ("discursive earrings and intellectual collars and ornaments for the neck and bosom").[25] Similarly, in a witty tercet composed as a retort to another tercet by an anonymous *grammatikos*, Theodore of Stoudios equates his verses, as well as those of his rival, with jewelry:

Τῇ τριστίχῳ σου χρυσομαργάρῳ φράσει
σμαραγδότιμον ἀντεπεξάγω χρέος·
αὐτὸς δ' ᾄδοις μοι μουσικοπρεπῶς πάλιν.[26]

In response to your three-verse discourse of gold and pearls, I bring my dues made of precious stones. Now sing for me again according to the laws of art!

Precious stones are, in fact, a uniquely felicitous simile for Theodore's iambs, which are not only prosodically polished, but sparkle with rare, recondite words such as *chrysomargaros* and

23 I use the term *logos* in the broad sense defined by Lauxtermann, *Byzantine Poetry*, 69: "The word λόγος denotes any text that appears to be structured according to the rules of rhetoric and that appears to have a certain literary quality. And hence it does not matter whether a λόγος is in prose or in verse, as long as it is worth reading."

24 Marc de Groote, ed., *Christophori Mitylenaii Versuum variorum Collectio Cryptensis* (Turnhout, 2012), 137, no. 141: Ναὶ μαργαρῖται χειλέων σῶν οἱ λόγοι, / οὐκ αὐχένας κοσμοῦντες, οὐ στέρνων πλάτη, / μορφὰς δὲ μᾶλλον, Ἰωάννη, τὰς ἔσω· / ψυχῶν γάρ εἰσι κόσμος, οὐχὶ σωμάτων.

25 Letter no. 7 to the *kaisar* John Doukas, in Paul Gautier, "Quelques lettres de Psellos inédites ou déjà éditées," *REB* 44 (1986): 111–97, at 135–36.

26 Paul Speck, *Theodoros Studites: Jamben auf verschiedene Gegenstände* (Berlin, 1968), 306–7, no. CXXIII.

mousikoprepos mined from lexica or perhaps, as in the case of *smaragdotimos*, crystallized in the poet's mind.[27]

The inscription on the San Marco casket may not qualify as great poetry, but its prosody is for the most part correct and its diction sufficiently elevated. Besides, the very choice of poetic form distinguished this text from countless pedestrian prose dedications, something that an informed viewer would not have failed to recognize. The literariness of the inscription, its status as logos, invested the casket with a distinct aura. It served to both enhance and reveal the preciousness of the relics lodged inside.

The remains of the Trapezuntine saints were adorned by the inscribed poem not only in its verbal, but also in its aesthetic dimension. The verses running along the sides of the casket are forceful in their material presence. Crisply incised into the precious-metal surface, their letters are filled with niello, a compound of sulfur, silver, and other metals, which, when fired and polished, creates an enamel-like effect. The black color of niello stands out vividly against the gilded background. Further enhancing the visual impact of the epigram is the restrained ornamental elegance of its script. The letters produce a dense decorative pattern that is playful yet devoid of calligraphic exuberance, with each individual letter form clearly distinguished and graphically intelligible. Despite a high level of uniformity and regularity, the script does allow for variation in the size and shape of letters. The decision to display the epigram on the casket in such a way that each verse occupies exactly either the length of a shorter side or half the length of a longer side has necessitated slight changes in character spacing, with some letters packed together more densely than others. The occasional use of ligatures, however, does not seem to have been prompted only by the need to save space but also by a predilection for graphic complexity. Particularly notable on this account are combinations featuring the letter T, which at times shares its stem with P or grows out of Ω or ϒ. Contributing to the overall decorative effect is the presence of accents, breathing marks, and double dots that in most instances hover above

the letter I, as well as triple dots signaling the verse endings.

Yet there is more to the aesthetics of the epigram on the San Marco casket. The spatial and visual presentation of the epigram, I would argue, speaks to a degree of self-consciousness. The nielloed verses, in a sense, recognize their own aesthetic force. Working in concert with the imagery and design of the casket, they call attention to the idea of calligraphic script as a form of kosmos. Key in this regard is the motif of crowning. The scene on the casket's lid shows Christ presenting the Trapezuntine saints with crowns of martyrdom. There is, however, another crown with which the four martyrs are being rewarded here. In a gesture mirroring that of Christ, the anonymous commissioner honors his intercessors with a crown made of words. Indeed, the verses running along the sides of the casket once encircled quite literally, like a wreath, the relics deposited within. Introduced by a cross in the middle of the upper register on the reliquary's front side, to the right of the clasp, the inscription runs along its perimeter, making a full circuit, and then continues in the lower register retracing its route around the reliquary. The notion that the unfolding script represents a complementary crown for the martyrs, one fashioned with words, is strengthened by the characteristic design of the casket's exterior. Significantly, the superimposed ornamental bands on its sides, which frame and offset the two registers of the text, consist of highly stylized braids, twisted ropes, and foliage, all resembling wreaths.[28] This association between letters and wreath-like ornaments highlights the aesthetic dimension of writing and the material and visual aspects of the linguistic sign. By implication, it foregrounds the script itself, the nielloed lettering on gold, as a form of adornment in its own right.

The Byzantine epigram thus attains the status of kosmos in two complementary ways: as poetry, an instantiation of logos, and as a material artifact. I shall revisit the interplay between these two dimensions in the conclusion, but now we

---

27 See Speck's commentary in ibid.

28 Another wreath-like ornament on the reliquary (now lost) was a string of small pearls that once bordered the lid. Its presence is signaled by a series of hoops along the lid's perimeter, which were needed to secure it.

must return to Eugeneianos's monody and take a closer look at the manner in which he praises the epitaphs composed by Prodromos. Recall that in the relevant lines the author notices the power of these poetic inscriptions, which, in his account, have the ability to transform gloomy tombs into gorgeous bridegrooms, richly clad in garments fashioned with words. Eugeneianos's striking simile draws upon several sources. The figure of the bridegroom, for instance, evokes the imagery of the biblical Song of Songs. Underlying the comparison of the inscribed verses and garments is the notion of text as textile, a venerable motif in the Greek literary tradition.[29] To give but one example of the use of this motif, in a poem addressed to one of his patrons, Manuel Philes advertises his verbal artistry as follows:

Ἐγὼ δέ σοι πρέποντας ἀθροίσας μίτους
χλαμύδα λαμπρὰν τεχνικῶν πλέξω κρότων,
ἣν οὐδ' ὁ πᾶς δήπουθεν ἐκτρίψει χρόνος.[30]

Having strung together threads fitting for you, I shall skillfully knit a splendid cloak of beats/rhythms,[31] which not even all of time could destroy.

The idea of the tomb as a personified being, on the other hand, must have been informed by a common poetic device in Byzantine epitaphs, namely, the trope of the speaking object.[32] Prodromos, in fact, employed this device on several occasions.[33] In epitaphs featuring the trope, the tomb itself speaks in the first person, typically addressing the passerby and informing him or her about the identity of its occupant. Through this device, sepulchral inscriptions lend voice to inanimate memorials and, in a sense, endow them with life. Eugeneianos puts a twist on this notion of animation by claiming that Prodromos's epitaphs clothe the tombs they accompany.

The association between inscriptions and clothing in Byzantium was both metaphorical and real. Actual garments worn by the Byzantines bore texts, sometimes poetic in nature.[34] In the realm of painting, especially in monumental works, clothing was a common locus of epigraphic elaboration. Inscriptions of different kinds appear on the garments of holy figures, typically on collars, hems, cuffs, and decorative bands.[35] They may consist of quotations from Scripture, short invocations, or names, epithets, and initials. By and large, however, such sartorial inscriptions are completely nonsensical.[36] Leaving examples of the so-called Kufesque aside, pseudo-inscriptions on garments in Byzantine paintings usually combine identifiable Greek letters with fanciful letterlike forms, often reminiscent of Hebrew, Arabic, or Cyrillic writing. The figure of Saint Orestes in the Church of the Annunciation at Gračanica (ca. 1320), Kosovo, provides a characteristic example (fig. 3.5).[37] The

29 See Ann L. T. Bergren, "Language and the Female in Early Greek Thought," *Arethusa* 16 (1983): 69–96; and Beate Wagner-Hasel, "*Textus* und *texere*, *hýphos* und *hyphaínein*: Zur metaphorischen Bedeutung des Webens in der griechisch-römischen Antike," in *Textus im Mittelalter: Komponenten und Situationen des Wortgebrauchs im schriftsemantischen Feld*, ed. Ludolf Kuchenbuch and Uta Kleine (Göttingen, 2006), 15–42. See also Anna Caramico, "Policromatismo semantico nel *De animalium proprietate* di Manuele File," in *Vie per Bisanzio: VII Congresso Nazionale dell'Associazione Italiana di Studi Bizantini*, ed. Antonio Rigo et al. (Bari, 2013), 1:157–66.

30 Miller, ed., *Manuelis Philae carmina*, 1:195, no. XV, vv. 6–8.

31 The reference to κρότοι here alludes to the vocal recitation of Philes's verses.

32 For the ancient background of this trope, see Mario Burzachechi, "Oggetti parlanti nelle epigrafi greche," *Epigraphica* 24 (1962): 3–54; Jesper Svenbro, *Phrasikleia: An Anthropology of Reading in Ancient Greece*, trans. Janet Lloyd (Ithaca, N.Y., 1993), esp. chap. 2; and Michael A. Tueller, *Look Who's Talking: Innovations in Voice and Identity in Hellenistic Epigram* (Leuven, 2008), esp. chap. 1.

33 Hörandner, *Theodoros Prodromos*, nos. XXVIa, XXIX, LVIII, LXIVa.

34 See, e.g., the two epigrams composed by Manuel Straboromanos for a sumptuous cloak with an image of Saint Demetrios, which the emperor Alexios I Komnenos received as a gift from his wife, Irene Doukaina: Paul Gautier, "Le dossier d'un haut fonctionnaire d'Alexis Iᵉʳ Comnène, Manuel Straboromanos," *REB* 23 (1965): 168–204, at 201.

35 See especially Smiljka Gabelić, "Prophylactic and Other Inscriptions in Late Byzantine Fresco Painting," in *Byzantinische Malerei: Bildprogramme, Ikonographie, Stil*, ed. Guntram Koch (Wiesbaden, 2000), 57–72.

36 For nonsensical letters on clothing, see Soterios K. Kissas, "Ἡ Μονὴ Ἁγίων Ἀποστόλων Νερομάνας Αἰτωλίας," Ἐπ.Ἐτ.Στερ.Μελ. 3 (1971–72): 21–64, esp. 51–57; Gennadiĭ V. Popov, "Shriftovoĭ dekor rospisi Mikhailoarkhangel'skogo sobora v Staritse. 1406–1407 gg." in *Drevne-russkoe iskusstvo: Monumental'naia zhivopis' XI–XVII vv.* (Moscow, 1980), 274–96, esp. 282–90; and Gabelić, "Prophylactic and Other Inscriptions," 57–72.

37 Vladimir R. Petković, *La peinture serbe du Moyen Âge* (Belgrade, 1930–34), 2: pl. LXV.

FIG. 3.5.
Saint Orestes,
ca. 1320, Church of
the Annunciation,
Gračanica.

Photo courtesy of
BLAGO Fund.

saint sports a mantle embellished with a horizontal strip bearing a sequence of nonsensical characters, some of which resemble real letters. One can pick out, for instance, what looks like the ligature for OY in the segment on the right, as well as disparate elements of the letters K and Λ, and the Cyrillic letter Б, combined into a highly intricate and dynamic visual pattern.

Far from being merely a decorative form, pseudo-inscriptions could be variously construed as repositories of sacred power, marks of

the foreign and the exotic, indices of an otherworldly realm, or graphic traces of the no longer comprehensible language of a sacred past.[38] For the purposes of the present discussion, however, I would like to point to the indeterminacy of pseudo-inscriptions, their ambiguous status

38 For the phenomenon of pseudo-inscriptions, albeit in a different context, see the excellent discussion in Alexander Nagel, "Twenty-Five Notes on Pseudoscript in Italian Art," *RES: Anthropology and Aesthetics* 59–60 (2011): 229–48.

between the linguistic and the iconic, script and ornament. The graphic constellation on the mantle of Saint Orestes has an undeniable ornamental force. Yet its strokes, squiggles, and dots are also recognizable as elements of a script, that is, visual representations of language, even though their linguistic content eludes us. Thus, precisely because they are unintelligible, pseudo-inscriptions call attention to writing as a visual medium. By exposing the duality between verbal content and visual form immanent within any written text, they throw into relief the iconicity of the linguistic sign. Their association with dress makes this aesthetic dimension all the more apparent, since in Byzantine culture clothing was a common metaphor for material and visual elaboration, and also one of the standard figurative similes for kosmos.[39] This partially explains why, for instance, Eugeneianos in his monody on Prodromos likens the poet's learned epitaphs to gold-embroidered garments. Both dress and the inscribed word have the capacity to frame, embellish, amplify, and externalize, that is, to adorn, to function as kosmos.

The nexus of clothing, adornment, and writing finds a vivid visual articulation in a group of Marian images dating to the mid-fourteenth century and later in which the Virgin's *maphorion* ("veil") bears an inscription borrowed from the description of the royal bride in Psalm 44(45):14: "Πᾶσα ἡ δόξα αὐτῆς θυγατρὸς βασιλέως ἔσωθεν ἐν κροσσωτοῖς χρυσοῖς περιβεβλημένη πεποικιλμένη" ("The king's daughter is all glorious within, arrayed with golden fringes, intricately adorned").[40] The imposing icon of the Virgin

and Child from the treasury of the monastery *ton Blatadon* in Thessalonike, dated to ca. 1360–1380, is a fine representative of the group (fig. 3.6).[41] Written, or rather embroidered, in a stately calligraphic majuscule, the psalmic verse runs along the luxuriant tasselled fringe that adorns the hem of Mary's maphorion, elegantly draped over her right shoulder. Since the king's daughter of Psalm 44(45)—the beautiful and sumptuously appointed bride led to her royal bridegroom—was often interpreted as a prefiguration of the Virgin in the Byzantine exegetical tradition,[42] the purpose of the inscribed verse was clearly to extol Mary and allude to her mystical marriage with Christ. Without doubt, the choice of the decorative hem as a place for the inscription was dictated by the reference to "golden fringes" in the verse. Undulating gracefully with decorative golden bands, knots, and tassels, this type of hem became a distinctive feature of the Virgin's maphorion in post-Iconoclastic art, and was associated with Mary's royal ancestry and interpreted by reference to Psalm 44(45). Thus, an *ekphrasis* of an icon of the Mother of God, variously attributed to John and Mark Eugenikos, explains:

Ἡ δὲ παντάνασσα μήτηρ ἐκ κορυφῆς ἄνωθεν, ἡ τηνικαῦτα ταῖς Σύραις ξύνηθες, πορφυραυγεῖ χιτῶνι κατέσταλται, ἐξαλλάσσοντι καὶ πρὸς τὸ κυανοῦν κατὰ τὸ τῆς ἴριδος ἄνθος, ἐν ἱματισμῷ διαχρύσῳ περιβεβλημένη, πεποικιλμένη βασίλισσα, Δαυὶδ ἂν ᾖσε. Τὸ γὰρ πρὸς τοῖς τέρμασιν, ὅποι παρείποι, λῶμα καὶ οἱ ποικίλοι κρώβυλοι καὶ θύσανοι οἱ χρυσοῖ, καὶ ὅσα τοιάδε, τρυφῆς καὶ χάριτος μᾶλλον, καὶ ὡς βασιλικῆς ῥίζης ἡ θεόνυμφος ἐξέφυ τεκμήρια.[43]

39   For epigrammatic poetry, see, e.g., Horna, "Die Epigramme des Theodoros Balsamon," 189, no. XXIV.A; and Miller, ed., *Manuelis Philae carmina*, 1:214, no. XXXVIII, and 2:93, no. LII. In Modern Greek usage, precious-metal revetments affixed to icons are sometimes referred to as πουκάμισα ("shirts") or ποδιές ("aprons" or "skirts"): Giota Oikonomake-Papadopoulou, Ἐκκλησιαστικά ἀργυρά (Athens, 1980), 23. The standard term for icon revetment in Modern Greek is ἐπένδυση. Derived from ἐνδύω ("to put on" clothes), the term carries the connotation of "clothing" or "dressing": Demetrios Demetrakos, Μέγα λεξικὸν ὅλης τῆς ἑλληνικῆς γλώσσης (Athens, 1936–50), s.v. "ἐπένδυσις." In Church Slavonic, the word *riza*, meaning "garment," may also denote a precious-metal revetment: Sterligova, *Dragotsennyĭ ubor*, 46. For the affinity between garments and luxury book covers, see Atsalos, "Termes byzantins relatifs à la décoration des manuscrits grecs," 2:460–62.

40   On this group of Marian images, see Gordana Babić, "Le maphorion de la Vierge et le psaume 44(45) sur les images

du XIVᵉ siècle," in Εὐφρόσυνον: Ἀφιέρωμα στον Μανόλη Χατζιδάκη, ed. Evangelia Kypraiou (Athens, 1991–92), 1:57–64.

41   See Loula Kypraiou, ed., Βυζαντινή καὶ μεταβυζαντινή τέχνη (Athens, 1986), cat. no. 84 (Chrysanthe Mauropoulou-Tsioume); Babić, "Le maphorion," 57–58.

42   See, e.g., Pseudo-Athanasios, *In Annuntiationem*, PG 28:937A–C; Neophytos the Recluse, *Commentarius in Psalmos*, ed. T. E. Detorakes, in Ἁγίου Νεοφύτου τοῦ Ἐγκλείστου Συγγράμματα (Paphos, 1996–2005), 4:327; and Gregory Palamas, *In Dormitionem*, PG 151:465B–C, 469B.

43   Jean François Boissonade, ed., *Anecdota nova* (Paris, 1844), 338–39. As noted by Henry Maguire, "Originality in Byzantine Art Criticism," in *Originality in Byzantine Literature, Art and Music: A Collection of Essays*, ed. Antony R. Littlewood (Oxford, 1995), 101–14, at 109–10, the author's characterization of the changing color of the veil is couched in language borrowed from

FIG. 3.6.
Icon of the Virgin
and Christ Child,
ca. 1360–1380,
Monastery
ton Blatadon,
Thessalonike.

Photo courtesy of
Monastery ton Blatadon

As was customary among Syrian women of her time, the Mother and Queen of all wears over her head a bright purple veil, whose color changes to dark blue of the iris. As David would sing, she is the Queen "clothed in a golden robe, intricately adorned." The fringe lining the edge of the veil on all sides, various golden knots and tassels, and similar ornaments are tokens of delicacy and grace and sure signs that the divine bride sprang from a royal root.

Philostratos the Elder (cf. *Imagines* 2.2.2). Boissonade attributed the ekphrasis to John Eugenikos. For the attribution to Mark Eugenikos, see Irinej Bulović, *Τὸ μυστήριον τῆς ἐν τῇ Ἁγίᾳ Τριάδι διακρίσεως τῆς θείας οὐσίας καὶ ἐνεργείας κατὰ τὸν Ἅγιον Μάρκον Ἐφέσου τὸν Εὐγενικόν* (Thessalonike, 1983), 506, no. 12.

In the icon from Thessalonike, the psalmic verse serves as a kind of caption or gloss, declaring somewhat redundantly the hem's ornamental function and further signaling its symbolic associations. Yet the verse is also self-referential. It proclaims its own ornamental force insofar as its elegant majuscule letters are part and parcel of the hem's decorative exuberance. Much like the tasseled fringe, the verse itself is here to adorn the divine bride.

The visual presentation of the psalmic quotation in the icon from Thessalonike employs chrysography, or "writing in gold." Eugeneianos alludes to this mode of writing when he refers to Prodromos's epitaphs as "χρυσεπὴς στιχουργία"—literally, "gold-worded poetry." Granted, the image of golden words is meant primarily to indicate the literary quality of the verses penned by the dead poet, but to Eugeneianos's audience, the adjective *chrysepes* would inevitably have brought to mind the practice of chrysography.[44] In Byzantium, writing in gold was normally applied to sacred and authoritative texts, Scripture in particular. In sumptuous biblical manuscripts, the use of gold ink declared in the most palpable way the significance and authority of the copied text. Prodromos's epigrams, of course, cannot compete with the word of God, but their literary merit—so the reader of Eugeneianos's monody may surmise—renders them worthy of chrysography. As a matter of fact, Byzantine book epigrams, that is, epigrams attached to other texts in the form of introductions, dedications, colophons, or titles, are often written in gold ink. This is one of several strategies by which such poetic paratexts are distinguished from the main text in a manuscript as well as from other materials.[45]

The final opening of the so-called Theodore Psalter exemplifies the kind of visual elaboration reserved for epigrams in Byzantine books (fig. 3.7).[46] This profusely illustrated manuscript of Psalms and Odes takes its name from the archpriest and scribe Theodore, who copied and possibly also illuminated it in 1066 at the Stoudios monastery in Constantinople at the order of Michael, the monastery's abbot and *synkellos*. The upper half of folio 207v is occupied by the concluding lines of the Ode of Zachariah (Luke 1:75–79) written in minuscule letters in brown ink, with enlarged initials rendered in gold. The lower half of the folio features a scene of presentation. King David, dressed in Byzantine imperial regalia, is depicted holding a psaltery in the *bas de page*. In a medallion in the left margin is a bust of Christ, who appears to be blessing the nearly obliterated figure of Abbot Michael below him. With his gaze lifted toward Christ, Michael holds a codex, undoubtedly the Theodore Psalter itself, in his left hand, while with his right hand he seems to point to the figure of David. The accompanying label written in gold ink introduces him as follows: "Ὁ ἁγιώτατος πατὴρ ἡμῶν Μιχαὴλ ὁ καθηγούμενος καὶ σύγκελλος ὁ Στουδίτης λέγει" ("Our most holy father Michael, the abbot and synkellos, the Studite, says"). The words spoken by Michael are written in large gold capitals within the main text block of the folio. They are poetic in nature and represent a short, two-line, dedicatory epigram in dodecasyllable:

44 On chrysography in Byzantium, see especially Lauxtermann, *Byzantine Poetry*, 274–84. For the use of chrysography in manuscripts, see John M. Burnam, "The Early Gold and Silver Manuscripts," *CPh* 6.2 (1911): 144–55; and Herbert L. Kessler, "The Book as Icon," in *In the Beginning: Bibles before the Year 1000*, ed. Michelle P. Brown (Washington, D.C., 2006), 77–103, esp. 77–82. See also Atsalos, "Termes byzantins relatifs à la décoration des manuscrits grecs," 2:484–94. On chrysography as "painting in gold" in Byzantium, see Jaroslav Folda, "Sacred Objects with Holy Light: Byzantine Icons with Chrysography," in *Byzantine Religious Culture: Studies in Honor of Alice-Mary Talbot*, ed. Denis Sullivan et al. (Leiden, 2012), 155–71.

45 On book epigrams, see especially Lauxtermann, *Byzantine Poetry*, chap. 6; and Daniele Bianconi, "Et le livre s'est

fait poésie," in *'Doux remède . . .': Poésie et poétique à Byzance*, ed. Paolo Odorico et al. (Paris, 2009), 15–35. For the elaborate visual presentation of other kinds of paratexts in Byzantine manuscripts, see Irmgard Hutter, "Marginalia decorata," in *The Legacy of Bernard de Montfaucon: Three Hundred Years of Studies on Greek Handwriting*, ed. Antonio Bravo García and Inmaculada Pérez Martín (Turnhout, 2010), 1:97–106; 2:719–34; and Kallirroe Linardou, "An Alternative to Illustration: *Marginalia Figurata* in the Codex Coislin 88 of the Bibliothèque Nationale," Δελτ.Χριστ.Ἀρχ.Ἑτ. 34 (2013): 285–300.

46 London, British Library, Add. MS. 19,352, fols. 207v–208r. On the Theodore Psalter, see Sirarpie Der Nersessian, *L'illustration des Psautiers grecs du Moyen Âge*, vol. 2, *Londres, Add. 19.352* (Paris, 1970); Charles Barber, ed., *Theodore Psalter: Electronic Facsimile* (Champaign, Ill., 2000), with further bibliography. For the final opening, see also Charles Barber, "In the Presence of the Text: A Note on Writing, Speaking and Performing in the Theodore Psalter," in James, ed., *Art and Text in Byzantine Culture*, 83–99.

Αἰνῶ σε, Σῶτερ, τερματίσας τὴν βίβλον
τοῦ σοῦ προφήτου καὶ σοφοῦ βασιλέως.

I praise you, O Savior, having finished this book of your prophet and wise king [i.e., David].

Claiming the agency behind the executed work—which in Byzantine dedicatory epigrams is typically a prerogative of the patron rather than the work's actual maker—the abbot with these words offers the book to Christ.[47] On the facing folio, 208r, one encounters a similar juxtaposition of texts of different kind. The short Ode of Symeon (Luke 2:29–32) is in the upper third, accompanied by the scene of the Presentation of Christ in the Temple in the margin. The Ode, introduced by a title in gold capitals, is written

in minuscule letters with the use of carmine ink. Again, the biblical text features enlarged gold initials. Underneath the Ode is a prose colophon. Its first half, written in gold minuscule, reads:

Ἔσχεν οὖν τέλος ἡ τοιάδε τῶν θείων ψαλμῶν δέλτος κατὰ τὸν φεβρουάριον μῆνα τῆς δ' ἰνδικτιῶνος τοῦ ,ςφοδ' ἔτους· ἐπιταγῇ μὲν γεγενημένη τοῦ θεσπεσίου πατρὸς καὶ συγκέλλου Μιχαὴλ καὶ καθηγουμένου τῆς παναγεστάτης καὶ πανευφήμου μονῆς...

This book of the divine Psalms was completed in the month of February of the fourth indiction of the year 6574 [1066] at the order of the divinely inspired father and *synkellos* Michael, abbot of the all-holy and all-praiseworthy monastery [of Stoudios].[48]

The second half of the colophon, separated from the first by five gold asterisks, is rendered in

FIG. 3.7.
Theodore Psalter, fols. 207v–208r. London, British Library, Add. MS. 19,352.

Photo courtesy of British Library.

47 It is possible, however, that the phrase "τερματίσας τὴν βίβλον" is to be understood in the sense of "having finished reading this book." See Georgi R. Parpulov, "Psalters and Personal Piety in Byzantium," in *The Old Testament in Byzantium*, ed. Paul Magdalino and Robert Nelson (Washington, D.C., 2010), 93.

48 The name of the monastery has been erased.

carmine minuscule letters. It provides information about the scribe:

Χειρὶ δὲ γραφὲν καὶ χρυσογραφηθὲν Θεοδώρου πρωτοπρεσβυτέρου τῆς αὐτῆς μονῆς καὶ βιβλιογράφου τοῦ ἐκ Καισαρείας, ἣν ποιμὴν καὶ φωστὴρ ὁ κλεινὸς ὦπται καὶ λαμπρὸς Βασίλειος ὁ τῷ ὄντι μέγας καὶ ὢν καὶ καλούμενος.

Written and written in gold by the hand of Theodore, the archpriest of this monastery and scribe from Caesarea, whose shepherd and luminary was the glorious and brilliant Basil [i.e., Saint Basil the Great], who was truly great and was also so named.

Underneath another row of carmine asterisks is a dodecasyllable monostich, written in large gold capitals:

Χριστῷ ἄνακτι δόξα καὶ κράτος πρέπει.

Glory and power belong to Christ the King.

Through the use of different scripts and the presence or absence of gold, the final opening of the Theodore Psalter establishes a clear hierarchy of paratextual material. The two epigrams and the prose colophon are neatly and visually distinguished. The colophon is written in a fine yet less graphically elaborate minuscule script. Quite remarkably, a sort of internal hierarchy is even maintained within the colophon itself, with the use of gold in the section mentioning the patron of the manuscript and the simple carmine ink in that recording the name of the manuscript's producer. A much higher degree of graphic elaboration has been accorded to the poetic paratexts: the patron's dedicatory address and the short metrical doxology. The scribe has rendered these two epigrams in calligraphic gold capitals. This kind of display script represents a variant of what Herbert Hunger has termed *epigraphische Auszeichnungsmajuskel*, the type of writing that borrows its letter forms from monumental epigraphy.[49] Texts written in this highly stylized

epigraphic mode retain some of the grandeur, dignity, and decorative elegance of monumental stone inscriptions. In the Theodore Psalter the epigraphische Auszeichnungsmajuskel in gold has been reserved for titles, initial letters, and select passages from the Psalms. In the final opening, it has been employed to single out and emphasize the inscriptions in verse.[50] The emphatically ornate presentation of these texts effectively conveys their poetic nature.

The foregoing discussion of the Byzantine epigram as an aesthetic object allows us to draw some conclusions. The Byzantines were clearly sensitive to the extralinguistic aspects of verse inscriptions. The aesthetic dimension of epigrammatic poetry was not just recognized and admired; the inscribed verse, in fact, called for graphic and material elaboration. In a sense, the poetic nature of an inscription was expected to be communicated in the shape, materiality, and the spatial arrangement of its lettering. This is not to suggest that the Byzantines maintained a strict visual differentiation between poetic and nonpoetic texts. To be sure, in many, if not most, instances it is impossible to tell whether an inscription is in verse or in prose simply by looking at it.[51] And there are certainly a number of epigrams preserved in situ that feature strikingly careless and incompetent scripts. However, my concern in this essay has not been so much with the actual epigraphic practice, but rather with a larger discourse that defines the status, function, and effects of epigrammatic poetry in Byzantium.

As Eugeneianos's monody indicates, one of the ways in which the epigram was conceptualized in Byzantine culture was in relation to the notion of kosmos. The inscribed verse had what may be termed *kosmetic* potential. It could adorn the object to which it was attached

49 Herbert Hunger, "Epigraphische Auszeichnungsmajuskel: Beitrag zu einem bisher kaum beachteten Kapitel der

griechischen Paläographie," *JÖB* 26 (1977): 193–210; and idem, "Minuskel und Auszeichnungsschriften im 10.–12. Jahrhundert," in *La paléographie grecque et byzantine*, ed. Jean Glénisson et al. (Paris, 1977), 201–20.

50 On book epigrams in the epigraphische Auszeichnungsmajuskel, see Rudolf Stefec, "Anmerkungen zu einigen handschriftlich überlieferten Epigrammen in epigraphischer Auszeichnungsmajuskel," *JÖB* 59 (2009): 203–12; and idem, "Anmerkungen zu weiteren Epigrammen in epigraphischer Auszeichnungsmajuskel," *Byzantion* 81 (2011): 326–61.

51 Cf. Rhoby, *Byzantinische Epigramme auf Stein*, 77.

by virtue of its calligraphy, but also by virtue of its literary content, that is, its status as logos. In an intensely logocentric culture, such as that of Byzantium, the importance of this aspect cannot be sufficiently emphasized. In theory, if not always in practice, the verbal and aesthetic dimensions of the epigram were inseparable. One required and reinforced the other. If epigrammatic poetry, as Eugeneianos puts it, was "gold-worded," it glittered with a brilliance that was simultaneously interior and external, intellectual and material.

Rebus-Signatures

Béatrice Fraenkel

THE SIGNATURE HAS EVOLVED OVER A LONG PERIOD OF TIME. I HAVE SURVEYED the main stages of this long evolution in France, covering a period that stretches from the sixth to the sixteenth century.[1] I have traced the origin of the signature to the French Royal Chancery, whose archives served as the source of my historical investigation. These archives revealed that the signature's evolution was in fact a relatively complex phenomenon that was articulated in, and that incorporated aspects of, law, identity, and design.

Law is critical to the study of signatures, because the signature was an efficient sign imbued with the specific power of validating legal decrees. This power was regulated by normative texts that specified who must sign them and how. An example can be found in the 1554 Moulins Ordinance, which made the application of signatures on legal documents mandatory. Some offices, such as those of the notary, the chancellor, or the bailiff were actually subject to particular signing guidelines. The litigator, in particular, specifically warranted the authenticity of legal documents by affixing his personal mark. In this case, the signature was applied to a document after a series of judicial proceedings, and was meant to validate their due process and veracity. In other words, the signature contributed to a more efficient written law.

As a sign of identity, the signature also had to fulfill several obligations: it had to individualize and unmistakably refer to a specific person. The constraints of the autograph were a response to this demand for individualization. A signature could not be inked without one's own hand, so it required a personal, physical contact between the scribe and the document to be signed. The autograph, in other words, was a sort of ruse that forced the signer to present that most elementary proof of his being: his physical, corporeal person. But the graphic signature was not merely a simple mark. It had to be produced willingly, as a sign of personal agreement between oneself and others. It became the voice of a legal document, stating that the text—signed here and now by all parties involved—was both official and unique.

But personal handwriting was only one of the "individualizing factors" that was embedded in one's signature.[2] One's proper name was also of pivotal importance, as it represented the signer's identity, as it was rooted in the prevalent system of anthroponymy. The necessity of writing one's own name was at the linguistic basis of the sign, supported by the current definition of the word "signature" ("handwritten family name"): when we sign, we write our name.

1   Béatrice Fraenkel, *La signature: Genèse d'un signe* (Paris, 1992).

2   Paul Ricoeur, *Soi-même comme un autre* (Paris, 1990).

Name writing itself is a subcategory in the history and anthropology of writing. Depending on time and place, and its particular writing system(s), each literate society has developed new ways to write proper names that contradict the graphic standards applied to other elements of a written language. Furthermore, some proper names, such as those of kings and gods, received special treatment. This is particularly notable in Mesopotamia, where proper names appeared very early on seals, in ancient Egypt, where the use of cartouches is widely known, and in China with its calligraphic flourishes. Numerous examples may also be drawn from the large number of cultures shaped by alphabet-based writing systems.[3]

Rebus-signatures are of particular interest to me, as they sit on the cusp between the three constitutive elements of a signature: law, identity, and design. Law, because from the end of the twelfth century notaries started to use rebuses as signatures to validate their documents. Identity, because those rebuses encrypted the users' names and sometimes even their city of origin. And finally design, because the rebus is one of many ancient devices used to write a proper name. One might recall, for example, that just as cities in ancient Greece or in republican Rome used rebus heraldry to promulgate their names, so did numerous medieval European cities, as is corroborated by their coins and seals.[4]

From the late nineteenth century in France, a *rebusomaniac* era if ever there was one,[5] the rebus-signature phenomenon prompted many local intellectuals to compile and publish as many samples as they could find, albeit merely as curios. An exploration of those collections has generated a renewed interest in rebuses, fostering the dynamic research that has been carried out on the history of signatures and of notarization

over the last few decades.[6] I intend to follow the constructive evolution of notarial marks in particular, whose appeal revolves around an unexpected alliance between almost naive and clumsily drawn shapes, on the one hand, and designs that display an unabashed virtuosity, on the other hand. Both aspects, naïveté and virtuosity, appear in the eminently serious context of legal writings. Their uncanny combined presence should not preclude their analysis but, on the contrary, should encourage the application of deeper historical and anthropological approaches than those previously reserved for the study of signatures. Different words are used to refer to the personal marks used by notaries to validate their acts. In Latin the most common expressions are *signum manuale* and *signum manus consuetum*. The multilingual community of scholars uses different terms to designate these medieval professional signs. In German, for example, the term is *Notariatssignet*, in English it is referred to as a *notarial mark* or *notarial sign*, in French *seing manuel*, and in Italian *signum notarile*. In this chapter, I will use mark, signum (plur. *signa*), and also signature (even if the term corresponds to a modern phenomenon).[7]

First, I would like to present some of the research, both old and new, that has focused on the inventory and analysis of these handmade ciphers. I will set the rebus-signa back into the larger context of the handwritten marks used by notaries, the study of which traditionally belongs to the history of signs meant to convey both authority and identity. I will then explore how the process of transforming a proper name into a rebus evolved in parallel with the changes taking place in the anthroponymic system. The obvious correlations between heraldry ("canting

---

3 Anne-Marie Christin, ed., *L'écriture du nom propre* (Paris, 1998).

4 Léon Lacroix, "Les blasons des villes grecques," in *Études d'archéologie classique* I (1955–56), 89–115; and Brigitte Bedos-Rezak, *Sceaux des villes* (Paris, 1980).

5 I borrow this term from Valérie Sueur-Hermel, "Rébusomanie et estampes au XIXᵉ siècle," *Revue de la BNF* 18 (2004): 70.

6 For a comprehensive overview of studies about notary work, see Jean-Yves Sarazin, "L'historien et le notaire: Acquis et perspectives de l'étude des actes privés de la France moderne," *Bibliothèque de l'École des chartes* 161 (2000): 229–70. On the history of signature, see Fraenkel, *La signature*; Claude Jeay, *Signature et Pouvoir au Moyen Âge* (Paris, 2015); Béatrice Fraenkel, "La signature, Ce que signer veut dire," *Sociétés & Représentations* 25 (2008); and Frederick Bravo, ed., *La signature* (Bordeaux, 2011).

7 Maria Milagros Carcel Orti, ed., *Vocabulaire international de la Diplomatique* (Valencia, 1997).

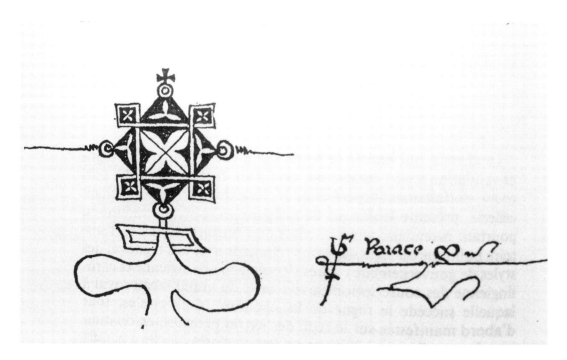

FIG. 4.1.

Large and small
signa (left and right,
respectively) of
Guillaume Raiace,
notary in Trevoux
around 1400.

After A. Giry, *Manuel
de diplomatique*, rev.
ed. (Paris, 1925), 607,
figs. 18–19.

arms")[8] and rebus-signa substantiates a theory
of interdependent emblems. I will then test
a hypothesis that links rebus-signa with the
broader universe of cryptography. Is it pertinent to place these devices within the lineage of
cryptographic practices? Finally, I will explore
the relevance of a new research trend that seeks
to interpret not only the enigmas embedded in
rebuses, but also the broader enigma of their use
as notarial signs. Was the selection of a rebus
simply a scholarly choice, or should one see it as
the conscious expression of a professional culture? How important were the rebus-signatures
in a period that was decisive for the history of
notaries? That is, the period during which the
character of the notary as a public figure invested
by local authorities was in full bloom. As Michel
Zimmerman has already summarized,

> the main innovation of the notarial profes-
> sion is the fact that the notary (*scriptor publi-
> cus, notarius*) is the custodian of the *fides
> publica*. In the hands of tenth- and eleventh-
> century scribes, good faith, sometimes con-
> trolled by the judge, replaces legal investiture

and handwriting ability constitutes legal
competence. The twelfth-century notary, for
his part, possesses an extrajudicial personal
authority that confers legality and authenticity to the documents that he writes. He
is a public officer and cannot refuse service
to anyone who agrees to pay the price. He
becomes the memory of his clients.[9]

We must wonder, then, what impact or role the
rebus signature had on this newfound authority.

Signum manuale and Rebus-Signa

Rebus-signa belong to a broader category of
signs that were marks of authentication used
from the twelfth to the sixteenth century to
certify the authenticity of a document. Arthur
Giry has noted that "the seing manuel or *signum*

8 "Those are coats of arms whose blazon, or verbal description in the language of heraldry, recalls the name (or, less
often, some attribute or function) of the holder of the arms."
See the Heraldica website by Françoise R. Velde, http://www.
heraldica.org/topics/canting.htm, accessed 1 March 2015.

9 "La grande nouveauté apportée par le notariat réside dans
le fait que le notaire (*scriptor publicus, notarius*) est dépositaire
de la fides publica. Chez les scribes des X et XI siècles, la bonne
foi, parfois contrôlée par le juge, remplace l'investiture légale
et la capacité graphologique tient lieu de compétence juridique.
Le notaire du 12 siècle, pour sa part, dispose d'une autorité personnelle extrajudiciaire qui confère légalité et authenticité aux
documents rédigés par ses soins. Il est officier public et ne peut
refuser ses services à quiconque accepte d'en payer le prix. Il
devient la mémoire de ses clients." Michel Zimmermann,
"Ecrire et lire en Catalogne (IXᵉ au XIIᵉ siècles)," *Bibliothèque
de la Casa de Velazquez* 23 (2002): 165.

PI IX

FIG. 4.2. Five rebus-signatures: (1) signum of Artaud Payen, cleric (1357); (2) signum of Pierre de l'Orme, notary in Lyons (1313); (3) signum of Teste, imperial and royal notary (1371); (4) signum of Hugues Verrier, notary in Forez (1277); and (5) signum of Jean Poulet de Montbrison, notary (1326).

From M.-C. Guigue, *De l'origine de la signature* (Paris, 1863), pl. IX.

or notarial mark is a sign of validation used by notaries."[10] This somewhat circular definition can be supplemented by Chantal Ammann-Doubliez's "personal pictorial mark,"[11] which has the advantage of highlighting the sign's iconic figurative feature. They were always autographed and came in various shapes. They could be geometric, realistic representations of diverse objects, letters, more or less complete renditions of a proper name, or a combination of these.

In some cities, the signa were filed in official registries as early as the thirteenth century, when notarial entities were just being established. In instances where a registered signum was changed or modified, the notary had to submit and register his new one. Toward the end of the Middle Ages, many notaries had two signa: a large one, reserved for more solemn documents, and a small one that was used more commonly and whose speed of execution made it a de facto signature (fig. 4.1). By the sixteenth century in France, it had become mandatory for a notary to sign legal documents only with his name, abandoning his drawn marks. This obligation slightly precedes the 1554 ordinance that also required private citizens to sign contracts by hand, without a seal.

Corpuses and Context

The first plates of collected signa appeared in Marie-Claude Guigue's opus on the history of signatures published in 1863.[12] It comprises twenty-three plates dedicated to signa, only four of which include rebus-signa (fig. 4.2). A few years later, in 1868, Emile Roschach published his first monograph on the authenticating seals used by the notaries of Toulouse from the thirteenth to the sixteenth century. In the city's

10 "Le signe manuel ou *signum* ou marque de notaire est un signe de validation utilisé par les notaires." Arthur Giry, *Manuel de diplomatique* (Paris, 1925), 603.

11 "Marque figurée personnelle," Chantal Ammann-Doubliez, "Les signes manuels des notaires dans le diocèse de Sion: De l'apparition du notariat public jusqu'en 1350," *Vallesia: Bulletin annuel de la Bibliothèque et des Archives cantonales du Valais, des Musées de Valère et de la Majorie / Jahrbuch der Walliser Kantonsbibliothek, des Staatsarchivs und der Museen von Valeria und Majoria* (2004): 281

12 Marie-Claude Guigue, *De l'origine de la signature* (Paris, 1863).

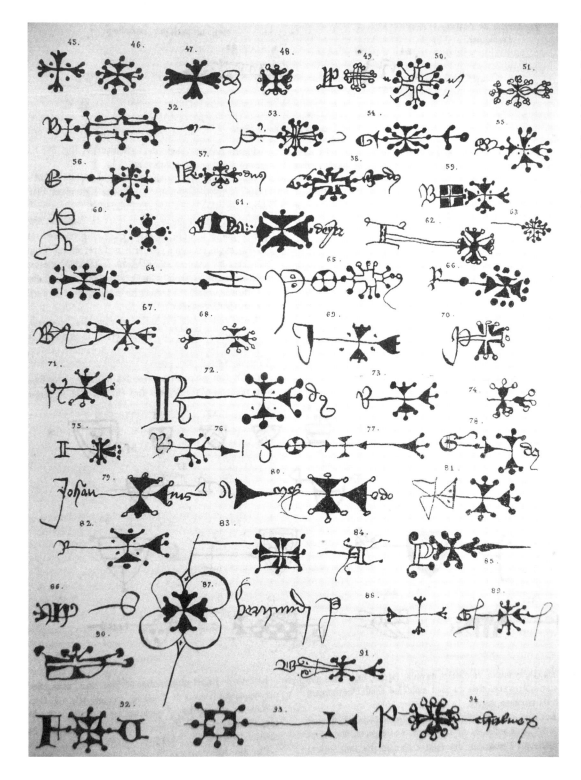

FIG. 4.3.

Signa of notaries
of Toulouse with
the Toulouse Cross.

From E. Roschach,
"Signets authentiques
des notaires de Toulouse
du XIIIe au XVIe siècle,"
*Revue archéologique
du midi de la France* 1
(1867): 147.

archives, Roschach found more than 11,000 notarial signs that were recorded between 1271 and 1536. He suggested dividing them into four categories, a classification system that is still in use today: two categories of signa refer to the proper name (the canting signa through the rebus and the alphabetical signa through the initials), while a third category is heraldic, and the fourth is geometric. Roschach's work incorporated reproductions of twenty-five rebus-signa paired with short commentaries, including the following definition:

The canting signets, plentiful during the thirteenth and fourteenth centuries yet extremely rare beyond then, are based on the same principle as heraldic canting arms. They are rebuses in their truest form that reproduce, with more or less perfect analogy, the way a name sounds.[13]

Roschach's analysis revealed semiotic devices other than analogy, such as synecdoche (used in alphabetical signa, for example, which include the letters of the notary's name) or metonymy (as in heraldic signa, which make multiple references to the city in which the notary practiced). He also observed some regional specificities, such as the pervasiveness of the Toulouse cross in the signa, which he believed epitomized the importance "of this essentially national emblem, the symbol of a vanquished civilization which, throughout centuries, would seek to restore its hegemony with a persistence usually reserved for hopeless causes" (fig. 4.3). He also identified cases in which a signum was transferred from father to son. This pioneering analysis established an enduring framework for the interpretation of manual signa, one in which the signs are scrutinized on their own terms, without consideration for the documents from which they were extracted. The analysis of these signs through this framework encourages both a semantic approach (to what are they referring?) and a rhetorical approach (how do they refer to that?).

However, a further examination of these inventories and modes of analysis raises several necessary criticisms. The first deals with the extent of the rebus-signature phenomenon. While revisiting the corpus in 2002, I was disappointed by the relative scarcity of rebus-signa. Contrary to Roschach's claim, they are in fact extremely rare; this fact has been further corroborated by many other sources. Thus, of the seven hundred notarial signa from the Dauphiné province cataloged by Edouard Maignien in 1878, not a single rebus is mentioned.[14] The same finding was made with regard to "the authentic notarial signets from the Tarn and Garonne" collected by Captain Poussy in 1890.[15] One must therefore acknowledge that rebus-signa are atypical at best among notarial signatures, and that late nineteenth-century intellectuals, always on the lookout for a new curiosity, exaggerated their importance.

Among recent inventories of signa, the *Catalog of Notarial Signa from the Diocese of Sion (13th Century to 1350)*, edited by Chantal Ammann-Doubliez, is of particular importance, but not for its quantity of rebuses. Ammann-Doubliez notes that only two of four hundred cataloged signs are rebuses, a fact that supports my own observations. Like many other scholars, she yearned for a science of signa comparable to sigillography and heraldry. Far from limiting herself to those pious wishes, though, Ammann-Doubliez actually innovated on several fronts. With regard to publishing, for example, she writes:

> it is not the reproductions of manual signa taken out of any context that one should be able to publish, for they have no inherent value, but indeed the documents on which they are affixed, in order to reveal the relationship between the text and the signa, their relative interdependent layout and size, the type and quality of the paper that binds them, etc. But this remains utopian in the traditional publishing world.[16]

The Double Inscription of the Proper Name: Subscription and Signa

Presenting the document in its entirety, favoring the whole over the signum, and abandoning the traditional presentation of signa in a section of plates, clearly changes our perception. The signum never appeared by itself; rather, it was inserted flush with the subscription, the short sentence handwritten by the notary to introduce himself, state his name, and often even his status and where he came from (fig. 4.4). The

13 Emile Roschach, "Signets authentiques des notaires de Toulouse du XIIIᵉ au XVIᵉ siècle," *Revue archéologique du midi de la France* 1 (1867): 145–52.

14 Edouard Maignien, "Les marques de notaires en Dauphiné," *Bulletin de l'Académie delphinale* 14 (1878): 46–57.

15 Captain Poussy, "Fac-similé du signet authentique des anciens notaires du département de Tarn-et-Garonne," *Bulletin archéologique du midi de la France* 1 (1890).

16 Ammann-Doubliez, "Les signes manuels" (n. 11 above), 287.

interaction between the signum and the sub-scription became preponderant because of the juxtaposition of the notary's surname with his signum. Our grasp of rebus signatures and of alphabetical signa is thus altered, for we simul-taneously see the enigma and its solution. The close proximity of the proper name and its rebus on the page suggests that deciphering is not what was expected from the reader or viewer. The rebus was not offering riddles, but served instead to transform a linguistic item into an image. It allowed a semiotic mutation that led to the creation of a drawing. The notary who chose a rebus-signum had to complete two different graphic tasks: he wrote his name in his subscrip-tion and he drew it in his signum.

These two tasks actually correspond with the different uses of the family name. In the subscription, the notary introduces himself. Sometimes he did this using the first person singular, as in "et ego Johanes Pomerii, notar-ius publicus ... feci publicum instrumentum et signo meo signavii inferius annotato" (see fig. 4.4), while at other times he used the third person singular, as in "N., scriptor Narbonensis publicus, scripsit."[17] In both cases the name was used as a mention.[18] On the other hand, with the rebus-signum the name that appeared as an image was used specifically to authenticate the act. The proper name can thus be seen twice, but in two different forms and with two different uses. The dual inscription of the proper name— the joint use of a drawn form and a written form—raises questions concerning the notary's decision to employ a rebus. In what working context did the rebus-signa make sense? It seems to me that while the hypothesis of a strong link between marks of authentication and of per-sonal and professional identity is reinforced, the relationships between the surname and rebus-signatures should be reconsidered. The act of writing the surname, and its subsequent trans-formation into an image, is perhaps more impor-tant than its simple enigma suggests.

FIG. 4.4. Rebus-signature of Jean Pommier, notarius publicus. Montpellier, Charte, 3 mars 1275, Archives nationales, Paris, AE/II/282.

Photo courtesy of Archives nationales, Paris.

17   Alain de Boûard, *Manuel de diplomatique française et pon-tificale: L'acte privé* (Paris, 1948), 219.
18   On the use-mention distinction, see *The Stanford Encyclo-pedia of Philosophy*, 2nd ed. (Stanford, 2005), s.v. "quotation."

Anthroponymic Systems and Rebus-Signa

The interpretation of the rebus-signum as a device through which a proper name was written can be fully understood only when the rebus-signum itself is reframed in its proper historical context, a context in which the graphic phenomena that I discussed above were established. The timeline here is particularly crucial: the various inventories that I have presented all agree that the signum flourished from the second half of the thirteenth century—when a 1270 ordinance issued by King Louis IX of France accredited notarial offices—to the sixteenth century. Claude Jeay's quantitative study on the evolution of notarial signa from Toulouse yields some critical information about the general evolution of all types of signa:[19]

	1288	1536
presence of letters	48%	3.6%
absence of letters	52%	0.9%
full name	0%	95.5%

It is clear that the proper name gradually evolved out of the signum between the late thirteenth and early sixteenth century. The initially sparse use of letters, typically initials that alluded to the notary's name, eventually became the complete formula that is used in signatures today: first name followed by surname. Rebus-signatures, as well as alphabetical signa, are thus connected to a different and major transformation that affected European societies: the anthroponymic system. It was indeed during the same period of time that the use of family names was becoming increasingly common. The notarial signa participated in this evolution, as did seals and coats of arms. Heraldry, which from its inception had favored emblems with geometric or organic figures, began to incorporate proper names. It is in this context that we see the rise of canting arms, whose vogue, according to Michel Pastoureau, paralleled that of the rebus-signatures.[20]

The relationships between the formation of proper names, rebus-signa, and canting arms are not coincidental. They all took part in the establishment of a new system that gave rise to the hereditary patronymic. For centuries, the first name alone had served as one's proper name; but a second element, which would become the surname, was added to complete it. As pointed out by Albert Dauzat in his treatise on French anthroponymy,

> the origin of family names can be divided into four categories: old baptismal names; names of origin, which evoke the provenance of a family, be it a town, a village, a landmark, or even a salient residential feature (Dupont [from the bridge], Duval [from the valley]); names describing an ethnicity (Picard [from Picardy], Lombard [from Lombardy]), a profession or a status (Mercier [mercer], Maître [master]), or a family relationship (Legendre [son-in-law]); and finally, the various types of nicknames.[21]

Dauzat's research sheds light on an all-too-often forgotten reality: proper names, for the most part, were created from common nouns. "The commoner," he wrote, "doesn't particularly care about his patronymic, until the day its original meaning gets somewhat lost."[22] We know that many nicknames were actually pejorative or ironic. The care taken to soften the sometimes humiliating connotations of one's own surname seems perfectly legitimate, but it is superseded by the desire for a semantic ambiguity of the proper name. The "Benoist," Dauzat remarked, are attached to the S in their name, just as the "Lefebvre" to their B. This propensity to keep complicated or archaic spellings comes from the "desire to distinguish, at least visually, the surname from its corresponding common noun or adjective."[23]

The original functional difference between proper name and common noun is uncertain. This distinction is sometimes expressed in the spelling, but may also manifest in other graphic

---

19   Jeay, *Signature et pouvoir au Moyen Âge*, 465.

20   Michel Pastoureau, *Heraldry: Its Origins and Meanings* (London, 1997).

21   Albert Dauzat, *Traité d'anthroponymie française, les noms de famille de France* (Paris, 1949), 39.

22   Ibid.

23   Ibid., 279–80.

elements: the rebus is one and the signature, which offers a personalized version of the way a name is written, is another. From that standpoint, rebus-signa are subtle apparatuses that morph common nouns into proper names. As we saw above, the notary's signum was included in the subscript—it was read first, then related back to the name it represented. The rebus can thus be deciphered. This back-and-forth process requires two separate actions: to read a word, for example "Auzels" ("bird" in the Occitan language), and then to name an image. Those two steps reveal the existence of significant layers of meaning; there is indeed a proper name and a common noun. Furthermore, continuing with the example of "Auzels," the somewhat derisive avian nickname loses its negative connotations in the drawing, which suggests a bird more than it represents one.

Were the rebus-signa part of the widespread trend among notaries to gradually adopt new anthroponyms in their writing? Alphabetical signa seem to have most directly preceded the signature, whose form gained prevalence in the sixteenth century alongside the generalization of writing one's full name. Yet should we go so far as to interpret the evolution of alphabetical signa as a progression by which a partial sign, one that merely contained a few letters of the name, gradually expanded until it reached the fullness of the signed name? Does the isolated letter not also generate an allusive process more complex than it would appear at first glance?

Transition through the Letter: The Cryptographic Hypothesis

To conclude this analysis of the impact of the anthroponymical evolution on the rebus-signum, I would like to go back to more general questions regarding the cryptographic function of signa. Rebus-signa concurrently reveal and hide a name. Alphabetical signa, inasmuch as they allude to a name more than they fully reveal it, offer another way to conceal the name. In both cases, as one might recall, the notary's name can be found in the subscription: we are thus not faced with solving an enigma, but rather with appreciating the name's transformation into a visual presentation. How can the

graphic elements of a signum be extracted from a name and then be imbued with certifying power? That is the critical question. To answer it, we must look at the more common processes involved in this transformation: the use of the initials, the design of a monogram, and the dispersion of the letters.

The use of a name's letters, and particularly its initials (that of either the first or the last name, but more commonly of both), is well demonstrated in signa. This use of letters perpetuated the practices already familiar to clerics and notaries of abbreviating a proper name, as was often the case with the names of popes, as a sign of respect.[24] Splitting up and reconstructing the letters of a name into figures seems to have been a privilege reserved for the mighty. Evidence of this trend can be seen in the monograms of kings and popes that were used to decorate coins and charters from the Carolingian period. Thus, one must consider with great care the checkered names collected by Maignien (fig. 4.5). Indeed, perhaps a certain solemnity should prevail where we see only graphic games. These examples suggest that alphabetical signa cannot be seen merely as precursors to signatures, and that showcasing some choice letters over a literal transcription required a very specific relation to the proper name. Notaries manipulated the letters of their names to strengthen the signa. Far from losing anything or being simple stylistic idiosyncrasies, the graphic figure actually gained some kind of symbolic power and added a significant level of authority and solemnity to the documents on which they were affixed.

Let us go back now to the general allusion principle at work in the few rebus-signa and in the more numerous alphabetical ones. The fact that notaries, diligent as they were in recording dates, places, and personal data, would introduce into their legal documents a cryptographic principle and allusive elements seems now to have been an undoubtedly pertinent strategy. The purpose of the signum was not to muddle the text of the document with ambiguity, but rather to include elements borrowed from other similarly formal and discursive spheres, such as

24 Jacques Stiennon, *Paléographie du Moyen-âge* (Paris, 1991), 317–18.

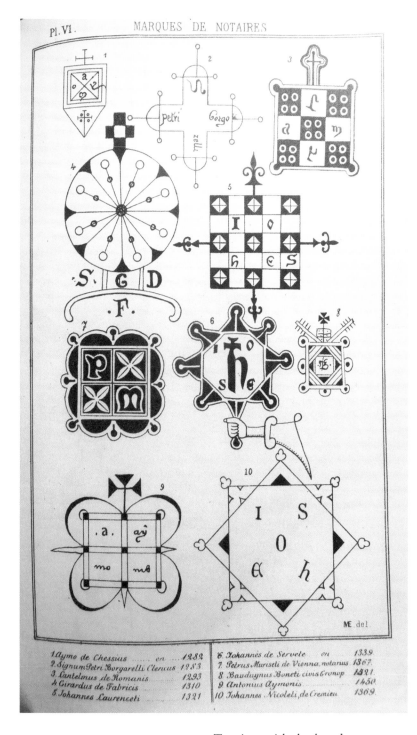

Pl. VI.   MARQUES DE NOTAIRES

1. Aymo de Chessius .... en ... 1282
2. Signum Petri Borgarelli Clericus 1283
3. Cantelmus de Romanis 1293
4. Girardus de Fabricis 1310
5. Johannes Laurenceti 1321
6. Johannès de Servete   en   1339
7. Petrus Muriseti de Vienna, notarius 1367
8. Bauduynus Boneti civis Gronop. 1321
9. Antonius Aymonis 1450
10. Johannes Nicoleti, de Cremieu 1369

FIG. 4.5.   Ten signa with checkered names.

From E. Maignien, "Les marques de notaires en Dauphiné XIIIᵉ–XIVᵉ siècle," *Bulletin de l'Académie delphinale* 14 (1878): pl. 6.

heraldry, cryptography, and scribal traditions. Those allusive forms, alphabetic and rebus-signa, break with the text while still being linked to it. The dual writing of the proper name in the subscription and in the signum graphically splits the power of the anthroponym to designate someone who had the power to validate the document. The signature ultimately subsumed both acts.

Rebus-Signa as Professional Cultural Marks

The Spirit of the Blazon: Imitation or Parody?

Everything leads to the understanding that rebus-signa not only followed the same process as canting arms, but were inspired by them. In both cases, a word had to be transformed into an image, and emblems drawn from a name had to convey one's personal identity. But just as the proper name became the foundation on which a coat of arms was designed, true to what Pastoureau calls the "spirit of the blazon,"[25] heraldry could also represent the origins of a name. This last point illuminates another aspect of the context in which rebus-signa evolved: they appeared during the period when heraldry became broadly disseminated (1180 to 1320). Seals, the other major tools of validation in parallel with signa, played a large part in the propagation of heraldry. They were its primary supports, they offered a wide gamut of secular motifs that inspired heraldry (canting arms in particular), and lent them a new legal authority. The proximity of signa, seals, and heraldry is thus both systemic and hereditary.

Nevertheless, the relation of notaries to heraldry and to rebuses could be even more specific than is suggested by this rather general overview. From a quantitative point of view, canting arms accounted for roughly twenty percent of all medieval heraldry. Furthermore, from the twelfth to the sixteenth century, their number increased. The same cannot be said with respect to rebus-signa, which were marginal among notarial marks and faded away as the signature imposed itself before the turn of the sixteenth century.

25 Michel Pastoureau, "Les armoiries parlantes," *Revue de la Bibliothèque de France* 18 (2004): 36–46.

From a qualitative point of view, one might also question the nature of the link between the model (the canting arms) and its imitation (the rebus-signa). Are we seeing imitation—notaries copying a prestigious model to dignify their marks—or parody—notaries mocking the nobility's pratices? Considering Jean Céard's and Jean-Claude Margolin's research on the history of the rebus and especially on the *Rébus de Picardie,* this last hypothesis is probably justified, although difficult to validate.[26] They demonstrate that the rebuses designed and exhibited each year by petty clerks who inhabited the parliaments, courts, and offices of notaries and lawyers were parodic. They belonged to a carnavalesque culture that did not hesitate to poke fun at important people. To craft pseudo-blazons was just one of the activities undertaken by many Basoche, the late medieval, professional, nonreligious communities of law clerks, who organized themselves in France through the thirteenth and fourteenth centuries.[27]

Nevertheless, rebuses were not used exclusively by these petty clerks. At the end of the Middle Ages, the taste for rebuses spread to men of letters attached to the great and powerful. Paul Zumthor has shown how sophisticated the rebuses of the Grands Rhétoriqueurs, a famous group of court poets from approximately 1450 to 1530, became within the princely courts. In this brilliant world, the carnival spirit was still there: such men as Gringoire, Baudet, and the notary Molinet were part of the Basoche.[28] As such, the popularity of rebus—be it in a popular and parodic vein or in a scholarly and ironic vein—coincided with the "notarial revolution" that started at the beginning of the thirteenth century.

The era of rebus-signa, or "canting-signets," that started in the thirteenth century continued through the fourteenth century and began to slowly vanish in the fifteenth century. This timeline, with the greatest proliferation of rebuses in the fourteenth century, differs greatly from Céard's and Margolin's research,

which ascertains that rebuses were particularly numerous more than a century later, from 1480 to 1530. Here again, as for the canting arms, the growing success of the rebus at the end of the Middle Ages both in heraldry and in the letters contrasts significantly with their fading away as notarial marks.

The Rebus-Signum: A Mark Apart

If we stick to observing notarial signs in their legal context, we must give attention to not only the signs themselves but also their layout. From the twelfth century, the signs tended to appear only at the bottom of legal documents, not embedded in the subscription. Thus, the notarial sign became more visible and its iconicity increased. More important, it was reinforced by its mode of presentation. The contrast between the scriptural world of the text and the signum manuale planted at the bottom of the document, clearly displaying its graphic shapes, was not accidental. Pastoureau's reflections on this are valuable: was there not a change in the value of the sign in this new scheme? Was the signum manuale not part of a vast revival of old marks "to which the fledgling art of heraldry gave impetus: family marks, workshop marks, artisan marks, merchant marks, usage marks, storage marks, etc. Medieval civilization is a civilization of the mark."[29] The visual assertion of the notarial signum in its natural environment, that of the legal act, relies on two opposing forces: the strength derived from the power of symbols—from their familiarity because they were part of a vast network of visual motifs that flooded medieval society—and the strength derived from the new salience given to these symbols by their new treatment in the graphic space of documents, particularly by their stylization as notarial marks. From this point of view, the notarial signs would have participated in a semiotic effervescence that affected professional emblems more broadly. It would be suitable,

---

26   Jean Céard and Jean-Claude Margolin, *Rébus de la Renaissance: Des images qui parlent* (Paris, 1986).

27   Marie Bouhaïk-Girones, *Les clercs de la Basoche et le théatre comique: Paris, 1420–1550* (Paris, 2007).

28   Paul Zumthor, *Le Masque et la Lumière: La Poétique des Grands Rhétoriqueurs* (Paris, 1978), 131.

29   "Auxquelles l'héraldique naissante a redonné vigueur: marques de familles, marques d'ateliers, marques d'artisans, marques de marchands, marques d'utilisation, marques de rangement etc. La civilisation médiévale est une civilisation de la marque." Michel Pastoureau, *Figures et couleurs* (Paris, 1986), 56.

then, to analyze graphic forms such as notarial marks as having been developed within the specific context of the notarial profession itself.

As an individual mark, the signum was placed on acts prepared by the same notary. The signum thus created a series of documents that were linked together by the same author, who was responsible for their quality, reliability, and validity. It quickly becomes clear that the initial design selected by a notary was modified over time, with changes of varying importance. As an individual, a notary could change his sign to reflect and advertise changes in his professional career. Thus, a fleur-de-lis or the keys of Saint Peter might appear in the sign, indicating a notary's newly acquired royal or imperial status. While this intrusion of personal elements into the signa loaded them with biographical depth, the seriality of the signs essentially highlighted the continuity of an activity and the permanence of an office, which the same notary might have held for up to fifty years. It is tempting to think that we can see, through the repeated use of a sign over a long period and in the same area, the anchoring of a man and his influential place in a community.

It is easy to see that the majority of notarial signs fell within graphic "families." Local features are prominent: in the registers of Toulouse, for example, many notarial signs display the footed cross, the city's emblem. Andreas Meyer's inventory also shows the strong presence of initial letters designating the name of the town that had hired a notary.[30] The elements included in notarial signs are easy to decode: the letters of the notary's name, the keys of Saint Peter, the fleur-de-lis, or aspects of family crests all functioned as symbols to be read. On the other hand, many regional markers retained a degree of mystery. If it is difficult to see a difference between the notarial signs of Sion and Geneva, it is because the styles and shapes were regularly borrowed. It is more risky to interpret obvious differences on a greater scale. The inventories developed by Ammann-Doubliez and by Martine Piguet and Dominique Torrione-Vouilloz show that

that the majority of signs had a square shape, typical of those seen in the acts of the diocese of Sion, and were affixed to the beginning and the end of a document.[31] In contrast, the signs listed by Poussy from Le Tarn and Garonne, like those collected from many Spanish cities, were predominantly shaped quite differently: symbols, motifs, and letters were woven onto a line straight as an arrow.

The rebus is clearly different from the main signa families. It does not display a belonging to a certain place, for instance by using the emblem of the city where the notary worked; it also does not make use of a single, common pattern, like the trilobe or the quadrilobe. The rebus-signum does not show where the source of its authority comes from, as do the marks integrating the keys of Saint Peter or the fleur-de-lis. The rebus refers to the notary's proper name in a way that could be parodic. Clearly the choice of a rebus as a notarial mark seems to go against the main graphic and semantic trends that model the majority of other contemporary signa.

Rebus-Signa and Fides publica

The notarial signa carried out a performative function in many ways. Notaries were responsible for the acts they signed: they guaranteed its due form and its authenticity, while also granting credibility through the *fides publica* that they conveyed. The term *fides publica* allows us to name—at least provisionally—an important yet elusive phenomenon that we can associate with documentary security: the conceptual referent that accompanied the emergence of the notary public's authority that was distinct from the authority traditionally assigned to the seal. As such, rebus-signa were also affected by the set of values with which the notary public profession was gradually invested: the values of expertise, reliability, and responsibility. As a professional mark endowed with a growing performativity, the notarial sign was subject to obligations, the most important of which, in the case of

30   Andreas Meyer, *Felix et inclitus notarius: Studien zum italienischen Notariat vom 7. bis zum 13. Jarhundert* (Tübingen, 2000).

31   Martine Piguet and Dominique Torrione-Vouilloz, "Les signes manuels des notaires à Genève," in *Graphische Symbole in mittelalterlichen Urkunden: Beiträge zur diplomatischen Semiotik*, ed. Peter Rück and Jan Thorbecke (Sigmaringen, 1996), 718.

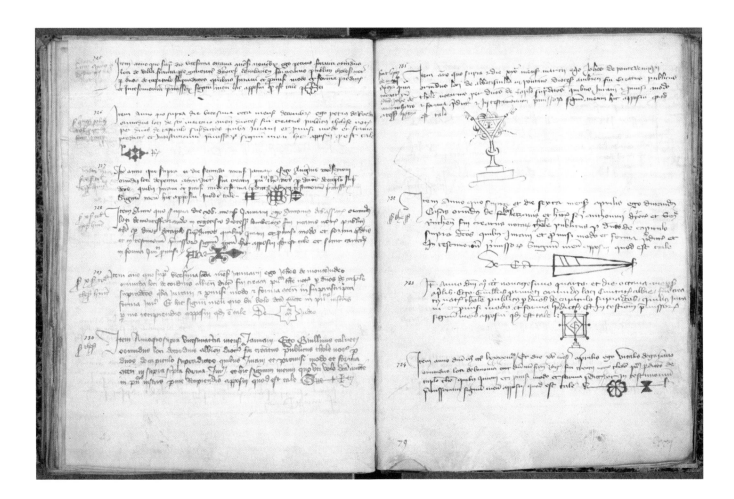

the notary public, was the creation of a record (fig. 4.6). The famous registry rolls of notaries in Toulouse offer a rare corpus of more than 10,000 such marks.

The analysis of the evolution of the notion of fides publica in the thirteenth century, put forward by Petra Schulte, brings a new perspective to this subject.[32] This notion, while difficult to grasp, remains essential for apprehending the value of the notarial marks and, consequently, for analyzing their design. According to Schulte, at the beginning of the thirteenth century the fides was mainly rooted in the notary's good reputation. Relying upon the archives of the city of Come, she shows how, progressively, the credibility of the acts also depended upon their conformity to discursive norms, upon the presence

of some mandatory elements, such as dates, the keeping of and their being recording in a register, and upon the quality of the witnesses. Checking procedures were established for the notary himself: he had to take an oath, prove his abilities by taking an examination, and pay a tax. The recording and control of notarial marks were part of broader regulatory provisions. It was no longer just a notary's good reputation that allowed him to be the depository of the fides publica; it was also a set of community measures which defined and evaluated his aptitude for the responsibility. These evolutions match the main graphic trends evident in the various corpora: the signa slowly changed to become standardized signatures and the use of images was withdrawn. That development, in turn, led to the disappearance of alphabetical, heraldic, geometrical, and rebus-signa.

Yet the design cannot fully be understood through technical aspects alone. It combined practical and aesthetic demands. In the case

FIG. 4.6.

Signa of notaries of Toulouse. *Livre des matricules des notaires créés par Messieurs les Capitouls, ubique terrarum 1357–1422*, Archives municipales, Toulouse, ms. BB206, fols. 78v–79r.

Cliché Atelier photographique des Archives nationales.

32   Petra Schulte, "Fides publica: Die Dekonstruktion eines Forschungsbegriffes," in *Strategies of Writing: Studies on Text and Trust in the Middle Ages,* ed. Petra Schulte, Marco Mostert, and Irene van Renswoude, Utrecht Studies in Medieval Literacy 13 (Turnhout, 2008), 15–36.

of rebus-signa, the sign contained a narrative. It sought to be deciphered with the help of the subscription, and it required that its relations with a web of emblems and signs, as well as the bonds that linked it to chains of festivals, discourses, and practices, be decrypted, grasped, and interpreted. Rebus-signa are rare, but alphabetical signa are numerous, and they seem to anticipate the signature and its future. As in all good designs, some emerging tendencies can be discerned that seem to foretell the separation of text from image within legal documents. But, as we have seen, like the rebus-signatures, they also announced the end of a world that bestowed upon letters and images a unique and singular power.

꧁ I would like to thank Lori Jones, Department of History, University of Ottawa, for her help in translating and preparing this article for publication.

From Many into One

The Transformation of Pre-Columbian Signs
into European Letters in the Sixteenth Century

THOMAS B. F. CUMMINS

The Alphabet and America

THE YEAR 1492 WAS PROPITIOUS, A YEAR WHEN AMERICA HAD NOT YET begun to learn its ABCs.[1] In that year, Antonio de Nebrija opened his prologue of the first published, European, vernacular grammar with a dedication to Queen Isabella of Castile and León.[2] Immediately following, he penned his famous observation:

---

1 "Our world has lately discovered another (and who can assure us that it is the last of its brothers, since the Daemons, the Sybils, and we ourselves have been ignorant of this till now?) as large, well peopled, and fruitful, as this whereon we live; and yet so raw and childish, that we are still teaching it its A B C; 'tis not above fifty years since it knew neither letters, weights, measures, vestments, corn nor vines; it was then quite naked in the mother's lap, and only lived upon what she gave it. If we rightly conclude of our ends, and this poet of the youthfulness of that age of his, that other world will only enter into the light when this of ours shall make its exit; the universe will fall into paralysis; one member will be useless, the other in vigor. I am very much afraid that we have greatly precipitated its declension and ruin by our contagion; and that we have sold it our opinions and our arts at a very dear rate. It was an infant world, and yet we have not whipped and subjected it to our discipline, by the advantage of our natural worth and force, neither have we won it by our justice and goodness, nor subdued it by our magnanimity. Most of their answers, and the negotiations we have had with them, witness that they were nothing behind us in pertinency and clearness of natural understanding. The astonishing magnificence of the cities of Cusco and Mexico, and among many other things, the garden of the king, where all the trees, fruits, and plants, according to the order and stature they have in a garden, were excellently formed in gold; as, in his cabinet, were all the animals bred upon his territory and in its seas; and the beauty of their manufactures, in jewels, feathers, cotton, and painting, gave ample proof that they were as little inferior to us in industry. But as to what concerns devotion, observance of the laws, goodness, liberality, loyalty, and plain dealing, it was of use to us that we had not so much as they; for they have lost, sold, and betrayed themselves by this advantage over us." M. de Montaigne, "On Couches," in *The Complete Essays*, trans. M. A. Screech (London, 1987), 330–31.
    The first known connection between a printer and the New World took place in 1512, when Jacobo Cromberger sold "some sheets of devotional woodcuts and two thousand ABCs to a Franciscan expedition, which was setting off under the leadership of Fray Alonso de Espinar to evangelize islands in the Caribbean." C. Griffin, *The Crombergers of Seville: The History of a Printing and Merchant Dynasty* (Oxford, 1988), 52.

2 There were earlier vernacular grammars, most importantly Leon Battista Alberti's *Grammatica della lingua toscana*, which was finished around 1443, but not published until 1908. Thus "Nebrija's *Grammatica de la lengua castellana* (1492) was in fact the first grammar of a vernacular to have a public influence." Werner Hüllen, "Characterization and Evaluation of Languages in the Renaissance and in the Early Modern Period," in *Language Typology and Language Universals: An International Handbook*, 2 vols., ed. Martin Haspelmath (Berlin, 2001), 1:243–44.

When I ponder [my] very honored queen and place before the eyes the long history of all things that are written for our recall and memory, I find and take as a very certain conclusion that language was always the companion of empire.[3]

His "very certain conclusion that language was always the companion of empire" addresses Ferdinand and Isabella's triumphant entrance on 2 January into Granada after the surrender by Muhammad XII (Boabdil) of the Emirate of Granada and the Alhambra, thus achieving the unification of the Iberian Peninsula as a Catholic and primarily Spanish world.

Columbus, of course, would depart later the same year for parts unknown and return in March of 1493. But for Nebrija and so many others, what was meant by his introduction was a Spain that was becoming unified as a nation and with a national, even imperial, language. That is, Spanish became hegemonic, even though there were multiple languages spoken in the newly unified nation, based upon an ancient and noble past.[4] What is just as important, but less

frequently cited, is Nebrija's point that written language places the antiquity of all things before the eyes of the present, because, through it, memory and recollection remain constant. Here, sign and the thing signified produce the historical bases of an imperial culture. Thus, it is not just the intimate relationship of spoken language to empire, but their combined connection to the alphabet, writing, and the materialization of history in the present and for the future, allowing a dialogue with the ancients.[5] As Spain expanded to become the first truly global empire, societies around the world were subjected to a critical and hegemonic comparison with Spain's cultural, hierarchical, lettered standards.[6] And while Spanish became the official language of a global empire, local languages were too numerous and too pervasive to be subsumed by Spanish.[7] Hence Spanish took the place of Latin as the empire's universal language, and indigenous languages were subsumed within it. But it was the alphabet and not the language that was recognized as a divine sign of cultural and spiritual supremacy by both Catholic and Protestant Europe. And as we shall see, as the alphabet subsumes all other systems within its "superior" capacity of economically transcribing the sounds of speech, it also becomes a subject of representation in the sixteenth century in Europe, culminating with a series of illustrated volumes about the genesis of the alphabet and its development up until the present that depicted the alphabets of the various nations and languages of Europe. The alphabet becomes aestheticized, a unified object of singular beauty that was most fully realized in the hands of some of the great Protestant illustrators

---

3   "Cuando bien comigo pienso mui esclarecida Reina: y pongo delante los ojos el antigüedad de todas las cosas: que para nuestra recordación e memoria quedaron escriptas: una cosa hallo y saco por conclusión mui cierta: que siempre la lengua fue compañera del imperio." Antonio de Nebrija, *Gramática sobre la lengua castellana* (Barcelona, 1492; repr. 2011), 1.

4   Of course other languages continued to be spoken and written throughout the Iberian Peninsula, including Catalan and Basque; however, most royal documents and laws were written either in Latin or Spanish. Moreover, the history of the New World conquest was understood to be accomplished by Spanish speakers and it was almost entirely written in Spanish. See Thomas B. F. Cummins, "De Bry and Herrera: 'Aguas Negras' or the Hundred Years War over an Image of America," in *Arte, historia e identidad en América: Visiones comparativas,* ed. G. Curiel, R. González Mello, and J. Gutiérrez Haces (Mexico City, 1994), 17–31. I. Illich wrote one of the first and finest critical essays that demonstrated the relationship between the rise of modernity, empire, and Nebrija's linguistic project: "Vernacular Values," *CoEvolution Quarterly* (summer 1980): 26–51. This was followed by Walter Mignolo's study that offered a fine-grained analysis of the relationship among Spanish-language texts, imperial formation, and the alphabet: "Nebrija in the New World: The Question of the Letter, the Colonization of American Languages, and the Discontinuity of the Classical Tradition," *L'Homme* 32, no. 122–24 (1992): 185–207; *The Darker Side of the Renaissance: Literacy, Territoriality, and Colonization* (Ann Arbor, 1992), 29–122. The present essay, in fact, is deeply influenced and is in many ways an elaboration on the work of Illich and Mignolo.

5   "La causa de la invención de las letras primeramente fue para nuestra memoria, y después para que por ellas pudiésemos hablar con los ausentes y los que están por venir." Antonio de Nebrija, "Capítulo tercero, de cómo las letras fueron halladas para representar las voces," in *Gramática sobre la lengua castellana.*

6   See Anthony Pagden's discussion of the evolution of some of the cultural theories in *The Fall of Natural Man* (Cambridge, 1982), 1–198.

7   In fact, a hierarchy developed that governed which languages passed through translation and were transcribed into alphabetic writing within the newly extended Spanish imperial documentation. Local languages were used to gather information, and these were termed *lengua maternal.* They were then translated into an officially recognized native language (*lengua general*).

of the Americas: Theodore de Bry and his sons. Through their sumptuous engravings of penned letters the alphabet becomes, as we shall see, a sign that in and of itself distinguishes between the most civilized and the rest in descending levels of social categories, a European fetish of cultural superiority.

This process of aestheticization begins with a new role for the alphabet in its economical means to represent sounds. And so, more important than what Nebrija says about the relation of language to empire, which both imperial Romans and Chinese long before understood, is the fact that Nebrijas's *Grammar* was printed. Language reproduced through the invention of this new technology of mechanical reproduction and moveable type, using meticulously carved tiny letters in mirrored reflection, appeared in Europe only just before the New World appeared on the horizon.[8] Through printing, Nebrija's *Grammar* was made available in cheap, plentiful copies throughout the world.[9] Printing, the codification of vernacular, and imperial global conquest are intimately connected. Thus, the printed books carried across the Atlantic and Pacific were not alone.[10] They were quickly accompanied by the printing press itself. Printing, as a merchant-capitalist venture, became one of the first international businesses as presses, movable type with individual metal letters, and woodblock plates were transported to the Americas.[11] Beginning in full scale in Mexico and then later in Peru, the first printings were directed toward evangelization and translation. Metatexts, such as bilingual dictionaries and grammars for Spanish-Nahuatl, Spanish-Quechua, and other native languages, were produced so that the bilingual Catholic religious texts could be instrumentalized.[12] Some of these doctrinal texts, such as bilingual sermons and catechisms, were further instrumentalized at a metalevel by offering the phonetic sounds transcribed into the Roman alphabet at the beginning of the texts.[13]

In sum, indigenous languages were recognized as locally useful for political and religious administration, but they were universally transcribed into Roman letters. In fact, as we shall see, it is the European alphabet, not the Spanish language, that became the sine qua non of cultural and therefore political performative superiority, i.e. alphabetic performance. All other systems of recording were first appraised, then used, but ultimately judged to fall short and therefore were subsumed by the efficacious superiority of writing with the Roman alphabet.

8   Thomas B. F. Cummins, "The Indulgent Image: Prints, Natives, and the New World," in *Contested Visions*, ed. Ilona Katzew (Los Angeles and New Haven, 2011), 201–23, 289–92.

9   For Nebrija's impact on the creation of grammars for the languages of New Spain, see the various essays in Ignacio Guzmán Betancourt and Eréndira Nansen Díaz, eds., *Memoria del Coloquio: La Obra de Antonio de Nebrija y su Recepción en la Nueva España; Quince estudios nebrisenses (1492–1992)* (Mexico City, 1997). For Quechua, see A. Durston, *Pastoral Quechua: The History of Christian Translation in Peru, 1550–1650* (Notre Dame, Ind., 2007). For a broader discussion see Thomas B. F. Cummins, "Town Planning, Marriage, and Free Will in the Colonial Andes," in *The Archaeology of Colonialism,* ed. C. Lyons and J. Papadopoulos (Los Angeles, 2002), 199–240.

10   For the market in books brought to the New World in the sixteenth century, see I. Leonard, *Books of the Brave: Being an Account of Books and of Men in the Spanish Conquest and Settlement of the Sixteenth-Century New World* (Berkeley, 1992).

11   Griffin, *Crombergers of Seville*, 82–97.

12   See J. Medina, *La Imprenta en Lima (1584–1824)* (Santiago de Chile, 1904); idem, *La Imprenta en México (1539–1821)* (Santiago de Chile, 1907); Durston, *Pastoral Quechua*; and M. Garone Gravier, "Historia de la tipografía colonial para lenguas indígenas" (Ph.D. diss., Universidad Nacional Autónoma de México, 2009).

13   For example, in 1542 the privileges awarded by Charles V to Juan Cromberger were renewed, stating that he "be allowed to make 100 per cent profit [from this export trade] . . . and that, if it were our royal wish, only he be allowed to export books, ABCs, and all other printed matter to New Spain and that he alone . . . be permitted to print there": document from AGN Mexico, Mercedes Libro 2, Expediente 120, fols. 46v–47v, as cited in Griffin, *Crombergers of Seville*, 93. The first book printed in Peru, *Doctrina christiana y catecismo para instruccion de los Indios y de las de mas personas que han de eseñadas en nuestra fé: Con confession y otras cosas necessarias para los que doctrinan que se contienen en las paginas siguiente* (Lima, 1585), which was composed by the Third Council of Lima, of which José de Acosta was a major contributor, has on folio 25r and 25v an alphabet and a syllabary to help teach. It appears at the end of *Platica Breve en que se contiene la Suma de lo que ha de saber el que se haze cristiano* and at the beginning of the *Catecismo Mayor*. The printing of the alphabet at the beginning of the catechism is not only a Spanish Catholic printing exercise in the Americas, but it also appears at the same time in English catechisms, such as in E. Dering, *A Short Catechisme for Housholders, with Prayers to the Same Adioying* (London, 1595), verso of the frontispiece. See Boone (this volume) for an alternative Mexican creation of catechisms that employed Mexican and European pictorialism for teaching Christian doctrine.

And what do I mean by alphabetic performance? It is the act of writing with letters and measuring what they can do against what other systems cannot do. It is also, as mentioned, the emergence of a sixteenth-century genre of illustrated books that historicize, aestheticize, and fetishize the alphabet as a sign in and of itself, standing for Christian civilization and its superiority. In other words, what I shall briefly argue is that just at the historical moment when the Roman alphabet becomes recognized as the perfect symbolic tool for transcribing the human sounds of all places newly conquered, it also becomes a divine sign whose historical transmission across time and space is aesthetically recognized as a critical element in Europe's rise to global, cultural, and political supremacy.

We can see this performance in its global entirety when José de Acosta, a Jesuit, sought to demonstrate in his *Historia Natural y Moral de Las Indias*, published in 1590, that the European system of letters was the only true system of writing.[14] He writes as proof that the Chinese system had great difficulty in transcribing proper names, especially foreign ones, as they included words and sounds that they had never seen or heard before, and so could not invent figures for them. Acosta writes that:

> Finding myself in Mexico with some Chinese, I asked them to write this statement, or something resembling it, in their language: "José de Acosta has come from Peru." And one Chinese thought for a great while, and finally wrote, and afterwards he and another read essentially the same thing, however there was great variety in the proper name. Because they use this system . . . they search for something in their language that has a resemblance to the name and place of that thing (and use that character), and as it is difficult in so many names to find similarity of things and sounds in their language, it is thus very hard to write such names.[15]

I shall return to Acosta's *Historia Natural y Moral de Las Indias* below, because his book became an immensely important and widely read source on the Americas and the cultures found there. More importantly, it is critical for several reasons to the arguments I develop about the fetishization of the alphabet through an aesthetic process. This particular passage, however, succinctly encapsulates the themes of Acosta's book, as it demonstrates a truly global condition in which a Spanish Jesuit, freshly arrived from Peru to Mexico City, meets several Chinese living there. Simultaneously, this short passage narrates the competitive performance of one form of sign system against another, a test of cultural symbolic technology. Acosta, in his own cross-cultural perspective, demonstrates through a personal encounter in Mexico with several Chinese how Chinese characters are inferior to the alphabet in their failure to capture the new sounds of his personal name in precise and flexible ways. This passage occurs within Acosta's general assessment of the sign systems of the Americas and Asia and their inherent inferiority to the Roman alphabet, something that Nebrija had already anticipated in his account of the sign value of the alphabet as representing sounds not things, based upon Aristotle's opening passage in *On Interpretation*.[16]

---

14 José de Acosta, *Historia Natural y Moral de Las Indias* (Seville, 1590).

15 "Mas dificultad tiene entender, como pueden escrivir en su lengua nombres proprios especialmente de estrangeros, pues son cosas nunca vieron, ni puedieron inventor figura para ellos, yo quise hazer experencia desto hallandome en Mexico con

unos Chinas, y pedi que escrivierssen en su lengua esta proposicion, Joseph de Acosta ha venido del Peru, o otra semejante. Y el China estuvo gran rato pensando, y al cabo escrivio, y despues el y otro leyeron en efecto la misma razon, aunque en le nombre proprio tanto variada. Porque usan deste artificio, tomando el nombre proprio, y busean alguna cosa en su lengua con que tenga semjança aquel nombre, y ponen la figura de aquella cosa, y como es deficil en tantos nombres hallar semejança de cosas y sonido de su lengua, asi les es muy trabajoso escrivir los tales nombres." Acosta, *Historia Natural*, book 6, chap. 5, 262. I have translated Acosta's term "China" as "Chinese," although those whom Acosta met in Mexico may have been Japanese. However, Acosta makes a distinction between Japan and China immediately before this passage and elsewhere in his book. So for his purposes, he is meeting Chinese and talking about their writing system, based upon a knowledge gathered in China by his fellow Jesuits.

16 "Ante que las letras fuesen halladas, por imágenes representaban las cosas de que querían hacer memoria: como por la figura de la mano diestra significaban la liberalidad, por una culebra enroscada significaban el año. Mas porque este negocio era infinito y muy confuso, el primer inventor de letras, quien quiera que fue, miró cuántas eran todas las diversidades de las voces en su lengua, y tantas figuras de voces hizo, por las cuales, puestas en cierta orden, representó las palabras que quiso. De manera

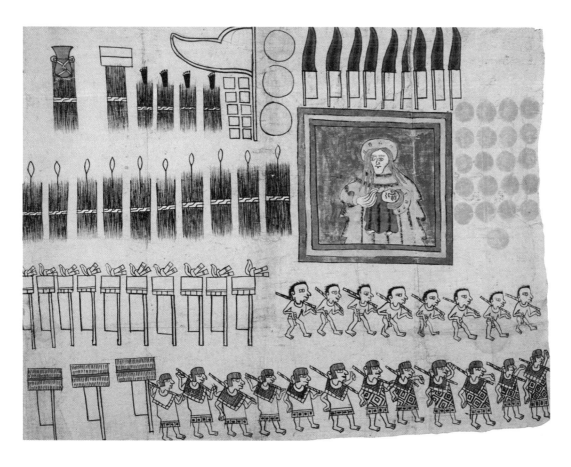

FIG. 5.1.

Drawing 7 of the
Codex Huejotzingo
(1531) on Maguey paper
recording the tribute,
including a feather
image of the Virgin and
Child, given to Nuño de
Guzman by the town of
Huejotzingo. Submitted
as evidence in a legal
dispute involving
Cortes in Mexico City.

Harkness Collection,
Library of Congress,
Washington, D.C.

But what exactly is Acosta describing in terms of the Americas in the preceding three chapters, the last of which is entitled "Que ninguna nacion de indios se ha descubierto que use de letras" [That No Nation of Indians Has Been Discovered That (know how to) Use Letters]? There are at least four kinds of American notational systems that Acosta directly mentions or implies, all of which he appreciates.[17] The first is the hieroglyphs used by the Maya, of which he was only dimly aware if he knew them at all;

the second is the type of glyphs and pictographs on *amate*, or native paper and sculpture used by the Aztecs (fig. 5.1); third is a tapestry weave textile with an Inca system of abstract symbols called *tocapu*;[18] and finally, an Andean recording system that is even more enigmatic, the Inca *khipu*, a series of twisted, knotted strings based on a decimal structure (fig. 5.2). The diversity of these sign systems was at times bewildering to the Spanish, and Acosta was the first to discuss them in a comparative framework. But for him and others the complexities and differences were something that could only be recognized and categorized so as to be reduced to their own more flexible and precise alphabetic equivalence as laid out by Nebrija. They could all be rendered in one and the same way because they were all found wanting in one way or another when compared to the alphabet's capacity to reproduce sounds.

---

que no es otra cosa la letra, sino figura por la cual se representa la voz; ni la voz es otra cosa sino el aire que respiramos, espesado en los pulmones, y herido después en el áspera arteria que llaman gargavero, y de allí comenzado a determinarse por la campanilla, lengua, paladar, dientes y beços. Así que las letras representan las voces, y las voces significan, como dice Aristóteles, los pensamientos que tenemos en el ánima." Nebrija, "Capítulo tercero, de cómo las letras fueron halladas para representar las voces" *Gramática sobre la lengua castellana*.

17   For succinct discussions and analyses of the various Pre-Columbian sign systems, see the essays in Elizabeth Boone and Gary Urton, eds., *Their Way of Writing: Scripts, Signs, and Pictographies in Pre-Columbian America* (Washington, D.C., 2011). See also W. Mignolo, *The Darker Side of the Renaissance* (Ann Arbor, 1995).

18   For images of and greater discussion about *tocapu* see Thomas B. F. Cummins, "Tocapu: What Is It, What Does It Do, and Why Is It Not a Knot?" in Boone and Urton, eds., *Their Way of Writing*, 277–317.

FIG. 5.2.
Inca khipu, wool
and cotton string.
CMA#628, from
Laguna de los
Cóndores.

Photo courtesy of
Gary Urton.

The most famous example, one that was probably unknown to Acosta, appears in Diego de Landa's *Relación de las Cosas de Yucatán,* composed around 1566, which has his transcription of a part of the Maya calendar and Maya "script," or logosyllabic Maya images, shown with their Roman alphabetic "equivalents" written above them. The fanatical Franciscan friar writes about the Maya sign system:

> These people also used certain characters or letters with which they wrote in their books about antiquities and their sciences with these and with figures and certain signs in the figures, they understood their matters, made them known, and taught them. We found a great number of books in these letters, and since they contain nothing but superstitions and falsehoods of the devil we burned them all, which they took most grievously and which gave them great pain.[19]

The conflagration of these Mayan "books," as well as almost all other pre-Hispanic Mexican codices, is famous for the completeness of its destruction. Only a handful of pre-Hispanic manuscripts survive.

Landa nonetheless calls these Maya signs "letters" and the objects that contain them "books," and he goes on to describe their letters and syllables and offers an example of the Mayan ABCs and their equivalent letters in the Roman alphabet (fig. 5.3).[20] He then notes that while the Maya alphabet lacked some of the letters of the

19 Diego de Landa, *Yucatan Before and After the Conquest* [ca. 1566], trans. W. Gates (New York, 1978), 82. The actual

manuscript may very well be a compilation from the late seventeenth to early eighteenth century of earlier sixteenth-century manuscripts. See M. Restall and J. Chuchiakb, "A Reevaluation of the Authenticity of Fray Diego de Landa's *Relación de las Cosas de Yucatán," Ethnohistory* 49, no. 3 (2002): 651–69.

20 The transcription of the Maya hieroglyphs by Landa and the Maya convert Gaspar Antonio Chi, a member of an elite and therefore erudite Yucatán family, was recognized by Yuri Knorosov as being a syllabary. Knorosov also realized that Maya informants had provided glyphs for the equivalent or at least closely approximate sounds represented by Spanish letters. This provided the key for the explosion in the decipherment of Maya hieroglyphic text, some from as early as 250 BCE; see Stephen Houston, "All Things Must Change: Maya

FIG. 5.3.
Maya syllabary in
Diego de Landa's
*Relación de las
Cosas de Yucatán*,
composed around
1566, pen, ink, and
European paper.

Photo courtesy of
George Stewart.

Roman alphabet, it also had additional letters. Landa ends by saying that "they no longer use any of the characters, especially the young people who have learned ours." In other words, there once was, for Landa, a Mayan writing system of sorts, but it gave way to the universal adaptability of the Roman alphabet within a generation after the conquest. And as Stephen Houston has observed, this process began with the transcription of Maya by Landa, because "they are written as though in Latin ordering, one after the other in linear sequence. No self-respecting scribe would [have] ever created a text like this."[21] This to say that a Mayan scribe would have presented the glyphs in compressed glyph blocks. It is a "clue that the system had begun to unravel at that time [1566] or, at least, that Gaspar Antonio Chi

or some other informant of Landa's understood the writing but was not terribly practiced in it."[22]

Yet, as Landa indicates, the Mayan world was in every sense a world of signs writ large and small and from about 900 BCE until well after the conquest. The keys to the phonetics of some Maya signs as registered in Landa's *Relación* allowed for the decipherment by late twentieth-century scholars of many sculpted and painted texts. What is significant, however, is that while the Mayan language continued to be used throughout the colonial period in official documents, printed books, and local histories, it was by and large written in Roman alphabetic letters, sometimes supplemented with pictographs.[23] That is, despite the fact that Maya hieroglyphs were in part phonetic, cable of capturing Spanish words and being rendered as a syllabary, they were hardly ever used to write the words of Nebrija's

Writing over Time and Space," in Boone and Urton, eds., *Their Way of Writing*, 21–76.

21 Stephen Houston, personal communication, 16 October 2003. See also Stephen Houston, "The Small Deaths of Maya Writing," in *The Disappearance of Writing Systems*, ed. John Baines, John Bennett, and Stephen Houston (London, 2010).

22 Idem, personal communication, 16 October 2003.

23 See W. Hanks, *Converting Words: Maya in the Age of the Cross* (Berkeley, 2010).

"companion of empire," and certainly never by the Spaniards.

The transcription of Maya glyphs into the Roman alphabet was not an isolated act that occurred naturally due to their phonetic capacity. Each Pre-Columbian sign system was in some fashion or other quickly rendered into alphabetic text so that it could be understood at least in part and therefore explained. Some systems offered easier modes of representation for Spanish attempts at commensurability. For example, Aztec pictographs and glyphs were also quickly transcribed or explained through alphabetic writing. One of the earliest examples is a 1528 pictorial tribute account from Huejotzingo in central Mexico that was made on native paper (see fig. 5.1). The pictographs have almost no alphabetic glosses; rather their meaning was carefully transcribed from oral testimony into the handwritten legal document. That is, the glyphs were first described in terms of their form, then what the forms generally signified in terms of number and species, and finally what this specific image meant in terms of the exact amounts for two years of tribute.[24]

A second example appears on folio 1v of the Codex Mendoza, a complex manuscript detailing Aztec dynastic history, tribute lists of conquered towns, and social customs. The manuscript was commissioned circa 1541 by the first viceroy of Mexico and was intended for Emperor Charles V. The text reads:

> [Here] begins the history and foundation of the city of Mexico founded and inhabited by the Mexicans who at that time were called meçiti; this brief and summary history of the origin of how they became overlords and of their deeds and lives is recounted through the following paintings and figures.[25]

The text proceeds to detail the early history of the Aztecs and gives an account of the layout of their city in the lake, which in fact is an ekphrastic description of the image on folio 2r. This famous image depicts the diagrammatic layout of Tenochitlan as a cosmogram, framed by the year glyphs of the reign of the first Aztec emperor. So that the intended viewer, the Holy Roman Emperor Charles V, could interpret the pictorial conventions used in the codex, the historical narrative is interrupted with an explanatory text of how and what the year glyphs mean: "What is depicted in blue in each small compartment or division in the margins of this history is a year sign and together they represent the number of years in the reign of lives of each Aztec ruler." However, this written explanation is deemed insufficient, so the author later writes: "To understand this and to help, the names with their interpretation are shown here." Thus, the first image that appears in the manuscript is an explanatory diagram of the Aztec calendar system, interfaced with an alphabetic text (fig. 5.4). There is a blue horizontal bar divided into thirteen squares, each one representing one year. The individual year is marked with one of four symbols—rabbit, reed, flint knife, or house—and a numerical sign, represented by one to thirteen dots. Combined, these provide a cycle of fifty-two distinct year names that define the Aztec century: One Rabbit, Two Reed, Three Flint Knife, Four House, Five Rabbit, Six Reed, and so forth. Above the Aztec glyphs are the Nahuatl words for them, written in red roman letters; below and in black letters the Nahuatl terms are translated into their Spanish equivalents. The different colors of the alphabetic words may not be incidental. The two colors, when combined in Nahuatl speech, signify the Aztec scribe/painter, the *tlacuilo* or master of the red and black. It is he who then goes on to paint the rest of the manuscript, while a Spaniard, probably, discreetly places written glosses with some of the images.

Such juxtapositions and transpositions of Aztec signs into alphabetic texts take place throughout the sixteenth century, such as in the mid-sixteenth-century manuscript called the Codex Telleriano-Remensis, created on

---

24 See Thomas B. F. Cummins, "The Madonna and the Horse: Alternative Readings of Colonial Images," in *Native Artists and Patrons in Colonial Latin America*, ed. E. Umberger and Thomas B. F. Cummins, special issue, *Phoebus* 7 (1995): 52–83.

25 "Comiença la ystoria y fundaçion de la çibdad de mexico fundada E pobalada por los mexicanos que en aquella Sazon se nonbauan meçiti. Los quales el origen que tubieron de ser señores y de sus hechos y vidas / beuye y sumaariamente en esta historia se declara / segun que por las pinturas e figuras sucçeiuamente van signifcadas." P. Anawalt, ed., *The Codex Mendoza* (Berkeley, 1992), fol. 1r.

European paper.[26] The third part of this colonial manuscript presents a mixed pictorial, pictographic, and glyphic history of the Aztecs from the fourteenth to the mid-sixteenth century. It is clear that the pictorial and glyphic conventions follow the pre-Hispanic sign system. A band of year glyphs, glossed in Arabic numerals, flows across the tops of the pages in a temporal narrative sequence. Pictographs of historical events and individuals are attached by a line to the approximate year in which events occurred. Name glyphs of the political actors appear behind their heads; however, they are also glossed alphabetically. These year glyphs and the events and personages attached to them correlate to Aztec imperial stone monuments, such as the sculpture known as the "coronation stone." This monument shows the year glyph 11 Reed, or 1503, which is the second of the two years shown in the Telleriano-Remensis on folio 41r. The Aztec imperial sculpture marks the transition between the death of Ahuitzotl and the ascension of Moctezuma on 15 July, as indicated by 2 Crocodile, which is the date of the event also depicted in the painted image.

The point is that very quickly these glyphic, pictorial, and pictographic systems were first used independently, then glossed, and finally rendered solely by alphabetic writing, often with explicit instructions as to how they were to be or had been read. If we look again at folio 30r from the Telleriano-Remensis, we can see this most tellingly (fig. 5.5). At the bottom of the page we see the Aztec ruler Huitzilihuitl, identified by his name glyph. Behind is one of his wives, known as *la pintora*, "the painter." Her name is not placed behind her head and attached by a line to a glyph, as are the names of other persons, including Huitzilihuitl. Rather, she is shown in the act of painting, quill in hand, and she draws the glyphic sign for the term *tlacuilo* or "painter," hence the words in alphabetic form come from the tablet upon which she paints and are related to the Aztec sign for the name.

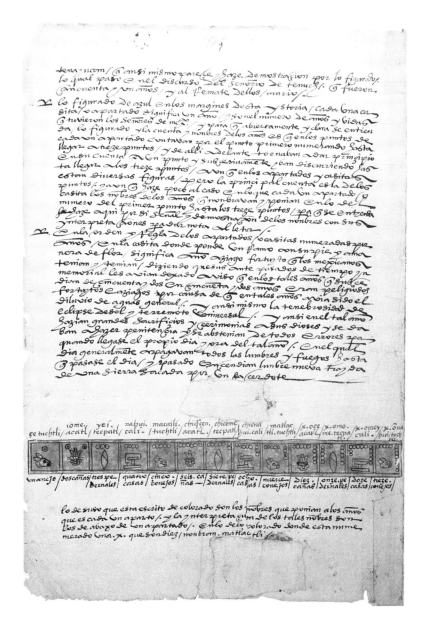

FIG. 5.4.
Fol. 1v with introductory text and explanation of year glyphs, Codex Mendoza, ca. 1542, pen, ink, and European paper.

Bodleian Library, Oxford University.

The same attempt to gloss and explain transpired in Peru, but not as rigorously or precisely, which has much to do with the media and systems used in the Andes. By and large, the systems used by the Inca were abstract, mnemonic devices, mostly produced in some form of textile.[27] Therefore, commensurability

26   For a description of the manuscript, see E. Quiñones Keber, *Codex Telleriano-Remensis: Ritual, Divination, and History in a Pictorial Aztec Manuscript* (Austin, 1995). For an in-depth study of Aztec and colonial Aztec historical manuscripts, see Elizabeth Boone, *Stories in Red and Black: Pictorial Histories of the Aztec and Mixtec* (Austin, 2000).

27   José de Acosta is insistent that the Inca had no form of writing whatsoever, and that their sign system was not at the level of the Chinese or even the Aztecs: "Los indios del Peru antes de venir Españoles, ningun genero de escritura tuvieron, ni por letras, ni por caracteres, o cifras, o figurillas, como los de la China y los de Mexico, mas no por esso conservaron menos la memoria de sus antiguallas, ni tuvieron menos su cuenta para todos los negocios de paz, y guerra, y gobierno. Porque en la tradicion de unos a otros fueron muy diligentes, como cosa

fingen que ban

buet pense

vichilobuitl

la pintora

Vitzilihuitl

Σ ote vitzili huitl se caso con una nieta ~~de la tixa~~ se a coma pichi tl
fixa dela senora de coafuchian dela qual no hubo hijos hubo ou eman
çebas. la Vna que se dezia la pintura y la otra fa mos que a avsuca
y pestas vuo hixos

khipu, to be discussed below, is the best-known Incan recording device, as it was the acknowledged source for many Spanish texts about Peru in the same way that pictographic manuscripts were in Mexico.[29] The khipu was an entirely different mode of recording—a kinetic set of knotted strings that required physical manipulation and oral recitation to be encoded and decoded, as indicated in the only three illustrated manuscripts dealing with Incan history. There are, in fact, neither early colonial images that depict nor texts that describe precisely how the khipu or any other Andean sign system was actually manipulated, and thus they remain unreadable until today. Unlike Mexican and Mayan colonial illustrated manuscripts, in which the pages carry a means of understanding and interpreting the native signs, the few colonial Andean images of the khipu portray them simply as objects, either as a closed object held in the hand while being carried from one place to the next, or stretched open in the arms of a man so that all the strings can be seen (see fig. 5.2).[30] There are no glosses either, as the knots correspond to numbers and not to sounds.

It seems, nonetheless, that object manipulation and vocal recitation, either poetry or song, were key simultaneous components of Incan communicative devices. Spanish chroniclers consistently remark that songs or poems about religious or historical events were recited as objects were brought out and used.[31] Moreover the information was keyed into the objects, such as the khipu, as they were being produced. This amounts

Tovar responded both in writing and by commissioning a pictorial manuscript demonstrating how the Mexican system could be used so accurately. See Thomas B. F. Cummins, "From Lies to Truth: Colonial Ekphrasis and the Act of Crosscultural Translation," in *Cultural Migrations: Reframing the Renaissance*, ed. Claire Farago (New Haven, 1995), 164–69.

29 See the essays and texts in M. Pärssinen and J. Kivihaju, *Textos Andinos: Corpus de Textos Khipu Incaicos y Coloniales*, vol. 1 (Madrid, 2004); and Jeffrey Quilter and Gary Urton, eds., *Narrative Threads: Accounting and Recounting in Andean Khipu* (Austin, 2002).

30 For images of and greater discussion about *tocapu* see Cummins, "Tocapu" (n. 18 above).

31 R. Harrison, *Signs, Songs, and Memory in the Andes: Translating Quechua Language and Culture* (Austin, 1989); and R. Howard-Malverde, *The Speaking of History: 'Willapaakushayki' or Quechua Ways of Telling the Past* (London, 1990).

FIG. 5.5.
Detail, fol. 30r depicting the Aztec ruler Huitzilhuitl and his wife "la Pintora," identified by written name and glyph for *tlacuilo* (scribe), Codex Telleriano-Remensis, ca. 1563, European paper.

Photo courtesy of Bibliothèque nationale de France.

between Andean and European sign systems never reached the level of transparency found in Mesoamerica, despite repeated attempts.[28] The

sagrada reciben, y guardaban los moços, lo que sus mayores les referian, y con el mismo cuydado lo enseñaban a sus sucessores. Fuera desta diligencia suplian la falta de escritura y letras: parte con pinturas como los de Mexico, aunque las del Peru eran muy grosseras y toscas: parte y lo mas con Quipos." Acosta, *Historia Natural*, book 6, chap. 8, 265–66.

28 This difference is exemplified in the exchange of letters between two Jesuits in 1586. José de Acosta, after his experiences in Peru gathering information through oral testimonies based on khipus and other devices, arrived in Mexico to continue his studies. There he encountered a different symbolic system, and wrote to his fellow Jesuit Juan de Tovar asking how it was that the Indians of Mexico could remember the long and detailed history of their ancient past without writing.

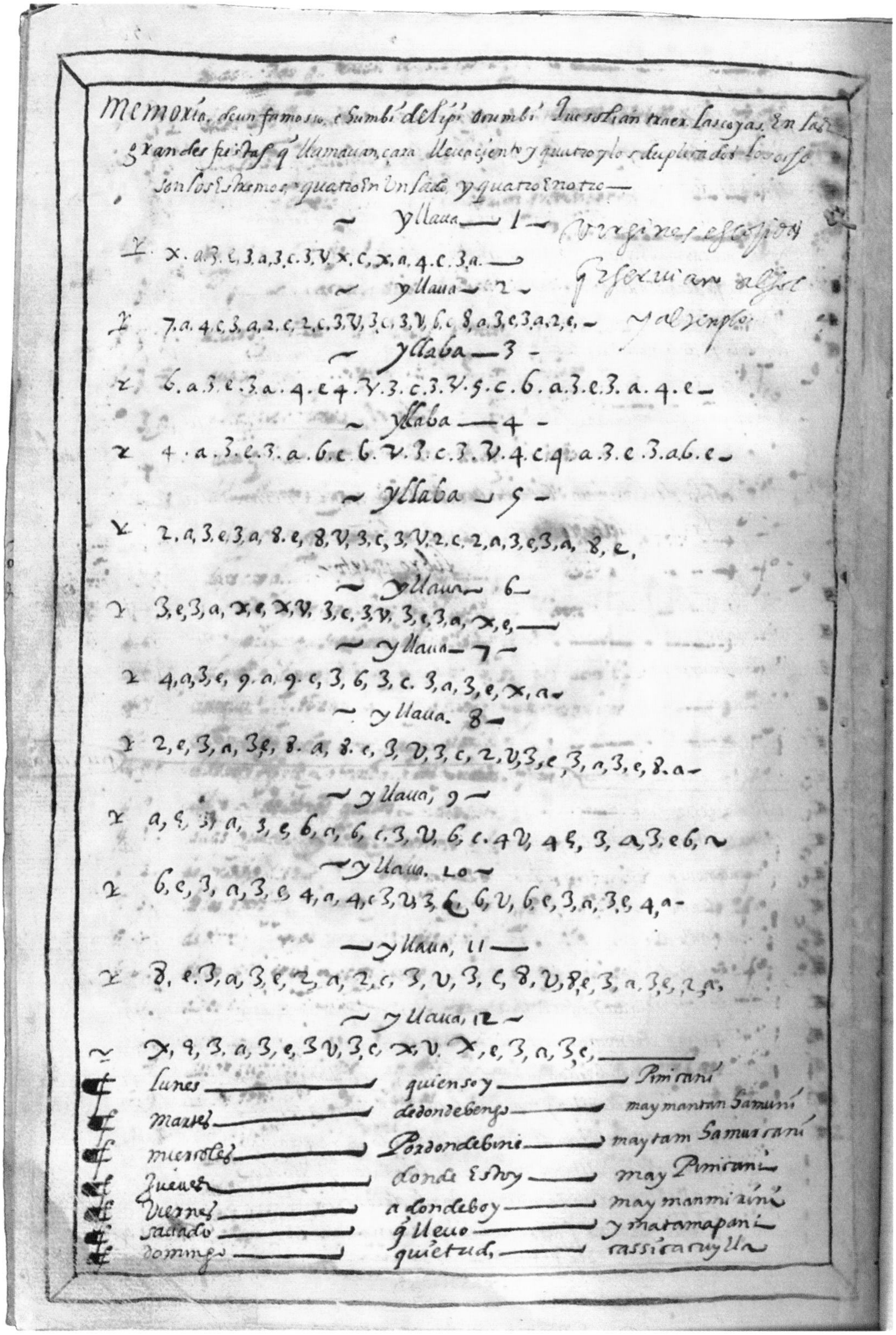
Memoria de un famoso chumbi del piru de cumbi que solian traer las coyas en las grandes fiestas q llamauan capa ...

yllaua — 1 —
x. a. 3. e. 3. a. 3. c. 3. v. x. c. x. a. 4. c. 3. a. —
yllaua — 2 —
7. a. 4. c. 3. a. 2. c. 2. c. 3. v. 3. c. 3. v. 6. c. 8. a. 3. c. 3. a. 2. e. —
yllaba — 3 —
6. a. 3. e. 3. a. 4. e. 4. v. 3. c. 3. v. 5. c. 6. a. 3. e. 3. a. 4. e —
yllaba — 4 —
4. a. 3. e. 3. a. 6. e. 6. v. 3. c. 3. v. 4. c. 4. a. 3. e. 3. a. 6. e —
yllaba — 5 —
2. a. 3. e. 3. a. 8. e. 8. v. 3. c. 3. v. 2. c. 2. a. 3. e. 3. a. 8. e.
yllaua — 6 —
3. e. 3. a. x. e. x. v. 3. c. 3. v. 3. e. 3. a. x. e. —
yllaua — 7 —
4. a. 3. e. 9. a. 9. c. 3. 6. 3. c. 3. a. 3. e. x. a —
yllaua. 8 —
2. e. 3. a. 3. e. 8. a. 8. e. 3. v. 3. c. 2. v. 3. e. 3. a. 3. e. 8. a —
yllaua, 9 —
a. e. 3. a. 3. e. 6. a. 6. c. 3. v. 6. c. 4. v. 4. e. 3. a. 3. e. 6. —
yllaua. 10 —
6. e. 3. a. 3. e. 4. a. 4. c. 3. v. 3. 6. 6. v. 6. e. 3. a. 3. e. 4. a —
yllaua, 11 —
8. e. 3. a. 3. e. 2. a. 2. c. 3. v. 3. c. 8. v. 8. e. 3. a. 3. e. 2. a.
yllaua, 12 —
x. e. 3. a. 3. e. 3. v. 3. c. x. v. x. e. 3. a. 3. e. —

lunes	quien soy	Pimicani
martes	de donde bengo	may mantan samumi
miercoles	por donde bine	maytam samucani
jueves	donde estoy	may pimicani
viernes	a donde boy	may manmi rini
sabado	q lleuo	y maramapani
domingo	quietud	rassicaruylla

FIG. 5.6. Martín de Murúa, "Memoria de un famoso chumbi del Piru de cumbi," *Historia del Origen y Genealogía Real de los Reyes Ingas del Piru. De sus hechos. costumbres, trajes, maneras de gobierno*, 1590–1605, book 4, folio 150v.

Private Collection, Dublin.

to a phenomenology of creation that is quite different from the act of painting and writing onto an already prepared surface, because information is embodied within the object and the creator(s). This is different from meaning produced through the figure-ground relationship of a Mexican or Mayan painting—a process that was much easier for the Spaniards to understand and transcribe. Nonetheless, there is at least one specific attempt to render the significance of this Andean process into alphabetic form, which is parallel in some sense to Landa's transcription of Maya hieroglyphs. It appears on the last manuscript page of a 1590–1613 illustrated history of the Inca written by Martín de Murúa, a Spanish-born Mercedarian monk (fig. 5.6). Unlike the pictorial images in the same manuscript that tell us next to nothing about the khipu other than what it looks like, this page gives the transcription or *memoria* of the weaving process for making a special cloth (*cumbi*) for a belt (*chumpi*) worn by royal women (*coyas*) in the great corn feasts. The text states that the belt has 104 double threads, including eight threads at the edges and four at each side. Below the introductory text are twelve lines numbered 1 Yllaba through 12 Yllaba. *Yllaba* means "heddle rod of a loom" in Quechua, and the numbers and letters enumerate the actual steps of passing the different color warp through the weft to produce a complementary warp weave belt. Below this are three columns that give the days of the weeks and lyrics in Quechua and Spanish. It is unclear why this last text is included here, but perhaps the lyrics were sung as the weaving took place. The important point is that the embodied act of weaving, in which song and memory are produced, has been here distilled into a diagram of European letters and numbers, accurate enough that textile experts can today recognize the process and reproduce it.[32] This rather enigmatic diagram, however, only indicates the kinesthetic relationship between song and technical

movement of weaving and cannot be used as an interpretive key.

The khipu (see fig. 5.2) was never transcribed as such in the sixteenth century, so there is no Rosetta Stone or Landa manuscript. Rather, the data recorded by the khipu were transcribed directly from the oral reading of the numerically coded knots into alphabetically written legal testimony, confession, and historical deeds. Garcilaso de la Vega, el Inca, offers the most descriptive account in two different chapters of his *Commentarios Reales*, published in 1609. One chapter concerns a rather straightforward account of how the Inca used the khipu as an inventory for the numerical recording of population and things. The second chapter is more relevant to the subject of this essay, as it discusses the poetry and history of the Inca, which he says, citing the lost manuscript of the mestizo Jesuit Blas Valera, were recorded on khipus as words and syllables.[33] It is probable that this system was a Jesuit or even a Franciscan invention, not dissimilar to the manuscripts developed in Mexico (see Boone, chapter 2). Whatever the case, the early eighteenth-century French edition of *Commentarios Reales* was one of the sources used for the first analytical illustration of the khipu. It is in fact only in the eighteenth century that we get a description of the workings of the khipu and a fanciful attempt at seeing it as an alphabetic device in Prince Raimondo di Sangro of Sansevero's *Lettera apologetica*.[34] As the title suggests, Sangro's book is a defense of the 1747 French novel *Les lettres d'une Péruvienne*, written in the popular eighteenth-century epistolary genre by Françoise de Graffigny. Based upon a reading of the French edition of the *Commentarios Reales*, Graffigny constructs a romance between two young Inca nobles, Zilia and Aza, who are separated by the Spaniards. Zilia ends up in Paris, and they communicate by written letters and khipus. The entire work is just as fictitious as Montesquieu's *Lettres persanes*.

32 See Sophie Desrosiers's analysis of this text and her comparison with archaeological examples as well as contemporary Andean weaving practices: "An Interpretation of Technical Weaving Data Found in an Early Seventeenth-Century Chronicle," in *The Junius B. Bird Conference on Andean Textiles*, ed. A. Pollard Rowe (Washington, D.C., 1986), 219–42.

33 Garcilaso de la Vega, *Commentarios Reales de Los Incas* (Madrid, 1723), 66–69; 181–83.

34 Raimondo di Sangro, Principe di Sansevero, *Lettera apologetica dell'Esercitato accademico della Crusca contenente la difesa del libro intitolato Lettere d'una peruana per rispetto alla supposizione de'quipu scritta alla duchessa di S**** e dalla medesima fatta pubblicare* (Naples, 1751).

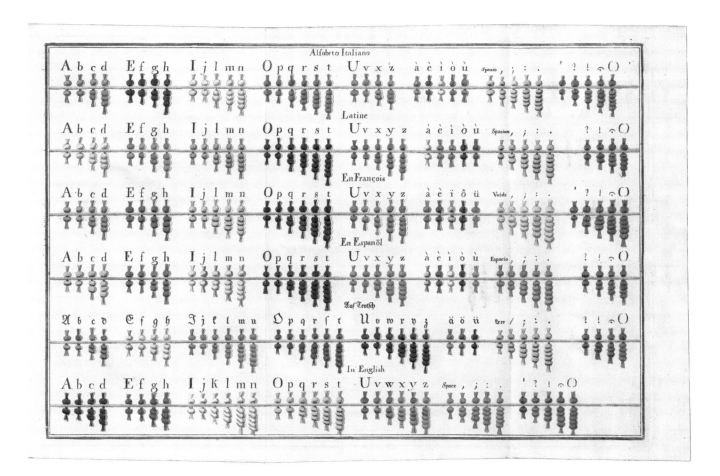

The epistolary style of the novel gives a certain authenticity to its fictional story. In the case of *Les lettres d'une Péruvienne,* Sangro proposes that there are "master words" that are keyed to a certain number of signs in the khipu that were important to the daily exercise of the office of the khipu master (*khipucamayoc*).[35] These master words then can be used to represent syllables. Thus, Sangro presents two types of khipus in his book. The first khipu is iconic and able to represent precise master words by abstract images tied into the knots. He then uses these symbols to demonstrate how the poem that Garcilaso de la Vega says he transcribed from a khipu was actually represented by this type of khipu.[36] The

second type of khipu is one that Sangro invents to show that through color and knots the khipu could be used phonetically, such that the knots are equivalent to the sounds of the Latin, Italian, French, Spanish, German, and English alphabets. That is, there is a different khipu that corresponds to the various alphabets as represented in a one-to-one comparison (fig. 5.7). As one of the first Freemasons in Naples, Sangro's aim was to create equality between these systems and to demonstrate that Graffigny was correct.[37]

We can perhaps imagine Sangro's intentions if we turn back to Nebrija and his dedication and to Acosta's arguments in the *Historia Natural y*

35   After Sangro's letter to the reader introducing *Lettere d'una peruana* and the khipu as its source, there is a long introduction about writing and biblical, ancient philosophical (Aristotle for example), and modern sources that is written by Sangro to introduce the khipu as an equivalent system to the alphabet.

36   Sangro also cites Cieza de León and Acosta, after which he then takes up the question that his reader might ask: were Peruvians capable of expressing their sentiments through khipus as Graffigny writes? To which he responds that although she uses artistic license in her novel, she was not so off the mark, as he will demonstrate.

37   For an analysis of the complicated relationship between Sangro's presentation of the khipu and his sources in the sixteenth and seventeenth centuries, see S. Hyland, "Woven Words: The Royal Khipu of Blas Valera," in Quilter and Urton, *Narrative Threads,* 150–70. See also J. E. Burucúa and L. A. Burucúa, *Carta Apológetica Raimondo: Estudio Introductorio* (Buenos Aires, 2010), 9–52.

FIG. 5.7.
Folding, colored, engraved plate of alphabet/khipu from Raimondo di Sangro, Prince of Sansevero, *Lettera apologetica dell'Esercitato accademico della Crusca contenente la difesa del libro intitolato Lettere d'una peruana per rispetto alla supposizione de'quipu scritta alla duchessa di S****e dalla medesima fatta pubblicare,* Naples, 1751.

Photo courtesy of Houghton Library, Harvard University.

Moral about the lack of alphabetic writing in the Americas. But more importantly, Sangro uses his publication to demonstrate his own printing invention. The title page is printed in four colors with a single turn of the press, a major typological innovation. There is a recursive set of references that move from the printing process to the content of the book, implying the inventive capacity of the author/printer Sangro himself, which he then demonstrates in the foldout, full-page, color illustrations of the khipus. At the same time, as we shall see, Sangro's desire to give a precise sound for each individual knot of the khipus by assigning them the sound of alphabetic letters used to write modern European languages has precedence in the sixteenth-century aesthetic presentation of the history of the alphabet in printed books.

Alphabetic writing and the transliteration of native languages and sign systems are, however, more than simply the transcription of sounds (words) and actions (narrative). Writing places the past before the present in a way that no other system supposedly could. This is what Nebrija says in the dedication of his grammar: writing conserves the memory of the ancient past. And as the power of this symbolic technology was pressed upon the peoples of America, it was slowly internalized so that the absence of letters began to be a sign of weakness.[38] We can see this expressed in the introduction of the only Andean oral myths written in Quechua, the language of the Inca. Known as the Huarochiri Manuscript and written down around 1611–1613, it begins:

> Runa yndio ñiscap machoncuna ñaupa pacha
> quilcata carca chayca hinatin cusacancunpas
> manam cananca mapas chincaycuc hincho
> canancam.

If the ancestors of the people called Indians had known writing in earlier times then the lives they lived would not have faded from view until now.[39]

This opening text was added later, but why would Andean myths, recorded in Quechua, begin with such a phrase? It echoes both Nebrija and Acosta, and there are two words in the sentence that are instructive. The first is *yndio* or "Indian" that modifies the Quechua term *runa*, "people"; the second is the neologism for writing, *quilcata*. Together their appearance marks the colonial intersection of the mythic Andean past with the present, and indicates how the Andean past was once remembered. Orality and the khipu were inadequate for recording that past, but only an yndio who experienced alphabetic quilcata and the capacities of the written word would realize this.

And what does this fully mean? It is critical to return to Acosta's discussion of alphabetic writing in relation to American, Chinese, and Japanese systems. Acosta's *Historia Natural y Moral* was not just another sixteenth-century text. It was translated into English, French, Dutch, Italian, Latin, and German within twelve years of its appearance in Seville in 1590. In fact it is probably one of most widely read and influential early modern books written about the Americas. Acosta begins his chapter four, entitled "Que ninguna nacion de Indios se ha descubierto que use de letras," by following Nebrija:

> According to the philosopher, letters were invented to refer to and immediately signify the words that we pronounce, just as words and terms themselves are immediate signs of men's concepts and thoughts.[40] And one as well as the other (by this I mean both letters and words) were established to make us understand things: words for

38 This process of coming to define one's culture in the terms of the dominant, inquisitorial culture is similar to what is analyzed by Carlos Ginsburg, *The Night Battles: Witchcraft and Agrarian Cults in the Sixteenth and Seventeenth Centuries* (Baltimore, 1983).

39 J. I. Úziquiza Gonzalez, ed., *Manuscrito de Huarochirí, Libro Sagrado de los Andes Peruanos: Versión bilingüe Quechua-Castellano de José María Arguedas, Facsímil del Manuscrito* (Madrid, 2011). English translation by Frank Salomon and George L. Urioste, ed. and trans., *The Huarochirí Manuscript: A Testament of Ancient and Colonial Andean Religion* (Austin, 1991), 41.

40 Acosta is referring to Aristotle and in particular *On Interpretation,* referring to the same passage as Nebrija. See n. 16 above for a comparison of Acosta's text with that of Nebrija.

present things and letters for those that are absent or still to come. Signs that are not arranged in such a way as to signify words, but only things, they are not called letters, nor are they truly letters even though they are written, just as a picture of the sun cannot be called writing, or letters representing the sun, but is a simple picture. Nor can other signs that have no resemblance to the thing but serve only as reminders be described as writing, for the person who invented them did not do so to represent words but simply to denote that thing. Such signs are not called, nor are they properly speaking, letters or writing but ciphers or memory devices. . . . Letters do not do this, for, although they denote things, they do so through words, and thus only those who know the language can understand them. For example, the word *sol* is written: neither Greek nor Hebrew knows what it means, for these languages do not know the Latin word itself. So that writing and letters are used only by those who signify words with them, and if they immediately signify the same things then they are not letters or writing but pictures and ciphers. From this we may draw two important conclusions. One is that the remembrance of history and of ancient times can persist among men in one of three ways: either by letters and writing, as the Romans, Greeks, and Hebrews use, as well as many other nations; or by pictures, as has been used almost everywhere in the world (since as was said in the second Nicene Council, pictures are a book for the illiterate); or by ciphers or characters, just as an arithmetical figure can stand for the numbers one hundred, one thousand, and so on, without necessarily meaning the word *hundred* or *thousand*. The other important conclusion to be drawn is the one stated in the title of this chapter, namely, that no nation of the Indians discovered in our time uses letters or writing but employs the other two methods, which are images or figures. And by this I mean not only the Indians of Peru and New Spain but also in part the Japanese and Chinese; although what I have said may seem very wrong to some, since there have

been so many accounts of great libraries and places of study in China and Japan and of their printed blocks and writing supplies. But it is the plain truth, as will be understood in the following chapter.[41]

Acosta articulates two critical points about the place of writing and the alphabet in the subjugation of the New World. The first is in agreement with Nebrija: that writing allows direct contact with the ancients in a form that no other system can provide. Second, images are the books of the illiterate, as articulated by Pope Gregory in his letter to Serenus, Bishop of Marseilles, at the end of the sixth century and

---

41 "Las letras se inventaron para referir y significar immediatamente las palabras que pronunciamos, asi como mismas palabras, y vocabulos, segun el Philosopho son señales immediatamente de los conceptos y pensamientos de los hombres. Y lo uno y otro (digo las letras y las vozes) se ordenaron para da a entender las cosas: las vozes a los presentes; las letras a los ausentes y futuros. Las señales que no se ordenan de proximo a significar palabras sino cosa, no se llaman, ni son en realidad de verdad letras; aunque esten escritas, asi como una imagen del Sol pintada no se puede dezir, que es escritura, o letras, sino pintura ni mas ni menos otros señales que no tienen semejança con la cosa, sino solamente sirve para memoria, por que el que invento, no las ordeno para significar palabras, sino para denotar aquellas cosa. Estas tales señales no se dizen, ni son propiamente letras, ni escritura, sino cifras, o memoriales. . . . lo qual no hazen las letras, que aunque denotan las cosas en mediante las palabras, y asi no las entienden, sino los que saben aquella lengua. *Verbi gratia.* Está escrita esta palabra Sol, no percibe el Griego, ni el Hebreo que significa, porque ygnora el mismo vocablo Latino. De manera que escritura y letras, solamente las usan los con ellas significan vocablos, y si immediatamente significan las mismas cosas, no son ya letras, ni escritura, sino pinturas y cifras. De aqui, se sacan dos cosas bien notables: la una es, que la memoria de historias y antiguedad, puede permanecer en los hombres por una de tres maneras: o por letras y escritura, como lo usan Los Latinos, y Griegos, y Hebreos, otras muchas naciones por pintura, como en todo el mundo ha usado pues como se dize en el Concilio Niceno Segundo, la pintura es libro para los ydiotas, que no sabe leer; o por cifras y caracteres, como el guarismo significa los numeros de ciento, de mil, y los demas, sin significar esta palabra ciento, ni la otra mil. El otro notable que se infiere es, el que en este capitulo se ha propuesto, es a saber que ninguna nacion de Indios que se ha descubierto en nuestro tiempos usa de letras ni escriptura, sino de otras dos maneras, que son ymagenes o figuras, y entiendo esto no solo de los Indios de Peru, y de los de Nueva España, sino en parte tambien de los Japones y Chinas. Y aunque parecera a algunos muy falso lo que digo, por aver tanta relacion de las grandes librerias y estudios de la China, y del Japon, y de sus chapas, y provisiones, y cartas, pero es muy llana de verdad, como se entendera en el discurso siguinete." Acosta, *Historia Natural y Moral de Las Indias,* book 6, chap. 4, 260–61.

rearticulated in the Council of Trent.[42] Acosta then mentions Mexican pictographs and glyphs, as well as Inca khipus. And he clearly and definitively states that none of the symbolic technologies of the newly discovered cultures measure up to the capabilities of the alphabetic letter. Therefore, their histories are neither as exact nor as profound as those of Europe because they have no true alphabetic writing. This is what is implied in the opening passage of the Huarochiri Manuscript.

In truth, Acosta's entire *Historia* is a demonstration of the inferiority of non-western cultures. It was written as the historical part of his *De procuranda Indorum salute*, published just two years earlier. In that work, Acosta demonstrates the radical cultural differences between Europe and the Americas in terms of the different histories of evangelical conversion. Acosta says that when Christ's disciples began their apostolic mission in antiquity, God needed to provide miracles, because the people of that time, the Greeks and the Romans, were at the height of reason and intellect. Moreover, Christianity was a new religion by comparison to the pagan practices of the Mediterranean world. The ancients could therefore not be persuaded by mere words, but required prodigious signs so that "the Christian religion was founded by God with miracles because human agency was completely lacking in effect because the early Christians did not have the power."[43] But the idolaters of Acosta's day, the Mexicans, Andeans, and others, were quite different. In his words "the situation of our era is very distinct. Those to whom the priests announce the faith are inferior in everything: in reason, in culture, and in power, and those who announce the Gospel are superior in terms of the great age of Christianity by the number of its faithful, their wisdom and erudition and all other means of persuasion."[44] The Indians, according

to Acosta's logic, lacked both the wisdom and the intelligence of the ancients.[45] Therefore only one miracle was needed, and that miracle was embodied by those who had come with the written word to the Americas to preach the word of God made possible by the military force of Spain. The miraculous in the New World was manifested in the righteous life of the evangelizing priest, who, simply through example and teaching, could lead the Indians into the Christian community.[46] Only the power of their piety was required for conversion in light of the simplicity of the Indians and their weak intellect and culture. The "Word" preached was sufficient and complete; the "Word" spoken and written was the sacred sign of conquest, just as it had been for Constantine. However, it did not appear miraculously in the sky; it was written and printed on paper and cloth. Nonetheless, the "Word" in the form of the monograms of Mary and Jesus contained mystical presence, and these were writ (painted) large in the mural programs of sixteenth-century Mexico and incorporated into the fine tapestry weaves of *uncus* (tunics) of Peru, created for devotional statues of Christ dressed as the Inca.[47] Here painted or woven images are blended seamlessly with written letters, signifying tremendous magical power.[48] After all, the incarnation (the Word become man) was real (Christ became flesh).[49] Thus the written word, by means of

42 Gregory the Great, "Letter 9," in *The Letters of Gregory the Great*, 2 vols., trans. John R. C. Martyn (Toronto, 2004), 1:209; and Henry Joseph Schroeder, *The Canons and Decrees of the Council of Trent* (Rockford, Ill., 1978), 217.

43 José de Acosta, *De Natura Novi Orbis Libri duo et de Promulgatione Evangelii, apud Barbaros, sive de Procuranda Indorum salute* (Salamanca, 1588), 244.

44 Ibid., 245.

45 Here Acosta is also refuting Bartolomé de Las Casas's paralleling of antiquity and the New World, a strategy through which Las Casas attempted to demonstrate the rationality of the Indians: Bartolomé de Las Casas, *Apologética historia sumaria*, ed. E. O'Gorman (Mexico City, 1967).

46 Acosta's argument for why there was a lack of miracles in the New World of the kind produced for the conversion of the ancient world is followed very closely by Grijalva in his chapter entitled "De la poca razon con que algunos dizen, q no vuo milagros en la conuersion de los Indios," in *Croníca de la Orden de n. p. s. Augustin en las prouincias de la Nueva España, en quatro edades desde el año de 1533 hasta el de 1592. Por el p. m. f. Ioan de Grijalua, prior del Conuento de n. p. s. Augustin de México* (Mexico City, 1624; repr. 1924), 132–37.

47 J. Berenbeim, "Script after Print: Juan de Yciar and the Art of Writing," *Word & Image* 26, no. 3 (2010): 231–43.

48 Estrada de Gerlero, "La epigrafía en el arte novohispano del siglo XVI," in *World Art, Themes of Unity and Diversity: Acts of the XXVth International Congress of the History of Art* (University Park, Pa., 1989), 349–54.

49 The Second Council of Nicea of 787, to which Acosta refers (see lengthy quote above), articulated this position when

the alphabet, is also the physical manifestation of God.[50] Also, in the New World, especially in Mexico, murals in the monasteries built in indigenous communities (Alcoman, Actopan, Tlayacapan, Culhuacan, and Malinalco) abound with images of the Church Fathers writing and reading as well as the mystical names of Mary and Jesus.

America's Effect: The New Aesthetic of the Alphabet in Europe

The alphabet, as already noted, came to represent more than just the abstract sign of sound as Aristotle had described. It came to denote the great moral divide between Christian civilization and savage barbarism as the European world became more global in the sixteenth century. The moral imperative of the alphabet was based on the notion that it was one of God's signs and gifts to his chosen people.[51] The precedent for the sixteenth-century fetishization of the letter and word can be found in the Bible. In Exodus, for example, the tablets received by Moses were written by God's finger in the Hebrew alphabet, and the Gospel of John opens with, "In the beginning was the Word, and the Word was with God, and the Word was God." But it was not just the written word's importance in the Bible, but also the discovery of so many other inferior systems used by peoples deceived by the devil that made the alphabet a sign in and of itself of God's divine will.

Two beautifully produced and illustrated alphabetic books manifest by their text and image how the alphabet came to be appreciated in and of itself, and therefore how it became almost a transubstantial sign of European cultural supremacy. It is the aesthetic appreciation of the alphabet in relation to its interpretation as a sign of divine cultural superiority that transforms the alphabet into a fetish.[52] The reification of the image of the alphabet as sign and as discourse of savage/civilized occurs in two editions of a book printed in Germany by a Protestant family of engravers and printers at the end of the sixteenth and beginning of the seventeenth century. Here the ability of the alphabet to record the history of the ancients, as mentioned by Aristotle and Acosta, is applied to the alphabet itself. The first is *Alphabeten vnd aller Art Characteren*, published by Theodor and Johann Theodor de Bry in 1596; the second is the English version, *Caracters and Diversitie of Letters Vsed by Divers Nations in the World: The Antiquity, Manifold Vse and Varietie Thereof; With Exemplary Descriptions of Very Many Strange Alphabets Curiously Cutt in Brasse by Iohn Theod de Bry Deceased*, published in 1628 and commissioned by William Fitzer. A Latin version, which I have not been able to consult, was published simultaneously with the German edition, and together the three volumes comprise some of the most luxurious editions of a relatively new genre of printed, illustrated books: the alphabet, ancient and modern.[53] For example, the illustrations of ancient alphabets featured in these two books include Chaldean, Greek, Phoenician, Syrian, Hebrew (Moses), and others. Modern alphabets of Arabic, German, Spanish, Greek, etc., came later.

There had been medieval illuminated letters and, by the fourteenth century, fully illustrated alphabets. The de Brys had participated in that tradition with the 1596 publication of a book of historiated letters called *Nova alphati effictio historiis ad sigulas literas correspondētibus, et toreumate Bryanaeo artificiose in aes incisis illustrata:*

---

the members distinguished between absolute and relative worship and the role of images in the church. See D. Sahas, *Icon and Logos: Sources in Eighth-Century Iconoclasm* (Toronto, 1986), 178–79.

50   Mexican pictorial glyphs, pictographs, and hieroglyphics, as well as Andean khipus and tocapus, continued to be used by indigenous communities well into the nineteenth century, and some are still in use today. They were sometimes used in official documents, religious practices, and teaching. See the various essays in Boone and Urton, eds., *Their Way of Writing*; and Elizabeth Hill Boone's contribution to this volume. However, alphabetic writing was always placed above these indigenous systems in terms of value and importance.

51   The moral imperative precedes the technical imperative of the alphabet as articulated by Jack Goody, *The Logic of Writing and the Organization of Society* (Cambridge, 1986).

52   I use the understanding of fetish as developed by William Pietz, "The Problem of the Fetish I," *RES: Anthropology and Aesthetics* 9 (Spring 1985): 5–17; and "The Problem of the Fetish II: The Origin of the Fetish," *RES: Anthropology and Aesthetics* 13 (Spring 1987): 23–45.

53   There are differences between the German and English editions. However, aside from the texts of the two editions, this is not the place for a comparative study.

versibus insuper latinis et rithmis germanicis nō omnino inconditis. In this book, the letters are keyed to the first word in the poem that appears on the facing page written in Latin and German. These words, and thus the initials, are either Old or New Testament names and subjects, such that the letter A contains the figure of Adam and the poem in Latin and German begins with his name. The letter T contains the figure of Thomas the apostle.[54]

There is a difference in the new genre of alphabet books. Letters neither are keyed to words nor refer to sounds. Instead, toward the end of the sixteenth century, the alphabet as an entity comes to be a subject in and of itself. This reevaluation of the alphabet goes beyond the Aristotelian assessment of its sign value in part because the Roman alphabet was critical to the print revolution itself. The mechanical reproduction of writing was invented by the Chinese some four hundred years prior to Gutenberg's innovation. However, the flexibility of the twenty-four letters of the Roman alphabet made it feasible to produce a movable type that was efficient. This difference between Chinese characters and the alphabet was also at the heart of Acosta's demonstration of the efficiency of the alphabet. And if Acosta's argument were true for the facility of the transcription of words, then it was most certainly true for printing. The limited number of metal type pieces for the alphabet, as opposed to the thousands of characters needed

for Chinese, Korean, and Japanese, made printing practical, cheap, and global.

The alphabet books produced by Theodor and his son Johann Theodor de Bry at the end of the sixteenth century might be seen as simply crystallizing the industrial importance of the alphabet by bringing different modern examples together.[55] After all, de Bry's images show many influences from earlier printed alphabets. For example, Peter Flötner (ca. 1485–1546), who published a complete figurative alphabet in 1534, is directly copied by de Bry in an engraving that appears toward the end of the German edition. In Flötner's alphabet, naked or nearly naked figures pose singly or in pairs to form the various letters. These letters seem to be animated images of human sound as it becomes sign. This animation is different from the more rational use of the human figure as the means of demonstrating a design strategy, such as in Albrecht Dürer's letters in his 1525 *Art of Measurement*. That is, the alphabet, whether drawn, cut, and so forth, was shown in its entirety so as to be *the* paradigmatic image of all that writing could be and do, just as Nebrija implied that it should be. Here, the alphabet becomes a sign in and of itself and the key component within the new technology of printing. One need only think of the word of God written and then printed by Gutenberg to understand the intimate relationship. But these new alphabet books are not just about the joyful melding of European symbolic and mechanical technologies. If that were the case, why do we find the same strategy in the 1579 *Rhetorica Christiana* published in Perugia by the Mexican Diego? This book deals with conversion and the use of artificial memory in the Americas. There are three illustrations of two Roman alphabets, using either formal or aural keys to remember them. That is, one alphabet is based upon the similarity of the shape of a letter to a thing and the other to the initial sound of the thing represented. In the former alphabet there is at least one human form for the letter V that is similar to that found in Flötner's alphabet. In fact the shapes are European things, while those that

---

54 Fourteen preparatory drawings for the letters still exist. The drawings do not have these biblical figures, rather they are classical mythological figures. These classical figures are replaced in the engravings by the biblical images. For example, the figure of Abel offering his sacrifice in the engraving for the letter B replaces the figure of a satyr depicted in the drawing of that letter. Otherwise, the drawing is a rather faithful copy of the engraving. This engraving is followed by the letter C, in which Cain holds aloft the jaw of an ass. Just as Abel has the same pose as the satyr, Cain's pose derives from a nude classical figure he replaces. See *Original Drawings for Fourteen Historiated Initials*, ca. 1595, Houghton Library, Harvard University, drawing 1 (letter C), drawing 5 (letter B). It appears that the drawings were altered to conform to the poems and their biblical content. The book is dedicated to the French Protestant antiquarian and poet Jean-Jacques Boissard, who may have written the poems, and in return, Boissard gives an extravagant appraisal of the talents of the de Brys in the preface of his *Theatrum vite humane* (1595). See Auguste Castan, *Jean Jacques Boissard poète latin, dessinateur et antiquaire enfant de Besançon et citoyen de Metz: Etude sur sa vie, les ouvrages et ses portraits* (Besançon, 1875), 14 n. 1.

55 Theodor de Bry (1528–1598) moved to Frankfurt am Main in 1588, where he and his sons Johann Theodor (1560–1623) and Johann Israel (1565–1611) established their publishing house.

correspond to the initial sound are a combination of New World and Old World figures. For example the letter E is cued by the Spanish word *edificio* (building); however, the Aztec glyph of a profile façade is used to represent the sound.

The three alphabet books by de Bry family are much less well known than their famous intergenerational series of thirteen volumes on the Americas and Asia, sometimes known as *Les grands voyages*, or *The Great Travels*.[56] The American volumes are, by and large, translated accounts of previously printed works, and many are about the Spanish and Portuguese conquest of the Americas, such as in volumes four through six, which are Latin and German translations of Girolomo Benzoni's *La historia*

de mondo nuovo.[57] First published in Venice in 1565, *La historia* was translated several times into French, Latin, and English before 1594, when it was republished and illustrated as part of *Les grands voyages*. The de Bry volumes are luxury books in which the illustrations compete with the printed text for the attention of the viewer. The first part of volume nine, published in 1602, is an edited version of Acosta's *Historia Natural y Moral de las Indias*.[58] This illustrated volume demonstrates the de Brys' close working relationship with Acosta's text and his chapters about writing, the alphabet, and its superiority to other sign forms.

So let us return to the alphabet books by the de Bry family and what they imply. Their texts are brief, just a few pages (nine in the German edition and twelve in the English edition), and the majority of the books are

56   See Theodor de Bry, *Collectiones peregrinationum in Indiam orientalem et Indiam occidentalem, XIII partibus comprehenso a Theodoro, Joan-Theodoro de Bry, et a Matheo Merian publicatae*, ed. and ill. Theodor de Bry (parts 1–6), Johann Theodor and Johann Israel (parts 7–9), Johann Theodor (parts 10–12), and M. Merian (part 13) (Frankfurt am Main, 1590–1634).

57   G. Benzoni, *La Historia de Mondo Nvovo* (Venice, 1565).
58   Johann Theodor de Bry, *Americae nona & postrema pars* (Frankfurt-am-Main, 1602).

FIG. 5.8.
Greek alphabet, *Alphabeten vnd aller Art Charactere*, published by Theodor and Johann Theodor de Bry, 1596.

Houghton Library, Harvard University.

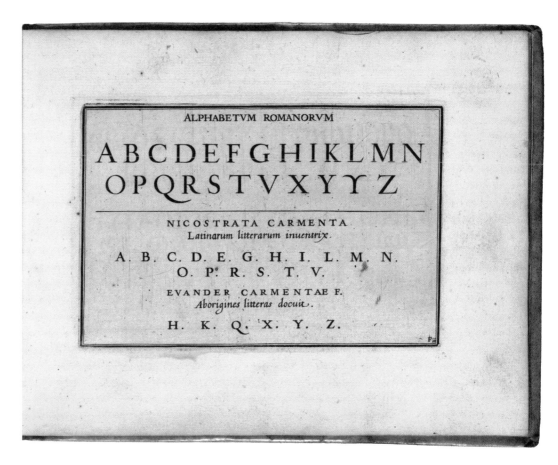

composed of different historical alphabets. For example, there are plates of ancient, or non-Christian, and modern alphabets, divided by the appearance of the Roman alphabet. Thus, first come the plates of the Phoenician, Hebrew, Chaldean, Armenian, Greek, and Arabic alphabets (fig. 5.8). The printing and binding of the book are horizontally oriented and thus accommodate visually and spatially the integrity of the horizontal image of all the alphabets. This first set of alphabets is also given sound equivalents by combinations of consonants and vowels from the Roman alphabet placed above each ancient letter, much like the sounds indicated for the knots in Sansevero's khipu book. The modern reader can reproduce the sounds for which each of the different ancient letters were signs. These ancient alphabets are set off from what follows by the appearance of the *Alphabetum Romanorum* and the name of Nicostrata Carmenta, who is glossed as the inventor of the Latin alphabet (*Latinarum litterarum inuentrix*), and the name of her son Evander, who gave the people their letters

(*Aborigines litteras docuit*) (fig. 5.9). This noble lineage of the alphabet is then followed by engravings of the different modern alphabets used in German, Flemish, Italian, French, and Spanish. The engravings of modern-language alphabets are slightly different from the ancient ones, since they do not require a key to their sounds. The modern letters are self-sufficient, standing as pure or transparent sound signs for their modern audience.

The series of ancient and modern alphabets is followed by an alphabet of two historiated capital letters per page. It is unclear what relation the letters have to the images, whether it is sound or concept. No one language seems to be the cue of the initial letter in terms of the names of the things depicted within the letters. It is clear, however that such references were used in de Bry's 1596 *Nova alphati effictio historiis,* in which, as described above, each letter has images depicting the first word of both the Latin and German poems. It may be that the historiated letters in *Alphabeten und aller art Characteren* are keyed to the different alphabets and languages that precede this series.[59] There is one pair of letters that seems to juxtapose the two worlds of America and Europe. The letter P is adorned with a peacock followed by the letter Q, which is adorned with what looks very much to be a turkey. In Spanish, at least, the two birds are seen in a hierarchical relationship of turkey to peacock, or *pavo* to *pavo real*. More interesting, perhaps, is that a grasshopper appears below the turkey, and this is a painted sign for the Nahuatl name glyph of Chapultepec, a famous site just outside of Mexico City where Moctezuma and Cortes had their palaces.

But it is in the text of both English and German editions that the hierarchical differentiation between the cultures of these two worlds is made explicit. Both editions mention "the variety and differing forms" that the Mexicans, Peruvians, Japanese, and Chinese use. In particular the Mexicans use pictures and the Peruvians use khipus, each "expressing a word or thing, but not a letter." This is clearly derived from Acosta, as is the following passage from de Bry's English edition:

And indeed much is the literall advantage; by speech we utter our minds once, at the present, to the present, as present occasions move (and perhaps unadvisedly transport) us: but by writing Man seems immortal, conuerseth and consulteth with the Patriarkes, Prophets, Apostles, Fathers, Philosophers, Historians and learners of the wisdom of the sages which have been in all times before him, yea by translations or learning Languages, in all places and Regions of the world; and lastly, by his owne writings, suruiueth, himselfe, remains (*litera scripta manet*) through all ages a Teacher and Counseller to the last of men, yea hereby God holds conference with men, and in his sacred Scriptures; as at first in the *Tablets of Stone*, speakes to all. And whereas speech pierceth the Eare (pierceth indeede and passeth often, in at the one and out the other) Writing also entertaineth the Eyes; and so long, by our owne or others readings, speekes to either of

those nobler senses, as wee will, and whereof we will ourselves; husht and silent at our pleasure; always free from fear, flattery and other humane passions. Therefore the dead were esteemed the best companions and faithful Counsellors, *Alfonsus* his opinion, namely, in their Writings still living to perfume those Offices, and want of Letters hath made some so seely [silly] as to think the Letter itself could speake, so much did *Americans* herein admire the *Spaniards* seeming in comparison of the others as speaking Apes.[60]

The German text clarifies that this incident is given to the reader so as to show what an exalted place letters and characters have when first encountered:

Let us turn to something new and demonstrate the reputation that the art of writing and the letters have, even among those who, because they are unfamiliar with them, can hold them for witchcraft and necromancy, like many of the savages in the New World do, which is rather bemusing and entertaining to hear, even though we cannot digress too much. So we will have to be brief.

The savages on the island of Hispaniola, when the Spanish first came to them, were of just this opinion. The historian who relays this particular history recounts it with these words:

When the Americans heard that the Spanish could talk with one another, even though they were not together, they assumed that they either had a soothsayer's spirit with them, or that the characters and letters could talk. From then on, the savages were concerned that when they did wrong, it would be exposed in this way. So they kept all the more quiet and demure, so that from that time onward, they

---

59 In one instance, that of the letter F, the figure of the pelican piercing its breast appears, allegorically referring to Christ's sacrifice and the sacrament of the Eucharist, and therefore, perhaps, to the word "faith."

60 Theodor de Bry, *Caracters and Diversitie of Letters Vsed by Divers Nations in the World: The Antiquity, Manifold Use and Varietie Thereof; With Exemplary Descriptions of Very Many Strang Alphabets Curiously Cutt in Brasse by Iohn Theod de Bry Deceased* (Frankfurt am Main, 1628), 3–4.

neither lied, nor wrangled the smallest thing from the Spanish.[61]

The "want of letters" in the New World places the reader in a privileged position in relation to the silly *Americans* who "think the Letter itself could speake."[62] For the European, the letter is read, silent or aloud, bringing the past and the physically absent into the present, but for the savage it does so in a magical way. As such, the alphabetic letter has a qualifying effect on Amerindians that goes well beyond the content of what is written about them.

De Bry's German text is also much more precise in its account. He says that a native servant from the Darien recounted to his Spanish master named Corales that when he saw the printed books of the Spanish and how they could read, he was reminded of similar things in his community, which were made of leaves gathered together.

> Script and books are, moreover, also in use in some places in the New World; this can be deduced from the fact that their books have been sent to us in our times.

> A lawyer by the name of Corales, the municipal governor of the Darien, writes to the King of Spain and recounts among other things that he has been sent a servant who escaped his master and fled from the heart of the land toward the solid ground in the west. This servant, upon observing that a letter was read to the governor, came closer to see what it was; he was duly surprised and told that his old lord, whom he had escaped, and his fellow countrymen also had books, but that these consisted of foliage and leaves that were fixed and bound together. Some of these

books have been sent to Spain by Cortes from the land of Calluacana (Culhuacan). They are also mentioned by Peter Martyr (d'Anhiera).[63] For curiosity's sake and to further commend the art of writing, we did not want to pass this over silently.[64]

These anecdotes only enliven for the reader what is already culturally assured precisely because they can read. Moreover, the introduction places him or her in a different cultural world from those without writing, just as Acosta had placed the alphabet as the index of all registers of society.[65] The 1628 English edition opens thusly:

> God hath added herein a further grace, that as Men by the former (reason) exceed Beasts, hereby one man may excel another; and amongst Man, some are accounted Civil, and more both Sociable and Religious, by the use of letters and Writing, which others wanting are esteemed Brutish, Savage, Barbarous.[66]

What then follows in this book can be understood as an expression of divine will as the text comes toward an end with the vision of Constantine at the Milvian bridge:

> I had rather mention that which Eusebius in the life of Constantine recordeth written by Divine hand, which some say was the cross, but by his description appeareth rather to have been the two first letters of Christ's

---

61   I thank Hugo Van der Velden and Benjamin Buchloh for helping with the translation of this text.

62   The cultural misunderstanding of writing and the printed book by nonwestern societies is a common European trope. The most famous historical account is the first encounter between the conquistador Pedro Pizarro and the Inca ruler Atahualpa. All Spanish accounts describe how a religious book was offered to him, which he threw to the ground because it did not speak to him. Told from an Andean point of view, this is not what happened. See Thomas B. F. Cummins, *Toasts with the Inca: Andean Abstraction and Colonial Images on Kero Vessels* (Ann Arbor, 2002), 15–20.

63   This seems to be a reference to the passage in book 8, decade 4 of Pietro Martire d'Anghiera, *De orbe nouo*, first published in 1530. It describes the Mexican characters as resembling the hieroglyphs of Egypt.

64   De Bry and de Bry, *Alphabeten vnd aller Art Characteren*, 9.

65   It is clear that Johann Theodor de Bry read Acosta, at least in the preparation for the English edition, as chapter 9 of book 6 is cited almost verbatim regarding the directions that different writing has in comparison to the left-to-right orientation of the Roman alphabet. Acosta writes about Mexican "writing": "Aunque quando escrivian en sus reuedas, o signos, començaban de en medio donde pinturaban al sol, y de alli yban subiendo por sus años hasta la vuelta de la rueda." *Historia Natural y Moral*, 263. In de Bry, we find "The Mexicans had writings in the forme of a wheel, which were read from the Center upwards to the Cirfumfrance." Johan Theodor de Bry, *Caracters and Diversitie of Letters*, 12.

66   Ibid., 3.

name X [chi] and P [rho] combined [☧], with promise of victory to the pious Emperor, not in that figure sifne [of the cross] but in Christ himslefe [*sic*], to whom be glory himself.[67]

That is, God writes by "Divine hand" in Greek letters for Constantine just as he had written the ten Commandments for Moses by his "Divine hand" in Exodus 24:12.

Most of the de Brys' other volumes have some such laden connotation. Most obvious are the texts on the Americas that are, in part, to be understood through their images as a sociopolitical Protestant strategy for dehumanizing the Catholic Spanish world by depicting as graphically as possible the atrocities visited upon the natives.[68] The 1598 publication in Latin by de Bry of Bartolomé de Las Casas's *Brevísima relación de la destrucción de las Indias* is the most explicit example. This famous text, originally written to argue in Spain among Spaniards for more humane dealings with the Indians by pointing out the abuses committed against them, is subverted by the de Brys' engravings so as to become the most horrific depictions of cruelty and torture by Spaniards and, by extension, the Catholic church. The engravings exaggerate, amplify, and even falsify Spanish actions so that they become images of unspeakable atrocities toward mankind in general.[69]

The de Brys' meticulous and beautiful books about the alphabet would seem to be a counterpoint to the dark side of European civilization that is so horrendously depicted in the plates illustrating their 1592 edition of Las Casas's *The Short History of the Destruction of the Indies*. But in truth, these beautiful books must be understood in relation to other publications about the New World, else why make reference to the Americas, and to Acosta in particular? Therefore, the reader can go on after reading these accounts to contemplate the beautiful plates that trace the history of letters and their demonstration of cultural superiority.

———ɱ———

As we have seen, the alphabet enabled the writing and, more importantly, the printing of Nebrija's famous "language is the companion of empire." As Nebrija understood and Mignolo has analyzed, writing with the alphabet was a symbolic technology that was as mighty as the steel sword.[70] The realization that writing demonstrated the intellectual superiority of western civilization changed the alphabet from a set of signs to a sign in and of itself, a secular fetish with divine origins. Acosta is one of the great proponents of the alphabet's power to be a defining marker in the hierarchy of cultures. This transference of value (i.e., fetishization) endowed the alphabet with an abstract signification above and beyond sound. The changed or enhanced nature of the alphabet meant that it became a subject of representation as opposed to being just illustration.

The alphabetic books of the de Brys are a logical extension of this new objectification. They are enacted through the reading of their text and, more importantly, the visual contemplation of the plates. They offer pleasure in the beauty of each character in relation to the whole. But they are the signs of the western tradition, and so dehumanize the rest of the world by their lack of pure signs, which are instantiated in the beautiful prints. That is, the letters of movable type that form the text of this historical relationship are rendered aesthetically by the beautiful engravings of each alphabet. Historically arranged into two periods, they also situate the reader in real time, the time of the global expansion of the European world. As one contemplates the beauty of one's own lettered history, one performs, by reading, viewing, and pronouncing, the letters of empire, letters to which all else is to be subsumed and/or destroyed.

67 Ibid., 12.

68 See Thomas B. F. Cummins, "De Bry and Herrera: 'Aguas Negras' or the Hundred Years War over an Image of America," in *Arte, historia e identidad en América: Visiones comparativas,* ed. G. Curiel, R. González Mello, and J. Gutiérrez Haces (Mexico City, 1994), 17–31.

69 See Tom Conely, "De Bry's Las Casas," in *Amerindian Images and the Legacy of Columbus,* ed. René Jara and Nicholas Spadaccini (Minneapolis, 1992), 103–31; and E. Shaskan Bumas, "The Cannibal Butcher Shop: Protestant Uses of Las Casas's *Brevísima relación* in Europe and the American Colonies," *Early American Literature* 35 (2000): 107–36.

70 Nebrija, *Gramática*, 1–3; Mignolo, "Nebrija in the New World," 185–207; and idem, *Darker Side of the Renaissance,* 29–122.

Text: Imaging the Ineffable

Dynamic Signs and Spiritual Designs

Herbert L. Kessler

In principio

OPENING JOHN'S FIRST EPISTLE IN THE MOUTIER-GRANDVAL BIBLE, an initial Q constructs a relationship between its circular bowl and the oculus at its center, that is, between the letter and its figural equivalent (fig. 6.1).[1] Initially, the relationship seems to be a simple one. Much larger than the letters that follow and wrapped in vine tendrils, the Q introduces the Scripture that begins "Quod fuit ab initio" and, at the same time, serves as a window through which the reader/viewer peers at another smaller circle within it. The letter belongs emphatically to the world, at least to the sacred world of the Bible inscribed on porous animal skin, five lines of which it embraces with its tail; and it is made of silver, which is precious and lustrous but degrades and turns black when exposed to air.[2] At the same time, the Q seems to generate its cosmic counterpart rendered in incorruptible matter and pure shape: a gold circle filled with magenta that frames a hand, the traditional symbol of God's disembodied presence, proffering a third ring.[3] The hand of God itself provides a transition between the world of spirit and the world of matter created by the materials and ornamentation, and even engenders the round letterform itself. The smaller gold ring in its grasp creates an intermediary field where it overlaps the central circle, transforming the magenta into light aqua green-blue and seeming to move outward toward the initial and text. Letter, word, and sign thus seem to produce one another in a circular process of origination and generation.[4]

1   London, British Library, Add. MS. 10,546, fol. 406r. See Wilhelm Koehler et al., *Die karolingischen Miniaturen* (Berlin and Wiesbaden, 1933–2009), 1.1:386–87 et passim; Ellen Beer, "Die Buchkunst, die Initialen," in *Die Bibel von Moutier-Grandval*, ed. Johannes Duft et al. (Bern, 1971), 121–85, at 129; Christine Jakobi-Mirwald, *Text-Buchstabe-Bild: Studien zur historisierten Initiale im 8. und 9. Jahrhundert* (Berlin, 1998); and Kathrin Müller, *Visuelle Weltaneignung: Astronomische und kosmologische Diagramme in Handschriften des Mittelalters* (Göttingen, 2008), 49–58. Unless otherwise noted, the translations in this article are my own.

2   Psalm 11 (12):6 identifies silver with divine communication: "The promises of the Lord are promises that are pure, silver refined in a furnace on the ground, purified seven times." On this and other meanings of the metal, see Herbert L. Kessler, "The Eloquence of Silver," in *L'allégorie dans l'art du Moyen Age: Formes et fonctions; Héritages, créations, mutations*, ed. Christian Heck (Turnhout, 2011), 49–64.

3   See Herbert L. Kessler, "'Hoc visibile imaginatum figurat illud invisibile verum': Imagining God in Pictures of Christ," in *Seeing the Invisible in Late Antiquity and the Early Middle Ages: Papers from "Verbal and Pictorial Representations of the Invisible, 400 to 1000" (Utrecht, 11–13 December 2003)*, ed. Giselle De Nie et al. (Turnhout, 2005), 293–328.

4   In other Touronian manuscript illuminations, e.g., the Majestas Domini page in a Gospel book in Paris (BnF, Cod. lat. 261 and Cod. lat. 9385, fol. 179v), a similar color progression indicates movement from the central divinity toward the terrestrial realm; see Koehler, *Die karolingischen miniaturen*, 1.1:279–86, 320–21; and Marie-Pierre Laffitte and Charlotte Denoël, eds., *Trésors carolingiens: Livres manuscrits de Charlemagne à Charles le Chauve* (Paris, 2007), 155–56.

FIG. 6.1.

1 John from the
Moutier-Grandval
Bible. London, British
Library, Add. MS.
10,546, fol. 406r.

Photo courtesy of
the British Library.

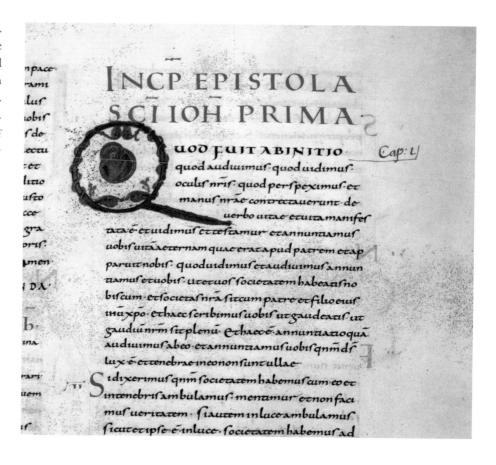

Painted around 840 at the abbey of Saint Martin's in Tours, the initial is a rare though not unique instance of a Touronian illuminator's transforming a letter into a cosmological diagram.[5] In a slightly later cognate manuscript, the First Bible of Charles the Bald of 845, the D that opens Jerome's defense of his Vulgate translation that begins "Desiderii mei" is conceived as an enormous zodiac with the sun at its center rising in a chariot above a setting moon.[6] Based on a planisphere of fixed stars and orbiting planets of the type found, for instance, in the

contemporary Leiden *Aratea*,[7] the zodiac initial has no obvious relationship to the words it adorns; rather, it introduces the creation of the world recounted in the text that follows it immediately and provides a prologue to the pictured account of the creation of Adam and Eve and the fall of humankind that is the subject of the frontispiece to the book of Genesis on folio 10v.[8]

Moreover, the borrowed cosmological motif at the start of the single-volume Moutier-Grandval Bible in London has a precedent in

5   On the pictorial functions of Carolingian letters, see, notably, Beat Brenk, "Schriftlichkeit und Bildlichkeit in der Hofschule Karls d. Gr.," in *Testo e imagine nell'alto medioevo (Settimane di studio del Centro italiano di studi sull'alto medioevo, 15–21 aprile 1993)* (Spoleto, 1994), 2:631–91; Jakobi-Mirwald, *Text-Buchstabe-Bild*; and Müller, *Visuelle Weltaneignung*. See also Laura Kendrick, *Animating the Letter: The Figurative Embodiment of Writing from Late Antiquity to the Renaissance* (Columbus, Ohio, 1999).

6   Paris, BnF, lat. 1, fol. 8r. Koehler, *Die karolingischen Miniaturen*, 1.1:396–401 et passim. See also Paul E. Dutton and Herbert L. Kessler, *The Poetry and Paintings of the First Bible of Charles the Bald* (Ann Arbor, 1997); Laffitte and Denoël, eds., *Trésors carolingiens*, 103–15.

7   Universiteitsbibliotheek VLQ 79, fol. 93v. Florentine Mütherich, "Die Bilder," in *Aratea: Commentar zum Aratus Germanicus, Ms. Voss. Lat. Q 79, Bibliotheek der Rijksuniversiteit Leiden* (Luzern, 1979); Naomi R. Kline, *Maps of Medieval Thought* (Woodbridge, 2001); Bianca Kühnel, *The End of Time in the Order of Things: Science and Eschatology in Early Medieval Art* (Regensburg, 2003); and Eric Ramírez-Weaver, "Classical Constellations in Carolingian Codices: Investigating the Celestial Imagery of Madrid, Biblioteca Nacional, MS 3307," in *Negotiating Secular and Sacred in Medieval Art: Christian, Islamic, and Buddhist* (Aldershot, 2009), 103–28.

8   Like the Leiden zodiac, the First Bible initial lacks the sign of Virgo, the presence of which may be implied by the sun's passing through Pisces; the Annunciation occurred on 25 March.

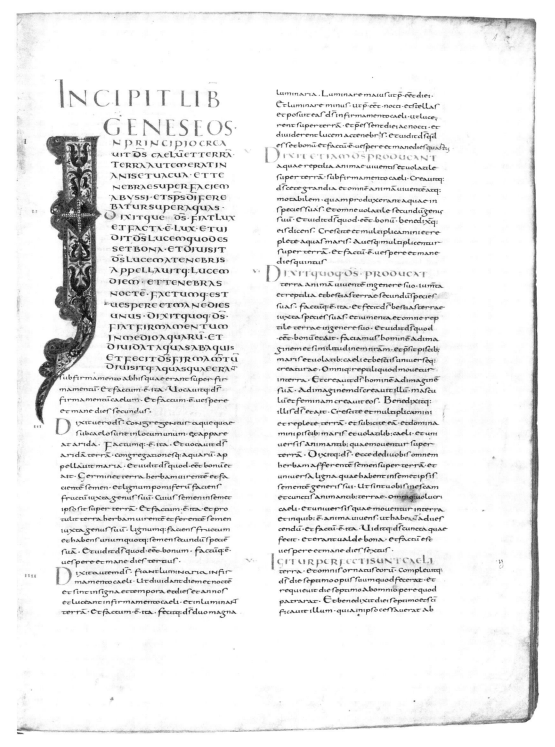

FIG. 6.2.

Genesis from
a Touronian
Bible. Zurich,
Zentralbibliothek,
Cod. Car CI, fol. 6r.

Photo courtesy of
Zentralbibliothek Zurich

the diamond-shaped lozenge in a slightly earlier Touronian Bible in Zurich (fig. 6.2).[9] It, too, is a diagram that serves as an organizing feature—the *tetragonus mundi* found in such astronomical tracts as the early ninth-century miscellany preserved in Vienna.[10] And, inscribed with a cross on a deep blue ground, the ideograph depends directly on the tradition of *carmina figurata*

9 Zentralbibliothek, Cod. Car CI, fol. 6r. Koehler, *Die karolingischen Miniaturen*, 1.1:374–75 et passim.

10 Nationalbibliothek, Cod. 387, fol. 134r. Herbert L. Kessler, *The Illustrated Bibles from Tours* (Princeton, 1977).

Dynamic Signs and Spiritual Designs   113

beloved by Carolingians, including Alcuin, who served as abbot of Saint Martin's from 796 until his death in 804.[11] Alcuin's own *Versus de sancta* *cruce ad Carolum* in Bern includes a similar figure described in the pictographic text as the world (*mundus, orbis*) "sealed" by the "salvation that the

---

11   For a recent discussion of the use of the lozenge form in the Book of Kells (Dublin, Trinity College Library, MS. A. I. [58]), see Benjamin C. Tilghman, "The Shape of the Word:

Extralinguistic Meaning in Insular Display Lettering," *Word & Image* 27 (2011): 292–308.

earth's ruler has provided."[12] Incorporated into the letter I of "In principio creavit Deus caelum et terram" (Gen. 1:1), the inscribed lozenge in the Zurich Bible not only evokes the creation of the terrestrial world, but also glosses the text of Hebrew Scripture with the assertion that Christ preexisted time. Incorporating letter and letter-like diagram, the figure-text ligature transforms the opening word of Hebrew Scripture into an image of the cosmos created by the Word made flesh and redeemed by his sacrifice. In so doing, it demonstrates the essential harmony believed to exist between the world, the word through which it was made, and the incarnate God who brought it into existence. The design is, itself, the sign.

The "In principio" initial in the Zurich Bible is, in turn, an antecedent of the cross from which the alpha and omega are suspended that marks Christ's eternal presence at the beginning of the titulus on the Genesis frontispiece in the Moutier-Grandval Bible itself,[13] and, more important, of the Genesis initial in the First Bible of Charles the Bald, which in the same place actually portrays the anthropomorphic Deity (fol. 11r; fig. 6.3).[14] Shown half-length within a circle colored light magenta, the Creator is pictured displaying an open book in one hand and a gold ring filled with blue in the other, the "caelum et terra" he brought into being through his word. The Creator is portrayed as Christ the Logos, whom Alcuin called "gubernator in totius mundi naturis"[15] and whom the First Bible's own dedicatory verses characterize in Trinitarian terms: "Creator of heaven, and earth, and sea, and the one born of that one, and the Holy Spirit."[16] In this case, the letter's stem filled with vines evokes the earthly realm; but near the oculus, abstracted

versions of the organic patterns effect a transition to the view of heaven.

The imagery introduced in the opening letter of Scripture in the First Bible of Charles the Bald is recapitulated and greatly amplified in the Majestas Domini that serves as the New Testament frontispiece in the great one-volume Bible (fig. 6.4). Derived from depictions of Christ returning at the end of time, the Majestas Domini depicts Christ full length and enclosed by a figure-eight mandorla set inside the lozenge of the tetragonus mundi, again holding a disk in one hand and a book in the other. Positioned at the hinge of Old Testament and New in a manuscript containing all of Scripture, the Christ of the Second Coming is presented both as the fulfillment in his very person of Hebrew prophecy (represented by Isaiah, Ezekiel, Daniel, and

FIG. 6.4.
Majestas Domini, frontispiece to the New Testament of the First Bible of Charles the Bald. Paris, Bibliothèque nationale de France, lat. 1, fol. 329v.

Photo courtesy of the Bibliothèque nationale de France.

12 Burgerbibliothek, Cod. 212, fol. 123r. Ulrich Ernst, *Carmen Figuratum: Geschichte des Figurengedichts von den antiken Ursprüngen bis zum Ausgang des Mittelalters* (Cologne, Weimar, and Vienna, 1991), 168–78; and Celia Chazelle, *The Crucified God in the Carolingian Era: Theology and Art of Christ's Passion* (Cambridge, 2001), 14–16.

13 Kessler, *Illustrated Bibles*, 13–35.

14 Henri Omont, *Peintures et initiales de la première Bible de Charles le Chauve* (Paris, 1911); Dutton and Kessler, *Poetry and Paintings.*

15 *Interrogationes et responsiones in Genesin*; PL 101:517.

16 "In primis caeli terraeque marisque creator, ipsius et natus, spiritus atque agius"; Dutton and Kessler, *Poetry and Paintings*, 110–11.

Jeremiah) and as the subject of the account of his life transcribed by the Four Evangelists. He is also conceived as the source of the four streams shown beneath Matthew, Mark, Luke, and John, a reference to the fountain in the Garden of Eden (Gen. 2:10–14), as Jerome maintained in his "Plures fuisse" preface included in the Bible.[17] The Majestas Domini thus refers to the creation of the world described at the beginning of Scripture and also to the return to Paradise promised the faithful when Christ returns at the end of time. It thereby represents visually the process of reading and rereading advocated in the Bible's dedicatory verses.[18] Expanding on the tiny figure presenting the primordial cosmos inserted into the first initial, it presents the full-length Christ enthroned on a star-filled, blue orb ringed in gold and divided into heaven and earth, so that he is pictured quite literally as the "gubernator in totius mundi naturis."

The Mysterious Orb

If the Majestas Domini in the First Bible of Charles the Bald is understood, at least to a certain extent, as an elaboration of the vignette within the initial that opens the book of Genesis, then the disk Christ is shown holding (see fig. 6.4) might productively be interpreted as the cosmos he is pictured creating at the beginning of time (see fig. 6.3), that is, as a form of the world. Absent from the parallel page in the Moutier-Grandval, with which the later Majestas Domini frontispiece shares a titulus and basic iconographic elements, the gold disk has been much discussed. Primarily on the basis of comparisons with later versions of the same subject derived from Touronian exemplars in which the object Christ holds between his fingers is labeled "mundus" or "terra," the small gold disk has, in fact, sometimes been understood as the cosmos.[19] That identification, and with it a direct

connection to the cosmic orb in the Genesis initial, seems to be confirmed by tituli in two cognate Carolingian pictures produced for Charles the Bald around 870, one in the San Paolo Bible in Rome, which refers to Christ's "weighing the world,"[20] and another in the Codex Aureus of Saint Emmeram in Munich describing Christ's "balancing the four-cornered earth with wondrous discernment."[21]

However, in an article on paired eleventh-century leaves from Tours in Auxerre (now on deposit in the Bibliothèque municipale) published some sixty years ago, Meyer Schapiro argued persuasively that the disk in the First Bible of Charles the Bald (and its slightly later analogues) is not a representation of the world but rather a depiction of a Eucharistic wafer. Schapiro cited a sacramentary still in Tours, where it was made during the third quarter of the ninth century, which pictures a priest consecrating the sacred species, represented as a golden wafer atop a silver paten alongside a chalice.[22] Even more important for the object's

initial grasps the orb firmly in a way that invites comparison with a personification on the diptych of Rufus Gennadius Probus Orestes in London (Victoria and Albert Museum), whose orb, inscribed with the letter A designating the city of Constantinople, refers to the earthly domain in much the same way. Wolfgang F. Volbach, *Elfenbeinarbeiten der spätantike und des frühen Mittelalters*, 3rd ed. (Mainz am Rhein, 1976), 40–41, and also 24–25 and 35; and Paul Williamson, *Medieval Ivory Carvings: Early Christian to Romanesque* (London, 2010), 46–49.

20 "Sede throni residens, mundum qui ponderat." Monastero di San Paolo fuori le mura, fol. 259r; Girolamo Arnaldi, ed., *Commentario storico paleografico artistico critico della Bibbia di San Paolo fuori le Mura (Codex membranaceus saeculi IX)* (Rome, 1993), 166.

21 "Liberat tetragonum miro discrimine mundum." Staatsbibliothek, Clm 14000, fol. 6r; Koehler, *Die karolingischen Miniaturen*, 5:175–98; and Michael Herren, ed., *Iohannis Scotti Eriugenae Carmina* (Dublin, 1993), 130–31. The notion of weighing is reinforced by Christ's fingers, which conjure up contemporary depictions of the *computus digitalis* in Bede's *De temporum ratione*. See Moritz Wedell, "*Actio—Loquela Digitorum—Computatio*: Zur Frage nach dem *Numerus* zwischen Ordnungsangeboten, Gebrauchsformen und Erfahrungsmodalitäten (Einleitung II)," in *Was Zählt: Ordnungsangebote, Gebrauchsformen und Erfahrungsmodalitäten des 'numerus' im Mittelalter*, ed. idem (Vienna, 2012), 15–63.

22 Bm, ms. 184, fol. 3r. Meyer Schapiro, "Two Romanesque Drawings in Auxerre and Some Iconographic Problems," in *Studies in Art and Literature for Belle Da Costa Greene*, ed. Dorothy Miner (Princeton, 1954), 331–49, reprinted in idem, *Romanesque Art* (New York, 1977), 306–27. See also

17 "Quattuor flumina paradisi instar eructans"; Donatien de Bruyne, *Les préfaces de la Bible* (Namur, 1920), 155.

18 "Testamenta duo quod relegenda gerit"; Dutton and Kessler, *Poetry and Paintings*, 104.

19 Herbert Schade, "Hinweise zur frühmittelalterliche Iconographie," *Das Münster* 11 (1958): 375–92; and Hans B. Meyer, "Zur Symbolik frühmittelalterlichen Majestasbilder," *Das Münster* 14 (1961): 73–88. The Creator in the Genesis

FIG. 6.5.

Vere dignum from a
Touronian sacramentary
made during the third
quarter of the ninth
century. Tours, Bm,
ms. 184, fol. 2r.

Photo courtesy of the
Bibliothèque municipale
de Tours

idem, "A Relief in Rodez and the Beginnings of Romanesque
Sculpture in Southern France," in *Studies in Western Art: Acts
of the Twentieth International Congress of the History of Art*,
ed. Millard Meiss et al. (Princeton, 1963), 1:40–66. Koehler,
Die karolingischen Miniaturen, vol. 1, part 1: 423–25 et passim;
Franz Rademacher, *Der thronende Christus der Chorschranken
aus Gustorf* (Cologne, 1964); Søren Kaspersen, "Majestas
Domini—Regnum et Sacerdotium: Zu Entstehung und Leben
des Motivs bis zum Investiturstreit," *Hafnia: Copenhagen
Papers in the History of Art* 8 (1981): 83–146; Martin Büchsel,
Die Entstehung des Christusporträts (Mainz am Rhein, 2003),
146–49; Anne-Orange Poilpré, *Maiestas Domini: Une image
de l'Église en Occident V^e–IXe siècle* (Paris, 2005); Jakobi-
Mirwald, *Text-Buchstabe-Bild*, 52; and Elizabeth Saxon, *The
Eucharist in Romanesque France: Iconography and Theology*
(Woodbridge, 2006), 149–53. Gold disks inscribed with
Christological monograms appear, tellingly, on the *In principio*
page of John's Gospel in the Lothar Gospels (Paris, BnF, Lat.
266, fol. 172r), a more or less contemporary manuscript that
also pictures Christ in Majesty; Koehler, *Die karolingischen
Miniaturen*, vol. 1, part 1: 403–5; Laffitte and Denoël, eds.,
Trésors carolingiens, 103.

identification is an initial in the same manuscript that, within the V of *Vere dignum*, represents the Hand of God in a gold-framed magenta
circle holding between the thumb and forefinger
a red-ringed gold disk very much like the one in
the First Bible of Charles the Bald (fig. 6.5).[23] The
context of the preface to the Canon of the Mass
leaves little doubt that in the later Touronian
book the disk is the sacramental wafer, albeit a
gold one, that is, the archetypal host that God
sent to earth to redeem humankind.[24]

23   Fol. 2r. In the depiction of Saint Denis receiving the host
in an eleventh- or twelfth-century sacramentary in Paris (BnF,
lat. 9436, fol. 106v), Christ holds the tiny gold wafer with his
thumb and forefinger in much the same way; see Rademacher,
Thronende Christus, fig. 106.

24   On the liturgical underpinning of Majestas Domini pictures, particularly their relationship to the Vere dignum, see

Eucharistic species are not frequently pictured in Carolingian art. In the Stuttgart Psalter of circa 820–30 (Württembergische Landesbibliothek, Cod. bibl. fol. 23), the miniature accompanying Psalm 115(116):4 (fol. 130v) includes an altar on which four circles representing the sanctified bread are white in contrast to the nearby gold cup, candlestick, and cross.[25] In the depiction of Christ at Emmaus in the more-or-less contemporary purple Gospels from Augsburg, however, the Eucharistic bread is as gold as the chalice beside it.[26] Most important, in the Marmoutier Sacramentary in Autun,[27] illuminated at Tours in 844–45, the very period when the Moutier-Grandval Bible and the First Bible of Charles the Bald were being produced there, the picture of the Last Supper includes both a round white loaf marked for division on the table, surrounded by a paten, chalice, and liturgical knife and spoons, and a gold bread in Christ's hand above (scored as in the Munich Gospels). In distinguishing the liturgical bread from the historical one, the illuminator of the Marmoutier Sacramentary may have been inspired by Augustine's conceit in his reading of Psalm 33 (34) that, at the Last Supper, "Christ carried himself in his own hands, entrusting his own body when he said 'This is my body.' He carried his body in his hands."[28] The

gold wafer Christ is shown handing the apostles in person would then represent the archetype of the real, white eucharist that the priest offers the faithful at Mass.

Inscribed with the chi-rho, the disk in the Majestas Domini of the First Bible of Charles the Bald (see fig. 6.4) is a different kind, an unleavened or azyme wafer that also evoked a coin and, hence, the eternal Sovereign's offering to redeem humankind's sin.[29] A short tract composed allegedly by one "Eldefonsus of Spain" and finished just two months before the Bible, perhaps at Corbie, begins by noting that the waffle-iron–like molds used to produce hosts are inscribed with circles on both sides, creating single wafers with two impressions, in the same way that coins are minted. It then asks about Eucharistic wafers: "if coins of the earthly king in circulation everywhere are valued, why is the coin of the heavenly king not better, which is always everywhere?"[30] The disk Christ

Marcello Angheben, "Théophanies absidales et liturgie eucharistique: L'exemple des peintures romanes de Catalogne et du nord des Pyrénés comportant un séraphin et un chérubin," in *Les fonts de la pintura romànica*, ed. J. Milagros Guardia and Carles Mancho (Barcelona, 2008), 57–96; and idem, "Les théophanies composites des arcs absidaux et la liturgie eucharistique," *CahCM* 54 (2011): 113–42.

25 Bernhard Bischoff et al., eds., *Der Stuttgarter Bilderpsalter: Bibl. Fol. 23 Württembergische Landesbibliothek Stuttgart* (Stuttgart, 1965), 2:133. See also Tobias Frese, *Aktual- und Realpräsenz: Das eucharistische Christusbild von der Spätantike bis ins Mittelalter* (Berlin, 2013), 141–206. On the appearance of the host in later medieval representations, see Maurice Vloberg, *L'eucharistie dans l'art* (Paris, 1946); Saxon, *Eucharist*; and Aden Kumler, "The Multiplication of the Species: Eucharistic Morphology in the Middle Ages," *RES: Anthropology and Aesthetics* 59–60 (2011): 179–91.

26 Munich, Staatsbibliothek, Clm 23631, fol. 197v. Katharina Bierbrauer, *Die vorkarolingischen und karolingischen Handschriften der Bayerischen Staatsbibliothek* (Wiesbaden, 1990), no. 97.

27 Bm, ms. 19bis, fol. 8r. Koehler, *Die karolingischen Miniaturen*, vol. 1, part 1: 393–96.

28 "Ferebatur enim Christus in manibus suis, quando commendans ipsum corpus suum, ait: *Hoc est corpus meum*. Ferebat enim illud corpus in manibus suis." Eligius Dekkers and

Johannes Fraipont, eds., *Enarrationes in Psalmos*, CCSL 38 (Turnhout, 1956), 281. On the Carolingian history of Augustine's text, including its use by Alcuin and, around the time the First Bible was being produced, by Hincmar of Reims, see Janet Nelson, "The Intellectual in Politics: Context, Content, and Authorship in the Capitulary of Coulaines, November 843," in *Intellectual Life in the Middle Ages: Essays Presented to Margaret Gibson* (London, 1992), 1–14; Chazelle, *Crucified God*, 249–50; and Henry Mayr-Harting, "Augustine of Hippo, Chelles, and the Carolingian Renaissance: Cologne Cathedral Manuscript 63," *Frühmittelalterliche Studien* 45 (2011): 51–75. The scribe of Cologne, Erzb. Dombibl., Cod. 63, the nun Gislildis, marked Psalm 33 with two marginal signs. Other Carolingian copies of the *Enarrationes* from Fleury and Corbie are preserved in Orléans (Bm, ms. 45) and Paris (BnF, lat. 12171–73).

29 The gesture may, in turn, have been intended to allude to the worldly rulers' largesse pictured on late antique consular diptychs that show servants pouring coins from bags into heaps on the ground (see n. 19). The inscribed christogram in the Majestas Domini does not subvert this interpretation; it was frequently impressed on coins and seals at that time to convey the ruler's authority. See Ildar Garipzanov, "Metamorphoses of the Early Medieval *signum* of a Ruler in the Carolingian World," *EME* 15 (2006): 419–64.

30 "Si valens ubique discurrit moneta terreni regis, cur non melius valens discurrat semper ubique moneta caelestis regis?" *Revelatio quae ostensa est venerabili viro Hispaniensi Eldefonso Episcopo*; Roger Reynolds, "Vetera analecta," *Peregrinations: Journal of Medieval Art and Architecture* 4 (2013): 154–72, at 155; idem, "Christ's Money: Eucharistic Azyme Hosts in the Ninth Century According to Bishop Eldefonsus of Spain; Observations on the Origin, Meaning, and Context of a Mysterious Revelation," *Peregrinations: Journal of Medieval Art and Architecture* 4 (2013): 1–69; and idem, "Eucharistic Adoration in the Carolingian Era? Exposition of Christ in the Host," *Peregrinations: Journal of Medieval Art and*

is shown holding in the First Bible of Charles the Bald (and later manuscripts) is thus a visual parallel to an idea found, for instance, in Bede's *Commentaries on Ezra and Nehemiah*, that claims the sacrifices described in the Hebrew Bible prefigure the coming of Christ, who, in offering his own flesh and blood, purchased the whole world.[31] The little disk is a dynamic sign of the world, the Eucharist, and a token of redemption, functioning simultaneously—as so many other details do in the Touronian Bibles—to construct Scripture's unity through pictorial cross-referencing.[32]

Schapiro rightly makes a similar point, noting that the disk introduced into the Majestas Domini pictures might, in fact, be identified as either the world or the sacramental wafer because of the analogous shape and two-part construction. However, he hypothesizes that the meanings were interchanged from the eleventh century, not the ninth; and he does not cite the initial in the First Bible of Charles the Bald, with its parallels to the Majestas Domini frontispiece in the same manuscript. All of this suggests that the exchange of meaning Schapiro imagines had, in fact, occurred first in Carolingian Tours, and that the "confusion"

of forms is in fact an intentional succession. In the historiated initial at the start of Genesis, the co-eternal Logos creates the universe, pictured as an orb; then, enthroned on the cosmos at the Second Coming, he offers his own body in the form of the sacramental species to save humankind by restoring its pre-lapsarian condition.

As Elizabeth Saxon has observed, "the hand-held host does not seem to appear in art until Paschasius [Radbertus] presented Charles the Bald with a revised version [of the *De corpore et sanguine Domini*] in 844."[33] It is indeed hard to believe that the introduction of the gold disk into the Majestas Domini of the First Bible of Charles the Bald produced one year later is not related to the particularly active Eucharistic debates involving Ratramnus of Corbie, Paschasius, Hincmar, and others, at the very moment the frontispiece was being painted. The spotty records of these debates do in fact yield such significant, albeit often oblique, parallels to the Touronian imagery as Ratramnus of Corbie's claim that the Eucharist offers the faithful a foretaste of their eventual meeting with God at the end of time.[34] The records may also help to explain the monogram painted on the disk Christ proffers. Paschasius, for example, explains the Eucharist in terms of an impressed seal.[35] Most pertinent to the visual argument made by the relationship of the Genesis initial and Majestas Domini frontispiece in the First Bible of Charles the Bald, it would seem, is Paschasius's and, in turn, Hincmar's arguments that just as Christ created the world from nothing, so, too, could he change wine and bread into his blood and body.[36] A few years after the Bible was completed in 845, Hincmar summed up the ideas perfectly in his (fragmentary) *Ferculum Salomonis*, even alluding to profit exchange.[37]

Architecture 4 (2013): 70–153. See also Herbert L. Kessler, "Medietas/Mediator and the Geometry of Incarnation," in *Incarnation*, ed. Walter Melion and Lee Palmer Wandel (Leiden, 2015), 17–75.

31 "Quae cuncta in figuram praecesserunt eius qui in sexta aetate uenturus in carne et hostia eiusdem suae carnis ac sanguinis totum orbem erat redempturus"; Bede, *In Ezram et Neemiam*, ed. David Hurst, CCSL 119A (Turnhout, 1969), 271–72. Eldefonsus projected the idea onto the Eucharistic wafers arranged in a cross pattern on the altar: "et in medio quinque in crucis modum ad significandos Evangelistas, et unicum Filium, quem testantur quasi undique sustinentes, pro redemptione generis humani olim crucifixum" (Reynolds, "Vetera analecta," 157–58). In his linear interpretation of his *Carmen* 22 (= *In honorem S. Crucis*), Hrabanus Maurus conjures up the Second Coming from the chi-rho and describes the "bene meriti tunc accepta talenta cum lucro reportant ad Dominum"; *Rabani Mauri in Honorem Sanctae Crucis*, CCCM 100, ed. Michel Perrin (Turnhout, 1997), 271–73. I wish to thank Aden Kumler for urging me to consider the possibility that the disk also refers to a coin. On the chi-rho, see Vincent Debiais's chapter in this volume.

32 See Herbert L. Kessler, "'Facies bibliothecae revelata': Carolingian Art as Spiritual Seeing," in *Testo e immagine nell'alto medioevo (XLI Settimana internazionale di studi)* (Spoleto, 1994), 533–94, reprinted in idem, *Spiritual Seeing: Picturing God's Invisibility in Medieval Art* (Philadelphia, 2000), 173–79.

33 Saxon, *Eucharist*, 148, n. 3. The first picture Saxon cites is the Majestas Domini of the First Bible of Charles the Bald.

34 Chazelle, *Crucified God*, 234.

35 Ibid., 222–23; and idem, "Figure, Character, and the Glorified Body in the Carolingian Eucharistic Controversy," *Traditio* 47 (1992): 1–36.

36 E.g., Pascasius Radbertus, *De corpore et sanguine Domini*, ed. Beda Paulus, CCCM 16 (Turnhout, 1969), 13–17 and 92–96. Chazelle, *Crucified God*, 221–23.

37 "Hic deus omnipotens, per quem pater omnia fecit / Naturas rerum mutat, ut ipse velit. / Hic cruce nostra creat, propriis et munera verbis / Fitque caro ac sanguis pane liquore

Whatever the precise historical origins, both the disk Christ is shown holding in the Genesis initial of the First Bible of Charles the Bald and the one he is offering in the Majestas Domini frontispiece rely on geometry, the circle itself, to activate the multivalence. Connoting unity within multiplicity—of heaven and earth in the first and spirit and body in the second—the circle draws on a tradition of mapping meaning onto that most basic of letter forms: the O. Thus, one of the earliest figured initials that has come down to us, the O that begins book six in the sixth-century manuscript of Orosius's *Historia adversum paganos* in Florence, depicts the concordance of Christ in the four Gospels.[38] Inspired by the text's account of the Savior's coming into the world and the word *omnes*, of which it is a part, the manuscript's sole figured letter uses the circle's multivalence to convey the unity of the four Gospels.[39] Just before the Touronian Bibles were adorned, moreover, Beatus of Liébana provided an extended reading of Christ's declaration "I am the alpha and omega" (Rev. 1:8), in which he interpreted the O of the omega in much the same fashion, seeing God's comprehensiveness and divinity revealed in its circular form and, playing on the words *medietas* (the circle's center point) and *mediator*, to read in the letter's pure geometry a means for anagogical ascent from humankind to God through Jesus Christ (cf. Tim. 1:2, 5).[40] The illustrated Beatus manuscripts themselves

do not realize the author's play between the omega's design and Christ's person,[41] but early Carolingian pictures do. Hrabanus Maurus's *In honorem sanctae crucis* of 810, as represented in a manuscript in Rome, opens with a picture-poem of the crucified Christ in which the final letter O of "ordo iustus deo" forms Christ's umbilicus.[42]

The circle's flexibility as letter and sign was frequently used later. In a late tenth-century sacramentary in Udine, for instance, an O functions as part of the word *omnipotens* and, filled with blue, also as the mandorla of a Christ in Majesty flanked by the alpha and omega.[43] The letter's perfect geometrical shape is deployed several times in the tenth-century Benedictional of Saint Aethelwold to stand for Trinitarian unity. Pairing divine and human, for instance, the O of *omnipotens* faces the depiction of the Annunciation (fols. 5v–6r); and with the same notion of word-image harmony, the letter doubles as a mandorla on both the Trinity frontispiece (fol. 70r) and the omnipotens page (fol. 91r).[44] And in the twelfth-century *Libellus capitulorum* from Zweifalten, the O of "O altitudo divitiarum sapientiae et scientiae" (Rom. 11:33) serves as the aureole surrounding a depiction of the Trinity, represented as a youthful God bearing a cruciform halo and holding two circular disks, one inscribed with a lamb and the other with a dove.[45]

The interpretation of the circle's basic shape as a sign of the all-encompassing triune God, albeit without a secondary allusion to the letter O, is explicitly articulated in the caption accompanying a depiction of the Trinity on the

suus. / In cruce nam corpus fixum est, sanguis quoque fusus / Christi, quae in cena iam dedit ante suis. / Cum nos indigni haec memoramus, redemptor / Emptorum pretium munera nostra fecit"; MGH Poetae, 3, 414–15. On the dating to 846–56, see Franz Brunhölzl, *Histoire de la litterature latine du Moyen Age*, vol. 1, part 2 (Turnhout, 1975), 199–200; Chazelle, *Crucified God*, 155.

38 Biblioteca Laurenziana, Cod. Plut LXV. 1, fol. 102. Carl Nordenfalk, *Spätantike Zierbuchstaben* (Stockholm, 1970).

39 Ibid., 144. Tellingly, the subject was also developed at Tours, for example, in the Nancy Cathedral Gospels, which also includes a Majestas Agni built around the tetragonus mundi; Koehler, *Die karolingischen Miniaturen*, 1.1:383–84.

40 "In latino O quadam circuli rotunditate concluditur; nam et in hac conclusione continens omnia et protegens divinitas declaratus. Porro quod ad elementorum hac litterarum pertinet rationem, elementa haec scientiae sunt initia et quaedam ars stultos ad sapientiam ducens…apud nos O medietas quaedam habetur, significat et initium sapientiae et complementum et medietatem ipsum esse dominum Iesum Christum, mediatorem Dei et hominum"; *Beati Liebanensis Tractatus de*

Apocalipsin, CCSL 107B, ed. Roger Gryson (Turnhout, 2012), 72; and Kessler, "Medietas/Mediator."

41 John Williams, *The Illustrated Beatus: The Eleventh and Twelfth Centuries* (London, 2002).

42 Vatican, BAV, Cod. Reg. lat. 124, fol. 8v. See *In Honorem sancti crucis*, pl. B1; and Michele Ferrari, *Il "Liber sanctae crucis" di Rabano Mauro: Testo–immagine–contesto* (Bern, 1999).

43 Archivio Capitolare, ms. 1, fol. 83r. See Christoph Winterer, *Das Fuldaer Sakramentar in Göttingen* (Petersberg, 2009), 206.

44 London, British Library, Add. MS. 49,598. See Robert Deshman, *The Benedictional of Æthelwold* (Princeton, 1995), 97–107 and 156–57.

45 Stuttgart, Württembergische Landesbibliothek, Cod. brev. 128, fol. 49v. François Boespflug and Yolanta Załuska, "Le dogme trinitaire et l'essor de son iconographie en Occident de l'époque carolingienne au IVe Concile du Latran (1215)," *CahCM* 37 (1994): 181–240, at 192–93.

tenth-century ivory book cover in the Museum Meermanno-Westreenianum, The Hague (fig. 6.6):[46] "Here the Unity [God] is shown in a diagram comprising three signs."[47] A hand descending from a fiery cloud on the ivory cover not only symbolizes the invisible Father but also, as it is assimilated into the Son's halo, becomes part of the sequence of circular elements that includes, most notably, the oval shield emblazoned with the dove of the Holy Spirit. The formal interplay of the three "sc[h]emat[a]e," as the accompanying titulus has it, and encompassing sign of "unitas" also contributes to the descent illustrated through the overlapping of Christ's left hand and the Holy Spirit's oval with the circular frame, which, as in the Touronian initial, is opened in a field filled with vines (set over a blue ground) symbolizing the physical world. The interpretation of the fundamental design persisted. Honorius Augustodunensis incorporated the idea into his allegorical interpretation of the thurible: "the circle, in which all these things are interconnected, is the Divine which contains all these things, whose majesty is enclosed by no end."[48] Sicardus of Cremona, in turn, quoted Honorius in his influential *Mitrale, sive de Officiis ecclesiasticis summa*, paraphrasing him slightly and referring to the fire and incense within the thurible as God's Holy Spirit, divinity, and body: "The circle, in which all these things are interconnected, is the Divine which is enclosed by no boundary, in which all these things are formed and operate."[49]

Generative Designs

The interplay of meaning and geometry in these texts and depictions returns the discussion to the seemingly simple initial that opens the First Epistle of John in the Moutier-Grandval Bible (see fig. 6.1).[50] As the bowl of the letter Q of "Quod fuit ab initio," the circle extends polysemic potential to the words themselves:

> We declare to you what was from the beginning, what we have heard, what we have seen with our eyes, what we have looked at and touched with our hands, concerning the word of life, this life was revealed, and we have seen it and testify to it, and declare to

46 Adolph Goldschmidt, *Elfenbeinskulpturen aus der Zeit karolingischen und sächsischen Kaiser, VIII.–XII. Jahrhundert* (Berlin, 1914), 1:154; Petrus C. Boeren, *Catalogus van de Handschriften van het Rijksmuseum Meermanno-Westreenianum* (The Hague, 1979), 33; Boespflug and Załuska, "Dogme trinitaire"; and Alexander Patschovsky, "Die Trinitätsdiagramme Joachims von Fiore: Ihre Herkunft und semantische Struktur im Rahmen der Trinitätsikonographie, von deren Anfängen bis ca. 1200," in *Die Bildwelt der Diagramme Joachims von Fiore: Zur Medialität religiös-politischer Programme im Mittelalter*, ed. idem (Ostfildern, 2003), 55–114, at 89.

47 "Hic unitas ternis monstratur scemate signis."

48 "Circulus, cui haec omnia innectuntur, est divinitas a qua haec omnia continentur, cujus majestas nullo termino clauditur"; *Gemma animae*, book 1, chap. 22; PL 172:548.

49 "Circulus, cui haec omnia innectuntur, est divinitas quae nullo termino clauditur, a qua haec omnia continentur et operantur"; chap. 13; PL 213:49.

50 For an examination of John's importance, particularly in relation to the opening text of Genesis and his Gospel, see Jeffrey F. Hamburger, *St. John the Divine: The Deified Evangelist in Medieval Art and Theology* (Berkeley and Los Angeles, 2002).

you the eternal life that was with the Father and was revealed to us.[51]

Repeating the shape not as a discrete element but overlapping the other circle, the design within the initial connects the opening text of 1 John to geometric diagrams that used overlapping arcs to demonstrate how a third field can be created from the intersection of the original two. It was an aspect of geometry well known to the Carolingians. Intersecting arcs are used to imagine the essence of natural things in Boethius's *De arithmetica*, preserved in a mid-ninth-century manuscript in Saint Gall,[52] a late tenth-century manuscript in Lund,[53] and, most significant, a luxury edition produced at Tours at the time the great Bibles were being illuminated there.[54]

A feature of an astronomical diagram in the so-called Eudoxus papyrus, a second-century fragment in the Louvre (Papyrus 1), the diagram of overlapping circles was transmitted to the Carolingians in Calcidius's fourth-century commentary on Plato's *Timaeus*.[55] It also survives in such ninth-century manuscripts as that in Valenciennes (fig. 6.7) and Lyons (Bm, ms. 324, fol. 38r), where the map of the orbits of fixed stars and moveable planets is reduced to this basic geometry.[56] Moreover, in the scientific text, as in the initial, the schema of the universe is intimately connected to letter forms. Commenting on *Timaeus* 36b6–36c2, Calcidius explains that the straight line (A–B), when cut in half, generates the X (ΓΔEZ), which, when curved back on itself, forms two interlocking circles (HΘKΛ and HKMN), "duos innexosos sibi inuicem circulos faciat."[57] In other words, the sign within the letter Q at the beginning of 1 John not only imitates the way in which Calcidius's diagram begins with a form that operates as a letter and generates another letter—"speciam chi Graecae litterae coartauit"—but also engages the process through which the accompanying text cues the transformation of these letterforms.[58]

---

51 It is not, as Ellen Beer proposed, a simple, literal realization of the words: "what we have looked at and touched with our hands, concerning the word of life"; "Die Buchkunst, die Initialen," 129.

52 MS 248, fol. 55v.

53 University Library, Medeltidshandskrift 1, fols. 5r and 11r. Elisabeth Pellegrin, "Manuscrits d'auteurs latins de l'époque classique conservés dans les bibliothèques publiques de Suède," *Bulletin d'information de l'institut de recherches et d'histoire des textes* (1954): 28–31. See, more generally, the important essay by Kathrin Müller, "Theorie und Materialisierung der Zahl in Boethius' *De institutione arithmetica*," in *Was Zählt*, 81–102.

54 Bamberg, Staatsbibliothek, Msc.Class. 5 [H J IV 12], fol. 73r. Koehler, *Die karolingischen Miniaturen*, 1.1:235–36, 401–2.

55 Jan H. Waszink, ed., *Timaeus a Calcidio translatus commentarioque instructus*, 2nd ed. (London and Leiden, 1975); Michel Huglo, "La reception de Calcidius et des *Commentarii* de Macrobe à l'époque carolingienne," *Scriptorium* 44 (1990): 3–20; Rosamond McKitterick, "Knowledge of Plato's *Timaeus* in the Ninth Century and the Implications of Valenciennes, Bibliothèque municipale MS 293," in *From Athens to Chartres: Neoplatonism and Medieval Thought; Studies in Honour of Edouard Jeauneau*, ed. Haijo J. Westra (Leiden, 1992), 85–95; Paul E. Dutton, "Material Remains of the Study of the *Timaeus* in the Later Middle Ages," in *L'enseignement de la philosophie au XIIIᵉ siècle*, ed. Claude Lafleur (Turnhout, 1996), 203–30; Anna Somfai, "The Nature of Daemons: A Theological Application of the Concept of Geometrical Proportion in Calcidius' *Commentary* to Plato's *Timaeus* (40d–41a)," in *Ancient Approaches to the "Timaeus,"* ed. Robert Sharples and Anne Sheppard (London, 2003), 129–42; Peter Dronke, *The Spell of Calcidius: Platonic Concepts and Images in the Medieval*

West (Florence, 2008), xviii–xix; Colette Dufossé, "La tradition gréco-latine de l'optique médiévale, de Calcidius jusqu'au XIIᵉ siècle" (Ph.D. diss., Sorbonne, 2008); Anna Somfai, "Calcidius' *Commentary* on Plato's *Timaeus* and Its Place in the Commentary Tradition: The Concept of *Analogia* in Text and Diagrams," *Bulletin of the Institute of Classical Studies* 47 (2004): 203–20; and Calcidius, *Commentaire au Timée de Platon*, ed. and trans. Béatrice Bakhouche (Paris, 2011).

56 The diagrams are also assembled in such compendia as those in Leiden (Universiteitsbibliotheek, VLF 48 and BPL 168, fol. 35v) and Paris (BnF, lat. 14754). Beginning with Herbert Schade, modern scholars have interpreted the Majestas Domini frontispiece in the First Bible of Charles the Bald in terms of such Calcidian orbits, seeing the Savior's body itself as being assimilated into the universe through the figure-eight mandorla, with the umbilicus at the point of intersection. No one has introduced the initial of 1 John in the Moutier-Grandval Bible into the discussion, however, and it is there that the earliest and most interesting application of the cosmic geometry occurs. See Schade, "Hinweise"; Meyer, "Symbolik"; Schapiro, "A Relief from Rodez" (reprint), 292; Kaspersen, "Majestas Domini"; Kühnel, *End of Time*; Kessler, "'Hoc visibile imaginatum'."

57 Oscar Velásquez, "The X of the Universe (*Timaeus* 36b6 sq.)," in *Concentus ex Dissonis: Scritti in onore di Aldo Setaioli*, ed. Carlo Santini, Loriano Zurli, and Luca Cardinali (Naples, 2006), 751–57; Müller, *Visuelle Weltaneignung*, 62.

58 Much has been written on diagrams generally. See Anna C. Esmeijer, *Divina Quaternitas een onderzoek naar methode en toepassing der visuele exegese* (Rotterdam, 1973); Madeline Caviness, "Images of the Divine Order and the Third Mode of Seeing," *Gesta* 22 (1983): 99–120; Lina Bolzoni, *La rete delle immagini: Predicazione in volgare dalle origini a Bernardino da Siena* (Turin, 2002); and Patschovsky, "Trinitätsdiagramme." More recently, see Ramirez-Weaver, "Classical Constellations in Carolingian Codices" (n. 7 above); Bruno Reudenbach, "Ein Weltbild im Diagramm—Ein Diagramm als Weltbild: Das Mikrokosmos-Makrokosmos-Schema des Isidor von Sevilla,"

The Moutier-Grandval initial deploys the Calcidian diagram to gloss 1 John specifically as a demonstration of trinitarian convolution, prompted no doubt by the prologue to the Catholic Epistles attributed to Jerome that is included four folios earlier in the manuscript (402r): "in that text particularly where we read the unity of the trinity is placed in the first letter of John.... In which the Catholic faith is especially strengthened and the unity of substance of Father, Son, and Holy Spirit is attested."[59] The pseudo-Hieronyman prologue is a reduction of the argument found in Jerome's tract *De spiritu sancto*: "The same circle of unity and of the substance of the Holy Spirit ... arising out of that which is the spirit of wisdom and truth, we see dwelling with the Son, and again the Son to be in no way separate from the substance of the Father."[60] Accordingly, the hand in the initial is the Father, the ring is the "substance of the Holy Spirit," and the intersection is the incarnate Son.[61]

Calcidius's *Commentary* was known in Alcuin's circle; and it is perhaps no mere coincidence that a paraphrase from it was integrated into a composite ninth-century text now in Munich that focuses on the Trinity and includes, among other excerpts, passages from Augustine's *De trinitate*, Boethius's *De trinitate*, and the *Dicta Candidi* attributed to Alcuin's student, Candidus Wizo.[62] Labeled "A Certain Platonist's

Reasoning about How to Discover the Artificer of the Universe," the short paraphrase from the commentary concludes with the Platonic claim: "[God's] Mind composed what is called the sensible universe by rationally harmonizing the similarities of the elements of this immense body."[63] The Moutier-Grandval initial seems to pick up on this idea and on Calcidius's other meditations on the relationship between the temporal world and God, who existed from the beginning,[64] by inserting the diagram's interlocking circles into the Evangelist John's claim at the beginning of his First Letter that the human Christ existed with the Father from eternity.[65]

Moutier-Grandval Bible was illuminated. See Christine E. Ineichen-Eder, "Theologisches und philosophisches Lehrmaterial aus dem Alcuin-Kreise," *Deutsches Archiv für Erforschung des Mittelalters* 34 (1978): 192–201; John Marenbon, *From the Circle of Alcuin to the School of Auxerre: Logic, Theology and Philosophy in the Early Middle Ages* (Cambridge, 1981), 161–70 et passim; and Huglo, "La reception." On Candidus Wizo, see Christopher A. Jones, "The Sermons Attributed to Candidus Wizo," in *Latin Learning and English Lore: Studies in Anglo-Saxon Literature for Michael Lapidge*, ed. Katherine O'Brien O'Keefe et al. (Toronto, 2005), 260–83.

The Calcidius interpolation can be separated from the various questions that have arisen from Marenbon's attribution to Alcuin and Candidus of the composite text known as *De dignitate conditionis humanae*. Introduced by Donald Bullough in *Carolingian Renewal: Sources and Heritage* (Manchester, 1991), 178–81, these questions have recently been elaborated by Mette Lebech and James McEvoy, with John Flood, "*De dignitate conditionis humanae*: Translation, Commentary, and Reception History of the *Dicta Albini* (Ps.-Alcuin) and the *Dicta Candidi*," *Viator* 40 (2009): 1–34. Peter Dronke seems to accept Marenbon's claims, concluding that "Calcidius's commentary was already being carefully studied, in Alcuin's circle, before 800," *Spell*, xix; and Ineichen-Eder's conclusion based on a study of Munich 18961 still holds that: "Es kann nicht bezweifelt werden, daß der gesamte Inhalt der bretonischen Handschrift ursprünglich zum Lehrmaterial von Alkuins Unterricht gehörte, der sich nicht nur an der Hofschule, sonder später auch in Tours abgespielt hatte" ("Lehrmaterial," 200). A short tract on seeing Christ with corporeal vision has also been attributed to Candidus Wizo: MGH Ep, 4:557–61; Brunhölzl, *Histoire*, 287.

in *Atlas der Weltbilder,* ed. Christoph Markschies et al. (Berlin, 2011), 32–39; and, for an overall analysis, John Bender and Michael Marrinan, *The Culture of Diagram* (Stanford, 2010).

59 "Illo praecipue loco ubi de unitate trinitatis in prima iohannis epistula positum legimus.... In quo maxime et fides catholica roboratur et patris et filii et spiritus sancti una divinitatis substantia conprobatur"; De Bruyne, *Préfaces,* 255.

60 "Eumdem circulum unitatis atque substantiae Spiritus sancti [*read*: Spiritum sanctum], secundum id quod sapientiae et veritatis est spiritus, videmus habere cum Filio: et rursum Filium a Patris non discrepare substantia." Chap. 22; PL 23:122.

61 This exegesis had a continuous resonance. Bede cited the passage to argue Christ's coeternity with the Father (*Super epistolas catholicas expositio,* chap. 1; PL 93:85); and shortly before the initial was constructed, Benedict of Aniane read it the same way: "Denique hanc vitam aeternam apud Patrem ab initio, quam sibi apparuisse testatur, nisi Verbum caro fieret, neque vidisset, neque manibus contrectasset"; *Second Disputation against Felicianus*; PL 103:1401–2.

62 This manuscript, now in Munich, was produced during the second half of the ninth century in Brittany (Munich, Bayerische Staatsbibliothek, Clm 18961), that is, just after the

63 "Rationabiliter elementorum congruentias coaptando huius immensi corporis, quod mundus sensibilis dicitur, composuit"; Marenbon, *Circle of Alcuin,* 167. See Bakhouche, *Commentaire au Timée,* 532.

64 *In Timaeum comm.,* 23; Bakhouche, *Commentaire au Timée,* 230–31.

65 As an ideograph of Christ's dual nature, the motif of interlocking circles was mapped onto this exegesis after the Carolingian period. Applying Calcidius's diagram to gloss Bede's *De temporum ratione* at the end of the tenth century, Byrhtferth of Ramsey understood the intersecting orbits as representing "de una essentia innectuntur sibi duo circuli." See

FIG. 6.7.
Calcidius's
commentary on
Plato's *Timaeus*.
Valenciennes, Bm,
ms. 293, fol. 54r.

Photo courtesy of
Bibliothèque municipale
de Valenciennes

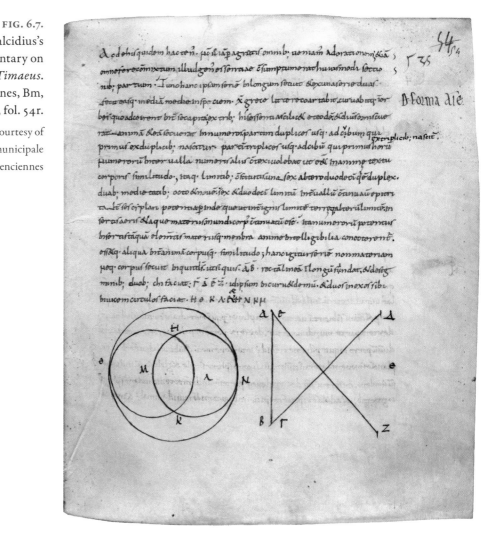

In filling the Q of 1 John with intersecting circles derived from geometric diagrams, the illuminator of the Moutier-Grandval Bible was certainly inspired by one of the most important figured letters of his time, which already

had engaged the same abstract concept. In Carolingian sacramentaries, including, most notably, the contemporary Touronian manuscript in Autun in which the golden bread also appears, the VD ligature introducing the Vere dignum in the preface to the Mass comprises uncial letters that share a central descender, with the abbreviation mark elaborated as a cross (fig. 6.8). Unlike the pointed V framing the orb in the later sacramentary (see fig. 6.5) that aided in the comprehension of the meaning of the gold orb in God's hand, here two circular forms are used to create a third field through their joining, a linking that is possible only by reducing *vere* and *dignum* to single initials and by signaling the collapsing of the two separate words with the element that, at the intersection, creates a third figure, namely the cross.

Michael Gorman, "The *Glosses* on Bede's *De temporum ratione* Attributed to Byrhtferth of Ramsey," *Anglo-Saxon England* 25 (1996): 209–32. Unfortunately, the manuscript of the glosses published in the PL has vanished, but Michael Lapidge has argued that Byrhtferth may have used texts brought to him by Abbo of Fleury, which could well have included Carolingian elements already attached to Bede, and so the form may go back to the ninth century. See Michael Lapidge, "Byrhtferth of Ramsey and the *Glossae Bridferti in Bedam*," *Journal of Medieval Latin* 17 (2007): 384–400. Byrhtferth, it should be noted, was the author of a famous diagram with strong links to the Touronian Majestas frontispieces. See Caviness, "Images of the Divine Order," 107–8; and also Melanie Holcomb, ed., *Pen and Parchment: Drawing in the Middle Ages* (New York, 2009), 106–10.

FIG. 6.8.

Vere dignum from a Touronian sacramentary. Autun, Bm, ms. 19bis, fol. 142r.

Photo courtesy of the Bibliothèque municipale d'Autun

This form of VD ligature was not invented in Tours; it is found already in the Gellone Sacramentary in Paris, dating from the end of the eighth century, which is adorned with dozens of similar VD ideographs.[66] In the Gellone Sacramentary, the decorated ligature not only replaces the opening words but also, in most cases, replaces the entire passage "Vere dignum et iustum est, aequum et salutare, nos tibi semper et ubique gratias agere, domine, sancte Pater, omnipotens aeterne Deus." Variants range from simple pictograms of the sort found in the Marmoutier Sacramentary to elaborate animated forms. Having nothing to do with the literal meaning of the words "it is truly meet and right" as such, the ideographs must have functioned as prompts for priests celebrating Mass, who had memorized the text of the "secreta." Indeed, creating a cross from interlocking circular forms, the

66   BnF, lat. 12048. Jean Deshusses, "Le sacramentaire de Gellone dans son contexte historique," *EphL* 75 (1961): 193–210; *Liber Sacramentorium Gellonensis*, ed. Antoine Dumas and Jean Deshusses, CCSL 159 (Turnhout, 1981); Gianluca Millesole, "Il vere dignum tra simbolo grafico e simbolo concettuale," in *Dal libro manuscritto al libro stampato*, ed. Outi Merisalo and Caterina Tristano (Spoleto, 2010), 133–51.

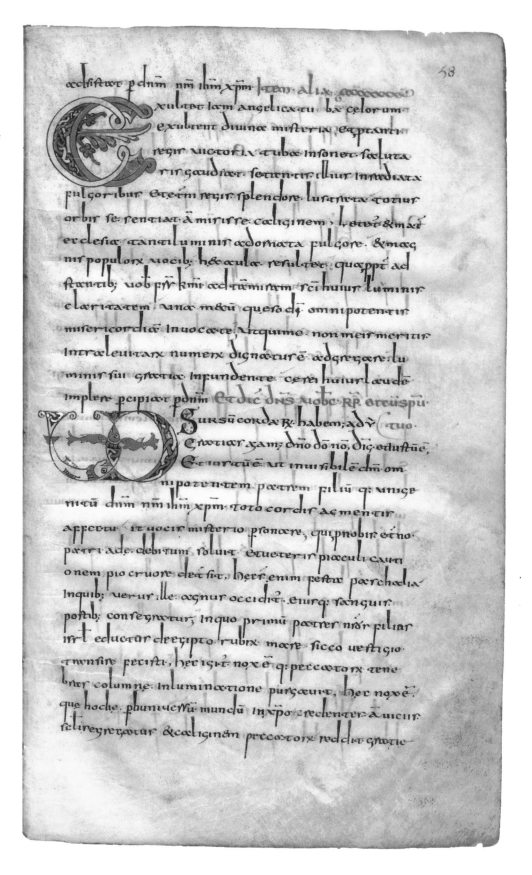

FIG. 6.9.
Vere dignum from the
Gellone Sacramentary.
Paris, Bibliothèque
nationale de France,
lat. 12048, fol. 58r.

Photo courtesy of
the Bibliothèque
nationale de France.

ligature mimics the transformation of the bread and wine through the speech-act of uttering the text the letters adorn, which were already in the priest's memory and person. Just as the celebrant transformed word into sacred presence when he consecrated the Eucharistic species with his benediction, so too the dynamic ideograph makes visible God's becoming visible in the world.

The least geometrical ligature in the Gellone Sacramentary (fol. 51v) renders the pictorial argument explicit in its playful elaboration. The V is figured as a mermaid with long, seductive hair discreetly covering her bosom—the epitome of carnality—transformed into an only vaguely organic form as her serpentine tail becomes the letter D. A fish—perhaps symbolizing Christ—creates a cross from the shared descender formed by the mermaid's body. The figured letter is not a symbol of Christ himself, of course, but expresses the integration of carnal and spiritual in his person. The simpler ligature on folio 58r (fig. 6.9) is, however, even more important for the Touronian initials. It, too, distinguishes the organic V from the more abstract D; but, echoing the double E above, its bowls are compass-drawn circles, strict geometric shapes that create a perfect *vesica piscis* (to use a postmedieval term), with two fish attached to the central descender. Pisciform letters were common in the preceding centuries, e.g., in the seventh-century Gregory manuscript from Luxeuil in New York.[67] But the geometry of the Gellone Sacramentary also engages illustrations in such manuscripts as Boethius's *De arithmetica* as diagrammed in the Lund exemplar, which inserts the final diagrams of book 2:54, "Concerning the Greatest and Most Perfect Symphony Shown in Three Intervals" (i.e., geometry, arithmetic, harmonics, and consonances) into a cruciform frame.[68] The Lund colophon page (fol. 23r), derived, perhaps, from an eighth- or ninth-century insular prototype, demonstrates the congruence of cosmological geometry and the sign of Christ's sacrifice.[69]

The VD initials in the Gellone and Marmoutier sacramentaries thus operate the way monograms do, as Hrabanus Maurus defined them, namely, as a collection of letters that reveals the hidden meaning by means of a few marks,[70] or, in the case of the christogram, a grouping of letters that construct a single sign, the cross.[71] Their very form conveys the meaning of the prayer of consecration, revealing in the interplay of letter and sign, that is, in the merging of the V elaborated with living creatures joined by a cross to an abstract D, the fusion of carnal and spiritual natures in Christ's death asserted in the preface and, in turn, in the Eucharist.[72] Even more than in the mysterious disk in later Majestas Domini pictures, the essential belief in transubstantiation is thus visualized: just as God had created the world from nothing, so too can he, even against the laws of nature, transform wine and bread into his blood and body.

Although clearly embedded already in the Carolingian initials and later versions of them,[73] the meaning of this imagery was first explicitly articulated in words four hundred years later by the French theologian John Beleth:

signs on the other: the sun and moon with a cross formed of interlaced ornament; see *Thronende Christus*, 97.

70 "Cum congerie litterarum, unum characterem pictores facere soliti sunt, quod monogramma dicitur: quorum significatio subtus per pauca adnotata monstratur"; *De inventione linguarum*, PL 112:1583; René Derolez, *Runica manuscripta* (Bruges, 1954), 279–83. Hrabanus's emphasis on the pictorial origin and nature of the monogram is striking.

71 "Sed maiore dignitate nunc a Christianis ad exprimendum nomen Christi assumitur, quasi duae litterae primae nominis eius uno monogrammate simul sint conprehensae, id est, X et P"; *Rabani Mauri In honorem sanctae crucis*, book 22, 173; Garipzanov, "Metamorphoses," 450.

72 In the Drogo Sacramentary, a laboratory of experimentation in historiated initials, the pointed V prevails, but the combined form is used for several initials (e.g., fols. 9r and 66r). Folio 66r provides the perfect counterpart to the Doubting Thomas scene directly above by imagining Christ's two natures. The letter M on folio 21 of the Cathac of Saint Columba (Dublin, Royal Irish Academy [unnumbered]) offers an antecedent, comprising two circles joined by a stem that evokes the shape of a cross: Jonathan J. G. Alexander, *Insular Manuscripts: 6th to the 9th Century* (London, 1974), 28–29, fig. 4. The seventh-century *Lex romana visigothorum* in León (Archivo Catedralicio, MS 15) includes an uncial initial M with a central descender figured as a cross flanked by an alpha and omega; Nordenfalk, *Spätantiken Zierbuchstaben*, pl. 74, fig. C.

73 For instance, Le Mans, Bm, ms. 77, fol. 8r; and Verona, Biblioteca Capitolare, Cod. 87, fol. 13v.

67 Pierpont Morgan Library, MS. M.334, fol. 2r. Nordenfalk, *Zierbuchstaben*, 212, fig. 68.

68 Michael Masi, *Boethian Number Theory: A Translation of the* De institutione arithmetica (Amsterdam, 1983), 185–88.

69 Pellegrin, "Manuscrits." Rademacher published an interesting Merovingian amulet in the Fries Museum in Leeuwarden that portrays the Majestas Domini on one side and cosmological

One finds at this point [in the Missal] a figure which is like our Delta or D, wholly enclosed; in front of it, there is an outline of a V, open at the top; the middle is crossed by a horizontal stroke which joins both these in the manner of a cross. This is not without deeper meaning. The Delta, enclosed on all sides, signifies the divine nature, which has neither beginning or end; V stands for Christ's human nature, which originated in the Virgin but is without end. The hyphen in the middle, however, which links the two parts, is the cross, signifying the tie between mankind and God.[74]

A century after Beleth, Durandus of Mende captured the dynamics of the ligature even more expressively in his influential *Rationale divinorum officiorum*, and explained the relationship to the priest's intoning of the Vere dignum:

> Before the Preface, a figure is transcribed in the books which represents the letter V in front and the letter D behind, and these two letters joined together are placed there for the Vere dignum; they are the initial letters for speaking the words. The letter V, open above and closed below, symbolizes Christ's humanity and human nature, who descends from an ancient line, and who originated in the Virgin but is without end. The D, which encloses a circle, is the figure of the divinity or Christ's divine nature. The drawing in the middle, fusing both parts, is the cross, through which the humanity and divinity are united. This figure is placed at the beginning of the Preface because, through the mystery of this union, both shall men be reconciled to angels through the Lord's Passion,

and the human be joined with the divine in praise of the Savior.[75]

Geometry of the Ineffable

The Touronian illuminators did not invent the remarkable abstract design enclosed in the initial of 1 John in the Moutier-Grandval Bible, then; rather, they transformed a formula underlying the VD ideographs of the Gellone Sacramentary according to the geometrical principles found in Calcidius and Boethius. The process is particularly evident in the full-page frontispiece devoted to the Vere dignum in the Marmoutier Sacramentary, where the inherited formula is elaborated upon by depicting the terminals of the uncial V as lions, the sign of Christ's carnal nature, and an explicit reference is made to the Eucharist by picturing the chalice and paten beneath the cross formed by the merger with the letter D in gold and aqua blue-green. Indeed, the precise geometrical rendering of these forms recalls nothing so much as the elaborate diagrams of the Bamberg Boethius, the Marmoutier Sacramentary's closest relative among surviving Touronian books (so close, indeed, that Wilhelm Koehler dated it on the basis of its similarities with the datable manuscript in Autun).[76] The most complex of the diagrams, visualizing the products of the multiplication of even numbers described in *De arithmetica*, book 1, chapter 12 (fig. 6.10), is, like the Sacramentary frontispiece, organized around a cross of golden bands punctuated by medallion portraits. It, too, engenders a dynamic process of visual reading—correlating

---

74 "Inuenitur autem quedam figura ibi continens Delta, scilicet undique clausum et ex parte precedenti U in summo apertum et in media linea per transuersum tractulus utramque in modo crucis partem copulans, quod non sine causa factum est. Per D circulariter clausam diuina figuratur natura, que nec principium nec finem habet; per U humanam Christi naturam, que in uirgine principium habuit, sed fine carebit. Tractulus in medio utramque copulans partem crux est, per quam humana sociantur diuinis"; *Iohannis Beleth Summa de ecclesiasticis officiis*, ed. Herbert Douteil, CCCM 41A (Turnhout, 1976), 80; Patschovsky, "Trinitätsdiagramme," 83, n. 111.

75 "Ante prefationem describitur in libris quedam figura representans ex parte anteriori litteram V, ex parte uero posteriori litteram D; que due littere coniuncte pro 'Vere dignum' pronuntur, littera uidelicet pro dictione. Sane per litteram V, que inferius clausa et superius aperta est, habens initium a linea longiori, humanitas siue humana Christi natura que in Virgine principium habuit sed fine carebit; per D, uero circulariter clausum diuinitas seu diuina natura, que nec principium nec finem habet, figuratur. Tractus autem in medio, utramque copulans partem, crux est, per quam diuinis sociantur et uniuntur humana. Ideo ergo hec figura in prefationis principio ponitur, quia per mysterium unionis et dominice passionis pacificantur homines angelis, sociantur humana diuinis in preconio Saluatoris" (book 4, chap. 33). *Rationale divinorum officiorum*, CCCM 140, ed. Anselm Davril and Timothy M. Thibodeau (Turnhout, 1998), 2:401.

76 Koehler, *Die karolingischen Miniaturen*, 1.1:235–36.

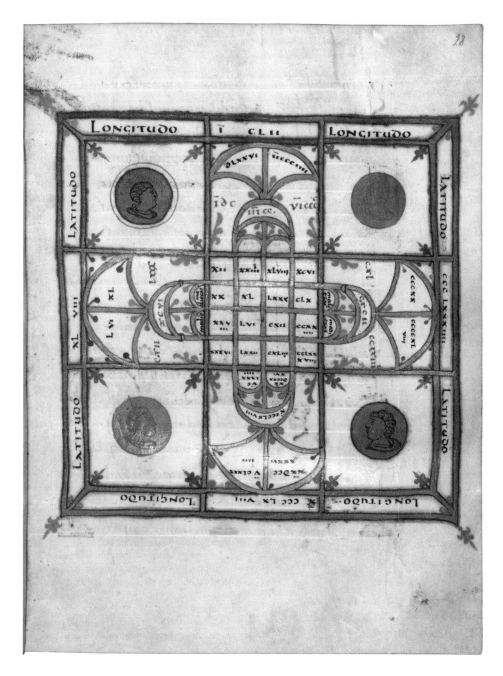

FIG. 6.10.

Multiplication of even numbers from *De arithmetica*, book 1, chapter 12. Bamberg, Staatsbibliothek, Msc.Class. 5 [H J IV 12], fol. 28r.

Photo courtesy of the Staatsbibliothek Bamberg

the numbers in one part with those in another. Moreover, the diagrams evoke compass and straightedge, the very tools with which the scribes organized the vellum pages on which the text and elaborate initials are adorned.

The Moutier-Grandval initial, however, deploys the sources derived from contemporary manuscripts produced at Tours not only to represent Christ's two natures but also, as suggested by the exegesis of the accompanying text, to integrate his person with the Trinity. Augustine had already used circles as a figure of this greatest of Christian mysteries; quoting Ecclesiasticus, he, in fact, introduced the notion of the planetary orbit into theological meditation: "For neither has the Son separated the Father from himself, because he himself, speaking elsewhere with the voice of wisdom (for he himself is the Wisdom of God), says, 'I alone compassed the circuit of heaven.'"[77]

77 "Nec sic inde separatum filium oporteret intellegi. Neque enim quia ipse filius alibi loquens uoce sapientiae (ipse est enim *sapientia dei*) ait: Gyrum caeli circuiui sola, separauit a se patrem"; *De trinitate libri XV*, 1.6.10, ed. W. J. Mountain and Fr. Glorie, CCSL 50 (Turnhout, 1968), 39.

The short but important text known as the *Dicta Albini*, which was known at Tours and from the ninth century associated with the *Dicta Candidi*, reiterated Augustine's argument and expanded it to include other metaphors of generation.[78] The mapping of arithmetic principles onto an image of the Trinity may, however, have been inspired by Boethius himself, who, in his own highly influential *De sancta trinitate*, had already integrated number theory into his understanding of the triune God, noting, for instance, that: "If 'God' is predicated thrice of Father, Son, and Holy Ghost, it does not follow that this triple predication produces a plural number."[79]

Alcuin's enigmatic epigone, Candidus Wizo, was apparently fascinated by the idea that the Trinity might be understood as a mathematical progression. Following Augustine and Boethius, a text attributed to him underscored the claim, also found in Calcidius, that the mean created by two extremes (i.e., three brought about by one and two) allows the cosmos to function:

> Is three none other than three ones, and one three? For that reason, it is also a beginning because it is the first perfection, coming from one and two: the first one gives birth; two is the first to be born; and three is the first perfection of that which gives birth and which is born. On that account, one cannot exist alone, since it would not be giving birth unless something were born. But nor can there be just two because the existence of two implies the existence of one and two. Therefore there must be three. However, to make three, one and two must be joined together. And, like love, this joining makes three things of two. Unless they are one, they are not three.... See, therefore, that all perfection is a trinity, and indeed this alone; and that everything consists of a beginning, a middle, and an end. And the beginning cannot exist without the middle and the end; nor the middle without the beginning and the

end, nor the end without the beginning and the middle. And one thing said, all things said; all things said, one perfection is said.[80]

Two centuries later, inserting the speculation into the creation of the world, Byrhtferth translated the arithmetic progression into geometry:

> The first number, the second, and the third, are known to be sanctified in the name of the Father, Son, and Holy Ghost. The first person was created from nothing, the second was born of the Father and Son, just as Holy Scripture declares. This Trinity and undivided unity permeates all things in the majesty of its divinity, and by permeating, encircles them, and by encircling, fills them, and by filling, governs them, and by governing, rules all created things; it is said, concerning the distinction of this glory, that "he created all things in measure, and number, and weight" (Wisdom 11:21).[81]

---

78 See n. 63; Marenbon, *Circle of Alcuin*, 158–61.

79 "Nam quod tertio repetitur Deus, cum Pater ac Filius et Spiritus sanctus nuncupatur, tres unitates non faciunt pluralitatem numeri in eo quod ipsae sunt," chap. 3; Boethius, *De consolatione philosophiae, Opuscula theologica*, ed. C. Moreschini (Munich and Leipzig, 2005), 171.

80 "Tres quid sunt nisi tria unum et unum tria? Et hoc ideo principium quia prima perfectio est ex uno et duobus ueniens: unum primum gignens, duo primo genitus, tres prima perfectio gignentis et geniti. Ideo non solum unum, quia non esset gignens nisi generaret. Ideo non sola duo, quia non aliter fieri potest nisi unum et duo aliquid sint. Sunt ergo tria. Non sunt autem tria nisi iungas unum et duo. Nam unam per se et duo per se non sunt tria; si iungis, tria sunt. Et ipsa eorum iunctio, quasi amor quidam, facit ea duo secum tria esse. Fitque mirabiliter: si in unum sunt, tria sunt; si tria divisa sunt, non sunt tria. Et, si sic dici queat, si unum sunt, tria sunt; si tres sunt, tria non sunt. Unum enim, cum gignit ipsum quod est, gignit duo. Autem considera quid sint, scilicet duo unum aequalia. Non potest hoc unum plus unum esse quam illud unum. Aequalis ergo potentiae duo unum sunt. Vide ergo quod omnis perfectio trinitas est, immo haec sola: primo, media, fine stare omnia. Et primum non esse sine medio et fine; et medium non esse sine primo et fine, et finem non esse sine primo et medio. Et uno dicto, omnia dicta; et omnibus dictis, unam perfectionem dictam"; Marenbon, *Circle of Alcuin*, 169–70. Attributed to Wizo by Germain Morin ("Un saint de Maestricht rendu à l'histoire," *RBén* 8 [1891]: 176–83), the passage occurs in a manuscript written in northeastern France at the start of the ninth century (British Library, Harley MS. 3034).

81 "Primus numerus, secundus et tertius sacratus esse dinoscitur in nomine patris et filii et spiritus sancti. Prima persona a nullo est facta, secunda a patre genita, tertia a patre et filio processit, sicut diuinus promulgat apex. Ista trinitas et indiuidua unitas sua maiestate deitatis omnia penetrat, et penetrando circumdat et circumdando adimplet et adimplendo gubernat et gubernando cuncta creata regit (supera scilicet, media et ima), de cuius laudis preconio dictum est: Omnia in mensura et in numero et pondere creauit." Peter S. Baker and Michael Lapidge, eds., *Byrhtferth's Enchiridion* (Oxford, 1995), 196–97.

A little later, Peter Damian condensed the idea in a few words: "However, in a single and ineffable moment God contemplates everything simultaneously and, contemplating, distinguishes them; he penetrates everything surrounding them and, in penetrating, surrounds them."[82]

The Moutier-Grandval Bible initial was not the first attempt in art to conceive the Trinity by means of geometry. The fifth- or sixth-century mosaic in the Baptistery of Albenga was an early attempt to visualize the idea of Trinitarian interpenetration, known as *perichoresis*, using circles and symbols.[83] And, as Jean-Claude Bonne has demonstrated, the diagram at the end of Matthew's Gospel in the mid-seventh-century Gospel book in Durham deploys letter forms and abstract ornament to convey the mystery.[84] But the Touronian letter does seem to be the first purely mathematical realization, dependent on Calcidius and on the arguments written down in various early ninth-century tracts associated with Alcuin and his followers to imagine the Trinity in the world "ab initio."

Continuation

The potential of interlocking circles to visualize the Trinity's dynamic unity was also realized in later works. The manuscript of Hrabanus Maurus's *De natura rerum* illustrated at Montecassino in 1023,[85] for instance, uses a variant of the diagram that deploys three circles instead of two and inserts a representation of each person in its own space. Although the elements are different, the concept and structure are quite the same as the VD ideograph in the Marmoutier Sacramentary, with the human at the left, the spirit at the right, and the fusion of the two in the center—pictured as a frontal, bust-length God the Father fully encircled by an aqua blue circle.[86] In this case, the depiction is not an initial, though it may perhaps be understood to function with the letter T below, in a prediction of the Throne of Mercy—the Trinitarian trope par excellence—introducing the Son's sacrifice in this world just as the chalice and paten do in the earlier Autun Sacramentary.

The cosmological and Trinitarian meanings of intersecting circles were never lost, but they were continuously modified as they were filtered through contemporary theology. In the letter of postulation of Edmund of Abingdon (1241) incorporated by Matthew Paris into the saint's life, the story of Edmund's dead mother appearing to him draws on the relationship between arithmetic diagram and Trinitarian speculation:

> While he was giving cursory lectures on arithmetic... his most pious mother said to him: "My son, what are those shapes to which you are giving such earnest attention?" "These are the subject of my lecture," he said, and showed her the diagrams which are commonly used in that faculty; she promptly seized his right hand and painted three circles in it, and in the circles she wrote these three names: Father,

Catherine E. Karkov introduced this text in connection with the semicircles in the creation pictures in the so-called Caedmon Paraphrase (Oxford, Bodleian Library, MS. Junius 11); see *Text and Picture in Anglo-Saxon England: Narrative Strategies in the Junius 11 Manuscript* (Cambridge, 2001), 37–38.

82 "Deus autem uno atque ineffabili suae contemplationis ictu simul omnia conspicit et conspiciendo distinguit, omnia circumdando penetrat et penetrando circumdat"; *De divina omnipotentia*, 606b; ed. Alfredo Gatti (Padua, 2013), 243–44. Later parallels include the opening miniature of the Tiberius Psalter (London, British Library, Cotton MS. Tiberius C. vi, fols. 7v and 8r) and the Uta Codex Hand of God frontispiece (Munich, Staatsbibliothek, Clm. 13601, fol. 1v). See Barbara C. Raw, *Trinity and Incarnation in Anglo-Saxon Art and Thought* (Cambridge, 1997), 106–7 et passim; Adam S. Cohen, *The Uta Codex* (University Park, Pa., 2000), 32–33; Patschovsky, "Trinitätsdiagramme," 82–83.

83 C. Musso Casalone, "Nota sul Battistero di Albenga," *ArtLomb* 8 (1963): 103–10; Josef Engemann, "Zu den *Dreifaltigkeitsdarstellungen* der frühchristlichen Kunst: Gab es im 4. Jahrhundert anthropomorphe Trinitätsbilder?" *JbAC* 19 (1976): 157–72; Patschovsky, "Trinitätsdiagramme," 80.

84 Cathedral Library, MS. A.II.10, fol. 3v. "Noeuds d'écritures (le fragment 1 de l'Evangéliaire de Durham)," in *Texte-Image, Bild-Text*, ed. Sybil Dümchen and Michael Nerlich (Berlin, 1990), 85–105.

85 Abbazia, Cod. 132, p. 13. See *Rabano Mauro, De rerum naturis: Codex Casin. 132, Archivio dell'Abbazia di Montecassino, Commentari*, ed. Guglielmo Cavallo (Scarmagno, 1994); and Giulia Orofino, *I codici decorati dell'archivio di Montecassino* (Rome, 2000), 2.2:50–86.

86 The central portrait recalls depictions of the Majestas Domini in Touronian manuscripts, but whether or not the illustrator of the eleventh-century encyclopedia actually drew on an illustrated Carolingian original is not at all certain. For the manuscript's pictorial genealogy in general, see Marianne Reuter, *Metodi illustrativi nel Medioevo: Testo e immagine nel codice 132 di Montecassino "Liber Rabani de originibus rerum"* (Naples, 1993); and the essays by Cavallo and Orofino in *Rabano Mauro, De rerum naturis*.

Son, Holy Spirit. This done, she said, "My dearest son, henceforth direct your attention to these figures and to no others."[87]

The connection made in these later works between the mathematical diagram and the Trinity may well have developed independently of the Carolingian initials,[88] as certainly seems to be the case of Trinitarian diagrams developed by Peter Alfonsi (after 1106)[89] and, most extensively, by Joachim da Fiore. The latter possibly owe something to the earlier tradition, but they are largely new creations.[90] A planetary schema comprising three overlapping circles that occurs already in the ninth-century Macrobius in Leiden, for instance, may have provided an independent foundation for Joachim's "Venn diagram."[91] Likewise, what is perhaps the most famous expression of the concept seems to derive from cosmic schemata independent of the ninth-century experiments, that is, Dante's description of the Trinity as "three rings of three colors and one circumference."[92]

The same is true of an elaborate figured initial in the late twelfth-century Breviary from Montiéramey in the Tours diocese.[93] To decorate Augustine's *Homily on John's Gospel* (tractate 74), the illuminator followed the exegesis by picturing the Pentecost, integrating the well-known subject within intersecting circles (fol. 182r). Largely obscuring the initial A of "Audivimus fratres," he inserted Mary (as Ecclesia) accompanied by the twelve apostles into the lower orb and the Holy Spirit in the form of a dove into the mandorla-shaped field created by two overlapping circles, each held by an angel. Seen from below entering into the earthly Church, the dove is painted against a blue background—the sky—in contrast to the pure gold and light of heaven behind the angels. In this way, the image is also made to illustrate Augustine's reading of the passage from John as evidence that "worldly love does not possess the invisible eyes, with which, except in an invisible way, the Holy Spirit cannot be seen."[94] The historiated initial thus conceives the Pentecost imagery in the same way Calcidius's mathematical understanding did as the mean between God and man "as God is to the angel, the angel is to man."[95] Though it is not directly connected to it, the depiction in the Breviary from Montiéramey may be seen as a fleshing out of the concept underlying the Moutier-Grandval initial. Functioning as a bridge to the sacred text, the lower ring represents God's communication with humankind; and the inner/upper intersection of two circles figures the Divinity's transformation through cosmic geometry into a substance that can penetrate the human realm.[96]

Only one later example appears to stem directly from the Touronian developments, the VD initial in the late twelfth-century

---

87   "Apparuit ei in sompnis piissima mater eius paulo ante defuncta dicens, 'Fili, quid legis? Que sunt ille figure quibus tam studiose intendis?' Quo respondente, 'Talia lego,' ostensis protraccionibus que in illa solent fieri facultate, illa mox dexteram manum eius arripuit et in ea tres circulos depinxit. In ipsis quoque hec tria nomina per ordinem scripsit: 'Pater, Filius, Spiritus Sanctus.' Et hoc facto sic ait, 'Fili karissime, talibus figuris et non aliis amoduo intende'"; *Vita S. Edmundi auctore Matthaei Parisiensi,* in *St. Edmund of Abingdon: A Study in Hagiography and History,* ed. Clifford H. Lawrence (Oxford, 1960), 229–30; trans. Lawrence, *The Life of St. Edmund* (Oxford, 1996), 124.

88   In the Odbert Psalter (Boulogne-sur-Mer, Bm, ms. 20), the initial of Psalm 100 (fol. 108r) is organized the same way but for purely formal reasons: Judas Kissing Christ is framed at the center, while Roman soldiers and Christ's disciples are separated from the two principal figures in the bowls of the letter M (*misericordiam*); see Rainer Kahsnitz, "Der christologische Zyklus im Odbert-Psalter," *ZKunstg* 51 (1988): 33–125, fig. 20.

89   Patschovsky, "Trinitätsdiagramme."

90   Ibid. and Alessandro Ghisalberti, ed., *Pensare per figure: Diagrammi e simboli in Gioacchino da Fiore* (Rome, 2010).

91   Universiteitsbibliotheek, BPL 168, fol. 35v. See Bruce Eastwood and Gerd Graßhoff, *Planetary Diagrams for Roman Astronomy in Medieval Europe, ca. 800–1500* (Philadelphia, 2004), 55–58.

92   "Tre giri di tre colori e d'una contenenza"; *Paradiso,* 33.115–17. See also Beatrice Hirsch-Reich, "Die Quelle der Trinitätskreise von Joachim von Fiore und Dante," *Sophia* 22 (1954): 170–78.

93   Paris, BnF, lat. 796, fol. 182r. Jakobi-Mirwald, *Text-Buchstabe-Bild,* 87; and Stephan Waldhoff, "Synagoga im Sakramentar zur *revelatio synagogae* in der Handschrift 193 der Bibliothèque municipale in Tours," *FS* 43 (2009): 215–70.

94   "Non enim habet inuisibiles oculos mundana dilectio, per quos uideri Spiritus sanctus, nisi inuisibiliter non potest"; *In Iohannem Evangelium tractatus,* 74, chap. 14, paragraph 4; ed. Willems Radbod, CCSL 36 (Turnhout, 1954), 515.

95   Chap. 132; *Timaeus a Calcidio translatus,* 368–70.

96   Honorius Augustodunensis, applying the principle he introduced in his symbolic interpretation of the thurible, made a parallel argument in the interpretation of the circular candelabrum suspended in churches: "Catena, qua corona in altum continetur, est spes, qua Ecclesia a terrenis ad coelestia suspenditur. Supremus circulus cui innectitur, est Deus a quo omnia continentur" (*Gemma animae* 1.141); PL 172:588.

sacramentary of Saint Martin's. Recently studied by Cecile Voyer and in greater depth by Stephan Waldhoff,[97] the ligature prefacing the Vere dignum frames an essentially new iconography featuring Ecclesia bringing in the wine and bread (stamped with IHC) as the counterpart of Synagoga, holding the tablets of the laws and being unveiled by God's hand. As is appropriate in a sacramentary, the initial conceives of Christ as replacing the Jewish sacrifices with his eternal one instituted in the Eucharist. In doing so, it apparently draws on traditions established three centuries before, such as the inscribed wafer and also, most likely, the unveiling of Judaism found in the First Bible of Charles the Bald.[98] Most important, the later initial channels the VD formula through geometric diagrams that picture the incarnate God as the essence at the juncture of the letter-signs, demonstrating the unity of all sacred Scripture in the incarnate Deity (whose facial features have been rubbed away), a point of fusion that Hrabanus had already made in his commentary on Ezekiel's figure of "a wheel within a wheel," that is, the joining of the two testaments,[99] or "the Gospels, whose

course and stature, clinging to each other, head toward heaven."[100]

The Moutier-Grandval initial may be understood first and foremost in the context of ninth-century Tours and the two English theologians Alcuin and Candidus, who seem to have brought insular traditions of textual embellishment with them to the Monastery of Saint Martin.[101] Far more abstract even than the micro/macrocosmic relationship manifested, for example, in the Majestas Domini pictures,[102] the "science" inserted into the letter Q of 1 John in the Moutier-Grandval Bible serves the fundamental purpose of engaging the eternal processes instituted to govern the world by the "Creator of heaven, and earth, and sea, and to one born of that one, and the Holy Spirit."[103] Essentially visual, the initial derives its meaning not only from the analogy between signs and designs reduced to basic geometrical shapes, but also from the demonstration that one sort of knowledge generates others—Scripture, Calcidius's late antique mathematical science, and biblical exegesis. However precocious, the attempt to represent the Trinity as interlocking circles is thus a part of a much broader and continuing interest in integrating science and theology with visual forms of diverse sorts—letters, diagrams, and pictures.

The Carolingian initial functions in much the same way as modern cosmology, as Sarah Bakewell recently explained.[104] Writing alongside a photograph of the light echo from star V838 in the constellation Monoceros taken by the Hubble Space Telescope, Blakewell concluded: "Perhaps everything exists because . . . an initial zero separated itself into +1 and -1, forming matter and antimatter. Perhaps only mathematical entities are real, and our physical world is an

97 Tours, Bm, ms. 193, fol. 71r. Cecile Voyer, "L'allégorie de la Synagogue: Une représentation ambivalente du judaïsme," in L'allégorie, ed. Heck, 2:95–109; Waldhoff, "Synagoga."

98 See Kessler, "'Facies bibliothecae revelata'."

99 "Rota ergo in medio rotae est, quia inest Testamento veteri Testamentum novum. Et, sicut saepe jam diximus, quod testamentum vetus promisit, hoc novum exhibuit. Et quod illud occulte adnuntiat, hoc istud exhibitum aperte clamat.... Rotas quippe significare Testamenta diximus. Et Testamentum Vetus ambulavit quidem, cum per praedicationem ad mentes hominum venit; sed post semetipsum reversum est, quia juxta litteram in praeceptis suis et sacrificiis usque ad finem servari non potuit. Non enim sine immutatione permansit cum in eo spiritalis intelligentia defuit. Sed cum Redemptor noster in mundum venit hoc spiritaliter fecit intelligi, quod carnaliter invenit teneri. Itaque dum spiritaliter littera ejus intelligitur, omnis in eo illa carnalis exhibitio vivificat. Testamentum vero novum, etiam per testamenti veteris paginas, testamentum aeternum appellatum est, quia intellectus illius nunquam mutatur. Bene ergo dicitur quod 'rotae euntes ibant, et non revertebantur cum ambularent.' Quia dum novum Testamentum non rescinditur, dum vetus jam spiritaliter intellectum tenetur: post se non redeunt, quae usque ad finem mundi immutabilia persistent"; Commentaria in Ezechielem, chap. 1; PL 110:528. In the apse of Santa Maria d'Aneu (Barcelona, Museu Nacional d'Art de Catalunya) the wheels of Ezekiel's vision are pictured as intersecting circles of the type found in Calcidius.

100 ". . . vel evangelia sibi cohaerentia, quorum rursus et statura tendit ad coelum"; PL 110:526.

101 See Tilghman, "Shape of the Word"; Malgorzata Krasnodebska-d'Aughton, "Decoration of the In principio Initials in Early Insular Manuscripts: Christ as a Visible Image of the Invisible God," Word & Image 18 (2002): 105–22.

102 See Kaspersen, "Majestas Domini."

103 See Jeffrey F. Hamburger, "Idol Curiosity," in Curiositas: Welterfahrung und ästhetische Neugierde in Mittelalter und früher Neuzeit, ed. Klaus Krüger (Göttingen, 2002), 19–58.

104 Review of Steven Gimbel, Einstein's Jewish Science (Baltimore, 2012) in New York Times Book Review, 5 August 2012, 1 and 15.

'outcropping' of mathematics." Starting with "an initial zero" that generates other forms, the letter Q of 1 John in the Moutier-Grandval Bible offers a startling, albeit pseudomorphic, analogue to the circular nebula framing a red orb used to illustrate the review. More significant, the initial and the related images analyzed in this paper demonstrate the possibility of visualizing what Bakewell calls "the interzone between philosophy and scientific cosmology," not only in the fields they create through the overlapping of circular forms or even in the application of Calcidius's mathematical physics to Trinitarian theology, but also in the very intersecting of the letters of holy Scripture and the geometry that governs the universe. Each in its own way attests to God's involvement in the world; but operating together in a spiritual design, the two generate a unique space that is neither theology nor science, but rather a third field that is different from both and yet the same,[105] a dynamic sign of the invisible triune Deity who constructed the universe *ab initio* and then "outcropped" as a man in time.

105 Müller, *Visuelle Weltaneignung*. For the parallel but independent eastern tradition, see Joel Kalvesmaki, *The Theology of Arithmetic: Number Symbolism in Platonism and Early Christianity* (Washington, D.C., 2013).

I wish to thank Christopher Lakey, whose own work on the relationship of science and geometry to artistic practice has taught me much, for his thoughtful reading of a draft of this paper. Brigitte M. Bedos-Rezak's comments on the draft version of this paper were particularly productive.

From Christ's Monogram to God's Presence

An Epigraphic Contribution to the Study of Chrismons in Romanesque Sculpture

Vincent Debiais

THE CHRISMON IS OMNIPRESENT IN ARTISTIC AND CULTURAL PRODUCTIONS of the western middle ages.[1] It was carved in the tympanum of Romanesque churches, engraved on sarcophagi, drawn in charters and diplomas, and inscribed on seals and coins. It holds a special place in monumental sculpture, particularly in the south of France and the north of Spain, where it participates in the decoration and visual organization of buildings.[2]

The purpose of this chapter is not to propose a history of chrismons, but to explore how this symbol can be interpreted as a "hybrid sign, not necessarily bound to any specific language."[3] There is actually a rich bibliography on the subject; but despite such omnipresence, the abundant studies on this topic (since the end of nineteenth century) rarely concern art history, and those that do fail to submit the chrismon to a formal analysis or interpretation of its meaning. Actually, medieval epigraphers have produced the most studies on the chrismon, seeing it as a special part of medieval written manifestations.[4] Apart from these epigraphic studies, most of the works about chrismons take an evolutionary

1   In this essay *chrismon* must be understood as the medieval version of the chi-rho symbol, inscribed in a circle and frequently completed by the Greek letters alpha and omega. The chrismon was not the only christogram used during the Middle Ages, but it seems to have been the only monogram. In some cases, especially when the vertical stroke of the rho is crossed by a horizontal line, the chrismon can also be considered as a *staurogram* (i.e., an iconic sign for the Holy Cross).

2   The great number of chrismons in Pyrenean churches has deterred scholars from attempting an exhaustive corpus, although there is a website providing good pictures of most of the chrismons from the Pyrenees, mainly for Spain. For the examples mentioned but not reproduced in this paper, see http://www.claustro.com/ (accessed 5 January 2015). The examples that appear in this essay have been selected for their monumental coexistence with epigraphic inscriptions; they do not provide a representative overview of the production of the Pyrenean chrismons.

3   Quote from the conference announcement written by Brigitte M. Bedos-Rezak and Jeffrey Hamburger. I wish to thank the organizers for their invitation and for all their comments on this essay. I also want to express appreciation for the great work of the reviewers, and the friendly and accurate reading by Herbert L. Kessler, Eric Palazzo, and Daniel Rico.

4   Volume 10 of the *Corpus des inscriptions de la France médiévale* (*CIFM*), released in 1985, includes all the chrismons of southern France (Gironde, Landes, Lot-et-Garonne, Aveyron, Gers, Pyrénées-Atlantiques, Hautes-Pyrénées, Haute-Garonne, and Ariège). In short records, the authors make a formal analysis of the sign and interpret possible inscriptions accompanying it. This publication remains to this day the most important bibliographic reference for the study of chrismons in epigraphy. The introduction (pp. 5–12) provides an overview of the existing scholarship on chrismons, returns to patristic texts that explain the chrismon, and gives a few guidelines to explain its significance. Even if *CIFM* does not propose a general interpretation of the chrismon, the reader will find its

perspective and try to point out formal and semantic transformations, from Constantine's labarum[5] to Romanesque chrismon.[6]

Studies on chrismons in ancient and late antique manuscripts and on coins have established first that the symbol may not consistently or exclusively relate to the sign associated with Constantine's victory, because its monogrammatic formulation allows connections with wide range of semantic content.[7] The chrismon, in essence a christogram, can also be considered as a staurogram in its simplest compositions. In all cases there is a true porosity between the form composed of letters and the iconic sign of some material (the cross) or intangible (the victory granted by the deity) reality. By seeking meanings and formal evolutions of the chrismon—a mutable sign, in its form and signification—such studies have ignored the definition of the nature of this sign. From a semiotic point of view, there have been no genetic analyses of the signifier, but only attempts to extract a signified meaning from the graphic choices. As noted by Henri Leclercq, Ludwig Traube, and Larry Hurtado, the chrismon existed as a manuscript and epigraphic abbreviation long before it was used

by Constantine as a monogrammatic military or religious sign.[8] The chrismon then received the Greek letters alpha and omega; this essential addition and its subsequent developments (from fifth century onward) transform its semiotic nature. Through many enrichments of its initial monogrammatic structure, the chrismon became isolated and no longer factored into the composition of a sentence, as it used to when it was an abbreviation.[9] It acquired a real individuality and became an autonomous sign, enabling a wide range of iconic and symbolic meanings, such as peace, the Trinity, victory, protection, and divine figuration.[10]

Local Context

Almost all the monumental chrismons concerned in this study come from France and Spain and can be dated from the eleventh to thirteenth centuries, although there are some rare exceptions from the Carolingian period. From a geographic point of view, the sample of chrismons is found exclusively in the Pyrenees on both sides of the current border between France and Spain, with a higher density in the center of this area.[11] The chrismon adopts there a particular form that incorporates the Greek letters chi and rho of the labarum inscribed in a circle, completed by alpha and omega, to which is added a Latin S or a Greek sigma. These signs come in more-or-less complex compositions giving the motif particular values within the panorama of christological themes. Such variations on Christ exposed in the stone of the tympanum of Romanesque churches are often accompanied by epigraphic texts. They allow us to approach the value and

synthesis most interesting and accessible. See also Bernadette Leplant-Mora, "Réflexions sur le chrisme: Symbole et extension en Gascogne," *Bulletin de la société archéologique, histoire, littéraire et scientifique du Gers* 88 (1977): 22–33. The most complete analysis of a monumental chrismon deals with a Spanish example, that of Jaca cathedral in Aragón. In 1996, Robert Favreau analyzed the inscriptions that accompany the monumental chrismon carved between two lions in the tympanum of the cathedral; see "Les inscriptions du tympan de la cathédrale de Jaca," *Comptes-rendus de l'académie des Inscriptions et Belles-Lettres* (1996): 535–60; and idem, "Note complémentaire à propos d'une inscription du tympan de la cathédrale de Jaca," *Comptes-rendus de l'académie des Inscription et Belles-Lettres* (2004): 7–10.

5 "Labarum," *DACL* 8.1:927–62. See William Seston, "La vision païenne de 310 et les origines du chrisme constantinien," in *Mélanges Franz Cumont: Annuaire de l'Institut de philologie et d'histoire orientales et slaves* 4 (1936): 374–95.

6 The most complete reference on this evolution remains the "chrisme" entry of the *Dictionnaire d'archéologie chrétienne et de liturgie*, which reviews the state of the question and gives many epigraphic examples; *DACL* 3.1:1481–1534. See also Alain Sené, "Quelques remarques sur les tympans romans à chrisme en Aragon et en Navarre," in *Mélanges offerts à R. Crozet*, ed. P. Galais and Y. J. Riou (Poitiers, 1966), 1:365–81. Though this paper gives a very useful first approach to monumental chrismons, its conclusions are quite difficult to follow.

7 Patrick Bruun, "The Victorious Signs of Constantine: A Reappraisal," *NC* 157 (1997): 41–59.

8 *DACL* 3.1:1486; Ludwig Traube, *Nomina Sacra: Versuch einer Geschichte der christlichen Kurzung* (Munich, 1907); and Larry Hurtado, "The Origin of the Nomina Sacra: A Proposal," *JBL* 117 (1998): 655–73.

9 *DACL* 3.1:1504.

10 The need to understand the meaning of the chrismon and an evolutionary approach have sometimes led to the proposal of theories that seem difficult to apply to epigraphic medieval examples. See for example the hypothesis of Anne Lombard-Jourdan, *Fleur de lis et oriflammes: Signes célestes du royaume de France* (Paris, 1991). For examples of the chrismon's various iconic and symbolic meanings, see *CIFM* 10:8.

11 French departments of Hautes-Pyrénées, Gers, and Pyrénées-Atlantiques, and Spanish autonomous communities of Aragon and Navarre.

meaning of these graphic constructions, but also to appreciate its semiotic nature.

A question arises from the mapping and statistical analysis of the Pyrenean chrismons: how can we explain their geographic and chronological concentration? No satisfactory answer has ever been formulated on this subject, and it is difficult to say more than the bare facts: they are monumental chrismons from between the Basque country and Catalonia. The concerned areas were, during the twelfth and thirteenth centuries, very different at political, artistic, and linguistic levels, and it is therefore impossible to reduce such graphic practice to a unique theological or historical explanation. The graphic culture in which Pyrenean chrismons were created was not homogeneous, and documentary or epigraphic practices varied considerably throughout the Pyrenees.

Starting from such changeability of intellectual and graphic contexts, it is tempting to envisage some diffusion of a model, of a figurative tradition from an initial spot, located for the most ancient examples in the northern part of the ancient kingdom of Navarre. This solution is possible even if it remains difficult to explain influences and choices that led Romanesque artists to reproduce this symbol on both sides of Pyrenees in the tympana of churches of wholly variable status, size, and location. How can we connect, whatever relationships we envisage, the portal of Jaca cathedral, that of Armentia church, the chrismon of Eusa gallery, and the portal of Oloron-Sainte-Marie cathedral? Even in the case of a dynamic diffusion (which would be a *difficilior* reading of this artistic phenomenon), it would still remain hard to explain the appearance of the chrismon in Navarre.

Dulce Ocón Alonso, who made a prodigious study of Pyrenean chrismons, proposed that the symbol be read as a sign of the Pamplonan monarchy and its fidelity to Rome.[12] Her explanation is appealing, but it does not seem to apply to all Pyrenean chrismons. Nevertheless, it allows us to explain the diffusion of the chrismon thanks to an endogenous phenomenon; its limit also allows us to infer the vast range of meaning in this motif, as the inscriptions that accompany numerous chrismons show.

By analyzing these inscriptions and seeking unity amid very marked formal and functional differences, this paper tries to propose some guidelines for the interpretation of Pyrenean chrismons, their semantic value, and their role in monumental sculptural decoration.

Giving and Hiding Christ's Name: Monogram, Abbreviation, Description

The explanation of the chrismon as Christ's name is the more common one among the Church Fathers and medieval authors, especially Paulinus of Nola and Orens, bishop of Auch.[13] Eusebius, in his *Vita Constantini*, describes the labarum as "a monogram giving this Holy Name by the first two letters, joined in a unique form with the P in the center of the X."[14] So, first of all, the chrismon is a name, reduced or extended thanks to its monogrammatic shape.[15] This is the explanation we find in an inscription that once accompanied Christ's monogram at the church of Saint Thecla in Milan; its formulation is complex, sometimes inelegant, but explains all the letters in a simple way: "This circle gives the High King's name who sees without beginning nor end. Alpha and omega shows that you are at the same time the beginning and the end. X and P gather Christ's holy name."[16]

With the introduction of two additional letters, alpha and omega, it becomes difficult to consider the chrismon as a monogram, because these two signs are not part of the monogram's solution of *Christos* in Greek, or *Christus* in

12 Dulce Ocón Alonso, "El sello de dios sobre la iglesia: Tímpanos con crismón en Navarra y Aragón," in *El tímpano románico: Imágenes, estructuras y audiencias* (Santiago de Compostela, 2003), 76–101. For a reading of Alonso's conclusions see Aiskoa Pérez Alonso, "Una nueva interpretación de la escultura del pórtico de Armentia," *Estudios Alaveses* 28 (2008): 129–56.

13 Paulinus of Nola, *Poema* 19, PL 61:544–49; Orens, *Item plus de trinitate*, PL 61:1002. See *CIFM* 10:7.

14 Eusebius, *Vita Constantini*, 1:26; ed. B. Bleckmann (Turnhout, 2007).

15 For more on the links between chrismons and monograms, see Antony Eastmond's contribution to this volume (chap. 11).

16 Edmond Le Blant, *Inscriptions chrétiennes de la Gaule* (Paris, 1856), no. 48 (105).

Latin.[17] Inscriptions that accompany chrismons do not miss that point and, in France as in Spain, try from the beginning of the thirteenth century to emphasize the essential relation to Christ that may have been obscured by the enrichment of the monogram. The addition of the letters alpha and omega is, in that sense, a confirmation of the meaning of the motif, insofar as they suggest God's omnipotence (thanks to Saint John's Revelation).[18]

Such enrichment can also be seen in the addition of the four monosyllabic words *lux, rex, lex,* and *pax,* which designated, throughout the middle ages, Christ in the paraphrases *rex regum, lux mundi, pax aeterna,* etc. Their association seems to have started in an epitaph composed for himself by Angilbert, Abbot of Saint-Riquier.[19] The association continued for a long time, even entering the iconography of the Holy Cross, which frequently carries the words on its four arms.[20] On the square chrismon drawn above the west door of Saint Orens church at Bostens (Landes), placed on each side of the rho, we read *lux* and *lex,* and on each side of the S, *pax* and *rex.*[21] The final X of both *rex* and *lex* is formed by the ends of the two lines that form the chi (fig. 7.1). It is a detail, of course, but it also manifests in stone the unity between the chrismon and its textual supplements, all participating in the definition of Christ's complex reality. At the base of the rho, a hand is physically holding the cross made of letters, which is constructed by crossing and tying alphabetic signs. The horizontal stroke bisecting the chi contributes to the construction of the cross and shows the similarity between christogram and staurogram on the one hand, and on the other hand demonstrates the inextricable intertwining of visual and linguistic dimensions of the chrismon.

The square shape of the Bostens chrismon is unique, and it may be associated with the desire to create in stone the shape of a particular object. Chrismons are more usually inscribed in a circle that contains the monogram letters and possible supplements, thus isolating the figure from its surroundings. The medallion type, and more generally the idea of inclusion, concerns a large number of signs referring to Christ's figure, in particular his bust or his hand, which appear in circular medallions from late antiquity on architecture or jewelry. The enclosing shape of the medallion, like that of the mandorla, allows the artist to create a division between the inside and outside of the circle. Thus, the chrismon, like Christ's bust or God's hand, is sacred and divine, separated from the world of men; the circle and the mandorla are doors that open onto the infinity of the Deity.

The chrismon at Lème (Pyrénées-Atlantiques) is very similar to the previous one in its construction and its graphic choices (fig. 7.2): *rex* and *lex* use the chi lines; a hand holds the vertical stroke of the rho; the letters V and X are joined in the word *lux*; and the letters alpha and omega are drawn on horizontal stroke of the rho.[22] Despite the obvious differences between these two chrismons, we must recognize a common desire to create a complex object using effects of plan and background to show an unbreakable unity among all the components of the chrismon. The constituent lines of each complementary sign (alpha, omega, sigma) seem to pass sometimes ahead, sometimes behind the written plan of the chi and rho.

The chrismon of Peyraube church in Lamayou (Pyrénées-Atlantiques) shows that the search for unity (by the use of common elements in a chrismon and its additions) is not systematic. The words *lex* and *lux* are indeed engraved independently on both sides of the chi, in the

17   The first Christian symbols, however, often offer complex compositions in which letters can display all words of a nominal group or sentence. See Luc Renault, "La croix aux premiers siècles chrétiens," in *Le supplice et la Gloire* (Saintes, 2000), 12–22.

18   Rev. 1:8: "Ego sum alpha et omega, principium et finis." Anne-Orange Poilpré says that "le Christ, spécifiquement présent dans la lettre *chi,* contient également en sa personne l'intégralité du monde": Anne-Orange Poilpré, *Maiestas Domini: Une image de l'Église en Occident* (Paris, 2005), 165.

19   MGH SS, 15.1 (Hanover, 1887), 179.

20   See, for example, folio 4v of Ferdinand's *Beatus* (Madrid, Biblioteca nacional, ms. B.31 [olim Vit. 14.2]), on which appears a full-page Asturian victory cross flanked by the words *pax* and *lux* in the upper part, and *rex* and *lex* in the lower part. As is always the case in this type of Asturian cross, the letters alpha and omega hang from the horizontal arm of the cross, making a complex visual construction in which Christ is manifested by the image of the cross, the letters (individual elements and manifestation of his omniscience), and by the words, a paraphrase of his power: Mireille Mentré, *Spanische Buchmalerei des Mittelalters* (Wiesbaden, 2006), pl. 57.

21   *CIFM* 10:127.

22   Ibid., 170.

FIG. 7.1.

Chrismon, west portal, Saint-Orens Church, Bostens (Landes).

Photo © CESM.

lower part of the chrismon, which becomes an epigraphic support for the definition of Christ's nature.[23] But one should note that this chrismon lacks a circle or another square form enclosing the letters. Is there a connection between these two characteristics? This chrismon carries, in addition to the words *lex* and *lux*, the two christograms IHS and XPS used as abbreviations for *Ihesus Christus*. These two *nomina sacra* do not use signs or letters from the original chrismon and thus can be considered as complements to the monogram. Does the lack of a unique construction lead to redundancy in the presence of the chrismon *and* the XPS abbreviation? Actually, they can be considered as two modes of expression for the same reality, each one with a specific function of what Jean-Claude Bonne calls "ornementalité" and "littéralité."[24]

As seen in Peyraube, the association of the four words *lux*, *rex*, *lex*, and *pax* with the chrismon is not necessarily complete. A few more examples are needed to demonstrate that relationship. At Lacassagne (Hautes-Pyrénées), only the word *lex* was transcribed:[25] L and E are placed on either side of the chrismon, and the chi is used as the final X. In the tympanum of Gellenave church (in Bouzon-Gellenave, in Gers),[26] the word *rex* has been set up in the same way, with the chi used as final X. In Castillon-Debats (Gers), a reused bas-relief outside the south wall has a more complex form, in which the words *rex*, *lux*, and *lex* can be read. Using the alpha that hangs under the chi, we can also compose the word *pax*.[27] In this case, the stonecutter has chosen to use letter games to make visible the play on the four monosyllabic nouns. This complex chrismon could be considered a monogram containing not only the letters of

23 Ibid., 167; http://www.claustro.com/Crismones/Webpages/Catalogo_crismon.htm (accessed 5 January 2015).

24 Jean-Claude Bonne, "Les ornements de l'histoire (à propos de l'ivoire carolingien de saint Remi)," *Annales Histoire Sciences Sociales* 51 (1996): 37–70.

25 *CIFM* 10:232.

26 Ibid., 71.

27 Ibid., 76.

FIG. 7.2.
Chrismon,
east wall above
sacristy door,
Lème (Pyrénées-
Atlantiques).

Photo by author.

FIG. 7.3.
Chrismon, west
tympanum, Saint-
Michel Church,
Lamaguère (Gers).

Photo © CESM.

Christ's name but also those of its definition by the monosyllabic words used by Angilbert in his epitaph.

In the tympanum of Azuelo church, IHS and XPS (featuring a stroke that really shows their sacred nature and excludes the christograms from the construction of a unique graphic system) are placed on both parts of the chi.[28] Some examples show however that the border between the chrismon monogram and the XPS abbreviation is very thin. The west portal of Saint-Christophe de Montsaunès (Haute-Garonne) carries a beautiful Pyrenean

28 María Concepción García Gaínza, ed., *Catalogo monumental de Navarra* (Pamplona, 1980–97), 2.1:337.

chrismon, in which rho is surmounted by a large tilde (increasing the crosslike shape of the chrismon).[29] Such implementation differs from the abbreviation XPS only by the juxtaposition of letters, an aesthetic phenomenon that affects many abbreviations or complete words in epigraphic practice, and which is not exclusively reserved for the composition of monograms.

Other examples would confirm that the chrismon can be, in a few cases, a monumental epigraphic and manuscript abbreviation for Christ's name. Let us take the example of the chrismon carved in the tympanum of the west door of Saint-Michel of Lamaguère church (Gers; fig. 7.3).[30] It presents a chi and rho, and the alpha and omega, but it is also supplemented with an I and an S inscribed on the middle stroke, and with an H traced where one would have expected the usual S. These letters build the christogram IHS, used alone in the epigraphic world only from the end of thirteenth century. The Lamaguère chrismon dates to the twelfth century, so one is tempted to look for the christogram XPS appearing with IHS. It is found easily in the chrismon, another form of monumental abbreviation for Christus, where a single S is used to complete both forms.

Letters as Voices
Proclaiming Christ's Peace

If the chrismon can be regarded as a monogram—that is, as a figure composed of all the letters or the main letters of a name ("ligature of ligatures" according to Otto Pächt)[31]—two possibilities must be considered: (1) the chrismon uses the Greek characters chi, rho, and sigma, and refers to the Greek name Christos, giving a monogrammatic form to the manuscript abbreviation XPS; (2) the Greek characters alpha, chi, and rho are exchanged for the Latin letters P, A, and X to make a new monogram for the word *pax*.

Associations between the chrismon and peace have been repeatedly highlighted throughout the corpus of scholarship on monumental chrismons.[32] These cross-references can take various forms, but the tympanum of Jaca cathedral, in Aragon, may offer the most comprehensive explanation of such relationship (fig. 7.4).[33]

29 *CIFM* 10:43.

30 Ibid., 83.

31 Otto Pächt, *L'enluminure médiévale: Une introduction* (Paris, 1997), 67.

32 *CIFM* 10:8: "There are clear interferences between the chrismon and the word *pax* . . . also used in a monogrammatic form."

33 On the Jaca tympanum, see the important studies by David Simon, "El tímpano de la catedral de Jaca," in *XV congreso de historia de la corona de Aragón*, vol. 3, *Jaca en la corona de Aragón siglos XII–XVIII* (Saragossa, 1996), 405–19; and Calvin

FIG. 7.4.
Chrismon, tympanum, Jaca cathedral (Aragón).

Photo © CESM.

FIG. 7.5.
Chrismon,
tympanum of the
gallery door, church
of Eusa (Navarra).

Photo by author.

A famous inscription on the circle around the chrismon, located between two lions, gives the following text: "In this sculpture, take care to recognize, you reader: P is the Father, A is the Son, the double [letter] is the Holy Spirit. These three are truly one single Lord."[34] Many interpretations can be found in the extensive bibliography about this beautiful piece from the end of twelfth century. The French scholar in medieval epigraphy Robert Favreau found the source of Jaca's inscription in the commentary on Saint Paul's Letter to the Ephesians by Atto of Vercelli.[35] It brings together the three Latin letters P, A, and X in the word *pax*, "symbol of the Trinity, composed of three inseparable letters."[36] If the chrismon can be linked to the Trinity, it is because the combination of letters into the word *pax* forms a Trinitarian symbol (and not because it adds to Christ's monogram the letter S symbolizing the Holy Spirit).

Spanish scholars have seen in the chrismon a way for graphic medieval culture to represent the mystery of the Trinity, interpreting each letter as a single person gathered into a unique motif.[37] The inscription written around the chrismon at Jaca evokes "These three are truly one single Lord," but it does so in order to develop the concept of peace and actually ignores the letter S. Jaca's chrismon is the most complex monumental example of associations between Christ's monogram and the idea of peace; the very rough metrical construction of the inscription's third verse is a reflection of this complexity. This verse also raises significant difficulties in understanding the semiotic definition of the symbol. If the three Latin letters are really gathered into a monogram at Jaca's tympanum, each of them simultaneously possesses an individual semantic existence, insofar as they refer to something other than the word they begin (the Father for P, the Son for A, and the Holy Spirit for X). Jaca's chrismon therefore offers the viewer a very rich range of meanings and, at the same time, very different ways to reach them: the decomposition of Christ's monogram, the reconstruction of the word *pax*, the theological realities of symbolic letters, an iconic reading of the chrismon, and so forth. However, Jaca's chrismon also shows a strong principle of unity in its construction; the addition of ornamental devices to the circle enclosing the letters engages all the alphabetic components in a single paradigm.

The connection between the chrismon and the word *pax* transforms the Greek letters into Latin letters, and results in a monogram that possesses all the letters to form a complete word. This association is still more common from the eleventh century, especially thanks to the success, in epigraphy as in manuscripts, of the word play on *rex*, *lex*, *lux*, and *pax*.[38] In the tympanum of the gallery of the church of Eusa (near Pamplona, Navarra), there is a classical chrismon with alpha and omega hanging from the

Kendall, "The Verse Inscriptions of the Tympanum of Jaca and the Pax Anagram," *Mediaevalia* 19 (1996): 405–34.

34   "Hac in sculptura lector si gnoscere cura / P pater, A genitus, duplex est spiritus almus / Hii tres jure quidem Dominus sunt unus et idem." Favreau, "Les inscriptions du tympan," 536.

35   PL 134:554–55.

36   Favreau, "Les inscriptions du tympan," 551.

37   See, for example, Dulce Ocón Alonso, "Problemática del crismón trinitario," *Archivo español de arte* 233 (1983): 242–63.

38   Robert Favreau, "*Rex, lex, lux, pax*: Jeux de mots et jeux de lettres dans les inscriptions médiévales," in *Bibliothèque de l'École des chartes* 161 (2003): 625–35.

upper arms of chi (fig. 7.5).[39] Inside a circle, the word *vobis* completes the word *pax* drawn in a monogrammatic form. Though Eusa's chrismon is much simpler than Jaca's, it also transforms in a particularly explicit way Christ's monogram into an original, graphic form of the word *pax*. In such compact and voluntarily elliptical form, the motif refers to Christ's words "pax vobis," related in his successive appearances to the disciples;[40] it also makes reference to the verse "pax Domini sit semper vobiscum."[41] In this sense, the appearance of the monogram of *pax* does not sever the chrismon from its christological meaning. On the contrary, "peace" on the tympanum of churches is Christ's peace, the one that is proclaimed in one of the antiphons of the Paschal season: "Pax vobis, ego sum, alleluia, nolite timere, alleluia."[42] The chrismon is a monumental depiction of Christ's voice.[43]

In certain cases, the conventional monogrammatic form of the chrismon can disappear for the benefit of the word *pax*. Near the south door of Bon-Encontre church a relief has been reused, in which the letters rho and chi are placed side-by-side, followed by a straight line that might be an I. The letters A and X are also drawn vertically under the center of the chi. The editors of the *Corpus des inscriptions de la France médiévale* (*CIFM*) convincingly read in these two groups of signs (the first one horizontal, the second one vertical) an abbreviation for *Christi* (XPI) and then the word *pax*. The bas-relief then forms the expression *pax Christi*, which is commonly found, for example, in benedictions engraved at the entrances of churches.[44]

With the partial dissolution of the monogram—partial because the stone-cutter clearly sought to gather the three letters of christic abbreviation—a more complex syntactic construction becomes possible. This is the case with the bas-relief placed above the west entrance of Saint-Pierre-de-Cazeaux chapel, in Laplume. The form and general composition of this relief is described by the authors of the *CIFM* as a "symbolic wheel" that reminds one of contemporary chrismons, even if no letter of the monogram can be read.[45] However, in the circle divided into eight parts (just as the Greek letters chi and rho would do in a chrismon) the same formula as in Eusa was engraved: "pax vobis."[46] In some churches, such inscriptions can be read without any chrismon in a "visual evocation" of Christ's monogram, showing how deep the associations between this motif and peace were in medieval visual culture. At the west portal of the chapel of Saint John in Chancelade, four circles contain, from left to right, the letters P, A, a cross, and the letter X (fig. 7.6).[47] There is no monogrammatic construction, each sign is isolated from others within individual circles. The cross carved at the top is, however, an image of Christ, so all the signs can therefore be said to form part of a unique composition proclaiming Christ's peace at the entrance of the church.[48] Here, the chrismon has been excluded, and the analogy stands in the location of the text, and in the combination of the word *pax* and a christological symbol. Topographic analogies between chrismons and these inscriptions, and obvious semantic relationships between the chrismon and the *pax* formulae, invite us to ask whether the claveau inscribed with the formula "pax huic domui" in the church of Merlande has the same

39 http://www.claustro.com/Crismones/Webpages/Catalogo_crismon.htm (accessed 5 January 2015).

40 Jn 20:21: "Et, cum hoc dixisset, ostendit eis manus et medio et dixit eis: pax vobis." Jn 20:26: "Venit Iesus, ianuis clausis, et stetit in medio et dixit: pax vobis."

41 Christine Mohrmann and Bernard Botte, *L'ordinaire de la messe* (Paris, 1953), 124.

42 *Corpus antiphonalium officii* (Rome, 1966), 3: no. 4254; Lk 24:36.

43 The association between Christ and peace is also evident in some monumental chrismons where the word *pax* is fully transcribed. This is the case in the tympanum of the portal of Sainte-Engrâce church, where the circle is inscribed with the formula "pax tecum." This inscription could give the meaning of the motive, as the words *cherubin* and *seraphin* identify the two sculptures nearby the chrismon. *CIFM* 10:187 and 6:PA18, 166.

44 *CIFM* 6:PA13, 124–25.

45 *CIFM* 6:PA14, 126–27.

46 At the church of Eusa, one can see two more christograms presenting original shapes similar to the Laplume chrismon. These are reminiscent of old Christian symbols like stars and wheels, which were also used in antique pagan or medieval magic. See Don C. Skemer, *Binding Words: Textual Amulets in Middle Ages* (University Park, Pa., 2006); and idem, "Written Amulets and the Medieval Book," *Scrittura e civiltà* 23 (1999): 253–305.

47 *CIFM* 5:D6, 11–12.

48 In Chancelade, the superior arch is surmounted by a blessing hand designating the whole building as the recipient of the protection of Christ's peace.

status and fulfills the same space-creating function in the building, even in the absence of any explicit reference to Christ.[49]

Despite significant semiotic differences between Christ's monogram and the word *pax*, both elements present such similar content that they could be interchangeable from time to time, as on a tenth-century ivory now in the British Museum, on which an inscription gives the incipit of the Gloria.[50] Within the inscription, Christ's monogram becomes an image of the word *pax* in a complex syntactic sequence, in some ideographic use of alphabetic signs. Where the word *pax* would have been carved in the response "et in terra pax hominibus bonae voluntatis," a very simple chrismon (in an early-Christian form composed of the two original Greek letters) appears instead.[51] Proclaiming

peace through Christ's monogram allows a reinforcement of its essential christological origin, according to John's Gospel.[52] So, the link between the word *pax* and the chrismon in monumental sculpture does not mean the end of any graphic reference to Christ's name, but participates in its affirmation, thanks to a semantic expansion of the monogram.

Chrismon and Trinity

In Spanish scholarship on the chrismon, the adjective "Trinitarian" is applied to the Pyrenean forms with the three letters X, P, and S supplemented by alpha and omega.[53] The very existence of the word "Trinitarian" is a sign of the persistence of some historiographic trend that has made the chrismon the medieval solution for representing the Trinity mystery. Though this explanation seems attractive and cannot

49   *CIFM* 5:D10, 17–18.

50   Adolph Goldschmidt, *Die Elfenbeinskulpturen aus der Zeit der karolingischen und sächsischen Kaiser: VIII.–XI. Jahrhundert* (Berlin, 1969–1970), no. 159, 78, pl. 70.

51   In the first Christian epitaphs including a chrismon, the monogram appears near the word *pax* in the formula "in pace Christi"; Bruun, "The Victorious Signs of Constantine," plate 17.

52   Jn 14:27: "Pacem relinquo vobis, pacem meam do vobis: non, quomodo mundus dat, ego do vobis."

53   For an overview of this important bibliography, see the recent article by Francisco García García, "El tímpano de Jaca y la escenificación de la ortodoxia," *Anales de Historia del Arte* 2 (2011): 123–46.

FIG. 7.7.
North portal,
Saint-Miguel
Church, Estella
(Navarra).

Photo © CESM

be totally excluded, it has been strongly questioned since Robert Favreau's article on the Jaca cathedral in 1996, in which he concludes that a Trinitarian meaning must have been given to epigraphic chrismons in very few instances, in France as in northern Spain.[54]

There is actually no inscription with a chrismon giving any explicit Trinitarian description, even if the reference to the Trinity is evident in the text inscribed around the chrismon of Saint-Sauveur church at Saint-Macaire, which reads "in honor of the triune and only Lord" ("in onore trini et unius Domini").[55] The expression "trinus et unus," inherited from Saint Augustine[56] and very common in medieval epigraphy,[57] certainly takes a particular meaning in its association with the chrismon, and could become, in this exceptional case, a graphic representation of Trinity. Yet the monogram at Saint-Macaire does not contain the letter S, which normally leads to the Trinitarian interpretation. The lack of S shows that the semantic relationship between the chrismon and Trinity is not located in any monogrammatic structure nor construction of specific

signs (in order to build an abbreviation or a complete word), but rather in the capacity of the overall shape of the chrismon to visually signify (as an image or symbol) a complex reality through an iconic method of perception and restitution.

Let us try to go further in this direction. If the chrismon enters the world of representations (in a broad sense of the medieval concept of *representatio*), it cannot answer to a strictly lexical approach. The letter games have from now on no ambition to form a word semantically associated with a given intellectual reality, an abbreviation, or a monogram. The chrismon becomes an autonomous representation, part of a possible visual discourse.

We find the word "sign" in the inscription placed around the chrismon in Saint-Maixant church (Gironde), which gives the metric caption "qui confidit in hoc signo speret in Deo" ("let him who has faith in this sign hope in God"), making the chrismon a representation of the whole faith.[58] Christ's monogram acquires a figurative dimension that exceeds the association of Greek or Latin letters. At the portal of San Miguel church at Estella, there are two representations of the chrismon. The first one is located at the top of the upper archivolt; the second is engraved on the object held by Jesus Christ, who is represented in a mandorla on the tympanum (fig. 7.7). According

54   Favreau, "Les inscriptions du tympan," 553, 555.

55   *CIFM* 10:124; see also *CIFM* 5:G33, 121.

56   Augustine, *De moribus ecclesiae catholicae*, 1.1, ch. 14; PL 32:1321.

57   On that point, see Robert Favreau, "Épigraphie et théologie," in *Épigraphie et iconographie* (Poitiers, 1996), 37–49.

58   *CIFM* 10:125.

FIG. 7.8.
Chrismon, west
wall of the tower,
Camparan church
(Hautes-Pyrénées).

Photo by author.

to Christ's iconographic type in this sculpture, this object should be a book, but its shape does not fit with this interpretation.[59] It is perfectly square and also too thick; it actually looks more like a stone! The object is as original as the chrismon's location: the symbol that rarely enters complex visual compositions, here in association with other representations. The text around the edge of the mandorla offers this commentary: "Nec Deus est nec homo presens quam cernis imago, sed Deus est et homo quem sacra figurat imago."[60] Very common in epigraphy, this formula synthesizes the noticeable tension in medieval art between a thirst for visual depictions and the transcendence of the represented contents.[61] It offers an attempt at defining Christ's nature and proposes a perspective on medieval implications of image theory.

The novel location of the chrismon at Estella invites us to wonder whether the epigraphic message does not deal also with the monogram carved on the object held by Christ. In the limited context of the tympanum at San Miguel, what does the expression "sacra imago" refer to? To the enthroned and blessing Christ or to the chrismon he presents to the believers entering

the church? There could be a complementarity between the two representations, in which Christ's human figuration is accompanied with a divine one thanks to the chrismon. We should notice in this sense the proximity between the monogram and the word *sacra* of the inscription. The chrismon could be considered one of the representations of Christ's divine nature.

In the case of Estella, the chrismon, as the mandorla and throne, excludes the human figuration represented in the tympanum of the world of men and instead depicts only the divine, in a very medieval sense of what sacredness is.[62] After reading some medieval texts, one might go further and ask whether the monogrammatic structure of certain nomina sacra or formulae related to Christ are the best graphical constructions to testify to his dual nature. Otto Pächt reports the interpretation given by Jean Beleth of the monogram bringing together, in liturgical manuscripts, the letters V and D of the Vere dignum preface: "Closed from all sides, delta is indeed an image of the divine nature which has no beginning and no end"; the *V* expresses instead Christ's human nature, which finds its origin in the Virgin but knows no end (see Kessler, chap. 6). "The line bringing together the two elements in the center represents the Cross, by what human existence seems to be linked to divine one."[63]

There is a strong correlation between the shape of the chrismon, its location, and contemporary graphic practices in the consecration of the church, unction of the altar, chrismation of the dying, and so forth. Placed in the tympana of church doors, the chrismon is an image of sacredness projected on the outside of the building that designates its function, in the same way as liturgical dedication ceremony and crosses on the church walls do. As such a generic symbol, the chrismon might then have been part of nonceremonial events after the consecration of the church. Such local or historical uses may have caused the chrismon to be fixed in stone

59 In any case, this object does not look like the books held by the Evangelists on the Estella tympanum.

60 Gaínza, ed., *Catalogo monumental*, 2.1:486.

61 On these verses, see the great book by Herbert L. Kessler, *Neither God nor Man: Words, Images, and the Medieval Anxiety about Art* (Berlin, 2007). The author offers a great analysis of Estella's image. My own reflections on this topic were inspired by Kessler's conclusions.

62 Jean-Claude Schmitt, "La notion de sacré et son application à l'histoire du christianisme medieval," *Cahiers du Centre de recherches historiques* 9 (1992): 19–29; see also Michel Lauwers, "Le cimetière au Moyen Age: Lieu sacré, saint et religieux," *Annales Histoire Sciences Sociales* 5 (1999): 1047–72.

63 Jean Beleth, *Rationale divinorum officiorum*, chap. 43; PL 205:53; quoted by Pächt, *L'enluminure*, 44.

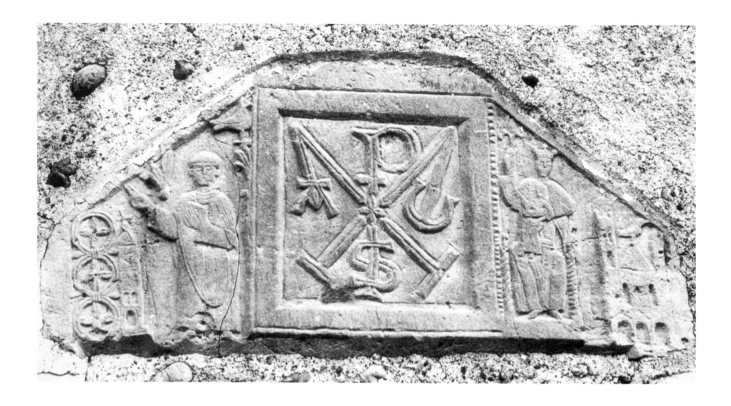

more often in the Pyrenees than elsewhere. This hypothesis is suggested by the inscription accompanying the monogram in the tympanum of Camparan church (Hautes-Pyrénées), which reads, on both sides of the circle: "olea sacra."[64] The very stylized chrismon (fig. 7.8) has certain similarities to a cross of dedication found as evidence of the dedication ceremony. The episcopal ritual says, in the *Pontifical romano-Germanique* as in Guillaume Durand, that twelve crosses traced by the bishop's auxiliaries were anointed.[65] The inscription of Camparan's chrismon also has a ceremonial aspect; associated with the church dedication (which gives sanctity to the building), it also transforms this motif into a sacred mark, a sculptural demonstration of the transcendental nature of God's house. During the ceremony of

church dedication, the bishop would have pronounced this prayer while entering the building: "Pax huic domui." It can be found in several medieval inscriptions occupying similar positions to those occupied by chrismons in southwest France.

The friction between the motif and its theological and symbolic background generates the precise meaning of each monumental chrismon; that is why a global study of this graphic phenomenon would be so complicated. The tympanum of Sedze-Maubecq illustrates the impossibility of systematizing the study of all chrismons (fig. 7.9). The Sedze-Maubecq example deserves a long and precise study of the interrelations among letters, images, locations, and meanings. Near the chrismon are bas-reliefs of the Virgin and Child, the Holy Spirit, and the *manus Dei*. The clearly Trinitarian meaning of these images is translated in the chrismon in a literal way. This double representation allows the passage of the earthly dedicated church (which contains three flagships, signs of the Trinity) to the celestial church, throne of the Divine. How not to notice the contact between the cross and the chrismon near the deisis, and the dove on earth, upon the church? An object of mediation, the chrismon translates sculpturally what

64   *CIFM* 10:214.

65   One can find a good description of the ritual of church dedication (gesture, prayers, liturgical texts, etc.) in Jean Michaud, "Les inscriptions de consécration d'autels et de dédicace d'églises en France du VIIIe au XIIIe siècle: Épigraphie et liturgie" (Ph.D. diss., Université de Poitiers, 1978). See also Cyrille Vogel, ed., *Le pontifical romano-germanique* (Rome, 1963), 83: "Deinde in circuitu ecclesiae per parietes de dextro usque in dextrum faciat cruces cum pollice de chrismate in duodecim locis, dicens: sanctificetur hoc templum in nomine Patris et Filii et Spiritus sancti."

FIG. 7.9. Chrismon, tympanum of the cemetery door, south wall, church of Sedze-Maubecq.

Photo by author.

can neither be said nor represented, and allows the passage from one world to another. The alphabetical signs are no longer the instruments of linguistic expression, but the means for the Logos to take physical form.

The Chrismon: Sign (Seal) of Protection

Since Christ's monogram loses its lexical dimension when converted into a figurative representation, it is often used for protective purposes, to preserve churches from danger and say that here is the house of the Lord. That is what we find, for example, in the inscription that accompanies a chrismon formerly located at the door of the Hospitalers church in Toulouse. The text reads: "Here we pray to God, and this House is called his home."[66] The chrismon below might refer to the word *Deus* or to *domus ejus*, confirming the link with the church dedication.[67] The association between text and image reveals the desire to ensure the identification of the building, making the chrismon act like a seal, as a guarantee of authenticity.[68] The psalm verse engraved under the chrismon in the tympanum of Aguilar de Codés hermitage serves the same function by declaring: "I will enter your house, Lord; with fear of you I will worship at your holy temple" (fig. 7.10).[69] In this composition (as in many

other examples), the chrismon is a projection of sanctity at the entrance of the building; it guarantees the security and integrity of the church by a kind of proclamation *ad limine* of the special status of sacred space.[70]

A fragment of the former portal of Saint-Pé-de-Bigorre church (Hautes-Pyrénées) is now reused in the northern wall of the building. On the arch of the tympanum that formerly carried a chrismon, two verses are engraved in a beautiful script from the beginning of the twelfth century.[71] The first hexameter has a very close meaning to that of previously mentioned texts: "Here is God's house, the way to heaven and pilgrim's hope." The second verse not only identifies God's house, but also offers protection against evil: "This door is given to Peter. You are removed, Devil." In the monumental arrangement at Saint-Pé-de-Bigorre, as at Aguilar de Codés (where this aspect of protection is reinforced by the expression "in timore tuo"), the linguistic values of letters disappear in the construction of a prophylactic sign like the cross.

Actually, the alpha and omega in the chrismon can remind us of some early medieval Asturian crosses, symbols of protection and victory.[72] Let us refer to the chrismon located in the tympanum of the small Romanesque church of Otazu (near Pamplona). In this beautiful piece, we see the two letters of the Apocalypse hanging from the upper arms of the chi, as in Asturian examples or images from Beatus codices.[73] Otazu's chrismon is reminiscent of the one from Fredenandus's epitaph preserved in the church

---

66 "Hic Deus oratur domus ejus et ista vocatur." *CIFM* 10:62 and *CIFM* 7:57, 96. It should be noted that there is a play between the foreground and background, just as we observed in Bostens. The principle of unity is also present here through the node in the center that seems to connect all of the constituent parts of the chrismon.

67 On the relationship between epigraphic inscription and church dedication, see the great article by Cécile Treffort, "Une consécration à la lettre: Place, rôle et autorité des textes inscrits dans la sacralisation de l'église," in *Mises en scène et mémoire de la consécration de l'église dans l'Occident medieval* (Turnhout, 2008), 219–51.

68 The use of chrismons as seals of protection has been studied conveniently in diplomatics; see, for example, the stimulating remarks by Robert Maxwell, "Sealing Signs and the Art of Transcribing in the Vierzon Cartulary," *ArtB* 81, no. 4 (1999): 576–97. Regarding magic uses, an important question remains: does the prophylactic action lie in the chrismon's graphic existence, beyond any performance, or in the marking, reading, spelling, or touching of the sign? For monumental chrismons, and according to the inscriptions, this prophylactic efficiency lies in both presence and vision.

69 "Introibo in domum tuam Domine. Adorabo ad templum sanctum tuum in timore tuo." Gaínza, ed., *Catalogo monumental*, 2, pt. 1: 59–60; for a detailed study of this tympanum,

see José Esteban Uranga Galdiano, "El tímpano de la puerta de la ermita de San Bartolomé en Aguilar de Codés," *Príncipe de Viana* (1942): 249; see also Javier Martínez de Aguirre, ed., *Enciclopedia del Románico en Navarra* (Aguilar de Campoo, 2008), 164–68.

70 These ideas have been formulated by Calvin Kendall, "The Gate of Heaven and the Fountain of Life: Speech-Act Theory and Portal Inscriptions," *Essays in Medieval Studies* 10 (1993): 111–28; and idem, *The Allegory of Church: Romanesque Portals and their Verse Inscriptions* (Toronto, 1998).

71 *CIFM* 10:263; *CIFM* 8:HP13, 104–5. "Est domus hic domini, via caeli, spes peregrini."

72 On the question of Asturian crosses, see Robert Favreau, "La croix victorieuse des rois des Asturies (VIIIᵉ–Xᵉ s.): Inscriptions et communication du pouvoir," in *L'écriture publique du pouvoir: Table-ronde Bordeaux (14–15 mars 2002)* (Bordeaux, 2002), 195–212.

73 See ibid.

FIG. 7.10.
North portal,
hermitage, Saint-
Bartholomeo, Aguilar
de Codés (Navarra).

Photo © CESM.

of Saint Peter of Teverga. The inscription, dated to 1076, is located under the protective symbol of the cross, recalling that symbol's power in the preservation of the deceased and burial: "I wear the sign of the kindly cross: flee, demon."[74] Even if there is not, strictly speaking, a chrismon in this Asturian example, we can envisage that victory crosses and Christ's monograms played a comparable prophylactic role. This connection confirms that the chrismon is an iconic sign, an image beyond any lexical development.

In the marking, identification, or protection of buildings, the chrismon possesses a form of efficiency, an operating strength.[75] The monogram makes, acts, transforms, or generates sacred qualities—maybe even sacramental ones—and its realization in stone on churches transmits these qualities to buildings or larger spaces. Where does this operating strength come from? What gives chrismons their effective power? Certainly, we can suggest the obvious

fact of its contents: Christ, whose name is fixed and exposed in his monogram, intervenes himself to transform a building made of stone into a spiritual one, excluded from the time of men but, at the same time, the locus of their community. In the same way that the letters of Holy Scripture, from alpha to omega, contain by synecdoche all of creation, the initials of Christ's name combined in his monumental monogram contain the totality of his sacramental efficiency. The active and immediate strength of the name is added to the mechanical value of lettering, an instrument of creation by making language visible, to create a way for the name to have a participative existence in the world.

From Letters to Images

The assimilation between chrismons and images is particularly clear in the case of some elaborate pieces in which alphabetical structures have been dissolved, as in the southern tympanum of Ardanaz church. This chrismon is quite original: the chi lines end in floral elements on the circle that surrounds the chrismon, leaving very little blank space for lettering. The S is carved horizontally and the belly of the rho is reduced; and a small cross replaces the alpha. Even if the aesthetic result is beautiful, it is difficult to consider the Ardanaz chrismon as a monogram. Similarly, the southern door of the small church of Janariz (Navarre) was engraved with a complex but small chrismon (now destroyed): the

74 "Crucis alme fero signum: fuge, demon." Francisco Diego Santos, *Inscripciones medievales de Asturias* (Oviedo, 1993), no. 183, 178.

75 The location of a chrismon and its efficiency has been studied in charters; its role cannot be separated from the presence and the role of monograms and seals. On that topic, see Olivier Guyotjeannin, "Le monogramme dans l'acte royal français (X^e–début XIVe siècle)," in *Graphische Symbole in mittelalterlichen Urkunden: Beiträge zu einer diplomatischen Semiotik*, ed. Peter Rück (Sigmaringen, 1996), 293–318; Jean-Baptiste Renault, "Le monogramme dans les chartes épiscopales en Lorraine et Champagne (X^e–début XIIe s.)," *Annales de l'Est* 59 (2009): 55–90; and Brigitte M. Bedos-Rezak, *When Ego Was Imago: Signs of Identity in Middle Ages* (Leiden, 2011).

letters were composed of double lines and the stone cutter deliberately increased the size of the ornamental elements, forming a complex pattern of interlacing. O. Pächt wrote of chrismons: "The Holy Monogram no longer seeks to be decrypted or to be read; it must spontaneously be perceived as the *signum Crucis*."[76]

Above the southern door of the church of Santiago in Puente la Reina, a chrismon is sculpted with a figure that resembles a prophet carrying a snake in his hand and a frog on his shoulder.[77] The sculpture hides the letters P and S of the chrismon; only alpha and omega can be seen. This representation is unusual, but it also confirms the iconographic value of the chrismon. In Puente la Reina, it can probably be interpreted as showing the opposition between good and evil from a passage of Saint John's Revelation.[78] In any case, a part of the chrismon has been voluntarily sacrificed to represent another image. The chrismon was most often a support for writing, but here we see it also as a support for iconography. The center of a chrismon from the church of Olóriz (preserved in the Museum of Navarra in Pamplona) depicts a wheel. In the center of one of the chrismons from Irache church, there is a floral motif and a hand of God.

The Holy Lamb is one of the most frequently added motifs, as in the tympanum of Aguilar de Codés hermitage (see fig. 7.10), where the chrismon is clearly relegated to second place, and serves as the background for the sculpture of a lamb. Christ's sacrificial destiny is based on the complex nature of God as man, as it appears in this chrismon motif. The quality of the sculpture allows a harmonious composition, but gives prominence to the lamb, as confirmed by the inscription on the circle: "He is worthy, the lamb who was sacrificed, to receive power, wealth, wisdom, strength,

glory, honor, and blessing."[79] The text ignores completely the monogram (probably associated with the other inscription referencing the church dedication), which becomes simply a figurative support for another image. There are complex interactions between these two representations of the same subject. This is suggested by the two inscriptions, in which the evocation of the sacrificed lamb is the very sign of the *templum* mentioned at the bottom of the tympanum: "I will enter your house, O Lord. I will worship in your holy temple fearing you."[80]

To conclude, consider the rich figuration carved on the facade of the Church of La Oliva monastery (in Carcastillo, Navarra) (fig. 7.11).[81] In the center of the monogram, which has lost an alpha to the iconographic development, the depiction of the Lamb of God is associated with lions, griffins, and stars. Outside the circle, sculptures of the Pantocrator and the Tetramorph (a motif depicting symbols of the Four Evangelists) on the right and a Nativity on the left participate in the creation of a complex visual discourse. The interpretation of the tympanum is indeed quite difficult.[82] If we consider the chrismon as an iconic object, we see that it forms a junction between the scene of Christ's birth, when his humanity is proclaimed to the world, and a representation of the Pantocrator, a reference to his divinity. Lions and griffins, symbols of the Resurrection, are placed within the chrismon to link the two scenes. In its implementation within the iconographic discourse, there is no semiotic difference between the chrismon and the other images of the tympanum. Therefore it could be considered as a synthetic image of God's humanity and deity, and thus as a symbol of his dual nature. This hypothesis for the interpretation of Carcastillo adds weight to my discussion following Herbert Kessler regarding the tympanum of Saint Miguel in Estella: the sacred image of the chrismon contains both God's human and divine natures.[83]

76 *Medieval Illumination: An Introduction* (Paris, 1997), 68.

77 Javier Martínez de Aguirre and Asunción de Orbe Sivatte, "Consideraciones acerca de las portadas lobuladas medievales in Navarra: Santiago de Puente la Reina, San Pedro de la Rua de Estella y San Román de Cirauqui," *Príncipe de Viana* (1987): 41–59.

78 Rev. 16:13–14: "Et vidi de ore draconis et de ore bestiae et de ore pseudoprophetae spiritus tres inmundos in modum ranarum sunt enim spiritus daemoniorum facientes signa et procedunt ad reges totius terrae congregare illos in proelium ad diem magnum Dei omnipotentis."

79 "Dignus est agnus qui occisus est accipere virtutem divinitatem sapientiam fortitudinem honorem gloriam benedictionem," Rev. 5:12.

80 "Introibo in domum tuam, Domine. Adorabo ad templum sanctum tuum in timore tuo."

81 Gaínza, ed., *Catalogo monumental*, 1:205.

82 See Sené, "Quelques remarques," 372.

83 Kessler, *Neither God nor Man.*

FIG. 7.11.
Chrismon, north
portal, La Oliva
monastery church,
Carcastillo
(Navarra).

Photo by author.

Due to its diversity of forms and functions, the chrismon cannot be reduced to a simple monogram using the first two letters of Christ's Greek name. Monumental examples and their epigraphic complements show that people of the Middle Ages played with the plurality of interpretations of the sign to make a full word, an abbreviation, sometimes a monogram, but especially an image, an iconic sign referring to complex notions.[84] The transcendence of these notions leads to its use as a semiotic paradigm, the nature of which is often difficult to determine. The chrismon shows that the borders between letter and image are not impervious in medieval graphic culture. The epigraphic examples (in contrast to letters or charters) allow us to consider this motif in relation to specific spaces and to approach the "archaeological" relationships between writing and sanctity.

The graphic build-up around the chrismon is constant. This phenomenon might certainly be explained by a graphic tropism, in which

writing attracts writing (an omnipresent fact in written cultures). A second explanation lies in the medieval practice of *titulus*, the simultaneous functioning within the same paradigm of a text and an image, both complementing visual and semantic plans. Though some inscriptions actually give an explanatory reading of chrismons, more likely they contribute to, as in most tituli, semantic expansion, considerably enriching the motif. The inscription does not make the chrismon more accessible or more understandable, but increases its layers of representational meaning.

Finally, we must understand that monumental chrismons, like those in charters or manuscripts, have a capacity to introduce and promote writing; the chrismon is no longer just a name, but an invocation, and places writing in a range of action, in the shade of sanctity or, at least, of solemnity. Inscriptions are not found near chrismons because they channel their meaning or make them explicit; on the contrary, the motif gives to the inscription a part of its sacramental efficiency. Gathered within the same monumental paradigm, chrismon and inscription are both aspects of the same effective system that gives the building and its community to Christ's name, friendship, and protection, and that creates an encounter with God's image.

84 On the subject of full-page monograms in Irish manuscripts of the early Middle Ages, Otto Pächt wrote in 1984 that it is a "typical medieval approach, which gives rise to a sign full of expressiveness of a simple initial, a meaningful visual form, and which replaces symbolic abstraction by real physiognomy": *L'enluminure*, 39.

8

The Role of Hebrew Letters
in Making the Divine Visible

KATRIN KOGMAN-APPEL

WHEN JEWISH FIGURAL BOOK ART BEGAN TO DEVELOP IN CENTRAL
Europe around the middle of the thirteenth century, the patrons and artists of Hebrew
liturgical books easily opened up to the tastes, fashions, and conventions of Latin illuminated manuscripts and other forms of Christian art. Jewish book designers dealt with the visual
culture they encountered in the environment in which they lived with a complex process of transmission, adaptation, and translation. Among the wealth of Christian visual themes, however, there was
one that the Jews could not integrate into their religious culture: they were not prepared to create
anthropomorphic representations of God. This stand does not imply that Jewish imagery never met
the challenge involved in representing the Divine. Among the most lavish medieval Hebrew manuscripts is a group of prayer books that contain the liturgical hymns that were commonly part of central
European prayer rites. Many of these hymns address God by means of lavish golden initial words that
refer to the Divine. These initials were integrated into the overall imagery of decorated initial panels,
their frames, and entire page layouts in manifold ways to be analyzed in what follows. Jewish artists
and patrons developed interesting strategies to cope with the need to avoid anthropomorphism and
still to give way to visually powerful manifestations of the divine presence.

Among the standard themes in medieval Ashkenazi illuminated Hebrew prayer books
(*mahzorim*)[1] we find images of Moses receiving the tablets of the Law on Mount Sinai (Exodus 31:18,
34), commemorated during the holiday of Shavuot, the Feast of Weeks (fig. 8.1). Ashkenazi mahzorim,
usually made up of two very large volumes, do not contain the statutory prayers, but rather include a
set of liturgical embellishments (*piyyutim*), which became a key feature of the Ashkenazi prayer rites
during the Middle Ages. As is common for the iconographic programs of most mahzorim, the first
piyyut of each holiday's liturgy was the most lavishly adorned. The Shavuot liturgy begins with the
piyyut *adon imnani* ("The Lord Has Nourished Me").[2] This hymn, sung, so to speak, by the Torah,

---

1   In the following a simplified system of transliteration is used (similar to what is common in the *Encyclopedia Judaica*): there
is no distinction between the letters ה (he) and ח (het), both are transliterated as h (*mahzor*); א (aleph) has no extra mark (*adon*);
ע ('ayin) is marked by an inverted apostrophe (*'anfehem*); ק (quf) appears as q, whereas כ (k(h)af) appears as k or kh (*ashkenaz,
bekhol*); פ (peh or feh) appears either as p or f (*sefer*); there is no distinction between ש (sin) and ס (samekh), both are transliterated
as s (*sefer*); ז (zayin) appears as z (*mahzor*).

2   Israel Davidson, *Thesaurus of Hebrew Poems and Liturgical Hymns from the Canonization of Scripture to the Emancipation*
(New York, 1924), 1:24, no. 484; Jonah Fraenkel, ed., *Mahzor shavuot lefi minhage bene ashkenaz lekhol 'anfehem* (Jerusalem,
2000), 97–101.

deals poetically with the role of the Law in Israel. Hence, the most common iconography for this poem and the entire Shavuot service in medieval mahzorim from the German lands is a narrative representation of the giving of the Law.[3]

We find the same piyyut, "The Lord Has Nourished Me," illustrated in the so-called Laud Mahzor, now held in Oxford, written and illuminated around 1250 in the southern German lands, but the imagery there is slightly different (fig. 8.2).[4] The transmission of the Law is squeezed into a small section near the upper

3   For a short overview of the Ashkenazi mahzorim and basic iconographic treatment, see Gabrielle Sed-Rajna, *Le mahzor enluminé: Les voies de formation d'un programme iconographique* (Leiden, 1983).

4   For basic information on the manuscript and its pictorial program, see ibid., 14, 64–66.

FIG. 8.2.
Opening page
for the Shavuot
service, Laud
Mahzor, southern
Germany, ca. 1250.
Oxford, Bodleian
Library, MS. Or.
Laud 321.

Photo courtesy of the
Bodleian Library,
Oxford.

edge of the miniature, where an angel holds the two tablets; on the right, the Law is passed on to three bird-headed representatives of the people of Israel in the form of a Torah scroll. Unlike parallels elsewhere, the focus of the Laud Mahzor image seems to shift away from the giving of the Law to the large architectural structure that occupies most of the picture space. A large arch circumscribes the initial word of the liturgical hymn, *adon* (the Lord), which is set between two horizontal beams that support the arch.[5] The space between the beams and the

5 The embellishment of initial words is as popular in Hebrew manuscript painting as is the decoration of initial letters in Christian book art. Some of these initial words simply appear enlarged or written in silver and gold. Other, more elaborate words were embedded in full-fledged painted compositions. In most cases these words do not have any particular iconographic significance, but in the few examples discussed here, I submit, they do.

whereas the half-moon top represents the flat lid, the *kapporet*, with the two cherubim above it (echoed in the curved line).[7] This basic structure developed into yet more abstract and stylized shapes in the Middle Ages, turning into a widespread convention communicating the message of messianic (and political) hope.[8]

In the Middle Ages this symbol, which was also adopted in Christian art, occasionally took on a different form. We find it in several examples from Iberia, in both Christian and Jewish contexts, where it appears as an arch functioning, so to speak, as a gateway opening onto the space where a sacrifice is taking place or the Ark is on display. In the Sarajevo Haggadah from circa 1330, for example, the arch opens onto the Holy of Holies (fig. 8.4).[9] The Laud Mahzor (see fig. 8.2) uses the arch in a similar way, and its upper edge appears to represent the curved line of Mount Sinai, as if to identify the arch with that mountain. The small, stylized, green plant set on the apex of the arch seems to turn it into a part of nature—a mountain. Several rabbinic commentaries identify Mount Sinai with both the site of the Binding of Isaac and the Temple Mount.[10] The arch, which also functions as a framing device creating cohesion between the different iconographic elements, should be understood as a symbol, not as a reference to an actual physical space.

7   Exod. 25:17–18.

8   Elisabeth Revel-Neher, *Le témoignage de l'absence: Les objets du sanctuaire à Byzance et dans l'art juif du XIe au XVe siècle* (Paris, 1998); Shulamit Laderman, *Images of Cosmology in Jewish and Byzantine Art: God's Blueprint of Creation* (Leiden and Boston, 2013).

9   Katrin Kogman-Appel and Shulamit Laderman, "The Sarajevo Haggadah: The Concept of *Creatio ex nihilo* and the Hermeneutical School Behind It," *Studies in Iconography* 25 (2004): 85–128, esp. 103–6. Arches appear in numerous forms as organizing compositional devices, especially as framing decoration; in most cases they bear no iconographic significance. However, given the earlier history of the ark shape and the fact that the arch in the Laud Mahzor appears in conjunction with the sacrificial theme, I suggest that this particular arch refers to the Temple/Tabernacle theme. The horizontal beams further underline this echo of the ark symbol known from earlier Jewish art.

10   For example, Solomon Buber, ed., *Midrash tehillim hamekhune shoher tov* on Ps. 68:15 (Vilnius, 1890), 320; for an English translation, see William G. Braude, ed. and trans., *Midrash on Psalms* (New Haven, 1959), 1:544.

FIG. 8.3.
Coin issued during the Bar-Kokhba revolt, Palestine, 132–135 CE. Jerusalem, Israel Museum, the Temple and the Ark of Covenant.

Photo © The Israel Museum, Jerusalem.

arch is devoted to a depiction of a sacrificial rite. The representation of an arch of that particular shape and appearance with the portrayal of a sacrifice beneath it links this imagery with one of the most common symbols of Jewish art since late antiquity. The image suggests the Temple in Jerusalem, the desert Tabernacle, and the Ark of the Covenant—or, rather, all three notions combined. After the destruction of the Temple in 70 CE, a schematic shape, rectangular at the base with a curved top, developed into a symbol of the Tabernacle/Temple implying the eschatological hope that the sanctuary will be rebuilt in messianic times. An early example of this imagery is a coin minted by Bar-Kokhba during the revolt of 132–135 CE showing that shape within a small temple-like structure (fig. 8.3).[6] The rectangular lower part is a graphic symbol that developed from the shape of the Ark,

6   Elisabeth Revel-Neher, *L'Arche d'Alliance dans l'art juif et chrétien du second au dixième siècles: Le signe de la rencontre* (Paris, 1984).

Diverging from the straightforward approach of other Ashkenazi prayer books with their narratives of the giving of the Law, the Laud image juxtaposes the Law and the sacrificial cult. What we see here is, in fact, the initiation of the sacrificial cult described in Exodus, chapter twenty-nine; the meeting place of the cult, the Temple (and initially the Tabernacle), is indicated by the large arch, columns, and the two horizontal beams. The arch thus takes us beyond the plain biblical narrative into the more complex layers of this imagery.[11] The sacrifice takes place in either the Tabernacle or the Temple, two concepts—one referencing the temporary movable sanctuary and the other the permanent structure in Jerusalem—that cannot be separated. The appearance of the arch and beams in the color of limestone, with realistic architectural features, suggests that the designer of the composition intended to represent the Temple. The large initial word *adon* ("the Lord") between the two horizontal beams, which are integral parts of the architectural structure, seems to emphasize the notion of the Temple as God's dwelling place.[12] As is well known, a pictorial representation of God as a figure is unthinkable of in Jewish art.

In another, slightly later mahzor produced in Worms in the middle Rhine region, but now held in the University Library at Leipzig, we find another example of an iconographic use of letters to represent the Divine (fig. 8.5). The Sabbaths before Purim and before Passover are considered "special Sabbaths," and are characterized by extra reading portions in addition to the regular pericopes that follow the order of the Bible. The opening page of the liturgy for the morning service of *shabbat sheqalim* shows the text of the first piyyut to be recited during that service. Entitled *el mitnasse* ("God, the mighty one"), the poem refers repeatedly to the extra Torah reading (*sheqalim*).[13] The sheqalim reading describes the Israelites each

offering half a sheqel for the construction of the Tabernacle. The sum is referred to as a ransom "to avert plague breaking out among them," and the Israelites are promised expiation and atonement.[14] The wording of the hymn tightly links the ransom with the atonement for sins. However, the first part of the poem also refers repeatedly to the glory of God and concludes with an allusion to the divine throne as it is described in the first chapter of the book of Ezekiel:

And above the firmament that was over their [the four living creatures'] heads was the

FIG. 8.4.
Messianic Temple, Sarajevo Haggadah, Aragon, ca. 1330, fol. 32r. Sarajevo, National Museum of Bosnia and Herzegovina.

Photo courtesy the Jewish community, Sarajevo.

11   For a more extensive discussion of the Temple imagery on this page, see Katrin Kogman-Appel, "The Temple of Jerusalem and the Hebrew Millennium in a Thirteenth-Century Jewish Prayer Book," in *Jerusalem as Narrative Space: Erzählraum Jerusalem*, ed. Annette Hoffmann and Gerhard Wolf (Leiden, 2012), 187–208.

12   Exod. 25–29.

13   Davidson, *Thesaurus*, 1:178, no. 3853.

14   Exod. 30:11–16.

FIG. 8.5.
Sheqalim pericope,
Leipzig Mahzor, Worms,
ca. 1310, fol. 31v. Leipzig,
Universitätsbibliothek,
Ms. V. 1102/I.

Photo courtesy of the
Universitätsbibliothek,
Leipzig.

likeness of a throne, as the appearance of a sapphire stone; and upon the likeness of the throne was a likeness as the appearance of a man upon it above (1:26).[15]

The opening word, *el*, "God," is shown within a large panel, written in gold and bordered by medallions with Ezekiel's four creatures, two on each side.[16] We also see a balance scale in the center of the composition, flanked by two dragons that seem to be toying with the weight on the balance.[17] The balance refers to the sheqel contributions of the Israelites, but as I have shown elsewhere, the scales are also a common symbol

15 Translations from the Bible are based on the *Jewish Publication Society Bible* (Philadelphia, 1917).

16 Ezek. 1:5–11.

17 On dragons as symbols of evil, see Ilia Rodov, "Dragons: A Symbol of Evil in European Synagogue Decoration?" *Ars Judaica* 1 (2005): 63–84.

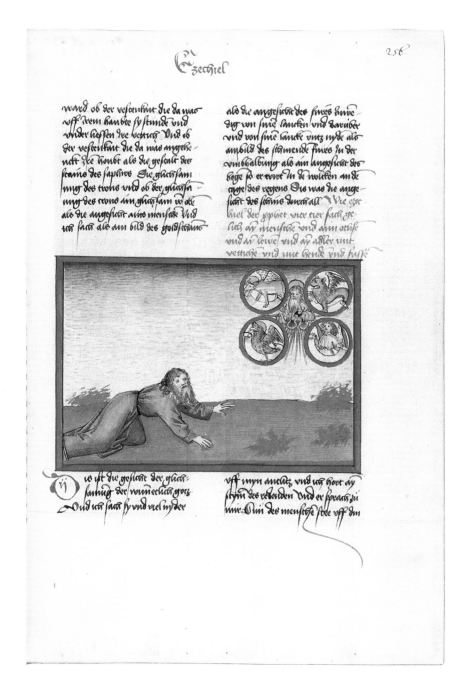

FIG. 8.6.
Ezekiel's vision,
Bible in German,
Swabia 1477, fol.
256r. Heidelberg,
Universitätsbibliothek,
cpg 18.

Photo courtesy of the
Universitätsbibliothek,
Heidelberg.

for the atonement of sin.[18] The scales, which are attached to the upper frame by a hook, appear to be balanced. The vertical pole of the balance rests upon the lamed of the alef-lamed ligature standing for *el*, thus suggesting that it is God who holds the balance. According to several penitential traditions, it is God between the four living creatures who receives the repentant.[19]

A brief look at a similar composition in a Christian Bible lets us understand that the gold letters that form the word *el* are in place of the figure of God in the center between the medallions. Ezekiel's vision, a prominent theme in

18 Katrin Kogman-Appel, "The Scales in the Leipzig Mahzor: Penance and Eschatology in Fourteenth-Century Germany," in *Between Judaism and Christianity: Art Historical Essays in Honor of Elisheva (Elisabeth) Revel-Neher*, ed. Mati Meyer and Katrin Kogman-Appel (Leiden, 2009), 307–18; eadem, *A Mahzor from Worms: Art and Religion in a Medieval Jewish Community* (Cambridge, Mass., 2012), chap. 5.

19 For details, see ibid.

medieval Christian art, is depicted for example in a fifteenth-century German Bible in an image that makes this point particularly clear (fig. 8.6). The fact that the balance scales hang from the letters shows vividly that the word not only replaces the Christian image of God, but that it is actively integrated into the overall meaning of the imagery. The word is not merely a decorative element, but has turned into a definitive part of the iconography to become an active agent in the communication of the message being conveyed. Furthermore, the ligature merges the two letters into a single entity, one sign—there are two letters, but only one iconographic agent.

Divine intervention is also alluded to at the beginning of the piyyut *ata he'arta or* ("You [= God] Lit the Light")[20] for the last day of Passover in the Laud Mahzor (fig. 8.7). The initial word "you," addressing God, stands between the Israelites departing from Egypt and the pursuing Egyptians, as if to protect the former from the latter. I shall return to the narrative of the Departure from Egypt and divine protection further on.

These examples demonstrate that in Jewish iconography words such as "God," "the Lord," and "you" not only replace the anthropomorphic representation of God often found in Christian iconography, but unacceptable in a Jewish context, but also can be actively integrated into the overall imagery. They represent God's residence in the Temple, his presence at the Last Judgment, holding the balance scale, and divine protection.

Whether the biblical prohibition "you shall not make a graven image"[21] is understood broadly, in the sense that no created being should be depicted in any form, or more specifically as restricting three-dimensional figurations, one point is unquestionable: God is beyond representation.[22] Indeed, the commandment, which came out of the need to counter polytheistic idol worship, clearly was not directed at mere artistic

production, but focused rather on the aspect of worship. Hence during the late antique period the approach to the biblical prohibition was slightly altered and allowed for the possibility of two-dimensional portrayals of plants, animals, and human figures. Figural painting was widely practiced during the early Talmudic period, until about 550, but with the exception of several images of the hand of God, figural depictions within Jewish culture do not normally include a full or even a partial anthropomorphic representation of the Deity.

However, the Bible and the post-biblical tradition do tend to refer to God anthropomorphically. Not only did God create man in his own image, according to the book of Genesis,[23] but the Bible and Talmudic literature are replete with details such as the hand of God, God putting on phylacteries, and so on.[24] The description of the bridegroom in the Song of Songs is intensely anthropomorphic and, particularly in the Middle Ages, was usually understood as an allegorical representation of God offering his love to his people.[25] Allegory, in fact, grew into the most common method of coping with biblical anthropomorphism. Such descriptions were approached as allegories of theophany, rather than as references to revelations of an anthropomorphic God.

20 Davidson, *Thesaurus*, 1:396, no. 8745; Jonah Fraenkel, ed., *Mahzor pesah lefi minhage bene ashkenaz lekhol 'anfehem* (Jerusalem, 1993), 423–28.

21 Exod. 20:4.

22 The following section on anthropomorphism is based on my discussion of Pietist approaches to anthropomorphism in the context of a representation of the feminine *shekhinah*, in *Mahzor from Worms*, 147–51.

23 Gen. 1:26.

24 *bBer*, 6a.

25 Song of Songs, chap. 5. For some background on the literal and the allegorical interpretation of the Song of Songs, in particular on the anthropomorphic aspects, see Sarah Japhet, "The Literal Meaning of the Song of Songs: On Rashi and His Followers as Interpreters of the Literal Meaning [in Hebrew]," in *Collected Studies in Biblical Exegesis*, ed. Sarah Japhet (Jerusalem, 2008), 135–56; on allegorical interpretations vs. literal explanations of the Song of Songs, see eadem, "Description of the Body and Images of Beauty [in Hebrew]," in *Papers on the Interpretations of the Bible and the Quran in the Middle Ages Presented to Haggai Ben-Shammai*, ed. Meir Bar Asher, Simon Hopkins, Sarah Stroumsa, and Bruno Chiesa (Jerusalem, 2007), 133–62, repr. in eadem, *Collected Studies*, 54–84; for a list of medieval commentaries on the Song of Songs, see Barry D. Walfish, "Annotated Bibliography of Jewish Commentaries to the Song of Songs [in Hebrew]," in *The Bible in the Light of Its Commentators: Collective Volume in Memory of Sarah Kamin*, ed. Sarah Japhet (Jerusalem, 1994), 518–71; and Ivan G. Marcus, "The Song of Songs in German Hasidism and the School of Rashi: A Preliminary Comparison," in *The Frank Talmage Memorial Volume*, ed. Barry D. Walfish (Haifa, 1993), 1:181–89.

FIG. 8.7.
Last day of Passover, Egyptian army pursues the children of Israel, Laud Mahzor, southern Germany, ca. 1250, fol. 108r. Oxford, Bodleian Library, MS. Or. Laud 321.

Photo courtesy of the Bodleian Library, Oxford.

However, things were not always so clearcut. In the twelfth century the Sefardi philosopher Moses Maimonides noted "our Sages were far from the belief in the corporeality of God."[26] If anthropomorphism were indeed a taboo, then why would Maimonides have to underscore that the Talmudic Rabbis were "far from the belief in the corporeality of God?" His words must have been directed toward people who cast doubt on this assumption. Maimonides was clearly concerned with the possibility that some Jews held less radical views on anthropomorphism than his own. Furthermore, we now know that in his assumption about the Talmudic Rabbis Maimonides was somewhat misled,

26 *Moreh hanevuhim*, ed. and trans. Michael Schwarz (Tel Aviv, 2002), pt. 1, chap. 46; for an English version, see Maimonides, *Guide for the Perplexed*, trans. Michael Friedländer (London, 1904).

and Yair Lorberbaum has recently shown that late antique and medieval Jewish approaches to anthropomorphism varied greatly.[27] Not only are the Bible and rabbinic literature full of anthropomorphic references to God, but late antique mystical literature is also replete with such allusions. Time and time again the *Hekhalot* tradition, a group of late antique mystical texts about the heavenly shrines, refers to God anthropomorphically, and the so-called *Shi'ur Qomah* texts discuss the enormous size of God and his limbs.[28] Lorberbaum also suggests that clear anthropomorphic views can be observed in mainstream rabbinic thought.[29]

Whereas in the biblical tradition and in late antiquity verbal anthropomorphism was apparently quite common, Maimonides took a far more radical turn and condemned even an imagined picture of God. Verbal description of anthropomorphic features of the Divine, he argued, sets the imagination working and an imagined picture of God would, in fact, turn every prayer into a sinful act of idolatry.[30] The

difficulties medieval philosophers had with the essence of God and the resulting question of how to refer to prophetic revelation led to a variety of approaches. Maimonides's position is clearly one of radical anti-anthropomorphism. God is abstract at all times and can never be described in terms of human features; divine revelation can be understood only as a result of the Prophets' imagination. However, a controversy that shook the Sefardi intelligentsia for more than a hundred years after Maimonides's death shows that there was also opposition to his radical anti-anthropomorphism, particularly among scholars in northern France.[31] Neither of the two positions, however, was open to the possibility of a visual representation of the Divine in human form. The notion of an anthropomorphic God does not necessarily encourage the creation of a physical anthropomorphic image. On the contrary, the fear that verbal anthropomorphism might eventually generate visual representation meant that the prohibition of visual representation of the Divine was all the more serious a matter.

Issues of anthropomorphism were also a concern of a small group of scholars in the Rhineland, commonly referred to as the "Ashkenazi Pietists," active during the late twelfth and the early thirteenth centuries. The Pietists were a group of rabbis, mostly from one clan— the Qalonymide family of the Rhineland— who shared an ascetic attitude toward life, a rather complex set of ethical values, and an abiding interest in mysticism.[32] The Pietists

---

27 Yair Lorberbaum, *Image of God: Halakhah and Aggadah* [in Hebrew] (Tel Aviv, 2004).

28 These texts often reflect on the anthropomorphic descriptions in the Song of Songs; for more background, see the introduction to Rachel Elior, ed., *Hekhalot zutrati*, Mekhqare yerushalayim bemahshevet Israel, suppl. vol. 1 (1982); eadem, "The Uniqueness of the Religious Phenomenon in Hekhalot Literature: The Figure of God and the Limits of Its Perception [in Hebrew]," in *Early Jewish Mysticism*, ed. Joseph Dan, Jerusalem Studies in Jewish Thought 1–2 (Jerusalem, 1987), 13–64, with references to earlier literature. On the scholarship about Hekhalot literature in general, see the useful summary by Ra'anan Boustan, "The Study of Hekhalot Literature: Between Mystical Experience and Textual Artifacts," *Currents in Biblical Research* 6, no. 1 (2007): 130–60. Earlier scholarship has dated the beginning of Hekhalot literature to the second century; recent scholarship, however, tends to postdate it to the sixth or seventh; see ibid.

29 Lorberbaum, *Image*. For some earlier, less comprehensive treatments of possible rabbinic anthropomorphism, see, e.g., David Stern, "*Imitatio Hominis:* Anthropomorphism and the Character(s) of God in Rabbinic Literature," *Prooftexts* 12 (1992): 151–74; Moshe Halbertal, "Would It Not Be Written in the Bible [in Hebrew]," *Tarbiz* 68, no. 1 (1999): 39–59; and Alon Goshen-Gottstein, "The Body as Image of God in Rabbinic Literature," *HTR* 87, no. 2 (1994): 171–95, who goes so far as to claim that there is an anthropomorphic position to be found even in the literature of the Tannaim, the rabbis of Palestine in the first two centuries CE; Lorberbaum disagrees with this view and argues that reservations concerning anthropomorphism can be found in early rabbinic sources (*Image*, 27). For a full survey of past research on this matter, see ibid., chap. 1.

30 For more details, see Moshe Halbertal, "Of Pictures and Words: Visual and Verbal Representations of God," in *The*

Divine Image: Depicting God in Jewish and Israeli Art, exh. cat. (Jerusalem, 2006), 7–13.

31 For a detailed discussion of northern French Jewish ("Tosafist") approaches to these matters, see Ephraim Kanarfogel, "Varieties of Belief in Medieval Ashkenaz: The Case of Anthropomorphism," in *Rabbinic Culture and Its Critics: Jewish Authority, Dissent, and Heresy in Medieval and Early Modern Times*, ed. Daniel Frank and Matt Goldish (Detroit, 2008), 117–19.

32 Literature on the Pietists is extensive and cannot be listed in full here. Ivan Marcus's pioneer study has turned into a classic, as it defines the group in social and intellectual terms: *Piety and Society: The Jewish Pietists of Medieval Germany* (Leiden, 1981); see also idem, "Judah the Pietist and Eleazar of Worms: From Charismatic to Conventional Leadership," in *Jewish Mystical Leaders and Leadership in the 13th Century*, ed. Moshe Idel and Mortimer Ostow (Northvale, N.J., and Jerusalem, 1998), 97–127; idem, "The Historical Meaning of *Hasidei Ashkenaz*: Fact, Fiction or Cultural Self-Image?" in

wrote several treatises that targeted questions of anthropomorphism and divine revelation, but the picture we get from these writings is not entirely clear. In fact, whereas the Pietists certainly opposed anthropomorphism, they occupied themselves intensely with late antique anthropomorphic descriptions, so their overall attitude seems somewhat contradictory. Pietist thought implies, somewhat similarly to Maimonides's position described above, that the Creator is hidden from any human experience of the senses. He is abstract, has no material form or physical presence, and has never been revealed in any form. A central question in Maimonides's thought concerns the form of the divine revelations experienced by the Prophets. Similarly, the Pietists created a large corpus of writings, most of it esoteric, which addressed the apparent contradiction between biblical reports of these divine revelations and the objection to any anthropomorphic description of the Godhead. However, much of this material exists only in manuscript form; as it was intended only for somewhat seclusive groups of scholars who shared an interest in mystics, it was never published.[33]

Rabbinic sources from late antiquity occasionally refer to divine revelation in terms of *kavod* (literally: "glory"). In a treatise titled "Beliefs and Opinions" by Saadia Gaon, a tenth-century Babylonian scholar, divine revelation is described as an angel named Kavod.[34] Rabbinic scholars referred to it as the *shekhinah*, an appellation for the divine presence on earth (literally: "God's dwelling").[35] Whereas Saadia Gaon, similar to the medieval philosophers, described the kavod as a created being, according to Judah ben Samuel

the Pious (d. 1217), one of the leading Pietists, the kavod is related to God by emanation. It is identical with God and as such it emanates from the Creator, with successive emanations forming a chain, and it was the lowest linked member of that chain that was revealed to the Prophets. The Pietists occasionally distinguished between the upper and the revealed kavod.[36]

The distinction between the abstract Creator and the kavod of the prophetic revelations eventually opened the way to various visualizations of the imagined kavod, including depictions of the Glory with anthropomorphic features. By this the Pietists presumably did not mean an ontological being, but rather contended that God is revealed as a reflection of the upper kavod, as a visual equivalent without any physicality, and it is to this reflection that man turns in prayer.[37] On the other hand, it is concentration during prayer, and specifically concentration while uttering the letters of the tetragrammaton together with proper intention and the resulting contemplation, that leads to the visualization of an anthropomorphic image of the shekhinah. The human imagination, where the image is formed, is compared to a mirror in which the shekhinah appears as a reflection of the abstract Godhead.[38]

A mental image of the kavod as the result of a mystic experience could also mean visualization

---

Gershom Scholem's "Major Trends in Jewish Mysticism" 50 Years After: Proceedings of the Sixth International Conference on the History of Jewish Mysticism, ed. Joseph Dan and Peter Schäfer (Tübingen, 1993), 103–14. For a recent summary of the Pietists' mystical interests, see Joseph Dan, *History of Jewish Mysticism and Esotericism: The Middle Ages* [in Hebrew] (Jerusalem, 2011), vols. 5 and 6.

33 An entire corpus of Pietist literature, the so-called "Literature of Unity" (*sifrut hayihud*), deals with matters of divine revelation; for a detailed discussion, see Dan, *Jewish Mysticism*, vol. 5, *Circles of Esotericism in Medieval Germany: The Mystics of the Kalonymus Family*, 175–79.

34 On the reception of the Hebrew paraphrase of Saadia's work among the Pietists, see Joseph Dan, *The Esoteric Theology of Ashkenazi Hasidism* [in Hebrew] (Jerusalem, 1968), 22–24.

35 *Mishna, Avot*, chap. 3.

36 Pietist esoteric teachings about the kavod were first discussed by Gershom G. Scholem, *Major Trends in Jewish Mysticism* (New York, 1941), 107–18. See also idem, *Origins of the* Kabbalah (Princeton, 1987), 180–87; Dan, *Esoteric Theology*, 104–68; idem, "The Hidden kavod [in Hebrew]," in *Religion and Language: Papers in General and Jewish Philosophy*, ed. Moshe Halamish and Assa Kasher (Tel Aviv, 1982), 71–78; and Asi Farber-Ginat, "The Concept of the Merkavah in Thirteenth-Century Jewish Esotericism: 'Sod Ha-'Egoz' and Its Developments [in Hebrew]" (Ph.D. diss., The Hebrew University of Jerusalem, 1986), 401–32.

37 Moshe Hershler, ed., *Perush siddur hatefilah laroqeah* (Jerusalem, 1994), par. 326.

38 For further discussions of the Pietists' dealings with the kavod, see, e.g., Daniel Abrams, "'The Secret of All the Secrets': The Approach to the Glory and the Intention in Prayer in the Writings of Rabbi Eleazar of Worms and Its Echoes in Other Texts [in Hebrew]," *Da'at* 34 (1995): 64–65. Elliot R. Wolfson discusses the appearance of the shekhinah as a visualized human form on the throne of Glory, "Metatron and Shi'ur Qomah in the Writings of Haside Ashkenaz," in *Mysticism, Magic and Kabbalah in Ashkenazi Judaism*, ed. Karl E. Grözinger and Joseph Dan (Berlin and New York, 1995), 69, n. 43.

of the letters of the name of God.[39] In the Jewish tradition every letter equals a number and every word has a numerical value that is made up of the values of all of its letters. Hence a word and its letters carry a heavy exegetical burden. Using these numerical values as an exegetical device (*gematria*) has been practiced since antiquity. The Pietists, in particular, had a very strong interest in numerological exegesis.[40] Central to this line of thought, especially among the Pietists, was the numerological interpretation of the various names of God, words that circumscribe the not-to-be-spoken tetragrammaton, יהוה (YHVH). It was this aspect of the numerology that turned gematria into a favored tool for kabbalists and Pietists. Following up on observations made by Gershom Scholem, Elliot Wolfson points to the "failure" or the "unwillingness" of the Pietists "to recast the older mystical notions within a framework of a coherent metaphysics or ontology, despite their adaptation of a semi-philosophical theology."[41] Hence the Pietists preferred an exegetical method based on "a web of linguistic and numerological associations rather than abstract philosophical concepts."[42]

One of the leading Pietists, Eleazar ben Judah of Worms (d. 1232), a relative and student of Judah the Pious, authored a work titled *Sefer hashem* (The Book of the Name), which lists and interprets numerous designations for God that can serve as substitutes for the tetragrammaton.[43] There is a long list of such designations, including "the name," "Lord," *elohim*, and many more. At the beginning of his text Eleazar described a "secret ceremony of the transmission of the divine name," a ritual in which a master teacher reveals the secrets of the divine name to his pupil. He explained that both the teacher and the pupil, after a long period of learning, prepare themselves by dressing in white and immersing themselves in water, where they recite several blessings and a selection of biblical verses that create a link between the water and the name of God.[44] Thus the name of God served as a vehicle for mystical experience. Samuel of Speyer (twelfth century), the earliest of the Ashkenazi Pietists, was supposed to have ascended to heaven by means of the name of God.[45] In another account the same Samuel filled a schoolhouse with light with the help of the name of God.[46] Such practices were aimed at a visualization of the divine chariot, the heavenly throne, the light of the Glory, which can take on an anthropomorphic shape, or a visualization of the letters of the name of God.

Wolfson discussed the visual aspects of mystic experience in Pietist teachings and other schools in great detail.[47] The role of light in connection with visualizing the Divine is beyond question; moreover, the concept is shared by Islam and Christianity. The use of gold, not only as a symbol of sanctity but also as a device to underscore the presence of the Divine, is a well-known principle in medieval Christian, especially Byzantine, art and is, as such, deeply embedded in Christian theology. As Wolfson demonstrates, however, there are several features "unique to the Jewish mystics," primarily the "configuration of that light in terms of their respective theosophical structures,

39 Elliot R. Wolfson, *Through a Speculum That Shines: Vision and Imagination in Medieval Jewish Mysticism* (Princeton, 1994), chap. 5.

40 Gematria is strongly associated with the Pietists, but as Haym Soloveichik stresses clearly, by no means should it be seen as their invention: "Piety, Pietism and German Pietism: *Sefer hasidim I* and the Influence of Hasidei Ashkenaz," *JQR* 92 (2002): 455–98, esp. 470–71. There are, however, as Soloveichik points out, specific traits to Pietist numerology; see also Daniel Abrams, "From Germany to Spain: Numerology as a Mystical Technique," *JJS* 47 (1996): 85–101.

41 Wolfson, *Through a Speculum*, 189; see also Scholem, *Major Trends*, 86–87.

42 Wolfson, *Through a Speculum*, 189.

43 *Sefer Hashem*, in *Sifre Rabbi El'azar migermaiza ba'al haroqeah*, ed. R. Aharon Eisenbach (Jerusalem, 1994–96), vol. 1. For a discussion of this text, see Joseph Dan, "The Book of the Divine Name by Rabbi Eleazar of Worms," *Frankfurter Judaistische Beiträge* 22 (1995): 27–60.

44 *Sefer hashem*, 1. The ritual was first discussed by Gershom Scholem, "Tradition und Neuschöpfung im Ritus der Kabbalisten," *ErJb* 19 (1950): 121–80; for an English version of Scholem's paper, see idem, *On the Kabbalah and Its Symbolism* (New York, 1964); Dan, *Esoteric Theology*, 75–78; and recently idem, *Jewish Mysticism and Esotericism*, vol. 6, *Rabbi Eleazar of Worms and Thirteenth-Century Circles of Jewish Mysticism and Esotericism in Germany*, 560–62. According to Dan, the main concerns of this ceremony are theological and speculative, a thought that was challenged by other scholars who emphasize the magical elements; see, e.g., Moshe Idel, *Kabbalah: New Perspectives* (New Haven, 1988), 323, n. 171.

45 Scholem, *Major Trends*, 374 n. 77, discussing a textual tradition that is extant only in manuscripts.

46 Wolfson, *Through a Speculum*, 191.

47 Wolfson, *Through a Speculum*.

informed by specific religious and cultural patterns of thought and models of action."[48] There are numerous examples of numerological interpretations of words, such as *hashmal*, an expression used by Ezekiel to define the luminous form of the Glory (Ezekiel 1:4), *nogah* ("radiance"), and *zohar* ("splendor").[49] The fact that the various artists discussed here all used gold leaf for the large letters of the initial words in question cannot be overlooked. Even though the use of gold for initial words in the mahzorim was not reserved for names of God, it is reasonable to associate the use of gold also with the attempt to give visual expression to divine light. In fact, as a great number of medieval piyyutim begin with words that refer to God in one way or another, it follows that many initial words in the mahzorim also refer to God, which gives credence to such an association.

The Pietists distinguished between an abstract, hidden, incorporeal Creator and the kavod or shekhinah, an anthropomorphically envisioned entity that would occasionally reveal itself to the Prophets. In any event, we are speaking of verbal anthropomorphism and not of its application to visual representation, which was certainly not something the Pietists had in mind. It was a far cry from the Pietist discussions about the visualized kavod to the issue of such representation in manuscript illumination several decades after the death of the last of the Qalonymide Pietists, Eleazar ben Judah of Worms in 1232.

I am not arguing that the letters designating "the Lord" (*adon*) or "God" (*el*) are visual expressions of a Pietist mindset. These illuminated mahzorim are not pietistic works. But the Pietist concerns with anthropomorphism must have had an impact on the way Jewish illuminators a few decades later approached the representation of the Divine.[50] In the case of the

Leipzig Mahzor, the link to Pietism may be even stronger: Eleazar of Worms had lived in the city where the Leipzig Mahzor was produced. I have argued elsewhere that the imagery in that mahzor was a powerful vehicle of community identity and that those who shaped that identity in the early fourteenth century looked back at him as one of the key figures in their cultural history.[51] Eleazar, it should be stressed, was not just a strange, ascetic, sectarian, Pietist scholar, for he also functioned as a communal authority, his signature appearing, for example, on rabbinical decisions of the Rhineland rabbinic council.[52]

I suggest that these initial words in the panels of the Laud and the Leipzig mahzorim can be read against the background of concerns with anthropomorphism of both the Pietists and Sefardi philosophers. These initial words, as they are integrated with the imagery, can be seen as referring to the hidden Godhead as an abstract sign; they circumscribe the revealed kavod, which, although it could be imagined anthropomorphically, was not supposed to be represented pictorially in any form. In fact, we are dealing here with an artistic solution to a complex issue, a solution that did not come from the Pietists or the philosophers, but rather from the artists, who were very much aware of the concerns regarding anthropomorphism.

The tradition of numerological exegesis also helped artists craft solutions to the prohibition

---

48 Ibid., 228.

49 Ibid.

50 The question of how much influence the Pietists had on Ashkenazi Jewish culture, and perhaps beyond, is one of the main controversies in relevant modern scholarship. Some scholars of the past maintained that the Pietists had a crucial influence on the generations that followed and defined the teachings of Isaac ben Moses of Vienna, for example, who had studied with the Pietists, or his disciple Meir ben Baruch of Rothenburg, as basically Pietist. See, e.g., the classic contributions by Ephraim E. Urbach, *The Tosafists: Their History, Writings, and Methods* [in Hebrew] (Jerusalem,

1954; rev. ed. 1986), chaps. 8 and 10. For a more recent evaluation of the issue from the angle of interactions between Pietist and Tosafist scholarship, see Ephraim Kanarfogel, *Peering through the Lattices: Mystical, Magical, and Pietistic Dimensions in the Tosafist Period* (Detroit, 2000). The view that the Pietists had great influence on Ashkenazi society was challenged by Joseph Dan, "Ashkenazi Hasidim, 1941–1991: Was There Really a Hasidic Movement in Medieval Germany?" in *Gershom Scholem's "Major Trends,"* 87–101; see also Sari Halpert, "Elitism and Pietism: An Investigation into the Elitist Nature of the Hasidei Ashkenaz," *The Queens College Journal of Jewish Studies* 2 (2000): 1–7, who argues in favor of Pietist elitism, somewhat simplistically neglecting, however, the fact that Pietism was not a uniform mass of scholarship with a fully homogeneous worldview. Halpert's study is almost exclusively based on evidence from the *Sefer hasidim*. Most notably, the assumption that the Pietists had major influence was criticized by Soloveichik, "Piety, Pietism, and German Pietism"; see also idem, "Pietists and Kibbitzers," *JQR* 96, no. 1 (2006): 60–64.

51 Kogman-Appel, *A Mahzor from Worms*.

52 For details see ibid., 48.

of anthropomorphism. Examples of the Pietists' preoccupation with letters, words, and their numerical values are myriad, and discussing them in depth goes beyond the framework of this paper. As noted, I am not suggesting that they actively stood behind the visual concepts developed in the mahzorim. However, at the time these books were designed, their mystical teachings were no longer confined to the medium of oral transmission.[53] They had been written down, even though the texts were clearly not widely dispersed. However, once these teachings appeared on parchment, a process of diffusion must have started, and elements of even the Pietists' most esoteric thoughts became known beyond their narrow sectarian circles. We should not imagine Jewish artists creating complex visual concepts of the visualization of the Divine grounded in a full-fledged array of Pietist mysticism. However, by the early fourteenth century an awareness of those concepts might well have reached broader circles of Jewish patrons and artists, evolving into the inspiration for creative solutions to the prohibition against creating an image of God. The subject matters of the liturgical hymns that these particular panels embellish lend themselves easily to attempts to integrate the word panels as representatives of the divine presence into the overall imagery of the panels.

It appears, finally, that some of these ideas migrated beyond the realm of Ashkenazi scholarship. This can be demonstrated by yet another example, from Iberia, which creatively integrates letters and words into imagery. In 1366 a Jewish scribe and mapmaker in Mallorca by the name of Elisha Cresques ben Abraham began work on a richly illuminated Bible. On page 150 we find a painting of the menorah and in the adjacent text on page 151 he notes explicitly that he executed the painting himself. The entire project occupied him for more than sixteen years and the codex was not completed until 1383. The colophon also explains that the Bible was made for Elisha's own use and for that of his descendants.[54] The

biblical text is preceded by two hundred pages of various writings, which he chose to include in what we can describe as his own personal library. These works embrace a whole range of rabbinic and scientific interests, and enable us to define Elisha's intellectual and cultural profile in quite some detail. They discuss calendrical issues and contain short treatises on philology and masorah, midrashic commentaries, excerpts from the major Hebrew chronographic texts, such as *Seder olam, Seder olam zutta,* and Abraham ibn Daud's *Sefer qabbalah* (ca. 1160), extensive lists of biblical figures and rabbinic scholars, and a Hebrew-Occitan dictionary based largely on David Kimhi's *Sefer hashorashim* from the early thirteenth century. Elisha also clearly had a particular interest in gematria.

Toward the end of this preliminary section there are three openings representing various views of the Temple and its implements. The first of these is well embedded in the Sefardi pictorial tradition regarding the Temple and shows the implements as golden silhouettes spread on a diapered background.[55] There are numerous parallels to this arrangement, which has been widely discussed in research on Hebrew illuminated manuscripts. Scholars agree that these diagrams represent the messianic Temple, whereas the Bible itself, in the absence of a physical Temple, is referred to in Jewish culture as the "minor Temple."[56]

Elisha Cresques went beyond this traditional Sefardi Temple image and offered a more elaborate view of the Temple theme in addition to the conventional depiction of the Sanctuary.

---

53 On the apparent contradiction between a tradition being esoteric and secret (and thus supposed to be only orally transmitted) and putting such teachings into writing, see Dan, "Book of Names," 33.

54 Farhi Codex, Sassoon Collection, MS 368, Mallorca, 1366–1383, pp. 2–4.

55 Bezalel Narkiss, *Hebrew Illuminated Manuscripts* [in Hebrew], expanded ed. (Jerusalem, 1984), pl. 16.

56 Revel-Neher, *Témoignage*; Katrin Kogman-Appel, *Jewish Book Art between Islam and Christianity: The Decoration of Hebrew Bibles in Spain* (Leiden and Boston, 2004), chap. 5; Eva Frojmovic, "Messianic Politic in Re-Christianized Spain: Images of the Sanctuary in Hebrew Bible Manuscripts," in *Imaging the Self, Imaging the Other: Visual Representation and Jewish-Christian Dynamics in the Middle Ages and Early Modern Period,* ed. eadem (Leiden and Boston, 2002), 91–128. For a recent summary of the scholarship, see Katrin Kogman-Appel, "Sephardic Ideas in Ashkenaz: Visualizing the Temple in Medieval Regensburg," in *Science and Philosophy in Ashkenazi Culture: Rejection, Toleration, and Accommodation,* Jahrbuch des Simon-Dubnow-Instituts; Simon Dubnow Institute Yearbook 8 (2009), ed. Israel Bartal and Gad Freudenthal (Leipzig, 2010), 247–53.

FIG. 8.8. The high priest's breastplate, Farhi Codex, Mallorca, 1366–83, p. 184. Sassoon Collection, MS. 368.

Photo courtesy R. David Sassoon, Jerusalem.

The Role of Hebrew Letters in Making the Divine Visible　　　167

The next opening shows a somewhat geometric scheme of the high priest's breastplate on the right (verso) (fig. 8.8) and a schematic diagram of the Ark of the Covenant, indicating its shape and its measurements on the left (recto). The breastplate consists of twelve small tablets schematically representing the precious stones inscribed with their names together with the names of the twelve tribes of Israel. Below the names of the tribes we can discern a few extra letters. "Ruben," consisting of five letters is accompanied by an aleph in the lower line; "Simon," five letters, is accompanied by a beth; "Levi," only three letters, is accompanied by resh, he, and mem. These extra letters together form the name אברהם, "Abraham." Similar letter arrangements appear in the other compartments, and altogether the additional letters beneath the names of the tribes form the sentence "Abraham, Isaac, Jacob, the tribes of Yeshurun."[57] Each tablet contains six letters, seventy-two altogether, not counting the names of the stones.

The earliest medieval text to refer to the seventy-two letters in the inscriptions on the breastplate is attributed to the previously mentioned Judah ben Samuel the Pious. Like other Pietists he was frequently occupied with gematria. In his *Sefer gematriot*, a numerological commentary to the Pentateuch, he linked the mystic notion of the seventy-two letters of the full divine name with the high priest's breastplate.[58] This tradition is based on the observation that three subsequent verses in Exodus (14:19–21), which

refer to the angel of God accompanying and protecting the people of Israel on their journey out of Egypt, all contain seventy-two letters each:

> And the angel of God, who went before the camp of Israel, removed and went behind them; and the pillar of cloud removed from before them, and stood behind them; and it came between the camp of Egypt and the camp of Israel; and there was the cloud and the darkness here, yet gave it light by night there; and the one came not near the other all the night. And Moses stretched out his hand over the sea; and the Lord caused the sea to go back by a strong east wind all the night, and made the sea dry land, and the waters were divided.

Owing to the focus on divine protection in these verses a tradition developed according to which the full name of God contains seventy-two letters. This brings us back to the attempt I described above to express divine protection during the Exodus visually (see fig. 8.7). Whether the artist who put the initial word *ata* ("you") between the Israelites and the Egyptians had this observation in mind cannot be said with any certainty. However, it is quite likely that he was familiar with the tradition of the full name of God.

Such traditions go back to late antique midrashim and were later expounded by medieval exegetes. The section in the *Sefer gematriot* is very short and only mentions the "seventy-two letters on the breastplate."[59] In a commentary to the Pentateuch by Eleazar of Worms, or perhaps by one of his students, we find a more explicit description:

> It is written in [the Talmud] twelve tribes, three fathers and the tribes of Yeshurun were inscribed on the breast shield. There were six letters inscribed on every stone.... There were seventy-two letters on the breastplate.[60]

Although this motif apparently originated in early thirteenth-century Ashkenazi Pietist

---

57 Yeshurun is a poetic expression for Israel, both the land and the people. See, e.g., Deut. 32:5. The Babylonian Talmud refers to the inscription "the tribes of Yeshurun" on the breastplate, *bYoma* 73b.

58 For a recent treatment of the *Sefer gematriot*, a version of which is included in the so-called London Miscellany, British Library, Add. MS. 11,639, on the margins of fols. 615–34, see Sara Offenberg, *Illuminated Piety: Pietistic Texts and Images in the North French Hebrew Miscellany* (Los Angeles, 2013), chap. 1 and appendix. For a facsimile version of the extant manuscript source, see Daniel Abrams and Israel Ta-Shema, eds., *Sefer gematriot of R. Judah the Pious: Facsimile Edition of a Unique Manuscript* (Los Angeles, 1998). For a recent edition, see Ya'akov I. Stall, ed., *Sefer gematriot lerabbi yehudah hehassid* (Jerusalem, 2005). The latter edition, which does not have a critical apparatus, presents the commentaries according to the flow of biblical narration, whereas in the original version the text follows a different, more associative arrangement. Interestingly, in the London Miscellany version the commentaries are already edited according to the biblical chronology.

59 *Sefer gematriot*, 1:501.

60 Yoel Klugmann, ed., *Perush haroqeah* on Exod. 28:17 (Bne Brak, 2001), 2:151–52.

FIG. 8.9.
Opening page
of the book
of Genesis,
Ashkenazi Bible,
southern Germany
(Ulm?), 1236,
vol. 1, fol. 1r.
Milan, Biblioteca
Ambrosiana, cod.
30-32/inf.

Photo © Veneranda
Biblioteca
Ambrosiana—
Milano/De Agostini
Picture Library.

circles, it also appeared in Aragon around the 1290s. There Bahye ben Asher of Saragossa, a scholar with great interest in early kabbalah, similarly linked the inscriptions on the breastplate with the tradition of the seventy-two letters of the full name of God. Eventually the motif became quite common, and is referred to time and again in early Sefardi kabbalah.

The section in Bahye's commentary offers a full description of all the stones with the inscribed letters and concludes as follows:

You have six letters on each stone; this is to show you that the six days of creation depend on the twelve tribes. And there were seventy-two letters on the breast shield, because twelve times six makes seventy-two; and they correspond to the seventy-two letters of the Great Name.[61]

These observations about Elisha Cresques's possible interest in kabbalistic teachings do not necessarily mean that he was an active kabbalist. He may not, in fact, have fully understood the exegetical implications of this motif and added the names of the stones, thus meddling with the precise number of seventy-two.[62] But he clearly must have had a notion of the motif as such. Hence one can argue that the integration of these letters into the design of the breastplate was meant to mark the divine presence in the Temple. This thought brings us back to the initial word in the Laud Mahzor, *adon*, which similarly refers to God's dwelling in the Temple. In the days of the Temple, the high priest, wearing the breastplate, was the only person who was permitted to utter the tetragrammaton and then only on the Day of Atonement.[63]

—※—

The anthropomorphic representation of the Divine is an absolute taboo in Jewish pictorial art. As Maimonides noted, even an imagined anthropomorphic appearance is unthinkable. The artists and scholars who conceived the images presented here sought iconographic solutions for the inclusion of the Divine in the imagery. They countered the prohibition against anthropomorphic representation by integrating opening words of piyyutim, such as "Lord," "God," "you," and "king," into the imagery of initial panels. In the case of the Ashkenazi mahzorim, this was possible because many of the Ashkenazi piyyutim begin with a word that designates "God" in one way or another. Hence, this particular type of initial word encourages a sort of iconographic use of letters. The same idea would not serve in biblical books with, for example, initial words such as *bereshit* ("in the

beginning") for Genesis; *ve'ele shmot* ("these are the names") for Exodus; and *vayedabber* ("he spoke") for Numbers. It is this particular feature of liturgical poetry—to begin a poem with the name of God—that makes the integration of letters and imagery possible.

By integration of the initial word into the imagery I mean more than simply the fact that letters or a word are juxtaposed with images. The design of any initial panel could fulfill that function, as one example from a Bible from Ulm demonstrates (fig. 8.9). However, even though word and image seem to be integrated formally and visually, there is no integration of meaning in this image. The iconography chosen depicts one of the stories told in the book, the Temptation of Adam and Eve. The figures of Adam and Eve flank the initial word in a highly attractive design, but the meaning of the imagery would be the same with and without the initial word. Moreover, the absence of the tree, which is replaced by the initial word, in fact, makes the overall iconography less obvious.

The cases from the Laud and Leipzig mahzorim introduced here are different. In these images the words *adon*, *el*, or *ata* play an active role in communicating iconographic meaning. The word *adon* between the two beams of the sanctuary stands for the presence of the Divine within the Temple or the Tabernacle (see fig. 8.2). The word *el* onto which the balance scales are attached stands for God executing the Last Judgment, weighing the virtues and vices of the people of Israel (see fig. 8.5). The word *ata* between the escaping Israelites and the pursuing pharaonic army introduces divine protection into the imagery of the Departure from Egypt (see fig. 8.7). The high priest's physical breastplate reduced to an abstract shape with golden letters that reference the name of God speaks a similar visual language (see fig. 8.8).

There are different levels of integration. The Exodus image in the Laud Mahzor (see fig. 8.7) can be well understood against the background of the biblical narrative per se, but the integration of the initial word adds an extra layer of meaning stressing and underscoring divine protection. On the Shavuot page of the same book (see fig. 8.2), on the other hand, the level of integration seems to be much higher, and the

61 Hayyim Dov Chavel, ed., *Rabbenu Behaye: Bi'ur 'al ha-torah*, on Exod. 28:15 (Jerusalem, 1967), 2:298.

62 The breastplate is depicted similarly in an Ashkenazi Pentateuch in Jerusalem, Israel Museum, MS 180/52 from ca. 1300, fols. 155v–56r. For a discussion of this image, see Kogman-Appel, "Sephardic Ideas," 245–77.

63 Num. 6:22–27; *bYoma* 39b.

appearance of the initial word *adon* integrated within the architectural structure not only accentuates a particular aspect of the overall imagery but also goes beyond that to emphasize the essence of the Temple as God's dwelling place. Thus it becomes a centerpiece of the communicated message. The same is true to an even greater degree for the sheqalim picture in the Leipzig Mahzor, whose contents would by no means be the same without the initial word and its interaction with the other pictorial elements. The initial word, in fact, becomes the very key to the Pietist understanding of the balance scene. In the Farhi Codex, finally, the use of letters goes beyond this sort of integration of words and imagery and becomes the primary aspect of the overall design. The breastplate, in fact, is represented not as a physical object, but rather as an abstract piece of scribal design: a large square divided into twelve smaller panels all occupied with only the letters and surrounding filigree, which clearly belongs to the domain of scribal work. Calligraphy here turns into the main bearer of the visual message.

It would appear that this phenomenon of integrating words that refer to the Divine into imagery owes a double debt to Pietist scholarship: it constitutes a creative solution for concerns with anthropomorphism and is indebted to the Pietists' interest in numerological symbolism. The Pietist worldview dealt with issues of vision or visualization, but only within the realm of what we would call imagination and they would call mystic experience. By no means, however, did the Pietists' occupation with vision imply the option of visualization on parchment, that is, the creation of a physical image. It appears, however, that their ideas shaped the surrounding culture beyond the relatively tight borders of Pietist circles and eventually led to creative solutions for coping with the taboo of divine representation. It also seems that their ideas went beyond Ashkenazi culture and inspired Sephardi artists and commentators at a particularly interesting point of intersection between Pietist and kabbalist ideas, an intersection that eventually would be instrumental in shaping early modern mysticism.

❧ I would like to thank Brigitte Bedos-Rezak and Jeffrey Hamburger not only for the organization of the colloquium but also for the overall concept, which stimulated fresh thoughts on images that I had already considered in the past. I have worked and published on several of the images discussed here in earlier contexts, but the conceptual framework of the conference stimulated a fresh look and an alternative analytical tool, and offered a new common denominator for them all. My current research on Elisha Cresques, addressed in the last part of this paper, is funded by a grant from the Israel Science Foundation, no. 122/12.

The Content of Form

Islamic Calligraphy between Text and Representation

İRVİN CEMİL SCHICK

CALLIGRAPHY IS VIRTUALLY OMNIPRESENT IN ISLAMIC ART AND ARCHITECTURE. So much so, in fact, that it is generally thought of as the most "quintessentially Islamic" of all arts. This prominence is usually attributed to the supposed iconophobia of Islam, though this explanation is not satisfactory for a number of reasons. Rather than a substitute for figurative art, calligraphy is more productively viewed as a distinct artform with its own cultural genealogy and social function. That said, the fact remains that calligraphy is profoundly visual, and that its form adds to its content in a unique way. The intermediacy of Islamic calligraphy between its textual and pictorial dimensions is the subject of the present article.

While Islamic calligraphy has been the focus of some western scholarly attention, at least since the studies of Jacob Georg Christian Adler in the 1780s, it has been suggested recently that the word "calligraphy" itself is an eighteenth-century western term, and is thus inapplicable to the Islamic context.[1] This is manifestly untrue, however: the term *ḥusn al-khaṭṭ*, which in Arabic can mean either "beauty of script" or "beautiful script" and is the exact equivalent of the Greek *kalligraphia*, occurs in Islamic sources many centuries before the eighteenth. For example, there is a *ḥadīth*, a saying attributed to the Prophet Muḥammad, that goes as follows: "man kataba bismi Allāhi al-raḥmāni al-raḥīmi bi-ḥusni al-khaṭṭi dakhala al-jannata bi ghayri ḥisāb," that is, "whoever writes the Basmala [the formula 'in the name of God, the beneficient, the merciful'] with beautiful script [ḥusn al-khaṭṭ] shall enter paradise without accounting." Though it is likely that this ḥadīth is a later fabrication, as it does not appear in the canonical compilations, even so it certainly far antedates the eighteenth century, and its wide circulation and several extant versions suggest the existence of a certain tradition.[2] There is also another saying that is only slightly different, and goes as follows: "man kataba bismi Allāhi al-raḥmāni al-raḥīmi fa-jawwadahu ghafar Allāhu lahu," that is, "whoever writes the Basmala and beautifies it, God shall forgive him [for his sins]."[3] This one does not explicitly say "calligraphy," but it does have a stronger provenance, having been included in Imām Suyūṭī's (1445–1505) collection of ḥadīths.

---

1   Carol Garrett Fisher, "Introduction," in *Brocade of the Pen: The Art of Islamic Writing*, ed. eadem (East Lansing, Mich., 1991), ix, where private communications with Oleg Grabar and Heath Lowry are credited for the idea.

2   Several sayings along these lines appear in Nefes-zâde İbrahim, *Gülzarı Savab*, ed. Kilisli Muallim Rifat (İstanbul, 1939), 36–37. Nefes-zâde died in 1650.

3   Müstakīm-zâde Süleyman Sadeddin, *Tuhfe-i Hattâtîn*, ed. İbnülemin Mahmud Kemal [İnal] (İstanbul, 1928), 10, where the ḥadīth is attributed to the Imām Suyūṭī.

Even if we allow that the Prophet Muḥammad may have been entirely silent on the subject of calligraphy, still there is no doubt that the term *ḥusn al-khaṭṭ* was used in Islamic sources before the eighteenth century. For example, the celebrated poem *al-Qaṣīda al-rā'iyya* (Poem on the Letter Rā) by the great calligrapher Ibn Bawwāb (d. 1022) begins with the couplet "yā man yurīdu ijādata al-taḥrīri / wa yarawmu ḥusna al-khaṭṭi wa al-taṣwīri," roughly, "O you who aspire to beautifying writing / and desire beautiful script [*ḥusn al-khaṭṭ*] and drawing."[4] This poem was included by Ibn Khaldūn (1332–1406) in his *Muqaddimah*, and was widely read and commented upon in the centuries that followed. A couple of centuries later, the earliest known Ottoman treatise on the Islamic arts of the book, written by Mustafa Âlî of Gallipoli in 1587, begins with a discussion of "the essentialness of writing and the honorableness of calligraphy,"[5] a word that he renders precisely as *ḥusn al-khaṭṭ*.

In short, we can safely lay to rest the idea that the term "calligraphy" is not applicable to the Islamic context. If anything, looking at early Qur'ān manuscripts in chronological fashion makes it clear that beautiful writing was on the agenda from quite an early date. Arabic script at the time of the Prophet was anything but aesthetic. By the ninth century, however, barely two centuries later, scribes charged with writing down the Revelation were giving letters and groups of letters more and more refined forms, the only purpose of which was aesthetic (fig. 9.1). And as these forms became more standardized, writing acquired an increasingly pictorial character. Beginning in the tenth century, this pictoriality was enhanced through the development of several highly ornamented variants of Kūfī script. While the details of this process remain uncertain, it would appear that the elaboration of the apexes of some vertical letters gradually led to

plaited, foliated, and floriated scripts that, to a degree, sacrificed legibility for decorative effect.[6] In some manuscripts, and especially in architectural inscriptions such as the superb dome of the Seljuk-era Karatay *madrasa* in Konya (1251),[7] writing and ornamentation combined in ways that blurred the distinction between script and image.

This trend may be said to have reached its zenith in the anthropomorphic and zoomorphic inscriptions that became fashionable during the twelfth and thirteenth centuries, first emerging in Khorasan and spreading west into Mesopotamia.[8] As Richard Ettinghausen put it, this "rather remarkable phenomenon . . . seems to stem mainly from two converging impulses: the general tendency to elaborate the letters, and the tendency between the 10th and 13th centuries to develop floral and other ornament into birds, animals, or human beings."[9] D. S. Rice distinguished three main types of figural inscription.[10] In the first, ascenders end in human heads; according to Barbara Brend, this style was known as *waqwaq* after the legendary tree bearing humanlike fruits.[11] In the second, inscriptions are composed entirely of human or animal figures; Rice dubbed this "animated script." And in the third, which he aptly named "inhabited," animals fill in the spaces between individual letters.

---

4   For the Arabic text, see Muḥammad Bahjat al-Atharī, *Taḥqīqāt wa-ta'līqāt 'alā kitāb al-Khaṭṭāṭ al-Baghdādī 'Alī ibn Hilāl al-mashhūr bi-Ibn al-Bawwāb* ([Baghdad], 1958), 31–33; an English translation, though not one that I have followed here, is given in Ibn Khaldûn, *The Muqaddimah: An Introduction to History*, trans. Franz Rosenthal (Princeton, 1967), 2:388–89.

5   Mustafa Âlî, *Menâkıb-ı Hünerverân*, ed. İbnülemin Mahmud Kemal [İnal] (İstanbul, 1926), 8.

6   See, e.g., Adolf Grohmann, "The Origin and Early Development of Floriated Kufic," *BIE* 37, no. 2 (1954–55): 273–304, republished in *Ars Orientalis* 2 (1957): 183–213. It has been suggested recently that floriation was sometimes not purely decorative, but rather served to emphasize certain important words in architectural inscriptions, thus conveying public messages about spatial hierarchy in the urban realm. See Bahia Shehab, "Fāṭimid Kūfī Epigraphy on the Gates of Cairo: Between Royal Patronage and Civil Utility," in *Calligraphy and Architecture in the Muslim World*, ed. Mohammad Gharipour and İrvin Cemil Schick (Edinburgh, 2013), 275–89.

7   See, e.g., Mehmet (Emin) Eminoğlu, *Karatay Medresesi Yazı İncileri* (Konya, 1999), 54–85.

8   Adolf Grohmann, "Anthropomorphic and Zoomorphic Letters in the History of Arabic Writing," *BIE* 38, no. 1 (1955–56): 117–22; and Thérèse Bittar, "Les écritures animées," in *L'Étrange et le merveilleux en terres d'Islam: Paris, Musée du Louvre, 23 avril–23 juillet 2001*, ed. Laurence Posselle (Paris, 2001), 83–90.

9   Richard Ettinghausen, "Islamic Art," *BMMA* 33, no. 1 (1975): 50.

10   D. S. Rice, *The Wade Cup in the Cleveland Museum of Art* (Paris, 1955), 22.

11   Barbara Brend, *Islamic Art* (Cambridge, Mass., 1991), 92.

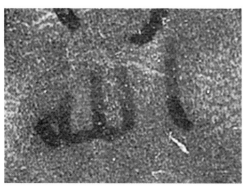 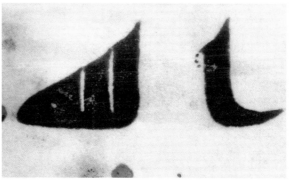

Figural inscriptions of this kind were used almost exclusively on metalwork, and to date several masterpieces bearing such inscriptions have come to light. These include the Bobrinsky bucket (1163) at the State Hermitage Museum, which is the earliest dated example; the Wade cup and Mosul ewer at the Cleveland Museum of Art; the Fano cup at the Cabinet des médailles in the Bibliothèque nationale de France; a bronze penbox (1210–1211) and a canteen at the Freer Gallery; the Zodiac ewer and a copper basin at the Musée du Louvre; and finally the Blacas ewer and another ewer at the British Museum.[12] Only a few of these are signed, and those signatures likely belong to the metalworkers, not the calligraphers. Whether or not the animated inscriptions were actually designed by the metalworkers themselves is unknown; indeed, even the precise identity of the metalworkers remains uncertain.[13] In his treatise *Gulistān-i hunar* (ca. 1606), Qāḍī Aḥmad b. Mīr Munshī al-Ḥusaynī mentioned

a calligrapher by the name of Maḥmūd Chapnivīs, also known as Majnūn, who "invented a style of writing in which combinations of letters formed images of men and beasts."[14] Given that Majnūn lived around the turn of the sixteenth century,[15] however, he was certainly not the originator of animated script.[16]

There is no denying that inscriptions in figural writing are difficult to decipher. Rice's pioneering study of the Wade cup and Yousif Mahmud Ghulam's more recent reconstruction of the inscriptions on a number of metallic objects have revealed the fact that animated inscriptions mainly feature "generic" content such as benedictions or prayers for the item's owner, often without explicitly naming him.[17] For example, on the top of one of the British Museum's ewers lies the inscription "al-ʿizz wa'l-baqāʾ wa'l-madḥa wa'l-sanaʾ wa'l-rifʿa wa'l-ʿalāʾ wa'l-ʿāfiya wa'l-shifāʾ wa'l-birr wa'l-ʿaṭāʾ li-ṣāḥibihi abadan" ("glory and endurance and praise and laudation and eminence and high standing and health and gratification and reverence and award to its

12 Richard Ettinghausen, "The Bobrinski 'Kettle': Patron and Style of an Islamic Bronze," *GBA* 24, no. 920 (1943): 193–208; Rice, *The Wade Cup*; Richard Ettinghausen, "The 'Wade Cup' in the Cleveland Museum of Art, Its Origin and Decorations," *Ars Orientalis* 2 (1957): 327–66; Ernst Herzfeld, "A Bronze Pen-Case," *AI* 3, no. 1 (1936): 35–43; Laura T. Schneider, "The Freer Canteen," *Ars Orientalis* 9 (1973): 137–56; D. S. Rice, "Inlaid Brasses from the Workshop of Aḥmad al-Dhakī al-Mawṣilī," *Ars Orientalis* 2 (1957): 283–326; Dorothy G. Shepherd, "An Early Inlaid Brass Ewer from Mesopotamia," *Bulletin of the Cleveland Museum of Art* 46, no. 1 (1959): 4–10; R. H. Pinder-Wilson, "An Islamic Bronze Bowl," *BMQ* 16, no. 3 (1951): 85–87; Esin Atıl, W. T. Chase, and Paul Jett, *Islamic Metalwork in the Freer Gallery of Art* (Washington, D.C., 1985), 102–10, 124–36; and Bittar, "Les écritures animées," 84–89.

13 Julian Raby, "The Principle of Parsimony and the Problem of the 'Mosul School of Metalwork'," in *Metalwork and Material Culture in the Islamic World: Art, Craft, and Text; Essays Presented to James W. Allan*, ed. Venetia Porter and Mariam Rosser-Owen (London and New York, 2012), 11–85.

14 *Calligraphers and Painters: A Treatise by Qāḍī Aḥmad, Son of Mīr-Munshī*, trans. V. Minorsky, with an introduction by B. N. Zakhoder, trans. T. Minorsky (Washington, D.C., 1959), 132–33.

15 Mehdī Bayānī, *Aḥvāl ve āsār-i khoshnivīsān* (Tehran, 1358), 3:611–16.

16 It is worth noting that the Turkish sociologist, pedagogue, and amateur calligrapher İsmayıl Hakkı Baltacıoğlu argued from 1904 onward that Arabic letters originally arose from the human form. See, e.g., "Türk Yazılarının Tedkikine Medhal," *Dârülfünûn İlâhiyât Fakültesi Mecmu'ası* 2, nos. 5–6 (1927): 119–20; and *Türklerde Yazı Sanatı* (Ankara, 1958), 17–19. Though certainly interesting, this hypothesis is without merit since the forms of Arabic letters as we now know them evolved over a long period of time.

17 Rice, *Wade Cup*, 21–33; and Yousif Mahmud Ghulam, *The Art of Arabic Calligraphy* ([Lafayette, Calif., 1982]), 300–379.

FIG. 9.1.
The name Allah in two documents written approximately two centuries apart. Left: in a letter reputed to have been sent in 628 by the Prophet Muḥammad to Mundhir b. Sāwā al-Tamīmī, ruler of Qatar (Chamber of the Holy Relics, Topkapı Palace Museum, 21/397); right: in a Qurʾān manuscript in Kūfī script, ninth century (The Nasser D. Khalili Collection of Islamic Art, KFQ 44).

Photos courtesy of Topkapı Palace Museum (left) and © The Nour Foundation, courtesy of the Khalili Family Trust (right).

owner, forever").[18] The waqwaq style, in which this inscription is written, is quite a bit easier to decipher than the animated inscription on the Wade cup (fig. 9.2), which, however, is very similar in content: "al-'izz wa'l-iqbāl wa'l-dawla wa'l-sa'āda wa'l-salāma wa'l-rāḥa wa'l-rutba wa'l-ni'ma wa'l-'āfiya wa'l-dawāma wa'l-ziyāda wa'l-kifāya wa'l-'ināya wa'l-baqā' dā'im li-ṣāḥibihi" ("glory and prosperity and fortune and happiness and soundness and comfort and rank and benefaction and health and permanence and plentifulness and sufficiency and providence and endurance everlasting to its owner").[19]

By contrast, inscriptions containing specific information, such as names and dates, were generally written in simpler and easier-to-read scripts. That would suggest that objects tended to be customized with legible scripts, while animated inscriptions may have followed standard models that were not necessarily intended to be read letter by letter. Indeed, Jonathan Bloom writes, "as artists explored the possibilities of animated inscriptions, they made the form of the inscription increasingly complex while allowing the content of the inscription to become increasingly banal. . . . Apparently, animated inscriptions were never designed to convey particularly significant information such as the names and titles of a patron or an artist: they were appropriate only for generalized good wishes."[20] This brings to mind the question as to whether or not the anthropomorphic and zoomorphic forms of the animated inscriptions had any discernible meaning at the time they were produced. In other words, were they simply ornamental, or did they contribute meaning to their textual content?

The answer to this question is not known with any certainty, but Bloom has suggested the following:

The content was intelligible even if the inscription was illegible, and a line of figures engaged in the hunt or revelry, for example, would immediately be understood as conveying good wishes, whether or not Arabic letters could be discerned among the limbs. . . . The form of the inscription signifies its content: one does not need to read the inscription to understand it, one only needs to recognize its form. . . . The decorative panels . . . should then be understood as signs rather than 'mere decoration.'[21]

In other words, the images of hunters and revelers represented the good life wished upon the object of the benediction. If this hypothesis is true, then we have here a fascinating example of *iconicity* in the sense used by Charles Sanders Peirce, for whom an icon signified its object by sharing certain attributes with it, that is, through resemblance and similarity—as, for instance, in the case of onomatopoeia.[22] To put it another way, if the form of the inscriptions did not necessarily *add* to the meaning of their textual content, it did convey that meaning graphically by conjuring the hoped-for good life.

Another example of the blending of writing and pictures is the so-called *gulzār* (flower-bed) style popular in nineteenth-century Iran, in which the outlines of letters are filled in with pictures.[23] This can also be related to inscriptions in *ghubārī* (dust) script, in which the outlines of letters or pictures are filled in with microcalligraphy.[24] In neither case, as a rule, do the pictures and writing constitute a semantic unit. To put it another way, the images and the textual content of the inscription do not share a common meaning, and therefore do not mutually reinforce each other. However there were, particularly in the Ottoman Empire, works of calligraphy in which form actually added to or enhanced the meaning of the text. Before discussing further the complex relationship

---

18 Ghulam, *Art of Arabic Calligraphy*, 313.

19 Rice, *Wade Cup*, 26. This inscription is also discussed by Ettinghausen ("'Wade Cup,'" 330–32 n. 4), who offers two alternative readings for Rice's al-raḥma (mercy): al-zīna (beauty, ornament) and al-rutba (rank, dignity). He suggests that the latter is more likely, and I agree wholeheartedly.

20 Jonathan M. Bloom, "A Mamluk Basin in the L. A. Mayer Memorial Institute," *Islamic Art* 2 (1987): 19.

21 Ibid., 19–20.

22 See *The Collected Papers of Charles Sanders Peirce*, ed. Charles Hartshorne and Paul Weiss (Cambridge, Mass., 1931–58), 2: §§247–49.

23 See, e.g., *Islamic Calligraphy/Calligraphie islamique*, exh. cat. (Geneva, 1988), 128–29.

24 For an Ottoman example dated 1573, see Filiz Çağman and Şule Aksoy, *Osmanlı Sanatında Hat* (Istanbul, 1998), 60–61.

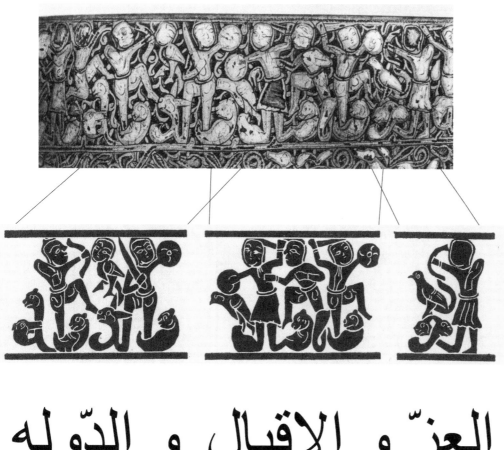

FIG. 9.2.
The first few words of the animated inscription on the Wade cup: "glory and prosperity and fortune." Seljuk Iran, early thirteenth century.

Illustration by the author after D. S. Rice, *The Wade Cup in the Cleveland Museum of Art* (Paris, 1955), pl. 2 and fig. 20.

العزّ و الاقبال و الدّوله

between form and content in such works, it will be useful to review briefly two basic concepts in the context of Islam: image and text.

Image: Figurative Art versus Iconophobia

Received opinion holds that the prominence of calligraphy in the Muslim world is due to a purported Islamic ban on representational art. This widely held (and thoroughly modern) view is problematic on many counts. First and foremost, it is exceptionally ethnocentric, in that it takes the European historical experience as normative. In fact, not even all European societies have produced figurative art: Cycladic art, for example, has a very important abstract component. Furthermore, this view fails to account for why abstract art emerged in western Europe around the turn of the twentieth century, when and where there was most assuredly no prohibition of images. And finally, it explains neither

the immense popularity of calligraphy in China and Japan, where there is no ban on figurative representation, nor the relative (and I emphasize "relative") unimportance of calligraphy in the Judaic tradition, given the extreme iconophobia of the Hebrew Bible.

Second, whether or not there is a prohibition of images in Islam, the fact remains that an enormous number of figurative images were produced throughout history, from the eighth-century wall paintings of Quṣayr ʿAmra (including nudes) to miniatures, textiles, and metalwork. Furthermore, the production of these works was not a marginal or illicit activity; quite to the contrary, it was heavily patronized by the ruling elite. Thus, it is not possible to attribute the prevalence of calligraphy to the absence of images, because there was no such absence in the first place. It is true, of course, that figurative images of humans or animals are generally not present in places of worship. However, there is a long history of objecting not only to images in mosques but also to inscriptions.[25] For example, a treatise entitled *Thimār al-maqāṣid fī dhikr al-masājid*, written in the second half of the fifteenth century by Yūsuf ibn Ḥasan ibn al-Mibrad, contains a chapter detailing the "abhorrence" of any decoration on a mosque that distracts one from prayer, specifying "gold or silver or pictures or colors or writing."[26] Thus, the unwillingness to decorate places of worship does not single out pictures.

There are, of course, floral decorations in mosques, which brings up the difference between images of animate and inanimate objects. Islam is generally said to prohibit images of animate objects only, a view that appears to be supported by the following ḥadīth: "Those who make these images will be punished on the Day of Judgment, and it will be said to them: 'Make alive what you have created.'"[27] Another ḥadīth says that he who makes pictures "will be in the fire of Hell. The soul will be breathed in every picture prepared by him and it shall punish him in Hell."[28] In fact, however, the distinction between animate and inanimate is quite foreign to Islam. For instance, it is said in the Qur'ān: "Have you not seen that, before God, prostrate themselves those that are in the heavens and those that are on the earth, and the sun, and the moon, and the stars, and the mountains, and the trees, and the animals, and many of mankind; and there are many too that deserve suffering. He whom God has scorned, no one can honor. Verily God does what He wills."[29] In other words, there is nothing fundamentally different between animals, trees, and mountains. They all bow down in worship before God. Therefore, distinguishing animate objects from inanimate ones is at best artificial, and the aforementioned ḥadīths call for a more nuanced interpretation.

The question that needs to be answered, therefore, is whether or not there really is a prohibition of images in Islam. This is a subject about which many volumes have been filled, and the present treatment will necessarily be cursory.[30] Contrary to the general view, which holds that Islam is fundamentally and unequivocally iconophobic, the licitness of figurative representation has been debated within the Muslim world since at least as early as the tenth century.[31] This debate has its roots in the fact that the Qur'ān does not prohibit such representations, and while the ḥadīths do betray some hostility toward them, their attitude is far from unambiguous.

The Qur'ān is by and large silent on the subject of figurative representation. Two verses may be construed as relevant to the issue. One says: "O ye who believe! Intoxicants and games of chance and idols and divining arrows are only an infamy of Satan's handiwork. Avoid it, so that you may succeed."[32] The word rendered here as "idols," *anṣāb*, specifically means "erected stones" and has sometimes been interpreted more generally as "statues," leading to a sweeping prohibition of all figurative representation. This is, however, only a minority opinion.

The other pertinent verse refers to jinns who were given license by God to serve Solomon. It goes as follows: "They made for him what he willed, of sanctuaries and representations and basins like wells and cauldrons firmly anchored.

---

25 See İrvin Cemil Schick and Mohammad Gharipour, "Introduction," in Gharipour and Schick, *Calligraphy and Architecture in the Muslim World*, 1.

26 Yūsuf ibn Ḥasan ibn al-Mibrad, *Thimār al-maqāṣid fī dhikr al-masājid*, ed. Muḥammad As'ad Ṭalas (Beirut, 1943), 170–72.

27 Bukhārī, *Libās*, 162, 173; Muslim, *Libās wa Ziynah*, 141, 148.

28 Muslim, *Libās wa Ziynah*, 147.

29 al-Ḥajj 22:18.

30 See, e.g., Sir Thomas W. Arnold, *Painting in Islam: A Study of the Place of Pictorial Art in Muslim Culture* (Oxford, 1928), 1–40; K. A. C. Creswell, "The Lawfulness of Painting in Early Islam," *AI* 11–12 (1946): 159–66; M. Ş. İpşiroğlu, *İslâmda Resim Yasağı ve Sonuçları* (İstanbul, 1973); Rudi Paret, *Schriften zum Islam*, ed. Josef van Ess (Stuttgart, 1981); G. R. D. King, "Islam, Iconoclasm, and the Declaration of Doctrine," *BSOAS* 48, no. 2 (1985): 267–77; Daan van Reenen, "The *Bilderverbot*: A New Survey," *Der Islam: Zeitschrift für Geschichte und Kultur des islamischen Orients* 67, no. 1 (1990): 27–77; Jean-François Clément, "L'Image dans le monde arabe: Interdit et possibilités," in *L'Image dans le monde arabe*, ed. G. Beaugé and Jean-François Clément (Paris, 1995), 11–42; Ahmad Mohammad Issa, *Painting in Islam: Between Prohibition and Aversion* (Istanbul, 1996); Yūsuf al-Qaraḍāwī, *al-Islām wa al-Fann* (Amman, 1996); Silvia Naef, *Y a-t-il une "Question de l'image" en Islam?* (Paris, 2004); and Almir Ibrić, *Das Bilderverbot im Islam: Eine Einführung* (Marburg, 2004).

31 See, e.g., Bishr Farès, "Philosophie et jurisprudence illustrées par les Arabes: La querelle des images en Islam," in *Mélanges Louis Massignon* ([Damascus], 1957), 77–109.

32 al-Mā'idah 5:90.

Labor, O House of David, with gratitude, [but] few among my servants are grateful."[33] Here, the word translated as "representations" is *tamāthīl*, which can also be rendered as "depictions," "images," or "statues." Since the verse states that the jinns had acted with God's permission, commentators wishing to support the prohibition of images resorted to arguing that while this may have been licit in Solomonic times, any such earlier authorization had been abrogated by Islamic law. That is a weak argument, however, and in any event it is clear that no explicit proscription of figurative representation exists in the Qur'ān.

By contrast, there are a number of ḥadīths (two of which are mentioned above) that show the Prophet Muḥammad's disapproval of at least some images in certain contexts. In the canonical ḥadīth collections, sayings that deal with pictures are mostly assembled in the sections dedicated to dress (*libās*). This is because in the Prophet's Arabia, the media on which pictures most often appeared were Byzantine, Coptic, or Persian textiles used either in clothing or as home furnishings. In a widely circulated account, the Prophet is reported to have said: "Angels do not enter a house in which there is a dog or there are pictures (*taṣāwīr*)."[34] In one version, factors that keep angels away also include a "man made impure by sexual defilement."[35] In these sayings, pictures are qualified by association as impure and polluting. This is somewhat curious, as the culprit in most versions of the story that occasions the ḥadīth, relating to the failure of the archangel Gabriel to meet the Prophet at the appointed time, turns out to be a dog; references to other polluting objects, notably images, seem gratuitous in this context. Nevertheless this ḥadīth has been systematically used as evidence of the unlawfulness of figurative representation in Islam.

The word *taṣāwīr* (singular: *taṣwīr*) is derived from a root that signifies "to form, fashion, or create," and the subject of such action, *muṣawwir*, can mean either "a painter or draftsman," or "one

who shapes or creates." In a number of ḥadīths, the Prophet is said to have stated that "the people who will receive the harshest punishment from God will be the muṣawwir."[36] To understand the extreme severity of this judgement, it is important to note that al-Muṣawwir is mentioned in the Qur'ān as one of the attributes/names of God: "He is Allāh, the Creator, the Maker out of naught, the Fashioner [al-Muṣawwir]. His are the most beautiful names. All that is in the heavens and in the earth glorifies Him. And He is the Mighty, the Wise."[37] In other verses, the related verb *ṣawara* is used to denote God's creative action, and the noun *ṣūrat* to denote its result: "He it is who fashions you [*yuṣawwirukum*] in the wombs as He pleases. There is no god but Him, the Mighty, the Wise";[38] "He created the heavens and the earth in accordance with truth. He has fashioned you [*ṣawwarakum*] and has made your shapes [*ṣuwarakum*] beautiful. And unto Him is the journeying";[39] "O Man! What is it that lures you away from your Lord, the Bountiful, who created you, then formed, then proportioned you into whatever shape [*ṣūratin*] your Lord pleased?"[40] Under these circumstances, it was but a short step to consider a *muṣawwir* one who arrogates to him/herself the creative act that is properly God's. According to the Prophet, "God has said: 'Who would be a greater evildoer than one who tries to create the like of My creatures? Let them create a seed, let them create an atom.'"[41] If figurative representations are at all prohibited in Islam, then they are so only to the extent that they attempt to imitate God's creation.

It is partly in this context that Islamic attitudes toward figurative representation must be considered, but matters are more complicated still. A well-known ḥadīth relates the story of a carpet or curtain that the Prophet's wife 'Ā'isha had hung at the door of her apartment.[42] The

33 Sabā' 34:13.

34 Bukhārī, *Libās*, 160, 167, 170, 171; Muslim, *Libās wa Ziynah*, 121, 123, 125; Abū Dāwūd, *Libās*, 132, 137, 138; Ibn Mājah, *Libās*, 100–2.

35 Abū Dāwūd, *Libās*, 132.

36 Bukhārī, *Libās*, 161; Muslim, *Libās wa Ziynah*, 145–47.

37 al-Ḥashr 59:24.

38 Āl 'Imrān 3:6.

39 al-Taghābun 64:3.

40 al-Infiṭār 82:6–8.

41 Bukhārī, *Libās*, 164; Muslim, *Libās wa Ziynah*, 150.

42 Bukhārī, *Libās*, 165, 166, 169; Muslim, *Libās wa Ziynah*, 130–41; Abū Dāwūd, *Libās*, 133, 135, 138; Ibn Mājah, *Libās*, 104.

curtain is said to have had pictures on it, and one version of the ḥadīth states that the Prophet complained: "Whenever I enter the room I see them and it brings to my mind worldly life."[43] Most noteworthy is what actually ended up happening to the curtain. According to several versions of the ḥadīth, ʿĀʾisha "made a pillow or two out of it" by cutting it up and stuffing it with date-palm fibers.[44] Indeed, in some versions, she even states "I saw the Prophet (prayers and blessings of God be upon him) reclining against one of them."[45] This clearly shows that it was not the pictures themselves that he had found objectionable, but their prominent display, particularly in the room in which he prayed. Most likely he felt that it uncomfortably harked back to the not-so-distant past of idolatry, when the Arabs of his tribe prostrated themselves before the effigies of various deities.

All this does not, of course, mean that there were no iconophobic interpretations of the scriptures. One of the most uncompromising is due to the Shāfiʿī scholar Muḥyi al-Dīn Abū Zakariyā Yaḥyā b. Sharaf al-Nawawī (1234–1278), who wrote in his commentary on *Ṣaḥīḥ Muslim*:

Painting a picture of any living thing is strictly forbidden, and it is among the capital sins, because it is threatened with severe punishment as mentioned in the ḥadīths, whether it is intended for ordinary everyday use or some other purpose. So the making of it is forbidden under every circumstance, because it implies a likeness to the creation of God (may He be exalted), whether it is on a garment, or a carpet, or a *dirham*, or a *dīnār*, or a *fals* [all three are coins], or a vessel, or a wall, or on anything else.... Similarly, it is forbidden to make use of any object on which a living thing is pictured, whether it is hung on a wall, or worn as a garment or a turban, or is on any other object of ordinary everyday use. But if it is on a carpet that is trampled on, or on a pillow or cushion, or another such object for ordinary everyday use, then it is not forbidden.[46]

Be that as it may, pictures—both figurative and otherwise—were produced in large numbers in the Muslim world. To be sure, this is not uniformly true everywhere, but one would be hard pressed to establish an inverse correlation between the presence of figurative art and the popularity of calligraphy. In short, hostility to images is not the source of the popularity of calligraphy. Then what is? Here, it is necessary to take a closer look at Islamic doctrine, which gives enormous importance to the written text.

Text: The Centrality of Writing

A saying attributed to the Prophet (on the authority of ʿUbādah ibn al-Ṣāmit) goes as follows: "The first thing that God created was the pen. And He said to it: 'Write!' It said: 'Lord, what should I write?' He said: 'Write down the destiny of all things until the final hour.'"[47] The pen is therefore in some sense the agent of God's will, for it is through it that all things—past, present, and future—were recorded and thereby made manifest. It is stated numerous times in the Qurʾān that "His command, when He intends a thing, is only that he says unto it 'Be!' and it is,"[48] and that is indeed the reason reference has been made to "the pen of the command 'Be!'" (Ottoman: "hâme-i emr-i kün").[49] Just as the writing pen represents the enactment of the Divine Will, so too is God's creation represented by a written text.

The ninety-sixth sura of the Qurʾān, al-ʿAlaq, begins as follows: "Read! In the name of thy Lord who has created—created man from a clot. Read! And thy Lord is the most bounteous, Who teaches by the pen, taught man that which he knew not."[50] The word "Read!" (*iqraʾ*, sometimes also translated as "Proclaim!" or "Recite!") is, according to tradition, the very first word of

43 Muslim, *Libās wa Ziynah*, 130.

44 Bukhārī, *Libās*, 165; Muslim, *Libās wa Ziynah*, 129, 136–40; Abū Dāwūd, *Libās*, 133, 138; Ibn Mājah, *Libās*, 104.

45 Ibn Mājah, *Libās*, 104; Muslim, *Libās wa Ziynah*, 142.

46 Muḥyi al-Dīn Abū Zakariyā Yaḥyā b. Sharaf al-Nawawī, *al-Minhāj fī Sharḥ Ṣaḥīḥ Muslim b. al-Ḥajjāj*, ed. Wahbah al-Zuḥaylī (Beirut and Damascus, 1994), 14:267.

47 Abū Dāwūd, *Sunnah*, 16.

48 Yā-Sīn 38:82.

49 Müstakīm-zâde, *Tuhfe-i Hattâtîn*, 7.

50 al-ʿAlaq 96:1–5.

the Divine Revelation. Based on the account of the Prophet's wife 'Ā'isha, it is related that Muḥammad would go into seclusion in a cave to meditate, when the archangel Gabriel appeared to him and ordered him to read.[51] It was the signs of God that the Prophet was enjoined to read—signs written with the Divine pen for the edification of humankind.

The motif of writing and reading is ever present in the foundational texts of Islam. At the beginning of the sixty-eighth chapter of the Qur'ān, significantly named al-Qalam or "the pen," God takes an oath "By the pen and that which they write (with it)"—an oath, in other words, by everything that has been, is, and will be, and by the very agent that makes them all happen.[52] The pronoun "they" in the verse is generally interpreted as referring to angels.[53] Indeed, angels engaged in the act of writing are alluded to more than once; for example, an account attributed to the Prophet (on the authority of Abū Dhar) describing his miraculous ascension to the heavens (Mi'rāj) includes the following fascinating detail: "Then Gabriel ascended with me to a place where I heard the creaking of the pens."[54] This was interpreted as angels busily recording the Divine Decrees, and anyone who has witnessed a scribe or calligrapher writing with a reed pen will know precisely what the verb "creaking" refers to.

It is stated in the Qur'ān, "Verily, over you are guardians, noble scribes, who know what you do."[55] A similar idea appears in a number of prophetic sayings, notably a hadīth qudsī (related by Abū Hurayra), according to which the Prophet reported that God said to the angels:

If My slave intends to do a bad deed, then do not write it [in his record] unless he does it; if he does it, then write it as it is, but if he refrains from doing it for My sake, then write it as a good deed. If he intends to do a good deed, but does not do it, then write a good deed; and if he does it, then write it for him as ten good deeds up to seven hundred times.[56]

Another saying attributed to the Prophet (on the authority of 'Abdullāh bin Mas'ūd) related the stages of development of an embryo in the womb; at a certain time, "God sends an angel who is ordered to write four things: he is ordered to write down his deeds, his livelihood, his death, and whether he will be blessed or wretched. Then the soul is breathed into him."[57] Such written records about a person transform his/her life into a text, one that shall speak either in his favor or against him on the Day of Judgment. Little wonder, under the circumstances, that the sentence "It was fated" is often rendered into Arabic as "written" (maktūb), and one's fate is described in Turkish as "the writing on the forehead" (alın yazısı).

The text implied in the verse "By the pen and that which they write (with it)" cited earlier is of a somewhat different nature, however, as it relates to the totality of events that are to take place between the moment of creation and the end of time. The very popular late fifteenth-century Qur'ānic commentary Tafsīr al-Jalālayn interprets the pen in this verse as that "with which He wrote the universe in the 'preserved tablet' [lawḥ al-maḥfūẓ]."[58] This interpretation was based in part upon a prophetic saying: according to 'Abdullāh ibn 'Abbās, the Prophet related that when God created the pen and ordered it to write, the pen immediately began to inscribe the "preserved tablet."[59] In turn, this term alludes to the Qur'ānic verses "Nay, this is a glorious Qur'ān in a preserved tablet."[60]

To make a very long story short, the concept of writing is fundamental to Islam. Indeed, although an individual Muslim can, of course, be illiterate, it is impossible to imagine Islam as a religious and cultural system without text, writing, and reading. Rather than attributing the popularity of calligraphy in the Muslim world to a negative cause, namely the Muslims' purported inability to make pictures, it is more appropriate

51 Bukhārī, Bad' al-Waḥiy, 3.

52 al-Qalam 68:1.

53 Jalāl al-dīn Muḥammad ibn Aḥmad al-Maḥallī and Jalāluddīn 'Abd al-Raḥman ibn Abī Bakr al-Suyūṭī, Tafsīr al-Qur'ān al-'aẓīm ([Cairo], AH 1342), 2:230.

54 Bukhārī, Salāt, 1.

55 al-Infiṭār 82:10–12.

56 Bukhārī, Tawḥīd, 124.

57 Bukhārī, Bad' al-Khalq, 18.

58 al-Maḥallī and al-Suyūṭī, Tafsīr al-Qur'ān al-'aẓīm, 2:230.

59 Nefes-zâde, Gülzarı Savab, 31.

60 al-Burūj 85:21–22.

to see calligraphy as a natural expression of the centrality of writing in Islamic culture.

Given the importance of written text within Islam, it should come as no surprise that it has also played a vital role in the daily lives of many Muslims. Indeed, the caliph ʿAlī ibn Abī Ṭālib is reported to have said, "Knowledge is fugitive; tie it down with writing," while his contemporary and rival Muʿāwīyah ibn Abī Sufyān similarly said, "He who relies on memory is deceived, and he who relies on the record is contented."[61] These are all forceful statements in support of textual practices in early Islam. Some rulers' awareness of the importance of written text is strikingly illustrated by a statement attributed to the ʿAbbāsid caliph al-Maʾmūn, son of the illustrious Hārūn al-Rashīd, who was quoted by Abū Ḥayyān al-Tawḥīdī as having said, "How wonderful is the reed pen! How it weaves the fine cloth of royal power, embroiders the ornamental borders of the garment of the ruling dynasty, and keeps up the standards of the caliphate."[62]

Since the Revelation was first set to writing, Arabic script has been charged with preserving it. Though it was hardly a worthy vessel when first recruited for this holy mission, it gradually became one, as efforts were made to beautify and standardize it. Eventually, the script that preserves the word of God came to be perceived as a Godly script. Arabic writing became a metonym for the Divine order, for the connection between God and His creation. In turn, inscribing objects with Arabic writing came to denote their enlistment in the divinely ordered system that is Islam. Far from simply serving an ornamental function, as some have suggested, such inscriptions represent a conscious effort at textually marking the man-made universe and reappropriating it in the name of God. Hence, inscribing objects with Arabic script actually amounts to making *explicit* their true nature (*fiṭrah*), their membership in the community of God.

This may also help answer the common question as to whether or not Islamic inscriptions were necessarily intended to be read. It has often been claimed that calligraphy is primarily ornamental; that texts are generally meaningless, full of errors, or illegible; and that those that do have a discernible meaning are usually haphazardly chosen or formulaic. For example, Ettinghausen wrote that "to be effective as a communication, an inscription has to appeal to a literate person in his own language with clear, legible characters without nearby distractions. . . . It is at once clear that Arabic inscriptions in often highly ornate mosques and other religious buildings throughout the Muslim world cannot be communications of the same nature—to be read by all and sundry."[63]

What is surprising about this argument and others like it is that they are so often binary: either calligraphy is meant to be read, or it is not; either it contains meaningful text or it is purely ornamental. In fact, of course, some lean one way and some the other. Many inscriptions are clear and eminently readable, and then again, others are fanciful with only the most tenuous ties to plain text—the animated writing discussed earlier being a case in point. Even more important, however, is the fact that such terms as "reading" and "legibility" are culturally specific at a very fundamental level; that is, they do not mean the same thing to everyone, in every location, and in every age. At a time when literacy was not as widespread, and when the division between orality and literacy not as firmly established, as they are today, an inscription would certainly have been processed differently. Many calligraphic inscriptions would have contained texts familiar to large segments of the population, who would have been able to "read" (that is, recognize) them after deciphering no more than a word or two. In particular, this would certainly have been true of Qurʾānic inscriptions on the walls of mosques and other sacred buildings. In addition, many inscriptions were meant to be talismanic or apotropaic; their purpose was not to be read by the average person, but to embody the power of the Word for an otherworldly audience.

61 Nefes-zâde İbrahim, *Gülzar-ı Savab*, 32, 38.

62 Franz Rosenthal, "Abū Ḥayyān at-Tawḥīdī on Penmanship," in *Four Essays on Art and Literature in Islam* (Leiden, 1971), 39.

63 Richard Ettinghausen, "Arabic Epigraphy: Communication or Symbolic Affirmation," in *Near Eastern Numismatics, Iconography, Epigraphy, and History: Studies in Honor of George C. Miles*, ed. Dickran K. Kouymjian (Beirut, 1974), 299–300.

In short, whether or not they can be read letter by letter, calligraphic inscriptions are very seldom purely decorative. On the contrary, they are repositories of meaning, and, as we shall see, the medium often adds to the message.

Beyond Text: The Content of Form[64]

The literal meaning of calligraphy is "beautiful writing," but Islamic calligraphy is sometimes more than that. A calligraphic composition sometimes entails a certain "value added" in the sense that it conveys more meaning than the same words would have if they had been recited or written as plain text.

There is a long tradition of letter symbolism in the literatures of Muslim societies.[65] Thus, in Ottoman poetry, the letter alif (١) was likened to the beloved's slender stature; mīm (م) to her mouth; jīm (ج) to a lock of hair curling around her ear; nūn (ن) to her eye and eyebrow; sīn (س) to her teeth; the dot (*nuqta*) to a mole on her fair skin, and so forth. These images were combined in countless ways, as in the following couplet by the poet Bâkî (1526–1600):

Dehânın mîm zülfün cîm kaşın nûn olmuştur
Seni ey zülfî Leylâ her gören Mecnûn
   olmuştur[66]

Your mouth becomes a mīm, your hair jīm,
   your eyebrows nūn

and anyone who lays eyes on you, O beauteous Leylā, becomes Majnūn.

Here, the lover's name—Majnūn, meaning "crazed, mad with passion"—is composed of letters that mime the beloved Leylā's features, offering a mystical interpretation of the well-known romance of Leylā and Majnūn. Just as the love of the lover is the mirror image of the beauty of the beloved, so too does Man's loving quest for God derive without mediation from His absolute beauty.

Another nice example is afforded by Sultan Süleyman I (1494/95–1566), known to Turks as "The Lawgiver" and to Europeans as "The Magnificent," who was a poet of some distinction writing under the pen name Muhibbî. In the following couplet, he teasingly refers to the beauty mark right above the lips of his beloved in terms of Arabic script:

Hâl-i müşkînün dehânun üzre düşmişdür
   galat
Komadı hattatlar âdet değül mîme nukat[67]

Your musk-black mole must have landed
   above your mouth by mistake
for it is not customary for calligraphers to
   dot the letter mīm.

Another use of the dot motif is the following playful reproach by Fuzûlî (1495–1556), a contemporary of Sultan Süleyman's:

Ham ettin kaametim tek terk-i ser kıldımsa
   mâ'zurum
Ne özrüm var eğer der olsa olmaz nokta dâl
   üzre[68]
You have bent my back, so if I took leave of
   my head, I must be forgiven
for what excuse would I give, were I told
   "the letter *dāl* does not take a dot"?

The image here is based upon a comparison of the letters dāl (د) and dhāl (ذ), which are identical

64 The resemblance between this subtitle and the title of Hayden White's well-known book is unintentional but fortuitous.

65 See, e.g., Dursun Ali Tokel, *Divan Şiirinde Harf Simgeciliği* (Istanbul, 2003); Annemarie Schimmel, *Mystical Dimensions of Islam* (Chapel Hill, 1975), 411–25; eadem, *Calligraphy and Islamic Culture* (New York and London, 1984), 115–47; eadem, *A Two-Colored Brocade: The Imagery of Persian Poetry* (Chapel Hill and London, 1992), 228–44; Shaker Laibi, *Soufisme et art visuel: Iconographie du sacré* (Paris, 1998), 74–86; Cheref-Eddîn Râmi [Ḥasan ibn Muḥammad Sharaf al-Dīn al-Rāmī], *Anîs el-'Ochchâq: Traité des termes figurés relatifs à la description de la beauté*, trans. Cl[ement] Huart (Paris, 1875); and Franz Rosenthal, "Significant Uses of Arabic Writing," text of a lecture presented at the meeting of the American Oriental Society in Ann Arbor, Mich., in April 1959, reprinted in *Ars Orientalis* 4 (1961): 15–23 and in Rosenthal, *Four Essays*, 50–62.

66 *Bâkî Dîvânı*, ed. Sadettin Nüzhet Ergun (Istanbul, 1935), 416.

67 *Muhibbî Dîvânı: İzahlı Metin*, ed. Coşkun Ak (Ankara, 1987), 410.

68 *Fuzûlî Dîvânı*, ed. Abdülbâkî Gölpınarlı (Istanbul, 1961), 139.

save for the dot. Because of the crooked shape of the letter dāl, the word *dâlî* ("dāl-like") was sometimes used in Ottoman to mean "hunchbacked"; this letter, moreover, was often contrasted to the upright alif, to indicate a stooped posture due to exhaustion, old age, or defeat. Hence the double entendre: unlike dhāl, the letter dāl is not dotted, hence the hunched ("dāl-like") poet must lose his head!

There are countless similar examples in Arabic, Persian, and Ottoman poetry, but lyric poetry was not the only area where the shape of letters provided a rich fount of metaphors; mysticism also made extensive use of letter symbolism. The Qur'ān proclaims: "And We shall show them Our signs in the horizons and in themselves,"[69] and some Muslim thinkers sought such signs in the appearance of human beings. For example, the seventeenth-century Ottoman mystic Oğlanlar Şeyhi İbrahim Efendi (d. 1655) taught that "from head to toe, the form of man exhibits the word of God; as such, instances of the shape of His proper name can be perceived in some of his features."[70] Note that it is the *word* of God that is manifested in the form of man, and not His image. Islamic tradition regards God as absolutely transcendent, and representing His form would have simply been inconceivable for a Muslim;[71] it is only through the mediation of text, that is, by means of his word, that God is manifested in the form of man.

The five fingers of the hand, for example, were likened by some mystics to the five vertical strokes in the name Allāh.[72] The positions taken by the body during daily prayers—standing, genuflection, and prostration—were likewise likened to the letters alif, dāl, and mīm, which, taken together, constitute the name Ādam (fig. 9.3). This was seen as illustrating the fact that prayer is a human being's central function.

Some mystics likened a man who has turned his back on all worldly possessions, devoting himself entirely to God, to the letter alif—the first letter of the alphabet, whose stark verticality and numerical value of one testify to the uniqueness of God. Relatedly, the posture of a Mawlawī ("whirling") dervish was interpreted as affirming the existence of God through a textual reference to the first part of the Muslim profession of faith, "lā ilāha illā Allāh" ("there is no god but God"). The letters lām and alif spell out the word *lā*, "there is not," but with the addition of another alif, they become *illā*, "except for." When superimposed, the compound lām-alif and the additional alif look very much like a Mawlawī dervish in his robes, performing the *semâ*.[73] Thus, the body of the dervish, corresponding to the additional alif, makes the difference between denial (lā) and re-affirmation (illā).

Such imagery also found its way into works of calligraphy, notably in pictorial calligraphies that abound throughout the Muslim world, particularly Turkey, Iran, and India.[74] Many of these are relatively modern, but not all. For example, a scroll dedicated to the Ottoman sultan Mehmed II (known as "The Conqueror") contains the Qur'ānic verse "fa Allāhu khayrun ḥāfiẓan wa huwa arḥamu al-rāḥimīn" ("but God is better at guarding, and He is the most merciful of those who show mercy")[75] in the form of a bird, and the invocation "Amīr al-mū'minīn 'Alī ibn Abī Ṭālib karam Allāhu wajhahu al-ghālib wa raḍī Allāhu 'anhu" ("prince of the believers,

69 Ḥā-mīm 41:53.

70 Cited (from a manuscript copy of *Sohbetnâme* in his personal library) byAbdülbâki Gölpınarlı, *Tasavvuf'tan Dilimize Geçen Deyimler ve Atasözleri* (Istanbul, 1977), 4.

71 This is not to say that anthropomorphist tendencies never existed in the Muslim world, but they were largely marginal. See, e.g., Michel Allard, *Le problème des attributs divins dans la doctrine d'al-Aš'arī et de ses premiers grands disciples* (Beirut, 1965); Binyamin Abrahamov, ed., *Anthropomorphism and Interpretation of the Qur'ān in the Theology of al-Qāsim ibn Ibrāhīm: Kitāb al-Mustarshid* (Leiden, 1996); Merlin Swartz, ed., *A Medieval Critique of Anthropomorphism: Ibn al-Jawzī's Kitāb Akhbār as-Sifāt* (Leiden, 2002); Abū Bakr Muḥammad ibn al-Ḥasan ibn Fūrak al-Isbahānī al-Ash'arī, *Kitāb Mushkil al-Ḥadīth; aw Ta'wīl al-Akhbār al-Mutashābiha*, ed. Daniel Gimaret (Damascus, 2003); Daniel Gimaret, *Dieu à l'image de l'homme: Les anthropomorphismes de la sunna et leur interprétation par les théologiens* (Paris, 1997); and Nedim Macit, *Kur'an'ın İnsan-Biçimci Dili* (Istanbul, 1996).

72 For illustrations of this and other examples described here, see İrvin Cemil Schick, *Bedeni, Toplumu, Kâinâtı Yazmak: İslâm, Cinsiyet ve Kültür Üzerine*, ed. and trans. Pelin Tünaydın (Istanbul, 2011), chap. 3.

73 The semâ is the ceremony that gave the "whirling" dervishes their name.

74 For examples, see Malik Aksel, *Türklerde Dinî Resimler: Yazı-Resim* (Istanbul, 1967); and Chaubey Bisvesvar Nath, "Calligraphy," *The Journal of Indian Art and Industry* 16, no. 124 (1913).

75 Yūsuf 12:64.

184   İRVİN CEMİL SCHICK

FIG. 9.3. The positions taken by the body during daily prayers—standing, genuflection, and prostration—likened to the letters alif, dāl, and mīm, spelling the name Ādam. Calligraphy by Mohamed Zakariya (2001).

Author's collection.

'Alī son of Abū Ṭālib, may the generosity of God be upon his victorious countenance, and may God be pleased with him") in the form of a lion (fig. 9.4). The scroll is the work of 'Aṭā Allāh Muḥammad of Tabriz, and is dated 1458.[76] A calligraphic horse formerly in the collection of Stuart Cary Welch contains the Throne Verse, one of the best known verses in the Qur'ān that describes God's absolute power.[77] It is undated, but was probably made in the late sixteenth century in India, possibly Bijapur in the Deccan.[78] An Ottoman calligraphic inscription in the form of a ship contains the names of the Seven Sleepers (aṣḥāb al-kahf) and their dog.[79] It is signed İsmail Derdi and dated 1690.[80]

Valérie Gonzalez has distinguished between works of pictorial calligraphy in which the text and image share a *single* referent, and those in which their referents are *distinct*.[81] The examples above include both cases. In the bird and the horse, for instance, there is no obvious relationship between form and content. On the other hand, the lion contains an invocation of the caliph 'Alī ibn Abī Ṭālib, whose nicknames were *khaydar* ("lion") and *asad Allāh* ("lion of God"); thus, the fact that the inscription is shaped like a lion emphasizes the caliph's nickname. Such lion-shaped calligraphic compositions were quite popular among Alevîs belonging to the Bektashi order.[82] Likewise, the fact that the ship contains the names of the Seven Sleepers is significant because the Ottoman navy was believed to have been entrusted to them, and their names were often written on the ships.[83]

It is not difficult to see the logic behind the latter category, where form and content enjoy a direct connection; the reason for writing a prayer, say, or a Qur'ānic verse in the form of a bird, a horse, a ewer, or a mosque is less obvious. It has been suggested that such pictorial calligraphic compositions were a way of getting around the prohibition of figurative representation—in other words, a means of licit cheating (*hile-i şeriyye*). This explanation is overly simplistic, however, and fails to understand the meaning

76 Topkapı Palace Museum, E.H. 2878, reproduced in David J. Roxburgh, ed., *Turks: A Journey of a Thousand Years, 600–1600* (London, 2005), 288–89.

77 "Allāhu lā ilāha illā huwa al-ḥayyu al-qayyumu lā ta'khudhuhu sinatun wa lā nawmun lahu mā fī al-samāwāti wa mā fī al-arḍi man dhā alladhī yashfa'u 'indahu illā bi'idhnihi ya'lamu mā bayna aydīhim wa mā khalfahum wa lā yuḥīṭūna bishayin min 'ilmihi illā bi-mā shā' wasi'a kursīyyuhu al-samāwāti wa al-arḍa wa lā ya'ūduhu ḥifẓuhumā wa huwa al-'aliyyu al-'aẓīmu" ("Allah! There is no God save Him, the Alive, the Eternal. Neither slumber nor sleep overtakes Him. Unto Him belongs whatsoever is in the heavens and whatsoever is in the earth. Who is he that intercedes with Him save by His leave? He knows that which is in front of them and that which is behind them, while they encompass nothing of His knowledge save what He will. His throne includes the heavens and the earth, and He is never weary of preserving them. He is the Sublime, the Tremendous.") al-Baqara 2:255.

78 This work is reproduced in Anthony Welch, *Calligraphy in the Arts of the Muslim World* (Folkestone, UK, 1979), 180–81. It was sold at Sotheby's, London, 6 April 2011, sale L11227, lot 99.

79 The story of the Seven Sleepers and their dog is told in the Qur'ān, al-Kahf 18:9–26. While their names do not appear in the Qur'ān, various versions were (and remain) popular in Turkey and elsewhere.

80 Topkapı Palace Museum, G.Y. 325/66, reproduced in Çağman and Aksoy, *Osmanlı Sanatında Hat*, 83.

81 Valérie Gonzalez, "The Double Ontology of Islamic Calligraphy: A Word-Image on a Folio from the Museum of Raqqada (Tunisia)," in *M. Uğur Derman 65th Birthday Festschrift*, ed. İrvin Cemil Schick (Istanbul, 2000), 313–40.

82 Aksel, *Türklerde Dinî Resimler*, 83–89; J. M. Rogers, *Empire of the Sultans: Ottoman Art from the Collection of Nasser D. Khalili* (London, 1995), 258–59.

83 See L[ouis] Massignon, "Les sept Dormants d'Éphèse (Ahl-al-Kahf) en Islam et en Chrétienté: Recueil documentaire et iconographique," Part 7, *REI* 29, no. 1 (1961): 9–11.

FIG. 9.4.
The invocation
"prince of the
believers, ʿAlī son of
Abū Ṭālib, may the
generosity of God be
upon his victorious
countenance, and
may God be pleased
with him" in the
form of a lion. From
a scroll signed ʿAṭā
Allāh Muḥammad
of Tabriz (1458).
Topkapı Palace
Museum, E.H. 2878.

Photo courtesy of
Topkapı Palace
Museum

of writing in the Islamic worldview. Moreover, it overlooks the fact that the societies where such works of pictorial calligraphy were most commonly produced—Turkey, Iran, and India—were precisely the societies in which figurative images were most plentiful. The question is why such works of pictorial calligraphy were made.

In the Qurʾān, mention is repeatedly made of God's signs, which provide incontrovertible proof of the existence of God and of the truth of His prophets. Yet, while these signs will confirm the faith of those capable of discernment, they can also reinforce unbelief on the part of those unwilling to be guided. Doubters who demanded special evidence from past prophets or from the Prophet Muḥammad were denied miracles, for God has placed his signs in plain sight for the wise to see:

> Behold! In the creation of the heavens and the earth; in the alternation of the night and the day; in the sailing of the ships through the ocean for the profit of mankind; in the rain which God sends down from the skies, and the life which He gives therewith to an earth that is dead; in the beasts of all kinds that He scatters through the earth; in the change of the winds, and the clouds which they trail like their slaves between the sky and the earth; [Here] indeed are signs for a people that are wise.[84]

In short, it is incumbent upon believers to read God's creation, to perceive His signs throughout, and to interpret them correctly as proof of both His power and His mercy. Calligraphic images are, in a way, akin to an x-ray image that exposes the normally invisible skeleton, which is in truth the supporting scaffolding of the human body, without which the latter would collapse. Calligraphic images foreground the "signs of God" that have been hidden in His creation, but are there as proof for those who can see them. They are, therefore, nothing less than visual confirmation of the Muslim faith, naturalizing the

84   al-Baqarah 2:164.

FIG. 9.5.
The Caliph ʿAlī
driving the camel
carrying his own
coffin, with his sons
Ḥasan and Ḥusayn
in tow. Anonymous
Alevī-Bektashī
calligraphy, Turkey,
nineteenth century.

Author's collection.

artist's belief system by projecting it onto the weft of daily existence.

As for the pictorial calligraphies in which text and image share a single referent, these are rarer but often much more interesting. An example is the stork-shaped inscription designed by the Ottoman calligrapher Abdülgani Efendi in 1763.[85] It survived as a stencil, from which several copies were subsequently made. The text forming the bird is a couplet about a certain dervish known in his day as Seyyid Hasan Leylek Dede. Here, Hasan was his given name, *seyyid* indicates that he was a direct descendant of the Prophet, *dede* is a title indicating that he had some seniority in the dervish order, and the word *leylek* is Turkish for "stork." It is said that the dervish earned this nickname because he was very tall and lanky. The poem that composes the image celebrates the devotion of this dervish to his master, Mawlānā Jalāluddīn al-Rūmī. It reads as follows:

Aşk-ı Mevlânâ ile hayretzede
Mevlevî Seyyid Hasan Leylek Dede

Ecstatic with love for Mawlānā
Mawlawī Sayyid Hasan Leylek Dede.

What is most important here is that the text and the image are related at a very basic level. The text speaks of a dervish known by the nickname "the Stork," and it is also written in the shape of a stork.

Another popular theme in pictorial calligraphy concerns a well-known story about Caliph ʿAlī.[86] He is said to have predicted his own assassination to his sons, Ḥasan and Ḥusayn. After the murder, he told them, a camel driver would arrive; they were to load his coffin onto the camel and follow the driver wherever he went (fig. 9.5). His predictions came true: a mysterious camel driver wearing a veil arrived, and the caliph's sons loaded the coffin and ʿAlī's famed sword, the *dhūlfiqār*, onto the camel. Then they followed the camel and its driver into the desert. Eventually they tired and begged the camel driver to stop and show his face. He lifted his veil and revealed himself to be their father, who

85   Aksel, *Türklerde Dinî Resimler*, 77–78; Schick, *Bedeni, Toplumu, Kâinâtı Yazmak*, 36–37.

86   See John Kingsley Birge, *The Bektashi Order of Dervishes* (London and Hartford, Conn., 1937), 139, 237; Aksel, *Türklerde Dinî Resimler*, 99–102; and Frederick De Jong, "The Iconography of Bektashiism: A Survey of Themes and Symbolism in Clerical Costume, Liturgical Objects and Pictorial Art," *Manuscripts of the Middle East* 4 (1989): 8.

FIG. 9.6.
"The well-being of
the hearts [depends
on] the coming-
together of the
lovers." Inscription
on the Sultan
Bâyezîd II Bridge on
the Sakarya River,
signed 'Abd Allāh,
1495/1496, Geyve,
Adapazarı, Turkey.

Photograph by
Mehmed Özçay

had risen from the dead. The panels illustrating this story are remarkably narrative: Caliph 'Alī himself is constituted by an invocation (here, "madad yā 'Alī" or "help, O 'Alī") or ḥadīth ("anā madīna al-'ilm wa 'Alīyun bābuhā" or "I am the city of knowledge and 'Alī is its gate"); his sons Ḥasan and Ḥusayn are made up of their own names; and so forth.[87]

Sometimes the pictorial calligraphy is quite subtle. A relatively early architectural example, this one from the late fifteenth century, is the inscription on the Sultan Bâyezîd II Bridge on

the Sakarya River in the town of Geyve, province of Adapazarı, in Turkey (fig. 9.6). It is dated 901 AH (1495/96 CE). The text is in Arabic, and says "shifā' al-qulūb liqā' al-maḥbūb" ("The well-being of the hearts [depends on] the coming-together of the lovers.") This is certainly an apt inscription for a bridge, but there is a very interesting detail in the calligraphy that deserves a more careful look. The inscription is written twice in mirror-images, a style that is called *muthannā* or "doubled." This in itself is not unusual. However, mirrored calligraphies are usually divided into left and right halves, that is, the axis of symmetry is usually vertical. Here, on the other hand, it is horizontal, which makes the calligraphy look very much like a bridge and its reflection in the river. Indeed,

---

87 For more on images of Caliph 'Alī and his camel, see İrvin Cemil Schick, "Hz. Ali ve Devesi Levhaları," in *Deve Kitabı*, ed. Emine Gürsoy Naskali and Erkan Demir (Istanbul, 2014), 5–40.

another curious detail about this inscription is that instead of beginning on the right-hand side, it begins on the left, and therefore the writing is upside-down. This may well be because the upside-down letters *bā* represent the arches of the bridge. In short, this is both text and picture.

A much more sophisticated example is a work by the Turkish calligrapher Mustafa Halim Özyazıcı (1898–1964) (fig. 9.7). Dated 1348 AH (1929/30 CE), this panel is composed of two parts. The text in the form of a hand is a well-known verse from the Qur'ān that reads: "wa mā arsalnāka illā raḥmatan li al-ʿālamīn" ("and we have not sent you but as mercy to the worlds").[88] It is spoken by God to the Prophet Muḥammad, and is taken to mean that the latter's mission is evidence of God's grace. Under the hand are two lines of poetry in Turkish, which say:

> Ne kadar müznib olsam da yine olmam
> gam-nâk
> Hüccet-i rahmet iken elde: "Ve mâ
> erselnâk(e)"

> No matter how great a sinner I may be, I do
> not grieve
> So long as proof of mercy is in hand: "And
> we have not sent you"

In other words, the Qur'ānic verse stating that the Prophet has been sent to humanity by God as an act of mercy is written in the form of a hand, just as the affirmation it represents is "in hand" by virtue of the sacred revelation. Here, the text and the image share a single referent, and the meaning of the text corresponds exactly to the meaning of the image into which the text has been woven. The same verse could have been written as plain script, and no matter how beautiful the script, it would not have conveyed the full range of meanings that this masterpiece embodies.

The examples discussed so far all have a rather discernible pictorial component, but in fact what at first sight appears to be plain text can also simultaneously be an image. A case in point is the genre known as *hilye-i şerîfe* or *hilye-i saadet*, apparently invented in the late seventeenth century by the Ottoman calligrapher

Hâfız Osman Efendi (1642–1689) (fig. 9.8).[89] These are "word portraits" of the Prophet Muḥammad, describing, within a recognizable composition, his physical and moral attributes. There are a number of recorded descriptions of the Prophet's appearance, of which the most popular is the one by Caliph ʿAlī as recorded in Tirmidhī's (824–892) *al-Shamāʾil*, a compilation of narratives relating to the Prophet. With slight variations, the central medallion contains the following text:

> [It is related] from ʿAlī (may God be pleased with him) that when he described the attributes of the Prophet (may prayers to God and peace be upon him), he said: He was not too tall, nor was he too short, he was of medium height amongst the nation. His hair was not short and curly, nor was it lank, it would hang down in waves. His face was not overly plump, nor was it fleshy, yet it was somewhat circular. His complexion was rosy white. His eyes were large and black, and his eyelashes were long. He was large boned and broad shouldered. His torso was hairless except for a thin line that stretched down his chest to his belly. His hands and feet were rather large. When he walked, he would lean forward as if going down a slope. When he looked at someone, he would turn his entire body toward him. Between his two shoulders was the Seal of Prophethood, and he was the last of the prophets.

That these panels were intended as portraits is clear not only from this descriptive text, but also from the fact that the components of the panel were named (from top to bottom) *başmakam* (head station), *göbek* (belly), *kuşak* (belt), and *etek* (skirt).

88 al-Anbiyā 21:107.

89 On the *hilye*, see M. Uğur Derman, *Letters in Gold: Ottoman Calligraphy from the Sakıp Sabancı Collection, Istanbul*, trans. Mohamed Zakariya (New York, 1998), 34–37; M. Uğur Derman, *Türk Hat Sanatının Şaheserleri* ([Ankara], 1982), pls. 18, 19, 42, 47, and 49; and Faruk Taşkale and Hüseyin Gündüz, *Hat sanatında hilye-i şerife / Characteristics of the Prophet Muhammed in Calligraphic Art* (Istanbul, 2006). On the calligrapher Hâfız Osman Efendi, see Derman, *Letters in Gold*, 72–74; and M. Uğur Derman, *The Art of Calligraphy in the Islamic Heritage*, trans. Mohamed Zakariya and Mohamed Asfour (Istanbul, 1998), 221.

FIG. 9.7.
"And we have
not sent you but
as mercy to the
worlds" (al-Anbiyā
21:107), followed by
a couplet in Turkish.
Mustafa Halim
Özyazıcı, dated
1929–1930, Turkey.

Author's collection.

The Arabic word *ḥilyah* refers to the features or appearance of a person, and the Ottoman compounds *hilye-i şerîfe* (noble hilye) and *hilye-i saadet* (felicitous hilye) denote the features or appearance of the Prophet Muḥammad. Tim Stanley has suggested that while the hilye may have arisen as the Muslim counterpart of the Orthodox Christian icon (in view of the fact that a figural representation of the Prophet would have been frowned upon in the Sunni tradition), it was most likely inspired by the celebrated poem known as *Hilye-i Hakānî*, written by the sixteenth-century Ottoman poet Hakānî

Mehmed Bey.[90] This poem was in turn based on a possibly spurious tradition, according to which the Prophet is reported to have said: "Whoever

90 Tim Stanley, "From Text to Art Form in the Ottoman *Hilye*," in *Studies in Islamic Art and Architecture in Honor of Filiz Çağman* (forthcoming). See also his "Sublimated Icons: The *Hilye-i Şerîfe* as an Image of the Prophet," paper read at the 21st Spring Symposium of Byzantine Studies on "The Byzantine Eye: Word and Perception," University of Birmingham, 21–24 March 1987. On the poet Hakanî Mehmed Bey (d. 1606), see E. J. W. Gibb, *A History of Ottoman Poetry* (London, 1900–1909), 3:193–98, where the name is transcribed as *Kháqání*; and Bursalı Mehmed Tâhir Bey, *Osmanlı Müellifleri*, ed. A. Fikri Yavuz and İsmail Özen (Istanbul, 1972?–75), 2:171–72.

FIG. 9.8.
Hilye-i Şerîfe
(word-portrait
of the Prophet).
Hafız Osman
Efendi, dated
1697/1698,
Turkey. Topkapı
Palace Museum
Library, G.Y.1430.

Photo courtesy of
Topkapı Palace
Museum

sees my hilye after me is as though he has seen me. And whoever is true to me, God will spare him the fire of Hell, and he will not experience the trials of the grave, and he will not be driven naked on the Day of Judgment."[91] If Hâfız

Osman did indeed draw his inspiration from the *Hilye-i Hakanî*, then he created his hilye panels primarily as objects of contemplation: "whoever sees my hilye," were the words reportedly spoken by the Prophet, not "whoever reads my hilye." As such, it is an image, albeit one made of plain text.

The four roundels at the corners often contain the names of the Four Rightly Guided

91 [Hakanî Mehmed Bey], *Hilye-i Hakanî* ([Istanbul], AH 1264), 12.

FIG. 9.9.
The names of the
Caliphs Abū Bakr and
'Umar placed between
captions. Anonymous
Ottoman devotional
manuscript, nineteenth
century, Turkey.
Private collection.

Photograph courtesy of
Atika Müzayede, Istanbul.

Caliphs of Sunni Islam. (Sometimes they contain the various titles of the Prophet Muḥammad.) Starting in the eighteenth century or so, we see an interesting new development. Devotional manuscripts began to feature pages with large medallions containing the names of God, the Prophet, the Rightly Guided Caliphs, sometimes the companions of the Prophet, and even the Seven Sleepers and their dog (fig. 9.9). What is so interesting is that often these medallions appear below (or are placed between) a caption that does nothing but state the obvious. For example, if the name Muḥammad appears in the central medallion, then the accompanying caption might say something like "This is the name of His Excellency Muḥammad, may prayers to God and peace be upon Him." If the name in the medallion is Abū Bakr, then the caption might say "This is the name of His Excellency Abū Bakr, may God be pleased with him." This is a common pattern, and begs the question, why

were the captions added in the first place? After all, if one can read the caption, then surely one can also read the central medallion.

The answer to this puzzle is that the caption refers in fact to two distinct objects: when it says "this," it is referring to the medallion below it; and when it says "the name of Muḥammad," it is referring to the proper name of the Prophet. In other words, the medallion is not identical to the name, it is an *image* of the name.[92] It is, in fact, an icon. Indeed, in many such books, virtually identical captions accompany pictures in the ordinary sense of the word, e.g., images of holy relics such as the mantle of the Prophet or his footprint. As the word for "picture," *rasmun*, is very similar to

92 With apologies to Derrida, might one perhaps refer to such inscriptions as "the signifier of the signifier of the signifier"? (Cf. Jacques Derrida, *Of Grammatology*, trans. Gayatri Chakravorty Spivak [Baltimore and London, 1976], chap. 1.)

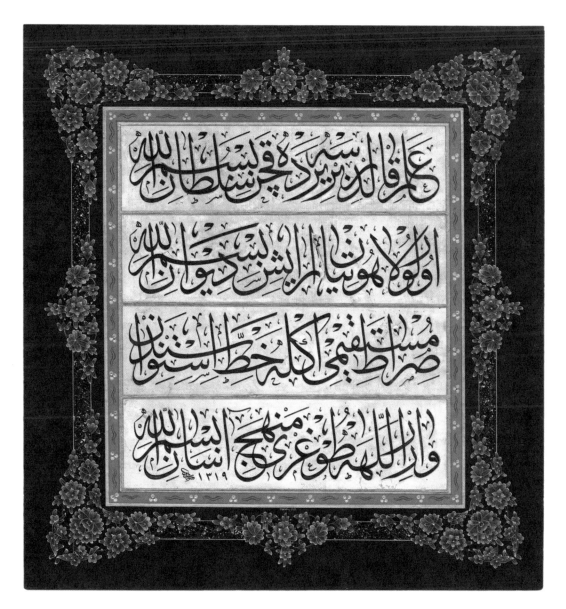

FIG. 9.10.

Poem in praise of the Basmala. Mehmed Nazif Bey, dated 1901/2, Turkey.

Author's collection.

the word for "name," *ismun*, the captions both look and sound almost exactly alike.

As a final example, it is instructive to consider a panel that produces meaning not only through its textual content but also through its form (fig. 9.10). It is by the great late Ottoman calligrapher *al-ḥajj* Mehmed Nazif Bey, who lived between 1846 and 1913. The panel is dated 1319 AH (1901/2 CE) and features a short poem in Turkish extolling the virtues of the Basmala. The poem is of no great literary value, and reads as follows:

Alem kaldırsa bir yerde kaçan sultân-ı
    Bismillâh

Olur lâhutiyân ârâyiş-i dîvân-ı Bismillâh
Sırât-ı Müstakıymi anla hatt-ı istivâsından
Varır Allâh'a doğru menhec-i âsân-ı
    Bismillâh
As soon as Sultan Bismillâh raises his flag
The angels become the pillars of the court
    of Bismillâh
Interpret its equator as al-Ṣirāṭ al-Mustaqīm
The short route of Bismillāh leads towards
    God.

The phrase "al-Ṣirāṭ al-Mustaqīm," or "the straight path," appears in the opening chapter of the Qur'ān, the Fātiḥa, and is taken to mean "the true faith," i.e., Islam. In addition, however,

Sufis believe that there is a bridge by this name that every soul is required to cross after death; it is "thinner than a hair and more trenchant than a sword," in the words of the poets, and those who fail to reach the other side will fall down into the eternal fires of Hell. Those who can cross the bridge, on the other hand, will reach the side of God.

In the poem, a visual analogy is drawn between the bridge of Ṣirāṭ and the words *Bismillāh*, by playing on the lengthened arc in the words *bismi*. In an ordinary text, these words would be written with a short arc; however, calligraphers traditionally lengthened the arc when writing this particular formula. With its lengthened arc, which the poet qualifies as an "equator" (*khaṭṭ al-istiwā*), the formula is likened to the bridge of Ṣirāṭ, which, going from right to left, leads straight to Allāh. So we have here a bit of visual iconicity. The formula Bismillāh leads the believer to God, and it actually looks like the very bridge over which the believer's soul is to reach God in the afterlife. But there is more: in the last line of the poem, where it refers to the Basmala as a "short route" that leads to God, the calligrapher has actually shortened the arc, so that once again the form of the writing echoes the meaning of the text itself.

Islamic calligraphy is beautiful to look at, and many who cannot read Arabic script enjoy it as abstract art. By the same token, many people who are perfectly fluent in Arabic, but do not have much of an appreciation for the art of calligraphy, look at this material as simple text. However, calligraphy is exclusively neither one nor the other. It is both. Form and content mutually inflect each other, and the only way to truly appreciate Islamic calligraphy is to look at it as standing between script and image, between text and representation.

Performativity:
Iconic Script and the Body

Text on/in Monuments

"Lapidary Style" in Ancient Mesopotamia

IRENE J. WINTER

ANCIENT MESOPOTAMIA DID NOT PLAY WITH ITS IDEOGRAPHIC SIGNS AND syllables. This does not mean that there was never wordplay. However, unlike the iconicized scripts of Islam, the historiated and embellished initials of the Western medieval world, or the animated hieroglyphs of pharaonic Egypt given agency by the addition of arms and legs, once Mesopotamian signs were stabilized into abstracted and legible forms, they retained their boundaries and their shapes within the scribal canon. With the possible exception of phonetic rebuses in the form of recognizable images early in the first millennium BCE,[1] distinctions between text signs and image figures were carefully maintained. And yet, there *are* things to be said about the relationship between verbal and visual representation throughout the three millennia of the Mesopotamian sequence—particularly for a volume exploring cultural and historical permutations on the relationship between textual signs and imagery.

It is my intention here to focus upon a particular subset of inscriptions in Sumerian and Akkadian, the languages of ancient Mesopotamia: those intended to be deployed and viewed in public. As a class, the works bearing inscriptions range in size from small cylinder seals, held in the hand and impressed upon clay tablets, bullae, and door and jar sealings, to large-scale, independent monuments and architecture. At both extremes, the inscribed works function "out there," in a domain where the carrier of the inscription has a material presence beyond the private exchange of information, as would have been the case in a letter from a father to a son scribed on a clay tablet, in which handwriting, that is, script-writing, could be individual and distinctive.

Because most of the examples I shall discuss are largely carved on stone rather than impressed into clay and were intended to be viewed by a public unfamiliar with the idiosyncrasies of personalized writing, the signs on monuments tend to be particularly well articulated and regular. As such, the signs both connote and contribute to legibility. They convey a formality that is seen to be part of the visual effect of the inscription. I shall refer to this group of texts on public works as executed in a "lapidary style" not unlike the regularized scripts employed on Roman triumphal arches and temples, or funerary markers from the classical world to the present. I would characterize such works, often

---

1   Irving L. Finkel and Julian E. Reade, "Assyrian Hieroglyphs," *Zeitschrift für Assyriologie* 86 (1996): 245–46, possibly derived from contact with ancient Egypt.

containing both texts and images, as expressly intended for display.[2]

In order to pursue this particular class of text inscription, I must first insist upon the distinction between sign and text. Early signs in the Mesopotamian writing system were ideographic and often pictographic, using standardized, recognizable forms to stand for substances or phenomena. In charts showing the evolution of signs from image-related to abstract (fig. 10.1), it is not difficult to see or infer the original referent—the head of an animal standing for the whole; a sheaf of wheat to indicate grain; a pair of feet to suggest motion, and thus the verb "to go"; a hand bringing a bowl to the mouth of a disembodied head as the verb "to eat."[3] Scholars who have dealt with the development of the script have noted, however, that within a relatively short period of time the written signs became "so abstract that they lost nearly all traces of their iconicity, and hence resemblance to the visual

representation."[4] Nevertheless, it is important to stress that the script began as iconic/ideographic, even if just a few centuries after the invention of writing in the fourth millennium BCE, the systems of imaging and notating had significantly and irrevocably diverged.

Jerrold Cooper, writing on the origins of writing in ancient Iraq, has defined writing as the "graphic representation of language."[5] Over the course of time, as individual signs shifted from more iconic to more abstract in order to accommodate phonemes and complex syntax, a number of signs continued to be read as whole concepts/ideas, such as the signs for "king" or "deity" and "city" or "land"; yet most also took on syllabic values that could be combined into longer words.

In distinguishing the signs employed in a writing system from legible text, the latter may be understood as content: a message in a given language inscribed using conventional signs, distinct from any pictorial accompaniment. When text and image appear together, there is a finite number of ways one may classify the relationship between the two. Relevant in the Mesopotamian case are instances that *replicate* (i.e., texts are parallel in content to accompanying imagery), *complement* (by adding additional or selected information), or *identify* (by use of an epigraphic label). Once juxtaposed, the whole becomes more than its individual parts, the message consisting of two communications, visual and verbal, both of which are part of the perception and, indeed, the nature of the overall monument.

2   Julian E. Reade, "Sargon's Campaigns of 720, 716, and 715 BC: Evidence from the Sculptures," *JNES* 35 (1976): 95–104, distinguishes two subgroups in wall texts for the reign of Sargon II of Assyria: annalistic and summary (or display) texts (on which, see below, note 36). See also John Malcolm Russell, *The Writing on the Wall: Studies in the Architectural Context of Late Assyrian Palace Inscriptions* (Winona Lake, Ind., 1999), 210; and Julian E. Reade, "Texts and Sculptures from the Northwest Palace, Nimrud," *Iraq* 47 (1985): 203–14. Yet, in a way, all texts incorporated onto palace walls have an inherent display function. This display aspect co-varies with but remains distinct from general bureaucratic uses of text. See J. N. Postgate, *Bronze Age Bureaucracy: Writing and the Practice of Government in Assyria* (New York and Cambridge, 2013), 14, for his observation that "Assyrian offers the richest material for the role of writing in Government"; also Russell, *Writing on the Wall*, 6–7, for the distinction between visible texts and hidden texts, as well as his definitions of "text" as composition, and "inscription" as applied text.

3   Ignace J. Gelb, *A Study of Writing*, rev. ed. (Chicago, 1963); C. B. F. Walker, *Cuneiform* (Berkeley and Los Angeles, 1987), 10; Béatrice André-Salvini, "L'écriture cunéiforme ou la naissance de l'écrit," in *L'Aventure des écritures: Naissances*, ed. Anne Zali and Annie Berthier (Paris, 1997), 22; Jean-Jacques Glassner, *The Invention of Writing: Cuneiform in Sumer* (Baltimore, 2003); idem, "Comment présenter l'invisible? Réflexions autour des termes *ṣalmu* et *uṣurtu*" (forthcoming). This does not mean that sign forms underwent no changes over the long Mesopotamian sequence. Rather, as with modern print fonts or tombstones, where one can differentiate the style of letterforms and spacing in 18th-, 19th-, or 20th-century inscriptions, the text nevertheless remains within a recognizable formal range of standardized, often capital, letters.

4   Jerrold S. Cooper, "Incongruent Corpora: Writing and Art in Ancient Iraq," in *Iconography without Texts*, Warburg Institute Colloquia 13 (London, 2008), 69; also Glassner, *Invention of Writing*.

5   Jerrold S. Cooper, "Babylonian Beginnings: The Origin of the Cuneiform Writing System," in *The First Writing: Script Invention as History and Process*, ed. Stephen D. Houston (Cambridge, 2004), 80–84. More recently, see Eva Cancik-Kirschbaum and Babette Schnitzlein, eds., *Keilschriftartefakte: Untersuchungen zur Materialität von Keilschriftdokumenten*, Berliner Beiträge zum Vorderen Orient 25 (Berlin, 2014); and more generally, Shai Gordin, ed., *Visualizing Knowledge and Creating Meaning in Ancient Writing Systems*, Berliner Beiträge zum Vorderen Orient 23 (Berlin, 2014). See also Anne-Marie Christin, *L'image écrite, ou la déraison graphique* (Paris, 1995), and chapter 1 of this volume for writing as the graphic representation of the spoken.

I address these points in sequence: instances of labeling, complementarity, parallelism, and bilingualism (even trilingualism) in the Mesopotamian repertoire, which I examine to illustrate how texts intended for the public sphere were operationalized. I close with observations on the need for a lapidary style in public scriptwriting. In so doing, I would like to note from the outset that whether the viewing public for such texts was literate or not, the very act/fact of writing on public works conveyed authority with respect to the monument in question and the putative author, precisely because literacy was not widely distributed within the general population. To this broader public, monumental inscriptions signaled authority by conveying the control of knowledge without actual knowledge of the text. Literacy was largely confined to cadres of specialists trained as scribes.[6] When rulers occasionally noted their being able to read and write themselves (which occurs in only two attested cases, of the third and first millennium respectively, although others may have existed),[7] it is clear that their claims were intended to imply learning, with the ruler's august status and authority augmented thereby. One must consider such elite—rulers, government officials, merchants and scribes, along with future readers and the gods—to have been the primary audience for the inscribed texts.

BIRD				
FISH				
DONKEY				
OX				
SUN				
GRAIN				
ORCHARD				
PLOUGH				
BOOMERANG				
FOOT				

FIG. 10.1.
Chart of the development of writing in Mesopotamia, after I. J. Gelb, *A Study of Writing*, rev. ed. (Chicago, 1963).

Photograph courtesy of the Oriental Institute Museum, University of Chicago.

Texts on Monuments: Labels

Given the present archaeological record, it would seem that signs used to represent words began pictorially sometime during the fourth millennium BCE.[8] As writing developed, one of the earliest uses of signs in conjunction with images was, apart from economic and lexical records, to provide labels for ambiguous scenes or figures, much like early Greek black-figure vase painting.[9] This is what Roland Barthes refers to as an anchor for otherwise generic or multivalent imagery.[10] Such a use in Mesopotamia may be seen on relief plaques of circa 2500 BCE that occasionally identify the principal figure—for example, the ruler Ur-Nanše of Lagash of the Early Dynastic III period (fig. 10.2).[11] The

6 On which, see Giuseppe Visicato, *The Power and the Writing: The Early Scribes of Mesopotamia* (Bethesda, Md., 2000), and a number of studies, such as Niek Veldhuis, *Elementary Education at Nippur* (Groningen, 1997), on scribal training in early Mesopotamia.

7 For example, Ashurbanipal in the 7th century BCE (on which see André-Salvini, "L'écriture cunéiforme," 23, and Russell, *Writing on the Wall*, 7).

8 See note 3, above, and also Holly Pittman, "Towards an Understanding of the Role of Glyptic Imagery in the Administrative Systems of Proto-literate Greater Mesopotamia," in *Archives Before Writing*, ed. Piera Ferioli (Rome, 1994), 177–203, for the relationship between early writing and imagery.

9 François Lissarague, "*Graphein*: Écrire et dessiner," in *L'image en jeu de l'antiquité à Paul Klee*, ed. Christiane Bron and Effy Kassapoglu (Yens-sur-morges, 1992), 189–202.

10 Roland Barthes, "Rhetoric of the Image," in *Image, Music, Text* (New York, 1977), 32–51.

11 See images in Anton Moortgat, *The Art of Ancient Mesopotamia: The Classical Art of the Near East* (London and New York, 1969), figs. 109–12. And for the continuing

principal figure is not only labeled in the sense of being named, but is also provided with epithets as, "the man who built a/the temple to the god Ningirsu." The text then "quickens the image," in Barthes's terms; and for some works, text is further used to identify additional characters, such as Ur-Nanše's sons, whose bodies are marked both by personal name and the logogram for "offspring." In this way, they, too, have a public presence on the plaque: both in the ruling lineage, and presumably as potential office holders.

This tradition of labeling images is a technique that persists over the following two thousand years. It has been discussed at length with respect to the use of epigraphic labels in

---

discussion that includes the "Standard of Ur" and the full depiction of the stela of Eannatum of Lagash, see also ibid., figs. 18–21 and Irene J. Winter, "After the Battle Is Over: The 'Stele of the Vultures' and the Beginning of Historical Narrative in the Ancient Near East," in *Pictorial Narrative in Antiquity to the Middle Ages*, ed. Herbert L. Kessler and Marianna Shreve Simpson (Washington, D.C., 1985), 11–32.

Neo-Assyrian narrative reliefs.[12] In one well-known example, the ruler Sennacherib (seventh century BCE) is clearly named and titled as King of Assyria on a relief image from the Southwest Palace at Nineveh, in which he receives prisoners and booty following the siege of Lachish in Palestine, modern Israel (fig. 10.3).[13]

12 Pamela Gerardi, "Epigraphs and Assyrian Palace Reliefs: The Development of the Epigraphic Text," *Journal of Cuneiform Studies* 40 (1988): 1–35; preceded by Julian E. Reade, "Narrative Composition in Assyrian Sculpture," *Baghdader Mitteilungen* 10 (1979): 52–110, esp. 96–101. See then the lengthy discussion by Russell, *Writing on the Wall*, 156–81, on the Assurbanipal reliefs and epigraphs recounting the king's battle against the Elamite ruler Teumman, from Room XXXIII of the Southwest Palace at Nineveh. There, it is clear that the complexity of the visual narrative virtually requires that clarification be provided by textual references. Note also that the increase of the use of epigraphic labels by Assurbanipal corresponds with a trend begun by his grandfather Sennacherib at Nineveh to curtail full-slab inscriptions in the palace, ending with their marked absence in the palace of Assurbanipal (ibid., 244).

13 Richard D. Barnett, Erika Bleibtreu, and Geoffrey Turner, *Sculptures from the Southwest Palace of Sennacherib at Nineveh,*

Other examples abound, but I discuss only two, in order to stress the importance of reducing ambiguity and heightening historical specificity through the use of such labels. First, in an attempt to underscore the importance of the introduction of text on the Ur-Nanše plaques, and on works of subsequent rulers of the city-state known as Lagash, it is useful to see them in the context of other mid-third-millennium images, such as those from Ur. On an inlaid trapezoidal box known as the "Standard of Ur" found in one of the royal tombs, a dominant figure likely to be the ruler is depicted on the front and back of each of the long sides—once in a battle context and again at banquet—with no attendant scriptural signs. From Lagash, however, on

the reverse of a relatively contemporary royal stela commemorating a victory over the neighboring city-state of Umma, the ruler Eannatum is clearly identified on the reverse (see detail, fig. 10.4b). He is shown in his chariot in the second register from the top, accompanied by proximate cuneiform signs located between his face and upraised left arm. These signs are distinct from the lengthy narrative account inscribed on the two faces of the stela. Contemporary audiences in Ur and Lagash would likely have been able to recognize the principal status of the male figures in each example, and perhaps even identify them immediately as rulers, due to known conventions of attributes and compositional dominance. However, the label on the Eannatum stela clearly serves to reduce uncertainty and provide historical specificity, which, I would argue, is a prime function of a text *on* an image.

The second instance of labels I want to note occurs on later Assyrian reliefs, when a battle

2 vols. (London, 1998), pl. 345 (slab 435c); Russell, *Writing on the Wall*, 287–88; also idem, "Sennacherib's Lachish Narratives," in *Narrative and Event in Ancient Art*, ed. Peter J. Holliday (Cambridge, 1993), 55–73. The text reads: "Sennacherib, king of the world, king of Assyria, sat on a *nemēdu*-throne and the booty of the city of Lachish passed in review before him."

scene is accompanied by text in order to identify enemy citadels. By these identifying rubrics, there is no question as to where the depicted event is taking place (see, e.g., fig. 10.3). This practice, too, constitutes a prime function of the epigraph-cum-label: the historical and topographical specificity of events and places represented. The desire for such specificity injects the element of time into the original conception of the life of the monument; that is, if the intended audience was not merely the contemporary generation but also a future generation, as is often stated explicitly in Mesopotamian royal inscriptions, then it was important to move beyond the generic figure of the Standard of Ur. There, the contemporary viewer might easily have seen a ruler, and even perhaps have identified the scene with recent history, but the written label on the stela of Eannatum allows the author to cast ahead into the future and the later viewer to look back at a particular moment/ruler from a time when specific identification might be uncertain or impossible. What this suggests to me is that conceptions of historical time necessitate the addition of label-like text on imagery as early as the third millennium BCE. The inclusion of a textual reference documents both the event and the patron, whose past achievements are thus remembered.[14]

What is more, the epigraphic identification follows a compositional pattern no less distinctive than the attributes, posture, and size of the principal figure. On Sumerian monuments, the identifying signs are placed immediately in front of the face of the individual and seem to issue directly from him (see fig. 10.4). In later periods, as discussed below, they often appear in the field immediately above the identified

entity. Such conventional placement makes clear to those reading the text, or even to those making the association of identification because of the closeness of text and visual attributes, that this was a label, not a dangling part of a longer narrative text.[15]

That labels have their own sets of conventions should come as no surprise. The category is clearly divided into several subcategories. With human figures, labels are used for the personal name of a represented figure or the name of a ruler; for titles of a given individual when an official role is part of the identity of the seal owner; or for epithets to indicate key achievements of the referent. With narrative images, the labels are used to designate the particular geographical locus, and sometimes to elaborate on action(s) taken at a site. In later Assyrian reliefs, as in those of Assurbanipal at Nineveh, multiple labels may be used to aid in following the narrative sequence in a single, complex scene (see, for example, fig. 10.10, which is a detail of a larger scene in which thirty-seven such epigraphs are included to anchor the sequence in a complex visual composition). As such, these labels offer identification, explication, and situational detail. The resultant historical specificity permits moving beyond generics to the particular and more historical narrative. The text incorporated onto the stela of Eannatum, then, marks the first preserved evidence for a continuum that extends from the third millennium BCE well into the first.[16]

14 This rather casts doubt on the evolutionary sequence provided in early studies of narrativity, which tends to assume that individuation and historical specificity began with the Greeks. Clearly the flow of ordered story beyond the merely annalistic and an anticipation of future consequences is already present in text-image relationships of Mesopotamia, well before texts claimed to be "true narrative" appear, such as that by Herodotus.

15 One such instance is seen in the identification of the ruler/patron Eannatum of Lagash on the stela also referred to as the Stela of the Vultures (fig. 10.4). It also serves as proof of the early misidentification of a figure at the bottom of the reverse of the stela, who was thought to be the ruler of a contemporary city-state of Kish by virtue of his proximity to the mention of that city in the accompanying narrative text. However, once it was seen that the juxtaposition of text to figure does *not* follow the compositional decorum of identifying labels, it had to be understood instead as part of the accompanying narrative that covers much of the obverse and reverse of the stela as a whole (on which, see Irene J. Winter, "Eannatum and the 'King of Kish'? Another Look at the Stele of the Vultures and 'Cartouches' in Early Sumerian Art," *Zeitschrift fur Assyriologie* 76, no. 2 [1986]: 205–12).

16 It is interesting to note that unlike Greek vase painting, where labels frequently are used to name objects and identify individuals from mythological and literary traditions (Lissarague, "*Graphein*: Écrire et dessiner"), in Mesopotamia they are used to identify deities, historical persons, and events.

b

FIG. 10.4.

(a) Reverse and (b) detail of second register on the reverse, Stela of Eannatum of Lagash, Telloh, Early Dynastic III period, limestone. Musée du Louvre, Paris, AO 50+2436+8+16109.

© RMN-Grand Palais / Art Resource, NY.

a

Texts on Monuments: Complementarity

The question of complementarity between textual inscription and imagery is also illustrated by the stela of Eannatum of Lagash, for identifying labels are not the only text applied to that monument. Both extended text and imagery were spread over the two sides of the stela, and may be seen in the detail illustrated here as forming the background behind the two registers (figs. 10.4a–b). The imagery on both obverse and reverse is drawn from a specific portion of the text: the antecedents to, enactment, and immediate consequences of the conflict between Lagash and Umma. On the obverse, one sees Ningirsu, the chief deity of the city-state of Lagash, as the icon of victory, holding the defeated enemy in a net; while on the reverse, we see the ruler enacting the story of the encounter through narrative time, to ultimate victory.[17] What is interesting here is not only that two different sorts of textual signs are deployed on the stela—labels and extended narrative—but also that the imagery represents only a selected portion of the action conveyed in the text. The two therefore overlap, but the latter is more inclusive.

17   Winter, "After the Battle Is Over."

A rather different circumstance of complementarity appears on the well-known Law Stela of Hammurabi of Babylon, dated to the first half of the second millennium BCE (figs. 10.5 and 10.6). The laws themselves, bracketed by a prologue and an epilogue, are inscribed in sequence around the entire stela. The imagery, by contrast, exists only on the upper part of the obverse (see fig. 10.5). Through the juxtaposition of the ruler Hammurabi with the sun-god, the deity governing justice and legal authority, the imagery seems to preface the laws. The iconic representation of divine and temporal authority makes clear to any viewer the divine sanction and thereby the legitimacy of the ruler to propound this particular body of laws. However, little attention has been given to the power ascribed to the imagery on the stela as a primary factor governing the laws below. In my view, the key to this relationship lies in the epilogue. The text reads: "Let any person [man] come before my image to verify the justice of the laws."[18] Initially, it was thought that the stela might have been placed in a public space in its likely city of origin, Sippar, with a statue or relief image of the king opposite—a sort of ritual replication of the ruler himself rendering judgments. However, the textual ambiguity has since been argued to suggest instead that the reference in the epilogue is to the imagery *on* the stela, and that the imagery indeed governs as well as references the authority of the laws, which have descended through the chain from deity to ruler to enactment.[19]

The combined roles of text and image may then be seen to be complementary in that the visualization of the relationship between the ruler and the divine authority is manifested in order to underscore the authority of the ruler

18 Epilogue, reverse, col. xxivb, 59–78: Martha T. Roth, *Law Collections from Mesopotamia and Asia Minor* (Atlanta, 1997); Béatrice André-Salvini, *Le code de Hammurabi* (Paris, 2008), esp. 80.

19 See Irene J. Winter, "Art *in* Empire: The Royal Image and the Visual Dimensions of Assyrian Ideology," in *Assyria 1995*, ed. Simo Parpola and Robert M. Whiting (Helsinki, 1997), 359–81; Kathryn E. Slanski, *The Babylonian Entitlement Narûs (Kudurrus): A Study of Their Form and Function* (Boston, 2003); Paolo Brusasco, *The Archaeology of Verbal and Nonverbal Meaning* (London, 2007); André-Salvini, *Le code de Hammurabi.* For a renewal of the former position, see Glassner, "Comment présenter l'invisible?"

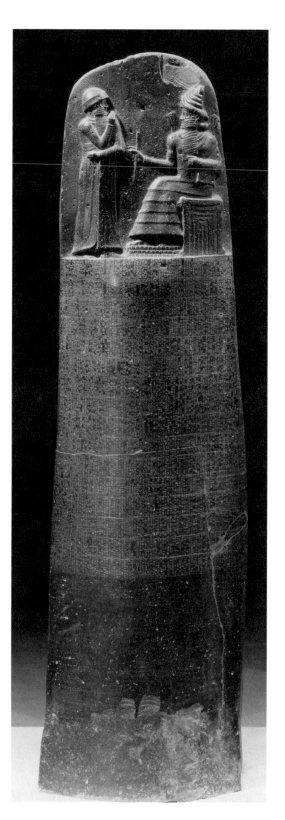

FIG. 10.5.

Law Stela of Hammurabi, Old Babylonian period, diorite. Musée du Louvre, Paris, Sb8.

© RMN-Grand Palais / Art Resource, NY.

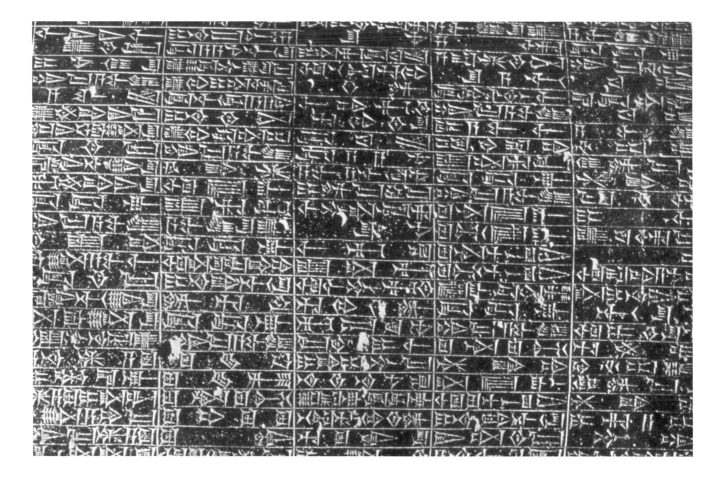

FIG. 10.6.
Detail of fig. 10.5.

in propounding the legal cases inscribed below. Neither would be sufficient in and of itself. The value and scale of the stone used conveys a sense of importance and lends to the stela all the sociopolitical weight of monument and monumentality. At the same time, the image validates both the ruler and his rules as acting with divine sanction, while the laws put forward justify the ascription to the ruler of the title "King of Justice" (Akkadian: *šar-mēšarim*), used frequently in the inscriptions of Hammurabi and other monarchs of the Old Babylonian period. Materiality, scale, imagery, and word are thus combined into the empowering of the monument and its contents at multiple levels.

As far as the material is concerned, the diorite stone of the stela does not come from the alluvial valley of ancient Mesopotamia. Scholarly debate has located its source either east, toward the coast of the South Asian subcontinent, or south, in the Gulf. What is clear is that the stone was considered to be of great value. Gudea of Lagash, ruler of the Neo-Sumerian period toward the

end of the third millennium (fig. 10.7), openly declares of his statuary: "This image is not of gold or of silver; it is of diorite!"[20] Diorite is a particularly hard stone, therefore difficult to carve. Mention of not only the name and titles of the ruler in the Gudea statues' texts, but also the precious material, underscores the status of the images, and by extension, of any work constructed of diorite.

In some examples, one sees the statuary of Gudea with the ruler's name and brief titles indicated on his shoulder. In others, a longer inscription is wrapped around the entire, usually seated, figure (e.g., fig. 10.7). And in yet others, an inscription identifying Gudea and his works is placed on his back. I have argued elsewhere that the reason for this placement is likely

20 Dietz Otto Edzard, *Gudea and His Dynasty*, The Royal Inscriptions of Mesopotamia: Early Periods 3, no. 1 (Toronto, 1997), 29–67, esp. 36: Statue B, col. vii 10–13. On the relationship between the diorite as material and the permanence/importance of the monument, see Girard and Zali, *L'aventure des écritures* (n. 3 above), 11.

FIG. 10.7.
Statue of Gudea of
Lagash, Neo-Sumerian
period, diorite. Musée
du Louvre, Paris, AO 2.

© RMN-Grand Palais /
Art Resource, NY

due to the fact that a standing image would have
been placed before a seated image of a deity in a
temple, and so the inscription would be visible
to others in the sanctuary from the rear.[21] What

seems operative here by analogy to other such
instances is that such labels are useful in two-
dimensional representations as well (such as in
some Indian miniature painting), when a figure
is seen from behind and needs to be identified
but no personal features are observable.

This is amply illustrated by the statue of
Enmetena, an earlier, mid-third-millennium

21   Irene J. Winter, "Idols of the King: Consecrated Images of
Rulers in Ancient Mesopotamia," *Journal of Ritual Studies* 7
(1992): 13–43.

ruler of Mesopotamian Lagash (fig. 10.8).[22] The band of inscription on the ruler's right arm is visible from the front, and not only identifies the ruler to the god Enlil, the deity in front of whom the image would have been placed, but it also articulates a dedication of lands to that deity, which would have been the intended communication to the god by the ruler's surrogate, the statue. A lengthier inscription is placed across the back, however, providing an extensive list of the pious building activities undertaken for various deities by Enmetena. The text identifies the ruler, provides his lineage, and includes a declaration that Enmetena has named and installed this image before the god Enlil.[23] This longer summary of activities would then have been visible (and legible) to literate priests and viewers, who by custom would have been proscribed from moving between the two dyadic images in the sanctuary, the seated god and the standing ruler.

The Gudea statues as a group, then, along with Enmetena and other examples of free-standing Sumerian sculpture, offer the complementarity of visual representation and textual identification. At the same time, however, the inscriptions can be seen as belonging to at least two subcategories: the one offering detailed information through labels that provide identification of the individual plus a brief synopsis of his credentials and achievements; the other offering expanded textual narrative relevant to the achievements of the ruler, and on occasion, details of the making and installation of, along with the ritual provisioning for, the image in the temple. In all cases, the carving of the attendant cuneiform signs is executed in the same lapidary script that conveys the formality, and hence the authority, of the content of the inscription for the public sphere.[24]

FIG. 10.8.
Frontal view, Statue of Enmetena of Lagash, Early Dynastic III period, diorite. Iraq Museum, Baghdad, IM5.

Photograph courtesy of John M. Russell.

22 Moortgat, *Art of Ancient Mesopotamia*, figs. 87–88. The present image I owe to the generosity of John Russell, who was instrumental in the return of the looted image of Enmetena to Iraq following events of 2003.

23 Jerrold S. Cooper, *Sumerian and Akkadian Royal Inscriptions*, vol. 1, *Presargonic Inscriptions* (New Haven, 1986), 63–64.

24 In those rare instances where an inscription is added later or seems an afterthought, as on the White Obelisk found at Nineveh naming "Assurnasirpal of Assyria" (Moortgat, *Art of Ancient Mesopotamia*, fig. 251), the anomaly has given rise to multiple theories of the origin and dating of the work to Assurnasirpal I, 14th c. BCE, Assurnasirpal II, 9th c. BCE, or

Texts in Palaces: Labels, Replication, and Complementarity

Materials related to this section have been the subject of considerable inquiry for the Neo-Assyrian period.[25] With respect to reliefs, on which most of the recovered texts have been found (see figs. 10.3, 10.9, and 10.11), the expanded visual field developed during the first millennium BCE in Assyria follows contact with the Neo-Hittite cultures of northern Syria and eastern Anatolia, where extensively carved stone orthostats were incorporated into the walls of the Assyrian palace or added to decorative bronze bands on doors and gates.[26] To the visual programs were added textual inscriptions that change and develop over the period from the ninth to the seventh century BCE. I shall make six brief points with respect to the palace texts associated with relief carving and free-standing sculpture in this period, as they are relevant to the current issue of the relationship between sign and design and the use of a lapidary script to regularize cuneiform inscriptions.

First, prior to the western campaigns of Assurnasirpal II (883–859 BCE) and the subsequent inclusion of sculptured stone reliefs in the decorative program of the palace, his father, Tukulti-Ninurta II, had employed a tradition in the capital city of Assur of decorating walls with glazed brick tiles, continuing a practice of wall painting and tile glazing from the Middle Assyrian period of the second millennium BCE. Most of these individual bricks or tiles also contained an inscription identifying the ruler, his patronym, and his title.[27] What is interesting here is how much these glazed tiles remind one of the use of Kufic script on glazed tiles of

considerably later Islamic monuments, as on the Chehel Dokhtar tower in Damghan.[28] In the Assyrian cases, the texts on the tiles seem to function as virtual labels for the associated image of the ruler in his chariot below, not unlike the labels on the bodies of Sumerian rulers such as Gudea and Ur-Nanše.

Second, in the Northwest Palace of Assurnasirpal II at Nimrud, the principal text known as the "Standard Inscription" occurs across the middle of virtually every relief slab, regardless of the visual content (fig. 10.9).[29] Organized in three parts, the text introduces the palace, the ruler, his genealogy, and his official titles, then proceeds with a narrative account of the territorial expansion of the polity during his reign, and closes with a mirror representation of the first part, giving a résumé once again of the ruler, his titles, and a statement concerning the construction of the palace.[30] Taken individually, this practice of laying the Standard Inscription over the imagery in full-figure slabs of approximately two meters in height, or creating a separate horizontal panel of text between two registers of imagery, would appear to be a good example of the autonomy of the inscribed text. The imagery varies, but the text remains the same in structure, with only small differences from room to room, depending upon sequential events in the reign of the ruler over the brief period of time during which the reliefs were created.[31]

The text could then be viewed as separate from the visual subject over which, or between the registers of which, it was inscribed. However, an ascription of textual autonomy would be misleading. For, as argued some thirty years ago, the entire visual program of the Northwest Palace's throne room (room B) and its façade in fact replicates the structure of the Standard Inscription, using all of the representational tropes—both

---

an earlier ascription of the imagery, but a later addition of the inscription (see, for example, Edmond Solberger, "The White Obelisk," *Iraq* 36 [1974]: 231–38; "Assurnasirpal I and the White Obelisk," *Iraq* 37 [1975]; Russell, *Writing on the Wall*, 59. In any one of these scenarios, it is usually the imagery rather than the inscription that seems to carry the argument.

25 See particularly, Russell, *Writing on the Wall*, esp. 220–45.

26 Ekrem Akurgal, *The Art of Greece: Its Origins in the Mediterranean and Near East* (New York, 1968), esp. 16–48 and 67–142.

27 Walter Andrae, *Farbige Keramik aus Assur* (Berlin, 1923); Davide Nadali, "Assyrian High-Relief Bricks from Nineveh and the Fragments of a Royal Name," *Iraq* 70 (2008): 87–104.

28 E.g., S. M. V. Mousavi Jazayeri, *Stone Inscriptions in Kufic Script: The Global Cultural Heritage* (Damghan, 2012), where design is often primary, the tile becoming a "calligraphic object" using a repeated word, such as "Mohammad," which then takes on a geometric pattern.

29 Russell, *Writing on the Wall*, 9–64.

30 Albert Kirk Grayson, *Assyrian Royal Inscriptions* (Wiesbaden, 1976) 2:164–67, no. 13: Standard Inscription; Russell, *Writing on the Wall*, 30–31.

31 Samuel M. Paley, *King of the World: Ashur-nasir-pal II of Assyria, 883–859 B.C.* (Brooklyn, N.Y., 1976).

FIG. 10.9.
Relief slab of
Assurnasirpal II with
Standard Inscription,
Neo-Assyrian period,
court D, Northwest
Palace, Nimrud/Kalah.
British Museum,
London, WA 124562.

Photograph © The
Trustees, The British
Museum.

iconic and narrative—that are present in the text.[32] Therefore, to limit our understanding of the function and content of the text to its association with individual slabs unrelated in content and themselves part of a whole would be a misunderstanding of the play between text and imagery throughout the entire reception suite. Russell has observed that the Standard Inscription complements, rather than duplicates, the visual program.[33] And yet, when taken together, the reception suite imagery and textual display work toward similar ends, introducing the ruler, his palace, and the achievements of his reign.

Third, further texts were often included in the palace: on the ruler's stone throne-base, on gateway colossi, and on the thresholds and pavement slabs of a number of rooms.[34] For Assurnasirpal II, the threshold inscriptions generally replicate the Standard Inscription; but the colossus inscriptions (fig. 10.10) placed beneath the legs and behind the protective figure are longer and contain more information. The close mirroring of the Standard Inscription

32 Irene J. Winter, "Royal Rhetoric and the Development of Historical Narrative in Neo-Assyrian Reliefs," *Studies in Visual Communication* 7 (1981): 2–38, esp. 18, 21–22.

33 Russell, *Writing on the Wall*, 41.

34 Ibid., 41–52.

Fourth, the particular use of texts in two distinct modes on the walls in the later palace of Sargon II (721–705 BCE) at Khorsabad has given rise to the distinction between inscribed, "annalistic texts" and what have been termed "summary texts."[36] In such cases, it is clear that the type of text panel has been carefully selected and juxtaposed with the associated visual panels, thus providing parallel complementary sources of information, largely related to historical events. The careful attention to execution of the texts in lapidary style signals the importance of the content, even for the nonliterate viewer. This virtual billboard demanded attention whatever the parsing capacities of the viewer might have been: i.e., here is a place where writing/text/the word itself is mastered and is being used to convey (something of) importance.

Fifth, as techniques and details for visual representation developed throughout the Neo-Assyrian period, signals to convey historical specificity through dress, landscape, and material attributes became more elaborate. At the same time, recognition of historical specificity is more and more often aided by labels that leave no ambiguity as to identification, as in the examples of labeling discussed above. The bronze Door Bands from Balawat attributed to Assurnasirpal II and Shalmaneser III in the ninth century BCE mark the beginning of this practice.[37] Along with other instances of labeling

reigning monarch at the time of construction, and occasionally also of the building under construction. Because these marks are hidden in the walls, not visible from the exterior, I have not discussed them here. However, like foundation deposits similarly found in building walls, their intended audiences were likely imagined to be both the deity invoked in the building project and future rulers who might come across the bricks in the process of restoring the building. Babylonian texts of the 7th–6th century BCE record kings finding such identifying features. Here, too, legibility would be important.

36 Reade, "Sargon's Campaigns," 95–104; and Russell, *Writing on the Wall*, 99–123. See also Andreas Fuchs, *Die Inschriften Sargons II. aus Khorsabad* (Göttingen, 1994); and Béatrice André-Salvini, "Remarques sur les inscriptions des reliefs du Palais de Khorsabad," in *Khorsabad, le palais de Sargon II, Roi d'Assyrie*, ed. Annie Caubet (Paris, 1995), 15–45. For the reliefs, see Pauline Albenda, *The Palace of Sargon, King of Assyria: Monumental Wall Reliefs at Dur-Sharrukin, from Original Drawings Made at the Time of their Discovery in 1843–44 by Botta and Flandin* (Paris, 1986).

37 J. E. Curtis and N. Tallis, *The Balawat Gates of Ashurnasirpal II* (London, 2008). I thank Yan Jia, who has worked on

FIG. 10.10.
Gateway Colossus of Assurnasirpal II, Northwest Palace, Nimrud/Kalah, doorway E, room Y. Metropolitan Museum of Art, MMA 321431, gift of John D. Rockefeller, Jr.

Photograph © The Metropolitan Museum of Art.

and the throne room suite's overall sculptural program was probably more direct and formal due to their placement on the wall slabs in such an important part of the palace. However, the Standard Inscription also appears on relief slabs throughout the building, reflecting the formal nature of the various suites at ground level. Clearly, textual signaling systems were equally appropriate to a wide array of palace spaces, in addition to the wall reliefs of the throne room.[35]

35 Ibid., 246–94. It should be noted that inscribed bricks are often part of the construction of temples and palaces. These inscriptions, generally produced using stamped clay or stone templates while the brick was still relatively malleable, are brief, providing the name, patronym, and title(s) of the

FIG. 10.11.
Detail of *Battle of the Ulai River*, relief of Assurbanipal, Neo-Assyrian period, Southwest Palace, Nineveh, room 33. British Museum, London, ME 124801.

Photograph
© The Trustees, The British Museum

in the reliefs of later rulers (as, for example the multiple epigraphs utilized on the seventh-century reliefs of Assurbanipal that narrate the sequence of his battle against Elamites at the Ulai River [e.g., fig. 10.11]), they seem to covary historically with the expansion of narrative complexity and a desire for greater historical specificity in imagery. This in itself is noteworthy as it attests to the relationship between verbal and visual signals in the Neo-Assyrian period.

Finally, sixth, the palaces were often furnished not only with luxury goods such as valued ivory furniture and textiles but also with free-standing monuments, such as the Banquet Stela of Assurnasirpal II found adjacent to the major courtyard D in the Northwest Palace. This particular stela commemorates the founding of the palace and the new capital at Nimrud in the later part of the king's reign.[38] While the upper portion of the stela shows an image of the

ruler in the company of divine emblems, the majority of the stone contains a lengthy account of the festivities associated with the construction and inauguration of the palace. Its presence in the palace suggests that textual display was not limited to the walls, floors, and colossi that constituted structurally engaged parts of the building.

Bilingual Texts: Monuments and Palaces

A number of instances occur during the sequence of the ancient near East, particularly in the first millennium BCE, in which inscriptions are provided in more than one language. These may be found on free-standing sculpture as well as on gateway walls or colossi. As with the palace texts, one could devote a long analysis to all such cases, but I will mention only two, as they are characteristic of my interest here in the power of the publicly inscribed word.

---

this material for her dissertation at Harvard University, for reminding me of this conjunction.

38 D. J. Wiseman, "A New Stela of Aššurnasirpal II," *Iraq* 14 (1952): 22–24; Grayson, *Assyrian Royal Inscriptions*, 2:17, 172–76; Nicolò Marchetti, "Texts Quoting Artworks: The

Banquet Stele and the Palace Reliefs of Assurnasirpal II," *Revue d'Assyrologie* 103 (2009): 85–90.

FIG. 10.12.
View of Gateway
Lion with Phoenician
Inscription, North
Gate, Karatepe.

Photograph courtesy
of Halet Çambel.

The first case is that of the gate inscriptions at Karatepe, located in southeastern Turkey above the Cilician plain. Note that this site is not within Assyria proper, nor does the installation, dated to the late eighth or early seventh century BCE, belie Assyrian style, content, or values, unlike the relentlessly Assyrian stelae and rock reliefs that are frequently placed in the periphery as testimony to Assyrian military campaigns. I cite Karatepe here because the bilingual nature of the texts affords an interesting corollary to signaling in public places. The texts occur in both the north and south gates of the citadel, and are almost identical in content: one in Semitic Phoenician (fig. 10.12), the other in Indo-European Neo-Hittite/Luwian.[39] At the

same time, there are two clearly different relief styles, generally parallel in subject matter, on the gateway reliefs: one relatively crude, with proportions in keeping with work of the ninth century; the other more refined and detailed, in keeping with work of the later eighth century.[40] The problem is that there are competing explanations for this relationship between text and image. One interpretation suggests separating the texts from the images, arguing that the earlier-style reliefs date from the ninth century, and have been secondarily (re)constructed into the gateway at the time of the parallel carving of the texts and the later style reliefs. An alternate reading suggests that the two sets are contemporary, the texts speaking to two different linguistic or cultural populations, the images executed in styles appropriate to the two linguistic redactions.[41]

39 Halet Çambel, *Corpus of Hieroglyphic Luwian Inscriptions*, vol. 2, *Karatepe-Arslantaş: The Inscriptions; Facsimile Edition* (Berlin, 1999); John David Hawkins, *Corpus of Hieroglyphic Luwian Inscriptions*, vol. 2 (Berlin, 2000); Aslı Özyar, "The Writing on the Wall: Reviewing Sculpture and Inscription on the Gates of the Iron Age Citadel of Azatiwataya (Karatepe-Aslantaş)," in *Cities and Citadels in Turkey: From the Iron Age to the Seljuks*, ed. Scott Redford and Nina Ergin (Leuven and Paris, 2013), 115–35; Annick Payne, "Multilingual Inscriptions and Their Audiences: Cilicia and Lycia," in *Margins of Writing, Origins of Cultures*, ed. Seth L. Sanders (Chicago, 2002), 125–40; idem, *Iron Age Hieroglyphic Luwian Inscriptions* (Atlanta, 2012), 20–42; K. Lawson Younger, Jr., "The Phoenician Inscription of Azatiwada: An Integrated Reading," *Journal of Semitic Studies* 43 (1998): 11–47. Note that the Phoenician inscription visible on the gateway lion of fig. 10.12 is decidedly *not* written in a distinctively lapidary style as here defined for cuneiform. Some peripheral inscriptions may be so identified,

in particular, those from the site of Zincirli just across the Amanus mountains. But the task of the present paper is not an in-depth study of inscription styles and co-variance with the presence of Assyrian works. Such a study might prove interesting, however.

40 This is apparent in particular on the two adjacent banquet scene slabs of the South Gate, one in each style, designated A and B.

41 Halet Çambel and Aslı Özyar, *Karatepe-Arslantaş: Azatiwataya; Die Bildwerke* (Mainz, 2003). See also the review by Stefania Mazzoni, "Review of *Karatepe-Aslantaş: Azatiwataya. Die Bildwerke*," *American Journal of Archaeology Online Book Review* (October 2008).

FIG. 10.13.

Bilingual Statue of Hadad-ʿIti, Tell Fakhariyeh. Archaeological Museum, Aleppo.

Photograph after Levtow, "Text Destruction and Iconoclasm in the Hebrew Bible and the Ancient Near East," in *Iconoclasm*, ed. N. May (Chicago, 2012), fig. 11.1.

However one reads the archaeological evidence, two distinct linguistic and scriptural signaling systems were clearly in play, together with two distinct stylistic renderings of related visual subject matter. And what is important is that all were deemed necessary in a place where an indigenous Anatolian tradition met a coastal, probably Phoenician, trading tradition of the eastern Mediterranean. The resultant bilingual-cum-bicultural statements were then placed at the very entrances to the site, in major gateways, implying either that separate ethnolinguistic audiences were envisioned, or that the broader inclusivity of the two scripts and two styles made a statement with respect to that very diversity.[42]

The second case of bilingual inscription is that of a statue found at the site of Tell Fakhariyeh, in the Habur River area of northeastern Syria (fig. 10.13).[43] In this case, text was written on the skirt of a male figure in both Assyrian-dialect cuneiform Akkadian and local, cursive Semitic Aramaean.[44] Once again, repetition

42   See Payne, "Multilingual Inscriptions"; and Hannes D. Galter, "Cuneiform Bilingual Royal Inscriptions," in *Language and Culture in the Near East*, ed. S. Izreʾel and R. Drory (Leiden, 1995), 25–50.

43   Ali Abou-Assaf et al., *La Statue de Tell Fekheriye et son inscription bilingue assyro-arraméene*, Études Assyriologiques, Cahiers 7 (Paris, 1982); and Stephen A. Kaufman, "Reflections on the Assyrian-Aramaic Bilingual from Tell Fakhariyeh," *MAARAV* 3, no. 2 (1982): 137–75. See also Nathaniel B. Levtow, "Text Destruction and Iconoclasm in the Hebrew Bible and the Ancient Near East," in *Iconoclasm and Text Destruction in the Ancient Near East and Beyond*, ed. Natalie N. May, Oriental Institute Seminars 8 (Chicago, 2012), 311–62.

44   One could also include here two recently discovered works inscribed with *three* different languages, one found at Tell Tayinat, in the Amuq Valley, the other from the site of Inçirli in eastern Anatolia (Lynn Swartz Dodd, "Squeezing Blood from a Stone: The Archaeological Context of the Incirli Inscription," in *Puzzling Out the Past: Studies in Northwest Semitic Languages and Literatures in Honor of Bruce Zuckerman*, ed. Marilyn J. Lundberg, Steven Fine, and Wayne T. Pitard [Leiden and Boston, 2012], 214–32. [See also the website on the Incirli Stela at humnet.ucla.edu/humnet/nelc/stelasite, and Balshanut.wordpress.com/2009/01/26 for

in more than one script and more than one language (not unlike the trilingual rock relief inscription of the Achaemenid ruler Darius at Behistun in western Iran two hundred years later, a true "billboard") suggests that there are instances when multiple audiences were anticipated. On the Tell Fakhariyeh statue, in fact, variants in the text signal slightly different audiences and cultural norms. For example, the ruler of the site is referred to as "governor" in the Assyrian Akkadian text and as "king" in Aramaic. This variant makes sense in light of Assyrian political dominance of the area in that period, where conflicting loyalties and traditions demanded that the hegemony of the Assyrian king be marked in the Assyrian text, the local ruler being but his governor, while in the indigenous language, the local ruler maintained the title and status of the supreme commander appropriate to an autonomous city-state.

In both of these cases, Karatepe and Tell Fakhariyeh, it is clear that whether built into architecture or laid onto sculpture, instances of bilingual or even trilingual inscriptions reflect specific historical conditions in which a multilinguistic or multiethnic audience was envisioned. When one language is local and the other refers to distant but hegemonical forces, issues of power, too, must enter into the interpretive equation. The message being sent was clearly visually multiplex, whatever the content of the text.[45]

The Anomalous Rebus

The imagery that has been identified as possible rebus writing of the names of two Assyrian rulers, Sargon II and Esarhaddon, of the eighth and seventh centuries BCE respectively, poses an interesting counterpoint to the assertion that ancient Mesopotamians did not play with their scripts. At the least, they may have played with the readability of signs, using an esoteric key not known to all readers/viewers. In the case of Sargon II at Khorsabad, glazed brick panels decorating the

exterior facade of the palace include registers of sequential, seemingly unrelated images that have been understood as picture-writing of the name of the corresponding ruler.[46] This does not seem to have been a widespread phenomenon, however. Scholars who have attempted to decipher the rebuses suggest that their occurrence toward the end of the Mesopotamian sequence may have been in part the result of contact with Egypt, where games with written text and images *were* played—particularly easy to do in a hieroglyphic writing system where images serve at once as pictorial referents and signs of language.[47] The public display of such imagery on palace and gateway walls of the later Neo-Assyrian period would have conveyed the identity of the patron and royal authority to the able decipherer in a manner not unlike the cuneiform banner inscriptions over arched entryways in the Khorsabad palace, while at the same time adding pictorial variation to the exterior of the building. As a short-lived phenomenon, the vagaries of the archaeological record notwithstanding, I do not think that it significantly changes the positions taken in the present chapter with respect to a regular lapidary style for public text. What is interesting for our purposes is that some texts may purposely obscure the boundaries between script and image, thereby deliberately resisting decipherment.

Texts on Cylinder Seals

One final example of the public use of inscriptions may be seen in the legends used on cylinder seals that are a hallmark of ancient Near Eastern scribal practice. Seals mark a quite different domain from palace walls, monuments, and sculpture, being considerably smaller in

inscription. My thanks to Elizabeth Carter, UCLA, for conveying access to the website and its imagery.])

45 For a broad view of this issue, see Alexander J. De Voogt and Joachim Friedrich Quack, eds., *The Idea of Writing: Writing across Borders* (Leiden and Boston, 2011).

46 Finkel and Reade, "Assyrian Hieroglyphs," 245–46. See also Michael Roaf and Annette Zgoll, "Assyrian Astroglyphs: Lord Aberdeen's Black Stone and the Prisms of Esarhaddon," *Zeitschrift für Assyriologie* 91 (2001): 264–95; Nadali, "Assyrian High-Relief Bricks," 96.

47 See discussion in Jerrold S. Cooper, "Incongruent Corpora: Writing and Art in Ancient Iraq," in *Iconography without Texts*, Warburg Institute Colloquia 13 (London, 2008), 80–81; Eckart Frahm, "Observations on the Name and Age of Sargon II," *NABU* (2005): 48; and Ludwig D. Morenz, "Neuassyrische visuell-poetische Bilder-Schrift und ihr Vor-Bild," in *Herrscherpräsentation und Kulturkontakte*, Alter Orient und Altes Testament 304, ed. Ludwig D. Morenz and Erich Bosshard-Nepustil (Münster, 2003), 197–229.

scale and intended for repeated use as signets of identity, office, and authority. Here, I would distinguish between the artifact, the seal itself, and the indexical impression of the seal, the so-called "sealing." Despite their relatively small scale, both the seals and their sealings functioned in a public domain when impressed upon clay tablets, bullae, or door closings. As such, both the seals and their impressions required recognition. It is not surprising, therefore, that those seals including inscriptions generally make use of the lapidary style in sign carving, at least from the Akkadian period onward (circa 2340 BCE). In the limited space offered by a cylindrical seal (or, even more so, a stamp seal), such inscriptions had to be relatively brief, but no less legible than the larger monumental inscriptions.[48]

Seals with well-integrated inscriptions are first attested during the Early Dynastic III period, circa 2600–2400 BCE. During the later part of the third and into the first half of the second millennium, concomitant with an expansion of state bureaucracies, seals and their impressed sealings enjoyed official prominence, their inscriptions incorporating increased personal information regarding the owner of the seal. This practice constituted a kind of epigraphic text not unlike the labels on Early Dynastic period sculptures discussed above. The inclusion on the seal of personal name, patronym, and office of the seal owner, often citing the ruler or deity in whose service the individual acted, occurred at the same time as a turn to greater literacy in the mercantile and administrative ranks (fig. 10.14). In political, administrative, or economic affairs, the authority of the sealing person had to be clear, and therefore both imagery and text on the seal had to enable recognition and attest to the legitimate authority of the seal owner when affixed to a clay document.

Not all seals were inscribed, nor were all inscribed seals executed with equal care and visual prominence. But in general, inscriptions were contained within boxes or columns set off from the imagery. By the end of the sequence, a devaluing of the accompanying imagery can be observed, not on the seal itself, which as a whole functioned in a way as a badge of office, but in the impressed mark of the seal as it was rolled on clay. Maria de Jong Ellis, some forty years ago, noticed an increase in partial rollings of seals on tablets during the Old Babylonian period of the early second millennium, with only the text

FIG. 10.14.
Seal and modern impression, Akkadian Period, ca. 2340 BCE. Musée du Louvre, Paris, AO22303.

© RMN-Grand Palais / Art Resource, NY

48 Although, note that in the Kassite period of the second half of the 2nd millennium BCE, the seals tended to be sufficiently tall and wide in circumference that seal cutters were able to include a lengthy prayer to a deity, which Edith Porada (*Corpus of Ancient Near Eastern Seals in North American Collections: The Collection of the Pierpont Morgan Library*, Bollingen Series 14 [Washington, D.C., 1948], 64) has suggested reflects the protective/amuletic function of the seal, in addition to its more practical, bureaucratic role.

portion of the seal being carefully impressed.[49] It was later observed that, indeed, the practice had begun earlier, in the Neo-Sumerian period of the rulers of the Third Dynasty of Ur, toward the end of the third millennium, at precisely the moment in which the state administrative bureaucracy was expanded.[50] For earlier seals, such as those of the Early Dynastic and Akkadian periods, while brief texts are included providing the name and title of the owner, the actual impressions on clay tend to be more complete, and must have required a combination of image-recognition and text-content as a means of identification. On seals of the Akkadian period in particular (ca. 2300–2100 BCE; see, e.g., fig. 10.14), it should be noted that the often beautifully rendered legend verges on the calligraphic. The text is not infrequently closed within a frame and made to play a role in the visual effect of the overall composition once the seal is rolled, thereby bringing the script into parity with the figural component—text *as* image; hence, text *in* the work, not merely *on* the work![51]

One could illustrate this section with a number of examples, including sealed tablets. The point I would stress here is that size is not the arbiter of either the use of the lapidary style or the inclusion of text with image. Instead, the public function of the vehicle—high-end, official seals no less than stelae, reliefs, and statues—all call forth the formal script.[52] In this regard, I would stress that works we as modern historians put into the scale-conscious category of "high art," as distinct from "minor art," in fact does not apply to Mesopotamia. Furthermore, as there was no official term for or category of art as such, the classificatory distinction is of our making. For Mesopotamia, the various works we group together as "art" were simply named according to object-type, often functioning within quite separate domains—political, economic, administrative, or religious. The place of the artifact we call art in the social and cultural system must therefore be factored into an understanding of the sign value of any accompanying text and its script.

The Need for a Lapidary Script: Sign and Design

In all of the cases discussed above, legibility would have been an essential factor whether or not the viewer was literate. For the literate, the textual portion of a public work was part of the overall program of the work, from the small in scale, as seals, to the great, as part of the palace façade or interior wall slabs. For the nonliterate, some basic ideographic signs may well have been identifiable, as for example the ideogram for "deity" or "king," while at the same time the "sign value" of the text qua text would have been understood as a part of the program. What I am suggesting, therefore, is that the very presence of the text marked the authority of the state and its access to knowledge (hence divine authority) beyond the empirical content of the inscription. Therefore, the very fact of the use of a lapidary style for an inscription visually conveys officialdom, authority, and power.

Such a distinction falls well into current discussions of the materiality of cross-cultural

49 Ellis, personal communication, 1978; also, D. Charpin, "Noms de personnes et légendes des sceaux en Babylonie ancienne," in *L'écriture du nom propre*, ed. Anne-Marie Christin (Paris, 1995), 43–55. This phenomenon is equally apparent in sealings of the Old Assyrian period (early 2nd millennium BCE) from Anatolia (A. Lassen, personal communication, gratefully acknowledged). Note also that cursory inscriptions did not disappear, and in the second half of the 2nd millennium, official texts were often replaced by lengthy prayers to the benefit of the seal owner, the best of which were rendered in the same lapidary style.

50 Most recently, Piotr Michalowski, "The Steward of Divine Gudea and his Family in Ur III Girsu," in *Beyond Hatti: A Tribute to Gary Beckman*, ed. Billie Jean Collins and Piotr Michalowski (Atlanta, 2013).

51 Henri Frankfort, *Cylinder Seals: A Documentary Essay on the Art and Religion of the Ancient Near East* (London, 1939), pl. 17c.

52 On the relationship between large and small scale with respect to reliefs and seals, see Irene J. Winter, "*Le Palais imaginaire*: Scale and Meaning in Neo-Assyrian Seals and Reliefs," in *Images as Media: Sources for the Cultural History of the Near East and the Eastern Mediterranean (1st Millennium BCE)*, ed. Christoph Uehlinger (Fribourg, 2000), 51–87. In another case, that of an ivory pyxis found at Nimrud (Georgina Herrmann, Stuart Laidlaw, and Helena Coffey, *Ivories from the North West Palace (1845–1992)*, Ivories from Nimrud 6 [Oxford, 2009], no. 213 = Iraq Museum 52418), the rim has been "carefully inscribed" (p. 178) in lapidary script, with a dedication to an Assyrian king by a prominent governor in the west in the late 9th to mid-8th century BCE. This example suggests that the script could also be used on formal, high-end, luxury goods not necessarily of stone, which had a public, presentational aspect.

writing practices.[53] The visual power of inscriptions would account for those instances of mutilation and iconoclasm applied to text as well as image in early Mesopotamian sources, as studied recently by Christopher Woods and Nathaniel Levtov.[54] Woods cites third millennium BCE curse formulae of the Akkadian period, in one of which it is said in no uncertain terms "whoever tears out this inscription, may Shamash [the sun god] uproot his foundations and pluck out his progeny."[55] Such formulae are repeated well into the end of the millennium in texts of Neo-Sumerian rulers, from Gudea to the kings of the Third Dynasty of Ur.[56] In particular, similar curses are frequently inscribed as part of the closure of texts on royal stelae, reliefs, and statuary. They articulate a warning not only against destroying the work, but also against substituting the name of another in the place of the original referent. These curses are in effect an attempt to avoid the usurping of images by modifying identifying labels. They also anticipate the possibility of purposeful destruction of images bearing texts, the *damnatio memoriae* of later periods. In prevention thereof, the curses threaten any vandal or usurper with erasure of his seed, hence his memory, as would have been perpetrated upon the image/work of the maker/original referent.[57]

Important here is the evidentiary nature of the text/name on the work in ancient Mesopotamia. It seems that works intended for public display were not complete without the complementary presence and subsequent preservation of both textual and visual representation. One is led, therefore, to the concluding observation that the affect of the work was determined by the physical, material aspect, the pictorial program, *and* the accompanying inscription(s).

Both word and image thus functioned as embedded and mutually related sign systems, the one sometimes, but not always, doubling the other. The texts may be studied separately for content and parsed grammatically by philologists, but it should be noted that there are few examples of texts standing alone in public space. When conjoined with imagery, the texts may be understood to have been composed with a conscious view to all of the variants mentioned above: label, parallel replication of the visual message, and complementarity. I argue, therefore, that the texts associated with monuments do not always, or even often, represent a discrete, closed domain in and of themselves. Rather, the inscribed public work/artifact is constituted by the particular combination of textual and visual signs, each in its own way representational, to which may be added the additional signaling values of material and skill appropriate to the object.[58] The script in which the text is executed, along with the additional intended function and placement of the work, all contribute to the effect of the whole, presumably as intended by its makers. Thus, the bilingual Karatepe inscriptions have to be understood as purposely set in gateways to the citadel; the seal inscription has to provide requisites of recognition for those in the active circle of official activities, along with the status of the owner/user; the sculpture has

53 See, for example, the papers included in Kathryn E. Piquette and Ruth D. Whitehouse, eds., *Writing as Material Practice: Substance, Surface and Medium* (London, 2013), particularly that of Roger Matthews, "Writing (and Reading) as Material Practice: The World of Cuneiform Culture as an Arena for Investigation," 65–74. Also, those in Sanders, *Margins of Writing*, particularly that of P. Zimansky, "Writing, Writers and Reading in the Kingdom of Van," 263–82. For ancient Egypt, see now John Baines, *Visual and Written Culture in Ancient Egypt* (Oxford, 2007), especially the prologue, 3–30, which also explores the relationship between the visual and the textual.

54 Christopher Woods, "Mutilation of Image and Text in Early Sumerian Sources," in May, *Iconoclasm* (n. 43 above), 33–51; Levtov, "Text Destruction," 311–62. Indeed, see the papers in the entire volume May, *Iconoclasm*.

55 Woods, "Mutilation," 41, citing the rulers Sargon and Rimush of the Akkadian period.

56 Ibid., 42–45.

57 On this, see Joan G. Westenholz, "*Damnatio Memoriae*: The Old Akkadian Evidence for Destruction of Name and Destruction of Person," in May, *Iconoclasm*, 71–95; and Levtov, "Text Destruction," where it is made clear that curses pertained equally to the defacement of images on monuments and their identifying inscriptions. See also Zainab Bahrani, "Assault and Abduction: The Fate of the Royal Image in the Ancient

Near East," *Art History* 18, no. 3 (1995): 363–83, for sculpture; JoAnn Scurlock, "Getting Smashed at the Victory Celebration, or What Happened to Esarhaddon's So-Called Vassal Treaties and Why," in May, *Iconoclasm*, 151–61, for texts.

58 For a recent study of the importance of material, hence materiality, see Nicole Boivin, *Material Cultures, Material Minds: The Impact of Things on Human Thought, Society, and Evolution* (Cambridge, 2008). And for the nature and historical function of modern public monuments, Sergiusz Michalski, *Public Monuments: Art in Political Bondage, 1870–1997* (London, 1998).

to be identifiable not as just "a king," but as "this (historically specific) king."

My objective in this essay has been to underscore the role of the text in public works—what Christin refers to as "l'espace inscrit"[59]—and also the fact that text and image work together, not separately, to constitute a monument.[60] Only then can the lapidary style of the inscription be understood as constituting part of the job of the work under scrutiny.

What is more, I have argued that the public text constitutes a particular mode of communication, articulating identity, authority, legitimacy, and even adding a dimension of intention with respect to the work in question. Such a perspective is consistent with Habermas's analysis of the public sphere preceding his historical moment of bourgeois transformation.[61] The logical consequences of this have yet to be fully studied, but what is suggested is that the presence of an inscription can affect, indeed change, the nature/meaning of a monument, building, site, or activity.[62] Under such conditions, a public demonstration of the control of writing in a particularly formal style would have signified social, political, and economic control, and hence the exercise of power, even without being read. The need for a clearly legible lapidary script becomes part of the semiotics of the public work. For it to be both affective and effective, for it to exercise agency in the public domain, the inscription must be no less recognizable than the image, whether or not it was intended to be read by the full complement of the viewing public.

For the purposes of the present volume, then, the public nature of the building, monument, or seal is augmented by, and indeed requires, the textual *sign*. The public nature of the sign requires regularization, which in turn becomes part of the *(de)sign* of the whole. And the *design of the sign* on/in the work—what has been called here the lapidary style—communicates in its own right, no less than the actual content of the text.

59   Christin, *L'image écrite*, 9, which I would argue may be understood to refer to both the space/place the inscription takes on the work as well as the space/place occupied by the work on which the text has been placed. Thus, I have referred several times to the "billboard effect," which holds particularly for rock reliefs and free-standing stelae, but also for doors and gates (on which see Jutta Börker-Klähn, *Altvorderasiatische Bildstelen und vergleichbare Felsreliefs*, Baghdader Vorschungen 4 [Mainz am Rhein, 1982]; Michelle I. Marcus, "Geography as an Organizing Principle in the Imperial Art of Shalmaneser III," *Iraq* 49 [1987]: 77–90; and Ann Shafer, "Assyrian Royal Monuments on the Periphery: Ritual and the Making of Imperial Space," in *Ancient Near Eastern Art in Context: Studies in Honor of Irene J. Winter by Her Students*, ed. Jack Cheng and Marian H. Feldman [Leiden and Boston, 2007], 133–59).

60   Note also that in ancient Greek, the verb *graphein* may be translated as both "to write" and "to draw" (Lissarague, "*Graphein*: Écrire et dessiner"), just as the various forms of the Akkadian verb *esēru* can be used to indicate both drawn and written plans (Glassner, "Comment présenter l'invisible?" 5, 8). *Both* verbal and visual, it would seem, constitute the necessary sign-making that in turn constitutes representation— both referring, in many cases, back to the same referent. In Heidegger's terms, then, the inscription contributes directly to the *work* of the work (of art). Martin Heidegger, "The Origin of the Work of Art," in *Martin Heidegger: The Basic Writings*, trans. David Farrell Krell (New York, 2008).

61   Jürgen Habermas, *The Structural Transformation of the Public Sphere: An Inquiry into a Category of Bourgeois Society* (Cambridge, Mass., 1991), 1–14, esp. 5, with reference to public space as an integral part of the public sphere, entirely distinct from private space, its organization and assigned functions/ components conveying the imperium.

62   The work of Tamara Sears on Hindu temple reliefs and monuments, particularly the Ranod inscription regarding the Dance of Shiva, has influenced my formulation of this issue by posing the question of whether or not the presence of an inscription can change the ontology of a work or a site. I am indebted to her for conversations on the topic. See also J. Kelly, "Writing and the State: China, India and General Definitions," in Sanders, *Margins of Writing* (n. 39 above), 15–32, for additional cases from India and China.

❧ My sincere thanks to Elisabeth Fontan, Musée du Louvre; Joan Aruz, Metropolitan Museum of Art; Jack Green, The Oriental Institute Museum, University of Chicago; and Jonathan Tubb, The British Museum for permission to reproduce images. I also thank Gojko Barjamovic, Jean-Jacques Glassner, Robert Hunt, Yan Jia, Afsaneh Najmabadi, John M. Russell, and the editors of this volume, for conversations that contributed to the present paper, while absolving them of any errors therein.

Monograms and the Art
of Unhelpful Writing in Late Antiquity

ANTONY EASTMOND

OUTSIDE THE CHURCH OF SAN MARCO IN VENICE STAND TWO GREAT,
monolithic, marble pillars. They are unlike anything else in the city, and over the past eight
hundred years their exotic appearance has attracted many myths and legends as to their
origins and meaning.[1] Much of their allure and mystery lies in their decoration: the delicate balance
between the flowing vine that scrolls across the front of the pier and the rigorous symmetry that
controls it (fig. 11.1). Within the details of the decoration a second battle between design and order
is fought, but this time with letters. Frames identical in thickness and diameter to the tendrils that
encircle the vine leaves contain monograms, densely meshed combinations of letters. These have long
attracted scholarly attention as a means to explain the columns, but equally they have defied analysis.
Before the columns were identified the monograms could be—and indeed were—read according to
their readers' desires, and were deciphered as everything from "Antioch" to "Manuel Komnenos."[2]
But even after the provenance of the columns was conclusively revealed, when excavations in Istanbul
proved them to be from the sixth-century Constantinopolitan Church of Saint Polyeuktos, the
monograms remained a visual and linguistic puzzle.[3] Even with knowledge of the name of the donor,
Cyril Mango and Ihor Ševčenko remained wary of trying to read her name into the monograms:
"None of the seven varieties appears to yield the name of Anicia Juliana, or those of her immediate
relatives."[4] Martin Harrison's otherwise comprehensive monograph on the church and its excavations
is totally silent about the monograms and their meanings.[5]

Monograms tantalize us with the prospect of revealing a name, only to withhold it from all but the
most tenacious (or imaginative) of scholars. Equally they tease us with their ambiguity as to whether
they belong to the world of words or that of images: are they part of the documentary archive of a
church, or part of its decoration? This chapter explores a series of ways of presenting words that seems
to undercut the basic premise of writing: to convey information. Monograms are the most obvious
cases that I will discuss, but this idea can also be applied to other forms of writing that at first sight

1   Robert S. Nelson, "The History of Legends and the Legends of History: The Pilastri Acritani in Venice," in *San Marco, Byzantium, and the Myths of Venice*, ed. Henry Maguire and Robert S. Nelson (Washington, D.C., 2010), 63–90.

2   Ibid., 73: "Antioch" in the case of Josef Strzygowski, "Manuel Komnenos" for Marinos Kalligas.

3   R. Martin Harrison and Nezih Firatlı, "Excavations at Saraçhane in Istanbul: First Preliminary Report," *DOP* 19 (1965): 234 n. 5.

4   Cyril Mango and Ihor Ševčenko, "Remains of the Church of St. Polyeuktos at Constantinople," *DOP* 15 (1961): 246.

5   R. Martin Harrison, *Excavations at Saraçhane in Istanbul* (Princeton, 1986), 1:162.

increases, the potential for secrecy or mystification in the service of status and cultural association increases.[6]

While I am interested in these ideas about secrecy and mystification, I am more concerned with their consequences for how people might react to such difficult-to-read texts. I will argue that they require viewers to consider them differently and to seek information in alternative ways. The meanings of some texts lie not within their contents, but actually within their contexts. They are designed to purvey meaning through their presence rather than the information they potentially contain.[7]

Revealing Names

The basis of this chapter lies in a world in which people could expect to encounter monograms and other texts in religious contexts. And with the expectation of presence came an expectation of content. The majority of surviving texts in early churches are votive in nature: evidence of piety and generosity; documents of vows fulfilled and promises made.[8] The frequency and the prominence of these votive texts are the legacy of the pagan Greco-Roman world and what has been called its "epigraphic habit."[9] They are

6   John Baines, "The Earliest Egyptian Writing: Development, Context, Purpose," in *The First Writing: Script Invention as History and Process*, ed. Stephen Houston (Cambridge, 2004), 151–52. My thanks to Scott Redford for bringing this to my attention.

7   Irene A. Bierman, *Writing Signs: The Fatimid Public Text* (Berkeley, 1998), 15.

8   See, for example, the extensive inscriptions recorded in Jean-Pierre Caillet, *L'évergétisme monumental chrétien en Italie et à ses marges: d'après l'épigraphie des pavements de mosaïque, IVe–VIIe s.*, Collection de l'Ecole française de Rome 175 (Rome, 1993); or Anne Michel, *Les églises d'époque byzantine et Umayyade de Jordanie (provinces d'Arabie et de Palestine): V^e–VIIe siècle: Typologie architecturale et aménagements liturgiques (avec catalogue des monuments)*, Bibliothèque de l'antiquité tardive 2 (Turnhout, 2001).

9   Ramsay Macmullen, "The Epigraphic Habit in the Roman Empire," *AJP* 103, no. 3 (1982): 233–46; Elisabeth A. Meyer, "Explaining the Epigraphic Habit in the Roman Empire: The Evidence of Epitaphs," *JRS* 80 (1990): 74–97; and Greg Woolf, "Monumental Writing and the Expansion of Roman Society in the Early Empire," *JRS* 86 (1996): 22–39.

FIG. 11.1.
Column from Saint Polyeuktos, Constantinople (524–527); known as one of the Pilastri Acritani in the Piazzetta of San Marco, Venice.

Photo courtesy of Stefania Gerevini.

appear more conventional. My paper is inspired by the comments of John Baines on some of the earliest writing in Egypt:

Knowledge that writing is present, that it is meaningful, and that it is exclusive may be as relevant for the actors as any specific verbal content or instrumental function it might possess. Exclusivity merges into secrecy, and writing systems can be used almost as easily to make things secret as to make them known. As the symbolic salience of writing

merely the Christian incarnation of a form of civic *euergetism* with a very long history.[10]

In early Byzantine churches the written word was a significant visual presence around the congregation and officiating clergy. Monumental inscriptions, whether painted, made in mosaic, or carved into wood and stone appeared on the floors, walls, and ceilings of churches.[11] On a smaller scale they were chased in precious metals on the instruments of the liturgy—on patens,[12] chalices,[13] and *rhipidia*.[14] Words were similarly inscribed on portable images, reliquaries, candelabra, and other objects.[15] These texts were not just isolated blocks of script, they were an integral element of larger visual environments. They acted as frames for images, and were themselves framed. They could be presented as documentary-like blocks of text set in a *tabula ansata* (the traditional Roman frame for inscriptions, a rectangle with dove-tail handles at each end), but they could also be presented as part of the decorative repertoire of interiors, whether through the artful arrangement of the text on the walls or floor of a church, or more abstractly. As monograms, names could be formal motifs in the pierced decorative system of polycandela (fig. 11.2) or could be woven into the foliage of church columns and capitals, where the letters echo symbols like the cross. Inscriptions were given extraordinary prominence in churches and were placed in key locations in the centers

of floors, around thresholds, and in apses. They could envelop viewers, surrounding them on all sides. Words engaged and accompanied the senses. They could be seen and touched and even trodden on or consumed, when branded into the Eucharistic bread.[16]

Yet we have become largely inured to the presence and significance of words. We separate them from their surroundings and deny their physical qualities, to consider only their contents in isolation. We treat them independently as evidence about a monument, rather than as a physical part of it.[17] The ways that many texts are presented seduces us into thinking that they are no more than a means to convey information and to commemorate names. Sometimes the texts are very simple, as in the seventh-century floor mosaic found in Santa Reparata in Florence:

FIG. 11.2.
Polycandelon from the Sion Treasure, sixth century.

Photo © Dumbarton Oaks, Byzantine Collection, Washington, DC.

10 For a general overview of the presence of votive texts, see Ann Marie Yasin, *Saints and Church Spaces in the Late Antique Mediterranean: Architecture, Cult and Community* (Cambridge, 2009); and Caillet, *L'évergétisme monumental.*

11 Just to take three examples, for floors, Madaba: Michele Piccirillo, *The Mosaics of Jordan*, American Center of Oriental Research Publications 1 (Amman, 1992); for walls, Santa Sabina, Rome: Erik Thunø, "Looking at Letters: 'Living Writing' in S. Sabina in Rome," *MarbJb* 34 (2007): 19–41; for ceilings, Sinai: George H. Forsyth and Kurt Weitzmann, *The Monastery of Saint Catherine at Mount Sinai: The Church and Fortress of Justinian; Plates* (Ann Arbor, 1973), pls. 80 and 81 C/D and E/F.

12 See the Paternus and Riha patens in Kurt Weitzmann, ed., *Age of Spirituality: Late Antique and Early Christian Art, Third to Seventh Centuries* (New York, 1979), 610–12, nos. 546–47.

13 See the Attarouthi treasure in Helen C. Evans and Brandie Ratliff, eds., *Byzantium and Islam: Age of Transition, 7th–9th Century* (New York, 2012), 41–44, no. 22 C, D, F, K, and L.

14 Ibid., 72–73, no. 44A, B.

15 See, for example, the Cross of Justin II in Jeffrey Spier, ed., *Picturing the Bible: The Earliest Christian Art* (New Haven and London, 2007), 283, no. 83.

16 Bread stamps in Weitzmann, *Age of Spirituality*, 627–28, no. 565; and George Galavaris, *Bread and the Liturgy: The Symbolism of Early Christian and Byzantine Bread Stamps* (Madison, Wisc., and London, 1970).

17 There is an analogy with the way in which footnotes, such as this one, are seen as important to the argument of a paper, yet distinct from it: Anthony Grafton, *The Footnote: A Curious History* (London, 1997).

MARIN[I]ANVS DIACON[VS]	Marinianus the deacon
FECIT P[ED]ES·CCC	gave [had made]·CCC feet
IOVIN[IA]NVS·FEC·P·CC	Iovinianvs·gv·CC ft
MARCELLVS·FEC·P·CC	Marcellus·gv·CC ft
G[A]VDENTIVS·FEC·P·CC	Gaudentius·gv·CC ft
O[P]TATVS·FEC·P·C	Optatus·gv·C ft
S[EP]TIMINVS·FEC·P·C	Septiminus·gv·C ft
E[V]RESIVS·FEC·P·LXV	Euresius·gv·LXV ft
V[E]RICVNDVS·F·P·LX	Vericundus·g·LX ft
[VIN]CENTIVS·F·P· . . .	Vincentius·g . . . ft
[DEL]MATIVS·F·P· . . .	Delmatius·g . . . ft
[LA]VRENTIVS·F·P· . . .	Laurentius·g . . . ft
I[O]VIAN[VS]·F·P· . . .	Iovianus·g . . . ft
F[O]RTV[NATVS] . . .	Fortunatus . . .
H[I]LAR[IVS] . . . [18]	Hilarius . . .

It is simply a list of names, each accompanied by the repeated formula "fecit pedes" and a Roman numeral ("gave X feet") to indicate the extent of paving funded by each individual.[19] The generosity of the donors is reflected in the hierarchy of the names, the use of a title for the lead figure, and the increasing extent of the abbreviation used for the donor formula, as Fecit Pedes becomes FecP and finally FP. On the roof beams of Saint Catherine's monastery on Mount Sinai, Justinian and Theodora's names are equally highlighted by the simple expedient of placing them as the final words.[20]

Longer and more complex inscriptions and poem texts could be visually manipulated to accentuate the donors' names, which would benefit identification for viewers with lesser degrees of literacy. Justinian's patronage of the Nea Ekklesia in Jerusalem in 524/25 was highlighted by ensuring that the emperor's name appeared in the very center of the tabula ansata placed in the cistern beneath the church:

K͜ϹTOVTOTOΕΡΓΟΝΕΦΙΛΟΤΙΜΗ
ϹΑΤΟΟΕVϹΕΒˢΗΜШΝΒΑϹΙ
ΛΕVϹΦΛˢΙꙊϹΤΙΝΙΑΝΟϹΠΡΟΝΟΙ
ΑΚϹΠΟVΔΙΚШΝϹΤΑΝΤΙΝΟV
ΟϹΙШΤᴬΠΡΕϹΒˢΚ͜ϹΗΓꙊΜᴱΙΝΔˢΙΓ+[21]

The extent of the abbreviations required to achieve this and the way that words break across lines makes the text itself harder to read, but this only serves to underline the completeness and centrality of the name Justinian.

A similar effect was achieved in the seven-line Latin foundation inscription placed on the west wall of Santa Sabina in Rome (422–32). But here the text was more carefully composed to place its founder's name, Petrus, in the center of the middle line of the poem without resorting to abbreviations:

18 Caillet, *L'évergétisme monumental*, 26–29.

19 Yasin, *Saints and Church Spaces*, 123–25.

20 Forsyth and Weitzmann, *The Monastery of Saint Catherine*, pl. 80a–f. For other examples of this, see John Higgit, "Design and Meaning in Early Medieval Inscriptions in Britain and Ireland," in *The Cross Goes North: Processes of Conversion in Northern Europe, AD 300–1300*, ed. Martin Carver (Bury St Edmunds, 2003), 327–38.

21 Nahman Avigad, "A Building Incription of the Emperor Justinian and the Nea in Jerusalem," *IEJ* 27, nos. 2–3 (1977): 145–51; and Yael Israeli and David Mevorah, eds., *Cradle of Christianity*, exh. cat. (Jerusalem, 2000), 192: "Κ(αὶ) τοῦτο τὸ ἔργον ἐφιλοτιμή|σατο ὁ εὐγεβ(έστατος) ἥμων βασιλεὺς Φλ(άουιος) Ἰουστινιάνος προνοί|α κ(αὶ) σπουδὶ Κωνσταντίνου | ὁσιωτά(του) πρεσβ(υτέρου) κ(αὶ) ἡγουμέ(νου) ἰνδ(ικτιῶνος) ιγ' +" ("And this is the work which our most pious Emperor Flavius Justinianus carried out with munificence, under the care and devotion of the most holy Constantinus, priest and hegoumen, in the thirteenth indiction. +."

CVLMENAPOSTOLICVMCVMCAELESTINVSHABERET
PRIMVSETINTOTOFVLGERETEPISCOPVSORBE
HAECQVAEMIRARISFVNDAVITPRESBYTERVRBIS
ILLYRICADEGENTE<u>PETRVS</u>VIRNOMINETANTO
DIGNVSABEXORTVCRHISTINVTRITVSINAVLA
PAVPERIBVSLOCVPLESSIBIPAVPERQVIBONAVITAE
PRAESENTISFVGIENSMERVITSPERAREFVTVRVM.[22]

An alternative approach was to draw attention to the donor's name through the arrangement of the inscription on the object, rather than through the construction of the text. This is evident in the dedicatory poem on the reliquary cross given by emperor Justin (565–578) to Rome. When the poem is written out, his name appears only half-way through the second hexameter: "+Ligno quo Christus humanum subdidit hostem | dat Romae Iustinus opem et socia decorem."[23] However, when inscribed on the object, everything that precedes the name is squeezed on the upright of the cross so that IUSTINUS occurs as the first word on the left arm of the cross. Here it is more instantly visible than the awkward division of words into blocks of one to three letters on the vertical:

```
                          +LI
                          GNO
                          QUO
                          CH
                          RI
                          ST
                          US
                          HU
                          MA
                          NU
                          M
    IUSTINUSOPEM    +    ETSOCIADECOREM
                          S
                          UB
                          DI
                          DI
                          TH
                          OS
                          TE
                          M
                          DA
                          TRO
                          MAE
```

<hr>

22 "When Celestinus held the highest apostolic throne and shone forth gloriously as the foremost bishop of the whole world, a presbyter of this city, Illyrian by birth, named Peter, and worthy of that great name, established this building at which you look in wonder. From his earliest years he was brought up in the hall of Christ—rich to the poor, poor to himself, one who shunned the good things of life on earth

and deserved to hope for the life to come." The placement of Petrus's name has already been highlighted by Thunø, "Looking at Letters," 32, who also notes the vertical alignment of FVNDAVIT | PETRVS | CRHISTI, evoking Matt. 16:18.

23 Spier, *Picturing the Bible*, 283: "Justin and his consort give to Rome a glorious treasure in the wood by which Christ subdued the enemy of mankind."

Equally, on the paten made for Paternus, usually identified as bishop of Tomis in Romania in the reign of Anastasios (491–518), the text that runs around the rim of the dish was manipulated by the increasing use of abbreviations in the second half of the text in order to ensure that Paternus's name remains central, immediately beneath the chi-rho symbol: "†EX ANTIQVIS RENOVATVM EST PER PATERNVM REVERENTISS(imum) EPISC(opum) NOSTRVM AMEN."[24]

A final example shows how more complex spaces could be manipulated. In the church of Saints Sergios and Bakchos in Constantinople (524–527), a twelve-line Greek hexameter poem encircles the nave at cornice level. Although each line of the poem is separated by a leaf motif (here represented by a dash), there are no spaces between words, and this combined with the many angled breaks in the cornice (here represented by line breaks), which do not correspond to divisions between words, results in a text that is very difficult to read, despite the relative size of the letters, and their closeness to the viewer:

ΑΛΛΟΙΜΕΝΒΑ
ΣΙΛΗΕΣΕΤΙΜΗΣΑΝΤΟΘΑΝΟΝΤΑΣ—ΑΝΕΡΑΣШΝΑΝΟΝΗΤΟΣΕΗΝ
ΠΟΝΟΣΗΜΕΤΕΡΟΣΔ
Ε—ΕΥΣΕΒΙΗΝΣΚΗΠΤΟΥΧΟΣΙΟΥΣΤΙΝΙΑΝΟ
ΣΑΕΖШΝ—ΣΕΡΓΙΟΝΑΙ
ΓΛΗΕΝΤΙΔΟΜШΙΘΕΡΑΠΟΝΤΑΓΕΡΑΙΡΕΙ—
ΧΡΙΣΤΟΥΠΑΓΓΕΝΕΤΑΟΤΟΝΟΥΠΥΡΟΣΑΤΜΟΣΑΝΑ
ΠΤШΝ—ΟΥΖΙΦΟΣΟΥΧΕΤΕ
ΡΗΒΑΣΑΝШΝΕΤΑΡΑΖΕΝΑΝΑΓΚΗ—ΑΛΛΑΘΕΟΥΤΕΤΛΗΚΕΝ
ΥΠΕΡΧΡΙΣΤΟΙΟΔΑΜΗΝΑΙ
—ΑΙΜΑΤΙΚΕΡΔΑΙΝШΝΔΟΜΟΝΟΥΡΑΝΟΝΑΛΛΕΝΙΠΑΣΙΝ—
ΚΟΙΡΑΙΗΝΒΑΣΙΛΗΟΣΑΚΟΙΜΗ
ΤΟΙΟΦΥΛΑΖΟΙ—ΚΑΙΚΡΑΤΟΣ
ΑΥΖΗΣΕΙΕΘΕΟΣΤΕΦΕΟΣΘΕΟΔШΡΗΣ—
ΗΣΝΟΟΣΕΥΣΕΒΙΗΙ

24 Alice V. Bank, *Byzantine Art in the Collections of Soviet Museums* (Leningrad, 1975), 66–68: date 491–518: "... Restored from the antique by Paternus, our most reverend bishop. Amen." See also Ruth Leader-Newby, *Silver and Society in Late Antiquity: Functions and Meanings of Silver Plate in the Fourth to Seventh Centuries* (Aldershot, 2004), 92.

ΦΑΙΔΡΥΝΕΤΑΙΗCΠΟΝΟCΑΙΕΙ—ΑΚΤΕΑΝωΝΘΡΕΠΤΗΡΕCΑΦΕΙΔΕΕCΕΙ
CΙΝΑΓωΝΕC.[25]

Ἄλλοι μὲν βα|σιλῆες ἐτιμήσαντο θανόντας
ἀνέρας ὧν ἀνόνητος ἔην | πόνος. Ἡμέτερος δ|ὲ
εὐσεβίην σκηπτοῦχος Ἰουστινιανὸ|ς ἀέξων
Σέργιον αἰ|γλήεντι δόμωι θεράποντα γεραίρει
Χριστοῦ παγγενέταο. Τὸν οὐ πυρὸς ἀτμὸς ἀνά|πτων,
οὐ ξίφος, οὐχ ἑτέ|ρη βασάνων ἐτάραξεν ἀνάγκη,
ἀλλὰ θεοῦ τέτληκεν | ὑπὲρ Χριστοῖο δαμῆναι
αἵματι κερδαίνων δόμον οὐρανόν. Ἀλλ' ἐνὶ πᾶσιν
κοιραίην βασιλῆος ἀκοιμή|τοιο φυλάξοι
καὶ κράτος | αὐξήσειε θεοστεφέος Θεοδώρης, |
ἧς νόος εὐσεβίηι | φαιδρύνεται, ἧς πόνος αἰεὶ
ἀκτεάνων θρεπτῆρες ἀφειδέες εἰ|σὶν ἀγῶνες.

Yet despite all these problems, the votive elements of the inscription were highlighted. The poem extols its builders Justinian and Theodora, but separates their names between the third and tenth lines of the poem. When carved into the cornice of the church, this resulted in the two names appearing opposite each other on the north and south sides of the nave. It is likely that this division corresponds to the gendered spaces in the church, where the two rulers stood during the liturgy.[26] If this were the case, then the names would have gained a visual prominence by appearing in conjunction with the emperor and empress when they attended the church (and could have been accentuated through the coloring of the words or background of the inscription).[27]

The ways in which names are emphasized in these examples means that they are accessible by those with a variety of levels and forms of literacy. Inscriptions were read and seen not just by the elite, well-educated, and cultured, but also by those with lesser degrees of literacy, whether just an ability to recognize the area of the wall or floor as writing, whether able to read individual letters but no more, or with some kind of functional or signature literacy. As we move down the literacy scale the visual properties of the text become increasingly important, as emphasis shifts from consideration of the information that the texts contain to a greater concern with the

25 Silvio G. Mercati, "Sulla tradizione manoscritta dell'inscrizione del fregio dei Santi Sergio e Bacco di Constantinopoli," *Atti della Pontificia Accademia Romana di Archeologia: Rendiconti* 3 (1925): 197–205; translated by Alexander Van Millingen, *Byzantine Churches in Constantinople: Their History and Architecture* (London, 1912), 74: "Other sovereigns, indeed, have honoured dead men whose labour was useless. But our sceptred Justinian, fostering piety, honours with a splendid abode the servant of Christ, creator of all things, Sergios; whom neither the burning breath of fire, nor the sword, nor other constraints of trials disturbed, but who endured for the sake of God Christ to be slain, gaining by his blood heaven as his home. May he in all things guard the rule of the ever-vigilant sovereign, and increase the power of the God-crowned Theodora, whose mind is bright with piety, whose constant toil ever is unsparing efforts to nourish the destitute." See Paul Saenger, *Space Between Words: The Origins of Silent Reading* (Stanford, 1997), for the implications of reading texts without spaces.

26 The problems of establishing the placement of women in the early Byzantine church are fully explored by Robert F. Taft, "Women at Church in Byzantium: Where, When—and Why?" *DOP* 52 (1998): 27–88. However, a gendered division between the north and south sides is supported by the split between images of men and women in the mosaics of the churches of San Vitale (Justinian on the north wall; Theodora on the south) and San Apollinare Nuovo (male martyrs on the north wall; female martyrs on the south), both in Ravenna.

For these see Deborah M. Deliyannis, *Ravenna in Late Antiquity* (Cambridge, 2010), 164–71; Charles Barber, "The Imperial Panels at San Vitale: A Reconsideration," *BMGS* 14 (1990): 19–42.

27 Evidence of polychromy has been lost in the recent cleaning of the church, but the contemporaneous inscription at Saint Polyeuktos was colored: R. Martin Harrison, *A Temple for Byzantium: The Discovery and Excavation of Anicia Juliana's Palace-Church in Istanbul* (Austin, 1989), 84. It is likely that similar care was taken at Saint Polyeuktos to highlight Anicia Juliana's name around the entrance to the church: Mary Whitby, "The St Polyeuktos Epigram (AP 1.10): A Literary Approach," in *Greek Literature in Late Antiquity: Dynamism, Didacticism, Classicism*, ed. Scott Fitzgerald Johnson (Aldershot, 2006), 159–88.

means by which that information is presented to the reader/viewer. This is a shift from the message to the medium, and its consequence is a shift in which texts become images, a shift most evident in monograms. How might writing be seen and interpreted by these different groups of people? While they were probably not the intended audience for the inscriptions in the minds of those that commissioned them,[28] they were undoubtedly part of the actual audience that viewed and interacted with them. The patterns of word placement that are visible in these inscriptions suggest an awareness on the part of the designers of these different modes of seeing and reading and a willingness to take them into account.

Studies of modern literacy acquisition and assessments of ancient forms of literacy all stress the importance of name recognition as a key first stage.[29] While the acquisition of literacy in late antiquity was no doubt taught differently than in modern schools, the surviving papyrus evidence of people with only signature literacy indicates a similar concentration on names as an elemental part of basic literacy.[30] With many votive texts only limited levels of literacy are required for them to be understood as relating to particular individuals: the ability to recognize a very restricted range of words (i.e., names) along with a visual sense for the hierarchy of the text. The frequent repetition of particular key words (such as the Greek Ὑπὲρ εὐχῆς, "as a prayer for," or Ὑπὲρ σωτηρίας, "for the salvation of"; or those in Latin that end *votum solvit* (abbreviated to VS; "in payment for a vow") converts these

words and phrases into pictographs that—like RIP on tombstones today—do not need to be read or expanded in order for their meaning to be recognized. However, even without these, the expectation of the content of such texts allows us to infer that the presence of a text mostly implied the memory of an individual or family. Texts become a form of identity marker.

The nature, location and design of these inscriptions all suggest that viewers were conditioned to search for names, and suggest that it was a practice open to a wider population than that we might describe as fully literate. The presence and readability of names seduces us into thinking that it was this commemorative element that was their central concern—that the name is the answer and that reading is the means to that answer. However, it is at this point that we should return to monograms and other inscriptions, which show that this expectation to find and to read names could often be undercut by the texts themselves. They could deliberately conceal their contents in order to turn even literate readers into viewers, and texts into images: things to be seen and apprehended, rather than read and comprehended.

Concealing Names

Many of the issues monograms raise can best be exemplified by Anicia Juliana's Church of Saint Polyeuktos, with which this chapter opened.[31] The building itself was in ruins by the twelfth century, but much of its carved marble decoration has been recovered. Monograms appear throughout her church. In addition to those on column shafts, they appear repeatedly on the cornice that once surrounded the nave (fig. 11.3). Here the monograms are integrated into the overall decorative program, appearing as just one of a sequence of four circular or almost circular devices, including palm trees and leaves enclosed in circles. As on the Venetian columns, the visual overlap between the monograms and the circular floral emblems and their rhythmic repetition is very strong. The tendency to view rather than to read the monograms is heightened by the stark contrast between them and

28   Although Averil Cameron, *Christianity and the Rhetoric of Empire: The Development of Christian Discourse*, Sather Classical Lectures 55 (Berkeley and London, 1991), 35, notes Augustine's "amazingly modern" concern to reach all sections of his audience.

29   See, as a starting point, Janet W. Bloodgood, "What's in a Name? Children's Name Writing and Literacy Acquisition," *Reading Research Quarterly* 34, no. 3 (1999): 342–67. Herbert C. Youtie, "ὑπογραφεύς: The Social Impact of Illiteracy in Graeco-Roman Egypt," *ZPapEpig* 17 (1975): 201–21, discusses evidence for differing degrees of literacy, including some implicit evidence about those with only signature literacy.

30   William V. Harris, *Ancient Literacy* (Cambridge, Mass., and London, 1989), 3–5; see also the discussion of Ann E. Hanson, "Ancient Illiteracy," in *Literacy in the Roman World*, ed. John H. Humphrey, *JRA*, Supplementary Series 3 (Ann Arbor, 1991): 159–98, at 164, although in general this is more concerned with writing than reading.

31   Harrison, *Excavations at Saraçhane*, 162, fig. L.

FIG. 11.3.

Cornice from
Saint Polyeuktos,
Constantinople
(524–527).

Harrison Archive,
Oxford, courtesy of
Marlia Mango.

the seventy-eight-line epigram that encircled the church just below this cornice.[32] The linear form of the inscription that wrapped itself around the interior of the church, the legibility of its individual letters, and its occasional punctuation all give the impression of readability (regardless of whether it can actually be achieved in the church).[33] These monograms seek to deny all the attributes of writing. They are of dubious legibility, hiding and overlapping letters within each other, omitting all duplicate letters, and undermining ideas of letter order by obscuring any evidence of directionality. There is no system by which to read the letters (much to many modern scholars' frustration).[34] Gustave Schlumberger complained that trying to decipher them was "a thankless task of no real utility."[35] Given that, I wonder whether we should read them at all. The monograms privilege the essence of the name over the ability or need for it to be deciphered.

Nevertheless, the apparent ubiquity of the monograms throughout the church shows the importance of attaching a name (or an emblem of a name) to the monument. At this level, it would seem that decipherment was essential. However, as we have already seen, it is one thing to attach a name to a church, and another thing for that name to be known or read. When monograms convey titles, or combine names and titles (as on the Justinianic dish in Berlin that has been read as "Nektarios Kandidatos"),[36] the ability to decipher them becomes harder still. Rather than seeing a monogram as something to be read, perhaps we should see it as something to be recognized and interpreted in a different, visual way. Monograms are familiar from seals and coins and even bricks.[37] In these contexts they act as markers of

32 Whitby, "St Polyeuktos Epigram."

33 An issue discussed in Liz James, "'And Shall These Mute Stones Speak?' Text as Art," in *Art and Text in Byzantine Culture*, ed. eadem (Cambridge, 2007), 188–206.

34 For the central concern of identifying monograms to collectors, see the popular book of Robert Feind, *Byzantinische Monogramme und Eigennamen: Alphabetisiertes Wörterbuch* (Regenstauf, 2010), 30–32.

35 Gustave L. Schlumberger, *Sigillographie de l'Empire byzantin* (Paris, 1884), 84; cited in Walter Fink, "Neue Deutungsvorschläge zu einigen byzantinischen Monogrammen," in *Buzantios: Festschrift für Herbert Hunger zum 70. Geburtstag*, ed. Wolfram Hörandner, Johannes Koder, Otto Kresten, and Erich

Trapp (Vienna, 1984), 85–94, at 86. See also Walter Fink and Werner Seibt, "Neue Wege zur Deutung der Monogramme," in *Akten der XVI. Internationalern Byzantinistenkongress* (Vienna, 1981), 1:1.

36 Arne Effenberger and Hans Georg Severin, *Das Museum für Spätantike und Byzantinische Kunst Berlin* (Berlin, 1992), 143, no. 55; and Erica C. Dodd, *Byzantine Silver Stamps*, DOS 7 (Washington, D.C., 1961), 77, no. 12.

37 Jonathan Bardill, *Brickstamps of Constantinople*, Oxford Monographs on Classical Archaeology 1–2 (Oxford, 2004).

FIG. II.4.
Lintel from the
south portico
of the kastron
at al-Anderin,
Syria, 558.

Photo courtesy of
Christine Strube.

identity, ownership, and validation with a quasi-legal status as a substitute for the presence of the actual person. The relationship between man (or woman) and seal is complex. In the fourth century, Quintus Aurelius Symmachus distinguished in one of his letters between the reading (*legi*) of his monogram and what he called the perceiving/comprehending (*intellegi*) of it. The second, he said, was much easier than the first.[38] For him the monogram was clearly as much a symbol through which a man could be recognized and understood as a name simply to be read.

The forms of monograms encourage these symbolic interpretations. Their design, particularly after the introduction of the cross monogram in the sixth century (in which all the letters are structured around a central cross), allows them to add additional layers of meaning through allusions and visual associations. In 558, a local governor named Thomas placed his monogram fifteen times on doorways and capitals around the *kastron* (fortified citadel) at Androna (al-Anderin) in Syria. On their own they acted as a significant and insistent proclamation of

ownership. However, they are frequently paired with other monograms, either the chi-rho monogram, or monograms made up of the words Φῶς Ζωή Θωμά ("Light [and] life [of] Thomas"). The three different monogram types are visually interlinked, and this encourages viewers to see them as equivalents, as on the south entrance to the kastron where all three types appear side by side on two neighboring monumental lintels, giving the name of Thomas a spiritual authority equivalent to that of the name of Christ (fig. 11.4).[39] The prominence of the A and Ω in Thomas's name further echoes the A and Ω in the chi-rho monogram.[40] That this was not simply a coincidence is revealed by the donor inscription Thomas set up on the west gate of the kastron, which explicitly likens Thomas the savior to God the Savior:

Νόμος τοῖς ἄλλοις ἐπιδόσει πλόυτου
θερ[απεύειν το]ὺς πλίονα[ς]
σὺ δέ, ὦ βέλτιστε καὶ θαυμάσιε Θωμᾶ,
καὶ [τῇ πόλει] φαιδρύνη καὶ τῇ πατρίδι
δι' ὧν εὐγνωμονεῖς. Ἀνεφάν[ης] σωτήρ,
Θ[εο]ῦ Σωτῆρος τοῖς σοῖς βουλεύμασει
συνλαμβάνιν φροντίζοντος.[41]

38 Quintus Aurelius Symmachus, *Lettres I (livres I–II)*, ed. J.-P. Callu (Paris, 1972), 2.12 (p. 160): "Non minore sane cura cupio cognoscere, an omnes obsignatas epistulas meas sumpseris eo anulo, quo nomen meum magis intellegi quam legi promptum est." I owe this reference to Walter Fink, "Das frühbyzantinische Monogramm: Untersuchungen zu Lösungsmöglichkeiten," *JÖB* 30 (1981): 83.

39 Christine Strube, "Androna / Al Andarin: Vorbericht über die Grabungskampagnen in den Jahren 1997–2001," *AA* 2003, no. 1 (2003): fig. 48

40 Ibid., figs. 5 and 8.

41 William K. Prentice, *Publications of the Princeton University Archaeological Expedition to Syria in 1904–1905: Division 3,*

a

b

c

d

e

f

It is the custom for others to court the masses by largess of their wealth; but you, O best and wonderful Thomas, shine to both your city and your fatherland, through your acts of prudence. You appear as a savior, God the Savior being minded to assist your plans.

It has similarly been suggested that the empress Theodora embodied meaning in the design of her monograms. She employed starkly different monograms in each of the churches with which she is linked. In the Church of Saints Sergios and Bakchos in Constantinople (ca. 530–33) her name is set in the form of a box monogram, but in Hagia Sophia (532–37) the letters appear around a cross monogram (figs. 11.5a–b).[42] The adoption of this different design has been linked by Walter Fink to Theodora's support for monophysitism, suggesting that what matters is not what is said, but how it is said: that the design rather than the deciphering of the name is the source of its real meaning. Unfortunately there is little concrete evidence to support one shape of monogram representing a particular theological belief.[43] The adoption by Theodora of such different monogram designs shows that they cannot simply be seen as a form of protoheraldic emblem. There are many cases that prove simple one-to-one correspondences were not always sought or desired. Areobindus (the husband of Anicia Juliana) created two completely different monograms of his

name for the ivory diptychs he produced to celebrate his consulship in Constantinople in 506 (figs. 11.5c–d);[44] and no two monograms in Saint Polyeuktos are identical.

Taking the opposite approach, the monograms of Justinian in Hagia Sophia replicate those used a few decades earlier by the emperor Anastasios (491–518) on his coins (figs. 11.5e–f).[45] Each emperor's monogram requires the same letters—A, I, N, O, C, T, and Y—and they chose to combine them in the same form.[46] On the one hand we can assume that neither of these emperors was concerned that they might be misidentified by their immediate circle, the limited audience with which each emperor was concerned. However, in a wider world, and over a longer time period, such knowledge could be, and indeed was, forgotten. While Anastasios could not look forward to anticipate imitators, Justinian must have been aware that his monograms simply replicated those of his predecessor; but he was clearly not

FIG. 11.5.
Monograms:
(a) Theodora, from Saints Sergios and Bakchos;
(b) Theodora, from Hagia Sophia;
(c) Areobindus, from ivory consular leaf of 506 (Lucca);
(d) Areobindus, from ivory consular leaf of 506 (Louvre);
(e) Anastasios, from nummus coin; and
(f) Justinian, from Hagia Sophia.

Greek and Latin Inscriptions in Syria; Section B, Northern Syria, pt. 2, *Il-Anderin, Kerrātîn, M'arâtâ* (Leiden, 1909), 45–47, no. 915; see now Strube, "Androna / Al Andarin," 69.

42   Harold Swainson, "Monograms on the Capitals of S. Sergius at Constantinople," *BZ* 4 (1895): 106–8.

43   Fink, "Neue Deutungsvorschläge." Werner Seibt, "Monogramm," in *RBK* 6: cols. 589–614, col. 593, says we should not disregard this reading, but he also considers the cross monogram as a more attractive design to suit the letters in Theodora's name.

44   Richard Delbrueck, *Die Consulardiptychen und verwandte Denkmäler* (Berlin, 1929), nos. 13–15; Wolfgang F. Volbach, *Elfenbeinarbeiten der Spätantike und des frühen Mittelalters,* Römisch-Germanisches Zentralmuseum zu Mainz, Katalog 7, 2nd ed. (Mainz, 1952), nos. 12–14; and Antony Eastmond, "Consular Diptychs, Rhetoric and the Languages of Art in Sixth-Century Constantinople," *AH* 33, no. 5 (2010): 742–65.

45   For coins of Anastasios, see Wolfgang Hahn and Michael A. Metlich, *Money of the Incipient Byzantium Empire,* vol. 1, *Anastasius I–Justinian I, 491–565,* Veröffentlichungen des Instituts für Numismatik und Geldgeschichte der Universität Wien 6 (Vienna, 2000), nos. 40² and 44. Hahn notes (p. 28) that it is possible that Justinian also revived the monogram on his coins, but none name Justinian on the obverse so this cannot be proven.

46   For Anastasios's monograms, see Alfred R. Bellinger and Philip Grierson, *Catalogue of the Byzantine Coins in the Dumbarton Oaks Collection and in the Whittemore Collection,* vol. 1, *Anastasius I to Maurice, 491–602* (Washington, D.C., 1966), 383. For the best drawings of the monograms, see Wolfgang Hahn and Michael A. Metlich, *Moneta Imperii Byzantini,* vol. 1, *Von Anastasius I. bis Justinianus I. (491–565),* Veröffentichungen der numismatischen Kommission 1 (Vienna, 1973), Prägetabelle 2:40, 44 (Anastasios); 6:53; 7:94; 9:253.

Monograms and the Art of Unhelpful Writing in Late Antiquity   229

concerned with the potential for misattribution. His reuse may indeed have had a political rationale: to present himself as the legitimate successor to Anastasios, whose family had been usurped when Justinian's uncle, Justin, took power in 518.[47] On coins Justinian also maintained a similar form of portrait bust to Anastasios.[48] This indicates that both the bust and the monogram represented the office of emperor rather than his person, and suggests that the symbols represent ideals rather than individuals.

Monograms indicate that words were not always designed to communicate meaning through their contents. Monograms are fundamentally unstable and inconsistent in the relationship between sign and referent. It is clear that they represent names and titles, but equally it is clear that they do not always facilitate decipherment. Rather, monograms ask you to accept them as an *idea* of a word that you do not need to read: they are essentially images that mark the presence of a donor or patron, who therefore becomes more of an abstract concept (as the overlap between Justinian and Anastasios implies). This shifts attention away from questions of identity to a consideration of the nature of the actual votive offering—the building in which they appear. The shift away from specific names to a more general notion that words imply ownership and mark presence can be applied more widely to other types of inscription.

This is apparent in the votive mosaics in the north inner aisle of the Church of Saint Demetrios in Thessalonike. Although largely destroyed by fire in 1917, the mosaics are well recorded in the watercolors of W. S. George, now in the British School at Athens.[49] At the right-hand end of the

sequence of mosaics Saint Demetrios stands in front of a representation of his ciborium (fig. 11.6). Three donors approach the saint, their hands covered in reverence. Two more saints appear in roundels in the top corners of the panel.

Names and identities were once overt in the panel: the two saints in roundels at the top seem originally to have been accompanied by inscriptions.[50] Demetrios, the patron saint of the church and city and the principal figure in the scene, has no inscription, but viewers would have been able to recognize him instantly. The first book of the *Miracula*, the text of the miracles performed by Saint Demetrios that was written circa 610 (i.e., after these mosaics were installed), makes frequent reference to the saint appearing to people in dreams and visions, and their being able to recognize him because he is "dressed as one sees him in the images."[51] Indeed, throughout the church Demetrios appears in the same guise, with short, straight, blond hair and wearing a *chlamys* gathered over his right shoulder. It is that consistency that enables us to distinguish him, the patron of the church, from other unnamed saints depicted elsewhere in the nave.

Given this emphasis on likeness in the identification of Saint Demetrios, we might expect a similar emphasis among the three donors. They are clearly portrayed as distinct individuals. All wear distinctive robes—each is unique in color, style, ornaments, and fringes—and all have distinct facial features, notably the receding hairline of the right-hand figure, leaving that distinctive central quiff of hair. These facial types are not generic and can be compared with equally distinct faces of donors elsewhere along the north inner aisle mosaics, indicating that a similar degree of recognizability (or at least, individuality) was envisaged for all of them. All these donors must have come from the wealthy

47   On Anicia Juliana's Saint Polyeuktos as a response to this usurpation, see Harrison, *Temple for Byzantium*, 36.

48   Hahn and Metlich, *Money*, 1:4.

49   Robin Cormack, *The Church of Saint Demetrios: The Watercolours and Drawings of W. S. George* (Thessalonike, 1985); idem, "The Mosaic Decoration of S. Demetrios, Thessaloniki: A Re-examination in the Light of the Drawings of W. S. George," *Annual of the British School at Athens* 64 (1969): 17–52; idem, "The Making of a Patron Saint: The Powers of Art and Ritual in Byzantine Thessaloniki," in *World Art: Themes of Unity in Diversity*, ed. I. Lavin (University Park, Pa., and London, 1986), 3:547–58. Leslie Brubaker, "Elites and Patronage in Early Byzantium: The Evidence from H. Demetrios at Thessaloniki," in *Elites Old and New in the Byzantine and Early Islamic Near East*, ed. John Haldon (Princeton, 2004), 63–90, argues that

the Maria cycle, the fourth set reading from west to east, is in fact more than one votive panel and refers to more than one person, despite the use of a unified frame around the full length of this section.

50   Only one inscription is recorded by George; this fragmentary inscription of the right-hand saint might be reconstructed as Alexandros: Ο ΑΓΙ[ος Ἀλέξαν]ΔΡΟΣ.

51   Paul Lemerle, *Les plus anciens recueils des miracles de saint Démétrius* (Paris, 1979), 1: VIII 70 (102:9); X 89 (115:16–17); XV, 167 (162:17); 2: VI 311 (239:5–7); all other references are collected in Brubaker, "Elites and Patronage in Early Byzantium," 80.

FIG. 11.6.
Mosaic of Saint Demetrios with anonymous donors, from Saint Demetrios, Thessalonike, spandrel H of the north inner aisle, ca. 600.

Watercolor by W. S. George. Photo reproduced with permission of the British School at Athens.

elite of the city to qualify for the dress that they wear and their ability to commission and erect mosaics so close to the ciborium of the saint.

However, they are not identified. The text reads only "Ὑπ[ὲρ ε]ὐχῆ[ς ο]ὗ οἶδ[εν] ὁ θ[εὸς τ]ὸ ὄνο[μα]" ("As a prayer for one whose name God knows").[52] The contents of the inscription seek to deny an earthly memory for the donor and so shift the importance of memory from the words to the image. On the one hand we might

be expected to recognize an important member of the city's elite; but on the other we are implicitly instructed to ignore such an identification, just as we might know of Justinian's responsibility for Hagia Sophia but be unsure how to read his monogram. This array of relationships is repeated in the panel at the western end of the north inner aisle arcade, which has the same anonymous inscription.[53]

52   Cormack, "Mosaic Decoration of S. Demetrios, Thessaloniki," 39.

53   Ibid., 25. One other example in Thessalonike appears in the Church of Hosios David, for which see Liz James, "Images of Text in Byzantine Art: The Apse Mosaic of Hosios David,

There is clearly a tension between the apparently distinctive identity of the individuals in the image and the ostentatious redundancy of the accompanying text.[54] So, what role does the text play? Why is it needed at all? The texts are structured to conform to general expectations of votive texts, with the standard opening Ὑπὲρ εὐχῆς (As a prayer for) only to confound them. When these anonymous inscriptions are discussed at all, it is to describe them as unremarkable examples of early Christian humility and modesty—a quirk that can safely be passed over without further discussion.[55] However, this text plays a particular role in the image, one which is separate from the consideration of its content. I argue that the inscription is designed to be understood as a caption, and as such highlights the image itself, which is the true votive offering and representation of the act of prayer.

The mosaics of Saint Demetrios draw a clear distinction between votive texts and inscriptions that represent the act of prayer. When direct prayers are intended, they are represented in a distinct manner that shows the words being conveyed to God. This is most evident in the mosaic on the south face of the north pier of the sanctuary, which shows the Mother of God and Saint Theodore praying to Christ, who appears above them (fig. 11.7). The panel is accompanied by two different types of text. Beneath the panel are the remains of the votive inscription that once explained its commissioning: "ἐν ἀνθρώποις ἀπελπισθεὶς παρὰ δὲ τῆς σῆς δυνάμεως ζωοποιηθεὶς εὐχαριστῶν ἀνεθέμην" ("discouraged by men, made alive by your strength, in thankfulness I dedicate [this]").[56] The second text appears on the scroll held by the Mother of God and

reads: "Κ[ύρι]ε ὁ Θ[εὸ]ς εἰσάκουσον τῆς φωνῆς τῆς δεήσεώς μου, ὅτι ὑπὲρ τοῦ κόσμου δέομαι" ("Lord God, hearken to the voice of my prayer, for I pray for the world").[57] The two texts are very different. The first is not a prayer, it is a caption that establishes the panel itself as the prayer. The content of that prayer is imagined as the intercessory plea of the Mother of God herself, and is visualized as the text on the scroll that she holds while gesturing up to God. In order to distinguish the two texts more clearly, the prayer is further emphasized by the appearance of a title on the upper roll of the scroll: "Δέησις" ("Supplication").

There is a clear divide here between texts that are designed to be seen as written versions of oral texts and texts which act as visual captions. The first of these present transcriptions of prayers: words to God that can be re-enacted every time they are pronounced (as in prayers with the form "Lord, help X").[58] The second is to mark out the status of what they accompany, in this case the intercessory mosaic image. These inscriptions have an indicative function rather than an intercessory one: as the inscription says, something is present "as a prayer for."[59] They are captions explaining the act of piety that they accompany. The fact that translations so often present these texts in the form of prepositional phrases ("As a prayer for," "For the salvation of," etc.) emphasizes that they simply ask the viewer to look elsewhere for the actual prayer itself, whether that be the whole building, part of its floor or wall decoration, or one of the instruments of the

Thessaloniki," in *Bild und Text im Mittelalter*, ed. Karin Krause and Barbara Schellewald (Cologne and Weimar, 2011), 255–66.

54 This redundancy is confirmed by the third panel, which also has unnamed donors but no other inscriptions.

55 As noted by Gordana Babić, "North Chapel of the Quatrefoil Church at Ohrid and Its Mosaic Floor," *ZRVI* 13 (1971): 263–75; Mary Beard, "The Function of the Written Word in Roman Religion," in *Literacy in the Roman World*, ed. John H. Humphrey, *JRA*, Supplementary Series 3 (Ann Arbor, 1991), 35–58; and Yasin, *Saints and Church Spaces*, 148 n. 106, have noted the exceptional nature of these inscriptions, but without further analysis.

56 Ralph F. Hoddinott, *Early Byzantine Churches in Macedonia and Southern Serbia: A Study of the Origins and the Initial*

Development of East Christian Art (London and New York, 1963), 154.

57 Ibid.

58 Primarily oral understandings of texts are proposed by Amy Papalexandrou, "Echoes of Orality in the Monumental Inscriptions of Byzantium," in James, *Art and Text* (n. 33 above), 139–60; and Amy Papalexandrou, "Text in Context: Eloquent Monuments and the Byzantine Beholder," *Word & Image* 17, no. 3 (2001): 259–83. See also Christina Maranci, "Performance and Church Exterior in Medieval Armenia," in *Visualizing Medieval Performance: Perspectives, Histories, Contexts*, ed. Elina Gertsman (Aldershot, 2008), 17–32. For an initial warning against texts as oral residues see Beard, "Function of the Written Word," 37–38.

59 Oleg Grabar, "Graffiti or Proclamations: Why Write on Buildings?" in *The Cairo Heritage*, ed. Doris Behrens-Abouseif (Cairo, 2006), 69–75, reprinted in his *Islamic Art and Beyond*, Constructing the Study of Islamic Art 3 (Aldershot, 2006), 239–44, at 239.

FIG. 11.7.   Mosaic of the Mother of God and Saint Theodore from Saint Demetrios, Thessalonike, south face of the north pier of the sanctuary, ca. 600.

Photo: C. Bakirtzis, E. Kourkoutidou-Nikolaidou, and C. Mavropoulou-Tsioumi, *Mosaics of Thessaloniki, 4th–14th Century* (Athens, 2012), fig. 42, with permission.

liturgy. The same intent was planned for monograms, which usually encode their names with genitive endings: "Of Justinian," "Of Theodora," and so forth.

A paten and chalice in the Benaki Museum bring these two elements together: the paten inscription proclaims it as an anonymous offering by people whose names are known only to God, but it is accompanied by a monogram that Anastasia Drandaki has deciphered as the name Maria.[60] The presence of a name and the claim of anonymity are not easily reconciled, which makes me think that we are not meant to understand the monogram as something to be read. These inscriptions point to meanings that lie elsewhere. The people who commissioned them were more concerned that the physical object be understood as a gift than they were that the acknowledgements for the gift be appreciated by those on earth.

Further corroboration of the importance of presence over content can be found in other examples in which the names in votive texts are concealed in more elaborate ways. The seventh-century church of Saint Sergios at Matiane in Cappadocia contains a number of votive texts placed in various locations around the church.[61] However, two are of particular interest. They appear in the standard tabula ansata format that so often denotes a foundation prayer, similar to Justinian's votive foundation text in the Nea Ekklesia in Jerusalem, and are written in a similarly bold (if considerably less elegant) majuscule script.[62] The frame and the script both evoke notions of legibility, clarity, and function; however, anyone trying to read the inscriptions faces problems. The texts cannot be read, they can only be deciphered. They are written in code using a substitution cipher. The most prominent of the inscriptions appears thus:

inscription	as deciphered	translation
+ ΘΖϟΕШꙀΖϟ	+ Ἅγιε Σέργι,	Saint Sergios, bring help
ΗΛΒΑΒШΛΝΨΛ	βοήθησον τὸ-	to your servant Longinos,
ΝϟΛΧΟΛΝШΛΧ	ν δοῦλόν σου	to your servant Maria,
ΟΛΝΖϟΝΛΝΠΘϟ	Λονγῖνον καὶ	and to...
ΨΒΝϟΛΧΟΕΝ	τὴν δούλεν	
ШΛΧΖΘΡϟΘΝ	σου Μαρίαν	
ΠΘϟΨΟΝΚΘΡΘΖΕΝ	καὶ τὸν παραμεν..	
ΛШ...Ο...Ν +	ος...λ...ν +	

The desire to conceal meaning here suggests a real concern with audience, in particular a desire to limit it by exclusion. Only a chosen few could bask in the (smug) satisfaction of being among the intimate group that could comprehend the words. For everyone else it was solely a text to be seen, and by that means it gained power.[63]

However, this deliberate mystification also hints at a more ambiguous world on the fringes of Christian orthodoxy, one that believed in the magical power of words. This could cut two ways. Some early Syrian churches employed cryptograms both to conceal the meaning of words and to retain their spiritual power, such as replacing ΑΜΗΝ with ΑΚΟΗ (ἀκοή, which means "hearing") or the letters ϟΘ. All have equivalence as they share an alphanumeric value of 99.[64]

On the other hand such practices could smack of something altogether darker and more suspicious. When Marianos, the eparch of

60 *Transition to Christianity: Art of Late Antiquity, 3rd–7th Century AD*, ed. Anastasia Lazaridou (New York, 2011), 143, cat. nos. 107, 108. Inscription: ΥΠΕΡ ΕΥΧΗΣ ΟΝ ΟΙΔΕΝ Ο Θ[εο]Σ ΤΑ ΟΝΟΜΑΤΑ + (As a prayer for those whose names God knows); monogram: ΜΑΡΙΑΣ (of Maria).

61 Catherine Jolivet-Lévy and Nicole Lemaigre Demesnil, "Saint-Serge de Matianè, son décor sculpté et ses inscriptions," *Travaux et Memoires* 15 (2005): 67–84. All that follows reproduces Demesnil's careful scholarship.

62 Israeli and Mevorah, *Cradle of Christianity*, 192.

63 Baines, "Earliest Egyptian Writing," 151–52.

64 William K. Prentice, "Magical Formulae on Lintels of the Christian Period in Syria," *AJA* 10, no. 2 (1906): 137–50, esp. 146–50.

Thessalonike, fell ill in about 620, one of his associates brought him a parchment to tie around his neck, on which were inscribed formulae and magical words that could not be read. Marianos refused, saying: "since its writer did not wish to make clear the force of what was written, is it not plain that nothing good has been inscribed upon it?"[65] Marianos was worried that the words on his parchment were imbued with power from non-Christian sources, and there must have been a concern that the coded inscriptions in Saint Sergios drew on a similar tradition.

The link between all these examples is their awareness of the power of the written word. They differ only in their attitudes as to its applicability and acceptability in different situations. What all share, however, is the need for the text to be physically present. These are not words to be spoken or read, they need to be seen, for then they accord power and authority to that with which they are associated.

In all these cases, the presence of the monogram or text was the most important element. It alerted the viewer to the fact that they were walking in or on a votive object, or viewing a votive offering to God. These texts were structured around an expectation of individual memory, but the very fact of that expectation allowed the memory to be circumvented. As Henry Maguire has argued with respect to the mosaic panels in Saint Demetrios with no inscriptions, the offering was between man and God, and so names were unnecessary because God knew them.[66] For Maguire the only audience was God, human viewers were not considered. However, this ignores the fact that a human audience was very much present, whether or not the text was meant for them. The texts and monograms that

I have considered here rely on that human presence for their meaning. It was by seeing these blocks of text or medallions of letters that the votive nature of mosaic floors or paintings could be made manifest. However, it is equally evident that meaning did not depend on comprehension. Few people could read the complete inscriptions in churches, either due to lack of literacy or to lack of readability (if, for example, the inscriptions were placed too high up or in an inaccessible location).[67] Rather, their meaning came from the confluence of the words, the locations, and the expectations of the viewers. The ultimate function of the inscriptions was to alert the viewer to the human agent behind the erection of a particular church or work of art. It was that fact that needed commemorating rather than the specific individual.

What these texts share is their intentional failure to reveal information that we modern readers consider crucial. Although the motives for this seem to have varied (a desire to conceal information from all, or a desire to limit access to that information to a select group) the results are the same: texts that are deliberately unhelpful, that present silent or invisible prayers to transfer attention to the real prayer embodied in the image, in the capital, in the floor, or in the whole church in which the text appears.

These inscriptions and monograms are evidence of a gradual shift away from the word and toward the image as the source for real engagement between man and God in the Byzantine world. Although all the inscriptions of this period owe their origins to the older Greco-Roman epigraphic habit, I think that they represent the beginning of a significant shift in the way this tradition is employed. The materiality and configuration of the words begin to overtake the content. There is a certain irony that this should take place in a religious culture that placed the idea of God as the Word at the heart of its theology.

65 Lemerle, *Miracles de saint Demetrius*, 1:61; cited in Henry Maguire, "Magic and the Christian Image," in *Byzantine Magic*, ed. idem (Washington, D.C., 1995), 51–71 at 62.

66 Henry Maguire, "Eufrasius and Friends: On Names and Their Absence in Byzantine Art," in James, *Art and Text*, 139–60.

67 James, "'And Shall These Mute Stones Speak?'"

The ideas in this paper were conceived during network meetings for a project titled *Viewing Texts: Word as Image and Ornament in Medieval Inscriptions*, funded by the Arts and Humanities Research Council in the UK: http://projects.beyondtext.ac.uk/wordasimage/ (accessed 3 February 2015).

The Performative Letter in the
Carolingian Sacramentary of Gellone

CYNTHIA HAHN

THE FAMED EARLY CAROLINGIAN MANUSCRIPT, THE GELLONE SACRAMEN-
tary (fig. 12.1), although not wanting for scholarly attention, benefits from a reexamination
in line with the concerns of this volume. In place of text-critical, stylistic, iconographic, or
historical approaches, we can reenvision the renowned liturgical manuscript as an innovative experiment of a quite particular "performative" kind. The striking images in the manuscript might be said
to serve not an illustrative, but rather a demonstrative function—they reach out to the viewer to
make contact, to instruct, and to rouse to faith. In other words, they do not "report" the liturgy of the
sacramentary, but instead facilitate its proper performance, helping to construct the ritual template
whereby the spiritual identity of the reader is shaped or affirmed.[1] From the very first image, introducing the text of the sacramentary, we encounter letters that enliven the page (see fig. 12.1). The figure
of Mary enacts both senses of the word "initial," not only serving as the letter I, but also creating an
environment for the beginning of the sacred text. She stimulates the viewer with the smell of incense
(swinging a censer and alerting us to divine presence), and she emphatically moves or "motivates" the
text by gesturing with a cross toward it.

Jean Porcher, the great manuscript scholar and art historian, makes an attempt to capture the
uniqueness of the Gellone manuscript and its initials in a uniquely spirited French passage:

> des initiales synthétiques, plantées en tête d'un chapitre comme une enseigne, comme des armoiries
> parlantes, une sorte de chiffre, à l'opposé du genre narratif antique, de l'illusion naturaliste.... Ces
> lettrines où se mêlent intimement texte et illustration, ces initiales synthétiques d'un genre inconnu,
> qui marquent de façon précise le confluent des courants meditérranéens et barbares.[2]

---

1 "A performative is that discursive practice that enacts or produces that which it names" (by reference to a code it repeats, enacted
with one's body): Judith Butler, *Bodies that Matter: On the Discursive Limits of "Sex"* (New York, 1993), 13. For performance,
see John Langshaw Austin, *How to Do Things with Words* (Cambridge, 1962); Judith Butler, *Gender Trouble: Feminism and the
Subversion of Identity* (New York, 1990); Geoff Boucher, "The Politics of Performativity: A Critique of Judith Butler," *Parrhesia* 1
(2006): 112–41; and many other studies. For medieval considerations, see Elina Geertsman, ed., *Visualizing Medieval Performance:
Perspectives, Histories, Contexts* (Aldershot, 2008); and Andrew Cowell, "Swords, Clubs, and Relics: Performance, Identity, and
the Sacred," *Yale French Studies* 110 (2006): 7–18. It is also of interest to remember Meyer Schapiro's discussion of the frontal as
opposed to profile in his *Words and Pictures: On the Literal and Symbolic in the Illustration of a Text* (The Hague, 1973).

2 Quoted by Deshusses combining various of Porcher's comments from Jean Porcher, "Les manuscrits à peintures," in *L'Europe
des invasions*, ed. Jean Hubert, Jean Porcher, and Wolfgang Fritz Volbach (Paris, 1967), at 188–206, at 188, 195, and 206; in Antoine
Dumas and Jean Deshusses, eds., *Liber sacramentorum Gellonensis*, CCSL (Turnhout, 1981), xi. Deshusses is responsible for the

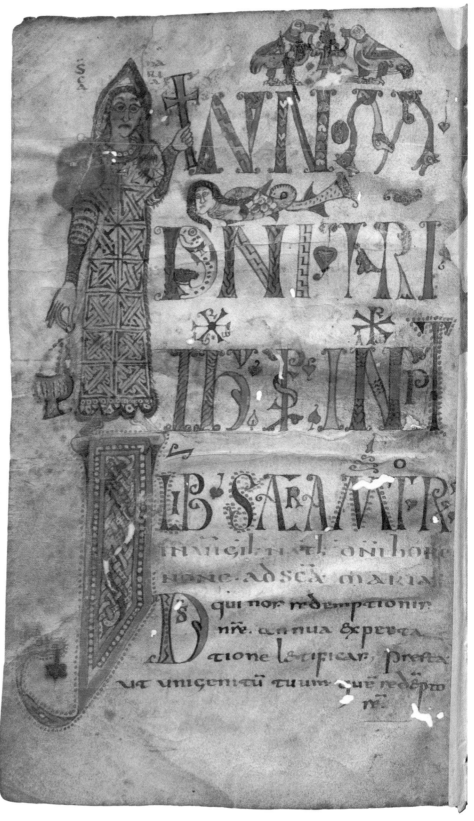

FIG. 12.1.

Letter I as "Maria." Gellone Sacramentary, Paris BnF, lat. 12048, fol. 1r.

Photo courtesy of the Bibliothèque nationale de France.

Porcher piles up terms such as "sign," "talking heraldry," and "a sort of code" in trying to describe the quality of the imagery of the "synthetic initials, planted at the head of each chapter like a sign," each of which is clearly opposed to "antique narrative" and most surely counter to "naturalist illusionism." Porcher seems to have felt that somehow the letters of the Gellone "intimately mix text and illustration" to create a "genre [as yet] unknown," fed by "currents flowing together from both the classical and barbarian traditions." Porcher was much concerned with understanding the workings of style in medieval art, and characterizes some of his perceptions in stylistic terms—Mediterranean versus northern and signlike as opposed to illusionistic. Although style will not be our primary concern here, this description serves to highlight an understanding that a mix of traditions—a combination of figurative narrative and flat signlike imagery—is important to the effect of the art of the Gellone Sacramentary.

Other characterizations of the manuscript have focused on iconography and have not only failed to capture the richness of the lively world of Gellone's animistic letters but have also fallen back on explaining some of the most compelling imagery only in terms of predecessors and precedents. In striking contrast, of illustrated sacramentaries in general Eric Palazzo has asked, "one may wonder whether such illustrations, joined to the text which the celebrant must speak, played any role in the act of praying itself."[3] I would argue this is precisely the

possibility we must investigate in the illustration of the Gellone Sacramentary. In refocusing our queries, we might once more proclaim wonder at the brash innovation of the Gellone artist and attempt to engage with the letters he produced as he seems to have intended. Perhaps we can even propose that this book is the very moment of innovation and can try to understand the artist—often identified as David because that name is inscribed in two initials in the manuscript—as an agent of considerable invention.[4]

There is one other book that can be properly compared to the Gellone Sacramentary as a product of the same milieu: a copy of the *De trinitate* of Augustine now in Cambrai (ms. 300).[5] Rather than contextualize and normalize the innovations of Gellone, however, the Cambrai Augustine only brings them into higher relief. The formation of the letters of the script, and even their ornamentation, are a precise match to examples in the Gellone, prompting scholars to attribute portions of both to the same scribe (and therefore identify one scribe among the four that have been discerned in the Gellone manuscript).[6] Because the two manuscripts are so alike in these features, it may be justified to conceptualize Cambrai as the baseline of manuscript production at the ecclesiastical center where both were made. In contrast to this norm, in many of its innovative elements Gellone makes a striking leap forward. In just one example of the extent of these innovations, it should be noted that there are no figures in the Cambrai manuscript, but many inhabit the pages of Gellone.

Other comparanda among early medieval manuscripts further highlight Gellone's novelty. What is often considered the greatest innovation

introductory essay, Dumas for the editing of the sacramentary text. I will not cite page numbers for the text when I supply folio numbers for initials. Other monographic studies of the manuscript include B. Teyssèdre, *Le sacramentaire de Gellone et la figure humaine dans les manuscrits francs du VIIIᵉ siècle: De l'enluminure à l'illustration* (Toulouse, 1959); Jean Nougaret, *L'iconographie du Sacramentaire de Gellone* (Montpellier, 1993); and Pierre de Puniet, ed., *Le Sacramentaire romain de Gellone*, Bibliotheca Ephemerides Liturgicae (Rome, 1939). See also Carl R. Baldwin, "The Scriptorium of the Sacramentary of Gellone," *Scriptorium* 25 (1971): 3–17; Jean Deshusses, "Le Sacramentaire de Gellone dans son contexte historique," *Ephemerides Liturgicae* 75 (1961): 193–210. And see more general work, including Christine Jacobi-Mirwald, *Text-Buchstabe-Bilde: Studien zur historisierten Initiale im 8. und 9. Jahrhundert* (Berlin, 1998). The manuscript is mentioned countless times in medieval surveys of history, art, and liturgy.

3   Eric Palazzo, *A History of Liturgical Books from the Beginning to the Thirteenth Century* (Collegeville, Minn., 1998), 60;

Cyrille Vogel, "Les échanges liturgiques entre Rome et les pays francs jusqu'à l'époque de Charlemagne," in *Le chiese nei regni dell'Europa occidentale e loro rapporti con Roma sino all'800, 7–13 aprile 1959* (Spoleto, 1960), 229–46.

4   Dumas and Deshusses, *Liber sacramentorum Gellonensis*, xii. On Carolingian artists see Lawrence Nees, "On Carolingian Book Painters: The Ottoboni Gospels and Its Transfiguration Master," *ArtB* 83 (2001): 209–39, esp. 211–12, where he suggests that David worked at Meaux and travelled to Cambrai.

5   Dumas and Deshusses, *Liber sacramentorum Gellonensis*, xi; Baldwin, "Scriptorium."

6   Dumas and Deshusses, *Liber sacramentorum Gellonensis*, xi; based on work by André Wilmart, "Le copiste du sacramentaire de Gellone au service du chapitre de Cambrai," *RBén* 42 (1930): 210–32.

of Carolingian manuscript production—the development of the historiated initial—occurs in unique form in the Gellone. Two Anglo-Saxon manuscripts of the eighth century, the Leningrad (or St. Petersburg) Bede and the Vespasian Psalter, most likely predate the Gellone in the use of historiated initials, but in those manuscripts the frame of the initial encloses a portrait or simple narrative story moment.[7] These reductive forms do not even begin to intimate the potential dynamism of the Gellone initials.[8] The Drogo Sacramentary of circa 870 also contains marvelous historiated initials, but in Benjamin Tilghman's words, the initials have by this time become frames for "narrative interventions."[9] The Drogo frames transport us to places decidedly separate from the text and its space, abandoning the unique signlike quality of the Gellone letters.[10] A more comparable quality in which letter and action are tightly unified and even respond to liturgical concerns can be found in the Corbie Psalter and to some degree in the Stuttgart Psalter, but both may postdate Gellone and do not create quite the same performative effect of what one might call "direct address."[11]

So, despite the occasional characterization of the vigorous drawings as childlike, the Gellone must be recognized as quite the contrary, an important creative move in the history of Carolingian manuscript production.

Indeed, by every indication, the Gellone is a very carefully produced manuscript. It consists of 259 folios of relatively small format (300 × 180 mm), but comparable to other Cambrai liturgical manuscripts.[12] Although the number of lines per page varies, its gatherings are entirely regular and the process of illustration is precise. In the first half of the book, the leading scribe (whom we will call David),[13] apparently drew the initials at the same moment the text was written.[14] In the second portion of the book, written by other scribes, spaces were left and notes appended for David and another rubricator to add initials and rubrics. Given that so few elaborated initials were added in the second half, perhaps the initials in that part can be considered as even more purposeful than those of the first half, added with no trace of the spontaneous "whimsy" that is often attributed to the initials of Gellone. For example, at the beginning of a special Mass to be said in time of war there is a small abbreviated notation to the left of the space set aside for the initial and rubric. The words read: "mis(sa) temp(o)r(um) belli," and match precisely those of the rubric itself. But if we allow ourselves to query the process of making, we can easily imagine that the note served as inspiration for the content of the initial. The initial takes the form of an uncial D, the tail formed by the body of a fully armed warrior on horseback. A second initial below, a P, shows an arm brandishing a weapon.

The Gellone Sacramentary is a liturgical book, and as such is filled with the proper and efficacious words for liturgical ceremony. As

7   For the Vespasian Psalter: David H. Wright, *The Vespasian Psalter: British Museum Cotton Vespasian A 1* (Copenhagen, 1967). For the Bede: Meyer Schapiro, "The Decoration of the Leningrad Manuscript of Bede," *Scriptorium* 12 (1958): 191–207.

8   Ulrich Rehm, "Der Körper der Stimme: Überlegungen zur historisierten Initiale karolingischer Zeit," *ZKunstg* 65 (2005): 441–59.

9   Benjamin C. Tilghman, "The Shape of the Word: Extralinguistic Meaning in Insular Display Lettering," *Word & Image* 27 (2011): 292–308.

10   Bibliothèque Nationale, *Drogo-Sakramentar, Ms. Lat. 9428, Bibliothèque Nationale* (Paris and Graz, Austria, 1974); and Robert G. Calkins, "Liturgical Sequence and Decorative Crescendo in the Drogo Sacramentary," *Gesta* 25 (1986): 17–23.

11   Rehm emphasizes the "voice" of the letter with its potential for both danger and salvation, "Der Körper der Stimme," 449 and passim. Heather Pulliam, "Exaltation and Humiliation: The Decorated Initials of the Corbie Psalter (Amiens, Bibliothèque municipale, MS 18)," *Gesta* 49 (2010): 97–115, esp. 106–7 discussing fol. 136v, which presents some parallels to my thesis here. See also eadem, "Eloquent Ornament: Exegesis and Entanglement in the Corbie Psalter," in *Studies in the Illustration of the Psalter*, St Andrews Studies in the History of Art, ed. Brendan Cassidy and Rosemary Muir Wright (Stamford, 2000), 24–33; and Felix Heinzer, *Wörtliche Bilder: Zur Funktion der Literal-Illustration im Stuttgarter Psalter (um 830)* (Berlin, 2005). Also, more generally Jean-Claude Schmitt, "Le rythme des images et de la voix," *Histoire de l'Art* 60 (2007): 43–56; and E. Pirotte, "La Parole est aux images: La lettre, l'espace et la voix dans les évangéliaires insulaires

(VII–IXème siècle)," in *Les images dans les sociétés médiévales: Pour une histoire comparée; Actes du colloque international*, ed. Jean-Claude Schmitt and Jean-Marie Sansterre, Bulletin de l'Institut Historique Belge de Rome 69 (Rome, 1999), 61–75.

12   Deshusses, "Le Sacramentaire," 197.

13   Although the name David does occur twice in the manuscript, we cannot be certain this is the artist's name. Nevertheless, there is a chance and I want to assert that the artist deserves "naming."

14   Dumas and Deshusses, *Liber sacramentorum Gellonensis*, xi; following Wilmart, "Le copiste."

Jean Deshusses has shown, however, the text of Gellone was creative and contested, and was quickly replaced with a more authoritative version worked out under the aegis of the Carolingian court as part of an effort of political unification. Liturgical scholars have argued that the Gellone is the best examplar of the Franco-Gelasian Sacramentary, a text that realized Pippin's directives to create a standard version of the sacramentary. The Gellone manuscript is monastic in origin and was only completed circa 760–770. Despite the fact that it is the best surviving witness to the Franco-Gelasian text, it also contains supplements that derive from the later Gregorian Sacramentary, and even elements from a specific version of the Gregorian Sacramentary, the *Hadrianum* (see below). These additions consist of adjustments to the baptismal ceremony and the addition of prayers that are useful only to a bishop—that is, episcopal blessings.[15]

We must, therefore, understand the production of the Gellone manuscript to have occurred not only in an environment passionately attentive to the text of the sacramentary but also during an era in which that text was contested. Indeed, when Charlemagne requested a better exemplar from Rome, the Gregorian Sacramentary that was sent, commonly called the *Hadrianum* and imported into the empire between 784 and 791,[16] quickly supplanted the Franco-Gelasian text. Ironically, the *Hadrianum* did not supply the necessary resolution to the need for a single unified text to be used throughout the Frankish empire. The *Hadrianum* was a festal sacramentary, more or less specific to Rome, and required further emendation and supplementation; subsequent modifications were not complete until circa 850.[17] Because it was made during such an active period of reform, the Gellone, as Marianne Besseyre is surely justified in arguing,

is a uniquely expressive product of a Carolingian "liturgical culture."[18]

Although not universally acknowledged, these observations about the liturgical text have led to an adjustment of the dating of Gellone from circa 780 to circa 790–804 (a later date that takes into account the presence of additions from the *Hadrianum*). Therefore, although many art historians still mention the monastery of Rebais in the diocese of Meaux as a possible site for the production of the manuscript,[19] the stylistic comparison to the Cambrai manuscript and the liturgical evidence make a compelling argument that the book was produced for the Cathedral of Notre Dame in Cambrai, whose bishop, Hildouard, was a man who seems to have been in the thick of Carolingian liturgical debates.[20] Indeed, he is thought to also be responsible for the best Carolingian copy of the *Hadrianum* (Cambrai, Bm, ms. 164).[21] Jean Deshusses confirms Hildouard's importance for other reforms and intellectual efforts dear to the Carolingian court.[22]

Although the authority of the Gellone liturgical text was quickly superseded, remarkably, the book itself did not lose its value or prestige and seems to have entered the Carolingian gift economy. Despite its small size and the modest materials of its ornamentation, it seems to have been considered something of a prize possession, even landing in the hands of a famous member

15 Dumas and Deshusses, *Liber sacramentorum Gellonensis*, xviii–xxiii.

16 Palazzo, *History of Liturgical Books*, 45–48.

17 Ibid., 52–53; Vogel, "Les échanges liturgiques." It is interesting to note that Teyssèdre calculates Easter dates from the *Hadrianum* and concludes that the manuscript was made in either 769 or 791, but rejects the latter as "too late": *Le sacramentaire*, 10.

18 Marianne Besseyre, "Une iconographie sacerdotale du Christ et des évangélistes dans les manuscrits bretons des IXᵉ et Xᵉ siècles," in *La Bretagne carolingienne: Entre influences insulaires et continentals*, ed. Jean-Luc Deuffic, special issue of *Pecia* 12 (2007): 7–26, esp. 13. For sacramentaries in the Carolingian culture as an instrument of unification, see Marie-Pierre Laffitte and Charlotte Denoël, *Trésors carolingiens: Livres manuscrits de Charlemagne à Charles le Chauve* (Paris, 2007), entry by Besseyre on the Gellone Sacramentary, 78–83. Also: Marie Anne Mayeski, "Reading the Word in a Eucharistic Context: The Shape and Methods of Early Medieval Exegesis," in *Medieval Liturgy: A Book of Essays*, ed. L. Larsen-Miller (New York, 1997), 61–84.

19 Teyssèdre, *Le sacramentaire*, 14.

20 Deshusses, intro., *Liber sacramentorum Gellonensis*, xx.

21 Patrick Périn and Laure-Charlotte Feffer, *La Neustrie: Les pays au nord de la Loire de Dagobert à Charles le Chauve (VIIᵉ–IXᵉ siècle)* (Rouen, 1985), 121, n. 19; cited by Palazzo, *History of Liturgical Books*, 51. See also Marie-Pierre Laffitte, "La politique religieuse et la réforme liturgique," in *Trésors carolingiens*, ed. Laffitte and Denoël, 43–47, esp. 46.

22 Deshusses, "Sacramentaire de Gellone," 198–99.

of the Carolingian court, William of Orange. Thereafter, it was apparently donated, along with "many other books," silver Eucharistic implements, and a golden reliquary containing a bit of the True Cross, to the monastery of Gellone by William.[23]

William of Orange was count of Toulouse and a cousin and favorite of Charlemagne. He founded the monastery of Gellone along with his former comrade in arms turned Carolingian monastic reformer, Benedict of Aniane. That Benedict had an interest in the monastery is of particular note because it is now believed that he was responsible for the Carolingian program of continuing emendations to the *Hadrianum* text (eventually completed in 850).[24] At the monastery, today called Saint-Guilhelm-le-Désert, it would seem that someone took care that the out-of-date liturgy in the Gellone manuscript was partially corrected and updated by means of marginal annotation and additions. It has been observed that its pristine condition indicates it was not used on a daily basis,[25] but its survival demonstrates its value as an object and perhaps, more specifically, as an artistic object. A later inscription on its "title page" marks it as William's gift; clearly it was a prestigious donation worthy of remembrance.[26]

It is not, however, the aesthetic, material, or iconographic value of the imagery of the Gellone that is its primary appeal, but again, what I would like to call its lively performative quality. It was meant to induce engagement with the text that would lead to a deeper understanding of sacred ritual. I believe the imagery was first and foremost addressed to the celebrant and others enacting the ceremony—bishop, priest, deacon, monk, and so forth—and that it was meant primarily for these eyes, or I should also

say, for these eyes, ears, lips, even these noses. Eric Palazzo has eloquently argued that the presence of a book during liturgical ritual signifies the presence of Christ and, in its multisensory claims on the viewer, creates a space of charged sacramental meaning.[27] He maintains that even the specific parts of the book had significance— the very texture of the parchment surface of the manuscript worked as a directive commanding that the skin of a believer was to be polished and perfected;[28] and the sculptural presence of the binding conveyed the presence of the body of Christ.[29] Consonant with this argument and important to our purposes here, contemporary writers asserted that the letters themselves were performative, and that they served as something more than mere signs. In some sense they were gateways or entry points into the text, and even into other more sacred realities.

The particularly charged nature of writing, and of initial letters specifically, has been amply demonstrated,[30] and Herbert Kessler supports similar ideas in his essay in this volume (chap. 6). Didier Méhu, among others in this publication, argues that sacramentaries, in particular from about 700, exhibit a new visuality expressed in graphic signs and indicative of a larger project of creating sanctified space (see chap. 13). Ivan Drpić writes of the poetic nature of the text that is revealed in the visual (chap. 3), and Anthony Eastmond and Vincent Debiais stress the multivalent nature and epigraphic use

23 Teyssèdre, *Le sacramentaire*, 12. Barbara Baert, "Le sacramentaire de Gellone (750–790) et l'invention de la Croix: L'image entre le symbole et l'histoire," *Arte cristiana* 86 (1998): 449–60, esp. 450, discusses the link to Charlemagne. See also Baldwin, "Scriptorium," 16.

24 Palazzo, *History of Liturgical Books*, 53. Similarly, the Godescalc Evangeliary left the court to be given to Saint-Sernin in Toulouse, perhaps before 814: Laffitte and Denoël, *Trésors carolingiens*, 93.

25 Deshusses, "Sacramentaire," 209.

26 Teyssèdre, *Le sacramentaire*, 11–12, added notes occur on fols. 1r, 123v–124r, 275v, and 276r.

27 Eric Palazzo, "Le Livre-corps à l'époque carolingienne et son rôle dans la liturgie de la messe et sa théologie," *Questiones Medii Aevi Novae* 15 (2010): 31–63, esp. 36.

28 Ibid., 36; Eric Palazzo, "Art, Liturgy, and the Five Senses in the Early Middle Ages," *Viator* 41, no. 1 (2010): 23–56; and Jean-Claude Bonne, "Rituel de la couleur: Fonctionnement et usage des images dans le Sacramentaire de Saint-Étienne de Limoges," in *Image et Signification: Rencontres de l'ecole du Louvre* (Paris, 1983), 129–39.

29 Susannah Fisher, "Materializing the Word: Ottonian Treasury Bindings and Viewer Reception" (Ph.D. diss., Rutgers University, 2012). Unfortunately, the Gellone does not retain its original binding.

30 Cynthia Hahn, "Letter and Spirit: The Power of the Letter, the Enlivenment of the Word in Medieval Art," in *Visible Writings: Cultures, Forms, Readings*, ed. Marija Dalbello and Mary Shaw (New Brunswick, N.J., 2011), 55–76; Laura Kendrick, *Animating the Letter: The Figurative Embodiment of Writing from Late Antiquity to the Renaissance* (Columbus, Ohio, 1999); and Carl Nordenfalk, *Die spätantiken Zierbuchstaben* (Stockholm, 1970).

of letters, even if in some cases they are illegible (chaps. 11 and 7, respectively).

To understand why this empowerment of physical letters occurred in the Christian text tradition, we can turn to the words of Second Corinthians 3:2–3, where we read that Christians and their faith were in some sense constituted by what one might call the act of spiritual writing made physical: "You show that you are a letter [epistle] from Christ, the result of our ministry, written not with ink but with the spirit of the living God, not on tablets of stone but on tablets of human hearts." If the individual Christian was constituted in the writing of words, the larger text, i.e., the whole, must be the Church as collective entity or even the spirit of God. Quite literally, text is a space of performance and faith.

But not every word or letter is equal, or even capable of reaching its full potential. Context matters. Letters that initiate the names or qualities of God, letters and words that initiate particular texts, even letters of particular shapes might be more efficacious in the pursuit of this project. David, the artist of the Gellone, seems to have preferred the letters O, Q, and D. It may be that these forms create enclosed frames that permit sight beyond or imaginative entry into spiritual spaces and particularly suited to his intentions.[31] He also liked Es and Fs, whose crossbars take an active stance and "reach out." Kessler demonstrates a wider appreciation in Carolingian manuscripts of some of these same letters and, similarly, Méhu, following Jean-Claude Bonne, argues that neumes, as a specific subcategory of scriptural marks, do not, as it might be supposed, signify a particular musical note, but instead indicate *qualities* of singing (see Kessler, chap. 6, and Méhu, chap. 13).[32]

This is a precise moment in the development of the letter as a mark, as a signifier, and as

an actant. David created initials that are based on the play of the surface of the text, but then abruptly allow a penetration beyond, both spatially and spiritually. In Gellone, circles are the only places that show "depth" or overlap, and the only places that allow the penetration of figures. However, these circles are also "pushed" by the tails of insular Ds and Qs. Arms extend; animals bite and eat and interact. The page is transformed into a menagerie filled with snakes, birds, and fish, the "sea" or "air" of the the vellum surface,[33] but at the same time it becomes a space that has the potential to create *alternative* spaces. Even the nonframed images create trajectories of meaning.

Marianne Besseyre has perhaps shown the most interpretive zest in terms of scholarly treatment of these initials. She calls attention to an angel holding a snake that bites its own tail used to form the D of *Deus* preceding a prayer of exorcism on folio 113v. As she argues, the image "anticipates the effect of the prayer to oblige the malevolent animal to 'say' the name of God."[34] With even more insight into matters liturgical, Besseyre explicates initial letters shaped as the figures of the Evangelists dressed as deacons, carrying books, and provided with the heads of Evangelical beasts. They occur in a section of the baptismal rite, the third scrutiny, also called the *Apertio aurium* ("opening of the ears"), in which the new Christians are introduced to the meanings of the Evangelists and the "good news" and mysteries of the faith. In the ceremony, the four Gospels are taken from the treasury and placed on the four corners of the altar (presumably as four separate manuscripts?) and the mystical meaning of the beasts is then explained. For example, the ox reveals the sacrificial nature of Luke. This particular section of the baptismal liturgy did not survive Carolingian reforms, and therefore Gellone is almost unique among Carolingian manuscripts in containing it. As Besseyre argues, "under our very eyes [is enacted] the sacramental actualization of the revelation of Christological message that inspired the liturgical act," that is, the vision of Ezekiel.[35] I

31   See examples on folios 4r, 27r, 30r, 38r, 54r, 56r, 65r, 77r, 78r, 79r, 83r, 113v, 208v, 209r, 227v, among many others. Dumas and Deshusses, *Liber sacramentorum Gellonensis*, reproduces many of the initials, and one can see the entire manuscript with notes at http://gallica.bnf.fr.

32   Jean-Claude Bonne and Eduardo H. Aubert, "Quand voir fait chanter: Images et neumes dans le tonaire du ms. BNF latin 1118; Entre performance et performativité," in *La performance des images*, ed. Alain Dierkens, Gil Bartholeyns, and Thomas Golsenne (Brussels, 2010), 225–40.

33   Kendrick, *Animating the Letter*, 57, 72.

34   Besseyre, *Trésors carolingiens*, 83.

35   Besseyre, "Une iconographie sacerdotale," 14.

would go even further. The beasts are vested as deacons with liturgically appropriate stoles (as Besseyre observed, note the narrow orange band on the eagle's shoulder), and deacons serve as the readers of the Gospel text during the liturgy, so it is as if the initials mirror or duplicate the actions of the participants in the liturgy. If, as in Second Corinthians, Christians are parts of the larger "text" of the Church, here the deacon-letters are shown to speak as the Evangelists, to merge with their being. In a remarkable way this is realized visually in the figure of John (fig. 12.2), in which the wings of the eagle wrap and enclose him, possibly even standing in for the human figure, and the beast-Evangelist-deacon clasps the book to his heart.

In a similar fashion, many other initials reference participants in the service. A letter D on folio 57r encloses two birds flanking a chalice and prefaces a text that describes the actions of a priest and an archdeacon. On folio 123v, an arm holding a cross emerges from a letter E and precedes a text that speaks of God inciting the devotee to find his full potential in faith. Often figures manipulate foliage—eating it, clearing it, and offering it—perhaps referring to the life-giving nourishment of the Gospels and the liturgy. In one case, on folio 40v, a shy rabbit seems to take comfort and refuge in the form of the O of *Omnipotens*, all the while feasting on foliage. The image precedes an address to catechumens. In the D for the word *Deus* on folio 227v, prefacing a blessing of animals, a lamb with a superimposed cross portrays the sacrificial lamb who seems to be nourished by the vegetation; the initial preceding a text which speaks of "accepting, indeed tasting this benediction."[36]

A series of heads, often taken as humorous, is also testimony to participation in the text. The heads are remarkable for the depiction of eyes and hairstyles; that is, the eyes are often enlarged to indicate the direction of the gaze, and the hairstyles differentiate monks and laymen, tonsured and shaven or not.[37] On folio 18r, in the O of *Omnipotens*, we see a monk's head,

shaven and tonsured, with large liquid eyes that sadly gaze heavenward (fig. 12.3). Below, an arm "pushes" a D for the abbreviation of *Deus*. The text these letters precede asks God to "make us always desirous of acting with devotion and serving your majesty with a sincere heart" and then continues "we offer the host." Similarly, on folio 234r with a prayer for a traveler's return, a bearded lay figure looks down, perhaps in humility; and on folio 173v a cowled, shaven figure humbly lowers his eyes, prefacing a prayer to be used during the scrutiny of a catechumen, asking that sin and the devil be expelled.

Finally, in this quick survey of the initials of the manuscript, I would call attention to the sequence of images on folios 54r and 55v, where the initial letter O of *oremus* and *omnipotens* alternates down the page, ornamenting prayers for use during the feast of the Passion.[38] Each of the seventeen circular (or polygonal) letters O is filled with cosmic imagery of a sort identified long ago by Otto Karl Werckmeister,[39] and further explicated in Kessler's essay in this volume (chap. 6). On folio 54v, the sequence progresses from a relatively simple floriate O with a surrounding wreath of cosmic "force" to other similar but simpler forms, then to a *tetragonus mundi* (a diamond-shaped O filled with interlace knots implying both a world map and a Greek letter);[40] to a complex shape filled with an image of a bird and snakes; and finally to a wreath enclosing a lamb and vegetation, surely a Christological image.[41] It is as if the artist is building upon and manipulating effects that are possible with the surfaces and "depths" of his letters, their movement, and their geometry. As Bonne has argued, it is the complexity of the ornament that serves as an invitation to look, to think, and, here, to react. Ornament takes a primary place because it works effectively as a supplement and completion to

36 Dumas and Deshusses, *Liber sacramentorum Gellonensis*, 421, 425.

37 Teyssèdre, *Le sacramentaire*, 29, discusses heads in the manuscript, comparing them to others from the period and noting the emotions of some of those in Gellone.

38 Dumas and Deshusses, *Liber sacramentorum Gellonensis*, 86–87.

39 Two of the seventeen have been cut out, so only fifteen survive. Otto Karl Werckmeister, *Irisch-northumbrische Buchmalerei des 8. Jahrhunderts und monastische Spiritualität* (Berlin, 1963). Also see the essay by Guibert de la Vaissière in Nougaret, *Iconographie*, 33–34, who mentions cosmic circles in Insular art.

40 Tilghman, "Shape of the Word," 292.

41 Teyssèdre, *Le sacramentaire*, 68 mentions this image along with other suggestive vegetation.

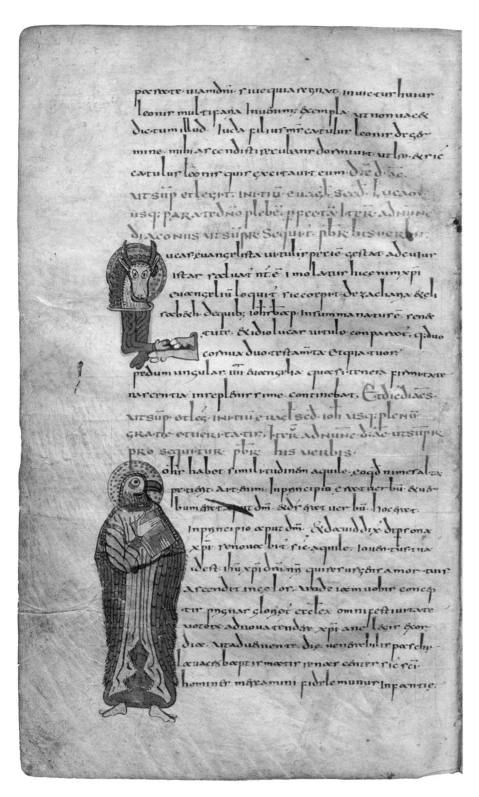

FIG. 12.2.

Letter I as Evangelist John. Gellone Sacramentary, Paris BnF, lat. 12048, fol. 42v.

Photo courtesy of the Bibliothèque nationale de France.

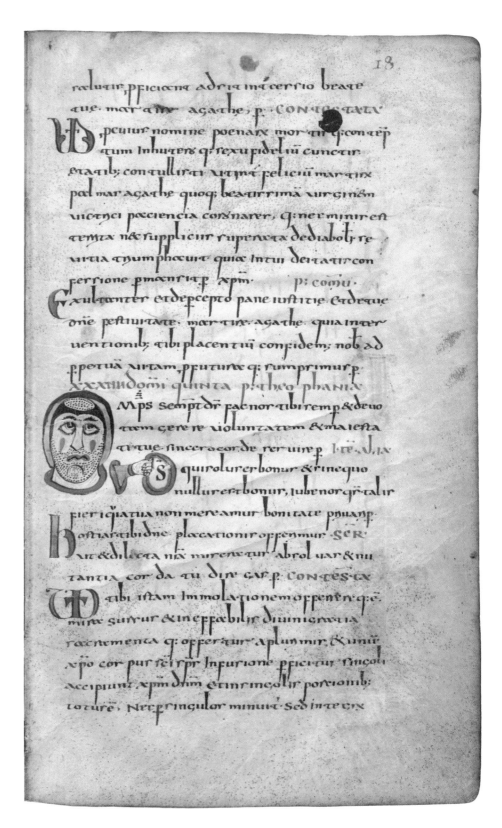

FIG. 12.3.

O of *Omnipotens*, D of *Deus*. Gellone Sacramentary, Paris BnF, lat. 12048, fol. 18r.

Photo courtesy of the Bibliothèque nationale de France.

CYNTHIA HAHN

the "bodies of the letters it celebrates."[42] This theme and variation continues for pages, in what amounts to the densest sequence of ornamented initials in the manuscript.

In a similar exploitation of the shapes of letters, Kessler discusses the potential and meaning of the "dynamic ideograph" of the Vere dignum, in which the linked letters V and D serve as an abbreviation of and substitution for the repeated liturgical phrase and prayer. The unification of the two letter shapes creates a third shape, a cross, and this specific construction may have originated in the Gellone manuscript, where it occurs frequently.[43] Kessler argues that the conjoined letters, as they occur in Gellone, show or perform the joining of body and soul, or even the miracle of transubstantiation (see Kessler, chap. 6).

Contemporary texts help us understand the environment within which such visual expression flourished. An anonymous text written at Fleury in the ninth century, *Expositio de litteris quomodo nominantur vel quale sonum habeant inter se*, explores the meaning of letter shapes.[44] The author writes: "We call the O the crown." He notes that O also signifies unity or Christ spread throughout the world by the Church. Q pushes out heretics and schismatics, presumably with its tail. T has two parts and signifies both body and soul, or two arms of Christ drawing all to him. In the Fleury text, each letter is given a meaning and even an action. Whether, as historians, we can take each of these meanings seriously or should dismiss the accumulation as a surfeit of symbolic "noise," nevertheless a message is delivered. It is apparent that letters qua letters might *signify* to readers of the Carolingian period and that a rich interface of meaning would have enlivened and animated the surface of the Gellone's pages for the medieval viewer.

We are investigating a historical milieu in which, as Martin Irvine argues, textual culture is material culture. He quotes an anonymous Carolingian author as writing: "Although letters and parts [of a statement] are heard, they are seen and can be touched in a book."[45] An author of the tenth century argues that "reading is established by seven foundations: sight, hearing, pen, hand, ink, wax, and parchment."[46] Or, finally, Isidore of Seville asserts that "the practice of letters was invented for the memory of things. Things would vanish into oblivion unless they were bound in letters."[47] The practice of literature, of writing letters, is in this conception tightly bound to physical inscription and a sustained interaction with that inscription that was multisensory and engaged with multiple media.

Indeed, in contrast to our own era's lack of respect for its discipline, during the Middle Ages, *grammatica*, based on a foundation in letters, was conceived of as the mother of writing and interpretation, the font of all medieval learning. Letters were the atoms or elements of writing, and of course *littera* is the etymological root of literature. Writing in its most elemental form, i.e., letters, was considered "the irreducible ground of knowledge and the vehicle of the Scriptures."[48] As opposed to vocalized *litterae*, which were termed *elementa*, written letters were called *figurae* or *notae*.[49] Just as grammar operates on two levels as the foundation as well as the potential for the interpretation of texts, so also letters, as the foundation of text, have two interrelated ontologies: physical form and potential meaning. And of course, as above, scripturally the people of the Church are in some sense also written texts, the foundation of the Church's "text" and yet also the source of action.

Within this general aura of meaning and performance among the letters of the Gellone and other manuscripts of the time, I would argue that David was emboldened to take yet another step, extending letters to a new and heightened level of signification. I will focus on an examination of four letters in the manuscript that

42 Jean-Claude Bonne, "Noeuds d'écritures (le fragment I de l'Evangeliaire de Durham)," in *Texte-Image, Bild-Text*, ed. Sybil Dumchen and Michael Nerlich (Berlin, 1990), 85–105, esp. 100, 101.

43 A suggestion made by Didier Méhu during the conference.

44 Hermann Hagen, ed., *Anecdota Helvetica*, Grammatici Latini (Leipzig, 1870): Bern, Stadtbibliothek 417, pp. 302–5 and cxiii–cxxxxvi.

45 Martin Irvine, *The Making of Textual Culture: "Grammatica" and Literary Theory, 350–1100* (Cambridge, 1994), 104.

46 Ibid.

47 Ibid., 214, quoting the *Etymologiae* I.3.

48 Ibid., 100–103.

49 Ibid., 97.

push the boundaries of the text and its potential through visual expression.

The first letter, the I we have already seen, occurs on the opening page of the manuscript (see fig. 12.1). It serves, as many I initials in manuscripts do (from as early as the first codices), as a sort of entry point, a column that supports and begins the textual structure, sometimes figured as the column of the Temple of Jerusalem.[50] Here, however, the I becomes a figure clearly identified by an inscription. This is "Maria" of the Vigil of the Feast of the Nativity; Mary, the patron saint of the cathedral in Cambrai for which the manuscript was originally made; Mary the patron of Santa Maria Maggiore in Rome, the Roman station for this feast; and Mary, the mother of Christ not yet born. She is the gate of heaven and the entry point to the text in the most universal sense.[51] As the text notes, Christ is expected, soon to be visible in the flesh—a coming for which one must prepare the mind and the heart.[52]

Despite the necessity of his absence in this example, it is unusual for an image of this period to depict Mary without the Christ child. In place of holding the child, however, this Mary takes up a different action. She swings a censer and carries a liturgical cross, making an entrance like an attendant of the Temple, creating a smell, space, and an environment of movement and anticipation that introduces the liturgy. Furthermore, she literally pushes with the cross to initiate the text. Rather than an author's portrait at the beginning of our immersion into textuality, we are instead offered a saintly fellow participant.[53]

Our second example, the D on folio 76v, introduces the Mass for the Invention of the True Cross, an important new feast for the Western Church (fig. 12.4). Unlike another D on the same page, and unlike many of David's other hand-drawn circles and spheres, this circle is perfect, made with a compass in two precise, nested lines. The tail of this insular D, however, is anything but perfect or regular; it hardly seems to belong to the same letter. It is made up of a bit of scrub vegetation that swings off to the left, not this time "pushing" the letter, but itself being pushed aside by the busy figure who compositionally continues that tail and is depicted as excavating the contents of the circle. Unlike the depiction of Mary, this figure and this scene have a pictorial precedent.[54]

The Carolingians were greatly interested in this scene and knew it from texts that came from Jerusalem and the East, which told of Helena's discovery of the True Cross.[55] The narrative was illustrated more than once during this period. In the eighteen scenes of the so-called Wessobrunner Gebetbuch of 814, produced in Augsburg and illustrating the Cyriacus legend, the story is told at length.[56] In summary, Judas, a Jew with privileged information about the whereabouts of the Cross that was passed down through his family, was forced—thrown in a well and threatened with fire—by the Empress Helena to reveal its location and dig it up. Three crosses were discovered, but the miraculous resurrection of a dead criminal indicated which was the True Cross. The process and miracle converted Judas, who eventually became the bishop of Jerusalem and was responsible for discovering the nails of the Crucifixion and presenting them to Helena. In another Carolingian manuscript, the Vercelli *Canones conciliarum* circa 800 from Milan, the story occurs in an epitomized

50 Hahn, "Letter and Spirit," 65–66; Nordenfalk, *Die spätantiken Zierbuchstaben*, reproduces a number of Is made to look like columns, for example that in the *Evangelia*, from Split (Kapitelbibliothek, fol. 82).

51 Celia Chazelle, *The Crucified God in the Carolingian Era: Theology and Art of Christ's Passion* (Cambridge, 2001), 85.

52 Dumas and Deshusses, *Liber sacramentorum Gellonensis*, 1.

53 See Chazelle, *Crucified God*, 82–85; Besseyre, *Trésors carolingiens*; Nougaret, *L'iconographie*, 5–6; and Teyssèdre, *Le sacramentaire*, 78–82. All note that the figure is unusual. For Mary as "censer of sweet fragrance" in the East see L.-A. Hunt, "The Fine Incense of Virginity: A Late Twelfth-Century Wall Painting of the Annunciation at the Monastery of the Syrians, Egypt," *BMGS* 19 (1995): 182–233 (ref. courtesy Leslie MacCoull).

54 Barbara Baert, *A Heritage of Holy Wood: The Legend of the True Cross in Text and Image* (Leiden, 2004). See also eadem, "Le sacramentaire de Gellone."

55 Eadem, *Heritage of Holy Wood*, 59, n. 21 enumerates the extant contemporary manuscripts of the text of the Cyriacus legend, mostly Greek but including the Latin example at Saint Gall Stiftsbibl. Cod. 225, following Stephan Borgehammar, *How the Holy Cross Was Found: From the Event to Medieval Legend* (Stockholm, 1991), with Latin manuscripts on 210–13. Baert also notes the diversity of the text forms and concludes that this testifies to the legend's popularity, 74.

56 Carl von Kraus, *Die Handschriften des Wessobrunner Gebets* (Munich, 1922); and Baert, *Heritage of Holy Wood*, 72–76 with bibliography.

FIG. 12.4.

D for *Deus* of the Feast of the Invention of the True Cross. Gellone Sacramentary, Paris BnF, lat. 12048, fol. 76v.

Photo courtesy of the Bibliothèque nationale de France.

version, with Helen as a featured presence.[57] There, in superimposed registers, Judas digs up the crosses below and presents the True Cross to the enthroned empress above.

Although the Gellone image is clearly derivative of some sort of illustrative tradition rather than a new ad hoc creation, its correspondence to the images that survive is not precise. The representation in the Gellone is like the excavation scene in the lower register of the Vercelli codex in that Judas works alone, but it has the flavor of being one moment within an extended narrative as depicted in the Wessobrun prayer book. In most Carolingian iterations, Judas is a key player in the narrative, but his identification and even his presence is uncertain in the Gellone.

In the Gellone manuscript, the narrative is reduced to a minimum narrative unit of a single figure and a sparse setting. However, two scenes are in some sense depicted: the discovery of the cross and the discovery of the nails. In the Cyriacus legend, the digger is Judas who, as the text of the legend notes, acts voluntarily, *accepto fossorio*, "accepting the capacity of digger." Such a digger is a laborer of a particular type. His title is identical to those other diggers so important to Christian cult who excavated the catacombs and who are sometimes represented as heroic figures in catacomb frescoes.[58]

Furthermore, as Barbara Baert notes, the story is one that casts the discovery of the True Cross as the bringing of a state of order to the wilderness through the removal of the scrub vegetation.[59] The Gellone digger is alone in this wilderness, and other people or witnesses, notably Helena or any fellow workers, are missing. Additionally, most surprising and contrary to narrative sense, rather than an earthen pit, the void of the letter becomes a *corona triumphalis*, a perfectly circular celebratory wreath to honor the cross, very comparable to a similar O in a late antique Orosius manuscript in Florence.[60]

57   Ibid., 76–77; and Christopher Walter, "Les Dessins carolingiens dans un manuscrit de Verceil," *CahArch* 18 (1969): 99–107.

58   Baert, *Heritage of Holy Wood*, 67–68, esp. n. 49; Teyssèdre, *Le sacramentaire*, 159.

59   Baert, *Heritage of Holy Wood*, 68.

60   The manuscript is Paulus Orosius, *Historia adversus paganos*, Bibliotheca Medicea Laurenziana, Cod. Plut. LXV. 1, fol. 102. Cited by Nordenfalk, *Zierbuchstaben*, 143–44.

FIG. 12.5.
T of *Te igitur* and
I of *In primis*.
Gellone Sacramentary,
Paris BnF, lat. 12048,
fols. 143v and 144r.

Photos courtesy
of the Bibliothèque
nationale de France.

n primis q̄ tibi offe
rimus p ecclesia tua
scā catholica quam
pacificare custodire
adunare et regere
digneris toto orbe
terrarū unacūpamu
lo tuo papa nro ill
et antestite nro ill
et omnib; orto doxis
adq; apostolice fidei
cultorib;
Memento dñe famulor
famularū q; tuarum
et omnium circū ad
stantiū Quorū tibi
fides cognita ē et no
ta denocio. Qui tibi
offerū hoc sacrificiū
laud. p se suis q; om
nib; p redemptione
animarū suar. p spe
salutis et incol. om
nitatis suae. Tibi
reddunt uota sua
et nodo uiuo et uero
Communicantes et me
moria uenerantes
n primis gloriose
semp uirginis mariae
genetricis dī et dñi nri
ihu xpi. Sed et beatorū
apostulorū hac ō ...

Petri
Pauli
Andree
Iacobi
Iohannis
Thome
Iacobi
philippi
Bartholomei
mathei
Symonis
et taddei
Lini
cleti
clementis
xisti
corneli
cybriani
Laurenti
crisogoni
Iohannis
et pauli
cosme
et damiani
helari
martini
agustini
gregori
geronimi
Benedicti
Et omnium sconctorū
quorū meritis pcib;
que concedas

Finally, the cross of Christ in the Gellone initial is not a large wooden one, but a ceremonial cross (likely metal) with the alpha and omega (additional powerful letters) hanging from its crossbeam (cf. John 21:6).[61]

Rather than read this initial as the deposit of a tremendously complex iconography, I would suggest that the features of its representation originate in other concerns. One liturgical scholar has suggested that the Feast of the Invention is one that has a distinctively performative aspect.[62] That is, it is not a reiteration of a historical event (remember, Helena is not depicted in the Gellone image), but instead a moment when, through the words of the liturgy and the way that they repeat portions of the narrative of the Invention, the Christian "discovers" the True Cross (read: faith) for him- or herself. Such an approach fits very well with the tremendous interest in this text—visual, literary, and liturgical—exhibited during the Carolingian period.[63] Perhaps then we can reimagine this initial in line with others in the Gellone. The digger is not Judas but in some sense a reflection of the viewer or celebrant: he sweeps away the scrub, the brush of the site, of daily life, and of spiritual wilderness, to discover the perfect revelation of the True Cross. He "excavates" the meaning of the cross for himself each time the feast is performed.

Our third example is a culmination of the cycle, although it does not occur at the end. Perhaps even more innovative, and certainly more impressive than the I and the D (although marked by a certain crude vigor in its execution), is the envisioning of the letter T of *Te igitur* (fig. 12.5, left).[64] This is one of the first Carolingian depictions of the crucified Christ, and is unprecedented in its divergence from any norm that might be established before or after for the representation of the Crucifixion.[65] Although the side wound spurts blood, as do the wounds of the nails, Christ is not yet dead, and stares out of the page with wide eyes.[66] Rather than John and Mary, who usually appear in images of the Crucifixion, we see to either side of the cross angels with wings carpeted with eyes, who present the cross to us, holding it forward. The cross itself is not wood but an unearthly blue (the only use of blue in the manuscript!), studded with encrustations of pearls and rubies.[67] One might profitably compare the ornamentation depicted in this image to a reliquary (fig. 12.6). Furthermore, this image, a liturgical vision induced by the Eucharistic sacrifice of the Mass, might also be compared to the poetic imagery of the Anglo-Saxon *Dream of the Rood*. That poem describes gazing upon the cross and seeing a fluctuation or shimmering—the dreamer's vision flashes from treasure to bloody sacrifice and back again, "sometimes [the cross] was made moist with blood . . . sometimes adorned with treasure."[68] In the Gellone initial, the crucifix is both wet with vivid red blood *and* adorned with treasure. The equivalence of Christ's sacrifice and its ransom of man's sin, the meaning of the historical event and its manifestation in the "shining sign," are forcefully elided. The Te igitur image restages the paradoxical meaning of the Crucifixion, both the sacrifice that the Eucharist reenacts and the victory over death

61   Baert, *Heritage of Holy Wood*, and others have already noted this quality of the cross.

62   P. Regan, "Veneration of the Cross," *Worship* 52 (1978): 2–13.

63   Baert, *Heritage of Holy Wood*, and Louis Van Tongeren, *Exaltation of the Cross: Towards the Origins of the Feast of the Cross and the Meaning of the Cross in Early Medieval Liturgy* (Leuven, 2000).

64   Jacobi-Mirwold, *Text-Buchstabe-Bilde*, 43; Teyssèdre, *Le sacramentaire*, 108–21; Chazelle, *Crucified God*, 86–92.

65   For an excellent discussion of the Carolingian and earlier tradition of the crucified Christ, see Lawrence Nees, "On the Image of Christ Crucified in Early Medieval Art," in *Il Volto Santo in Europa: Culto e immagini del Crocifisso nel Medioevo; Atti del Convegno internazionale di Engelberg (13–16 settembre 2000)*, ed. Michele Camillo Ferrari and Andreas Meyer (Lucca, 2005), 345–85, esp. 366–69.

66   The lance wound is usually seen as the moment of death and initiation of the Church, even in the early Christian Church. See discussion in Rudolf Suntrup, "Te igitur-Initialen und Kanonbilder in mittelalterlichen Sakramentarhandschriften," in *Text und Bild: Aspekte des Zusammenwirkens zweier Künste im Mittelalter und früher Neuzeit*, ed. Christel Meier-Staubach and Uwe Ruberg (Wiesbaden, 1980), 278–382, esp. 313–20. Nees argues that in such images with open eyes, Christ is both living and dead: "Image of Christ Crucified," 354–56.

67   As noted by Nees, "Image of Christ Crucified," 366. Nees argues that this blue shows that Christ's body is equal to the "glorified body in heaven."

68   Cynthia Hahn, *Strange Beauty: Issues in the Making and Meaning of Reliquaries, 400–circa 1204* (University Park, Pa., 2012), 87–92.

FIG. 12.6.
Imperial reliquary
cross, 1024–1039,
Kaiserliche
Schatzkammer,
Vienna.

Photo by author.

that is simultaneously intimated and celebrated by the liturgy.[69]

This Mass in the Gellone Sacramentary begins with one of the most elaborate of the Vere dignum initials, along with large rubrics in capitals (143r). Turning the page, one sees another part of the text again written in red letters and, although in Latin, partially transposed into Greek letters, perhaps, Besseyre suggests, as a

reference to the *Trisagion* chanted in Greek, a sound of great mystery and divine presence.[70] The angels constitute the heavenly hosts summoned by the prayers to join in that chant, but we also note that in their presentation of the cross they resemble the golden Cherubim of the Ark of the Covenant. In this echo of that imagery, the sacrifice of Christ stands in for the Jewish

69 Christopher L. Chase, "'Christ III,' 'The Dream of the Rood,' and Early Christian Passion Piety," *Viator* 11 (1980): 11–33, esp. 13, links the *Dream* to another Old English poem, *Christ III*, which presents a suffering Christ who laments the torment of man's continuing sin.

70 Besseyre, *Trésors carolingiens*, 80. Nees, "Image of Christ Crucified," 369, argues that the elaborate letters emphasizes that the priest chants with the seraphim.

FIG. 12.7.   T of Te igitur, Carolingian Sacramentary. Tours, Bm, ms. 184, fol. 3r.
Photo courtesy of the Bibliothèque municipale de Tours.

offerings and occupies the place of propitiation, marking the space where one speaks to God.[71]

The celebrant surely did not need the physical text to say the words of the Canon of the Mass, he must have known them by heart. As Palazzo argues, the book, its text, and here its letters, are used because they evoke the divine presence.[72] They also represent, in the words that initiate the canon, "te igitur," a direct plea to God.[73] In confronting this page, the priest or bishop faced and addressed God, staring directly at the reality of the sacrifice bodied forth as Christ, feeling, perhaps even "smelling," the blood that shed and mixed with treasure. A dialogic moment is realized that emphatically embodies the meaning of the mass.

One further detail may clarify the artist's intention that the T of the Te igitur should serve not as a letter to be passed over as the text is read, but as an icon and a subject of contemplation. The Te igitur is on folio 143v. On folio 144r, facing the crucified Christ, a letter I inscribed with interlace and topped with a head turns toward the cross (fig. 12.6, right).[74] Like the heads we examined earlier that react to adjacent texts appropriately, the eyes on this face very clearly indicate a direction of the gaze and the face seems to be depicted as sad. In this instance, the figure is not clearly lay or ecclesiastic, but simply the figure of a young person, perhaps one of the "faithful" mentioned in the prayer, who contemplates the profound meaning of Christ's sacrifice.[75]

Finally, I would argue that a remarkable confirmation of the intended dialogic functioning of this image is supplied in a somewhat later Carolingian miniature. In a Te igitur miniature from a ninth-century Touronian sacramentary, an image illustrates the process I have described (but lacks much of the performative quality of the Gellone). In the only figurative image in the manuscript (fig. 12.7),[76] the T is a simple initial adorned with interlace, and its status and function as a letter is not challenged despite its insertion into an illusionistic image.[77] Nevertheless, the figure of a rapt celebrant added to the left of the letter, along with an altar and instruments of the Mass, makes it clear that the structure of the Gellone Te igitur is reiterated here, but in this case is enacted within the "space" of the page rather than directly between priest and initial. In the Tours manuscript, the celebrant is *depicted* as gazing upon the letter, upon the words of the Mass that have become the realization of the action of the sacrifice. It is as if we have a diagram of the intended function of the letter in the Gellone.

In this vein, one more initial in the Gellone demands our attention (indeed is the culmination of the process begun with the T). Although it is not a large or even striking letter—it might be easily missed—nor is it the last decorated letter in the manuscript, although it appears in the more sparsely decorated second half, it is a letter that reiterates the interactions we have discussed. It is the final initial on folio 152v (fig. 12.8), along with a benediction (to be said by the bishop) for the *Cena D(omi)ni*, which blesses the populace who have come to the table of the Lord asking for protection from torment and defense against the "ire" of the serpent by means of the Lord's "shield." The text on the page also mentions the ablutions of the feet of the Apostles. The D itself prefaces the subsequent prayer for the Vigil of Easter, referencing the sacrifice of Christ's death, the cleansing of Baptism, and the triumph of Christ over his enemies. The physical letter D is badly damaged. Whether by some sort of ritual washing, or by kissing, as Celia Chazelle has suggested, the figure of Christ is all but destroyed.[78] No matter what has caused

71 Elizabeth Saxon claims the angels are lifting the cross to the "heavenly altar": "Carolingian, Ottonian, and Romanesque Art and the Eucharist," in *A Companion to the Eucharist in the Middle Ages*, ed. Ian Levy, Gary Macy, and Kristen Van Ausdall (Leiden, 2011), 251–326, esp. 261.

72 Palazzo, *History of Liturgical Books*, 37.

73 I want to thank Joshua O'Driscoll for a discussion of this material.

74 Lawrence Nees, "Words and Images, Texts and Commentaries," in *Irish Historical Studies in Honour of Peter Harbison*, ed. Colum Hourihane (Dublin, 2004), 47–69, has already noted this figure, as has Saxon. She believes the figure is Ecclesia: "Carolingian, Ottonian," 262.

75 Nees has wondered whether this is Ecclesia or a "witness": "Image of Christ Crucified," 370.

76 Although the hand of God occurs in the Vere dignum intial on folio 2r.

77 Tours, Bm, ms. 184, fol. 3r.

78 Chazelle, *Crucified God*, 96.

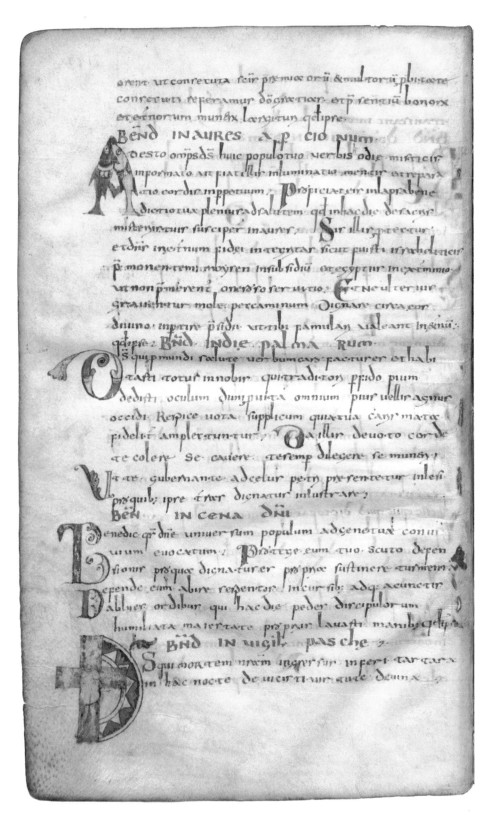

FIG. 12.8. D of *Deus*. Gellone Sacramentary, Paris BnF, lat. 12048, fol. 152v.

Photo courtesy of the Bibliothèque nationale de France.

the damage, the near obliteration of the figure of Christ clearly demonstrates a historical interaction with the manuscript that was fully and passionately physical.

Ultimately, what I hope to have shown in this essay is that the historiated initials of the Gellone Sacramentary are neither historical nor mimetic. They are neither simply narrative nor complexly iconographic. Instead, they range from animations of the page, to lively fragments, to reactions, to fully realized scenes that interact with their viewers and interlocutors. Rather than letters that are simply part of the text, they represent distinctively creative processes of imagination and ritual. The quail attends, the cock crows to wake us (both folio 34r). As grammar begins with letters and progresses to text and meaning, as individual members of the Church join together to make a larger spiritual body, these letters are read and performed as the experience of divine presence and the Christian need and desire to seek it. Hrabanus Maurus wrote of the experience of the liturgy:

[We] do our best to match ourselves to the ritual that we cultivate in our hearts; so that just as with the decorated walls of this very church, with many lighted candles, with voices variously raised through litanies and prayers, through reading and sound we can more earnestly offer praise to God: so we should always decorate the recesses of our hearts with the essential ornaments of good works ... always in the interior of our breast the holy sweetness of heavenly sayings and of Gospel praise should resonate in memory.[79]

Méhu also cites texts that speak to the creation of a "church" in the heart, and it is clear that in the Gellone, the artist aims for this effect, but rather than metaphoric and cumulative, the Gellone experience is an intimate, face-to-face encounter between priest and book. As Larry Nees emphasized, Gellone is both "liturgical and personal."[80] As the performance of the Mass requires the celebrant to experience an internal process provoked by the pronouncement of prayers and the experience of the materials of the Mass, here that performance is expanded through the viewing of a cross and a materialized letter. Whether as part of the liturgy or located within, as an individual's meditation, the effect is powerful. These letters not only perform on the page but also compose a "letter" [epistle] that is deeply impressed upon the heart (2 Corinthians 3:2–3).

79 PL 110:73–74, trans. Mary Carruthers, *The Craft of Thought: Meditation, Rhetoric, and the Making of Images, 400–1200* (Cambridge, 1998), 275.

80 Nees, "Image of Christ Crucified," 362.

The Colors of the Ritual

Description and Inscription of Church Dedication in Liturgical Manuscripts (10th–11th Centuries)

DIDIER MÉHU

THIS CHAPTER FOCUSES ON THE MODES AND THE MEANINGS CONCERNING the visuality of script in western liturgical manuscripts dating from the tenth and eleventh centuries. By *visuality*, I mean the potential of imagination and conceptualization provoked by the visible characters of the script. The understanding of written words proceeds from the recognition of the form of the letters, of the sounds to which this form refers, and of the meaning associated with each phoneme. This is the *legible form* of the word that the Latin grammarians call its *figura*, made visible as soon as words are distinguished from each other on the page by space, initials, or punctuation.[1] In a manuscript *figura* is associated with a word's *visible form*, which means all the formal processes by which the words are presented and organized on the parchment: the size and ornamentation of the letters, the arrangement of space on the page, the ink colors, the graphics and monograms, and so forth. These visible signs do not have any intrinsic meaning, but they confer on the text a cognitive dimension which is not included in its literality.[2]

These notions of visible form and visuality refer to the medieval concept of *visio*, as defined by Christian clerics from the time of Augustine of Hippo. *Visio* means spiritual understanding, insight, or conceptualization. It is a progressive cognitive process. Its outcome is the *visio Dei* ("God's vision"), which means the complete understanding of the truth (*veritas*). The *visio Dei* will no longer need sensorial mediation, and will not occur before the end of time. The terrestrial and human *visio* is a partial and veiled understanding, which uses formal mediations and sensory perceptions as a means of

---

1 Separated script was invented by Irish scribes in the 7th century. Irish and English grammatical treatises of the 7th and 8th centuries emphasize how the *figura* of words and sentences helps comprehension: Paul Saenger, *Space between Words: The Origins of Silent Reading* (Stanford, 1997), 83.

2 For a useful panorama on the visuality of medieval script in the Carolingian period, see Rosamond McKitterick, "Text and Image in the Carolingian World," in *The Uses of Literacy in Early Medieval Europe*, ed. eadem (Cambridge, 1990), 297–318. On Irish and English liturgical manuscripts from the 7th to 9th centuries, see Ben C. Tilghman, "The Shape of the Word: Extralinguistic Meaning in Insular Display Lettering," *Word & Image* 27, no. 3 (2011): 292–308. On different uses of colored script in medieval manuscripts, see Ulrich Ernst, "Farbe und Schrift im Mittelalter: Unter Berücksichtigung antiker Grundlagen und neuzeitlicher Rezeptionsformen," in *Testo e immagine nell'alto medioevo, Settimane di studio del Centro italiano di studi sull'alto medioevo* 41, 2 vols. (Spoleto, 1994), 1:343–415. For an anthropological approach to medieval script, including materiality and visuality of the text, see Joseph Morsel, "Ce qu'écrire veut dire au Moyen Âge: Observations préliminaires à une étude de la scripturalité médiévale," in *Écrire, compter, mesurer*, vol. 2, *Vers une histoire des rationalités pratiques*, ed. N. Coquery, F. Menant, and F. Weber (Paris, 2006), 4–32.

transcendence.[3] Reading is the paradigm of this cognitive progress. It uses visible signs understandable by the mediation of the body (the eye, or the voice when reading aloud); it becomes intelligible through the action of the mind; and it points the way to an imagination whose paths are not limited by the literality of the text.[4]

The question I will settle here is that of the role of formal characters in the cognitive experiment of the *visio*. Liturgical manuscripts are good starting points because they contain rites intended to spiritualize men, places, and objects. Nevertheless they are generally studied for their textual content or for their illuminations, but not as visual objects whose script, color, size, musical notes, and graphic signs are meaningful components. I will focus on the liturgical pieces of the church dedication ceremony because of the spectacular and multisensory nature of the rite, and also because of its particularly strong visual value.[5] This essay is part of a large survey that begins with the oldest dedication texts provided by liturgical manuscripts of the western Church, that is, those dating back to the beginning of the seventh century, and ends with those dating from the last quarter of the thirteenth century. During this long period, the western dedication rite (*ordo*) acquired its specific characteristics, became more and more complex and ceremonial, and provoked commentaries before reaching an established form with the Pontifical of Willelmus Durandus, circa 1290.[6] I will not

consider all seven centuries in this chapter. After a brief look at the modes of script visualization in liturgical manuscripts of the eighth to tenth centuries, I will focus on the so-called Lanaleth Pontifical, a manuscript composed in southwest England around the year 1000, which presents a striking visualization of the dedication ordo.

The Visuality of Script in Liturgical Manuscripts of the Eighth to Tenth Centuries

The oldest liturgical manuscripts, such as the so-called Leonine Sacramentary composed in Verona at the beginning of the seventh century, are written with Roman uncial script and do not present any ornament.[7] The sacramentaries and lectionaries composed in eastern Gaul in the first half of the eighth century present a new visuality, in which I have recognized five types of modulations.[8] Colored letters, most frequently

---

3 A very good collection of papers on the medieval *visio* is presented in *La visione e lo sguardo nel Medio Evo / View and Vision in the Middle Ages*, Micrologus 5–6 (Sismel, 1997–98). On the Latin tradition of the *visio Dei* from Augustine to the 13th century, see Olivier Boulnois, *Au-delà de l'image: Une archéologie du visuel au Moyen Âge, V^e–XVIe siècle* (Paris, 2008). For a stimulating reflection on the structural role of the *visio* in medieval society, see Alain Guerreau, "Stabilità, via, visione: Le creature e il creatore nello spazio medievale," in *Arti e storia nel Medioevo*, vol. 3, *Del vedere: Pubblici, forme e funzioni*, ed. Enrico Castelnuovo and Giuseppe Sergi (Turin, 2004), 167–97.

4 Ivan Illich, *Du lisible au visible: La naissance du texte; Sur L'art de lire de Hugues de Saint-Victor* (Paris, 1991).

5 On the multisensory nature of the church dedication ritual, see Didier Méhu, "Images, signes et figures de la consécration de l'église dans l'Occident médiéval: Les fonts baptismaux de l'église Saint-Boniface de Freckenhorst (XIIe siècle)," in *Mises en scène et mémoires et de la consécration de l'église dans l'Occident médiéval*, ed. idem (Turnhout, 2007), 285–326.

6 On the evolution of the ritual before the Carolingian period, see Miriam Czock, *Gottes Haus: Untersuchungen zur Kirche*

als heiligen Raum von der Spätantike bis ins Frühmittelalter (Berlin and Boston, 2012). For a useful panorama of the evolution of the western ritual from the 4th to the 16th century, including the Byzantine rite, see Peter Wünsche, "'Quomodo ecclesia debeat dedicari': Zur Feiergestalt der westlichen Kirchweihliturgie vom Frühmittelalter bis zum nachtridentinischen Pontifikale von 1596," in *"Das Haus Gottes, das seid ihr selbst": Mittelalterliches und barockes Kirchenverständnis im Spiegel der Kirchweihe*, ed. R. M. W. Stammberger and C. Sticher (Berlin, 2006), 113–41. On the different texts related to the ritual produced from the 5th to the 13th century, see Didier Méhu, "*Historiae* et *imagines* de la consécration de l'église au Moyen Âge," in idem, ed., *Mises en scène*, 15–48.

7 Verona, Bibl. Cap., Cod. 85 (olim 80), ed. Leo Cunibert Mohlberg, Leo Eizenhöfer, and Pierre Siffrin, *Sacramentarium Veronense (Cod. Bibl. Capit. Veron. LXXXV [80])*, Rerum ecclesiasticarum documenta: Series maior, Fontes 1, 2nd rev. ed. (Rome, 1966). The text is written in black uncial without any ornament, except some titles in red.

8 There are five well-known manuscripts. The Luxeuil Lectionary, composed in Luxeuil ca. 700 for the bishop of Langres: Paris, BnF, lat. 9427, http://gallica.bnf.fr/ark:/12148/btv1b84516388.r=latin+9427.langFR (accessed 27 March 2015); Pierre Salmon, ed., *Le lectionnaire de Luxeuil (Paris, ms. lat. 9427)*, 2 vols. (Rome, 1944–53). The Missale Gothicum, a Burgundian sacramentary composed in Luxeuil at the end of the 7th cent.: BAV, Cod. Reg. lat. 317; facsimile: Leo Cunibert Molberg, ed., *Missale gothicum: Faksimile-Ausgabe* (Augsburg, 1929); Els Rose, ed., *Missale Gothicum: E codice Vaticano Reginensi Latino 317 editum*, CCSL 159D (Turnhout, 2005). The Bobbio Missal, a lectionary-sacramentary composed ca. 700, probably in Vienna: Paris, BnF, lat. 13246; facsimile: J. W. Legg, E. A. Lowe, A. Wilmart, and H. A. Wilson, eds., *The Bobbio Missal, a Gallican Mass-book (ms. Paris, Lat. 13246)*, 3 vols., Henry Bradshaw Society 53, 58, 61 (London, 1917–24); Yitzhak Hen and Rob Meens, eds., *The Bobbio Missal: Liturgy*

in red, yellow, and green are introduced in titles and incipit (Luxeuil Lectionary, Missale Gothicum, Bobbio Missal, Missale Gallicanum vetus, Missale Francorum). The size of the letters varies, with those of the titles generally twice as large as those in the texts. The case of the letters also varies, sometimes alternating between two modes, with Roman capital in titles and uncial in the body text (Missale Gallicanum vetus); sometimes between three modes (Luxeuil Lectionary), with Roman capital in titles (names of the feasts) and in the incipit of the *lectiones*, uncial in subtitles (names of the lectiones), and "Merovingian minuscule" in the lectiones. Ornamented initials whose forms associate the classical *figura* of a letter with vegetal or animal motifs (such as fish or birds), and whose bodies are painted and inhabited by interlaces, circles, and roses, are the oldest known in western liturgical manuscripts (Luxeuil Lectionary, Missale Gallicanum vetus, Missale Gothicum).[9] The last innovation is the introduction of an iconicity of script. The Bobbio Missal presents the oldest ornamented *Te igitur* in the beginning of the canon of the mass: the T is a six-line-high initial painted in red and green, with a bird on the top whose body and tail form the horizontal part of the letter.[10] The Luxeuil Lectionary and the Missale Gothicum present full-page images associating oversized colored letters, arcades, birds, ornamented circles, and rosettes.[11]

These visual variations have a tripartite function. The first is didactic: they help to locate and identify the various pieces of the codex because the letters of the titles, the subtitles, and the incipit differ from the ordinary letters. The second is hierarchical: the most important pieces of text can be distinguished by specific ornaments, colors, and letter sizes (e.g., Easter in the Missale Gothicum and the Feast of Saint Julian in the Luxeuil Lectionary). And finally, the third function is rhythmical: the manuscript is poetized by the non-functional colored alternation of the letters in the titles, and by the colored initials throughout the codex. Two Gallican manuscripts produced at the end of the eighth century, the Old Gelasian and the Gellone sacramentaries, present a fourth mode of ornamented script, which I call "annunciative." In this type, the frontispiece of the manuscript or the beginning of a new codicological section is distinguished by a visual composition that announces the textual and ornamental structure of the book by associating all the ornamental modes used in the following pages, and by symbols (e.g., fish, cross, chrismon, arcades, and alpha and omega). These symbols feature the living Church.[12]

and Religious Culture in Merovingian Gaul (Cambridge, 2004). The Missale Gallicanum vetus, a sacramentary whose oldest part was composed in Burgundy in the first half of the 8th century: BAV, Cod. Pal. lat. 493; no facsimile; Leo Cunibert Mohlberg, Leo Eizenhöfer, and Pierre Siffrin, eds., *Missale gallicanum vetus (Cod. Vat. Palat. lat. 493)*, Rerum ecclesiasticarum documenta: Series maior, Fontes 3 (Rome, 1958). And the Missale Francorum, a Gallican sacramentary (Poitiers?, first half of the 8th century): BAV, Cod. Reg. lat. 257; no facsimile; Leo Cunibert Mohlberg, Leo Eizenhöfer, and Pierre Siffrin, eds., *Missale Francorum (Cod. Vat. Reg. Lat. 257)*, Rerum ecclesiasticarum documenta: Series maior, Fontes 2 (Rome, 1957).

9 On the three manuscripts, see Babette Tewes, *Die Handschriften der Schule von Luxeuil: Kunst und Ikonographie eines frühmittelalterlichen Skriptoriums*, Wolfenbütteler Mittelalter-Studien 22 (Wiesbaden, 2011), passim.

10 Bobbio, 11v. The T of the Te igitur is the only colored letter of this manuscript. Its form is much more simple than the "classical" one, which will emerge at the end of the 8th century in the Gellone Sacramentary (Paris, BnF, lat. 10248, 143v), which transforms the T into a cross or a crucified Christ. See Rudolf Suntrup, "*Te igitur*-Initialen und Kanonbilder in mittelalterlichen Sakramentarhandschriften," in *Text und Bild: Aspekte des Zusammenwirkens zweier Künste im Mittelalter und früher Neuzeit*, ed. Christel Meier and Uwe Ruberg (Wiesbaden, 1980), 278–382; also Hahn, chap. 12 above.

11 Luxeuil, 32v: triple-ornamented arcade with birds, which covers the title of the *Vita sancti Iuliani* and should be read for the Epiphany's vigil. Saint Julian was honored in the cathedral of Langres, for which the manuscript was probably written, according to Salmon, *Lectionnaire de Luxeuil*, 1:XCIII–XCVIII, 2:64–75. Missale Gothicum, 169v: double arcade in the opening of the Easter section with geometric figures (Rose, *Missale Gothicum*, pl. 3; *Biblioteca Apostolica Vaticana: Liturgie und Andacht im Mittelalter* [Cologne, 1992], 63). On the arcades in Merovingian manuscripts, see Tewes, *Die Handschriften*, 49–51, 79–82.

12 The so-called Old Gelasian Sacramentary (Chelles, mid-8th cent.) presents three openings introducing the temporal (3v–4v), the sanctoral (131v–132v), and the mass section (172v–173): BAV, Reg. lat. 316; facsimile, *Sacramentarium Gelasianum e codice Vaticano Reginensis Latino 316* (Vatican City, 1975). The so-called Gellone Sacramentary (Cambrai or Meaux, end of the 8th cent.) is introduced by a feminine veiled figure (*sancta Maria*) blessing and incensing an ornamented invocation of Christ: Paris, BnF, lat. 12048, 1v: http://gallica.bnf.fr/ark:/12148/btv1b60000317/f10.image.r=12048.langFR (accessed 27 March 2015); also Hahn, chap. 12 above.

The Visual Treatment of Church Dedication Pieces in Liturgical Manuscripts of the Eighth to Tenth Centuries

The Gallican sacramentaries and lectionaries of the eighth century do not seem to grant any specific ornamentation to the dedication texts. They do not take part in any particular codicological section, and their ornamentation is strictly identical to that used for the ordinary feasts.[13]

The sacramentaries and pontificals composed in the ninth and tenth centuries in Italian, Frankish, and German countries display some noticeable variations.[14] The first novelty concerns the textual structure of the dedication pieces, which by this time are integrated into a complete ordo, which articulates stage directions (didascalies) and euchological pieces (that is, prayers, benedictions, antiphons, and responses). We can observe two sorts of ordines. The first presents separately the laying of the relics in the altar (ordo romanus 42) and the dedication of the church building (ordo romanus 41). These are found in fourteen manuscripts prior to the year 1000, dating back to the first years of the ninth century.[15] The second

type is an integrated ordo, which articulates in a unique text didascalies and prayers for both the laying of the relics and the dedication of the building, usually taken from ordines 41 and 42. I have identified eight different ordines provided by a unique Frankish, German, or Italian manuscript of the 9th or 10th century.[16] Another one was copied out in five manuscripts in Aquitaine or northern France.[17] Furthermore, the Romano-German Pontifical (PRG) written in Mainz around 960 contains two dedication ordines (33 and 40), whose oldest exemplar is in a pontifical from Lucca of the late tenth century. The longer version, the *Ordo ad benedicendam*

---

13 This is the case for the five *lectiones* for the dedication in Luxeuil (236–39), for the prayers, *lectiones*, and dedication mass in Bobbio (183r–183v, 186v–193v), and for the 77 dedication pieces in Gellone (199v–208v). I have not yet seen the dedication pieces of the Missale Francorum (76v–88r), nor the forty-eight of the Old Gelasian (108v–117r), but according to their editors there is no specific ornamentation in those sections of the manuscript. There are no dedication pieces in the Gallicanum vetus or in the Gothicum. The Angoulême Sacramentary, another Gallic manuscript written ca. 780–800, contains thirty-four dedication pieces but no ornament: Paris, BnF, lat. 816, 140v–145v.

14 For a general survey on early pontificals, see Niels Kogh Rasmussen and Michel Haverals, *Les pontificaux du haut Moyen Âge: Genèse du livre de l'évêque* (Leuven, 1998).

15 The ordines romani (OR) 41 and 42 are edited by Michel Andrieu, *Les ordines romani du haut Moyen Âge*, 5 vols. (Leuven, 1931–61), 4:339–47, 397–402. Andrieu indicates six manuscripts from the 9th and 10th centuries that contain both the ordines romani 41 and 42: Verona, Bibl. Cap., Cod. 92 (ca. 820), 49–54; Munich, Bayerische Staatsbibl. 14510, 59v–62v; Cologne, Erzb. Dombibl., Cod. 138 (beginning 9th cent.), 36v–39v; Saint Gall, Stiftsbibl., Cod. 446 (ca. 845–870), 135–38; Wolfenbüttel, Herzog August Bibl., Wolfenbüttel 4175 (beginning 9th cent.), 83r–86v (OR 42 incomplete); Zürich, Stiftsbibl. 102 (9th–10th cent.), 24–27v. Three more contain only OR 42: Montpellier, Fac. Médecine, ms. 412 (9th cent.), 128r–128v; Copenhagen, Kongelige Bibl.,

GKS 3443 8° (beginning 10th cent.), 42v–46r; Albi, Bm, ms. 42 (end 9th cent.), 71v–72r. Five other manuscripts must be added to Andrieu's list: a pontifical from Sens, ca. 900, Saint Petersburg, MS. Q.v.I, no. 35, 35–43 (OR 41 and 42); the Autun Sacramentary, Berlin, Staatsbibliothek, Ms. Phill. 1667 (ca. 800), 117v–119v (OR 41); an Italian *libellum* of ordines, mid-9th cent., BAV, Cod. lat. 7701, 14v–18 (OR 41); a Basel Pontifical, Freiburg i. Br., Universitätsbibl. Hs. 363 (mid-9th cent.), 17v–24r; and the Constance Pontifical, Donaueschingen, Furstenberg. Bibl., ms. 192 (end 9th cent.), 1r–23v, ed. Max Josef Metzger, *Zwei karolingische Pontifikalien vom Oberrhein* (Freiburg im Breisgau, 1914), 25*–36* (OR 41).

16 The first is OR 43, known from a collection of ordines composed in Saint-Amand in the 9th century: Paris, BnF, lat. 974, 119v–120r; ed. Andrieu, *Ordines romani*, 4:411–13. There are also four dedication ordines, known from 9th-century sacramentaries: the Padua Sacramentary, Padua, Bibl. Cap., cod. D47, 105–113; the Saint-Vaast of Arras Sacramentary, Cambrai, Bm, ms. 163, 60r–76v; the Saint-Alban of Mainz Sacramentary, Mainz, Martinusbibl. Hs. 1, 156v–164r; and the Florence Sacramentary, Florence, Bibl. Medicea Laurenziana, Edili 121, 159v–165v. These four ordines are edited by Jean Deshusses, *Le sacramentaire grégorien: Ses principales formes d'après les plus anciens manuscrits*, 3 vols. (Fribourg, 1971–82), 3: nos. 449*–53, 195–99, 204–8. Two other ordines are known from 9th- or 10th-century manuscripts: the Drogo Sacramentary (Metz, ca. 844–855), Paris, BnF, lat. 9428, 100–105, ed. Léon Duchesne, *Origines du culte chrétien: Étude sur la liturgie latine avant Charlemagne* (Paris, 1925), 498–99; the Reims Pontifical, Reims, Bm, ms. 340 (10th cent.), 40v–56v, ed. Edmond Marène, in *AER*, 2.13:722–25. Although it was composed ca. 1036, I would also add the ordo of the Langres Pontifical, Dijon, Bm, ms. 122 (89), 15–28, ed. *AER*, 2.13:747–57.

17 The *Ordo ad ecclesiam dedicandam* from the Saint-Denis Sacramentary (Saint-Amand), Paris, BnF, lat. 2290, 139v–151r, ed. Deshusses, *Le sacramentaire grégorien*, 3: no. 452, 200–204. It was copied out in two Aquitanian manuscripts of ca. 900: the "Cahors" Pontifical (Moissac?), Paris, BnF, lat. 1217, 1–30; and the Pontifical of Albi, unknown origin, Albi, Bm, ms. 20 (olim 34), 30r–33v, 18r–25v, 34r–39r. It is also in a pontifical from Beauvais (9th–10th cent.), Leiden, Univ. Lib., BPL 111:2, 11r–31v, and in the Sacramentary of Figeac-Moissac (end of the 11th cent.), Paris, BnF, lat. 2293, 145–155.

ecclesiam (ordo 40) spread throughout Europe in the eleventh century.[18]

Formally speaking, we cannot say that these different ordines are distinguished by a neat ornamental treatment, but some signs testify to their new visual importance (I have noticed four). The dedication ordines can be located at the head of the supplementary section in a sacramentary, eventually after a codicological break (e.g., Saint-Denis Sacramentary, fols. 139v–140r). The supplementary section may appear at the opening of a codex, as for instance in the Cahors and the Constance pontificals. We can also find a distinguishing feature at the beginning of a dedication ordo, such as an initial taller or more adorned than the others in the manuscript. In the Cologne Pontifical from the first quarter of the ninth century, the D introducing the ordo for the laying of the relics is bigger than other initials and is the only one in the manuscript that contains two colors (Cologne, Erzb. Dombibl., Cod. 138, fol. 36v). However, this is not a rule. For instance, the dedication ordo of the Drogo Sacramentary has no specific ornament (fol. 100r). Its initials are among the most ordinary in the manuscript, although numerous temporal or sanctoral feasts are introduced by historiated initials of exceptional quality.

Another innovation is the distinction between two different kinds of script within an ordo. Colored uncial (generally red) is used for titles and didascalies; and black or brown minuscule for the recited, declaimed, or sung pieces. This seems to be an innovation of the second half of the ninth century when, after first passing through a variety of different states, the text reached a standardized form at the beginning of the tenth century. The Saint-Denis Sacramentary, composed in the last years of the ninth century, presents interesting modulations that seem to be specific to this transitional period: didascalies initiated in red uncial and followed by brown minuscule (fol. 140v); alternated red-brown didascalies (fol. 143r); and red didascalies and brown minuscule for prayer texts. Worth noting as well are the small,

interlinear cross signs that indicate the moment when the celebrant should make the sign of the cross during a benediction. I have not seen this kind of graphic sign in texts before the Saint-Denis Sacramentary and the Cahors Pontifical of circa 900.

The Visuality of the Church Dedication Ordines in the English Pontificals around the Year 1000

Pontificals composed in southern England from the middle of the tenth century to the beginning of the eleventh present a third evolutionary step.[19] I have focused my observations on four manuscripts: the Sherborne Pontifical (ca. 960–988), the "Lanaleth" Pontifical (ca. 1000), the Egbert's Pontifical (ca. 1000), and the Winchester Pontifical (ca. 1020), also called the Benedictional-Pontifical of Archbishop Robert of Jumièges.[20] Their dedication ordines proceed from an original articulation of the ordines romani 41 and 42. They generally open the manuscripts and present original visualizations of the script with ink drawings and images.[21] I will consider here the so-called Lanaleth Pontifical, which was composed in

18 Lucca, Bibl. Cap., Cod. 607, 41v–43v, 50v–67v; Cyrille Vogel and Reinhard Elze, eds., *Le Pontifical romano-germanique du dixième siècle*, 3 vols. (Vatican City, 1963–72), 1:82–89, 124–73.

19 On these manuscripts, see David N. Dumville, "Liturgical Books for the Anglo-Saxon Episcopate: A Reconsideration," in idem, *Liturgy and the Ecclesiastical History of Late Anglo-Saxon England: Four Studies* (Woodbridge, 1992), 66–95; Janet Nelson and Richard Pfaff, "Pontificals and Benedictionals," in *The Liturgical Books of Anglo-Saxon England*, ed. Richard Pfaff (Kalamazoo, 1995), 87–98; Sarah Hamilton, "The Early Pontificals: The Anglo-Saxon Evidence Reconsidered from a Continental Perspective" (paper presented at the international workshop "Interpreting Medieval Liturgy c. 500–1500: Text and Performance; Writing and Revising Medieval Rites," University of Exeter, 5–7 January 2010). For a masterly survey on late Anglo-Saxon liturgy, see Richard W. Pfaff, *The Liturgy in Medieval England: A History* (Cambridge, 2009), 62–96. On the church dedication rite in Anglo-Saxon England, see Helen Gittos, *Liturgy, Architecture and Sacred Places in Anglo-Saxon England* (Oxford, 2013), 212–56.

20 Sherborne Pontifical, Paris, BnF, lat. 943; Lanaleth Pontifical, Rouen, Bm, ms. 368 (A27); Egbert's Pontifical, Paris, BnF, lat. 10575; and Winchester Pontifical, Rouen, Bm, ms. 369 (Y7). I follow the dates given by David N. Dumville, "On the Dating of Some Late Anglo-Saxon Liturgical Manuscripts," *Transactions of the Cambridge Bibliographical Society* 10 (1991): 40–57.

21 On the place of English manuscripts in the development of the Pontifical's illustration, see Eric Palazzo, *L'évêque et son image: L'illustration du Pontifical au Moyen Âge* (Turnhout, 1999), 128–41.

FIG. 13.1.

Ink drawing introducing the Lanaleth Pontifical. Rouen, Bm, ms. 368 (A27), 1v–2r.

Photo courtesy of Collections de la Bibliothèque municipale de Rouen.

Wells or St Germans, Cornwall, around the year 1000, most likely for Lyfing, bishop of Wells. During the eleventh century, the manuscript was used in Canterbury and Jumièges, where it remained until the French Revolution (thus it is sometimes called the Jumièges Pontifical).[22]

22 Rouen, Bm, ms. 368 (A 27); Gilbert H. Doble, ed., *Pontificale Lanaletense (Bibliothèque de la ville de Rouen A. 27. Cat. 368): A Pontifical Formerly in Use at St. Germans, Cornwall* (London, 1937). The dedication ordo was previously edited and analysed by John Gage, "The Anglo-Saxon Ceremonial of the Dedication and Consecration of Churches, Illustrated from a Pontifical in the Public Library at Rouen," *Archaeologia* 25 (1834): 235–74. On the manuscript, see also Victor Leroquais, *Les Pontificaux manuscrits des bibliothèques publiques de France*, 3 vols. (Paris, 1937), 2:287–300. On the date and provenance of the manuscript, see Doble, *Pontificale Lanaletense*, xi–xiii, and Dumville, "Liturgical Books," 87. The name Lanaleth, which is mentioned in a benediction's formula, refers to Lannaled, the old name of the place where the St Germans monastery was built.

The manuscript contains two main sections. The first is a pontifical (fols. 3–93), the second a benedictional (fols. 93v–161), to which is added a third *varia* section with benedictions, ordines, and malediction pieces (fols. 162–196). Two singletons are located before the first quaternion. Their versos present ink drawings. The first presents two standing men (fig. 13.1). The taller man is a bishop. Drawn with red ink, his arms open in a prayer position and his feet rest on a pedestal; he is tonsured, dressed with the chasuble, holding the stole, the maniple, the *pallium* and the super-humeral, and he looks to his right, where a priest, drawn in black ink and almost half his size, holds an open book. The stole of the priest and the internal sewing of the book are drawn in red ink. This distinguishes them hierarchically and associates them with the episcopal authority, which is itself suggested by the red ink.

The drawing of folio 2v is entirely traced with black ink (fig. 13.2).[23] It presents a vision of the church dedication at once literate and emblematic. The church is a completed building located on a pedestal with three steps and shown with all its constitutive parts that could be seen from the outside. The knotted cloth visible through the apse window reveals the mystery accomplished by the dedication, that is, the invisible incarnation of Christ in the body of the building.[24] An

undulating line drawn below the church signifies the unified level on which the building and the clerics stand. In front of them, a bishop is knocking at the church door with his pastoral staff. Behind him is a group of tonsured or mitered clerics; the first holds the stole and a closed book. Two barrels are presented below on a second level. One is filled with a clear substance, the other with a dark one. They probably indicate the offerings of the lay people, which occur before the dedication. They could also represent the transitive species, water, salt, ashes, and wine, which are necessary to create the anointing water. Laymen are depicted on the lower level.

23 This drawing has often been reproduced and sometimes described, but never in terms of the visuality of the text it faces: Gage, "The Anglo-Saxon Ceremonial," 245, pl. XXIX; Leroquais, *Pontificaux*, pl. 1; Doble, *Pontificale Lanalatense*, pl. 2; Jane Rosenthal, "Three Drawings in an Anglo-Saxon Pontifical: Anthropomorphic or Threefold Christ?" *ArtB* 63, no. 4 (1981): 547–62, esp. 558–59; Palazzo, *L'évêque*, 318–19; Gittos, *Liturgy*, 213.

24 On the signification of the rent or open veil according to the Incarnation and Passion of Christ, see Jeffrey Hamburger,

"Body vs. Book: The Trope of Visibility in Images of Christian-Jewish Polemic," in *Ästhetik des Unsichtbaren: Bildtheorie und Bildgebrauch in der Vormoderne*, ed. David Ganz and Thomas Lentes (Berlin, 2004), 113–45, at 118–28.

FIG. 13.2.
Ink drawing facing the beginning of the dedication ordo in the Lanaleth Pontifical. Rouen, Bm, ms. 368 (A27), 2v–3r.

Photo courtesy of Collections de la Bibliothèque municipale de Rouen.

Introducing them in a position equal to that of the bishop is a bearded man wearing an embroidered tunic and holding a rough staff of office.

The two drawings may have originally been conceived to introduce the two main sections of the manuscript (pontifical and benedictional).[25] They were ultimately placed at the beginning, where they form a visual announcement of the overall structure of the manuscript. They present together a figuration of the whole ecclesiastic structure, as did, by other means, the arcades of the Gallican sacramentaries. The novelty here is the emphasis on the bishop's body, which is the unavoidable mediator of the ecclesiastic construction, and on the material dimension of the *ecclesia* (church), with the construction of the edifice and its endowment by the laymen. The representation of the bishop's entrance underlines the initiatory and fruitful virtue of the whole ritual.

Facing the illustration of the church, the *Ordo qualiter domus dei consecranda est* is shown (fol. 3r) in a visual form which alternates between three cases of letters, four colors, two different sizes and colors of initials, long lines and double columns of script, marginal notes, and musical signs (see fig. 13.2). This ornament of the text— that is to say, of the words by which the church building becomes a consecrated place—helps to signify the visual meaning of the rite. We first observe a six-line block of text written in colored uncials. The first line is the title, the second introduces the rubric that announces the clothing of the celebrants and their arrival in front of the church door. The text block presents lines with a three-color alternation: red, green, and blue. The red, which is the traditional color for rubrics and titles, forms the structure of the block. It occurs every two lines. The two other colors create rhythmic variations. They have no didactic meaning, but they adorn and make the didascalical rubrics dance. This first trichromatic rubric is both rhythmic and annunciative: it announces the trichromatic alternation of the initials that introduce all the pieces in the manuscript. All other rubrics in the *Ordo dedicationis* present a red-blue alternation, though those of the other ordines in the manuscript adopt only the red or orange color. These last rubrics simply state; they do not dance.

In the codex as a whole, black ink is reserved for the vocalized sections, either recited or sung. In the dedication ordo, both are distinguished. The sung parts (here introduced by "cantando antiphonam") are written in small Anglo-Carolingian minuscules, so that neumes could be traced above them.[26] The pieces are introduced by a painted initial much smaller than the ones that announce rubrics and prayers. These are little red signs that designate without any doubt the beginning of a sung text. Neumes do not fix the exact pitch; they show rhythm, accentuation, and indicate whether a word should be sung higher or lower than its predecessor. They are the visual signs of the chant that signify the vocalization of the rite and recall it to memory. They play on the same register as the colors and the changing characters of the letters, distinguishing pieces from one another and allowing the reader/viewer to mentally represent the multisensory course of the ritual.[27]

Here, the first sung piece is the antiphon *Zachee festinans*, created from Luke 19:1–9. Since the seventh century, Roman and Gallican lectionaries have testified to the reading of the pericope during the dedication Mass, but the English pontificals of the year 1000 are, to my knowledge, the oldest use of *Zachee festinans*

25   For the codicology of the manuscript, see Doble, *Pontificale Lanalatense*, v–ix.

26   It is very difficult to prove whether or not manuscripts were prepared for musical notation. Notation appears in English manuscripts at the end of the 10th century, and the distinction between small minuscule for sung pieces and ordinary minuscule for recited pieces also seems to appear at that time, perhaps in English manuscripts. Nevertheless the small script does not prove the preparation for neumatic notation, because it was often used without it. Even without notation the small script remained a visual sign of vocal variations. On the use of Anglo-Saxon neumes, see Susan Rankin, "From Memory to Record: Musical Notations in Manuscripts from Exeter," *Anglo-Saxon England* 13 (1984): 91–112; eadem, "Neumatic Notations in Anglo-Saxon England," in *Musicologie médiévale: Notations et séquences; Actes de la table ronde du CNRS à l'IRHT, 6–7 septembre 1982*, ed. Michel Huglo (Paris, 1987), 129–44.

27   Susan Rankin, *The Winchester Troper: Facsimile Edition and Introduction* (London, 2007), 24–25; Jean-Claude Bonne and Eduardo H. Aubert, "Quand voir fait chanter: Images et neumes dans le tonaire du ms. BNF latin 1118; Entre performance et performativité," in *La performance des images*, ed. Alain Dierkens, Gil Bartholeyns, and Thomas Golsenne (Brussels, 2010), 225–40.

as an antiphon during the dedication ordo.[28] The text invites the people to delight in Christ's entrance (*adventus*) into the house. The benefit that Zaccheus received when Christ came into his house in Jericho will now be extended to the faithful on the occasion of the church dedication. The English pontificals of the year 1000 mention the song of this antiphon right at the beginning of the ritual, although it takes place after the bishop enters the church in Roman pontificals of the twelfth and thirteenth centuries.[29] We may have here another sign of the initiatory value of the dedication on which English pontificals insist.

Afterward, the prayer *Deus qui nos pastores* is pronounced in a different tone (*dicatur*).[30] Like all other vocalized pieces, it is written in black ink, but to distinguish it from sung pieces, its characters are bigger and have the same size as the rubrics' letters. The first line is written in uncial, so that the incipit can be easily located. The rest is in Anglo-Carolingian minuscule. The *Deus qui nos pastores* is the prayer in which the bishop asks God to make human utterances worthy.[31] Thus, he implores the spiritual transformation of the vocalized letter.

The following rubric, written in alternating red and blue uncial, indicates the first gestures that the celebrant should perform in the church: illuminating twelve candles around the building and imploring the saints' intercession while singing their litany and walking three times around the edifice. The visual rhythm of the words on the parchment announces the dance of the ecclesiastic choir around the building. The triple circuit is a delimitation and a foundation. It also becomes an exorcism thanks to the power of the saints whose names are invoked (fig. 13.3). On the parchment, the constructive strength of the saints is suggested by the columns of their names, in which we can see the building of the harmonious Church, whose rhythm is given by the chromatic alternation of the red and blue initials.[32]

Then come four prayers introduced by red titles written in the middle of the column: *Sequatur oratio*, *Alia*, *Alia*, and *Alia* (fol. 4v, fig. 13.4). The four prayers are intended to provoke the ascension of the words toward God through the mediation of the saints.[33]

---

28 *Corpus antiphonalium officii* (*CAO* 5515), ed. R.-J. Hesbert, 6 vols. (Rome, 1963–78), 3:550. The recitation of *Zachee festinans* during the dedication Mass is already mentioned in *Luxeuil*, 237v–238r. It takes part in the Lauds office in the Compiègne antiphonary, ca. 870, Paris, BnF, lat. 17436, and in other antiphonaries of the *cursus romanus* in the 11th century: *CAO* 3:376–77 (127c). I have not seen it in the Carolingian ordines, but in other English pontificals of the 10th–11th centuries: Sherborne, 102; Egbert's, 41–41v; and Winchester, 95. It is not in the ordines 33 and 40 of the PRG.

29 Michel Andrieu, *Le Pontifical romain au Moyen Âge*, 4 vols. (Vatican City, 1938–41), 1:180; 2:426–27.

30 *Dicere* and *cantare* are the two principal modes of liturgical vocalization, which cannot be reduced to our modern "say" and "chant," and whose specific connotations seem to be linked with different perceptions of speech: creative speech (*dicere*) and communicative speech (*cantare*): Eduardo H. Aubert, "Le son et ses sens: L'*Ordo ad consecrandum et coronandum regem* (v. 1250)," in *Annales: Histoire, Sciences Sociales* 62 (2007): 2:387–411. A specific study should be initiated on the sound vocabulary in the church dedication ordo, in accordance with the colors of the script and the neumatic notations. Such an inquiry has been partially done by Eduardo Aubert in his unpublished master's thesis, "Intento sensu et vigilanti mente: Esboço de uma problemática histórica do som no Ocidente medieval" (master's thesis, Universidade de São Paulo, 2007), 312–78.

31 "Deus qui nos pastores in populo uocari uoluisti presta quaesumus ut hoc quod humano ore dicimur in tuis oculis

esse ualeamus. Per." ("God, who wanted us to be called shepherds among the people, grant we beseech you that what we are said by the human mouth to be we may be able to be in your eyes.") This prayer comes from the Gregorian Sacramentary, Hadrianum version of 811–812 (Cambrai, Bm, ms. 164), but it is not used there for the dedication ritual: *Corpus orationum* (*CO*), ed. E. Moeller and J.-M. Clément, 11 vols., CCSL 160, 160A–J (Turnhout, 1992–99), 3: no. 1902, pp. 94–95.

32 I know texts have long been written in columns in medieval manuscripts without there being an architectural allusion, but I suggest that this opening with the saints' names in columns could have been seen as a figura of the terrestrial Church, whose pillars are the saints.

33 "Preueniat nos quaesumus domine misericordia tua et intercedentibus omnibus sanctis tuis uoces nostras clementia tue propitiationis anticipet. Ascendant ad te domine praeces nostre et ab ecclesia tua cunctam repelle nequitiam. Per. Deus caeli terreque dominator auxilium nobis tuę defensionis benignus inpende. Per dominum. Actiones nostras quaesumus domine et aspirando preueni et adiuuando prosequere ut cuncta nostra operatio et a te semper incipiat et per te cepta finiatur. Per." ("Lord, we pray that your mercy may go before us and, with all your saints interceding, anticipate our voices with the mildness of your propitiation. Through [the Lord]. May our prayers ascend to you, Lord, and drive away all evil from your church. O God, ruler of heaven and earth, kindly send us the help of your defense. Through the Lord. We beseech you, Lord, both by favoring go before and by helping follow up our doings so that everything we do may both always begin from you and, having been begun, be completed through you. Through [the Lord].") *CO* 4595. This prayer comes from the Gelasian Sacramentary (Ge 2159) and is found in many

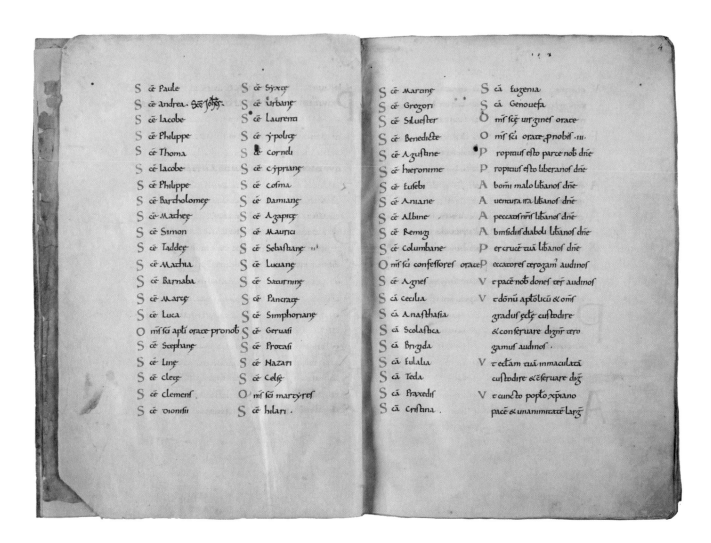

FIG. 13.3.
Folios 3v–4r of
the Lanaleth
Pontifical: the
litany of the saints.
Rouen Bm, ms.
368 (A27).

Photo courtesy
of Collections de
la Bibliothèque
municipale de Rouen

After these prayers comes the important sequence of the entrance into the church. A long red and blue uncial rubric highlights this text (fols. 4v–5v, figs. 13.4–5). From time to time, these didascalical indications are interrupted by the singing of an antiphon (black minuscule) and by some words written in orange uncial, in an as-yet unobserved style. Let us try to understand it, following the ritual and its visualization in the codex. A deacon enters the church and closes the door. The other clerics stay outside. The bishop approaches the door and sings the antiphon *Tollite portas principes uestras et eleuamini porte eternales*, created from Psalm 23 (24). The description of the entrance is in red and blue uncial, the text of the antiphon is written in black minuscule, then come again the red

and blue didascalies (fol. 5r line 2). The bishop walks around the church, versifying (*versificando*) Psalm 23 (24), from which the antiphon is derived, *Domini est terra*. The scribe did not write its incipit, leaving an incongruous blank on the parchment after the word *psalmum* (fol. 5r line 3).[34] Ending at the front of the door, the bishop strikes it with his pastoral staff and repeats the antiphon *Tollite portas*, this time with the authoritative tone (*dicat directe*). The deacon who is standing inside answers the bishop with a question: "Quis est iste rex gloriae?" Rather than the usual black minuscule, the scribe visualized

continental manuscripts from the 8th to 11th century, but it is not usually used for the dedication ritual.

34 The psalm can be rendered by the dedication ordo of Winchester, 96. I see no contradiction in the preparation of a specific and precise framework for the whole manuscript (script, color, placement on the page) and the omission of some pieces. These are two separate actions, and small omissions or mistakes are common in medieval manuscripts, even in the most precious.

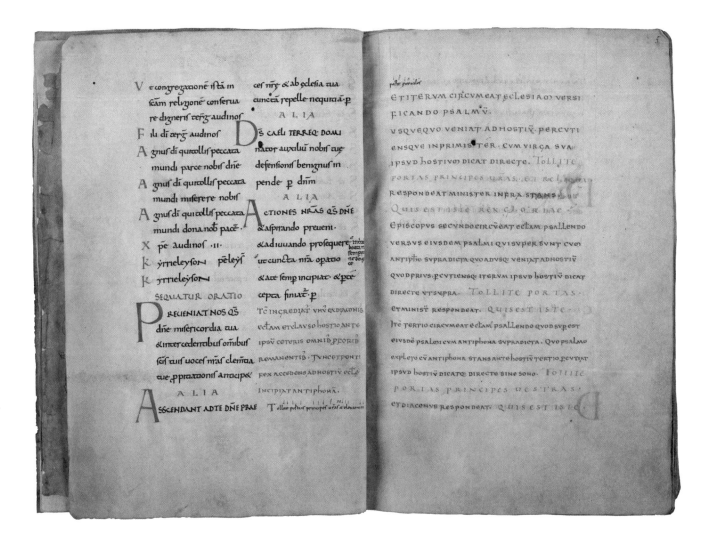

this dialogue with orange uncial, which is quite a lot bigger than the didascaly's letters. Then the bishop circles the church once again, chanting (*psallendo*) the same psalm and singing its antiphon, until he comes back to the front door and repeats the oral exchange with the deacon. The dialogue is again distinguished by big, orange uncial. After a third turn around the church and a third dialogue pronounced without the chant (*sine sono*) and written with the same orange uncial, the entire choir and the bishop answer "Dominus uirtutum ipse est rex glorie" (fol. 5v line 2, see fig. 13.5).[35] The deacon immediately opens the door. Entering the church, the bishop, personifying the King of Glory, is now vested to play Christ and to inscribe his presence in the

building. This initiation has been realized by the circuits around the church, the vocalization of the divine Word, whose complex and veiled meaning requires the use of variant vocal modes (annunciation, versification, psalmody, singing), and by a dramatic play whose performance was audible and partially visible to the audience. The long didascaly with its changing colors and characters suggests visually the inflections of the spectacle, independent of its ephemeral effects.

Following the entrance sequence, we observe two blank lines on the parchment, where there should be written the versicle of the prayer *Dominus vobiscum*, in big black minuscule and its response "et cum spiritu tuo." The scribe did not write them, leaving only a red R announcing the response (fol. 5v lines 5–6).

The next sequence does not show any visual novelty. It is presented with the three main writing styles: red and blue uncial for didascalies,

FIG. 13.4.
Folios 4v–5r of the Lanaleth Pontifical. Rouen, Bm, ms. 368 (A27).

Photo courtesy of Collections de la Bibliothèque municipale de Rouen.

35   We read "omnis clerus episcopo" rather than "omnis clerus cum episcopo," which can be rendered by the Winchester Pontifical, 96v.

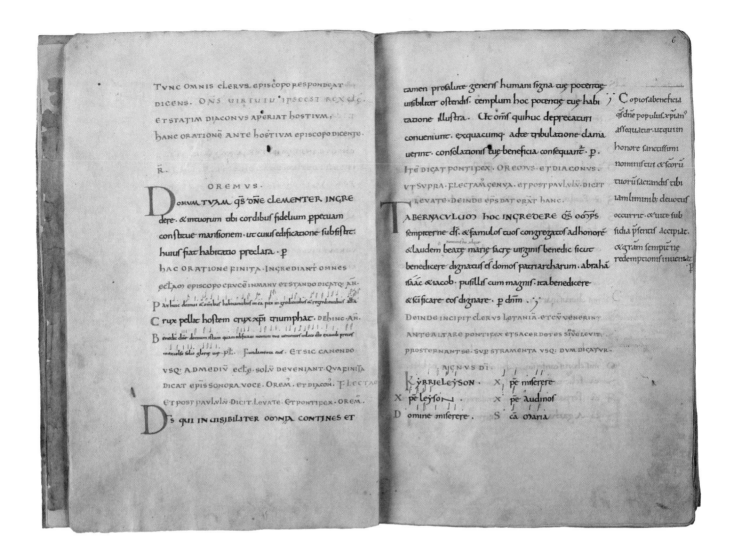

FIG. 13.5.
Folios 5v–6r of the
Lanaleth Pontifical.
Rouen, Bm, ms. 368
(A27).

Photo courtesy of
Collections de la
Bibliothèque
municipale de Rouen.

large black minuscule for spoken orisons, and a small black minuscule for sung pieces. First, the prayer. *Domum tuam quaesumus domine*, introduced by the red rubric *Oremus*, is written in big black minuscule, its incipit in uncial, like previous prayer. This one deepens the introductory and constructive dimension of the rite. The choir prays to the Lord to enter his church (*domus*), and to build in the heart of the faithful a perpetual house (*perpetua mansio*), which will be his dwelling place (*habitatio*) and from which he will direct the building (*edificatio*) of the faithful.[36] We can speculate here on the idea

36 "Domum tuam quaesumus domine clementer ingredere et in tuorum tibi cordibus fidelium perpetuam constitue mansionem, ut cuius edificatione subsistit huius fiat habitatio preclara. Per." This prayer is a mix of *CO* 2378a and *CO* 2378b. It comes from the Gregorian Sacramentary, where it was already used for the dedication ritual.

of the double temple of Christ, which is edified in the church building and in the most secret and most spiritual part of the faithful body, its "heart" (*cor*). The dedication of the church is considered to be the exact moment when the spirit is simultaneously vivified in this double temple. The pronunciation of the prayer *Domum tuam* achieves this vivification.

At the end of the prayer, all the clerics come into the church led by the bishop, who holds the cross, standing and speaking in an attitude of authority (*stando dicatque*). He sings the *Pax huic domui* for all those who will dwell in the *domus* and for all those who will enter and exit (this is written in small black minuscule). Singing the *Pax huic domui* means singing about the ideal harmony of a community established by the Passion of Christ, ruled by the sign of the cross, constituted by two social orders, welded together by the mediation of the saints, and led by the clerics. The choir then pronounces the *Crux pellit hostem, crux Christi triumphat* in a solemn tone that the large minuscule visualizes on the parchment (see fig. 13.5, left). Then the choir sings the antiphon *Benedic domine*, which is a call to the Lord to protect the church built in his name. The antiphon symbolically creates the vertical communication between the terrestrial church and the celestial dwelling place of God. It is followed by Psalm 86 (87) *Fundamenta eius*, which underlines the typological relationship between the newly edified church and the holy city of Zion. Both pieces are written in small black minuscule, the antiphon with neumes, the psalm without.

The next rubric (fol. 5v lines 17–20) announces a dramatic sequence that takes place in the middle of the nave in a rhythm of changing gestures and tones. First, the bishop invites with a strong voice the choir to pray (*dicat episcopus sonora voce oremus*). The deacon orders the choir to kneel down (*flectamus*) and then to get up (*levate*), as the bishop orders the recital (*oremus*) of the prayer *Deus qui invisibiliter*. Then the same gestures are repeated (fol. 6r lines 6–8): the praying, kneeling, getting up, and this time the recitation of the prayer *Tabernaculum hoc ingredere*. These alternations of standing and kneeling positions, of authority and supplicatory tones, highlight the mediatory role of the bishop, who is at once a guide leading the people by his authority and a man who submits himself to the Lord from whom he begs mercy. The way the scribe depicts these gestures is fascinating. The first *oremus* and *levate* are not distinguished from the didascaly, though the word *flectamus* and the second *oremus* are written in a different way, with orange uncials for the first, red ones for the second. The appearance of the prayer *Deus qui invisibiliter* is classical: large black minuscule with an incipit in uncial. Then, in the next sequence, the scribe plays only with the red and blue alternation. The didascaly begins in red; the first pronounced word, *oremus*, follows in blue; and the rubric carries on in red with the didascaly *Et diaconus ut supra*. In accordance with the style adopted at the beginning of the manuscript, the color of the didascaly changes every line: the red *et diaconus*, at the end of the line, is

followed by a blue *ut supra* at the beginning of the next line. The pronounced speech that follows, *Flectamus genua*, is therefore in red, and the next rubric in blue: *Et post paululum dicit*. The scribe again reverses the colors in the next line: dialogue in red (*Levate*), didascaly in blue (*Deinde episcopus dat orationem hanc*), so that the color alternation respects at once the change of line and the distinction between dialogues and didascalies. What a nice "exercice de style"!

The two prayers pronounced during this play (*Deus qui invisibiliter*[37] and *Tabernaculum hoc ingredere*[38]) further deepen the visual meaning of the ritual. The first is a wonderful expression of the cognitive value of visible things and of their intrinsic inferiority regarding the invisible truth. God has kept complete knowledge invisible, but he has presented visible signs to facilitate human salvation. The present church (*templum*) is one of them. It allows those who come to pray to find *consolatio*, that is, the way to wisdom. The second prayer recalls the typological relation between the church and the Old Testament Temple. The church is a *tabernaculum* in which God dwells and protects the faithful assembled there in honor of the Virgin, as he did for those assembled in the houses of the Patriarchs.

Then a second litany is sung, which is accompanied by prostrations in front of the altar (fol. 6r line 15 – fol. 7r line 1, fig. 13.6). The names of the saints and prayers are in black lowercase letters. The incipits are distinguished by alternating red and blue initials. Neumes are written above the collective prayers (*Omnis chorus angelorum*, *Omnis chorus confessorum*, and so forth), but not above the saints' names. Afterward, another sequence of standing and kneeling gestures with short speeches is visualized in the same manner

37 "Deus qui inuisibiliter omnia continens et tamen pro salute generis humani signa tuę potentię uisibiliter ostendis, templum hoc potentię tuę habitatione illustra, ut omnis qui huc deprecaturi conueniunt, ex quacumque ad te tribulatione clamauerint, consolationis tuę beneficia consequantur. Per." *CO* 1762. This prayer comes from the Gregorian Sacramentary, where it was already used for the dedication rite.

38 "Tabernaculum hoc ingredere quaesumus omnipotens sempiterne deus, et famulos tuos congregatos ad honorem et laudem beatę Marię sacrę uirginis benedic sicut benedicere dignatus es domos patriarcharum Abraham Isaac et Iacob pusillis cum magnis ita benedicere et sanctificare eos dignare. Per dominum." This prayer is not included in the *CO*. It seems to have been used only in English rituals.

as before, by the rhythmic and didactic blue-red alternation. The prayer *Magnificare domine deus* follows in the usual style.

The next sequence details the inscription of the alphabet on the pavement of the church. The Lanaleth Pontifical and other English pontificals of the year 1000 present a rite with the Latin alphabet written twice in a cruciform drawing on the pavement, starting in the corners of the nave.[39] The first alphabet is written while chanting verse 3:11 of First Corinthians, "Fundamentum aliud nemo potest," which declares Christ to be the only foundation; and then Psalm 86 (87), *Fundamenta eius*, already mentioned. The second alphabet is traced while singing the antiphon *Haec aula*, which declares that the church receives grace, benediction, and mercy from Christ.[40] It is followed by Psalm 47 (48), *Magnus dominus*, which praises the power of the Lord.

39 On the alphabet ritual, see Klaus Schreiner, "Abecedarium: Die Symbolik des Alphabets in der Liturgie der mittelalterlichen und frühneuzeitlichen Kirchweihe," in Stammberger and Sticher, eds., *"Das Haus Gottes,"* 143–87; Cécile Treffort, *"Opus litterarum*: L'inscription alphabétique et le rite de consécration de l'église (IXe–XIIe siècle)," *CahCM* 53 (2010): 153–80. The alphabet's ritual is unknown in Byzantine and old Roman rituals, and it probably comes from an old Irish dedication rite (5th–6th century?): Dominique Barbet-Massin, "Le rituel irlandais de consécration des églises au Moyen Âge: Le témoignage des sources irlandaises et bretonnes," *Annales*

de Bretagne et des Pays de l'Ouest 118, no. 2 (June 2011): 7–39; Patricia Stirneman, "L'inscription alphabétique: De la consécration de l'église à l'apprentissage de la lecture et autres usages," *Bulletin Monumental* 169, no. 1 (2011): 73–76. It formed part of the Gallic-Roman rites with the OR 41.

40 "Haec aula accipiat a deo gratiam benedictionem et misericordiam a Christo Ihesu." ("Let this house receive from God grace, benediction, and mercy from Jesus Christ.") This antiphon is not included in the *CAO*. It is probably specific to the English rituals.

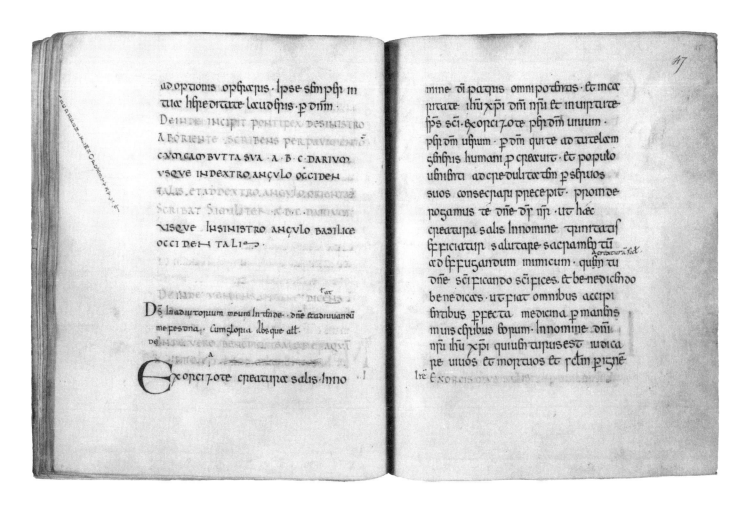

The writing of the alphabet is expressed in the following words: "pontifex de sinistro angulo ab oriente scribens per pavimentum cum cambuta sua A.B.C.darium usque in dexterum angulum occidentalis ... et a dextro angulo orientalis scribat similiter A.B.C.darium usque in sinistrum angulum occidentalem basilica."[41] The word *ABCdarium* is written in the same color of the didascaly, but it is visually distinguished by the separation of the first three capital letters with periods. Written this way *ABCdarium* is not only the word meaning "the alphabet," but also a visualization of the letters that constitute the alphabet. This writing of the three letters in the manuscript partly visualizes the writing of the letters on the church floor. The ways the

"word" *ABCdarium* is written in other manuscripts present interesting variations. In the Saint-Denis Sacramentary, the word is expressed only by the three letters A, B, and C, each separated by a point and written in red capitals within a black lowercase rubric.[42] The same style is observed in a pontifical from Langres of 1036, and in the Pontifical-Benedictional of Hugh of Nevers (ca. 1013–1066), where the beginning of the sequence is also distinguished by the red

FIG. 13.7.
Description of the inscription of the alphabet during church dedication, Egbert's Pontifical. Paris, BnF, lat. 10575, 46v.

Photo courtesy of the Bibliothèque nationale de France.

41 "The bishop writes the alphabet (*ABCdarium*) on the pavement with its staff, beginning from the left angle on the east up to the right angle on the west ... and he similarly writes the alphabet from the right angle of the east to the left angle of the west of the basilica."

42 Paris, BnF, lat. 2290, 140v: "Deinde pontifex incipiat de sinistro angulo ab oriente scribens per pauimentum cum cambotta sua A. B. C. usque in dextrum angulum occidentalis. Incipiens iterum similiter a dextro angulo orientalis A. B. C. scribens usque in sinistrum occidentalis basilicae." ("Then, the bishop begins from the left angle of the east to write on the pavement with his stick the ABC, up to the right angle of the west. A second time, he begins in the same way to write the ABC from the right angle of the east up to the left angle of the west of the church." In the Cahors Pontifical, which proceeds from the Saint-Denis Sacramentary, the letters A, B, and C are not distinguished by a red color: Paris, BnF, lat. 1217, 3.

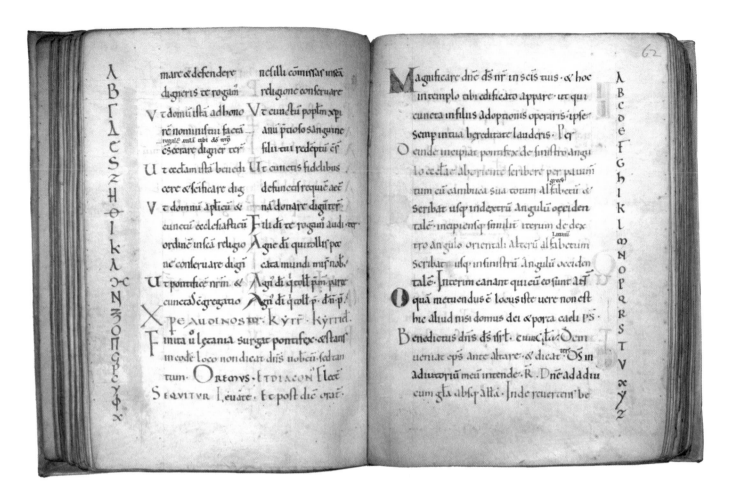

FIG. 13.8.
Mid-eleventh-century pontifical from Arras and Cambrai showing both Greek and Latin alphabets in the ordo of the dedication of the church. Cologne, Erzb. Dombibl., Cod. 138, 147v–148r.

Photo: Codices Electronici Ecclesiae Coloniensis

color, as if it were a title.[43] The visualization of the alphabet is still clearer in the Egbert's Pontifical (fig. 13.7). In the margin facing the section of the *ABCdarium*'s inscription, the Latin alphabet is written in a diagonal line from top left to bottom right, illustrating the start of the cruciform layout of the alphabet on the church pavement.

While Carolingian and English manuscripts of the year 1000 indicate the inscription of only the Latin alphabet, ordo 40 of the PRG recommends writing both the Greek and Latin alphabets.[44] The practice may have spread in England and France during the eleventh century, to the extent that older pontificals were adapted. A complete Greek alphabet is added at the end of the Winchester Pontifical; another one is written at the beginning of the pontifical

from Langres.[45] In the Winchester Pontifical the Greek alphabet is not only a range of letters but also a picture made of big letter signs, neatly arranged in lines and columns on a blank page. Such a visual arrangement becomes common in Romano-German pontificals of the late tenth and eleventh centuries.[46] As some manuscripts indicate the writing of both alphabets without listing all the letters, they are sometimes added in the margins. This is the case in a mid-eleventh-century pontifical from Arras and Cambrai, in which the capital letters of both alphabets form two columns that frame the main text (fig. 13.8). The same presentation appears in a contemporary pontifical from Trier adapted for the church of Cambrai (fig. 13.9). When rubrics spell out each Greek and Latin letter, these are indicated

---

43 Langres: Dijon, Bm, ms. 122, 16v. Nevers: Paris, BnF, lat. 17333, 35r. A libellus of ordines composed in Saint-Gall ca. 845–870 presents a similar rubric where the alphabet is called *a.b.c.d.durius*. The word is written without capitals in the same brown ink as the rubric: Saint-Gall, Stiftsbibl. 446, 133r.

44 Vogel and Elze, *Le Pontifical romano-germanique*, 1:136.

45 Rouen, Bm, ms. 369 (Y7), 198v. Dijon, Bm, ms. 122, 4v.

46 See Treffort, *Opus litterarum*, 158, n. 32, who indicates three PRGs of the 10th and 11th centuries in which alphabets are written in the rubric: Lucca, Bibl. Cap., Cod. 607, 33v–34r; Eichstätt, Diözesanarchiv, Cod. B4, Pontifical of Gondekar II, 53r (only Greek alphabet); Vienna, Nationalbibl., Cod. lat. 701, 51v–52r.

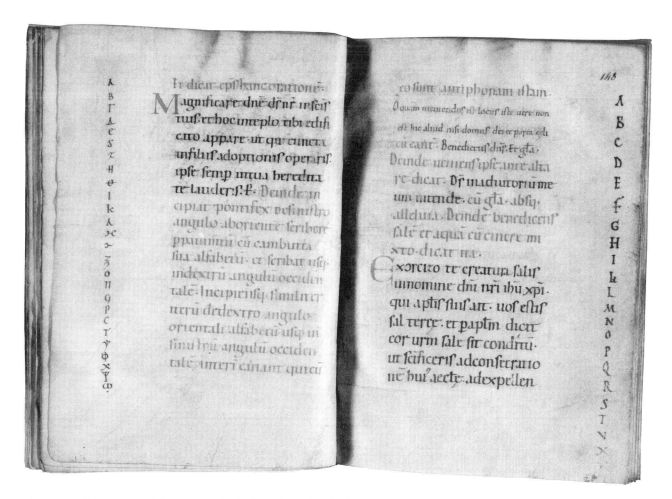

by a special design. A Salzburg pontifical adapted for the use of Sées (ca. 1025–1050) presents a very simple graphic style, where all the text is written with black ink, including the didascalies: only the titles are red. But the alphabet is enhanced by colors. The Latin letters are red uncials, each separated by a point and discretely highlighted by green painting. Greek letters are black majuscules, slightly bigger than the other ones, and enhanced by red and green colors. Another complete Greek alphabet, partly cut by the modern binding, is drawn in the head margin of the folio right above the section of the alphabet. Its special script and the brown ink differ from those of the main text, and it is undoubtedly an addition. The Otto von Riedenburg Pontifical (ca. 1060–1089) and the Monte Cassino Pontifical (before 1086) are other manuscripts in which the only visualization of the script takes place in the alphabet section. In the von Riedenburg Pontifical, the Latin and Greek letters are distinguished by brown majuscules within a red lowercase rubric. In order to start each alphabet at the head of a new line, the scribe has increased the space between the letters of the previous line.[47] In the Cassino manuscript, both alphabets are majuscule in a lowercase rubric. Latin letters are black with tiny green and yellow highlights (green and red for the letter A), all separated by a point. Greek ones are bigger and are more adorned. They are written in an alternation of black and red ink, with red, green, and yellow highlights.[48] In the twelfth-century Pontifical of Chieti, a Greek alphabet with capital letters twice as large as those of the text is written in the top margin above the alphabet's rubric. In this one, the complete Greek and Latin alphabets are written with black capitals highlighted with red.[49]

Writing the two alphabets in the codex has a didactic function, especially concerning the Greek letters, of which many clerics were

FIG. 13.9.
Mid-eleventh-century pontifical from Trier showing both Greek and Latin alphabets. Paris, BnF, lat. 13313, 147v–148r.

Photo courtesy of Bibliothèque nationale de France.

47   Paris, BnF, lat. 1231, 40v.

48   BAV, Cod. Barb. lat. 631, 6r–6v.

49   BAV, Cod. lat. 7818, p. 58–59/fol. 29v–30r.

probably ignorant. But it also gives a representation of the rite and displays the letters as ornamental signs. These displayed alphabets appear to be the synthetic image of the church dedication. Signs by which the Word was made intelligible, they construct the place where they are inscribed (either the book or the dedicating church building) as a locus from which the cognitive journey will emerge. This is completely assumed by the middle of the twelfth century, when pontificals present real pictures of large ornamented Greek and Latin capital letters.[50] Later, thirteenth-century pontificals present wonderful painted and ornamented alphabets, with oversized, colored, and golden capitals.[51]

Let us conclude with these letters. The alphabet rite is probably the act that signifies most explicitly the saving insemination of the Word. It *literally* inscribes the Word onto the church building, while the letters depict the Christian initiation. They are first written on the ground of the church, where they do not remain (according to later rituals, the writing is made on two lines of ashes spread on the floor).[52] They define the invisible dimensions of the church: here in the domus, there and then in the human heart and in God's presence. Echoing this ephemeral and almost invisible scripture, letters are sometimes carved or painted on the church walls. In this way the building is shown as the real place of the indwelling Word.[53] The circuits and the entrance

sequences, the prayers, antiphons, and psalms also figure the incarnation of the Word in the church body, and simultaneously in the spirit of the faithful, whose church building is the figure.

The ritual does not end with the alphabet's inscription. It carries on with other significant markings (cross signs on the walls and on the altar), purifying lustrations, consecrating unction on the constituent parts of the building (outside and inside walls, pavement, and altars), the spreading of incense, more circuits through the building, and the burying of relics and parts of a consecrated host in the altar. It ends with fantastic displays of visualization. The laymen are gradually shown into the building. They stay in the nave as a veil separates them from the sanctuary, where the clerics are. They can only hear what is said or sung during the burying of the relics. Then the veil is removed, the church is illuminated and prepared to proceed with the first consecration of the Eucharist.

The anthropological and social value of these rites is significant. Let us try to sum up. God created Man in his image.[54] In order to carry out his existential progress toward the model who created him, but from whom he has been separated by original sin, he has to welcome into his heart/spirit (*cor*) the divine Word. Then, gradually, his "flesh" (*caro*) will become "spirit" (*spiritus*), awaiting for and looking to the final visio, which will be a spiritual and eternal pleasure. The baptism is the starting point of such an insemination of the Word into the heart (*cor*) of the faithful. All throughout one's life, sacraments and virtues confirm and deepen this original transformation, and they are further steps toward the visio. The dedication produces in the body of the church the same effect as baptism. The building itself will not follow any progress, but it becomes, through the dedication, a place where man in peregrination for his salvation

50 The oldest examples I know are pontificals composed ca. 1140–50: the Sens Pontifical, Sens, Bm, ms. 9, 71; the Cologne PRG: Cologne, Erzb. Dombibl., Cod. 139, 66v–67r (this one reproduced by Klaus Schreiner, "Das Buch im Nacken: Bücher und Buchstaben als zeichenhafte Kommunkationsmedien in rituellen Handlungen der mittelalterlichen Kirche," in *Audiovisualität vor und nach Gutenberg: Zur Kulturgeschichte medialer Umbrüche*, ed. H. Wenzel, W. Seipel, and G. Wunberg [Vienna, 2001], 88; and Treffort, *Opus litterarum*, 161).

51 For instance the Pontifical from Auch (1268), BAV, Cod. lat. 7114, 10v. See also the Pontifical of Reims (mid- or late 13th cent.), Rouen, Bm, ms. 370 (A34), 103r–103v; Pontifical of Amiens (13th cent.), Amiens, Bm, ms. 196, 23.

52 See Treffort, *Opus litterarum*, 159, 172, who quotes an Ambrosian ritual of the 11th century, the sermon of Adhémar of Chabannes written for the dedication of the church of Saint-Martial in Limoges in 1028 and the *Ordo ad benedicendam ecclesiam* of the 12th-century Roman Pontifical (ordo 17).

53 Some astonishing monumental alphabets have recently been observed on churches in Provence and Aquitaine; certainly others have yet to be discovered. Treffort, *Opus litterarum*, 165–70; Yann Codou, "La consécration du lieu de culte et ses

traditions graphiques: Inscriptions et marques lapidaires dans la Provence des XIᵉ–XIIᵉ siècles," in *Mises en scène et mémoires de la consécration de l'église*, 254–82, esp. 259–62; Didier Méhu, "Les marques lapidaires de la cathédrale de Chartres," in *Chartres: Construire et restaurer la cathédrale, XIᵉ–XXIᵉ s.*, ed Arnaud Timbert (Rennes, 2013), 383–95.

54 Gen. 1:26–27: "Et ait: Faciamus hominem ad imaginem et similitudinem nostram. Et creavit Deus hominem ad imaginem suam."

(*homo viator*) can realize his existential progress. The dedication is not a sacrament, but it is the matrix of all sacraments. During the rite, the church building is inseminated by the saving Word. Its body is marked, incised, and anointed by signs of the divine Word. According to this architectural and spatial creation, the dedication of the church is also the social vivification of the faithful community. Christians are the living stones (1 Peter 2:5) of the Church. Inhabited by the divine Word, they build together a social and spiritual temple whose church building is the material and visible image. The idea of the simultaneous vivification of the church and of the spirit of the faithful during the dedication is conceived by the time of Augustine of Hippo, who mentions it in his church dedication sermons.[55] The idea is reinforced during the eighth century in England, and especially with Bede in his *De templo* or in two homilies on the dedication.[56]

Such a meaning asserts itself in the writings of the Carolingian clerics. Accordingly, the Church is no longer an immaterial temple but rather the temple of stones erected before our eyes, which is to be consecrated, adorned, and emphasized as the locus of every spiritual transformation (*transitus*) and as the fruit of the harmonious collaboration of the two social orders.

The dedication ordo in the Lanaleth Pontifical stages such a transformation of the church building. The frontispiece drawing of folio 2 portrays it. Like the *cor humanum* and the stone's *templum*, the manuscript codex is conceived of as a locus where the inscription of the divine Word allows the generation of the cognitive process. This process, I insist, is a gradual visualization. And I suppose that the various and dancing forms of the script suggest this visualization. It is never done in a literal way, neither with a systematic code, but with visual signs that open the letters and invite one to see beyond them. Their only clear declaration is that of imagination, poetry, ornament, vision, and dream as the most powerful engines of creation and knowledge.

55 Augustine of Hippo, *Sermones* 163, 336–38, PL 38:889–95, 1471–80; Gert Partoens, "Le sermon 163 de saint Augustin: Introduction et édition," *RBén* 115 (2005): 251–85; Hubertus R. Droebner, *Augustin von Hippo: Predigten zu Kirch- und Bischofsweihe (Sermones 336–340A); Einleitung, revidierter Mauriner-Text, Übersetzung und Anmerkungen* (Bern, et al., 2010).

56 Bede, *Homiliae* 2:24–25, in *Bedae Venerabilis opera III–IV: Opera homiletica, opera rhythmica*, ed. David Hurst (Turnhout, 1955), 358–78. *De tabernaculo: De templo, In Ezram et Neemiam*, in *Bedae Venerabilis Opera II.2ᵃ*, ed. David Hurst (Turnhout, 1969).

CONTRIBUTORS

BRIGITTE MIRIAM BEDOS-REZAK, professor of history at New York University, has published extensively on medieval seals as conceptual tools, markers of identity, and social agents, including *Form as Order in Medieval France* (1993), "Medieval Identity: A Sign and a Concept" (*American Historical Review*, 2000), *When Ego was Imago* (2011), "Semiotic Anthropology: The Twelfth-Century Experiment" (in *European Transformations 950–1200*, ed. Thomas F. X. Noble and John Van Engen [Notre Dame, 2011]), and "Outcast: Seals of the Medieval West and Their Epistemological Frameworks (12th–21st centuries)" (in *From Minor to Major: The Minor Arts in Medieval Art History*, ed. Colum Hourihane [Princeton, 2012]).

ELIZABETH HILL BOONE holds the Martha and Donald Robertson Chair in Latin American Art at Tulane University. Formerly Director of Pre-Columbian Studies at Dumbarton Oaks (1983–1995), she has edited or coedited eleven books, including *The Aztec Templo Mayor* (1987), *Writing without Words* (1994, with Walter Mignolo), and most recently *Their Way of Writing: Scripts, Signs, and Pictographies in Pre-Columbian America* (2011, with Gary Urton). Among her monographs are *The Codex Magliabechiano* (1983), *Stories in Red and Black: Pictorial Histories of the Aztecs and Mixtecs* (2000), and *Cycles of Time and Meaning in the Mexican Books of Fate* (2007). She is a fellow of the American Academy of Art and Sciences and a corresponding member of the Academia Mexicana de la Historia. She was awarded the Order of the Aztec Eagle by Mexico in 1990. Her current research examines changes in the indigenous tradition of pictography and manuscript painting after the conquest.

ANNE-MARIE CHRISTIN was professor emerita at l'Universite Paris Diderot 7, where she taught for over forty years. She founded the Centre d'étude de l'écriture et de l'image (CEEI) in 1982 and remained the center's director until her premature death on July 20th, 2014. She specialized in the relationship between writing and the image, publishing numerous articles, collected volumes, and monographs, notably *L'Image écrite ou la déraison graphique* (1995, repr. 2001 and 2009), *Poétique du blanc: Vide et intervalle dans la civilisation de l'alphabet* (2000, repr. 2009), *L'Invention de la figure* (2011), and the forthcoming *Par la brèche des nuages: Les paravents japonais*. Her work touches on diverse subjects, from prehistoric cave painting to Japanese kanga, and moves in fields as far ranging as typography, anthropology, ethnography, linguistics, philosophy, and literary, art, and multimedia studies. Anne-Marie Christin was awarded the distinguished title of Chevalier de la Légion d'Honneur on July 3rd, 2014, which proved to be a final salute to a scholar whose brilliant intellectual trajectory led the study of writing into previously uncharted territories. As Roger Chartier emphasized in bestowing the award, Christin was being honored for exploring the implications of her fundamental insight that writing had both linguistic and visual poles. Appropriately, her contribution opens the present volume with the fruits of her life-long reflection upon the iconicity of script.

THOMAS B. F. CUMMINS is the Dumbarton Oaks Professor of the History of Pre-Columbian and Colonial Art in the department of the history of art and architecture at Harvard University. His research and teaching focuses on Pre-Columbian and Latin American colonial art. He recently coedited *The Getty Murúa: Essays on the Making of Martín de Murúa's "Historia General del Piru"* (2008) and *Manuscript Cultures of Colonial Mexico and Peru: New Questions and Approaches* (2014). His most recent monograph, *Beyond the Lettered City: Indigenous Literacies in the Andes*, coauthored with Joanne Rappaport, was published by Duke University Press in 2012.

VINCENT DEBIAIS (PhD in medieval history, University of Poitiers, 2004) is full researcher at the Centre national de la recherche scientifique (France), Centre d'études supérieures de civilisation médiévale, University of Poitiers, where he leads the research team on medieval epigraphy (Corpus des inscriptions de la France médiévale). His PhD was published in 2009 ("Messages de pierre: La lecture des inscriptions dans la communication médiévale"). He has also published many articles about medieval epigraphy and art history: "L'écriture dans l'image peinte romane: Questions de méthodes et perspectives," *Viator* 41 (2010): 95–125; "Lieu d'image et lieu du texte: Les inscriptions dans les peintures murales de la voûte de la nef de Saint-Savin," *L'image médiévale: Fonctions dans l'espace sacré et structuration de l'espace cultuel*, ed. E. Sparhubert and C. Voyer (Turnhout, 2011); "La vue des autres: L'ekphrasis au risque de la littérature médiolatine," *Cahiers de civilisation médiévale* 55 (2012): 393–404; and "La poétique de l'image, entre littérature classique et épigraphie médiévale," *Veleia: Revista de Prehistoria, Historia antigua, arqueología y filología clásicas* 29 (2012): 43–53. He is now working on the relationships between text and image in Romanesque works of art, and on Latin ekphrasis. His current research explores the concept of silence and its use in the material and artistic culture of the tenth to the thirteenth centuries.

IVAN DRPIĆ is assistant professor of Byzantine and western medieval art at the University of Washington in Seattle. He received his PhD (2011) from Harvard University. Drpić has held fellowships at Dumbarton Oaks and the Center for Advanced Study in the Visual Arts at the National Gallery of Art in Washington, D.C. His articles have appeared in *Byzantinische Zeitschrift*, *Dumbarton Oaks Papers*, *Speculum*, *Word & Image*, and *Zograf*. His first book, *Epigram, Art,*

and Devotion in Later Byzantium, forthcoming from Cambridge University Press, explores the interplay between art and personal piety in the last centuries of Byzantium through the lens of this period's epigrammatic poetry.

ANTONY EASTMOND is AG Leventis Reader in the History of Byzantine Art at the Courtauld Institute of Art, University of London. He has written extensively on the art and culture of medieval Georgia and its relations with Byzantium. He is the editor of *Viewing Inscriptions in the Late Antique and Medieval World* (2015), and has just completed a study of cultural interaction in eastern Anatolia on the eve of the Mongol invasions. His books include *The Glory of Byzantium and Early Christendom* (2013), as well as *Art and Identity in Thirteenth-Century Byzantium: Hagia Sophia and the Empire of Trebizond* (2008) and *Royal Imagery in Medieval Georgia* (1998).

BÉATRICE FRAENKEL, Director of Studies at the École des Hautes Études en Sciences Sociales (Paris), teaches the anthropology of writing. She values a pragmatic approach in research and in teaching. Her early work, *La Signature: Genèse d'un signe* (Gallimard, 1992), deals with the history of the performativity of a sign. She has widely researched the use of writing in workplaces and coedited *Langage et Travail, Communication, Cognition, Action* (2001 with Anni Borzeix). Her monograph *Les écrits de Septembre: New York 2001* (Paris, 2002) is the result of a field survey in Manhattan in September 2001. She has co-curated *Affiche-Action, Quand la politique s'écrit dans la rue*, an exhibition at the Bibliothèque de Documentation Internationale Contemporaine (Hôtel national des Invalides, Nov. 2012–Feb. 2013) and has co-written the exhibition catalogue (2012). She currently directs research projects on displayed writings ("écritures exposées") in public spaces.

CYNTHIA HAHN began her scholarly work in the field of manuscripts, publishing *Portrayed on the Heart: Narrative Effect in Pictorial Lives of the Saints from the Tenth through the Thirteenth Century* (2001), many articles, and a facsimile volume concerned with the subject of illustrated saints' lives and their narratives. Since that time, she has turned to the study of reliquaries and has been particularly interested in the liturgical use of such objects and their reception by medieval audiences. Her most recent book is *Strange Beauty: Origins and Issues in the Making of Medieval Reliquaries 400–circa 1204* (2012). The contribution to this volume, along with a few other similar works, represents her return to manuscript studies and a new interest in the performative qualities of books. She is full professor at Hunter College and the Graduate Center CUNY.

Educated at Yale University (BA 1979, PhD 1987), JEFFREY F. HAMBURGER, currently the Kuno Francke Professor of German Art and Culture in the department of the history of art and architecture at Harvard University, taught at Oberlin College and the University of Toronto before joining the faculty of Harvard in 2000. His research interests include the history of the medieval book, with special emphasis on medieval manuscript illumination, the art patronage of female monasticism, medieval theology, mysticism and devotional practices, German religious literature of the Middle Ages, and the history of attitudes toward imagery. His most recent books include '*Haec figura demonstrat': Diagramme in einem Pariser Exemplar von Lothars von Segni, De missarum mysteriis' aus dem frühen 13. Jahrhundert* (2013), *Script as Image* (2014), and *The Prayer Book of Ursula Begerin* (2015), coauthored with Nigel F. Palmer (Oxford University). A fellow of the Medieval Academy of America and a member of both the American Philosophical Society and the American Academy of Arts and Sciences, Professor Hamburger is currently working on a book on the medieval diagrammatic tradition.

Educated at the University of Chicago (BA 1961) and Princeton University (MFA 1963, PhD 1965), HERBERT L. KESSLER taught at the University of Chicago beginning in 1965 and at the Johns Hopkins University from 1976 to 2013. He has been a visiting professor at Harvard University, Emory University, and Williams College, was the first Richard Krautheimer Professor at the Bibliotheca Hertziana in Rome, and is currently an invited professor at the Masaryk University in Brno. A fellow of the

American Academy of Arts and Sciences and of the Medieval Academy of America, he has published nearly two hundred articles and reviews and is the author or editor of sixteen books.

KATRIN KOGMAN-APPEL, Alexander von Humboldt–Professur für Jüdische Studien, Institut für Jüdische Studien, Westfälische Wilhelms-Universität Münster focuses on the relationship between Jewish and Christian art and on Hebrew manuscript painting. She is the author of *Jewish Book Art Between Islam and Christianity* (2004), *Illuminated Haggadot from Medieval Spain* (2007), and *A Mahzor from Worms: Art and Religion in a Medieval Jewish Community*, a monograph on the Leipzig Mahzor (2012). She is currently working on a study of Elisha Cresques ben Abraham, a fourteenth-century Jewish scribe, illuminator, and mapmaker in Mallorca.

DIDIER MÉHU is professor of medieval history and art history at Laval University, Québec, Canada. His research focuses on the history of the Church from the fourth to the thirteenth century. He has published books and articles especially on the history of Cluny, medieval liturgy, papal voyages, and the relationship between architecture and images in the medieval West. He is now preparing a book on the figural and narrative discourses of church dedication in the western Church, from the fourth through the ninth century.

İRVİN CEMİL SCHICK holds a PhD from the Massachusetts Institute of Technology (MIT) and has taught at Harvard University, MIT, and İstanbul Şehir University. He is the author of *The Erotic Margin: Sexuality and Spatiality in Alteritist Discourse* (1999), *The Fair Circassian: Adventures of an Orientalist Motif* (in Turkish, 2004), and *Writing the Body, Society, and the Universe: On Islam, Gender, and Culture* (in Turkish, 2011). He is also the editor of *The M. Uğur Derman 65th Birthday Festschrift* (2000) and *European Female Captives and their Muslim Masters: Narratives of Captivity in "Turkish" Lands* (in Turkish, 2005), and the coeditor of *Turkey in Transition: New Perspectives* (with E. Ahmet Tonak, 1987), *Women in the Ottoman Balkans: Gender, Culture and History* (with

Amila Buturović, 2007), and *Calligraphy and Architecture in the Muslim World* (with Mohammad Gharipour, 2013).

IRENE J. WINTER recently retired as Boardman Professor of Fine Arts, Harvard University. In 1997 she was Slade Professor at Cambridge University, and in spring 2005 delivered the Mellon Lectures at the National Gallery in Washington, D.C. She has excavated in Iran and Iraq. Her awards include a MacArthur Foundation Fellowship (1983–88), election to the American Academy of Arts and Sciences (1999) and The Austrian Academy of Sciences, Vienna (2005), and she was named an Honorary Fellow of the Institute of Fine Arts, New York University (2013). Research interests focus on the art of Ancient Mesopotamia, particularly aesthetic experience.

INDEX OF MANUSCRIPTS

GENERAL INDEX

Objects will be found under their geographic location if they do not have a specific name. See the Manuscript Index for manuscripts by location, under city and institution or under "private collections." Book titles will be found under the author's name. Page numbers in *italics* indicate illustrations.

Abbo of Fleury, 124n65
ABCdarium, in church dedication rites, 272–76, *273–75*
Abdülgani Efendi, 187
Abdullāh bin Mas'ūd, 181
Abdullāh ibn 'Abbās, 181
Abraham ibn Daud, *Sefer qabbalah* (ca. 1160), 166
Abū Bakr (caliph), *192*
Abū Dhar, 181
Abū Ḥayyān al-Tawḥīdī, 182
Abū Hurayra, 181
Acolhua, 44
Acosta, José de, 7, 87n13, 94n28, 97–98, 97n36, 101
    De procuranda Indorum salute (1588), 100
    Historia Natural y Moral de Las Indies (1590), 88–90, 93–94n27, 98–100, 103, 105, 106, 107
Adhémar of Chabannes, 276n52
Adler, Jacob Georg Christian, 173
Saint Aethelwold, Benedictional of (London, British Library, Add. MS. 49,598), 120
agglutination, 33
Aguilar de Codés (Navarra), hermitage of Saint-Bartholomeo, tympanum, 148, *149,* 150
Ahuitzotl (Water Beast), 34–36, *35,* 38, 41
'Ā'isha (wife of prophet), 179–80, 181
Akkadian, 197, 205, 213–14, 218n60
Albenga, mosaic in baptistery of, 131
Alberti, Leon Battista
    De pictura (1435), 19–20
    Grammatica della lingua tuscana (1443), 85n2
Alcuin, 114–15, 118n28, 123, 130, 131, 133
    Versus de sancta cruce ad Carolum (Berne, Burgerbibliothek, Cod. 212), 114–15
Aleppo, Archaeological Museum, bilingual statue of Hadad-'Iti, Tell Fakhariyeh, *213,* 213–14
Alexios I Komnenos (Byzantine emperor), 62n34

'Alī (caliph), *187,* 187–88
'Alī ibn Abī Ṭālib (caliph), 182, 184–85, *186*
Alonso, Dulce Ocón, 137
alphabet ritual, in church dedication rites, 272–76, *273–75*
alphabetic scripts. *See also* encounter of Pre-Columbian graphic systems with alphabetic system
    aesthetization/fetishization of, 86–87, 88, 101–7, *103, 104*
    Greek alphabet, 13, 14, 19, 20, 26, *103, 274,* 274–76, *275*
    iconoclastic theory of writing and, 6
    ideograms compared, 2, 6, 15, 20
    Latin alphabet, 13, 14, 19, 20, 26, *104, 274,* 274–76, *275*
    as second-generation writing systems, 26
    in typography/history of script as image, 19–21
alphabets, monumental, 276n53
Amman-Doubliez, Chantal, 74, 76, 82
Anastasios (Byzantine emperor), *229,* 229–30
Anders, Ferdinand, 38n14
Andrieu, Michel, 262n15
Androna (al-Anderin, Syria), lintel from south portico of kastron, *228,* 228–29
Angilbert (Abbot of Saint-Riquier), epitaph of, 138, 140
Anglo-Carolingian minuscule, 266, 267
Angoulême Sacramentary (Paris, BnF, lat. 816), 262n15
Anicia Juliana (founder of Saint Polyeuktos, Constantinople), 219, 225n27, 226, 229, 230n47
animated letters, 15
    figural writing in Islamic calligraphy, 174–77, *177*
    historiated initials, 8, *15,* 16, 237, *238,* 240, 242–47, *245, 246*
    pictorial Islamic calligraphies, 184–89, *186, 187, 190*
Anthony IV (patriarch of Constantinople), 57n17
anthropomorphism
    Hebrew letters in *mahzorim* and, 153, 157, 160–66, 170–71
    Islamic calligraphy and, 184n71
anthroponymic systems and rebus-signatures, 78–80, *80*
Apertio audium (opening of the ears), baptismal rite, 243–44

Aramaean, 213–14
arch representation of Temple/Tabernacle/Ark in *mahzorim,* 155, 155–57, *156, 157*
Areobindus, consular diptych of (Paris, Louvre), 229
Aristotle, *On Interpretation,* 88, 98n40, 101, 102
Ark of the Covenant
    arch representation of Temple/Tabernacle/Ark, in *mahzorim,* 155, 155–57, *156, 157*
    in Farhi Codex, 168
    golden Cherubim of, Gellone Sacramentary, 253
Armentia church, 137
ashide, 27n25
Ashkenazi *mahzorim. See* Hebrew letters in *mahzorim*
Assurbanipal [Ashurbanipal] (Assyrian ruler), 199n7, 200n12, 201, *211*
Assurnasirpal I (Assyrian ruler), 207n24
Assurnasirpal II (Assyrian ruler), 207n24, 208–10, *209, 210,* 211
'Aṭā Allāh Muḥammad of Tabriz, 184–85, *186*
Atahualpa (Inca ruler), 106n62
Athens, Benaki Museum, paten and chalice, 234
Attarouthi treasure, 221n13
Atton de Vercelli, commentary on Ephesians, 142
Aubert, Eduardo, 267n30
Aubin Codex (London, British Library), 38n13
Auch, Pontifical of (Vatican, BAV, Cod. lat. 7114), 276n51
Augsburg Gospels (Munich, Staatsbibliothek, Clm 23631), 118
Augustine of Hippo
    De doctrina christiana, 15, 16
    De moribus ecclesiae catholicae, 145
    De trinitate, 123, 129–30, 239
    Ennarationes in Psalmos, 118
    iconoclastic theory of writing and, 6
    In Iohannem Evangelium tractatus, 132
    intended audience, 226n28
    Sermones, 277
    on *visio,* 259
Codex Aureus of Saint Emmeram (Munich, Staatsbibliothek, Clm 14000), 116
automatic writing, surrealist, 4
Autun Sacramentary (Berlin, Staatsbibliothek, Ms Phill. 1667), 262n15
Aztec pictography. *See* Mexican Pre-Columbian pictography
Azuelo church, tympanum, 140

Baert, Barbara, 249

Baghdad, Iraq Museum
    Enmetana of Lagash, statue of, 206–7, *207*
Bahye ben Asher of Saragossa, 169–70
Baine, John, 220
Bâkî, 183
Balawat, bronze Door Bands, 210
Baltacıoğlu, İsmayıl Hakkı, 175n16
Bambara, 25
Banquet Stela of Assurnasirpal II, 211
Bar-Kokhba coin (Jerusalem, Israel Museum),
    156
Barcelona, Museu Nacional d'Art de Catalunya,
    apse of Santa Maria d'Aneu, 133n99
Barthes, Roland, 199
Basel, Pontifical of (Freiburg im Breisgau,
    Universitatsbibl. Hs. 363), 262n15
Basil of Caesarea, 68
the Basmala (caliph), *193*, 193–94
Basoche, 81
Battle of the Ulai River relief, Nineveh, South-
    west Palace (London, British Museum),
    211
Beatus of Ferdinand (Madrid, Biblioteca
    nacional, MS Vit. 14.2), 138n20
Beatus of Liebana, 120
Bede
    De templo, 277
    De temporum ratione, 124n65
    Homiliae, 277
    St. Petersburg manuscript, 240
    Super epistolas catholicas expositio, 123n61
Bedos-Rezak, Brigitte Miriam, 1, 41, 279
Behistun, inscription of Darius (Achaemenid
    ruler), 214
Belching Mountain, 36n12
Beleth, Jean
    Rationale divinorum officiorum, 146
    Summa de ecclesiasticis officiis, 127–28
Benedict of Aniane, 242
    Second Disputation against Felicianus, 123n61
Benzoni, Girolomo, *La historia del mondo
    nvovo* (1565), 103
Berlin, Museum für Spätantike und Byzan-
    nische Kunst, Justinianic dish, 227
Besseyre, Marianne, 241, 243–44, 253
bilingual texts and images in ancient
    Mesopotamia, 199, 211–14, *212, 213*
Blacas ewer (London, British Museum), 175–76
Blakewell, Sarah, 133, *134*
Bloom, Jonathan, 177
Boabdil (Muhammad XII; emir of Granada),
    86
Boas, Franz, 20
Bobbio Missal (Paris, BnF, lat. 13246), 260n8,
    261, 262n13
Bobrinsky bucket (St. Peterburg, State
    Hermitage Museum), 175
Codex Bodley (Oxford, Bodleian Library,
    MS. Mex. d. 1), 39n17, 41n20
body, letters taking on, 12
Boethius
    De arithmetica, 122, 127, 128–29, *129*
    De consolatione philosophiae, 129n79
    De sancta trinitate, 123, 130
Boissard, Jean-Jacques, 102n54

Bon-Encontre church, chrismon, 143
Bonne, Jean-Claude, 131, 139, 243, 244
Book of Kells (Dublin, Trinity College
    Library, MS. A. I. [58]), 114n11
Boone, Elizabeth Hill, 7, 31, 87n13, 101n50, 279
Codex Borbonicus (Paris, Bibliothèque de
    l'Assemblée nationale française, ms.
    Y.120), 33–34, *34,* 36, 38–39, *40,* 40–41, 49
Codex Borgia (Vatican, BAV), 39n17
Bostens (Landes), Saint Orens church at, 138, *139*
Codex Boturini (Mexico City, Biblioteca
    Nacional de Antropología, Colección de
    Codices 35–38), 38n13, 42–43, *43,* 44
Boulogne-sur-Mer, Bm, ms. 20 (Odbert
    Psalter), 132n88
Bouzon-Gellenave (Gers), tympanum of
    Gellenave church, 139
breastplate of high priest, seventy-two letters
    on, *167,* 168–70, 171
Brend, Barbara, 174
British Museum. *See* London, British Museum
Brubaker, Leslie, 230n49
Brunel, Ghislain, 9, 13–14
Butler, Judith, 237n1
Byrhtferth of Ramsey, 124n65, 130
Byzantine epigrams, 51–69
    aesthetic dimension of, 54–56, 61, 68–69
    in books, 66–68, *67*
    chrysography, *65,* 66, 67, 68
    defined, 51–52
    in dodecasyllable, 51
    epigraphische Auszeichnungsmajuskel, 68
    hierarchy of paratextual material in, 68
    iconicity of script and, 8
    jewelry, literary works compared with,
        60–61
    as *kosmos* (adornment), 8, 56–61, *58, 60,* 68
    legibility of, 55–56
    as literary composition and material artifact,
        52–54, *53, 54,* 61, 69
    Mexican pictography compared, 32, 47
    orality of, 54
    performativity of script and, 12
    pseudoscript, 62–64, *63*
    textile, text as, 62–66, *63, 65*
Byzantine monograms, 219–35
    concealing names, 226–35, *227–29, 231, 233*
    as cryptography, 234–35
    iconicity of script and, 8
    legibility of, 8, 219, 227–28
    performativity of script and, 12
    votive texts and name recognition, 220–26,
        221
Byzantine votive texts
    concealing names in, 226–35, *227–29, 231, 233*
    name recognition in, 220–26, *221*

Caedmon Paraphrase (Oxford, Bodleian, MS.
    Junius 11), 131n81
Cahors, Pontifical of (Paris, BnF, lat. 1217),
    262n17, 263
Calame-Griaule, Geneviève, 24–25
Calcidius and Calcidian diagram, 122–23, *124,*
    128, 130, 131, 132, 133, 134
calligraphy, 15, 25, 27, 171, 177. *See also* Islamic
    calligraphy

Cambrai, Cathedral of Notre Dame, 241
Cameron, Averil, 226n28
Camparan church (Hautes-Pyrénées), west
    wall of tower, *146,* 147
Candidus Wizo, 130
    Dicta Candidi, 123
canting arms. *See* heraldry
Carcastillo (Navarra), Church of La Oliva
    monastery, 150, *151*
Carmenta, Nicostrata and Evander, 104
carmina figurata, 113–15
Castillon-Debats (Gers), church in, 139
catechism, pictorial (Paris, BnF, mexicain 399)
    47–48, *48*
Cathac of Saint Columba (Dublin, Royal Irish
    Academy [unnumbered]), 127n72
Céard, Jean, 81
Celestinus (pope), 223n22
Chalchiutlicue (Jade Her Skirt), 33–34, *34,* 36,
    38, 41
Chancelade (Dordogne), chapel of Saint John,
    west portal, 143, *144*
Charlemagne, 241, 242
Charles II the Bald (king of West Francia)
    First Bible of (Paris, BnF, lat. 1), 112, *114, 115,*
        115–17, 118–20, 122n56, 133
    presented with Paschasius's *De corpore et
        sanguine Domini,* 119
Charles V (king of France), charter of (Paris,
    Archives nationales, AE II 393), *13,* 14
Charles V (king of Spain and Holy Roman
    emperor), 87n13, 92
charters, royal, French. *See* French royal
    charters
Chase, Christopher L., 253n69
Chazelle, Celia, 255
Chi, Gaspar Antonio, 90n20, 91
Chieti, Pontifical of (Vatican, BAV, Cod.
    lat. 7818), 275
Chinese writing, 3, 20, 25, 26, 27, 72, 88, 102,
    105, 177
chrismons in Pyrenean Romanesque sculpture
    135–51
    as abbreviation of Christ's name, 136, 137–38
        140, 141
    alpha and omega, 137–38, 148, 149
    assimilation between letter and image in,
        149, 149–50, *151*
    as autonomous sign, 136, 138
    defined, 10, 135n1
    IHS and XPS, 140–41
    ineffable, imaging, 10
    local context of, 136–37, 146–47
    lux, rex, lex, and *pax,* 138–40, *139, 140*
    Mexican pictography compared, 32
    omnipresence of, 135
    origins and evolution, 136
    peace, as sign of, *141,* 141–44, *142, 144*
    protection, as sign or seal of, 148–49, *149*
    Trinity, as sign of, 142, 144–48, *145–47*
    typology and characteristics, 137–41, *139, 14*
Christ III (Anglo-Saxon poem), 253n69
Christin, Anne-Marie, 2–3, 5–6, 15–16n34, 19,
    22, 32, 279
Christopher of Mitylene, 60
chrysography, *65,* 66, 67, 68

church dedication rites in liturgical manuscripts, 259–77
ABCdarium, 272–76, *273–75*
alphabet ritual, 272–76, *273–75*
anthropological and social value of, 276–77
colored script, use of, 260–61, 263, 268–70,
271, 273–74, 275, 276
continental pontificals, after ca. 1000,
262n15, 262n17, 263, 273–76, *274, 275*
eighth to tenth centuries, 260–63
English pontificals, ca. 1000, 263–77, *264,*
265, 268–70, 272, 273
performativity of script and, 13
sound and vocalization modes, 266–67
visio, medieval concept of, 259–60
Cleveland Museum of Art
Mosul ewer, 175
Wade cup, 175, 176, *177*
clothing, Byzantine epigrams as, 62–66, *63, 65*
Codex Aubin (London, British Library), 38n13
Codex Aureus of Saint Emmeram (Munich,
Staatsbibliothek, Clm 14000), 116
Codex Bodley (Oxford, Bodleian Library, MS
Mex. d. 1), 39n17, 41n20
Codex Borbonicus (Paris, Bibliothèque de
l'Assemblée nationale française Y.120),
33–34, *34,* 36, 38–39, *40,* 40–41, 49
Codex Borgia (Vatican, BAV), 39n17
Codex Boturini (Mexico City, Biblioteca
Nacional de Antropología, Colección de
Códices 35–38), 38n13, 42–43, *43,* 44
Codex Colombino (Mexico City, Biblioteca
Nacional de Antropología), 41n20
Codex Dresden, *3*
Codex Huejotzingo (Washington, D.C.,
Library of Congress, Harkness Collection),
89, 92
Codex Mendoza (Oxford, Bodleian Library
3134, Arch Selden A.1), 34–36, *35,* 38, 92, *93*
Codex Osuna (Madrid, Biblioteca nacional),
38n13
Codex Selden (Oxford, Bodleian Library 3135,
Arch Selden A.2), 36–38, *37,* 39n17, 41–42,
42, 44, 49–50
Codex Telleriano-Remensis (Paris, BnF, Fonds
mexicain 40), 92–93, *94*
Codex Upsaliensis Graecus (Uppsala,
University Library, Cod. gr. 28), 52, *53*
Codex Vaticanus B (Vatican, BAV, Cod.
gr. 1209), 39n17
Codex Vienna (Vienna, Österreichische
Nationalbibliothek, Codice
Vindobonensis Mexicanus 1), *39,* 39–40
Codex Xolotl (Paris, BnF, mexicain 1–10),
38n13, 43–45, *44,* 47
Codex Zouche-Nuttall (London, British
Library, Add. MS. 39,671), 41n20, 42n21
coins
of Anastasios (Byzantine emperor), *229*
Bar-Kokhba coin, Jerusalem, Israel Museum,
156
Collins, Rochelle, 45–46
colored script, use of, 260–61, 263, 268–70, 271,
273–74, 275, 276
Columbus, Christopher, 86
comic book, history of, *3,* 3–4

Compiègne antiphonary (Paris, BnF, lat.
17436), 267n28
Constance, Pontifical of (Donaueschingen,
Furstenberg. Bibl. 192), 262n15, 263
Constantine I the Great (Roman emperor),
106–7, 136
Constantinople
Bebaia Elpis convent, *typikon* of, 57n17
Hagia Sophia
inventory of, 57n17
monograms from, *229, 231*
Saint Polyeuktos, Church of
columns now in San Marco piazzetta,
Venice, 219, *220,* 226
monograms in, 219, *220,* 226–27, *227*
nave cornice, 226, *227*
polychrome inscription, 225n27
reason for building, 230n47
Saints Sergios and Bakchos, Church of
monograms from, *229*
poem, nave cornice, 224–25
Stoudios monastery, 66
Virgin *Pammakaristos,* monastery of, verse
inscription, 52–54, *54*
Cooper, Jerrold, 198
Corbie Psalter (Amiens, Bm, ms. 18), 240
Cortes, Hernan de, 106
Coxcoxtli, 42–43, *43*
Cromberger, Jacobo, 85n1, 87n13
cryptography, 79–80, *80,* 234–35
Cummins, Thomas, 6, 7–8, 32, 85, 279
cuneiform, 3. *See also* lapidary style in ancient
Mesopotamia
Cycladic art, 177
cylinder seal texts in ancient Mesopotamia,
214–16, *215*
Cyriacus legend, 248–52, *249*

Damghan, Chehel Dokhtar tower, 208
damnatio memoriae, 217
Dan, Joseph, 164n44, 165n50
Dante, *Paradiso,* 132
Darius (Achaemenid ruler), inscription at
Behistun, 214
Dauzat, Albert, 78
de Bry, Theodor and Johann Theodor
alphabet books of, 101–7, *103, 104*
Les grands voyages series, 103, 107
Debiais, Vincent, 10, 11, 32, 54, 135, 242, 280
Deblitzenos, Manuel, inventory of belongings
of, 57n17
dedication of churches. *See* church dedication
rites in liturgical manuscripts
Derdi, İsmail, 185
Dering, E., *A Short Catechisme for Housholders,*
with Prayers to the Same Adioying (1595),
87n13
Derrida, Jacques, 59
Deshusses, Jean, 241
Dicta Albini, 130
Diego, *Rhetorica Christiana* (1579), 102–3
digital media, 1–2, 28
diorite, 205
Doctrina christiana y catecismo para instruccion
de los Indios... (1585), 87n13
Dogon culture, 24–25

Doukas, John *(kaisar),* letter no. 7 to, 60n25
Drandaki, Anastasia, 234
Dream of the Rood (Anglo-Saxon poem), 252,
253n69
Dresden Codex, *3*
Drogo Sacramentary (Paris, BnF, lat. 9428),
127n72, 240, 262n16, 263
Dronke, Peter, 123n62
Drpić, Ivan, 8, 9, 12, 32, 47, 51, 242, 280
Durand, Guillaume (Willelmus Durandus;
Durandus of Mende), 147
Pontifical (c. 1290), 260
Rationale divinorum officiorum, 128
Durand, Jean-Marie, 25
Dürer, Albrecht, *Art of Measurement* (1525), 102

Eannatum of Lagash, stela of (Stela of the
Vultures; Paris, Louvre), 200n11, 201, 202,
203
Eastmond, Antony, 8, 12, 219, 242, 280
Ebbo Gospels (Épernay, Bm, ms. 1), Evangelist
Mark from, *4, 5*
Ecatepec, 44
Echternach Gospels (Paris, BnF, lat. 9389), 16
Edmund of Abbingdon, 131–32
Egbert's Pontifical (Paris, BnF, lat. 10575), 263,
267n28, *273, 274*
Egyptian hieroglyphs, *3,* 20, 24, 25–26, *27,* 33,
72, 220
ekphrasis, 2n4, 56n15, 64
Eldefonsus of Spain, 118
Eleazar ben Judah of Worms, 165, 168
Sefer hashem (The Book of the Name), 164
Elisha Cresques ben Abraham, Bible of, 166–
68, *167,* 170, 171
Ellis, Maria de Jong, 215–16
emblems, 28
encounter of Pre-Columbian graphic systems
with alphabetic system, 85–107
aesthetization/fetishization of alphabet in
Europe, 86–87, 88, 101–7, *103, 104*
iconicity of script and, 6–7
iconoclastic theory of writing and, 6
indigenous languages, Romanization of, 86,
87
iteration streams in pictorial catechism,
47–48, *48*
language and empire, relationship between,
85–87
performativity of script and, 87–88
printing and, 85n1, 87
Protestant depictions of Spanish Catholic
atrocities against Indians and, 107
Spanish descriptions of American notational
systems, *89–91,* 89–100, *93–95, 97*
superiority of alphabet, assertion of, 87–88,
98–101, 105–7
Enlil (Mesopotamian god), 207
Enmetana of Lagash, statue of (Baghdad, Iraq
Museum), 206–7, *207*
epigrams, Byzantine. *See* Byzantine epigrams
epigraphic habit, 220–21
epigraphische Auszeichnungsmajuskel, 68
Espinar, Alonso de, 85n1
Essarhaddon (Assyrian ruler), 214

Leeuwarden, Fries Museum, Merovingian amulet, 127n69
legibility
  of Byzantine epigrams, 55–56
  of Byzantine monograms, 8, 219, 227–28
  deliberately difficult-to-read/interpret texts, 219–20
  of Islamic calligraphy, 175–76, 182–83
  of lapidary style in ancient Mesopotamia, 197, 216
  in typology/history of script as image, 21–22
Lème (Pyrénées-Atlantiques), church of, 138, *140*
Leningrad. *See* St. Petersburg
Leonian Sacramentary (Verona, Bibl. Cap. 85 [olim 80]), 260
letter symbolism
  associated with Mawlawī ("whirling") dervish, 184
  in Gellone Sacramentary, *238, 247–57, 249, 250, 256*
  in Islamic calligraphy, 183–84, *185*
  in Islamic prayer, 184, *185*
letters. *See* animated letters, anthropomorphism, body, breastplate of high priest, geometric symbols, Hebrew letters in *mahzorim*, Islamic calligraphy, letter symbolism, lettristic letters
lettristic letters, 15
Levtov, Nathaniel, 217
Lex romana visigothorum (León, Archivo Catedralicio, MS 15), 127n72
literacy
  lapidary style in ancient Mesopotamia and, 199
  name recognition and, 226
  pictures as text for illiterate, 7–8, 99–100
  votive texts and, 226, 235
Literature of Unity, 163n33
Livre des matricules des notaires créés par Messieurs les Capitouls, ubique terrarum 1357–1422 (Toulouse, Archives municipales, ms. BB206), 83
London, British Museum
  Battle of the Ulai River relief, Nineveh, Southwest Palace, *211*
  Blacas ewer and another ewer, 175–76
  Codex Aubin, 38n13
  ivory inscribed with incipit of Gloria, 144
  Sennacherib, siege of Lachish, relief from palace at Nineveh, 200–201, *201*, 202
  "Standard Inscription," Nimrud/Kalah, Northwest Palace of Assurnasirpal II, 208–10, *209*
London, Victoria and Albert Museum (V&A), diptych of Rufus Gennadius Probus Orestes, 116n19
London Miscellany (London, British Library, Add. MS. 11,639), 168n58
Lorberbaum, Yair, 162
Lord 3 Lizard "Hair of Jade," 36
Lord 10 Eagle "Jaguar," 36–37
Lord 11 Wind "Bloody Jaguar," 41
l'Orme, Pierre de, 74
Lothar Gospels (Paris, BnF, lat. 266), 117n22
Louis IX (king of France), 78
Louvre. *See* Paris, Louvre

Luxeuil Lectionary (Paris, BnF, lat. 9427), 260n8, 261, 262n13, 267n28
Lyfing, bishop of Wells, 264

Macrobius, 132
Madaba mosaics, 221n11
Magritte, René, *Ceci n'est pas une pipe*, 14
Maguire, Henry, 235
mahzorim. See Hebrew letters in *mahzorim*
Maignien, Edouard, 76, 79, *80*
Maimonides (Moses ben Maimon), 161–63, 170
Majestas Domini
  First Bible of Charles the Bald, *115*, 115–16, 118, 119, 120, 122n56
  Lothar Gospels, 117n22
  Merovingian amulet with, 127n69
  Moutier-Grandval Bible, 116
  Paris, BnF, MS lat. 261 and MS lat. 9385, 111n4
Majnūn (Maḥmūd Chapnivīs), 175
Mallarmé, Stéphane, 21, 28
Mallorca, Farhi Codex from (Sassoon Collection, MS 368), 166–68, *167*, 170, 171
al-Ma'mūn (caliph), 182
Mango, Cyril, 219
manuscripts. *See Manuscript Index (pp. 283–84)*
Marcus, Ivan, 162n32
Marenbon, John, 123n62
Margolin, Jean-Claude, 81
Marianos (eparch of Thessalonike), 234–35
Marmoutier Sacramentary (Autun, Bm, ms. 19bis), 118, 124, *125*, 127, 128, 131
Matiane (Cappadocia), church of Saint Sergios, votive texts, 234–35
Matthew Paris, 131–32
Mawlānā Jalāluddīn al-Rūmī, 187
Mawlawī ("whirling") dervish, letter symbolism associated with, 184
Mayan glyphs, 3, 20, 24, 25–26, 89–92
McCloud, Scott, *Understanding Comics* (1993), 3, 3–4
medallion pages, in Islamic calligraphy, 191–93, *192*
Mehmed II (sultan), 184
Mehmed Nazif Bey, Poem in praise of the Basmala, *193*, 193–94
Méhu, Didier, 6, 13, 242, 243, 257, 259, 281
Meir ben Baruch of Rothenburg, 165n50
Melnik, inventory of monastery of Virgin *Spelaiotissa* at, 57n17
Codex Mendoza (Oxford, Bodleian Library, MS. Selden 3134), 34–36, *35*, 38, 92, *93*
Merlande, church of, claveau inscribed "pax huic domui," 143–44
Merovingian minuscule, 261
Mesopotamia. *See also* lapidary style in ancient Mesopotamia
  name writing in, 72
  [re]invention of writing in, 25
Mexican Pre-Columbian pictography, 31–50
  art and image making, relationship to, 32
  continued use of, 101n50
  dynamic and complex relationship to speech and language, 49–50
  genre distinctions, 34, 36, 37
  glottographic systems compared, 31–32

iconicity of, 7, 32
iteration, sequential streams of, 32–33, 43–49, *44–46, 48,* 50
  in McCloud, *Understanding Comics, 3*
  principle features, 33–38, *34, 35, 37*
  rulership, connection of speech scrolls to, *34,* 38–39
  Spanish conquest and encounter with alphabetic system, *89,* 92–93, *93,* 105
  speech acts, content of, 32, 38, 41–43, *42, 43,* 49–50
  speech scrolls, 32, *34,* 38–40, 38–41, 49
Michael the Studite, 66–67
Mignolo, Walter, 86n4, 107
Milan, Biblioteca Ambrosiana, cod. 30-32/inf., *169*
Milan, church of St. Thecla, 137
minuscule, 28, 66–68, 261, 263, 266–71, 266n26; see also Carolingian minuscule, Merovingian minuscule
Missale Francorum (Vatican, BAV, Reg. Cod. lat. 257), 261, 261n8, 262n13
Missale Gallicanum vetus (Vatican, BAV, Cod. Pal. lat. 493), 261n8
Missale Gothicum (Vatican, BAV, Cod. Reg. lat. 317), 260n8, 261
Mixtec pictography. *See* Mexican Pre-Columbian pictography
Moctezuma Ilhuicamina (Aztec ruler), 38n13, *45,* 45–47
moji-e, 27n25
monograms. *See also* Byzantine monograms; chrismons in Pyrenean Romanesque sculpture; Constantinople.
  ambiguous nature of, 219–20
  cryptography and rebus-signatures, 79
  defined, 127, 141
  of Mary and Jesus in Latin America, 100
monophysitism, 229
Montaigne, Michel de, 85n1
Monte Cassino, Pontifical of (Vatican, BAV, Barb. lat. 631), 275
Montesquieu, *Lettres persanes,* 96
Montiéramey Breviary (Paris, BnF, lat. 796), 132
Mosul ewer, Cleveland Museum of Art, 175
Motolinia (Toribio de Benavente), 31
Mount Athos
  Docheiariou monastery, testamentary rule of Abbot Neophytos at, 56n15
  Xenophon monastery, inventory of, 57n17
Moutier-Grandval Bible (London, British Library, Add. MS. 10,546), opening letter for first epistle of John, 111–34
  Calcidius and Calcidian diagram, 122–23, *124,* 128, 130, 131, 132, 133, 134
  continuation of ideas from, 131–34
  cosmology, diagramming, 112–16, 131, 133–34
  description of, 111, *112*
  iconicity of script and, 8
  ineffable, imaging, 9–10, 128–31, *129*
  mapping meaning onto letter forms/circles, 111, 120–22, *121*
  relationship between letter and figural equivalent, 111
  Trinity, imaging, 128–32, 133, 134
  VD ligature, *117,* 124–28, *125, 126,* 131, 132–33

rebus-signatures, 71–84
  anthroponymic systems and, 78–80, *80*
  cryptographic hypothesis, 79–80, *80*
  design and, 72, 81–82
  dual inscription of signum and signa, 76–77, *77*
  evolution of signatures and name writing, 71–72
  heraldry and, 9, 72–73, 75–76, 78, 80, 81, 83
  iconicity of script and, 8–9
  identity and, 71, 72
  as imitation versus parody, 81
  inventories, collections, and categorizations of, *74*, 74–76, *75*
  lapidary style in ancient Mesopotamia and, 197, 214
  law and, 71, 72, 81
  local signs, use of, 82
  modification over time, 82
  notarial signs and marks, 9, 72–77, *73–75*, *77*, 79, 80–83
  performativity and *fides publica*, 82–83, *83*
  presentation and layout, change in, 81–82
  princely use of, 79, 81
  relative rarity of, 76, 80, 81
  as third-generation writing system, 27–28
Reims, Pontifical of (10th century; Reims, Bm, ms. 340), 262n16
Reims, Pontifical of (13th century; Rouen, Bm, ms. 370 [A34]), 276n51
reliquaries
  Te igitur crucifixion (Gellone Sacramentary) viewed as, 252
  Venice, San Marco, reliquary casket of Four Martyrs of Trebizond, 59–61, *60*
  Vienna, Kaiserliche Schatzkammer, imperial reliquary cross, 252, *253*
revetments, 57, 64n39
Reyes García, Luis, 38n14
rhizomatic nature of script as image, 2
Rice, D. S., 174, 175
Riha paten, 221n12
Robert of Jumièges, 263
Romano-German Pontifical *(Pontifical Romano-Germanique* or PRG), 147, 262, 267n28, 274
Rome, Santa Sabina, west wall inscription, 221n11, 222–23
Roschach, Emile, 74–76, *75*
royal charters, French. See French royal charters
Rufus Gennadius Probus Orestes, diptych of (London, V&A), 116n19
Russell, John M., 209

Saadia Gaon, 163
sacrificial rite, initiation of, in *mahzorim, 155, 156,* 156–57, *157*
Saint-Alban of Mainz Sacramentary (Mainz, Martinusbibl., Hs. 1), 262n16
Saint-Christophe de Montsaunès (Haute-Garonne), church portal, 140–41
Saint-Denis Sacramentary (Paris, BnF, lat. 2290), 262n17, 263, 273
Sainte-Engrâce church, tympanum, 143n43
Saint-Macaire, Saint-Sauveur church at, 145

Saint-Maixant church (Gironde), chrismon, 145
Saint Martin's sacramentary (Tours, Bm, ms. 193), 132–33
Saint-Pé-de-Bigorre church (Hautes-Pyrénées), portal fragment, 148
St. Petersburg, State Hermitage Museum, Bobrinsky bucket, 175
Saint-Vaast of Arras Sacramentary (Cambrai, Bm, ms. 163), 262n16
Salzburg pontifical adapted for use of Sées, 275
Samuel of Speyer, 164
San Marco, Venice
  Pilastri Acritani, 219, *220,* 226
  reliquary casket of Four Martyrs of Trebizond, 59–61, *60*
San Paolo Bible (Rome, Monastero di San Paolo fuori le mura, *Codex membranaceus saeculi IX),* 116
Sangro of Sansevero, Prince Raimondo di, *Lettera apologetica* (1751), 96–98, *97,* 104
Sarajevo Haggadah (Sarajevo, National Museum of Bosnia and Herzegovina), 156, *157*
Sarantenos, Theodore, will of, 57n17
Sargon II (Assyrian ruler), 198n2, 210, 214
Saussure, Ferdinand de, 25
Saxon, Elizabeth, 119, 255n71, 255n74
Schapiro, Meyer, 116, 119, 237n1
Schick, İrvin Cemil, 11, 173, *187, 190,* 281
Schlumberger, Gustave, 227
Scholem, Gershom, 164
screen and fan painting in Japan, 26–27
script. *See also* Anglo-Carolingian minuscule, cryptography, cuneiform, *ghubarī,* ideograms, Mayan glyphs, Mexican pictography, Mixtec pictography, minuscule, pictorial writing systems, pseudo-script, typology/history of script, uncial
separated, 259
script as image, 1–16
  body, letters taking on, 12
  Byzantine epigrams, 51–69 (*See also* Byzantine epigrams)
  Byzantine monograms, 219–35 (*See also* Byzantine monograms)
  chrismons, 135–51 (*See also* chrismons in Pyrenean Romanesque sculpture)
  in church dedication rites, 257–79 (*See also* church dedication rites in liturgical manuscripts)
  in digital media age, 1–2, 28
  encounter of Pre-Columbian and alphabetic systems, 85–107 (*See also* encounter of Pre-Columbian graphic systems with alphabetic system)
  in Gellone Sacramentary, 237–57 (*See also* Gellone Sacramentary)
  Hebrew letters, 153–71 (*See also* Hebrew letters in *mahzorim*)
  iconicity of, 2–9, 32, 261
  iconoclastic theory of writing, 6–7
  of the ineffable, 9–11, 128–31
  Islamic calligraphy, 173–94 (*See also* Islamic calligraphy)

lapidary style, 197–218 (*See also* lapidary style in ancient Mesopotamia)
Mexican pictography, 31–50 (*See also* Mexican Pre-Columbian pictography)
in Moutier-Grandval Bible, 111–34 (*See also* Moutier-Grandval Bible, opening letter for first epistle of John)
performativity of, 11–14, 82–83, 87–88, 237, 242–43
printing, effects of, 1, 3–4, 28, 85n1, 87, 102
protean nature of, 14–16
rebus-signatures, 71–84 (*See also* rebus-signatures)
rhizomatic nature of, 2
typology/history of, 19–28 (*See also* typology/history of script)
seals, 13–14, 80, 214–16, *215,* 227; see also lapidary style in Mesopotomia
Sears, Tamara, 217n62
Seder olam and *Seder olam zutta,* 166
Sedze-Maubecq, church of, tympanum of cemetery door, *147,* 147–48
Sées, Salzburg pontifical adapted for use of, 275
Codex Selden (Oxford, Bodleian Library, MS. Selden 3135), 36–38, *37,* 39n17, 41–42, *42,* 44, 49–50
Seler, Eduard, 38n14
Sennacherib, siege of Lachish, relief from palace at Nineveh (London, British Museum), 200–201, *201,* 202
Sens, Pontifical of (Sens, Bm, ms. 9), 276n50
Serenus (bishop of Marseilles), 99
Serres, *ekphrasis* of the Metropolis at (Theodore Pediasimos), 56n15
Ševčenko, Ihor, 219
Seyyid Hasan Leylek Dede, 187
shabbat sheqalim, reading for, 10, 157–59, *158,* 171
Shalmaneser III (Assyrian ruler), 210
Shamash, 217
Shavuot (Feast of Weeks), 153–54, *154, 155,* 170–71
Sherborne, Pontifical of (Paris, BnF, lat. 943), 263, 267n28
Shi'ur Qomah texts, 162
Sicardus of Cremona, *Mitrale, sive de Officiis ecclesiasticis summa,* 121
signatures. See rebus-signatures
Sinai, monastery of St. Catherine, roof beam inscriptions, 221n11, 222
sinusoidal line (chevron band), 24, 42
Sion Treasure, polycandelon (Washington, D.C., Dumbarton Oaks), *221*
Six Gentlemen scroll (Ni Zan, 1345), 27
Solomon, *Ars Notoria,* 9
Soloveichik, Haym, 164n40, 165n50
Songs of Songs, allegorical interpretation of, 160
Spanish conquest of Latin America. *See* encounter of Pre-Columbian graphic systems with alphabetic system
speaking object, trope of, 62
speech acts, content of, in Mexican Pre-Columbian pictography, 32, 38, 41–43, *42, 43,* 49–50
speech scrolls, in Mexican Pre-Columbian pictography, 32, *34,* 38–40, 38–41, 49
Spier, Jeffrey, 223n23

"Standard Inscription," Nimrud/Kalah, Northwest Palace of Assurnasirpal II (London, British Museum), 208–10, *209*
Standard of Ur, 200n11, 201, 202
Stanley, Tim, 190
stoicheion, 20
Straboromanos, Manuel, 62n34
Stroumitza, inventory of monastery of Virgin *Eleousa* near, 57n17
Süleyman I the Magnificent (sultan; writing as Muhibbî), 183
Sumerian, 197, 202, 207, 208
Sun Stone of Moctezuma Ilhuicamina, *45*, 45–47, *46*, 50
surrealist automatic writing, 4
Suyūṭī, Imām, 173
Symmachus (Quintus Aurelius Symmachus), 228

Tabernacle/Temple/Ark, arch representations of, in *mahzorim*, *155*, 155–57, *156*, *157*
tabula ansata, 221, 222, 234
Tafsīr al-Jalālayn, 181
Tarchaneiotes Doukas Glabas, Michael, 52
Tarchaneiotissa, Maria Doukaina Komnene Branaina Palaiologina, 52, 54
Te igitur
 Bobbio Missal, 261
 Gellone Sacramentary, *250–51*, 252–55
 Tours, Bm, ms. 184, 116–17, *117*, 124, *254*, 255
Tell Tayinat trilingual inscription, 213n43
Codex Telleriano-Remensis (Paris, BnF, mexicain 40), 92–93, *94*
Temple
 arch representation of Temple/Tabernacle/Ark, in *mahzorim*, *155*, 155–57, *156*, *157*
 in church dedication rites, 271
 historiated Is as columns of, 248
 Maria in Gellone Sacramentary as attendant of, 248
 Sefardi representations of messianic Temple, 166–68
Tepeyolotl (jaguar manifestation), 38n14
Teste (imperial and royal notary), *74*
tetragrammaton, 164
Teverga (Asturia), Church of Saint Peter, epitaph of Fredenandus, 148–49
textile, text as, 62–66, *63*, *65*; *see also* Byzantine epigrams
Teyssèdre, B., 241n17, 244n37
Tezcatlipoca (patron of rulers), 46
Tezozomoc (Angry Stone), 43–45, *44*
Theodora (Byzantine empress of Justinian I), 222, 225, *229*
Theodore Psalter (London, British Library, Add. MS. 19,352), 66–68, *67*
Theodore of Stoudios, 60
Thessalonike
 Holy Trinity, monastery of, act of donation, 57n17
 Hosios David, church of, 231–32n53
 Monastery ton Blatadon, Icon of Virgin and Christ Child, 64–66, *65*
 Saint Demetrios, votive mosaics from church of, 230–32, *231*, *233*, 235
Thunø, Erik, 223n22

Tiberius Psalter (London, British Library, Cotton MS. Tiberius C. vi), 131n82
Tilghman, Benjamin C., 15n32, 240
Tirmidhī, *al-Shamā'il*, 189
titulus, 151
Tizoc, Stone of, 45
Tlaltecuhtli, 39n15
tocapu, 89, 101n50
Todorov, Tzvetan, *Dictionnaire encyclopédique des sciences du langage* (1972), 21
Tokovinine, Alexandre, 3n9
tombs, as personified beings, 62
Tonalamatl Aubin (Paris, BnF, mexicain 18–19), 39n15
Torrione Vouilloz, Doninique, 82
Toulouse, Hospitalers church, chrismon, 148
Toulouse cross, *75*, 76, 82
Tovar, Juan de, 94n28
transubstantiation, 127, 247
Traube, Ludwig, 136
trecena, 33, *34*, 38n14, *40*
Trent, Council of (1545-1563), 7, 100
Trier, Pontifical of (Paris, BnF, lat. 13313), 274, *275*
Trinity
 chrismons in Pyrenean Romanesque sculpture as sign of, 142, 144–48, *145–47*
 The Hague, Museum Meermanno-Westreenianum, ivory book cover depicting Trinity, 120–21, *121*
 Touronian manuscripts imaging, 128–32, 133, *134*
Trisagion, 253
True Cross
 French royal charter of Charles V gifting relic of, to John, duke of Berry, *13*, 14n25
 Mass for Invention of, in Gellone Sacramentary, 248–52, *249*
Tukulti-Ninurta II (Assyrian ruler), 208
Twombly, Cy, *Notes from Salalah* (2005-2007), *4*, 4–5
typikon of *Bebaia Elpis* convent, Constantinople, 57n17
typography and printing, effects of, 1, 3–4, 28, 85n11, 87, 102
typology/history of script, 19–28
 alphabetic scripts, place of, 19–21
 iconicity of writing, 2, 3
 ideograms and alphabetic scripts compared, 2, 6, 15, 20
 oral versus written cultures, 20–21
 origins of writing and first-generation systems, 2, 3, 23–26
 prehistoric painting and inscription, 22–23
 printing, effects of, 1, 3–4, 28
 second-generation writing systems, 25–27
 third-generation writing and the lettered imagination, 27–28
 visible/legible, 21–22

'Ubādah ibn al-Ṣāmit, 180
Udine, Archivio Capitolare, ms. 1 (Udine sacramentary), 120
'Umar (caliph), *192*
uncial, 55, 124, 127n72, 128, 240, 260, 261, 263, 266–71, 275

Ur-Nanše of Lagash, plaque of (Paris, Louvre), 199–200, *200*, 201, 208
ut pictura poesis, 2n4
Uta Codex (Munich, Bayerische Staatsbibliothek, Clm 13601), 131n82

Valenciennes, Bm, ms. 293 (Calcidius, commentary on Plato's *Timaeus*), 122, *124*
Valera, Blas, 96
Valéry, Paul, 22
VD *(Vere dignum)* ligature, *117*, 124–28, *125*, *126*, 131, 132–33, 247, 253, 255n76
Vega, Garcilaso de la, *Commentarios Reales* (1609), 96, 97
Velde, Françoise R., 73n8
Venice, San Marco
 Pilastri Acritani, 219, *220*, 226
 reliquary casket of Four Martyrs of Trebizond, 59–61, *60*
Vercelli *Canones conciliarum*, 248–49
Vere dignum (VD) ligature, *117*, 124–28, *125*, *126*, 131, 132–33, 247, 253, 255n76
Verlaine, Paul, 22
Vernus, Pascal, 25
Verrier, Hughues, *74*
Verworn, Max, 33
Vespasian Psalter (London, British Library, Cotton MS. Vespasian A 1), 240
Vialou, Denis, 22–23
Vienna, Kaiserliche Schatzkammer, imperial reliquary cross, 252, *253*
visio, medieval concept of, 259–60
Vodena, inventory of the monastery of the Virgin *Gabaliotissa* at, 57n17
von Riedenburg Pontifical (Paris, BnF, lat. 1231), *275*
votive texts, Byzantine
 concealing names in, 226–35, *227–29*, *231*, *233*
 name recognition in, 220–26, *221*
Voyer, Cecile, 133
Vulgate of Jerome, 112, 116, 123
Vultures, Stela of the (stela of Eannatum of Lagash; Paris, Louvre), 200n11, 201, 202, *203*

Wade cup, Cleveland Museum of Art, 175, 176, *177*
Waldhoff, Stephan, 133
waqwaq style, 176
Warburg, Aby, 20
Washington, D.C., Dumbarton Oaks, Sion Treasure, polycandelon, *221*
Washington, D.C., Freer Gallery, penbox and canteen, 175
Welch, Stuart Cary, 185
Werckmeister, Otto Karl, 244
Wessobrunner Gebetbuch, 248
White Obelisk, Nineveh, 207–8n24
William of Orange (count of Toulouse), 242
Winchester Pontifical (Benedictional-Pontifical of the archbishop Robert of Jumièges; Rouen, Bm, ms. 369 [Y7]), 263, 267n28, 268n34, 269n35, 274
Winter, Irene, 8, 11–12, 54, 197, 281–82

Wolfenbüttel, Herzog August Bibliothek, Wolfenbüttel 4175 (Ordo Romanus), 262n15
Wolfson, Elliot, 164
Woods, Christopher, 217
The Wounds of Christ, Psalter and Rosary of the Virgin (London, British Library, MS. Egerton 1821), 5, *6*
writing. *See* script, script as image, surrealist automatic writing

Xochimilca, 42–43, *43*
Xochiquetzal, 38n14
Xolotl, 38n14
Codex Xolotl (Paris, BnF, mexicain 1–10), 38n13, 43–45, *44, 47*

Yūsuf ibn Ḥasan ibn al-Mibrad, *Thimār al-maqāṣid fī dhikr al-masājid,* 178

Zachee festinans, 266–67
Zimmerman, Michel, 73
Zincirli inscriptions, 212n39
Zodiac ewer and copper basin (Paris, Louvre), 175
Codex Zouche-Nuttall (London, British Library, Add. MS. 39,671), 41n20, 42n21
Zumthor, Paul, 81
Zweifalten *Libellus capitulorum* (Stuttgart, Württembergische Landesbibliothek, Cod. brev. 128), 120